Veterans
of War,
Veterans
of Peace

Veterans
of War,
Veterans
of Peace

Edited by
Maxine Hong Kingston

Koa Books
Kihei, Hawai'i

Koa Books
P.O. Box 822
Kihei, Hawai‘i 96753

www.koabooks.com

Printed in the United States of America
Koa Books are distributed to the trade by Publishers Group West

For more information about *Veterans of War, Veterans of Peace* and the
writers in this book, please visit www.vowvop.org

Library of Congress Cataloging-in-Publication Data

Veterans of war, veterans of peace / edited and compiled by Maxine
Hong Kingston. — Kihei, Hawai‘i : Koa Books, 2006.
    p. ; cm.
    ISBN-13: 978-0-9773338-3-7
    ISBN-10: 0-9773338-3-3
    A collection of essays, poems, and stories of 82 veterans from five wars.

    1. War—Psychological aspects—Literary collections. 2. War
neuroses Literary collections. 3. Post-traumatic stress disorder
Literary collections. 4. Veterans' writings. 5. Authorship—
Psychological aspects. I. Kingston, Maxine Hong.

U22.3 .V48 2006
616.85/212—dc22   0610

2 3 4 5 6 7 8 9 / 10 09 08 07 06

Contents

MAXINE HONG KINGSTON

Introduction

Tell the Truth, and So Make Peace

All my life, I have wanted to keep soldiers safe from war. During
World War II, my cousins in uniform stayed at our house on their
way to and from military bases in California, the Pacific, and Europe.
I heard veterans—including my mother, a refugee, a medic—talk story
about the war that was killing and maiming right now as they spoke.
Listening to people who had lived to tell the tale, I believed that it was
the telling that kept them alive. They had survived hell and come back
to warn us at home.

As Odysseus, the archetypical warrior, made his way home, he nar-
rated his journey—setting off to war, waging the long war, coming
home—to listener after listener. The story grew until, finally home,
he could tell the whole tale and become whole. We tell stories and we
listen to stories in order to live. To stay conscious. To connect one
with another. To understand consequences. To keep history. To rebuild
civilization.

About twenty years after our war in Vietnam—the Fall of Saigon,
the Vietnam War, the American War—the Buddhist monk Thich Nhat
Hanh gathered war veterans and their family members in retreats for
making peace. In Noble Silence, they meditated: eating mindfully,
walking mindfully, hugging mindfully, and hearing the Bell of Mindfulness. Walking meditation is the specific antidote to the march that
soldiers learn in basic training. On hugging, Thich Nhat Hanh said,
"When you hug one Vietnamese person, you hug all Vietnamese
people." I thought, When you hug one American, you hug all of us.
In the circle of the community, someone would sing or speak or dance;
the entire sangha bowed to him or her.

Singing, hugging, dancing, we were a community. But it is in words
that each individual reveals a unique mind. The veterans needed to
write. They would write the unspeakable. Writing, they keep track of
their thinking; they leave a permanent record. Processing chaos through

1

story and poem, the writer shapes and forms experience, and thereby, I believe, changes the past and remakes the existing world. The writer becomes a new person after every story, every poem; and if the art is very good, perhaps the reader is changed, too. Miraculous transformations! So, I added writing meditation to Thich Nhat Hanh's program for veterans.

We practiced writing in community. We would not have to write alone. We had one another to write with, and to write for. If you felt like quitting, you'd look across the table or garden or terrace or grove, and see the others bowed over their notebooks and laptops, and you kept going.

People who care what we have to say surround us. They draw the stories out of us by their wanting to know. Toward the end of the day, I evoke Avalokiteshvara, the bodhisattva of compassionate listening: "We aspire to learn your way of listening in order to help relieve the suffering in the world." And each one reads aloud a new story, a new poem.

The veterans did their most dramatic writing when I presented the First Precept, which is a vow against killing: "I am determined not to kill, not to let others kill, and not to condone any act of killing in the world, in my thinking, and in my way of life." A moral ethic helps shape and form thoughts about the war chaos. The drama is not just in the battle scenes but in the moral conflict.

Worried that the veterans would not take instruction from me, a non-veteran, I invited writers who had had war experience to help me teach. Larry Heinemann. George Evans. Wayne Karlin. Ho Anh Thai. Le Minh Khue. Fred Marchant. Grace Paley. Every one of these good-hearted artists affirmed that the written word gives life.

As the writers became skilled in knowing others' points of view, they enlarged the definition of *veteran*. A veteran could be a woman; a veteran could be a deserter; a veteran could be a civilian who had served in war; a veteran could have been a member of a street gang; a veteran could be a survivor of domestic violence; a veteran could be a peace activist. All manner of persons identified themselves as veterans and came to join the regulars, who argued for a while, then let every one belong. Wars affect all of our lives.

Our workshop/community/sangha has been meeting for a dozen years. There have been about 500 participants, counting people who met in the retreats on the East Coast and in Southern California. Nowadays, about thirty of us (never quite the same thirty) will gather in Sebastopol, California, once each season. A veteran from the other end of the country will set his clock to Pacific Time and meditate when we meditate, write when we write. This book is a harvest of conversations among multitudes. Most of these writers have met one another face-to-face. Nearby or at a distance, we inspire and influence one another, reading one another, editing, translating, giving feedback. We even appear in one another's tales.

If there is one thing the writers in this book have in common, it is that they are rebels. They had been assigned to war; they had volunteered and almost lost their lives. No more volunteering. No more following assignments. Suspicious of institutions, they have no name for our group. So, in this book, various writers call us: The Veteran Writers Group, the Veteran Writers' Workshop, the Veterans Writing Sangha. I have not edited for uniformity. Let stand *Viet Nam* or *Vietnam* or *Viêt Nam, Tet* or *Têt, Danang* or *Da Nang, Ha Noi* or *Hanoi, Communist* or *communist, terrorist* or *Terrorist, Hell* or *hell, God* or *god.*

This community of writers began its work during Gulf War I and has continued meeting and writing to the present day—as the war against Iraq continues. All these years, these faithful writers have paid attention to wars past and to wars ongoing. Their stories and poems are immense in scope, and in heart, and—amazingly—full of life and laughter. They carried out our motto: Tell the truth.

And so make peace.

Pacific waves lulled me to sleep as a baby and I took my first swimming lessons in the rollers of the Atlantic. I remember my father's advice: "When a big wave knocks you down and pulls you under, relax and let the water take you. You'll pop back up. Struggling will only make it worse."

I graduated from college with a degree in wildlife science and began working as a biologist in remote field camps in the Northwestern Hawaiian Islands, surrounded by the clear blue ocean. From Hawai'i, I moved to the mountains of Idaho and lived in a two-room cabin buried in a sea of snow in winter.

The first excruciating attempts to untangle my deep silence and give voice to the fears and griefs of a military officer's daughter began at a veterans' writing workshop with Maxine Hong Kingston and Thich Nhat Hanh. This story and the healing that continues would not have been possible without the compassionate support of my partner. His willingness to tell his own stories of Vietnam gave me the courage to seek out other veterans and, with their encouragement, begin to give voice to the suffering of the families left at home.

One night while I was on watch aboard a sailboat crossing the Pacific Ocean, a blue whale surfaced alongside the boat, and rolled one enormous eye out of the water to have a look at me. I gazed into the whale's eye and knew in that moment that I had never truly been alone.

Finding My Heart

The Bridge (1973)

I don't remember if it was warm or cold, or even what time of year it was. I wore a sweater to protect me from the wind blowing across the great red span that traversed the Golden Gate. I had never walked across that bridge before. To me it was an awkward contraption, strung from the clouds and destined to collapse. As the wind howled through the massive steel girders, we took our first steps away from the safety of solid ground. A truck passed, and the giant red beast shook and moaned.

I grew up on the shores of the Atlantic and followed my father in the early mornings across sharp, sea-white rocks to a point of land where a lighthouse bellowed into the fog. Waves slapped against the breakers like popgun blasts. We braced ourselves against rogue waves that left us drenched and salty and longing for sun. For endless hours, I rode in my father's motorboat casting shiny metal spoons, strips of rubbery squid, chicken necks, anything that would lure bluefish to my line. Often the days ended with a mad dash to shore, hungry black thunderclouds chasing at our heels. But I never felt afraid with my father at the helm. Swimming with sea stars—*bioluminescence*—in the ink-dark sea, peering into the cardboard and foil contraption my father built to observe the solar eclipse, even during storms at sea, I trusted him. Or, perhaps it would be more accurate to say, I wanted to trust him. I even slipped quietly from the fishing boat into the dark ocean, letting the current take me a little beyond his reach, just to see if what he'd said was true: "Trust me, there's nothing to fear."

I'd arrived in the fog-drenched Bay Area a year earlier. It was October 1972, and I was dressed in bellbottoms so wide it looked as though a skirt was hitched at each knee, a seersucker smock with no hint of a waistline, and two tarnished metal bracelets repaired with dirty wraps of masking tape on my left wrist. I was a shy child, uprooted from the tomboy world of forest wandering and mucking in the stinking, gelatinous, black mud of the Chesapeake for one-clawed crabs. In the affluent California suburbs, middle-school girls talked about boys and fashion and never once mentioned the ravaging war in Vietnam. It didn't take me long to notice that no one else in my school wore platinum POW-MIA bracelets.

"What does your father do?" they asked.

"He's a fighter pilot in Vietnam," I repeated, as though those words were a mantra, a koan that explained everything and nothing. Deep down in my survivor's heart, I was waiting for an outburst or a beating, something to alleviate my sense of guilt.

My mother, my sister and brother, and I arrived at the Golden Gate Bridge with bouquets of red roses for what was supposed to be a happy occasion. After seven months of separation, the senior officers' families would walk to the center of the bridge and toss roses onto the flight deck of the USS *Enterprise* as it passed under the bridge into the bay. My father was executive officer aboard the ship, the world's largest nuclear-powered aircraft carrier at the time. But we were confronted by a crowd of angry protesters; their words echoed ones I'd heard at the air base in Virginia—"Baby Killer! Murderer!"—I felt as though I was walking a gangplank. I wanted the shouting to stop. I needed to know what was true. I wanted to believe in my father again. I wanted peace.

Trucks thundered past. The wind carried the cries of the protesters. My mother looked past all the commotion and marched on toward the center of the bridge. My older sister and brother walked apart from us in their necessary boredom and defiance, their roses held recklessly at their sides as though to say, "Can we just get on with it?" Suddenly, I froze! Just where the bridge leaves the last piling, I knelt down and gripped the rust-red railing so tightly that my hands turned white. I could not move a muscle. I could not speak. My mother looked back for me over the blood-red roses. After hours of teasing, pinning, and spraying, her blond hair had become a storm at sea. On the horizon I could see the captain's bridge of the *Enterprise* rising up out of the ocean. I knew my father was there, his eyes fixed on the Golden Gate, his family waiting.

Sandhill Cranes (1995)

I lowered my eyes from my father's face—before he dropped the jelly bombs at three hundred feet—and watched his hands. They wrapped a thin sheet of copper foil around a black sliver of glass that would become a sandhill crane's bill. He wrapped the foil with such precision that it overlapped evenly both sides of the rippled glass. In a sun-filled garden house, he transformed green glass into foothills, blue glass into rivers, and gray glass into the wings of a sandhill crane. The solder lines that joined the pieces of colored glass flowed as lyrically as the sounds of the foreign places he named: *Hanoi, Hai Phong, Da Nang, Nam Dinh Bridge.* I was in awe of his concentration, how he could tell a story about war and, at the same time, create a primordial bird from colored glass.

The same year that he flew combat missions off the USS *Independence,* an astronaut walked in space, draft cards burned, Janis Joplin teased her hair into a bouffant and registered for secretarial school, and my mother sent me off to preschool on a yellow bus so she could get some work done around the house without me clinging to her legs. But what she told me later wasn't true: "You were too young. You can't possibly remember the war." She didn't want to believe that her baby girl had soaked up her misery like a sponge.

I came to the garden house in search of stories—my parents' and my own. I was armed with a tape recorder and a list of questions. But I was in no shape to ask any of them. All my attempts to speak about the war or even say the word *Vietnam* left a taste of fear and shame in my throat, a steel gray hatch slammed shut against my vocal chords. I hadn't fathomed the depth of my silence.

Thirty years after my father's tour in Vietnam, as he pieced together chips of colored glass, he finally spoke about the war. He told me that he flew one combat tour and then spent the rest of the war—while protesters lined the entrance to the Navy base shouting "Baby Killer!" and I wore an ugly metal bracelet engraved with the name "Lt. Cmdr. David Wheat" on my left wrist—on carrier duty in the Mediterranean Sea. I thought he was at war. I hadn't understood the difference. All I knew was that some other fathers did not come home.

In one of my earliest memories, my father is sitting on the edge of his bed in our Chesapeake house. He is wearing his khaki pants and an undershirt yellowed by the ship's laundry. He has just come home from a tour at sea, and he looks tired. I sit beside him and lean into that missed warmth. He smells of the dark leather chairs, the cigarette and cigar smoke of the ship's Ready Room. I am six years old. I ask my father, "Daddy, do you kill babies?" His head falls into his hands. My mother shuffles me out of the bedroom, cooing in my ear, "Everything's fine, dear, your father's just tired." The way his head falls into his hands—my wounding—I fall into silence.

The Veterans (1993)

In October, I boarded a train at Union Station in Washington, D.C., bound for Rhinebeck, New York, to attend a meditation-and-writing retreat for veterans and their families. I had never been on a passenger train before. I stowed my backpack in the luggage rack and settled next to the window. As the train pulled away, leaving behind a subterranean world of shops and shoppers, I felt a profound loneliness and fear—that punishing wall of silence closing in around me. Did I actually expect to write my way out of misery? As the train hurled past sooty city buildings splashed with graffiti, I recalled the sidebar in a national

magazine's article about a Vietnamese monk named Thich Nhat Hanh
and the word *Peace*. That word got me on the train. But at every station along the way, I wanted to get off.

Gulf War I had been declared a victory for more than a year, but I
was still caught in the despair of that burial in sand. Those punishing
days and nights, I sat in the mauve chair where my husband's grandmother had rocked him to sleep as a baby, and watched squadrons of
fighter jets raking the hot desert with bombs, while January winds
hurled snow at the windows of our cabin. Alone in the howling, white
wind, all I could make out on our nine-inch black-and-white television were the bright, white flashes of bombs exploding. I felt ashamed
of my voyeurism, and yet I could do nothing but sit in that old chair
and weep, my thoughts lost to another war and the searing memory
of a young Vietnamese girl running toward me out of a napalm fire, a
jet fighter gaining altitude above the flames. That was the year I lost
my heart, and my voice.

How does a child navigate this tapestry of silence and make sense
of a world gone mad? What does a child know, really, about a father at
war? About the ache of worry etched on her mother's face? About the
black military car parked in front of a neighbor's house? About POW-
MIA bracelets engraved with the names of fathers worn on the wrists
of elementary school children? About the Vietnamese girl burned by
napalm? I don't even know which memories are my own any more
and which are a fiction pieced together from stories, photos, and television. I do know that, at any cost, I wanted my father home, alive.

Those days and nights of torturous snow and bombings, I begged
my husband for stories. He was inducted into the Army in 1968, during the largest draft call of the war, when soldiers were needed to replace
the ones killed during Tet. He applied for and received 1-A-O status—
conscientious objector—and served as a combat medic without a
weapon in the Mekong Delta. The stories he wanted to tell weren't
battle stories, although he has those, but about a young man from
Prineville, Oregon, who grew watermelons on the firebase from seeds
sent from home, and, when the melons were ripe, slung them in a sack
over his shoulder and gave them to the villagers living amid the wreckage. And about the night my husband waited out an incoming mortar
attack crammed inside a bank safe, his limbs entwined around a bony
Vietnamese carpenter whose knotted string for recording measurements

was wrapped around his wrist like prayer beads. I was drawn to these stories, how they erased the lines we draw to separate ourselves from an enemy. I asked him to repeat his stories again and again, pacifying hunger for my own. Mercy or old wiring—toward the end of one hundred days in the Persian Gulf, the picture tube on the nine-inch TV went black.

At each stop along the ride to Rhinebeck, I thought of escape. Silence had a noose around my neck. What could I offer a group of veterans besides my fear? Autumn winds fanned the wildfire of red and gold leaves along the Hudson. At home, the cold had already descended from the mountains into the valley. It was hunting season, and an early snow meant a treacherous journey for the elk moving out of the high country to lower ground. Outside the train, towns piled up on each other.

At a stop in Pennsylvania, I looked across the station platform and saw a white clapboard building with a sign hanging in the second-story window: "Weekly Rates." I re-counted the couple hundred dollars stuffed in my pocket. Who would know if I actually attended the retreat? I slung my backpack over my shoulder and walked off the train.

The air was fresh and cool. I felt at home in the changing season. I'd read about a man who crawled free from the wreckage of a derailed train and walked past the crowd of onlookers into a new life. The railings that led up the stairs to the parking lot and town beyond, the freedom of anonymity, were rusted. The station sign, the ticket machines, the light posts, the benches, even the cars parked in the parking lot— all were rusting. I looked up at the white clapboard house and the room where I could continue hiding and suddenly recognized the red rust of my own paralysis, the unexamined despair eating away at my heart. I felt weary, as though I'd been lugging the dead on my back. I turned and reboarded the train.

By the time I got to the retreat center, registered, and set up my tent far away from others, I was late. I followed the map along narrow, paved paths past small white cabins and meeting houses to the building where the veterans had gathered for the weekend, and I walked past it. I went back to my tent, unrolled my sleeping bag, and lay down.

On the second pass, I saw a group of men meeting outside on the porch. I wanted desperately to run and never stop running, but before I could, a man with a leather Harley-Davidson jacket and blond ponytail leaped off the porch, crossed the demarcation line I'd set up between the veterans and me, and introduced himself as Claude. He told me later that I looked like one of the frightened deer he sees caught in the glare of his motorcycle headlights. He was sure I'd bolt at any minute.

Compelled by something deeper than fear, I looked into the faces of the wounded men on the porch, and I finally stopped running. When Claude asked me to say a little something about why I was there, I couldn't give any details about my father's military service, because I didn't know them. I didn't know that he had been stationed aboard the USS *Independence* in 1965, that he flew bombing missions over North Vietnam as part of Operation Rolling Thunder. To introduce myself, I simply said, "My father was a fighter pilot in Vietnam."

The days settled into a schedule of meditation and writing. I knew nothing about Zen Buddhism or meditation, and I struggled my way through the thirty-minute sittings without a moment of ease, while torrential rains pounded the cabin's thin roof. Writer and peace activist Maxine Hong Kingston led the writing sessions. Her compassionate attention to everything that was written and shared, no matter how disturbing, allowed a slow string of sentences to appear on my writing paper.

One afternoon the sky cleared, and we went outside for walking meditation. Some of the men were visibly uncomfortable. They spread out and hung to the periphery. One even refused to walk. I shuffled recklessly through the loud red leaves. Later I learned that the walking meditation reminded them of the dangerous walks they'd taken in Vietnam.

The stories the men wrote and read aloud were raw, brutal, and devastating. The small, dimly lit room where we sat hunched on cushions on the floor was filled with the memories of young men cast into war—alone, afraid, angry, shattered. A combat medic was still haunted daily by the young men he could not save. A helicopter door gunner lived the terror of killing hundreds, trusting no one. An army grunt carted around the ghost and the snapshot of a lover of the young Vietnamese man he had shot and killed. They wrote and cried, bearing down hard with their pens on the pages of their notebooks. Each read his stories, and when there was a break, I rushed outside to gulp the wet, cool air.

In the scorching company of violence, betrayal, disillusionment, guilt, and abandonment, I wrote about casseroles—tuna casseroles and green bean casseroles. When I read aloud, I barely managed a whisper, the steel trap of silence had a stranglehold around my neck. Why should anyone care about casseroles, a crooked chair, a father who lived to come home? My hands shook, and I was soaked with sweat. Although I knew rationally that nothing would happen to me, unconsciously I was crossing a dangerous line. The pact of silence among the families had prevented our fears from spilling out, flooding the community and jinxing our fathers. When I finished reading I ran outside gasping for air, and the men followed me, awkwardly, and held me.

On the last night of the retreat, I sat with the veterans in three rows of cold metal folding chairs in front of hundreds of retreatants and the Vietnamese monk Thich Nhat Hanh. I didn't want to read. I wasn't sure I could. So many eyes in the crowd. When my turn came, I sat in the hard metal chair for a long time without speaking. The pages I held shook visibly. I became the deer again, the familiar urge to escape swelling inside me, but I was paralyzed. I looked into a sea of pinched expressions—an audience puzzled, I thought, by the presence of a young woman in this group of veterans. Then I felt a large rough hand reach for mine. I looked behind me and saw Billy wearing his blue bandana around his forehead, sullen, quiet, enraged. I had felt afraid of him the entire weekend, but now he reached out and took hold of my hand. "You're not alone," he said. "I'm here with you." Those days, when surely he could smell my fear, he had seen into my heart and recognized the net of silence, the grief. I looked from Billy to the audience and the beatific smile of Thich Nhat Hanh, and the word *Peace* rang in my ears. In a small and frightened voice, I read about silence and dead fathers and casseroles, Billy's kind hand never letting go of mine. My heart burst open.

Sandhill Cranes (1995)

My father still used aviator lingo to describe an air strike: *over the beach*—in enemy territory, and *seat wet*—safe over water. He said that at night flak looked like the Fourth of July. He evaded SAMs—surface-to-air missiles—in the dark because he could see them coming, but during the day he couldn't.

My father soldered glass into snow and river as he talked about war, and I wondered if he knew how important it was that I could finally picture him in his jet. If he looked over his shoulder for his wingman or to watch antiaircraft fire barely miss the fuselage of his jet, he only had a second. He flew too fast and too low over the Nam Dinh Bridge to make a mistake.

I stopped taking notes and relied on the tape recorder. I looked at my mother. She flinched when my father demonstrated how to *lower the curtain* and *punch out*—eject. She looked up from her sewing and watched as he described flying into a sea of flak over Hai Phong Harbor. My mother is good at making faces. She squinted behind her drugstore eyeglasses, forced her lips into a deep frown, and nodded, acknowledging each pilot who did not make it out.

Thinking about the missing and dead pilots led my mother into her own story. Her words came slowly, timed by each small stitch of her sewing needle. She sounded old inside her stories. She talked about casseroles—tuna-and-green-bean casseroles, macaroni and cheese, shepherd's pie.

"I tried to bake the kinds of casseroles the kids liked to eat," she said. "It was important to make it easier for the mothers."

"The first time a pilot was shot down, we wives got word on a Monday. The next Monday, we got word of another. And the next Monday, another. I was scared to death to answer the telephone on Mondays. I just stood beside the phone and listened to it ring."

For three Mondays in a row, my mother baked casseroles that we delivered to the families of dead or missing pilots off the USS *Independence*.

To survive an unpopular war, the air-wing wives stayed in close contact. They formed a calling tree for disaster. "The CO's wife was notified first if a pilot was . . ." My mother searched for the word that would encompass all possibilities, and finally settled on *lost*. Is that what she hated most about the military? That others might know about her husband's death before she did, while she was hanging the day's laundry on the line or tossing a stick for his dog or kissing their children goodnight?

In the last hour of daylight, my father soldered a thin bead of copper around the red cap on the sandhill crane's crown. Weariness showed in his eyes and in his stiff posture. My mother, bent close to her sewing in the dim light of dusk, looked up at my father, puckered her lips, and commented, "I thought you said there was a church."

"No," my father insisted. "But there *was* an old man near the Nam Dinh Bridge. These are difficult things to live with."

He recounted how he had planned that if he was ever called in for an air strike on a village, how the bombs would not disengage and how there probably would have been a court-martial.

Complicity and guilt began to reveal themselves. I needed to know these things about my father. The sun dipped behind the mountains, leaving the sky on fire, and out of that fire, a bird called, a rasping old-world cry that reminded me that the earth will go on without us.

"What bird?" my father asked.

I smiled. "Sandhills." And I asked the first direct question I ever asked him about Vietnam. I asked if he remembered the thin man's name, the ex-POW who sat on a crooked chair in my elementary school gym and spoke about imprisonment and war to an audience of children.

My father shook his head.

My mother said, "I don't remember such a thing."

Maybe the only memories not lost to amnesia are those we think we can survive. What I remembered was the chair. The ex-POW, agitated by the tip, tip, tipping of the uneven chair leg, sat in the hushed auditorium and described to the children a bamboo cage: "This big around. This high. This is how I lived."

When I was eleven, before the thin man came home from Vietnam, I had sat in the same chair. I rocked myself in that chair outside the principal's office, while I waited for my mother to come for me. No one in the school office would look at or speak to me, such disgust for my refusal to salute the flag and recite the Pledge of Allegiance in my sixth-grade class. Was it the Vietnamese girl on fire? Or another dead father? I cannot remember.

Fire (1996)

I hurried through hurricane winds into the dark shelter of the Library of Congress to search for photos and articles about the time my father was at war. There was one photograph I needed to find, one memory I needed to confront. The reference librarian looked up at me when water from my rain-soaked hair dripped on the newspaper she was reading. I asked for Nick Ut's photograph of the Vietnamese girl running from the napalm. "Oh, that one," she said, and began typing on her computer. "Here's an article written about the girl in the photo seventeen years after she was burned."

"She lived?" I gasped.

I'd carried that haunting image with me to every fire since I was a young girl. They are all fleeing, down a wet road. Her brother, in a white shirt, is in front of her, his mouth a black hole of agony. In the center of the photo was Kim Phuc, naked, one bare foot splashing in a rain puddle, the other in the air, her arms held away from the sides of her body, the way you hold yourself after a bad sunburn.

"Nong qua. Nong qua," the children scream. Too hot. Too hot.

On November 11, 1996, Phan Thi Kim Phuc placed a wreath at the Wall of the Vietnam Veterans Memorial. The sun glistened on the cold black stone. I rested the palm of my hand against the name David Wheat, and when I raised my hand, the frosted imprint remained. Veterans in fatigues milled about, searching for names. "Welcome home," they offered each other. Testimony and keepsake at their feet, the columns of names.

I sat in the center where the first dead greet the last, beside a friend who wore a purple heart and a Vietnamese service medal pinned to his farm clothes. Kim Phuc looked younger than I had imagined.

"We cannot change history," she said. "But we can do good things in the present and the future to promote peace."

As the colors were posted, I did not join in the Pledge of Allegiance. I could not raise my hand to my heart. But Kim Phuc did, after she had placed the wreath at the apex of the Wall, with the help of Colonel Norm McDaniel, a former prisoner of war. A lone soldier standing above the scarred black slate played taps. Kim Phuc raised her right hand. If she had ever lost her heart, she had found it.

Green. As deep and wet as a Northeaster swamping Chesapeake woods. The smoke and flames. The confusion. The camera moves in quick jolts, while Kim Phuc runs away from the temple and down the wet road. She looks my way from the television screen, and I touch her face. Behind her, a fighter jet rises above the plumes of fire.

The Bridge (2004)

I never made it to the center of the Golden Gate Bridge the blustery morning my father came home from sea in 1973. A police officer found me, white-knuckled, at the point where many people jump to their deaths. He carefully pried my fingers from the railing, put his arms around me, and led me off the bridge to safety.

For several months after my father's return, I skipped school once every week to go into the city alone. I walked the length of the waterfront and onto the haunting red bridge. Step by step I inched out over the water and, after four months, I made it to the center of the bridge and dropped a single red rose to the blue waves below. I sat on the cold concrete and thought about my father and the war and what a life without fear truly meant. As the sun began to set, a policeman, concerned about my intentions and the growing dark, escorted me from the bridge and safely back to a BART station.

After the fall of the World Trade Center towers, toward the end of the agonizing buildup to the war in Afghanistan, I woke up one morning and knew clearly that I could never know peace in the world until I knew it in my own heart. I began a series of intensive meditation retreats, during which I found myself revisiting childhood fears, buried memories, and paralyzing grief. Silence. I bought a bodhi-seed *mala* and began wearing it on my left wrist. At night I lay awake and felt the skin burn where I had once worn the broken and bandaged POW-MIA bracelets. I began to see the finely crafted walls I had built to protect myself from conflict. Late one evening during long hours of meditation, Kim Phuc appeared. She reached out and touched my face, the way I had touched hers on the television screen many years before. "You're not alone," she said. "You've never been alone," and she placed her hand over my heart.

YIGAL BEN HAIM

I was born and raised in Kibbutz Ramot Menashe in Israel. I lost my leg in the Yom Kippur War in 1973. Studying and working as a trauma psychologist in San Francisco, I treated many Vietnam veterans, helping them to come home again. Since 1998, I've been living with my family in Haifa, Israel.

שיר מחאה למות בלי מזל

במלחמה כמו במלחמה
לכל הרוג או ניצול יש מזל משלו
להרוג הראשון לא היה מזל
להרוג האחרון המזל חמק אף הוא
לניצול שחק המזל
הוא מזמן מסרב להיכנס לבושה הזאת
לפלסטינאי מאחורי הגדר הבית הרוס
הרוע לא ריחם גם כאן
כך בין הראשון לאחרון
ארבע שנים נלחמנו בעוד מערכה בחתונת הדמים הדפוקה שלנו
1000 הרוגים אצלנו
10000 הרוגים אצלם
דם על הידיים אצל מי ?
הודנה והפסקת אש נסעו לשארם
שתו לחיים על חשבון המזל

הוי יהודסטינאי שלי בכה בכי מר
בשוך האימה כסה את אחיך בעפר שחור
עמוק באדמה הצדק מתפורר לאט

יגאל בן חיים,

חורף,2005

Gallipoli Beach 1913

Translated by Michael Shuval

Australians,
fire, meat, cannon,
the kill—their broad
fluttering hat brims caught.
Breezy beach and
death for nothing.

It began with virgin military music,
women, the colors,
Australia, wines and
eternity
of not yet—
only the parting looks
of Mom and Dad
knowing what you couldn't
at the time.

Shipped off to lock
with menace and
do battle from which
no victors . . .
Oh, my John,
had you and flags
streamed faster,
but Fate brought death
to Gallipoli seas
and rocks.

An evening of
melancholy memory hauls
from me three ghostly tanks
and Group D on
that morning
barren Hamutal Hills
October '73, the assault
on Egyptian armor.

It stood fast
then hit Yossi's tank;
scorched it open,
torn tin left to witness
Final Days.

But fall back with me,
explore, feel desert winds
persist. They bury and exhume.
No stopping the will to remember,
conceal, expose, cover, reveal.

SHEPHERD BLISS

Born into the proud, military family that gave Fort Bliss, Texas, its name, I followed my father, his father, and our ancestors to enlist as an officer in the United States Army.

I was trained to fight from an early age. Even the way I played chess at home was to learn military strategy. As a boy I had to stand at attention before my father, salute him, and address him as "Sir." I remember being a teenager in the army. It was the time of the Vietnam War, and I wanted to defend my beloved country from the "evil empire" of Communism. Testosterone pumping through my body, the thought of war was exciting. Basic training with my buddies at Fort Riley, Kansas, was actually a good experience. Though demanding, it felt like playing with the guys in the woods and preparing to defend our country. I was a boy soldier, enjoying my buddies and the conditioning of my male body into that of a man.

Bliss men had fought in American wars for more than two centuries. Wanting to become another General Bliss, I requested assignment in Vietnam, hoping it would help me rise up the ranks quickly. But after hearing Dr. Martin Luther King, Jr., preach, I resigned my commission and enrolled in the University of Chicago Divinity School, where I received a Doctor of Ministry (D.Min.) degree and was then ordained as a United Methodist minister. I became active in the resistance to the Vietnam War and then went to Chile during the democratic government of Salvador Allende.

Since that time, I have held teaching and administrative posts at various colleges, including Harvard, New College of California, and the University of Hawai'i at Hilo, and have contributed to eighteen books, including coauthoring *A Quiet Strength*. In 1992, I established the organic Kokopelli Farm in Sonoma County, California, and in recent years I have divided my time between Hawai'i and California. My current writing focuses on Peak Oil and how the decline in petroleum supplies is changing the Earth.

I left the military forty years ago, and I have worked hard to demilitarize myself. I'm older now, and war is no longer exciting or glorious to me. I know that even if you return alive, battle scars are inevitable, not just on the body, but on the soul.

I enjoy receiving e-mails from readers. Feel free to contact me at sb3@pon.net.

Sound Shy

Yesterday morning my car beeped at me, again—beep, beep, beep. It kept yelling at me until I did what it wanted me to do. The gas pump—the automatic bank teller—the telephone as I dialed—the phone answering machine—they all beeped loudly at me. They told me what to do or what not to do. They wore me down, so I obeyed their orders.

That afternoon, my good friend Yoshi called. I like talking to Yoshi on the phone, but today he was talking while doing the dishes—clang, clang, clang. Then he started rustling papers. Multitasking, like a normal twenty-first century American. When he started eating, I had to ask, "Are you eating?" Yoshi replied, "Yes, do you mind?" I got the nerve to say, gently, "Why don't you finish eating and call me back?" He said goodbye, but I don't think he understood. The noise had exhausted me. Yoshi tends to be diffused in his attention, and I tend to be focused. He tends toward being scattered, and I tend toward being rigid, something that can happen to people raised in military families.

Phones magnify certain background sounds and my filter does not work well, so the words and the sounds become one, and I cannot follow what is being said. This confusion also happens in loud restaurants and in gatherings with lots of people. When I talk on the phone, I give my phone partner my undivided attention. Yoshi can split his consciousness; he thinks he can do a good job at doing many things at once. But then, he was born into the digital age, whereas I remember a time before cars, phones, ATM machines, and gas pumps beeped out orders. I wonder who is in charge: people or machines.

As a child, my military father was always barking orders. He shouted at us while we were eating at the dinner table, playing in the yard, vacationing in new places. We had to answer, "Yes, sir!" and salute him. The rule was No talking at the dinner table. We were supposed to get nutrition, not socialize. We five children were his little squad, and he marched us around. Our job was to be obedient and to do what he ordered.

Counting my mother, he had six in his squad. I don't do well when machines or people shout orders.

"Ready. Set. Drop your load." Those may not be the exact words.

I don't remember much from my childhood. It's sort of a blur. I do remember the loud B-52 bombers taking off. I also remember my father showing me shrunken heads. We were living in the Panama Canal Zone at Albrook Air Force Base. I had a child's curiosity about these other people—the dark Panamanians. But my father warned me not to go into the jungle, since headhunting cannibals lived there. He showed me this shriveled head.

As an adult I worked in Panama during the nationalist government of President Omar Torrijos, one of the three American colonies where I have worked to support self-determination, the others being Puerto Rico and now Hawai'i. I asked a Panamanian historian how the head-hunting cannibals were doing. He laughed and commented, "You must have been raised in the Zone." I responded, "How did you know?" Getting more serious, he said, "That is what military parents tell their children, to control them, frighten them, and reduce their natural curiosity." Stories can be used for many reasons, in this case to teach racism.

Maybe you read the book or saw the film *The Great Santini,* by Pat Conroy. That was like our family—a Southern fighting family with five kids. We even had a '55 Chevy station wagon, like in the movie. My Dad beat me (whom he called "Number One, front and center!" rather than my name), then beat my younger brother, then beat our youngest brother, then beat our dog Spot. I didn't get my father off my back until I was big enough to beat him up, like the teenager in the movie.

Back to the twenty-first century. Tired from a day of noises from my car and the telephone—and memories of childhood as a "military brat"—I watched an old Hallmark Hall of Fame film called *Miss Rose White.* A woman and her father flee the Nazis; her mother and sister remain in the Polish concentration camps. Years later the sisters are reunited in New York. I listened to the sounds that the former prisoner made in her sleep, sounds directed toward the father who'd abandoned her. I cried, aware that those sounds touched some universal, not just personal, part of me.

I have heard some very ugly sounds in my life—like the sound of a woman being tortured by the military. I lived in Chile, during the democratic government of Dr. Salvador Allende. I made it out, early on, but some friends did not.

I was in the U.S. Army during the Vietnam War, but I refused to go into battle. I resigned my commission to protest the war. I disappointed the entire Bliss military family, after which Fort Bliss, Texas, was named.

Naming is important. Writing and naming this essay reminded me of my first adult act. I finished writing this essay during July 4 celebrations, as hundreds of us gathered to celebrate a robust Inter-Dependence Day. I was reminded of what I consider my first adult act—resigning my U.S. Army officer's commission to protest the Vietnam War. My second adult act was to cease using my first name, Walter, which I learned means "warrior." I was born Walter Shepherd Bliss III, carrying the military legacy from my father and his father and further back. I did not want to have this warrior legacy evoked for the rest of my life, even if those calling me "Walter" were not doing so consciously.

So I decided to use my given middle name, which is my great-grandmother's last name, as my first name. I wanted to honor my matrilineal legacy. I think this has made a great difference in my life. It has helped give me the peace of a shepherd, rather than the trauma of being called a warrior. I appreciate having a warrior inside and available, but I do not want it to be always leading me.

Deciding what to entitle this essay has not been easy, nor has writing it been easy. This essay is more personal than most of my writing—closer to home. I know that I wanted the word "sound" in the title. The title originally included "Sound Sensitivity." Then it evolved into "The Sounds of Trauma." Then the title "Sound Shy" emerged from a reader on July 4th, evoking "Gun Shy." Though it did not immediately appeal to me, I soon realized that the essay had found its title with the help of a member of our Veterans' Writers Group—Earll Kingston.

I also learned good things from my military family and from being in the service myself: teamwork, developing a mission, and country love. I still believe in Duty, Honor, and Country and uphold the vow I took upon being commissioned to defend the American Constitution.

I know there are reasons for my dad's loudness. He was in World War II, where he lost part of his hearing by being next to antiaircraft guns. Musicians and people who go to many rock concerts and get close to amplified music also lose part of their hearing. I prefer the harp and acoustic music.

I am usually oversensitive to noise, but even more so when I am under stress. My stress is currently high because I am, once again, moving, after about three years in one place. Being raised in a military family, we moved about every three years. We did not get to know anyone well or establish deep relationships. My psyche now seems organized in a pattern such that every three years, I change jobs, homes, or relationships. When people talk about their "childhood friends," I feel that I missed something; my friends only date back to college. The military keeps its personnel mobile; they mustn't be a stationary target. My Dad would call attachment to close friends and the expression of deep and intimate feelings a "national security risk."

I remember an officer once telling me, "When you get your platoon, don't learn the first names of your men until you've been in combat awhile. Some of them are likely to die pretty soon, because they are not good soldiers. If you get too close to them, you will have to do lots of grief work, which is not easy." This grief work is indeed not easy.

As I prepare to move from Hawai'i back to Kokopelli Farm in Sonoma County, Northern California, I recall my twenty-fifth high school reunion in Omaha, Nebraska—Strategic Air Command headquarters. I won the award for moving the most times since graduating from high school.

Haven't you noticed how much louder things have gotten? Restaurants, movies, grocery stores, airports all the public places. Someone is often talking to you over a loudspeaker, telling you what to do or what not to do, or trying to sell you something. Where in the city can one go for peace and quiet? Even in libraries, people talk on their cell phones. I find it embarrassing overhearing someone having a conversation—loud, animated, personal—into a machine with some distant human on the other end. On an airplane, a guy next to me turned on his cell phone. I asked him to turn it off; he's violating aviation policy. He felt he was entitled to invade my sound-space with his loud cell phone talk.

Much of my behavior is sound-avoidant. I often feel a misfit in our increasingly noisy society. If I go into a room with a battery-powered clock, I can hear it ticking. If someone has an old, predigital watch on their wrist and is close enough, I can hear it ticking, ticking, ticking, so methodically. I leave such loud rooms. Those ambient sounds become magnified to me; they thunder and produce headaches. And most refrigerators are too loud for me. I usually build a little room outside the house to contain the refrigerator.

We had hundreds of clocks in our military family. My Dad was in the Air Force, which depends upon clocks to launch attacks and drop bombs. They call it precision bombing or smart bombing. (Since when do words like *smart* and *bomb* belong together?) Even a second off means that you could miss your target. Have you ever been a target? It is not much fun.

You might think I am strange. Wanting to know how others perceive me, and my wounds, I asked one of my teaching assistants, Sarah Sullivan, to comment on her experiences of my noise sensitivity and how it impacted our work together. She responded, "Your noise sensitivity can look like feelings of annoyance and intolerance." When I am triggered, I can be curt.

She added, "I remember noticing how you are really careful about where you sit, where you eat, where you meet people, where you go out, where you walk even to avoid noise. Your face changes, too, when you are overcome by noise. Your frown becomes pronounced, you look harsher and closed, like a headache is brewing or the lights are too bright. It's difficult to understand, the way it wanes and waxes. Sometimes you seem fine. Your noise sensitivity makes me very cautious around you, and somewhat protective of you. I also sometimes feel quite inhibited."

After a pleasant morning of writing and doing other homebound activities, sometimes I will crave human contact, so I venture out into one of the nearby small towns. Sometimes the interaction with people goes smoothly. But at other times a few sounds can touch me off, overwhelm me, and create a "Get me home!" feeling.

Among the sounds that can be particularly agitating to me are certain kinds of nervous laughter or giggling. Humor can be like a weapon or a cover-up. Giggling that seeks to conceal pain is disturbing. (I have a vague memory of being laughed at as a child.) Laughter can be so high-pitched that it is physically painful. Fortunately, I have also heard laughter that comes from real joy.

My former partner, a wonderful Japanese-American woman, does not make a lot of noise and has great containment. We've been apart for over a decade but continue to have a soulful connection. We separated mainly because she wanted children and I didn't. Children need to make noise, and I need not to be around too much noisemaking.

I also had the fear of having another Bliss boy and having him go to war. I wanted to break the Bliss legacy of sending men to war, which reaches back to 1776. Being a Southern fighting family, we were not always on the right side, defending slavery and fighting Mexicans and Native Americans. (Little did I realize that we would get to the point that we also send females to war.)

Most of the time I feel it was best for me not to have had children, especially since my father was not a good role model. But sometimes I wonder if this wasn't the biggest mistake of my life—to have been with a woman I loved who loved me and yet not to have taken the risk. Being childless in my sixties creates a certain lack of intimacy and loneliness, especially when I see a child of a friend or a child in a movie that I could imagine myself caring for. I do like being an uncle for the children of my brothers and sisters, and being called "Uncle" here in Hawai'i by my students and other young people. So I have expressed my generativity in other ways.

I do not remember much from being in the military during the Vietnam era, though I do remember that I did not engage in combat. I do not remember much from Chile, except that one of my closest American friends, Frank Terrugi, was tortured to death by the CIA-supported military after the September 11, 1973, coup. They call this loss of memory "psychic numbing." It can be protective. But sometimes something—often a sound—triggers me. I go to an uncomfortable place. But after years of counseling, rather than a flashback or disassociation, I tend to just go cold, chilly, distant, or numb. I've gotten better at managing these moments, though I try my best to avoid them.

Packing up to move from Hawai'i back to the mainland, I think over my life. I'm remembering the early years, and I'm mourning deaths. Moving is a kind of death. I had three wonderful years in Hawai'i. Now I am returning home—a better place to die, among my friends. I hope I'll live for many years in Sonoma County, a home where I belong.

I am mourning a friend, whose hospice Celebration of Life I just attended. I didn't make it to his memorial service, though. I pooped out. I remember my Mom's funeral, and my good friend Captain Ray

Gatchalian's. I got some measure of closure; they are still both with me. A reason I'm going back home is to honor my departing friends at their final events.

Being in the military can have a lot to do with death—like the little deaths of moving and the bigger deaths of watching people prepare to kill people, and yourself prepare to kill people. And killing and seeing killing.

Iraq. Though I try not to think about what is happening in Iraq too much, my mind goes there most days. I know what is happening there and feel it in my body and soul. It is not pretty. It is loud and ugly. Many Germans (like in *Miss Rose White*) said that they did not know what was happening in their own country to Jews, gypsies, gay people, and others. They should have known; they do not have a good excuse, in my opinion. Americans today should know. What are you going to tell your grandchildren or others when they ask what you did while America was torturing, wounding, and killing people in Iraq?

My wounds have taken much from me, but they have also become gifts that transformed me. I have made a life for myself in a natural setting with plants, animals, and rocks. I live in the country and cultivate solitude. I am drawn to work—writing and farming—that I can do alone away from "the madding crowd." Spending time with plants and animals, studying and appreciating them, and working with them has been a way for me to find peace and serenity. Some of my most creative, deep, and wonderful moments are spent in nature with the pleasant sounds of birds, insects, other animals, the wind and waves.

I love reading. Books give me peace and quiet, and inspiration. May Sarton's *Journal of Solitude* celebrates solitude and has helped me accept its benefits and rewards. I am drawn to authors who transform difficult lives into jewels that benefit others—Rilke, Kierkegaard, Dante. Byron Katie in *Loving What Is* teaches me that accepting the difficult can enhance one's life. Rainer Maria Rilke, who went to military school, refused his good friend Lou Andreas Salome's offer to get him into therapy with Freud. His fear was that if he dealt with his demons through counseling, his "angels," whom he wrote about often, would also leave. One's demons, indeed, are sometimes attended by angels.

It was a book that gave a name to my wound. I am HSP, a Highly Sensitive Person. Dr. Elaine Aron, in her book, *The Highly Sensitive Person: How to Thrive When the World Overwhelms You,* states: "Having a sensitive nervous system is normal, a basically neutral trait. You probably inherited it. It occurs in about 15-20 percent of the population. It means you are more easily overwhelmed when you have been out in a highly stimulating environment for too long, bombarded by sights and sounds until you are exhausted in a nervous-system sort of way." Some people are born HSPs; others become that way. Trauma can create stress, which can be triggered by many things, especially noise. People who were in combat or were yelled at as children are often especially sensitive to sound. Those of us who are part of military families often have post-traumatic stress, even if we did not continue the family tradition and go into the service.

When I get enough solitude, then contact with people can be especially meaningful.

I have participated in two communities that practice silence. I once lived in a monastery. The monks taught us to close doors quietly and even to eat quietly, so that we not bother other people's inner lives or distract them. Our Veterans Writers Group, which has its home in Sonoma County, values silence and meditation. There I learned that one can find solitude within a group. The long silences feed my soul. Writing, I transform the noise that can hurt me into poems and essays that communicate from within and possibly to others.

I like listening to pretty sounds, like the mourning doves, as I awaken. I like the way the wind takes up various dance partners—making the smaller blue verbena plants rustle, the palm tree fronds sound like harps, and the tall, thin 'ohi'a trees, now with their bright red lehua blossoms, move like hula dancers. Looking out my bedroom window here in Hawai'i, I see quiet, intense movement, and hear some sound.

Loving what is. Loving what is. Loving what is.

CARROLL PARROTT BLUE

The following story is from my book, *The Dawn at My Back: Memoir of a Black Texas Upbringing* (University of Texas Press). In 2004, the American Library Association selected *Dawn* as one of the thirty best American Association of University Press publications. *Dawn's* DVD-ROM won the 2004 Sundance Film Festival Jury Award, and I am now completing an interactive multimedia installation for Project Row Houses of Houston, Texas.

As a documentary filmmaker, I have won prizes for the following: *Dubai 2005, The Fern Street Circus, Mystery of the Senses: Vision, Nigerian Arts-Kindred Spirits, Conversations with Roy DeCarava, Varnette's World: A Story of a Young Artist,* and *Two Women.*

My recent work, *The Dubai Orlando Project,* was a virtual collaboration between media production students from University of Central Florida, USA and Dubai Women's College, U.A.E.

At the end of the war in Viet Nam, pro-American groups of Vietnamese, Cambodian, and Hmong relocated from Southeast Asia to the United States through Camp Pendleton, California. At the time, I was an aspiring photojournalist and asked a local San Diego newspaper for a press pass to photograph their arrival. Three days after the refugees landed, I photographed them throughout a makeshift tent city built by U.S. Marines on the base. Years later I discovered that because there is very little remaining documentation of this 1975 settlement and its participants, these images have historical value.

from *The Dawn at My Back: Memoir of a Black Texas Upbringing*

My mother and father had entirely different approaches to how they viewed films. My father didn't go to movies to look at them; he went to movies to hide inside them. He used films to distract himself from his problems. He did not discriminate between what was good and what was mediocre. So when I was with him, I saw everything that came during the 1950s from Hollywood to Houston's five or six Negro theaters. We seldom saw first-run films. This was because we couldn't go to white theaters. And why was that?

Well, Houston was a strange place. It was one of the most segregated cities in the South. There is a historical reason for this. Most people attributed the cause to Houston's 1917 Camp Logan incident. Camp Logan was Houston's first and last military base.

Black soldiers from the Twenty-fourth Infantry Regiment were assigned guard duty during the camp's construction. Much to white Houston's dismay, these men were not predictably meek Negroes. They were well-seasoned professional soldiers, and they had created a distinguished past for themselves.

In 1869, based on Black soldiers' valor and loyalty during the Civil War, Congress created four colored regiments: the Ninth and Tenth Cavalries and the Twenty-fourth and the Twenty-fifth Infantries. The Twenty-fourth is the oldest segregated unit in the U.S. military. Originally, the men who made up the Twenty-fourth Infantry fought in the Civil War. The unit lasted until it was officially disbanded in 1954, after the Korean War. The men of the Twenty-fourth Infantry were proud of their tradition as military pioneers and excellent soldiers.

Their first official assignment in 1869 in Texas and the Indian Territories lasted thirty years. At the time, even their Native American enemies honored them. The Plains Indians consider the buffalo sacred. Out of respect, they bestowed on the Black soldiers the title of "Buffalo Soldiers." In 1898, during the Spanish–American War in Cuba, the Twenty-fourth fought with distinction in the Santiago Campaign and alongside Theodore Roosevelt at San Juan Hill. Because of the success of these military campaigns, Roosevelt became a national hero and the president of the United States. But when he returned to the United States, he made the political decision to disparage the Black military contributions in the war in order to distance himself in his voters' eyes from African Americans. Between 1898 and 1915, the Twenty-fourth helped quell the Philippine Revolution. In 1916, they crossed the border with General John Pershing's Mexican Punitive Expedition in pursuit of Pancho Villa. Shortly after, in July 1917, they arrived in Houston, Texas, to pull guard duty during the construction of Camp Logan.

By this time, World War I had begun, and a few of the men had begun to look critically at their situation. Rejection, discrimination, contempt, and shabby treatment characterized the Black military existence. In 1868, after a year-long campaign against the Cheyenne, a dismayed Major John Bigelow described his men's situation as one in which "the colored men did all the fighting—sustained nearly all the casualties, and the white troops received the commendations." These soldiers first considered the enemy and then their employers, the United States military. Their enemy was colored; their employers were not. Although on opposing sides of the battlefield, both the soldiers and their enemies were fighting whites who were racist toward both foes. The soldiers' participation in the killing began to make less good sense.

The Black soldiers empathized with, befriended, and married their enemy. A few men even fought with this so-called enemy, first defecting in the Indian wars, then in Cuba, and later in the Philippines. In the Philippines, David Fagan was one Black U.S. soldier who taught the rebels how to fight his former army. When he began winning battles, he became a legend. The rebels rewarded him by naming him an officer in their army. The United States reacted by sending the Black units back home, where some of the Twenty-fourth Infantry Regiment ended up with General John Pershing in Mexico in 1916.

In July 1917, fresh from pursuing Pancho Villa, a 140-plus contingent of these men reported for guard duty during the construction of new camp in Houston, Texas. And in those days, Houston's whites were used to calling all Blacks "niggers." In turn, Houston's Blacks stayed "in their place." So Houston whites were not ready for these proud men.

Immediately, trouble started. At first, there were strong exchanges of cursing between the soldiers and local whites. These Black soldiers gave the whites back what they got. Then the men found themselves objects of abuse, insults, and beatings by Houston police and civilians. They were not the kind to roll over. Bitter street fights broke out when the soldiers continued to refuse to back down over any provocation, no matter how slight, by the whites.

In less than a month the Houston police, City Hall, and the all-white National Guard squared off against the all-Black Twenty-fourth regiment. Houston's white population resolved to break the very backs of these "niggers." The tensions intensified and exploded on August 23, 1917. In a furtive police chase of a Black male crap-shooting suspect, police wrongly entered the house of Mrs. Sara Travers, a respectable Black woman. Failing to find the suspect, one policeman slapped and arrested the woman, then forced her, partly clad, out into the street. In the uproar, Private Alonzo Edwards, a Black soldier in the crowd of onlookers, offered to pay her fine in exchange for her release. He too was beaten and arrested. In the words of one of the policemen: "I hit him until his heart got right. He was a good nigger when I got through with him."

Later, when Corporal Charles Baltimore, a Black military policeman performing his official duty, approached these same officers to inquire about Private Edwards's whereabouts, he was also beaten and arrested. In those days, Black people were not supposed to question *any* white under *any* circumstances.

Corporal Baltimore was a very popular soldier. Rapidly, the rumor flew through camp that the city policemen had beaten the two men to death. Hearing this, the Negro soldiers killed the white soldier guarding the arms and secured most of the base's guns, rifles, and ammunition.

Among the soldiers back at the camp, there was one highly respected leader, Sergeant Vida Henry, an eighteen-year veteran. He was a strong, fearless man who was known by reputation to take no prisoners in any battle.

Much later it was discovered that both soldiers were still alive. But by then it was too late. Sergeant Henry was leading the march into town, with the men shouting the slogan "On to the police station!" Over 140 armed and angry Black soldiers hurried into town, slaughtering anyone in their path who seemed to be a white official. With the killings, the march turned into a major revolt. Hordes of white men, upon hearing of the massacre, broke into gun shops, taking every available loaded weapon. Many whites mobbed the police headquarters, where they were hastily sworn in as deputies and given guns. These angry whites massed to attack the rebellious soldiers who were by this time moving through Houston's Fourth Ward, a Black part of town.

There the whites blocked off the area. Desperate, the soldiers regrouped in an empty ball field. They were surrounded. They had killed between seventeen and twenty whites, thirteen of them policemen. Their choice was elegantly simple. They could live long enough to be killed or they could die right then and there by their own hand. The core of loyal soldiers who had followed Sergeant Henry's lead that night chose to live. Henry was the only one to refuse. Regretfully, the group left him. As they walked into the night's darkness, one shot rang out. The sound of it pierced the men's hearts as they ran from the sounds of angry white voices moving closer.

At daybreak Sergeant Vida Henry was found cold, with the gun in his mouth and the back of his head blown to thick and bloody bits.

Chunks of his brain had fallen heavy beside his crumpled body. Rather than be taken, he had committed suicide.

Four months later, on November 30, 1917, 13 of 118 court-martialed men were sentenced to death. Subsequently, 19 of the soldiers were hung and 86 were jailed, some of whom were sentenced to life imprisonment. This trial remains the biggest and longest court-martial in U.S. military history. It is also the largest murder trial held to date in the United States. Its impact permanently changed both the military and the city of Houston.

On December 11, 1917, the day after the death sentence was read, thirteen men were awakened just before dawn. All of this—the trial, the hanging, and the burial—was done secretly. According to historian Robert V. Haynes's book *A Night of Violence: The Houston Riot of 1917,* it all ended in a secluded wooded area of scrubby mesquite trees. The men died along the bank of a narrow meandering creek choked with dense underbrush. This was a desolate, lonely spot on the banks of Salado Creek in Fort Sam Houston, some four miles east of San Antonio, Texas. The flickering light of bonfires illuminated a hastily built large wooden scaffold that held thirteen gallows hung above two large trapdoors on a twenty-four-by-eighteen-foot platform situated twelve feet above the ground. The bleak landscape appeared as streaks of daylight streamed through a blanketlike gray sky.

It was still and quiet. Spontaneously, a low guttural drone came from the doomed men's chests. The only eyewitness to write a description of the execution was a young white draftee, who wrote that he heard the men "droning a hymn, very low and soft." The only words he could make out were "I'm coming home, I'm coming home." In a sea of white men, there was one Black minister, there to give last rites. And yet, to the end, these Black soldiers never broke.

The force of these Black men's defiant voices singing a spiritual startled the 68 white onlookers. Then suddenly, it was again quiet. The nooses passed over the men's heads, quickly landing on their necks. In the heavy stillness that followed, the circles of rope tightened. The weight of the men's falling bodies made the strong cord squeeze up, snapping their necks. Their heads drooped sideways like fat, old wilted tulips, too heavy for their slender stems. It was an ugly death, made all the more terrible by the slow, agonizing pain, the bodily fluids oozing out. Tremors continued to rack the now lifeless bodies that swayed in the cold early morning air. The accumulations of many early morning frosts had made the ground's grass cover soggy and brown. The trees were stark and barren. It was, after all, winter in America.

Camp Pendleton, California
May 1975

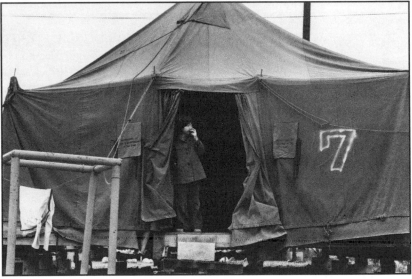

BONNIE BONNER

I am a native Northern Californian and graduated from the University of California at Berkeley. As a freelance writer and photographer, I contribute to such publications as: the *San Francisco Chronicle,* the *San Francisco Examiner Sunday Magazine,* the *Stockton Record, Rugby Magazine,* and *Poetry Flash.* Bonnie Bonner is the pen and maiden name for Joanne Palamountain, my stage and married name. When outdoors, I take pleasure in running, hiking, and snow skiing. When indoors, I paint botanical watercolors.

In 1968, I accompanied my late husband, Greg Palamountain, to military flight school and in 1969 to Korea, where he served as a helicopter pilot for the U.S. Army. Since then, I have traveled throughout Asia and have been writing about Vietnam with the Veterans Writing Group since 2000. A version of the following story, "For Soldiers Not Known," won the 1999 University of California Lilli Fabilli/ Eric Hoffer Essay Prize and is part of a novel in progress.

For Soldiers Not Known

In Hanoi near Hoan Kiem Lake, a barber shaves a man's neck with a blade that resembles a small machete. The barber's chair, ordinary and made of wood, flanks the outside of a cream-colored, moss-streaked, French colonial building. A small rectangular mirror hangs from a frangipani tree reflecting the face of a businessman, eyes closed in repose with a paper napkin cinched around his neck. Hundreds of bicycles and cyclos swirl noiselessly through the great wide boulevard, the quiet interrupted only by impatient motorbikes. The barber, switching on his miner's headlamp, bends looking intently into the businessman's ear. His industrious fingers twirl a long toothpick with a feather furball tip deep into the man's ear. His other bony hand holds a metal scoop the size of an ear canal.

A wrinkled man squats raggedly against the wall next to his rusty Sears & Roebuck foot scale. Check your weight. One *dong.* Two coins lie in a cracked porcelain bowl nearby.

At the corner a hardworking mother leans over her charcoal fired pho soup pot. She wears sandals and a conical hat tied beneath her jowls with a smudged pink ribbon. Perched on a six-inch teak footstool, she

39

cradles a babe in arms while a toddler seesaws over her knee, teasing a
scrawny puppy with a stick. The mother stuffs a bite of sticky rice into
her busy child's mouth, then ladles steamy pho into china bowls, handing one to each customer who waits squatting round her kettle. Into
every serving she tosses chopped greens, pungent garlic, red chilies;
she hands out chopsticks artfully folded in a paper napkin. Family,
friends, and neighbors slurp the comfort breakfast, bowls to mouths,
chopsticks clicking. They share jokes, gossip, and admonish the children with sharp words and gentle eyes. Smiles reveal betel nut–stained
teeth or no teeth at all.

Three white piglets ride silently to market caged tightly upon a
bicycle. Side by side they ride: head first, tail first, head first.

Around the corner a river of conical hats ripple through market
stalls. Chickens veer underfoot shackled to one another on the mud
track. Hanging upside down by webbed feet, ducks quack and flap
from a crooked woman's belt. One withered man peddles two-hundred-
year-old eggs. Six squatting women languidly slap the surface of six
tubs of water roiling with black fish, as water splashes over toes in
rubber sandals. Shuffling shoulder to shoulder amid the throng, an
overwhelming smell of fish seeps through the commotion. The snaggle-
toothed woman clenching a black cigar stub sells sugar crystals piled
in three-foot pyramids, alive with tunneling black ants. Bottles of coiled-
up snakes pickle in vinegar and skinned eels float in crimson water.
Baskets brimming brilliant with saffron illuminate an entire stall. Ten
cents a stem for fragrant ginger and lilies seems at once ridiculous and
fabulous.

I give the solicitous flower vendor, a woman younger than myself,
younger than the war, five one-dollar bills. "White flowers for the
Tomb of the Martyr please, *cam on nhew.*" With moistened brush, ink
block, and paper, the vendor deftly crafts characters in angular brush-
strokes. She fills my arms with lanky calla lilies and vanilla-scented ginger stalks, pressing a bouquet of joss incense sticks into my hand. "For
soldiers not known," she says, proffering the note looking directly into
my round blue eyes.

North Vietnam's Tomb of the Unknown Soldier stands in Ba Dinh
Square adjacent to the gray marble of Ho Chi Minh's mausoleum. The
red flag with its yellow star flaps in my peripheral vision while guards
scrutinize the scene.

My friend's request: "One day I'd like to lay flowers at Hanoi's NVA Memorial in all honor and respect." I am still trying to make sense of it twenty years later. Why North Vietnam? I light the joss sticks and swirl them in the air, struggling to recall what he had said: *Such a beautiful country . . . I'll never forget the children with their wide smiles . . . and the bodies littering the firebase like timber . . . my doing . . . tired and wet and knee-deep in NVA . . . children as soldiers thrown together . . . defending our countries . . . knocking at the unknown . . . my job was to kill . . . our duty . . . stop the capacity and will to wage war . . . hundreds of missions . . . before you know it, you're either dead or going home . . . longing to sleep deep as a child.*

On my knees I begin to understand. I am imagining forgiveness for all of the soldiers. I am like the women knee-deep in rice paddies still watching for their men to come home.

NANCY SUE BRINK

I was first invited to the Veterans Writers Group while working on a film about dog tags and was welcomed for all that I am—documentary filmmaker, writer, activist, and lover of birds, wilderness, good stories. I grew up during the Vietnam War and when I heard the courage of the veterans' voices—the depth of their stories, the risks they take in telling those stories—I had to ask myself, "If they can do that, what do *I* have to be afraid of? What stories do I need to tell?" The people in this group helped me find the courage to write without fear.

Some things that are important to me: My exceptional family and friends. My small independent film and video company, Present Tense Productions. Hiking in the mountains. Working with the Golden Gate Raptor Observatory, monitoring migrating hawks and falcons. (I take exception to the hawk–war metaphor.) Being a member of a Friends meeting (Quakers). Teaching filmmaking and writing to young people, with the hope that they will tell their stories and break open the heart of the world.

The Saturday after the Iraq War started in March 2003, I traveled to Sebastopol to join my friends in the Veteran Writers Group. The raw despair I felt about the war starting, about our inability to thwart the violent momentum of the Bush administration, took form in "The Night the War Begins in Iraq, We're Learning CPR."

"Wintering Cranes in the San Joaquin Valley" reflects for me another profound aspect of days spent with the group, writing and meditating: the search for healing and peace—not only for ourselves, but for as many as we can touch through our activities. On those days, we share with each other the beauty of a changing garden, walks through a eucalyptus grove, the seasons of birds, the California hills—the complex and intricately balanced relationships of the natural world—for me, the source of peace.

The Night the War Begins in Iraq, We're Learning CPR

We pull out the dummies.
A dozen people compress
and breathe, mannequins
scattered, gray and blue.
Begin CPR:
        fifteen compressions—
        two rescue breaths—
        fifteen compressions—
        two rescue breaths—
        one minute, check
        for signs of life—

We pull out infants,
plastic dolls with
accordion hearts.
Just two fingers
in the middle of the chest:
        five quick compressions,
        one rescue breath—
        one minute, check
        for signs of life—
repeat and repeat,
be sure we know
just what to do,
and as we repeat
the bombers begin
to fly overhead—repeat
and repeat, and as we
compress, the plastic infants
begin to breathe—
                        crackling
breath—like radio voices in the car,
war—

and the plastic infants begin to breathe:

They'll be dying on streets
in Baghdad, this time, they'll
cry with sirens and wailing
bombs, with night flayed open
by venomous light.

They'll be dying in diapers,
dying in rags, babies
in uniform, dressed for prayer, resting
in baptismal pools of blood, cradled
in fires that eat all truth—

      Merciless War, take your hands
      off those babies, let us breathe them
      back to life, let us turn their hard gray cheeks
      to pink—
               Merciful War, reach instead
      to grab the men who bless their babies
      off to kill, drag them here and make them
      see the blood that's running,
      make them hold the mothers
      who try to love their babies
      back from death, make them help that father
      find his child's leg, make them
      walk the streets
      between the bombs—

one rescue breath—
compress and breathe—
one rescue breath, I kneel
with babies, blue
and gray. We gather up
bodies, pack up
mannequins, bombs
begin to fall.

Wintering Cranes in the San Joaquin Valley

Sandhill cranes fly in against sunset,
I hear them rattling before they're more
than dotted lines oozing from clouds.

I sit on the hood of my car, lean back
to the windshield, heat of a turned-off engine
fading against my legs. I consider time, the way
it stops at sunset, the way it stopped just now, for just
a few seconds when the cranes appeared.
I think about silence at the edge
of a dirt road at the edge of a marsh,
which isn't silence at all. Marshwater,
greedy for light, pulls color
down from sky.

Sandhill cranes, their long great undulating wings
cupped back, slow themselves, stretch out their legs
and land. They dance and settle, dance again. This place
of water and cut cornfields is home, for now. Tonight,
they will come in strings of three or twenty, dance
settle, dance,

this is one of those edges
between dusk and night that forces your body open, almost
like longing for a love who isn't there, who may or may not
come back. This moment
will pass. Or you could choose to stay.

Fields just half a mile away are covered end to end
with snow geese. Their chatter
beds the creak and rattle and purr of cranes.

I tilt back my head. Nine sandhill cranes flap
ten feet above me, necks stretched out, bald heads
flickering red, redder than sky darkening
above the intercoastal range. Clouds embrace peaks,
as if in solace for all that mountains have witnessed, all
that could still be lost on these grass-bound plains
here, below.

Red-winged blackbirds, black-necked stilts, white-faced ibis rise
and pepper the sky. Sandhill cranes keep flying in, calling
to each other. I'd like to pretend they're calling me,
but I'm simply in the way
of evolution, thousands of years
of migration.

I slide off the car, take three steps toward water. I want
more than I am owed by this world of water and light,
of ancient birds, who each year claim their histories,
overcoming human intervention
with consistent flight.

I bend down, touch water, stand.
My feet are planting themselves in muck.
From not too far away, all the snow geese in my whole world
rise up, all at once, thousands thousands thousands
swirling in black silhouette. They move together, loud
and slowly toward the marsh. I hear nothing
but squawking geese, creaking cranes, the wildness
working its way out to the edge of my now
living body. They all come together, here, over my head,
over my arms, which have stretched themselves up and out,
dissolving in flight.

I was born in Bozeman, Montana, in 1918. After my father was shot to death, my mother married Rich Gex, a Basque cowboy. A Montana boyhood among cowboys, Indians, ranchers, rodeo hands, remittance men, gamblers, and survivors was her gift to me. Rich Gex raised me to ride horses, learn cowboy jobs and rules. In 1940, I graduated in literature and journalism from the University of Washington and took a job as a farmhand so I could write at night.

In World War II, I was commissioned directly from civil life as ensign, USNR. I volunteered for armed guard duty commanding a USN gun crew on armed Liberty ships and merchantmen in all three theaters of war. In 1945, I became an operations officer on the staff of Admiral Frank Jack Fletcher, Commander in Chief, Western Sea Frontier. After World War II, I moved to San Francisco, where I played roles with The Actors' Workshop. I was emcee on KPIX's *Art in Your Life* and KQED's *Discovery*. Also at this time I was enrolled in the San Francisco Conservatory of Music, and sang and acted in the San Francisco Opera Company, the Pacific Opera Company, and the San Francisco Little Symphony. During these years, 1950 to 1980, I also worked as a painter, exhibited in one-man shows at the de Young Museum, Seattle Art Museum, Phoenix Art Museum, Bennington College, and Cambridge University. I published poems in *Poetry* and had a story in *Best American Short Stories*.

In 1946, I married Mary Elisabeth Watts, of Seattle, Washington. She is mother of Shuah and Luke Brotherton. In 1982, I married Nam Kyong Hye, of Seoul, Korea. We lived in Kyoto, where I worked as a painter, studied Japanese art, and lectured at The Japan Foundation. In 1999, after a brief residence with Kyong Hye's family in Seoul, we returned to San Francisco.

Voyages of the SS Joshua Hendy

During our voyage from Capetown, South Africa, to Montevideo, Uruguay, we were escorted by a pair of dolphins cavorting acrobatically in and out of our bow wave. We were also blessed (or maybe cursed, like the Ancient Mariner) by a guardian albatross, ghostly white under the black heavens, his wingspan about twelve feet, soaring directly above us, motionless, held aloft by the updraft from the steadily fuming

stack. With us each night, by sunup he'd be gone. On encounters at
dawn and dusk, I thought I saw him crook his head, his beady black
eyes watching as I saluted him.

At 0400 hours, we arrived at Montevideo, the first metropolitan
port outside a war zone we had visited in nearly a year. "You don't
stare, you don't leer, you don't even glance at these *señoriters!*" the chief
warrant officer hollered at the gunners' drowsy but impatient heads.
"You hear what I'm saying? Keep your eyes front! This here is a Latin
country and you simple-minded peckerwoods have got no more notion
than a goony bird how careful these ladies are protected from the rude
stares of strangers, meaning anybody in long pants—meaning especially you woman-crazed sailor boys from Uncle Sam's Navy. You can
get yourselves shot at, get a knife stuck between your ribs by her
boyfriend, spend a year in the brig if she complains to the shore patrol.
For your own protection, I'm warning you—don't ever forget the first
order of the day on liberty in this port. Eyes Front!"

Later that morning, when I stepped ashore from the bumboat to
deliver my voyage report to the U.S. Naval Attaché, I was greeted by
one of these sheltered *señoriters,* one of the Medusas whose glance the
chief had warned us to avoid.

"Where is the fire?" she cried, taking my arm. "Let us rent a room
in that beautiful hotel, where we will become better acquainted!" She
pointed at a lowdown building not far up the street. I tried not to leer
at her, keeping the international insult and provocation of my gaze
fixed on the shabby hotel she proposed for the scene of our revels.

"Doggone the luck!" I exclaimed. "Ma'am, the admiral is waiting!
Forgive me!" I risked a glance. Although it was nigh onto 0900 hours,
she was wearing a stunning cocktail outfit: a picture hat, classic black
dress, pearls, and stiletto heels. Poor thing. Be careful, lootent! The
admiral is waiting, delegated far down the line. So stanch your bleeding heart.

She smiled. In excellent, colloquial English, using precise language
to describe the gyrations and juxtapositions she foresaw in the process
of our becoming better acquainted, she began to pant. "You are gurr-
juss!"—evidently an oft-croaked refrain in the many languages her
profession demanded. Devotedly, we pledged to meet outside her
shabby *palacio* at noon by the cathedral chime—an assignation which
somehow I knew both of us would forget. As we spoke, her eyes

appraised the other sailors debarking at the bumboat landing. I couldn't help but notice a bevy of cosseted Latin heroines in various man-killing costumes gathered at the landing or patrolling the street alongside the *Aduana.* I wished them well, observing the handful of jack tars slouching ashore from vessels of various registries. I wondered if the warrant officer from the Embassy had been a comedian or an impostor.

In the naval attaché's corner of the U.S. Embassy basement, I came face-to-face with another *señoriter,* this woman younger, blond, and spectacularly handsome, wearing headphones at the switchboard.

"Miss, your name wouldn't be Polly, by any chance?"

She stared at me with an expression I found hard to decipher. Adoring? Disdainful? Lustful? Then I realized, *"No habla Inglés?"*

"Polly, as in polylingual?" Still no response. Too bad. I'd meant to compliment her command of Spanish, Portuguese, German, all of which she seemed to speak at a full colloquial gallop, without a hitch. Except *Inglés?*

At that moment, the yeoman summoned me into the attaché's august presence, and I had to delay my foundering flirtation with the switchboard damsel.

Next morning, I arrived at the Embassy at 1000 hours, having commandeered Joel Marquez, Gunner's Mate, Third Class, to come as translator. There she was again, wearing earphones clamped around her pretty head.

"Marquez, ask the *señorita* if she would like to have lunch with me."

The gunner's mate stepped forward, holding his cap over his heart, placing one foot before the other in proper oratorical style. *"Señorita, el Señor Teniente . . ."*

I listened with satisfaction, catching phrases of a flowery elaboration of my simple request. At last, the gunner backed off center stage and put on his cap.

The girl smiled at him. "Guns," she said, "please tell the lieutenant that I can't have lunch with him today. I have to man the board here, to my regret. Ask him if I can redeem myself in his good books by inviting him to dinner this evening."

"You really are polylingual!" I replied. "English, Spanish, German, Portagee . . ."

". . . French, Italian, and Russian," she finished my sentence.

"I'd love to have dinner with you. On me, *Señorita.*"

"Shall we meet outside the Embassy gate at 1700 hours?"

"On the dot! I'll be waiting! Come along, Marquez."

I was elated. I thumped Marquez on the shoulder. "*Muchas gracias,* Guns," I bellowed. "You were terrific! Here, boost a few beers on me this evening."

Marquez put up his hands. "Turns out you didn't need me, lieutenant. I didn't do anything. You keep it."

"Man, you earned it! You were my luck." I watched him head up the street, away from the crowds downtown.

Then a terrible realization darkened the daylight for me. I'd expected to take a switchboard girl to lunch. I'd worn khakis, my clean fatigue uniform. My dress blues were rolled up in my sea bag, not even pressed. I'd have to zip back to the ship, change clothes, hustle back ashore, find a tailor to fumigate and press my blues—all by 1700.

In the water taxi en route to the ship, I had a notion that shivered my timbers. I'd never worn my summer whites. Another notion came to me. Gunner's Mate Third Class Harmon J. Gruber had served two hitches in the U.S. Navy before Pearl Harbor. His deck of fruit salad (service ribbons) was the pin-on kind. And he had the watch till 1600 hours.

"Gruber!" I pounded on his door and shoved it open. Sitting on his bunk with just a pair of skivvies, Gruber made feeble motions to upright himself. "In the name of God, at ease."

"Listen. Are you headed ashore after your watch this evening?"

"No, sir. I got the evening watch too. I traded duty with . . ."

"Okay, Guns. I got an important favor to ask you. Gruber, I remember seeing you headed for the beach in Karachi with General MacArthur's own sunrise array of campaign ribbons decorating your blouse. My question is, I'd like to borrow the entire fruit salad for tonight, so long as you're stayin' aboard. They pin on, right?"

"Yes, sir. They pin on real good. I'd be glad to lend 'em to you, Lootent Brotherington, sir. But they ain't mine. I reckon Flags has got himself about three dozen different assortments of them ribbons. You know he rents them to guys goin' ashore."

"Just my luck! Flags is on liberty today."

"Sir, I still got his ribbons pinned on my blouse. Lootent, I got to rent you them ribbons. No other way . . ."

"How many *pesetas?*"

"Buck a row, sir."

"How many rows has Flags got, in the name of God?"

"At least six, sir. I got three pinned onto my blouse."

"Okay, Gruber, tonight I step ashore with all three rows of your ribbons stuck on my whites. Cash on the barrelhead!"

When I arrived at the Embassy gate, the switchboard enchantress was already there. She kept her composure at the sight of me in my whites, slipped her hand companionably under my elbow, and steered me over to the bus stop.

"Now we must take a long bus ride. I should have asked you to come earlier. There are never any seats this late."

"Do you speak all languages this flawlessly?"

"Thank you. English is my native tongue."

She leaned on the strap and closed her eyes. Along the route she appeared to sleep standing up, hanging on, swaying gracefully with the gyrations of the bus. None of the courtly Spaniards or gallant Montevideanos stood up to offer her his seat. After an hour, I noticed that the bus, now nearly empty, skimmed along a broad floral thoroughfare of enormous villas surrounded by gardens. Still she snoozed, now seated on a bench, swaying against me. What was her name? Where was she taking me? Finally, we were the only passengers on the bus and she awoke, gripped my arm, led me to the largest villa of all the palaces beside the river.

"To the earthly Paradise!" I shouted.

She held my arm and rang the chimes. Both the mighty doors opened, and we were greeted by an unfriendly looking butler. "Good evening, Miss Andrea," he said.

As we entered, the intimate clamor of a festive gathering rose from the sunken living room.

Courage! I told myself.

"What are we celebrating tonight?" she asked the butler.

"Argentina declared war on the Axis today," he replied.

We entered the crowded room. "Ladies and gentlemen," she said. "Allow me to introduce Lieutenant Joseph Brotherton, Gunnery Officer on a U.S. flag merchant vessel." Several people raised a glass and then carried on with their drinking, smoking, and chattering, snatching canapés offered by housemaids.

"Who are the guests?" I asked her.

"Refugees from across the river, mostly former ministers of the Argentine government who opposed Perón's concordat with Hitler. Now they're hoping to be invited home as a symbol of the rapprochement with the Allies."

"All of them—everybody here, except yourself and His Excellency, your father, is a native speaker of Spanish, Portagee, Italian, or French, right?"

"Now that you mention it, yes. Why do you ask?"

"Then why are they all speaking English."

"Because one of our gallant fighting men is present."

"I can't imagine a gathering in the States where everyone would shift to Spanish the moment a Uruguayan sailor boy stuck his nose in the door."

"It's the diplomatist's faculty. Given a choice, I think I have more respect for the skills you bring to the table."

She smiled at me and put her hand on mine. "I'm afraid I owe you an apology, Lieutenant. If I'd known about this gathering, I would have suggested we go to one of the cafés downtown for a steak. But I am impressed by your prescience, wearing your whites! Papa must be green with envy. You're clearly the best-dressed man."

"Tell me about the house."

"It's the ambassadorial r-r-r-esidence," she shrugged. "In a country like Uruguay"—she squeezed my hand—"I hope you'll muzzle the firebrand when you have a word with Papa."

Of course she'd heard all my schoolboy objurgations—Perón, poverty, disorder, *descamisados* . . .

"Good luck, Lieutenant." She let go of my hand. "Now I must change for supper. If you please, bend down and kiss me, once for your safety and again for good fortune on the longer journey."

Clumsily, I leaned toward her and kissed her once on her cheek and again, chaotically, on her chin. "Like that?" I asked.

"Hush." She put her finger to my lips. "Don't say another word. I must go upstairs and change. I'll be down before supper. Please talk to my father. He is glaring at us."

Her father led me to a vacant corner of the room. To learn my intentions toward his daughter?

"Have you any idea where you're headed next, Lieutenant?"

"We're never supposed to know until the routing conference. But I'm harboring a strong suspicion."

"Which harbor is that?"

"Should I discuss it with you, sir? It's supposed to be classified."

"I'm familiar with your routing, Mister."

"Then let me guess. I think the *Hendy* is scheduled to pick up a cargo and head back into the war zone—West Africa, Morocco, Sicily. I can't imagine sending her all the way back to the States from here without a cargo."

"A hundred rounds for the four-inch fifty gun?"

"If you can spare them. I'm really impressed! You do look at the requisitions!"

"Of course I do. Why should you be surprised? It's what I'm paid to do. So tell me, why so many rounds for the main battery?"

"Ah, that sounds so impressive! Sir, after the last voyage, the shot locker is fairly well depleted."

"You were in action?"

"Oh, aye. Or at least the ship's master seems to think so. He insists that we were under attack twice—once by a raider, a Q-boat. Again by a submarine."

"You don't agree?"

"Well, sir, I have my doubts. But the Merchant Marine skipper is an ex-Navy three-striper, and who am I to contradict him? I believe all we did was discourage another merchantman who played chicken with us on a closing course longer than she should have. So we fired off several rounds in an easterly direction, being careful not to shoot across her bow. The U-boat I suspect was a fisherman off course—too far north of the fishing grounds off Tierra del Fuego, if there are fishing grounds off Tierra del Fuego. But I can't imagine why a submarine would venture into those waters."

"I can, easily. Until today's turnabout, Nazi submarines used Argentine seaports openly—stores, refitting, shore leave. You could easily have crossed one of them. I should think your routing instructions would have included this. Are you going to claim the submarine?"

"I don't know, sir. But I doubt if we came within a country mile."

"How did you happen to turn up as gunnery officer on a merchantman?"

"I'm Montana-born, sir. I had to get out and see the world. So I put in for the Armed Guard."

"I must say, I envy you your home country. I'd like nothing better than to end my days fishing trout in the Gallatin River."

"Sir, could you excuse me for a moment?" He pointed the way.

In the bathroom, I stumbled across a low, alien device new to my experience. The frog-shaped gold-plated spigots around the brim appeared to have been calibrated to jet six sprays in a pretty figure of falling arches intersecting several feet above the floor—truly an elegant conceit, no doubt a comfort on the hottest days. A *bidet!* That's what it must be! The first I'd ever seen.

As I stooped to inspect the mechanism, my heavy black brogan trod the floor pedal, and six sparkling jets raked me amidships. The geyser spouted high, sousing the target where he stooped. Bull's-eye!

I shook spray in haloes off my head, squishing and slopping across to the cool mirror. I saluted. "Mister Brothering-Brothelton, sir! The damage report if you please." I snarled at the tenant of the mirror as the water dripped and the reds, blues, and greens ran over my heart.

"Look at what's become of the confidant of ambassadors, the dinner companion of the beautiful Miss Andrea." If I'd had a gun, or a stone, even a dry shoe, I'd have smashed the mirror and the ridiculous image it reflected. "Front and center, Mister! Face the music!" Guiltily, gently as a felon, I cracked open the bathroom door, tiptoed out onto the platform a few feet above the level of the living room, a theater stage. I entered into one of those silences that follow now and then when the conversation lapses and the room falls still. In the hush, a new cynosure captures every eye.

The apparition facing the celebrants was wearing a clown's drenched motley—his uniform melted, the signalman's bold ribbons bled rainbows down the sodden tunic. Then the laughter began, discreetly at first, then full-bellied, gusty guffawing. Had the silly damn fool never seen a bidet before? I moved quickly around the raised platform to the French doors, jogged down the patio steps, crossed the shimmering lawn, and started to run. Breathing hard to the rhythm of my lumbering strides, I grunted "oaf," "lummox," "out of my depth." I ran faster, took a second wind, and my strides seemed to go more lightly. "Not running away," I panted. "Not escaping anything. Toward something!

Running toward youth, the fulfillment of promise toward the treasure and ecstasy of the world!"

I raised my fist high and leapt after it, feeling somehow as though I were racing to the bridge, racing to fire the guns in jubilation. "You lucky oaf! You clumsy blundering lummox! She kissed you, that sly bewitching switchboard goddess. She kissed you for good luck along the road you must travel!"

"I survived!" I bellowed. "Joseph Brotherington reporting! To the world and all its wealth and adventures! Reporting for duty! Gangway! Look lively! Clear the decks!"

Soon the bus overtook me and I climbed aboard, quite wet behind the ears.

I served in Episode I of the Gulf War as a Marine jet engine mechanic on Harriers. I helped our jets successfully drop more than two million pounds of ordnance, which killed thousands of people.

I don't need an alibi. I'm here to confess. I did it. I'm on the run from my own life. I ride on caffeine and fumes. I'm on the run from the Marines, from the charred bodies of young men, children, and women. Maxine and the other veterans of our workshop have given me the strength to stop running and begin healing. I found other veterans and people who understood the horrible tragedy and grief that war causes. I know now, as many Vietnam veterans have learned, that I will never be fully whole until I revisit Iraq and make peace with the people I once falsely believed were my enemies. I long for that day.

My prose poems, "Dear Commander in Chief," "Easter," and "Spin Drift," are fragments from my first novel, *Shrapnel,* which is a story about the weight of guilt, the levity of grace, and a soldier who struggles to make peace with the fragments of his past and finds his way home on America's black velvet highways. These poems are evidences of my distrust and disbelief in war as an option, as well as expressions of my personal experiences during and after Gulf War I.

Dear Commander in Chief

At an early age, our likenesses were taken prisoner at the last desert outpost called Iraq. Afterward, we were unrecognizable. We were young men on a mission, though we were never sure it was more than shooting gallery practice. And we have to admit, Sir, thanks to your commitment to technology, we had the best guns money can buy. We're sure they saved our hides more than once.

We boys are grateful for any semblance of our former lives, which is why we are writing to you now. We like waking at 3 A.M. with night sweats, or in the morning, discovering the left side of our face has gone numb; it makes us appreciate being alive. It's what Sartre meant when he said: *Existence is what I am afraid of.*

We've even got a pool going. We call it the Mystery Illness of the Day. All us guys at the VA Hospital cast our bets for what illness will surface next: strange red rash covering the right side of the groin and waist, a three-day migraine binge, involuntary muscle spasms and ticks, temporary loss of hearing in either ear (betting on the correct ear doubles down the bet and winnings).

Thank you, Mr. President, in your recent address to the American people, thank you for reminding us that signing our names on the dotted line meant we were indentured servants; we're sure you meant that in the best way. Us boys appreciate your honesty. Your Organization is doing a good job at whatever it is you do. Could you put in a good word for us with Beelzebub? We think he was pleased with our handiwork in the Gulf War, but it's been a long time since we've seen any action. You know how it goes: it doesn't hurt to have friends in the business.

We've sent you many letters over the years and invited you to countless parties. We've been looking forward to your response, but we're confident pressing business keeps you very busy and prevents you from writing. Thank you for your consideration and interest. Keep fighting the good fight.

Easter

On Easter, the girls dressed up in white hats with pink chiffon ribbons, pretty dresses with daisies and sunflowers, and us boys with new patent-leather shoes and freshly starched ironed shirts and off to church we would go and after come home to look for our Easter baskets with the sun still shining and father and mother there on the porch looking on and laughing. What good times. I hope God will bring me home so I can hunt for eggs in the field behind our barn, listen to the low short whistles of screech owls as they dive after mice while fireflies weave and bob like Lilliputian lanterns. But here there's only the high-pitched whine of sand flies in my ears, the twenty miles of switchbacks to hump before sundown, and we have to make the northern hill and no one knows why but when; it's Easter and we don't have any eggs but plenty of grenades, no white hats but Kevlar helmets, and no starched shirts but flak jackets. At night on the perimeter, when the rain clears and light from the moon shines across a field, I listen for low short whistles and the skitter of field mice across my boots, and watch for the phosphorescent glow of tracer fire streak red and orange through frozen air, like spring bonfires with winter wood, or lie prone in the mud, marking time, with nothing to do but wait for the sun.

Spin Drift

Take us the foxes, the little foxes,
that spoil the vines:
for our vines have tender grapes.
—SONG OF SOLOMON 2:15

Garrett sat on his bunk with an M16A2 rifle in his lap. The canvas door to his hooch flapped in the slow desert breeze. He had broken his foot a week ago while loading cluster bombs with the ordnance crew. The other men in his unit were away on exercises in the open desert ranges of Twenty-Nine Palms, and he was left to clean rifles.

He broke down the rifle with ease, dropped out the magazine, pulled back the bolt, locked it, and checked the chamber for rounds. He pulled out the take-down pin and wedged both hands around the slip ring and removed the hand guards.

Garrett knew the rifle's maximum effective distance is 550 yards for a point target, and at the 500-yard line the target looked like a small black gnat. Firing any distance greater than 500 yards required compensation for the force of gravity on a spinning bullet, known as spin drift. But Garrett wouldn't need to compensate, not at this range. He knew that the rifle weighed 8.79 pounds with a 30-round magazine and its cyclic rate-of-fire is 800 rounds per minute and after he pulled the trigger, the ball round would exit the chamber with a muzzle velocity of 3,100 feet per second. At close range a body provided little resistance to the two-and-a-half-inch bullet.

He separated the upper receiver from the lower and pulled out the charging handle and bolt. He lifted the barrel up to the light and inspected the bore. Through the barrel, everything shrunk. At its end, moths looked like dust specks hovering around the dirty halo of a distant and terrible sun. The bore was clear and clean. He reassembled the rifle, pulled back the charging handle and bolt, and released. The bullet shot forward in the chamber; the action was smooth. He sighted in and took aim at shadows.

One winter, when he was ten, Garrett and his father followed the tracks of a fox in the snow beyond their pasture and into the woods. They found the den just across Naaman's Creek near the dam Garrett had built for a swimming hole the previous summer. It was frozen over. They watched quietly as the mother poked out of the den, sniffed the air, and tilted her head as she looked at them. His father gave the order, Garrett raised his rifle, and the last thing he remembered, after he squeezed the trigger, was the fox's clear yellow eyes looking at him. She never blinked.

JIM CASTELLANOS

My military service began at Marine Corps Recruit Depot, San Diego, on August 13, 2001. Following boot camp, I started Marine combat training at the Camp Pendleton School of Infantry and subsequently trained as an aviation ordnance systems technician at the Naval Air Technical Training Center in Pensacola, Florida. I then trained at the Naval Air Maintenance Training Marine Unit in Cherry Point, North Carolina, where I specialized in helicopter weapons systems. Upon completing my training, I arrived at my permanent duty station, Marine Light Attack Helicopter Squadron 775, a UH-1 Huey and AH-1 Cobra helicopter squadron at Camp Pendleton, California. Since I was enlisted as a Marine reservist, I was immediately discharged from active duty and put on reserve status, which enabled me to begin academic studies at the University of La Verne in California. I completed only one semester before being activated from the reserves and deploying to Al Asad, Iraq, for a seven-month combat tour in support of Operation Iraqi Freedom. The following passage describes the events that prompted a two-year conscientious objector investigation by the Marine Corps.

Voluntary Disarmament in Iraq

July 24, 2004
Operation Iraqi Freedom, Al Asad, Iraq

Five months had passed since I first arrived in the Iraq combat theater and, as the weeks slowly blurred together, I felt more and more out of place among my fellow Marines. There were Marines from all walks of American life, from the backwoods of Virginia to the Louisiana bayous to the easygoing California beaches, yet I managed to feel uneasy among all of them. My lack of ease wasn't because of the vast diversity of socioeconomic backgrounds or political views. It was my conscience that kept me distanced.

I was sitting in an abandoned Iraqi one-story building, often called the "head shed" because it functioned as our headquarters, and could see Gunner Robins, a tall, balding Southerner who had attained the rank of warrant officer during twenty years of service. He was typing away at his laptop computer with his back toward me as I approached.

"Excuse me, Sir?" I asked nervously, standing at attention.

"Yes, Devil Dog," he answered in his South Carolina drawl.

"May I speak to you, Sir?" my voice faded off, uncertain, insecure.

"Yes, of course," he replied. He quickly finished his typing and turned around.

"What is it you want to speak about?" he asked.

"Well, Sir . . . I was wondering . . . if . . ." I discreetly rubbed my sweaty palms behind my back. "I hoped I could . . . go see the chaplain tomorrow?" I muttered.

A deafening silence overpowered the room. The gunner sensed there was something wrong. He sat quietly for a few seconds before answering.

"Yes, of course," he said, a puzzled look on his face. "I will have someone take you in the morning."

"Thank you, Sir."

I turned around and walked back to the break room across the hall, sat down on a cot, and began to think about our conversation. I wanted to smile, but I knew I had just raised a warning flag. I knew that someone would approach me tomorrow—either the warrant officer or another staff Marine—and inquire about my trip to the chaplain's office. Marines tend to look down on anyone who uses the chaplain's services. To them, seeking the chaplain's counsel is a form of weakness, a type of disability that threatens their Marine egos. I just hoped the chaplain could provide some guidance and insight in dealing with my ethical dilemma.

The next morning began like any other morning at Al Asad. The day crew, the Marines who work from 0600 to 1800, came in at their usual time and dispersed into working groups. Since I had an appointment with the chaplain, I had to sit around and wait until another Marine could drive me to mainside.

At 0900, after three hours of waiting, a Humvee picked me up at the ammunition supply point and drove me across the base to see the chaplain. His office was located at the headquarters for Marine Aviation Logistical Squadron 16. The building entrance was heavily fortified, and to reach the door, I had to walk through a winding pathway of sandbags. The chaplain was at his desk.

"Lance Corporal Castellanos?" he asked.

"Yes, Sir," I replied.

"Come in and have a seat."

The chaplain was a short, sunburned Vietnamese man with a strong accent and dark sunken eyes. On his chest, he wore various ribbons and decorations. On one collar was a silver oak leaf indicating the rank of naval commander, and on the other was a golden cross, designating that he was a chaplain.

"How may I help you today?"

"Well, Sir," I answered, "I'm not sure how to bring this up or even if you're the right person to talk to, but I've been having some problems on this deployment."

"Oh, what kinds of problems?" he asked curiously.

"Well, Sir. . ." I took a deep breath and began, "I've been in the Marine Corps for two years now, mostly on reserve status, and over these past two years . . . well . . . a lot of things in my life have changed. I enlisted when I was a senior in high school . . . I was only seventeen years old . . . and . . . well . . . I enlisted because I genuinely wanted to serve America and my community. At that time, the Marine Corps meant the world to me . . ."

I was uneasy, and my sentences were short and fragmented—I continued, "When I completed my training, I wanted to begin college and one day become a Marine officer . . . and . . . well . . . once I did start school I met students from different backgrounds . . . with different cultures . . . and with different viewpoints on the world. I began to realize that my training as a Marine was unique, but also narrow-minded. Boot camp had conditioned us to be machines, to not think or analyze independently, to follow orders without questioning, and to take tremendous pride in our Marine traditions."

Nervously, I shifted in my seat. I knew my words would not be taken lightly. The chaplain sat quietly without saying a word. My body was growing warmer, my palms drenched with sweat.

"Well, Sir, the more I interacted with my peers and the more educated I became, the more I began to question my Marine values and training. Then I realized why boot camp is structured the way it is . . . why our training is filled with psychological conditioning. Sir, I once strongly believed in these Marine values, but now I don't know if I can wear this uniform and take pride in myself. Education has opened my eyes to a new way of thinking and to new values . . ." I wanted to stop, but I knew it was too late. "Sir, every day I wake up and have to carry this rifle and a hundred fifty rounds of ammunition everywhere

I go. I don't take pride in myself or the job I am doing. I now live by different morals and values . . . I don't believe in shooting or killing anyone . . . I don't believe in waging war against another human being . . . I don't believe in carrying this weapon anymore . . . I've changed a lot in these past two years, and I don't think I can continue wearing this uniform. Sir, I want to be true to myself, and live by the values . . ."

"So if someone tried to kill you, you wouldn't kill them first?" he shouted, his interruption startling me.

"Sir, what I am trying to say is that I've changed and I don't . . ."

"So you wouldn't kill them?"

"Sir . . . I don't know what I would do," I mumbled.

"Are you stupid?" he reiterated. *"If someone tried to kill you, you wouldn't shoot them? So you would let them kill you?"*

"Sir, I don't think war or killing is the answer to solving problems. I don't plan on killing anyone because I don't believe we should settle our differences by killing one another. I've embraced different values now. I didn't ask to change. It just happened."

"You're stupid! You don't know anything!" His broken English and strong accent became more apparent. *"You are young and you don't know what you are doing. If you don't believe in it, then finish your tour and get out! We don't need people like you in the Marines!"*

For the first time I agreed with something he said. I could tell that he was infuriated and I felt incredibly uncomfortable. I figured that of all the service members, a chaplain would be more understanding of this type of situation. After all, his purpose is to comfort and guide Marines through hard times.

"Sir, I've been in Iraq for five months now," I continued, "and I didn't want to bring this up until the end of my deployment because I didn't want the other Marines to think that I was scared or trying to avoid a combat tour. Those are not my intentions. I am not asking to return home early. I am not asking for anything. I am just trying to explain my situation to you."

The chaplain kept nodding his head as I talked. I just wanted to leave the room. I wished I had not come to his office. To the chaplain, my situation may have seemed immature, pathetic, or perhaps idealistic. To me, this was an incredibly emotional subject that I rarely discussed. My face was moist with sweat, and my heart pounded as I continued.

"Sir, I have to be true to myself first. I want to live by the values that I embrace, and I can't do that because I am confined to military service by a contract I signed when I was seventeen years old. I don't want to hide my values or who I am any longer. I want to be myself and not have to worry about putting on this front as a Marine. This is not who I am. This is not who I want to be." I was making a desperate attempt to explain my situation, but my eyes began to water.

"Let me tell you something, Lance Corporal," he explained. "When I was a boy, I lived in Vietnam. I remember the Marines coming to my village and chasing out the Viet Cong. I remember I looked up to them. I told myself that I wanted to be a Marine. I have lived through war before. I have lived through four wars! I know more than you do. I think you don't know what you are doing. If someone came to your house and tried to kill your family, wouldn't you try to protect your family and kill them first?"

By this time I was in tears. Discussing such a sensitive subject wasn't easy for me, and I'd hoped he would be more understanding. I kept trying to explain my situation, but he would not listen to my words. He kept interrupting and telling me that my beliefs were wrong and immature. We continued discussing the issue for over an hour, and since all attempts to make any progress appeared futile, I decided to leave. I thanked the chaplain for his time and I walked out of his office with tears in my eyes.

When I returned to the ammunition supply point, I briefed the officers in charge, Warrant Officer Robins and Captain Edison, about my conversation with the chaplain. Until now, the officers and senior sergeants were unaware of my moral anguish, so my explanation may have seemed surprising. Captain Edison followed protocol and briefed the commanding officer, Lieutenant Colonel Bellington, who requested to see me immediately. Furthermore, Captain Edison instructed that I be taken off guard duty at the front gate of the ammunition supply point.

Once again, the Humvee drove me over to mainside and to Lieutenant Colonel Bellington's office, where we discussed my meeting with the chaplain. He felt the chaplain had disrespected me and treated me unfairly, so he arranged a meeting for the following day with Lieutenant Fawcett, the chaplain for a Marine infantry unit that was also stationed at Al Asad.

Overnight, rumors spread that I had undergone a "mental breakdown," that I was requesting to return to the United States because I couldn't withstand the stress involved with the deployment, and that I hated the Marines Corps and America as a whole. Where had these rumors originated? A few Marines began asking me questions and, as I explained my situation, they stood in silence. After a ten-minute explanation, Corporal Alberto Piedra, a Cuban-American Marine from Connecticut, volunteered to speak with Captain Edison and the commanding officer on my behalf. He told me that he had witnessed a change over the past few months and could tell that my feelings were not like those of the other Marines.

"Jimmy," he began, "you're not like the rest of us. We can all tell how you don't feel comfortable holding that rifle, and how you don't believe in what you are doing. Besides, you're our tree-hugging hippie!" We could always count on Piedra to lighten the mood.

I met with Lieutenant Fawcett that same morning. As I began speaking with him, I noticed something strange about him. He was different from the other chaplains. He seemed straightforward, and I sensed a higher level of confidence in his speech. I later learned that he was a former Marine grunt who had enlisted as a naval chaplain after completing his tour with the Marines. We sat down outside the head shed at the ammunition supply point and he began with a volley of questions regarding my beliefs, my religious upbringing, and how I had come to the realization that the military was no longer for me.

"When did you notice that you had changed? When did you first begin questioning your involvement in the Marine Corps?" he asked.

"During college, at the University of La Verne," I explained. "It was there that I met Dr. Andrea Labinger, a professor of Spanish and director of the Honors Program. She taught me to think differently, to think 'outside the box' as they say. I slowly began to see the world from a new perspective, and I began questioning my military training and everything I had learned during boot camp. Through her, my thinking matured. I matured."

Chaplain Fawcett continued, "Does the University of La Verne have any religious affiliation? Is it a religious school?"

"It was founded by the Church of the Brethren, a denomination traditionally known for its peaceful approach to life. However, the school no longer has any religious requirements, but we still have a chapel on campus," I answered.

"Were you raised in the Church of the Brethren?"

"No, sir. I was raised Catholic."

"Did you convert to the Church of the Brethren once you entered the university?" He began probing deeper into my religious affiliation.

"I did not convert, sir, but I do respect and value their teachings," I answered.

"But don't you also embrace your Marine training? After all, you are a Marine."

"I don't dislike the Marine Corps in any way. I just recognize that I no longer belong in this uniform, with this rifle, in this war or any war for that matter." I was once again trying to explain my beliefs, but I was choosing my words carefully. I knew the Marine Corps could misinterpret my language and use it to prosecute me for dereliction of duty or even treason. I just hoped Chaplain Fawcett could understand my moral philosophy.

"Well, let me tell you something," he continued. "I'm going to be honest with you. I disagree with your beliefs, but I respect them."

Chaplain Fawcett continued to listen attentively for roughly two hours. He explained that the commanding officer had ordered him to submit a written report explaining our conversation. Furthermore, he cautioned that I could be held in contempt and that I should be wary of any legal ramifications.

Later that evening I met with Captain Edison and Warrant Officer Robins to brief them on my meeting with the chaplain. Neither of them seemed particularly interested in my conversation with Lieutenant Fawcett. Throughout the deployment, I'd noticed they were emotionally detached from their troops and they never took interest in our personal lives.

"First things first," Captain Edison explained. "You will no longer stand guard at the front gate of the ammunition supply point. I don't want someone who might hesitate, even for one second, to be guarding my compound. I don't want to take that chance. I need Marines who will shoot."

His logic was understandable. As a Marine officer he was responsible for the safety of his troops, and he did not want to endanger the lives of other Marines. Keeping me on guard duty was a liability, and one that could be fatal. I was thankful for his decision.

He continued, "However, I am warning you. If something happens, you better shoot somebody!" Had Captain Edison not listened to a single word I'd said? How could he order me to shoot after everything that had just happened? It seemed apparent that either he did not care about my personal beliefs or that he did not believe my feelings were genuine. I needed to demonstrate the depth and sincerity of my convictions.

"Sir," I began, "I want to turn in my rifle. I want to finish my Iraq tour without a rifle."

The room fell silent.

———

Soon after these conversations, Colonel Bellington ordered an official investigation to probe the nature of my convictions and whether I should be honorably discharged from the Marine Corps. These investigations consisted of a battery of interrogations that lasted almost two years and took place in three states and in Iraq. In the end, my conscientious objector discharge file had official reports from one chaplain, four medical officers, two investigations officers, three commanding officers, and two commanding generals, all of whom requested that I be honorably discharged. Every interviewing officer felt that I was sincere in my convictions and that I had genuinely changed over the course my military career. Furthermore, I had letters of support from five University of La Verne professors and one signed by a number of students. In March 2006, my discharge case went before a judicial committee at Marine Corps Headquarters in Quantico, Virginia, where, despite unanimous support from officers and professors, my case was rejected and I was ordered to complete the remainder of my service contract.

After being activated from the reserves for two years in support of Operation Iraqi Freedom, I returned to the reserves and I am currently working as an aviation ordnance systems technician with Marine Light Attack Helicopter Squadron 775 at Camp Pendleton, California. My obligated military service contract terminates in August 2007, when I plan to be honorably discharged from the Marine Corps after six years of service.

Upon returning to reserve status, I left the University of La Verne and transferred to Claremont McKenna College, where I am majoring in biology and chemistry. I plan to continue public service through science and medicine and to use my combat experiences to educate others on peaceful, alternative means of conflict resolution.

Against my wishes and better judgment I reluctantly left the safety and comfort of my mother's womb and was propelled headlong kicking and screaming into this world on the eve of the Anzio beachhead and the invasion of Italy during the height of World War II, in which my father and all of my uncles proudly wore the uniforms of Army, Navy and Air Force (Army Air Corps then). I was raised in a military town and all my life I saw men go off to war. The sea called and during the Vietnam War I volunteered for the Navy and served aboard the aircraft carrier USS *Essex* on her last voyage. An illustrious ship. The flagship of the Atlantic fleet. I also served as a member of VC2 fighter squadron in Oceania, Virginia. Being somewhat of an impractical devil-may-care dreamer, I settled in Berkeley after my military service to live out my impossible dreams. So far my entire life has come true. The question of free will or predestination still remains unanswered. Life is more mysterious than ever—to my way of thinking at least.

Liberation Day

Now, somehow, the men worked on and on without saying a word. If you're not working, get the hell out of the way. Are you tired, soldier? Are you annoyed? The noise in the silent night is shocking. The mountain quakes. We shiver. The infantry takes out after the evacuating enemy, following the Germans through the blinding nightlong darkness. Hey? Give me a light, will you? The cigarette glows in the dark, a little pinnacle of triumph. I just want to see the Statue of Liberty again. Our conversation drifts back to other days as the whole war machine grew dirtier, tireder, and more smooth and capable. Still listening now? The oppressive drone, steady groan of the German night bombers. God, I'm so tired. Perpetual choking dust. Yesterday is tomorrow. Perpetual movement, one dull, dead pattern of emotion. The ceaselessness, the endlessness starts to devour us. Weariness and boredom, walking and fighting, fighting and walking. Don't you recognize me? Grimy, befogged, and deadly tired. Plain exhaustion.

Well, you've got to talk about something. I'd give my payroll for a pair of galoshes. You could take a shot of that lousy cognac they sell back in Naples. It will dry your socks as soon as it hits bottom. It rains and rains. Vehicles bogged down, bridges washed out. All day long, spitfires patrol above our fighting troops. Dark skies, forbidding ridges. Ghostlike clouds unveil and then quickly hide the enemy. The human spirit is an astonishing thing. An artillery shell bursts on the loose rock surface. Flying rock sounding like a windstorm comes down the mountainside. The moon is nearly full. You can see far up the trail and partway across the valley below. We talk soldier talk. The dead men lie all alone outside in the shadow of the wall. They just lie there in the shadows until somebody comes after them. Five dead men lie in a line, end to end, in the shadow of the low stone wall. And pretty soon, we were all asleep. The gun blasts make a continuous crashing in the night, the shells tearing above our heads. The trail was never straight, and our pace was miserably slow. Word came back that they were doing fine and that we could step up the pace if we wanted to.

One day, I wondered why I was there at all. I hated the whole damn business just as much as anybody did. I found no answer short of insanity, so I quit thinking about it, but I'm glad I was there. One day, he came up to me and smiled and handed me a rose. Little things like that do sort of make you feel good about the human race. American soldiers standing in doorways with their rifles at the ready. Gradually, a crowd of eager and curious people crushed in upon us, from babies to old women. On nice days, the sky is clear blue and the sun is out and everything seems wonderful, except for a hidden chill in the air. On dark days, on bad days, the whole universe is dark. It drizzles and sprinkles. The cold wind blows. Our bones and hearts are miserable. It is raining cats and dogs. We fight hard. There are heavy casualties. The general is cussing and fuming. Everybody is wet and miserable. Hey, soldier. Come and hold this light, will you? So General Eddy obediently squatted down and held the light. We all go through our share of hell.

Gradually, we move on, a few feet at a time. Came the day, we walked around a couple of hedgerows and captured the German generals commanding the Cherbourg area. The commanding general just threw up his hands and gave up. General Eddy had the appearance of the traditional cat that swallowed something wonderful. The soldiers did a lot of kidding as they sat around, taking rusty guns apart. Surely, history will give a name to the battle that sent us boiling out of Normandy. We had to dig them out. It was a slow and cautious business. Are you all right? Yes, quite, now that you chaps are here. He was in agony, yet, in his correct Oxford accent, he apologized for taking up our time to dig him out. He had been trapped there for days, lying there upside down in the cockpit.

Our jeep eased through the crowds. Paris. The women are all brightly dressed in white or red blouses and colorful peasant skirts, with flowers in their hair and big flashy earrings. Everybody was throwing flowers. Our jeep eases through the crowds. Frantic men, women, and children grab us and kiss us and shake our hands and beat our shoulders and slap our backs and shout their joy as we pass. The pandemonium of a free and lovable Paris reigned again. It was wonderful to be there.

It was over. I was still alive. Truthfully, I guess, I was the luckiest man in the house. By some pure miracle, I'm not dead. Frontline infantrymen survived because the fates were kind to them and because they had become hard and immensely wise in animal-like ways of self-preservation. Yet, they seemed just like ordinary men who now only wanted to go home.

The McGuffin

Walking point . . . your first kill.
Coming back to Camp, "How was it?"
"It was nothing."
Second and on and on. "How was it?"
"It was nothing." The McGuffin. 364 to go. 15 to go.
"How was it?" from the new guys.
"It was nothing."
The year is almost over. Extend another six months.
The first year was nothing.
Only hit once. Nothing. Stepped on a mine once,
blown backwards . . . freeflight (Something).
Made it through again (nothing). Take another six.
You have been here eighteen months.
You know every trail.
You've only killed the same guy over and over and over.
Keep the same face on every kill. Vengeance, personal . . .
it's all NOTHING.

How Low is It to Be a Mouse,
a Spider, a Snake?

"Denis, come here," my mother called me after school that day.
   "There is a mouse in the kitchen, KILL IT." At Catholic school I'm
taught, "Thou Shall Not Kill." I kill the mouse. "He has gone to a
better place," my mother says. Instead of saying someone is DEAD,
they use euphemisms. There's a code language all around me. Each
time it becomes easier for me. When I see a huge spider on the kitchen
table, with quick reflexes—SPLAT! I kill it.
   I was in the 1st Cavalry Division. Going in to Vietnam. I'm told,
"Kill the enemy."
   They're all the enemy.

On patrol, there are ARVN in front of us. If they come back through the pass, kill them. Thinking back . . . I killed the mouse, I killed the spider, I killed the man. Did I, in killing these beings, allow them to escape to a higher life force . . . The After Life? Is that figure in the tree—a roach, a (_____, you fill in the blank) whatever, take him out too. War Over. I become a vegetarian, because, "Thou Shall Not Kill."

A shriek in the night and I'm startled out of a dead sleep. "There's a spider on me, KILL IT."

IT NEVER ENDS

WHY DID I LET YOU LIVE?

On an S&D mission, the tall grass moves and the birds take
   flight, so I know something's coming. A VC? A farmer?
A person, probably of my age, comes into view, rifle slung over
   his shoulder, haphazardly.
Should I bayonet him? Lob a grenade? Shoot him?
He is whistling. There's no one behind him. He is not walking
   point.
He does have an AK–47. I decide, *mano a mano,* and spring from
   cover.
He falls to his knees and cries. I take the rifle. I let him live.
A week later, "Did you hear about Ski? Sniper took him out."
Is that the one I let go?
Years later, sitting on a Harley Davidson at a light, a car comes
   over the line on a left turn and just misses me. Is that him? I
   wonder again. Each time something happens, I wonder, Is that
   the one I let live?

Fred said, COMPASSIONATELY WITNESS TRIGGER ... DON'T SHOOT THE MESSENGER

I went with the advance party of the 1st Cavalry Division.
    To set up base camp.
I never compassionately witness anything.
You could only count so high. You had no time to reflect.
    (Be There Now.)
The only people you held were the ones who looked you in the
    eye and said,
"Shoot me ... If you can't do it, leave a gun with me."
It is very absolute with me that after the first, the wave never
    subsided.
Compassionate witnessing is very foreign to me.
There are no questions now. Only more absolutes.
Buddha, Dharma, Sangha.
Nihilistic, Great Doubt. The wake does not steer the boat, start
    by emptying.
Bodhisattva
Karma
"Remembering is thinking of the past without possibility of
    change.
Meditation is thinking of the Future for Change."
LET ME MEDITATE NOW.

I live on Main Street in Sebastopol, California, with my wife and our dog. We have a grown son living with us some of the time and a daughter who lives in San Francisco. Besides writing fiction and poetry, I also sing with a number of choirs and opera companies in Sonoma County.

Born in Benton Harbor, Michigan, in 1949, I lived in Washington, D.C., and Fort Wayne, Indiana, and moved to the San Joaquin Valley of California in 1956. After living in Bakersfield and Modesto, my parents moved the family to Riverside, in Southern California, where I grew up and tried college without success. I got drafted in 1970. I returned home from Vietnam in 1972 and was educated at Santa Barbara City College and Cal Poly in San Luis Obispo, where I studied English literature. I have done a variety of work that I used to think would make an interesting author note on the book jacket of my currently unfinished novel: laundry worker, bindery worker, landscaper, hospital page, typist, encyclopedia salesman, busboy, dishwasher, ice cream truck driver, construction laborer, bakery delivery man, disk jockey, greenhouse worker, office clerk, librarian, press operator, mail handler, tile factory worker, furniture mover, letter carrier, and more temporary occupations I have no doubt forgotten. Vietnam has had a profound effect on the rest of my life. I came back to the United States determined that I would always be a grower instead of a killer, a builder and not a destroyer. For the most part I have succeeded at what I have been trying to do. My love of music and poetry and beauty and the love of my family bring me joy.

Good Time

The rain is plenty loud as it hits the ground but this sheet metal roof amplifies the sound, so there's no point in trying to talk over it. It won't last too long. The staff sergeant up in front is pissed at everything and everybody. You can tell he resents this loud rain and he is too impatient to wait. He would rather fight it. He's a light-skinned black man, not very old for a lifer. His uniform is bright green with dark sweat streaks all through it. This sure is heavy rain. It must have been about six months since I've seen it rain this hard, but I don't think the sergeant has been in-country nearly that long. His job is to process soldiers in and out of Vietnam. He probably enjoys harassing the new guys. You can tell he hates the guys standing in sloppy formation in front of him now. Our fatigues are faded to no recognizable color at all. We have done our days here and we're going home. The rain keeps coming down, and we're standing on this concrete slab with a flat roof over it and looking at the sergeant trying to act real efficient. He is reading names from a computer printout and he won't wait for this downpour to slack off. He just keeps yelling louder into the microphone.

I'm on the edge of a group of black guys who have been cutting up the whole time the sergeant has been trying to read the list, and now that we can't understand what he's saying and he can't hear us, they aren't even pretending to pay attention anymore. They are joking and laughing and some of the things they say are pretty funny. This sergeant up in front is not a very impressive guy and he demands to be taken seriously. He is perfectly typecast to be the butt of rough humor. I'm sure he takes orders real well. These black guys don't like him. He's a lifer and he can't understand why everybody doesn't think he's hot shit. He sounds like he's trying to make his voice deep and it comes out sounding tight and nervous. "Listen up!" he says, "I'm only going to read each name one time only. Only one time, you hear? You miss the manifest and it's no skin off of my ass."

I know my name isn't on the list. This is just the second of these formations I have been to and there are hundreds of guys ahead of me. The sergeant is almost pleading into the mike, "Stop that bullshittin' around and let's get through the manifest." The black guys are growling at him now. Hissing, barking and howling, making gargling sounds. "All right," he says with a shrill edge in his voice, "I don't have to take this kind of shit. It don't make no never mind to me. I got lots of time if you guys want to fuck around all afternoon." He steps back from the microphone and folds his arms over his chest and scowls at us. Now he gets a lot of reaction. The black guys are taunting him and the white guys are yelling at the black guys to shut up so we can hear the list. The rain is pelting down.

The staff sergeant can't stand still and watch this. He looks like he is about to go into some kind of a fit. He rushes the microphone and screams over all the confusion, "I'm going to get the first sergeant out here!" The black guys next to me begin to whoop and cackle and break out of line all together and start doing the dap, slapping hands and

making symbolic motions in a ritual I've never seen so stylized anywhere but Vietnam. Doing the dap is something only the brothers do.
I've had them try to show me some of the moves but it takes practice
to do it right and they are the only ones who practice it. When black
guys meet and leave each other, they go through this complex ritual
that is basically the soul brother handshake but has a lot of extra moves
to it and requires improvisation and perfect timing. When they get in
big groups it takes them quite a while to go through the whole thing
with every other brother. Often you see them in the mess hall doing
the dap and their food is going cold.

The man up front is looking paler and paler. He's all alone up there
and the fact that the black guys hate him and nobody else likes him
either is plain to everyone, even him. He is beginning to shake a little
and his eyes are kind of bugging out. Too late, he tries to command
and calls out, "Attention!" Some guys snap to like robots and others
just shuffle their feet a little and stare impassively at the man behind
the microphone. These brothers next to me just laugh and keep on
doing the dap like a basketball team celebrating early an easy victory
with two minutes left in the final period. The sergeant is screaming
wildly, "No doing the dap! Straighten up! Get in line!" This is pathetic.
It reminds me of the kind of thing we used to do to poor substitute
teachers back in grade school. Sergeant Hot Shit leaves the microphone, turns his back on his tormenters, and stalks off in the rain like
he's going to get the principal.

The first sergeant doesn't appear right away. It's still raining hard
and under this metal roof there is a lot of angry yelling and some scuffling going on but nobody wants to fight very bad and the scufflers
are easily restrained. The shouting subsides and a low rumble takes its
place. The rain stops as abruptly as it began. Some people take off
immediately like they have something important to do. The original
troublemakers wander off among the bunkers at the edge of the perimeter. Most of the guys just stand around because there is really nowhere
to go and nothing more interesting than finding out if you're on the
next flight out of Vietnam.

I have mixed feelings about being back here in Long Binh at the
90th Replacement Station again. Of course, I have been counting my
days waiting for this, but now that I'm here I can't shake an awful sense

of uneasiness, almost a dread of returning to the United States. I feel something like a rat that has been kept in a cage and when somebody opens the gate to let him out he just sits there like he's afraid to do anything. Maybe he hates that cage but at least he is used to it. He knows what to expect in there. I have gotten used to Vietnam and it hasn't been as bad as I thought it would be since I don't know what I would do in California.

I wanted to get out of the Army in Vietnam and make my way back home through Asia and Europe. I sat in the little special services library at Tan Son Nhut and studied maps and atlases for hours some nights considering different routes and methods of transportation. Being halfway around the world, I would rather not turn around and go back home the same way I came. I could imagine flying to Thailand and starting there. I would have to skip over Cambodia because the war is too hot there. But from Thailand I could ride buses and trains through Burma and all across India and then into Pakistan. I might want to fly over some of the Middle East but certainly I would want to see Egypt and Israel and Turkey and then Yugoslavia and when I got to Greece what would I do then? There are a lot of possibilities from there. You see, I would rather not go home too fast. I have gotten too strange over here to feel like I can just turn up in Oakland tomorrow and head right down to LA and see people I know and talk about Vietnam and what I'm going to do. I would much rather be fresh from Europe, with Vietnam a more distant memory. Also, LA scares me more as I think about it now than Saigon does. I mean, I have been living in Saigon. I'm used to that.

I checked into it and found out that it's no problem. You can get your separation papers in Saigon and do whatever you want but what you give up is a return ride to your home of record. That flight is worth a lot of money that I don't have. I would still do it if I had the money. It would only take a couple of months to save a thousand dollars and I could go a long way on that, but with only two months left I got my orders for Oakland. It's an election year and Nixon is reducing American troop strength in Vietnam. American units are being moved out and South Vietnamese are replacing them. It's the Vietnamization of Vietnam. What it means to me is I'm back in Long Binh and I'm going to ride the freedom bird back to the U.S. like everyone else.

The sky is clearing. The few clouds are streaky white. I see an army-green bus in the distance on the road headed for Bien Hoa and it reminds me of my first morning here last May. There was a formation of all the new guys before breakfast and a sergeant read off the names of the people assigned to extra duty. My name was one of six guys on the Camp Alpha detail. This was bad luck. In Oakland I had managed to stay off of any extra duty, but here out of a huge crowd I had gotten picked for Camp Alpha. I didn't like the sound of that. I mean, Long Binh is a big installation with a lot of troops to defend it, but what was Camp Alpha? Was it way out in the boonies or what? I went up to the sergeant and asked him what the detail was, and he said it was KP, and I asked him where Camp Alpha was, and he said it was at Tan Son Nhut. My first day in-country and I get picked for KP. But what can I do about it?

After breakfast, I report to the place we are supposed to get on the bus and there are five other guys just like me who don't know what we're doing. As we get on the bus, I ask the driver where is Tan Son Nhut. He says it's in Saigon, which sounds good to me. I want to be sure and get a chance to see Saigon, so maybe this isn't such bad luck.

The bus makes a few stops around Long Binh picking up more passengers and then we drive right through the little town of Bien Hoa without stopping. It takes about an hour on a paved road through mostly defoliated brown countryside to get to the Saigon River, which we cross on a heavily guarded bridge high enough in the middle to let some pretty big ships go under. The bus is about half full and I watch the guys in faded uniforms to pick up any clues that I can about how to act. They don't seem too exotic to me. They are reading and smoking. They could be anywhere on a bus in any city. They don't act like they expect to be attacked at any minute.

As we come off the bridge, we can see what seems to be the main district of the city. The tallest buildings are to our left, and we veer right and take a narrow busy street through a newer part of town. The closest thing I have seen to this is Tijuana. The crazy traffic reminds me of that and the wild free-form building styles, which use any materials that are handy. But, unlike in Mexico, there are few big American cars here and the ones you see are usually taxis. There aren't many civilian cars at all. Mostly you see a great variety of military vehicles making their way through swarms of bicycles and motorcycles and thousands of pedestrians.

The people look just like they do in the *National Geographic,* only there are more of them. They lean against buildings in the shade or they squat on their haunches in the dirt on the side of the street with stuff that they have laid out to sell. Or they gossip in small groups and fan themselves. Or they carry huge loads in trailers behind their bicycles or in carts that they pull on foot and they lean out of upper-story windows and look at everything. Everywhere there are children in light-colored clothes running and laughing and playing and fighting and hanging out on the balconies and in the streets.

It is wartime. Most of the men are in uniform. Others wear tropical white shirts and baggy cotton pants or cone-shaped bamboo hats and the black silk pajama-like costume which is the traditional clothing of Vietnam. Some of the women wear white silk pants with colored or print dresses with slits all the way up the sides. Other women wear a variety of western clothes, particularly miniskirts with nylon stockings and high heels and bubble hairdos. You see some Americans in the crowd, mostly military but occasionally you might see a few hippie-looking guys with beards and long hair. Journalists, perhaps.

As we approach a large military base that looks almost stateside, we pass through a major business area that obviously caters to GIs. This is Plantation Road. There are many bars, restaurants, clothing stores, souvenir stands, massage parlors, and psychedelic shops. We slow down in the heavy traffic and I can hear the Beatles singing "All You Need Is Love." Army MPs wave us past the guard station at the gate of Tan Son Nhut Air Base.

Once we get inside the base, the bus again makes frequent stops and people get on and off. This place has a decidedly permanent look about it. There are miles of standard wooden military structures and a few imposing-looking buildings with white plaster walls that must date from French colonial days. We come to one area where there are a number of multi-story buildings made of concrete blocks with air conditioners hanging out of the windows. I am told that this is MACV headquarters, sometimes called the Pentagon of the Orient. This is where General Abrams has his office. Here also is the Saigon air terminal and at the other end of a long runway is a cluster of buildings, which is Camp Alpha. I learn that Camp Alpha handles the billeting of military transients who are waiting for planes to take them to their R & R destinations.

My fellow KPs and I get off the bus and are met by the mess hall sergeant who takes us over to the kitchen and shows us what to do. This turns out to be the easiest KP I have ever seen. They have Vietnamese doing all the hard work, and there are way too many people for the amount of work there is to do. I grab a mop right away and just keep working on the floor. When I get done with it, I start over. The cooks don't mind if you get yourself a snack once in a while. That's what they do. All in all, this is not bad duty.

After lunch, I figure it's OK to take a break and I fill a glass with orange juice and ice and find a tree to sit under near the chain-link fence behind the mess hall. On the other side of the fence are some Quonset huts with a lot of activity going on in them and around them. Children are playing some kind of a game with sticks and rocks in the dirt street, and women are hanging up washing and working in gardens. There is much jabbering in Vietnamese and the sound of many radios and televisions playing. From what I can make out, *Adam-12* is on TV. The children notice me, and they come to the fence and the smallest ones stick their hands through and say, "Give me money, GI. You give me money." I just sit where I am and smile and shake my head because I can't start handing out coins to these kids. There are too many of them. They finally believe me and go back to their game.

A young man wearing a Vietnamese Army uniform rides a red Honda 90 into the yard of the closest house. Some of the children run over to him and he greets them warmly and picks up the smallest and holds him in his arms and strides into the house. I can hear a number of voices engaged in a lively conversation, and then he emerges from the house and gets on his motorcycle. As he is kicking the starter, sudden excited cries issue from the house, and a woman and a teenaged boy come running out. The boy climbs on the back of the Honda, and the man and the boy take off down the street accompanied by a great deal of human and motorcycle noise.

I go back inside and give the floor another thorough scrubbing. When I return to the tree, I see an old Vietnamese man who works in the kitchen sitting there in the shade and smoking a ceramic pipe. He smiles toothlessly as I approach and sit down beside him. "It sure is hot," I say, and he smiles and nods. "Is it usually this hot?" I ask. He smiles and nods again. He is dressed in black silk and wears a standard Vietnamese bamboo hat. On his feet he has American GI jungle boots just like mine, only beat up. With his deep wrinkles and his thin white beard, he reminds me of pictures of Ho Chi Minh. His smile is much the same. "My name is Mark," I tell him and I hold out my hand and he grasps it the way young Army guys do—fingers high. Whatever I say he smiles but he never says anything so I have no idea how much English he understands. The smoke from his pipe intrigues me. It smells like tobacco and something else. I watch him as he takes a flat round tin from his pocket and fills his pipe with a black sticky mixture. I ask him if he will let me try what he has in his pipe, and he begins to laugh and cough. At first he thinks I'm joking, but I convince him at last, and he loads a bowl for me and lights it with his Zippo. I cough. I'm not used to smoking tobacco. He only laughs. We keep trading pipe loads back and forth and everything gets funnier and funnier. When I stand up to go back inside, my head feels like it is a long way from my feet. The sky is an impossible shade of blue and I am amazed at the intricate patterns of bird tracks in the dust as we make our way slowly back to the kitchen.

Back inside, I find my mop and get back to work. Every time I look at the old man, he grins with a sly look in his eyes, as if we share a terribly funny secret, and I suppose we do. I am mopping the floor with renewed vigor now, keeping the water in the bucket especially clean and steaming, and taking a real interest in the work. In my present state of mind, I find that I can think of songs that I know and hear them in my imagination played note for note, as if I were listening to the record. I'm following a Neil Young guitar solo on "Cowgirl in the Sand" when I look up to see a lifer beckoning me from a table in the rear of the mess hall. He is a sergeant major and he is having coffee with two E-7s. Maybe they want me to get them more coffee. I walk toward them still moving in time with the guitar in my head. Opium is surging through my brain, but I'm not paranoid. I feel terrific.

"Troop," says the sergeant major. "Your name is Williams." This is a statement. He is reading my name on my shirt. We look at each other through identical aviator sunglasses. I got mine at the main PX at Fort Sill. I wonder where he got his.

"Yes," I say.

"Where are you from, Williams?"

Now I grin broadly. I feel so far from home and I am pleased that he seems interested in me. "I'm from California," I say. "Where are you from?"

His expression has been neutral, but now he frowns. He shakes his head like a fly is buzzing him and I can see that this is not going to be a conversation. He ignores my question and asks, "What unit are you with?"

"I'm not in any unit yet," I tell him. "I just got here."

"Well, soldier, you need a haircut."

I need a haircut. This is what he wants to talk to me about. This is pretty silly. It hasn't been four days since I got a perfectly adequate haircut in Oakland before I left. I think of saying something like that but instead say, "OK, OK, as soon as I get a chance I'll get a haircut."

"No," says the sergeant major impatiently. "You need a haircut right now."

"But what about the floor?" I start to say.

He cuts me off with a calm but direct threat. "Williams," he says. "You're starting to aggravate me. I don't think you want to do that."

He directs me to a barbershop, and I turn around and walk straight out the door and leave my mop in the bucket. Outside in the bright sun, I am floating along through the heat toward some distant buildings and from habit I feel like I ought to be mad but I feel more like laughing. Why does the sergeant major think I need a haircut? He doesn't like the way I look. He doesn't like the way I was sort of dancing with the mop and singing to myself. What he would most like to change about me is the expression on my face. He probably hates the fact that people like me are allowed in the Army at all.

I'm preoccupied thinking about this stuff and not paying attention to my surroundings, when I look up to find that I have managed to blunder into the path of a captain who is approaching at a brisk pace. I can clearly see the black bars sewn on the collar of his fatigues and on his cap. My instinct is to salute, but I remember being told in basic training that you must always observe military courtesy, except when you are in a combat zone. There is only time to give what I hope will seem a friendly nod before he stops dead ahead of me and addresses me.

"Soldier."

"Yes, Sir."

"What do you do when you meet an officer?"

"Salute, Sir."

He points to his bars and says, "Don't you see I'm a captain?"

"Yes, Sir, but I thought you weren't supposed to salute when you're in a combat zone."

"This isn't a combat zone. This is Tan Son Nhut Air Base. You better get with it, soldier."

"Yes, Sir," I say and give him a salute which he returns and we go our different ways.

I find the barbershop right where I was told it would be. There are three chairs and no customers and three cheerful Vietnamese barbers. The place is air-conditioned. I say yes to the shine boy and yes to the manicure girl. I'm in no hurry. I have a lot of Vietnam time to do and this is good time.

I've published five books of poetry in the United States and England, including *The New World* (Curbstone Press) and *Sudden Dreams* (Coffee House Press), plus poetry, translations, fiction, and essays in magazines and anthologies in the United States, Australia, England, Ireland, France, Japan, and Vietnam. A recipient of writing fellowships from the National Endowment for the Arts, the California Arts Council, and the Lannan Foundation, I also received a Monbusho Fellowship from the Japanese government for the study of Japanese poetry. I was poetry and art editor of the national public arts project *Streetfare Journal,* which displayed contemporary world poetry, art, and photography on buses in cities throughout the United States; edited the two-volume work *Charles Olson & Cid Corman: Complete Correspondence* (National Poetry Foundation, University of Maine, Orono); translated *The Violent Foam: New and Selected Poems* (Curbstone Press) by Nicaraguan poet Daisy Zamora; and cotranslated, with writer Nguyen Qui Duc, *The Time Tree,* a collection of poetry by Vietnamese poet Huu Thinh.

In the late 1960s I served in the U.S. Air Force as a medical corpsman, stationed in Libya during the Six-Day War of 1967 and in Viet Nam in 1969 during the U.S.–Viet Nam War, where I worked in an emergency room and triage facility at a hospital in Cam Ranh Bay. In Viet Nam, I became involved in various forms of antiwar protest and was eventually court-martialed there for ostensibly disobeying orders, though actual motivations for the trial were rooted in war protest activities. The prosecution was unsuccessful, and I was honorably discharged in early 1970.

A Walk in the Garden of Heaven

A Letter to Viet Nam

1

They were talking when we entered the garden, two young people whispering with their hands, mist threads drifting from mountaintops on the raked gravel ocean. Islands afloat on the skin of infinity. The mind without its body.

"The moment I saw your face," he said, "was like walking into the Hall of a Thousand and One Bodhisattvas."

She had no idea what he meant, how it is to enter Sanjusangendo in Kyoto for even the fiftieth time and see row upon row of a thousand standing figures, carved, painted, and gold-leafed with a calm but stunned look of enlightenment, five hundred on each side of a larger, seated figure of their kind, miniature heads knotted to their scalps representing the fragments of a time when their heads exploded in dismay at the evil in this world, the way our heads exploded in the war, though we don't wear our histories where they can be seen.

Each statue has twenty pairs of arms to symbolize their actual 1,000 arms, these enlightened ones who choose to remain on earth and not end the cycle of death and rebirth some believe we go through until we get it right. They pause at the edge of nirvana to stay behind and help us all get through. It's easy to think they are foolish instead of holy.

But each hand holds twenty-five worlds it saves, and because each figure can multiply into thirty-three different figures, imagine the thirty-three thousand worlds they hold, how much distress there really is, then multiply that by a thousand and one and think of what it's like to stand in an ancient wooden temple with all that sparkling compassion, even for those of us who believe in almost nothing.

It is said, and it's true, that if you search the thousand faces, you will find the face of someone lost from your life.

Garden of Heaven refers to Tenshin-en, 天心園 *, the Japanese rock garden at the Museum of Fine Arts, Boston. I visited the garden with the North Vietnamese writers Ms. Le Minh Khue and Mr. Huu Thinh, both of Hanoi and both combat veterans of the U.S.–Viet Nam War. They were visiting the United States for the first time.*

But the young girl in the garden was bored and looked over her lover's shoulder at a twist of flowers. Then so did he. The spell was broken.

We are older. There are so many wasted lives between us that only beauty makes sense. Yet we are like them. We are. They are the way it is between our countries. One talking, one looking away. Both talking, both looking away.

2

We entered the garden by chance. We were like the rocks there, plucked from some other place to be translated by circumstance into another tongue. In the silent crashing of stone waterfalls, and the rising of inanimate objects into music, we remembered there was a time we would have killed each other.

In the future we will think of it again. We might get drunk beneath a great moon and see one another's eyes in a pool of water, or remember in a glance across a Formica table in a kitchen filled with friends and noisy children, or while walking down the street. But it will not be the same.

It is called realizing you have lived, and it happens only once.

3

During Vietnam, which we say because the name signifies more than a place—it is an epoch, a paradigm, a memory, a mistake— during Vietnam, things were the same as they are now for those who are young and poor. We were standing around. There was no work, it was the beginning of our times as men, we were looking to prove ourselves, or looking for a way out. Some were patriots, and many were the sons of men who had gone to another war and come back admired. I don't remember any mercenaries. We were crossing thresholds, starting to lie to ourselves about things, and because we were there and ambitious or desperate, when they passed out weapons, we took them. We didn't understand the disordered nature of the universe, so disordered humans must try to arrange it, and if they get you young enough, you will help.

I'm grieved but not guilty. Sad but not ashamed.

That does not mean I lack compassion. It does not mean I sleep at night, or don't sweat at night. It does not mean it is easy to live.

In parts of my country, I'm considered insane.

4

Thinking of it in terms of your country, I could say I was the son of peasants. We earned or made everything we had. I learned to honor people for what they do, not for their positions. I've never been able to escape the rightness of that. To explain it in terms of my country, it means: if I didn't have enemies here, I would choose to live in exile.

5

We want the bones. We want all the bones. You will hear this. Good people will say it. They are all good people. They say it. They say: *We want the bones.* And they mean it, they mean what they say. They carry it into sleep, into their children, into the voting booth. *We want the bones. That's what we want. We don't want the ghosts. You keep the ghosts. We don't want them. Just the bones.*

Your ghosts are driving us out of our minds.

6

In my country we shift blame. After the war, those who went became pariahs. Not the ones who started it, not the ones who carried it. And because not everyone can overlook rejection or memory, more who went have died by their own hand than by your mines or bullets. There are more suicides among us now than names on our monument in the capital, our broken dash against the landscape, scar that would span the city if it listed the actual dead, black river that would surge across the country if it listed everyone ruined on every side.

I want this remembering to end, yet cannot let it. It's like drinking the ocean, but someone must remember, someone refuse to be tethered.

I visited your country at the wrong time, but if I had not I still would not understand the nature of things, would still think my country is paradise, which in many ways it is, but which it is not. It is built on graves, on bones, on promises broken and nightmares kept, on graves that howl deep in the earth, on skulls crushed with religious objects, on human skin used as rugs, on graves upon graves of graves. And we are always busy conquering ourselves.

Whatever it is holds us in a spell of wonder when we are children, abandoned me when the war began. I don't mean just me or just youth, I mean something about this country. But I don't mean just this country, I mean the world. I've spent my time searching for what it is, like a suicide who refuses to die, an optimist who is empty, a buoy on the sea.

7

In the dry garden where we walked, where stone represents water as well as itself, the Chinese characters of which mean the center or heart of heaven (天 for heaven, 心 for center or heart), there is a mountain represented, Mount Sumeru, the highest peak of every world, every world a Bodhisattva holds in its hands, every world in the universe, and every world we live in, but it also represents the center of infinity, and because infinity has only centers, we were standing everywhere at once, and exchanged what could not be stated except in language which could never be spoken.

But we must speak it. The question is, how many heads do we have and how many arms and how many worlds do we hold, and just how far will we go to end our war.

8

The order of the universe is that there may be none, not like glasses lined up, each dish upon its shelf. And what we think is wild is not.

I want to be reasonable, it is something that interests, even haunts me, but given certain knowledge, how to be is more hellish.

The room here is small, and at times the way wind kicks up over the fence lip reminds me of animal howling and that in turn of an even smaller room, a box of sorts within a building stilted off the ground beneath a tin washboard roof hammered by rain in your country.

Our rooms there were like boxes really, perimeters not unlike the skin, and came to mean everything for each one, for each had the need to live in containment where there was none, to confine ourselves, as one might a crazed dog until it calms.

Perhaps it is not the past I should concern myself with, but not to speak of it and face what is still happening is not possible.

The double bonds of living for something and dying for something are ribbons that trail from us, drag behind or flap from us, and if I could understand it now or ever this business would be done.

I want to be reasonable, it is something I crave and wish I knew how to pray for but cannot pray, not having the faith of it, having seen.

We have friends, then we do not have them because we reach some border across which words cannot manage, across which silence will not bridge, and in the manner of children we stand without explanation or understanding, and there is no necessity that we question it. We learn to ignore those events which remove things in the way that we know of as "Before their time." It's another weapon we aim at our heads.

9

When we stood in the garden and looked at the stone bridges connecting islands on the gravel ocean, I felt the war lift from us in flames, inch by inch flowing into stone like a river on fire.

We ended something walking together, and started something.

I've read the war is over for you, but have never believed it. Victory is no balm for loss. Any of us may celebrate a moment, but we live a long time, and finality is not what we need, compassion is what we need. Let the future think about the war being over, because then it will be.

We can't afford to heal. If we do, we'll forget, and if we forget, it will start again.

We've destroyed too much to be sentimental. We know that those above and those below the jungle canopy killed anything that got in the way, and we're all guilty of something. Wars are always lost. Even if you win.

10

I returned to San Francisco sorry about some things I was unable to explain, especially the army of beggars in our streets, and how badly we treat the poor. The coldness of it, you see, is a symptom of killing nations at a distance, or even up against their breaths. It has also to do with how freedom can be like the end of a rope. It pollutes all notions of beauty, this living in the streets. My wife in those days pointed out that Americans do help one another during floods, earthquakes, and conflagrations. "That's not compassion," I said, "it's convenience—only generosity when there is no disaster counts." I'd become so wise, righteous anger made me happy. We sat in silence after that. Actually, one was washing dishes and one was peeling potatoes, we could hear the rattle of a bottle gleaner digging through the recycle bin on our sidewalk, a jet was passing over, John Lee Hooker was singing on the radio, the neighbors were having a horrible fight, there was a crash in the intersection, one of our cats spit at the other, and the phone rang but we ignored it, so it wasn't really silent. Then she said, "We would all be wealthy if people were born honest." So. Not all understanding comes from the barrel of a gun.

11

Stretched flat in deep grass   resolute about the sickness of
pursuits   watching a moth on a beer can lip swing its curled
tongue like an elephant trunk across the water dots.   The only
thing I know about fame and success is that they are stumbling
blocks when they commandeer my attention.   My real
function is to think about things and listen, drunk and lazy, to the
buzz in the grass, the millions of insects who do not care what I
think.   I'm tired of the world of people—they're not to be
trusted on the whole because they don't understand death.
It's not that they're unhappy, it's just that they don't understand
death.   I'm not above or beneath them, I'm just sometimes
not one of them.   I've seen too much to be fooled into
thinking we know what we are doing.   Maybe I'm getting too
arrogant for my own good, but even that sounds stupid in the
face of death.   I understand the insects in the deep grass, even
if I can't repeat what they say.

12

I've come out to the cliffs above the Pacific Ocean before sunset.
I told you my childhood friends were all killed in the war, and
you told me similar things. It wasn't difficult for me to also tell
you I was never angry at your country. What was difficult was to
tell you how angry I am at my own.

Pelicans overhead. The rose-colored hood of a finch in the
bushes. I sit on a railroad tie post on a high cliff at the edge of
North America.

Tourists drive up, take pictures, go home.

A cormorant. Sailboat. An Army gunship choppers over the
beach.

Behind me, an Army base. In front of me, the sea.

I'm waiting for the sun to set, but it will not.

Spring Dawn

The trees are talking.
Crows to everyone, migrant unknowns squabble,
jays fight over every inch,
mockingbird—lord of sound—says
everything, hummingbird swoops in
without care above the clover lanterns,
and blackbirds swarm
the sun-blasted window glass
electric in the rising
days before war.
                    –March 2003

DAN FAHEY

This story evolved from an entry in a journal I kept while serving with the Navy in the Persian Gulf. It was July 13, 1991, our ship was in port in Bahrain, and I was awaiting confirmation of my application for conscientious objector status. As I sat in the cramped stateroom I shared with five other officers, I wrote that day to preserve for my own memory the experience of being on watch on the bridge: the sights and the sounds, the activity and the boredom, the external vigilance and the internal reflection. Eleven days later, after my orders finally came through, I flew back to San Francisco. Two months after that, on September 20, 1991, I left the Navy with an honorable discharge and a $38,000 debt for my university scholarship.

In ways I could not then foresee, my experiences in the Navy shaped my future vocations and interests. For nearly six years I was a paralegal at Swords to Plowshares, a nonprofit veterans service organization in San Francisco, helping homeless and disabled veterans obtain health care and disability benefits. While at Swords, I became an advocate for veterans who developed health problems as a result of service during and after the 1991 Gulf War, and I served on the board of directors of the National Gulf War Resource Center, a veterans' advocacy group. I primarily investigated the scope and severity of exposures to depleted uranium (DU) ammunition, producing reports and providing testimony about DU for federal investigations of veterans' illnesses. Independently, I continue to promote expanded studies of veterans exposed to DU in the Gulf War and improved testing and health care for veterans exposed to DU during service in the wars in Iraq and Afghanistan.

My experience working on issues related to the Gulf War sparked my interest in understanding other post-conflict issues and debates. I obtained a master's degree in international relations from the Fletcher School of Law and Diplomacy at Tufts University, where I wrote my thesis on international responses to the environmental consequences of armed conflict. Currently I am pursuing a Ph.D. degree at the University of California at Berkeley, studying the social and environmental effects of conflict and development in the Great Lakes Region of Africa.

The 2 to 7 Watch

I'm standing on watch in the middle of the bridge, staring out across the bow of the ship into the endless black night. It's overcast, so neither the moon nor the stars are out to illuminate the passing sea. Even the gentle lapping of the water against the hull is obscured by the bulky headphones I am wearing. I normally enjoy the serenity and starry-night beauty of the two-to-seven A.M. watch, but tonight the shadowy darkness has taken my mind elsewhere.

A voice on the starboard side of the bridge breaks the silence. "Officer of the deck, next course is two-seven-zero at time three-five," says the quartermaster. He stands in the corner in front of a table covered in nautical charts that are softly lit by a dim red lamp. After his announcement, the quartermaster leans back over a chart to plot the next leg of our patrol.

"Very well," says the officer of the deck (OOD), who stands on the port side of the bridge. He lifts a pair of heavy black binoculars up to his bespectacled eyes and scans the horizon to our left, in the direction of our turn. "Conning officer, did you copy that?"

"Yes sir," I answer. I mark the new course and time to turn on a dimly illuminated glass board to my left. I glance down at the gyro repeater in front of me, which shows our present course, and then return my gaze forward.

During these night watches, a change in course or speed can be the only reminder of the passage of time. Between these changes, the solitude and peace of the night can make you forget we are halfway around the world from home, cruising the waters of the Persian Gulf on a nuclear-powered platform of missiles and guns.

The OOD is training a new officer in the fundamentals of the bridge watch. He stoops over the spot-25 radar repeater, notes the position of another ship somewhere in the distance, and moves to a table smoothly lit in red. He records the bearing and range marks on a maneuvering board, or moboard, and starts drawing lines and making calculations to determine the course, speed, and target angle of the unseen vessel.

Until we slid through the Straits of Hormuz into the Persian Gulf, I had worked the spot-25 and the moboards, keeping track of ships seen and unseen, in addition to being conning officer. I came to enjoy the challenge and activity of that position, along with the opportunity to ponder the freedom of the open sea by day, and the eternity of the endless stars at night. In the heightened state of security that our new location requires, additional people have been assigned to duty on the bridge. Now I just stand in the middle of the bridge in front of the gyro repeater, glancing down occasionally to make sure we are on course. I keep an eye out for other ships and floating objects, and give the commands to change the ship's course or speed.

As I gaze ahead, my thoughts drift back to California and the life that awaits me after I'm discharged. Oh how I want to get off this ship and go home!

It's hard to believe that just six months ago I was in school in San Diego learning to fire nuclear and conventional Tomahawk cruise missiles. I had only recently been assigned as the new missiles officer on the guided-missile cruiser USS *Arkansas,* based in Alameda, California, when I was sent to Tomahawk school. Over the course of three weeks in January 1991, I learned how to fire the different variants of the missile, which could carry cluster bombs, a high explosive charge, or a nuclear warhead.

Shooting a nuclear missile was not something I had given much thought to while I was in the Reserve Officers Training Corps (ROTC) during college. In 1986, at the age of seventeen, I accepted a four-year Navy scholarship to the University of Notre Dame, which required me to serve as a naval officer for four years after graduation. I was mainly attracted to the Navy by the money and the promise of travel and adventure, but I also believed that as part of the armed forces, I would be helping the United States promote freedom, democracy, and human rights around the world.

During my studies of government and international relations, however, I discovered the paradox of U.S. history: it is characterized by sublime idealism as well as profound hypocrisy. Sometimes the U.S. government supports democratic regimes; sometimes it overthrows them. Sometimes it assists freedom fighters; sometimes it coddles brutal dictators. I found myself becoming disillusioned with U.S. foreign policy, and I wondered what role I would play in it as a naval officer. But since thinking could lead to questioning and doubt, I coped by directing my thoughts to youthful distractions and sheltered places.

I graduated from Notre Dame in May 1990, fully prepared to fulfill my obligation to the Navy. A few months later, while I was at Surface Warfare Officers' School learning about weapons and navigation, the armed forces of Iraq invaded and occupied Kuwait. To my surprise, the anti-Soviet propaganda I had been fed for the previous four years was quickly replaced by anti-Arab and anti-Islam sentiment; the words *camel jockey, sand nigger,* and *raghead* entered daily discourse. Some officers openly joked about nuking the Middle East and turning it into a parking lot. I felt isolated and confused, but I found that a few other officers shared my doubts about the purpose of the war. Was it about resisting aggression, or ensuring the uninterrupted flow of cheap oil to industrialized countries?

I was in Tomahawk school the day Operation Desert Storm began. As I watched CNN's coverage of the cruise missiles exploding in Baghdad, a battle was raging inside me. I felt an acute tension between my obligation to the Navy and the obligation to my conscience, which was forcefully telling me that I could never fire a nuclear missile at anyone, regardless of the provocation or cause. And if I wouldn't fire a nuke, would I be willing to enforce U.S. foreign policy by firing a missile filled with cluster bombs or high explosives? I ended each day after Tomahawk school by trying to drown my confusion in a bottle of whiskey. I felt as if I had lost control over my life. Something had to give.

The warmth of the summer night and the pressing of the headphones bring me back into the present. I pick up the binoculars hanging around my neck and scan the void in front of the ship. I can barely tell where the horizon is as I look from left to right. Nothing . . . nothing . . . nothing . . . wait, yes, there's a faint light in the distance just off our starboard bow.

I grab the long cord attached to my headphones and walk around the helm to the contact status board at the back of the bridge. We have only three contacts at the moment. Two are moving away from us, and the other is designated "Skunk" Hotel. (A skunk is an unknown contact). The status board says Hotel is at 356 degrees true at 10,500 yards. Yep, that's him. We should have seen him earlier, but visibility is especially poor in this part of the northern Gulf. Humidity, airborne sand, and smoke from the Kuwaiti oil well fires combine to form an opaque haze. Even during the day, sometimes we don't see contacts until they are 6,000 yards away.

"Officer of the deck, we have Hotel visually now, at about zero-three-zero," I say as I walk back to the front of the bridge.

"Where?" he asks. He rushes up to the gyro repeater to check our course, and then looks ahead through his binoculars. "Yep . . . I see two masthead lights and a starboard running light."

I stand by the gyro while he scuttles back to the radar repeater to get another mark for the moboard. I watch the dim light on the horizon slowly drift to the right.

"He has a four-thousand-yard CPA (closest point of approach)," says the OOD as he rises from the moboard and hurries out to the starboard bridge wing to take another look.

I check my watch: it's one minute to turn. I place the right earpiece of the headphones behind my ear so that I can clearly hear the quartermaster when he marks the time to turn. I look again at the contact through my binoculars. He looks like a big merchant ship, probably an oil tanker, based on the distance between the white masthead lights. He's got a definite right-bearing drift.

PING . . . PING . . . PING. The metallic ring of sonar indicates that they have just gone active again, scanning the sea in front of us for floating and submerged objects.

"Officer of the deck, recommend coming left to two-seven-zero at this time," says the quartermaster. The OOD is still out on the bridge wing, so I acknowledge the quartermaster and give my command to the helmsman, who stands behind me.

"Helm, left standard rudder, steady on course two-seven-zero."

"Left standard rudder, coming to new course two-seven-zero, aye sir . . . Sir, my rudder is left standard coming to course two-seven-zero," the helmsman repeats back to me.

"Very well," I acknowledge.

Our change of course will clear the merchant ship's CPA way out, so we won't come anywhere near each other.

As we turn to the left, a refreshing breeze passes through the bridge. The ship starts to list heavily to port, and I shift my weight onto my left leg.

"Helm, ease your rudder to left ten degrees, steady on course two-seven-zero," I say. I want the helmsman to take some of the lean out of the ship to avoid rolling anyone out of his bunk.

"Sir, my rudder is left ten degrees coming to course two-seven-zero."

"Very well."

PING . . . PING . . . PING. While we are turning, sonar continues to sound. It's about five seconds between pings.

I stand, leaning on the gyro repeater, watching the merchant ship move into the distance and to the right as we turn. We see three types of ships here in the gulf: big oil tankers, small wooden dhow boats, and an array of warships. Our main concern these days is to avoid accidentally colliding with other ships or running into a mine. Things are pretty quiet here, at the moment.

"Sir, steady on course two-seven-zero, checking two-six-four."

"Very well."

I look again at my watch. It's 4:38 A.M. Only two hours to go until the next watch takes over. I take a deep breath, and my mind wanders again.

After Tomahawk school I returned to the *Arkansas* feeling utterly bewildered. I was considering filing an application for conscientious objector status, but I was concerned about the fallout from acting upon my change of heart. How will my family react? My friends? What will my shipmates think? What if the Navy turns down my application? What if the Navy approves it? How will I repay my scholarship if I am discharged? How will this experience affect my future? Should I just try to silence my doubts and stick it out for the next three years?

I threw myself into my work in the Missiles Division, hoping that activity would displace doubt. But I continued to think, and after several weeks of intense introspection, I decided my only recourse was to be honest with myself, my shipmates, and the Navy. I prepared a written statement asking to be recognized as a conscientious objector, and gathered letters of support from a priest at Notre Dame, a naval officer I knew from ROTC, and several friends. In addition, I consulted a lawyer who gave me invaluable tips on the process.

On a sunny day at the end of February—five months ago—I handed the application to my boss, the head of the Weapons Division. He was not pleased by my decision, but he was professional in the handling of my case. Some of the men on my ship shunned me as news of my action spread, but many respectfully asked me about what I was doing, and a few even inquired about the process, thinking it might be an easy way for them to get out of the Navy. In fact, it is one of the most difficult ways to get out. Being gay or testing positive for illicit drugs trigger quick discharges, but stating that you have a moral objection to nuclear weapons and war initiates a lengthy process in which you are judged by people who generally disagree with your action, and may even be openly hostile to you.

Up until now, the process has been relatively smooth, except that I now have to wait for the final decision while on patrol in the Persian Gulf. A couple of weeks after I submitted my application, two Navy chaplains interviewed me to evaluate the sincerity of my beliefs. Then an antagonistic Navy psychologist bombarded me with questions and administered four hours of psychological testing to quantify my change of heart and mind. Next my application was scrutinized during a formal hearing. Fortunately, everyone recommended that my application be granted, and my case was forwarded to the Pentagon for approval. As I waited for the final word, the captain decided I should help drive his ship to the Gulf. It's been almost two months now since we passed through the Golden Gate and charted a course to this distant outpost of the American empire.

"Officer of the deck, sonar reports an underwater contact bearing three-zero-zero true at seven hundred yards," says a voice from the back of the bridge. It's the status board operator, who communicates with the sonar and radar technicians in the combat information center.

"Very well," says the OOD as he scampers over to the starboard bridge wing.

I pick up my binoculars and look to the right of the bow, but all I can see is black. Sonar gets these "contacts" once or twice a watch, but they are usually just a school of fish or garbage. Sonar does serve a valuable purpose: it looks for floating mines the Iraqis dumped into the Gulf a few months back. Even now, in July, our minesweepers are still finding these bombs bobbing in the swell. I asked one of the nuclear engineers what would happen if we hit a mine below one of the two nuclear reactors powering our ship. He looked at me, shook his head, and said, "You don't want to know."

After a couple of minutes the OOD comes back into the bridge and heads over to the radar repeater to confer with the new officer about sonar. To my right, the quartermaster draws a line on the chart for our next course. I glance down at the gyro repeater to make sure the helmsman is on course, and then I look out into the night ahead. My mind starts to drift back to California again, and I wonder when I am going to get off this ship and go home.

JIM FAUSS
(1940–1996)

At a meditation retreat in the early 1990s, Jim came up to Therese Fitzgerald of the Community of Mindful Living, looked her in the face, and said, "Therese, give me something to do. I don't need to be here for myself. Let me help others. Let me do something for others."

When Therese and her husband Arnie Kotler, of Koa Books, visited Jim in the hospital in 1996, when he was dying of cancer, Therese asked if he'd like to read the Buddhist "Five Remembrances." He responded, "Sure, I'll read." After reading the First Remembrance, "I am of the nature to grow old. There is no way to escape growing old," he grinned his wide spread of a grin and said, "That sure sounds good to me."

The last time Arnie and Therese visited Jim in the hospital, he was completely lucid although in much pain. At that time, the almond blossoms were in full bloom. Therese bent down to Jim's ear and said, "Jim, the Almond Blossom Sangha is blooming beautifully now."

He had so much energy, joy, and love to share with others. He created places of refuge for people to come, sit themselves down, and try to make peace with all the stuff kickin' around inside. He set out on a course of meditation to center himself, to ready himself to meet death with as much ease as he could muster, with the help of all his wonderful family and friends—friends in the hospice movement, his veteran buddies, his friends in the Methodist Church, the Buddhist meditation hall, the Jewish synagogue, and many other places of prayer and contemplation that he made his home.

There is a nugget of inconsolable grief for the loss of Jim. But there is also mindfulness of his life and his teachings; his spirit lives on in us. We can let the Jim with his down-to-earth authenticity, the Jim who loved people all over the world, the Jim with a great compassionate soul—all these Jims help us look at our own pain and strife, and smile. We can smile, returning his smile.

How Can a Human Being
Learn to Love a People Then Kill Them?

Young and impatient,
Wanting adventure and independence.
Quit school and join the Army.
Take a test that says you get to learn a new language.
Out of thirty-two choices the fifth was Vietnamese.

How can a human being learn to love a people then kill them?
Viet Nam, the land of Dien Bien Phu and Dr. Tom Dooley.
I know where that is on the South China Sea,
Used to be French Indo-China.
Likely spot for trouble someday,
Army careers thrive on trouble.

How can a human being learn to love a people then kill them?
Youngest student at the Army Language School,
Seventeen and open to ideas,
John from Yale and Chapman from Harvard,
Don and Bruce from Cal, lots of schools all over,
These were my classmates sharing ideas, lots of ideas.
Castro was in the mountains,
Don and Kelley wanted to join him,
But they couldn't sell the hi-fi.
The first Monterey Jazz Festival was held,
The Kingston Trio was selling out on campuses.
We'd go to San Francisco, hang out and be beatniks for the
    weekend
in North Beach. We'd wear Levis and combat boots.

How can a human being learn to love a people then kill them?
The war came and many my age, old friends, classmates, and
    neighbors
went off to kill in that land where I had never been, physically.
I didn't watch the news,
I didn't have a television,
I marched and protested,
I led marches and protests,

I got arrested,
I became a leftist,
I thought the NLF was good and the government in Hanoi was
    bad.
I thought the "conventional war" after the Tet Offensive was
    evil,
I knew many thousands of lives were being wasted while the
    cynical
politicians in Hanoi and Washington, D.C., maneuvered to the
    bargaining table.

How can a human being learn to love a people then kill them?
I had few good feelings for those veterans who told me crude and
    ugly stories of Viet Nam that land I had learned to love.
They had not learned to love that land and those people.
Military training and war is not to teach love.
Military training is to teach hatred.
Military training and war does not want you to be a human
    being.
To be a human being, that is the question.
I met Mr. Hiep's daughter, Co Chau, "Pearl," and fell
    immediately in love.
They all loved their land which for various reasons they were
    separated from.
What was I supposed to learn?

How can a human being learn to love a people then kill them?
First thing I was told at my duty station, "You cannot associate
    with any Vietnamese."
I was stationed near Washington, D.C.
There were a few Vietnamese in D.C., but they were off limits.
Security, you know.
At work I was praised for being able to "think like a Vietnamese
    soldier."
I too was a young soldier.
That praise had a deep effect on my life.
A certain agency commended me for my work on their behalf
    and then
did a dastardly deed in Cambodia,

My mind said, "Enough."
My mouth said, "I will do this no more, make me a medic."
I was reading Gandhi.
They threatened to put me in jail and I said, "Do what you have
    to do."
I became a medic who spoke Vietnamese.
One day I had all the inside information on world events and the
    next day only what you read in the newspapers. This is the hook.

How can a human being learn to love a people then kill them?
Viet Nam language, culture, and history,
The main religion is Buddhism,
Most of the instructors are Christian.
Not many questions about Buddhism get answered.
Mr. Nhu is a Buddhist and the chair of the department.
Mr. Nhu wrote funny dialogues.
Mr. Nhu never answered my queries about Buddhism in Viet
    Nam.
The libraries had books on Buddhism in China and Japan but not
    Viet Nam.
Mr. Nghiem, Peter Nghiem was a Christian, a very good
    Christian.
Mr. Nghiem made jokes about Buddhists in Viet Nam and about
    the worship of ancestors.
Alan Watts and D. T. Suzuki had books about Zen and Tao.
Jack Kerouac had books about Zen.
I read the books on Zen, Taoism, Indian philosophy, Chinese
    Way of Thought
sitting crossed-legged on my bunk while my classmates were
    getting drunk.

How can a human being learn to love a people then kill them?
The instructors were homesick for their families and the land
    they loved.
Mr. Hiep and his son-in-law Mr. Hien, Mr. and Mrs. Toan,
Even Mr. Hoa, the playboy, got tears in his eyes when he talked.
Mrs. Toan was pregnant and every day became more beautiful
    glowing
with that special glow of pregnancy.

The Red Fox

On the road that goes under the freeway,
    about five blocks from the freeway, the road ends.
I pulled off, looking for a place to take a nap
    —a nap and a call of nature at the end of the road.
There at the end of the road is a dump
    —not an official dump, no fees to pay.
A dump, nevertheless.
Parts of cars and rubbish and garbage.
There at the end of the road I saw it.

There next to the dump I saw the fox.
Not just any fox but a red fox.
Not just any red fox but the super red fox.
The red fox that would put other foxes to shame.
You never see a picture of a red fox as pretty as this one.
Really, red and white, the model for the rest of the red foxes.

I've seen plenty of gray foxes.
I've seen my share of red foxes.
All the rest look scraggly and faded compared to this red fox.

At first I thought I was imagining it.
I blinked and it still stood there next to the dump.
I said, "Fox, you sure do look pretty."
The fox said, "I know."
"Fox, what are you doing here?"
"What do you mean, what am I doing here?"
"I mean, this is just a dump near the freeway."

"What are YOU doing here?"
"Well, I'm a human and I drive down the freeway."
"Why?"
"Because I have to go to and from work."
"Why do you work?"
"To support my family."
"Bring your family here to the dump and they'll be okay."

"Do you have a family?"

"Not yet, I haven't yet met a fox to raise a family with."

"Maybe if you moved away from the freeway and the dump,
  you'd find another nice fox."

"Life is easy here. The dump is full of mice, and sometimes I get
  fresh garbage."

"How did you get so pretty?"

"Mice are good for my coat. I take care of myself and I have good
  genes."

"Aren't you afraid of the people who live around here?"

"Why should I be?"

"They might think you're trying to eat their chickens."

"I do enjoy an occasional hen."

"They might think you're going to breed their French poodle."

"Poodles are not my cup of tea."

"Don't you worry about getting run over?"

"I stay off the freeway, and I'm a smart fox."

"But really, right here next to the freeway is no place for you.
You should be living where there are no roads—someplace really
  wild."

"How about you? How much time do you spend on the
  freeway?"

"Oh, about three or four hours a day."

"Do you like the freeway that much?"

"No, but that is how I make money."

"What is money?"

"It's what I buy things with."

"Like what?"

"Like this car."

"So you can drive on the freeway?"

"Yes, I also buy food with money."

"But the mice and the garbage are free."

My mother read me Longfellow's "Hiawatha" when I was little. My
dad came home from the war, having survived internment in a POW
camp after being shot down during the bombing of Dresden. A few
years later he joined the Air Force, and my two sisters and I were
raised as Air Force brats. In 1968 I was drafted and sent to Vietnam.
I came back in 1970 and finished college, graduating from San Francisco State University with a degree in creative writing. I lived off
the GI Bill until 1978, when I got a job at UC Berkeley. In 1986, I
started reading my Vietnam poems in public.

"Charlie Don't Surf" was inspired by a line from *Apocalypse Now.*
"Charlie" is a name we gave to the Viet Cong.

Brown Bread

they fed dad brown bread
in the german prison camp;
forever after that
he couldn't eat brown bread.
some experiences
scar us forever;
he was pulled by his parachute
across some ditches
and an open field.
seeing a farmer approach him
he threw down his weapon
and surrendered.
too far behind enemy lines.
they marched him thru a town
where people lined up
to spit at him
and call him nasty names.
one of his captors
said "good german name!"
and kicked him in the back.
he went to a dulag
which was a country club

compared to a stalag.
the international red cross
came to visit
and proclaim how well the prisoners
were being treated.
they must not have seen
the other prisoners—
the ones dad said they had
to feed every two hours
when patton's army came
and liberated them.
most of the guards had fled
by then; the rest cut a deal
with my dad in return for better
treatment—they were probably
afraid they'd be executed.
now that i've told his story
it sounds so much like vonnegut's
in slaughterhouse five
that it's almost the same story.
except for the science fiction
and dad was in the lead
bomber that bombed dresden
and not in the shelter
that vonnegut survived in.
they made a movie out of it—
slaughterhouse five i mean—
dad and i went to see it.
i don't recall him reacting
but then he always was
the great stone face.
maybe that was due to
all the brown bread they fed him
in the german prison,
that later he couldn't eat.

Cool Dad

my dad, who never blows his cool,
the day i left for vietnam
sat down to a stack of homemade buttermilk pancakes
and poured vinegar on them by mistake.

Charlie Don't Surf

charlie don't, charlie don't, charlie don't surf
charlie don't, charlie don't, charlie don't surf
charlie don't, charlie don't, charlie don't surf
    Charlie Don't Surf

when i went over to vietnam
after i got in that war-torn land
i met up with a guy named murf;
first thing he told me, is "charlie don't surf."

charlie don't, charlie don't, charlie don't surf
charlie don't, charlie don't, charlie don't surf
charlie don't, charlie don't, charlie don't surf
    Charlie Don't Surf

i was crawling on my belly thru the mud one day
after that morning it looked like play
there was shrapnel everywhere but me
i looked up and what did i see?

a funny little guy not five-foot-two
a thin white beard and a big stick too
he said "i'm uncle ho and i've come to see
if you yank surfers are as good as me."

he gestured left, and underneath a tree
was a brand-new surfboard, just right for me
i grabbed it up and he led the way
to what appeared to be the local bay

now many's the eye that may deceive
and a person's word may be hard to believe
but thirty-foot waves came crashing in
and i tell ya, they made one helluva din

he said, "you chicken?" and rushed on out
i followed him quick, for i had no doubt
for a california man, in his natural pride,
could show uncle ho one helluva ride

ho took off first; he was pretty quick
he did some things that were awful slick
like walking the nose and hanging ten
then he backed up and did them again

but i said nothing, and soon he did see
you can't beat a californian so easily
i was so hyped up when i did my show
i coulda sold ice to an eskimo

i did everything that'd ever been seen
till ho he was looking awful green
but he doubled his efforts, and soon i saw
that he was well-seasoned, he was not raw

he turned his head with a terrible smile
and showed me my tricks, hanoi style
he did at least one, to show he was boss,
while wolfing down rice with the local fish sauce

but i smiled too, i would not run
and did more tricks in the setting sun
and when at last the sun sank low
i could see we were in for one helluva blow

the storm came quickly, rain and wind
and uncle ho signaled that we should end
we'll take up again tomorrow said he
for you're pretty good for a yank, i see

i shook my head and i signaled no
and i rode right out in the teeth of the blow

and uncle ho followed, for he had pride,
but this time luck was not on his side

for there, in the middle of the final set,
came A FIFTY-FOOT WAVE, the biggest yet
ho wiped out in the crash and foam,
and me—i just rode the big wave home

so all you beach boys, i'll tell you free
a tip a short-timer once gave to me
if there's one thing we know on this God's Green Earth
it's Charlie Don't Surf

>   charlie don't, charlie don't, charlie don't surf
>   charlie don't, charlie don't, charlie don't surf
>   charlie don't, charlie don't, charlie don't surf
>   Charlie Don't Surf.

GARY GACH

I was born in 1947 in Los Angeles. I've worked as an actor, book designer and typographer, bookstore clerk, assistant hospital administrator, legal secretary, longshoreman, magazine editor in chief, office temp, and web weaver. I attained a B.A., in English, in 1970. I'd always shied away from writing workshops, until I happened upon Maxine Hong Kingston's veterans' writing sangha, in 1994. I currently teach haiku at Book Passage University, Stanford University, and the San Francisco Zen Center. And I facilitate mindfulness meditation at the Church for the Fellowship of All Peoples.

I am editor of *What Book!? Buddha Poems from Beat to Hiphop,* which includes works by a number of veterans; author of *The Complete Idiot's Guide to Understanding Buddhism;* and cotranslator of three books of poetry by Ko Un (*Flowers of a Moment, Songs for Tomorrow,* and *Ten Thousand Lives*). Homepage: http://word.to

Haiku

the old pawnbroker
pays not even one thin dime
for new war medals

kept from playing with toy guns
boys use their fingers instead

opera patrons pass by
the veteran leaning in trashcan
shadows in rain

Fathers and Sons

Recently, a stranger came up to me and spoke just one sentence, unexpectedly bringing much of my life story into focus. I was at the Church for the Fellowship of All Peoples, founded in 1944, in San Francisco, America's first interracial church. Its name might sound New Agey. I respect its congregation, the beloved community, as Dr. Martin Luther King, Jr., would put it. On rare occasions, I've been

honored to be asked to their podium. Me, a Jewish Buddhist, address-
ing a largely black congregation on Sunday—will somebody please say
Amen!?

Earlier this year, I'd suggested a book, *Engaged Spirituality,* for their
study group. The first selections are from the activist-minister-writer-
mystic Howard Thurman, cofounder of the Church for the Fellowship of All Peoples. The anthology continues with work by such
luminaries as Vine Deloria, Jr., Marian Wright Edelman, Thich Nhat
Hanh, Joanna Macy, Rabindranath Tagore, and Simone Weil. Its eclectic selections provided grist for the mill for ten sessions. Then the group
asked if I could come in for a month and continue their studies of
engaged Buddhism. Engaged, as in being actively involved in the world.

Well, on the third of those four Sundays, as I sat down with the five
or six members of the study group, about a dozen ladies suddenly filed
in. They were well into their seventies and beyond, all smartly dressed
as is customary in black churches, heads held high in Sunday go-to-
meetin' hats worn like crowns. They glided smoothly into empty seats
alongside us at our long table in the back of the large ground floor of
the church. Someone explained that they were visiting from Chicago
and were taking in our study group as part of their tour of the church.
Then, fine.

So, I continued, the focus of our attention would be motivation. If
our ultimate goal is enlightenment, awakening, liberation—what is
our initial intent, setting out upon the path? I could see faint, mute
question marks start to form on people's brows as they thought about
this. Obviously, the motivation here isn't money, though money
mobilizes many and much into action. Heads nodded. Is the motivation, then, personal salvation? Once I get mine, can everybody else
just go hang?

I was introducing the *bodhisattva* path, in which one sets out on the
Way for the sake of all beings. Some people had already heard of this.
After my introduction, I invited our extended study group to express
their own intentions. Why are we here? Many saw themselves as similar to the *bodhisattva.* One lady realized hers might even be considered
a kind of selfish altruism, wanting to live in a world in which others
were kind, as well as oneself. They were a pretty sharp crew.

And, as Rosa Parks had just died that week, one of the elder visitors,
a feminine, coffee-with-cream-complexioned buddha in a stylish dress

and a straw church hat with a broad ribbon, said she thought Rosa Parks was like the Buddha in daring to leave the high castle walls of accepted convention in quest for truth. We all nodded at that recognition, said Um-hmm, sipped coffee and tea together, and soon a meditative piano soloist could be heard, signaling time for the church service upstairs.

But one black woman, with thick glasses and an elegant, ebony walking stick, possibly in her eighties, lingering behind, was suddenly eye-to-eye close to me, our lives' differences momentarily negligible, and told me sadly but simply this one haunting sentence. The time when America's values collapsed was when both parents went out and worked, the children left free to come and go without guidance. That was all she said. I thanked her for her observation. And, as she walked away, I'd started to remember how both my parents worked. I'd never thought much of it before. Yet this familiar refrain, family values, watered the seed of a meditation that unfolded in my heart.

My meditation began by considering values and their roots in my family. Do some of our values come to us from our mothers but others from our fathers? Like an allowance, most boys receive training into manhood from fathers and father figures.

These bonds can be rosy, or rocky. How many males face the blank wall of an absent father? How many grow up with an invisible man for a father? How many with deadbeat dads? All the words never said. The missed opportunities. Me, I count my lucky stars.

I cherish my close, intimate relationship with my dad, from my childhood, but especially now, in maturity, as we've experienced the blessings of mutual forgiveness and reconciliation. The beneficial regrets ... the transformation of hurts ... the watering of the seeds within our hearts. He's now ninety-two, and (knock wood) with good health (an avid golfer) and all his marbles (plus a quick wit), a true blessing in my life. Of course, things were not always thus.

Things began to really fall apart when I'd crossed a line of value with him. It was a few months after my eighteenth birthday. He asked me if I'd registered for the draft. He asked it out of the blue, as it were, seemingly as a mere afterthought, home from work, before dinner, checking that everything in the household was in order. As simple as asking if I've washed my hands before dinner. I didn't mean my answer as anything personal, but I could see he took it so. I still remember the crestfallen look on his face, more than disappointment, a shock, when I said no.

I hadn't discussed my decision with anyone. I simply chose not to and had left it at that. But now that it was suddenly out in the open, it seemed to represent a widening rift between us. I'd been a child prodigy. My poor dad, truly a wise man, never dreamed of raising a kid who'd challenge his own formidable mind. Yet he trusted I'd turn out all right. Nevertheless, by this point in my own saga, I'd evolved into a latch-key kid with an extended family of artist types, actors, and free thinkers across town, part of the early '60s LA underground, if you will.

In those days, American values were being questioned beyond the known horizons of my family's home, and it sometimes seemed like everything not nailed down was shaking loose. In 1961, the country was riveted by rapidly escalating violence in the South. Although war was hardly mentioned in those days, it was pointed out to me by an artist that those "advisors"—American military personnel in Vietnam, from time to time reported in the daily newspaper, flown in by our government to some country few knew how to pronounce much less visualize—were there in preparation for an upcoming, major, all-out war. Wars don't always begin with a declaration nor end with an armistice.

My dad, on the other hand, was gung ho. He'd been raised at a military boarding school and served his country in the military, overseas—his induction delayed because he was still working on I Am an American Day. All citizens naturalized that year, as well as those who'd attained their majority, would be recognized and honored in special national, state, and local ceremonies, on Sunday, May 18, 1941. Two days later, he sent his draft board a dozen red roses, in appreciation for their granting him a temporary exemption from the Selective Service in order to complete his job. He was that patriotic.

He lived the American Dream. Yet he never had quite enough time, while being all he could be, to scrutinize my blossoming into a pacifist. While other parents were telling their kids to turn down the rock 'n' roll that was sweeping the nation, I was listening to the Weavers, Miles Davis, Ravi Shankar, and Bach, and he took quiet pride in my budding cultural awareness.

Once, after one of my periodic explorations of the dusty treasure troves of Hollywood Boulevard's secondhand bookstores, usually to buy science pocketbooks, science-fiction magazines, or poetry, I came home with a copy of *The Nation* in a brown paper bag. I shaded the nightlight by my bed as I stayed up and read Fred Cook's "Juggernaut: The Warfare State," a feature picking up where Eisenhower's farewell address had left off that year warning of the military-industrial complex. 1961: I was fourteen.

Two years later, people of my generation remember where they were on November 22, 1963, when they heard news of the assassination of the thirty-fifth president of the United States.

By age eighteen, I was supposed to register to be ready to serve my country in a battle that seemed dubious to me at the time, and would eventually prove a quagmire. Saying no and not registering proved far easier than facing the slippery slope of telling my dad about it. When he asked, I just said no, clenched my teeth, and prepared for the worst. My father's initial, silent expression of hurt, indignation, horror, and patient resolve melted away, and he quickly processed his reaction into words. When he found speech, he told me bluntly: I *had* to go register for the draft. It was my duty.

It was one of those many-feelings-all-welling-up-at-once moments for both of us. I dealt with my part by standing my ground, yet trying to give him ground too, asking him plain and simple, man to man: But why are we going to war in Vietnam?

Son, he replied, it's not for you to ask. There's no ifs, ands, or buts to this. The people in our government know far more than you or I about what's best for our country, and it's our duty to do what they say. Don't ask why.

I don't think either of us knew that much about Vietnam. But, in effect, he was saying he didn't have to know. Question authority? Him, or the government? I shouldn't go there. Dinner would be ready in less than an hour. We went our separate ways. Later that week, I registered with the draft board.

—

Questioning authority had been the order of the day for me and the whiz kids I hung out with at school. We'd take turns stopping class lectures and asking our teachers, Why?! New teachers would reply,

Because I say so! But then someone else would counter, Why do you say so?! Eventually they caught on that nothing less than Socratic dialogue would be the order of the day.

The worst of it, I think, befell a science teacher named Mr. Himmelman. Ordinarily a mild-mannered person, he had one very striking trait: namely, ordering more drop drills than any other teacher. This meant he'd unexpectedly shout *Drop!* at the top of his voice, and we had to drop down and crouch beneath our desks, heads tucked under folded hands, to rehearse protecting ourselves from the blinding flare and deadly radiation unleashed by an atomic bomb dropped on Los Angeles from Russia.

One day, in the middle of an especially boring lecture on cell meiosis or osmosis or halitosis, I opened my mouth and, without premeditation, shouted *Drop!!* Everyone ducked and covered, except for me and Mr. Himmelman. We remained sitting upright, regarding each other across the rows of empty desks. Then Mr. Himmelman, his gaze locked on me, spoke: OK, class, you can come back to your seats now. It's all right. Mr. Gach has just taught us a lesson . . . in how strongly we can all become indoctrinated . . . for which we can be very grateful and which is a lesson I presume none of us will have to ever experience again. He continued to look at me, as the class straightened their clothes, wiped off their knees, and returned to their seats, and I gave him a most grateful glance, as he returned to his lecture.

Nicely done, Mr. Himmelman, I thought. And thank you for not telling my dad. But Mr. Himmelman would also be relieved that it not leave the room, that he'd been shamed by a runt kid. Like Mr. Himmelman, my dad was left behind in my relentless questioning of this strange, new world we were inheriting from his generation, questioning received wisdom and accepted tradition, leaving him in what he later told me was awe at what my schoolteachers called my rare promise. They once told him a chance to teach someone like me came once in a lifetime. So here I was, this smart-aleck big brain who used big words that only widened the distance between my dad and me. Nor did he have an inkling that I didn't feel at all rewarded for whatever promise I might have held to my schoolteachers, receiving instead, all too often, an education in the absurd. So there was all the more reason for my dad to be so shocked to learn I wasn't big on what some might call blind faith. And all the more reason for me to feel estranged from him for wanting me to fight in a war that didn't make sense to me.

I didn't think of myself as a typical warrior and I didn't think the Army would miss just one more body if I didn't sign up for their war. In my way, I felt I was being patriotic. After all, I couldn't see myself charging over the top of a trench, pointing a bayonet on the end of my rifle as I ran into enemy lines. I felt I was being loyal to my flag by questioning the whole rationale for this unprecedented war. I did not see the clear and present danger, and wasn't that the reason for conscription? Like I say, I hadn't discussed my views nor my decision to say no, but when it came out, the brevity of the conversation somehow seemed a formal parting of the ways. I realize now that he's a very terse individual; but back then, it was as if he cared more about the Stars and Stripes than me possibly dying in a distant country about whose own history he seemed relatively indifferent. I felt as if I'd failed him, and from then on, as I was called more and more to make a way for myself as a man in the world, I felt his trust in me dwindling, like sands running out through an hourglass.

How many years did we say pass the salt to each other, at most, and that was it? I'd say please. He'd say thank you—nothing more. When in the same room, I felt myself doing the dance of shifty glances, with awkward body language, and silent palpable tension, as though the room weren't big enough for the two of us. I masqueraded as an adult, but knew I was still being yanked by the chain of my emotional reactions, so much so it would have been a luxury for me to even wonder if the same might be true of him. Finally, I put 300 miles between us, to chill out, and make a life for myself.

Over time, I learned there is no path to peace, that peace is the path, and that taking that path meant doing so step by step. It was along that path, with that grounding, I learned to walk with balance, a middle way between extremes. From there, I was able to reconnect with myself as a child, then feel my father as he too might have been as a child. Fragile, vulnerable, each of us bearing the difficulties of our father within us. Like all beings, we each wanted happiness. I learned to release the unnecessary suffering I'd felt between us, to look at it and let it go. Pain might be unavoidable, but suffering can be extra. I no longer conjured it up to let it pull me by the nose.

In coming home to the here and now, I came of age. I'd finally come home to take my place in the family of being. And now that I've grown old enough to claim a modicum of wisdom, I see how much of my father there is in me, and I'm grateful for how much of his own life he has given me, as well as life itself. And nurturing values, these too I cherish.

———

Stepping back from our particulars, for a moment, I wonder if father–son estrangement might not be inherent in our culture, where rites of passage are administered through school or the military or jail or the media. I've often thought of fathers and sons in terms of rites of passage. The onset of manhood kicks in with a fury at a certain age. It happens to any young boy. Not just his head but now his body grows hair. He suddenly gets pumped full of hormones rushing through his metabolism like a roaring whitewater river careening over uncharted falls. He tries to call out and hears his voice break, cracking open, to reveal a deeper voice. Beyond control. Then he wakes up one dawn, surprised to find his haunting breathless sexual arousal only a dream, in his own bed and not inside another person, his penis unfamiliarly hard as a rock, immense oceanic feeling spilling over with an intensely strange but weird pleasure. He soon bonds with others the same age, undergoing the same surge, as against the rest of the world for whom none of this immediate urgency seems of even the remotest interest.

Our ancestors understood. Wise elders of the tribe knew that their young boys, on approaching manhood, were gripped by outrageous demands of flesh and imagination, and that overnight the boy-men could kill the tribesmen in their sleep. And so they performed rites of passage, guiding the boys into adulthood, initiating them into a timeless vision of relationship with the universe, as interdependent beings, standing on their own two feet as members of a tribe that was itself part of a greater kinship of being beneath the stars.

Today, our young men are killing themselves as well as the tribe— inner cities staked out by gangs in growing networks of escalating violence; teen suicide an epidemic claiming almost as many lives as car accidents; and loner students coming to school one morning dressed in black, in mourning for themselves, armed and over the top, wasting everyone in sight. In each tragedy, each victim mourned by family, friends, the community, a widening chain reaction. (Ancestors, where are you?)

———

My own story had a happy outcome. Once there was a space in my life for reconciliation to take place, it did. An opportunity came for us to bury the hatchet. My father was now happily remarried to a woman who'd raised children of her own and then gone back to school and earned her degree in psychotherapy. She obviously saw the grand canyon between him and me. Sometimes the outsider sees the whole game. One afternoon, when I was visiting them, she staged an impromptu ritual over lunch. We'd gone out to a restaurant near the beach and sat in an outdoor patio, in the shade of its tall trees. The day was bright and clear, the air clean with the tangy smell of the sea. I say this was impromptu, but it was the perfect place, well chosen, and my dad clearly had rehearsed in advance. Midway in our sandwiches, at her cue, and with my full understanding, he retold for me, in a nutshell, the specific situations in which I had hurt him most. It was heartrending, really. I'd forgotten what an outrageous jerk I had been. Yet I had to admit, that was me in those days.

Surprised, listening deeply, I found I could identify with him, even after my writing us off as a failed pairing. After all, I still liked this guy, to say the least, and now I honored his courage to bring up out of the darkness, amid many other emotions surely being stirred up in their all-at-onceness, and speak in a spirit of reconciliation. I let myself feel his hurt from his own view. A blue jay in a palm tree scrawcked a reminder to me to remain in the present moment, as other diners clattered and chattered, and my dad and stepmom across from me awaited my response.

I admitted deep regret at having hurt him so gravely. It was as simple as that. Like joining palms, two hands together, we became pals again, ordered dessert, and have continued a wonderful relationship for the next twenty or more years.

Simple as that, but simple ain't easy. Life is lived forward and understood backwards. I had to go out on my own and develop as an individual, receptive and grounded enough for any chance of reconciliation. And it was necessary for there to be a chance to stop, for me to listen deeply.

Interesting that this peace treaty was initiated by a woman. And I suddenly thought of it years later because of what was said to me by the woman in church.

No doubt much in my own tale might well hold true for women. Yet women do have their own issues, and, looking back, I can see mine as very much "a guy thing." For example, this one ritual of reconciliation was so inextricably interwoven with another: the rite of passage, initiation of children, undergoing puberty, into the tribe.

My dad's coming of age was very much colored by the Great Depression, of making a way for himself in a world in upheaval and restarting from nearly zero. Then proving himself in military service. Next, raising a family.

My own coming of age was tested in the crucible of the 1960s. Like almost every other male my age, I did register for the draft. When my number was called and time came for me to be interviewed, I was classified 1-Y: qualified for service only in time of declared war or national emergency.

After the '60s' reevaluation of values, questioning not only war but just about everything else, I came away with seeds in my pocket dedicated for the renewal of spiritual traditions, which still nourish my life today. Back when I was thirteen, and *bar mitzvah* (come of age as a responsible adult), meditation meant bowing your head for one entire minute, in silence, while an invisible organist noodled away at some vague, slow, solemn filigree. Then in the 1960s, I reconnected with my roots through contact with what's now called the Jewish Renewal Movement, then just beginning, and was blessed to study with one of its founders, Rabbi Shlomo Carlebach of holy memory.

Back when I'd first sat in meditation, still in my preteens, there were more buddhas in the West sitting behind glass cases in museums than practicing on fresh cushions. But later, in the late '60s, I was fortunate to be introduced to *zazen,* Zen sitting meditation, by a living exponent of the art, relocated from Japan, himself a former kamikaze pilot. I cherish this daily practice of meditation. And I've had the honor of introducing my dad to meditation. Occasionally, now, he'll express a wish to practice meditation with me, and I practice golf with him. How sweet. Rites of passage, it seems, can be lifelong learnings.

Such estrangements as mine and my dad's may be inevitable—all the sad, wasted, unrealized potential; all the leaden silences, the clenched muscles, the seething or uncomprehending stares; and the seemingly narrow range of choices that to the actors appear as fixed as railroad tracks, stretching as far as the eyes can see. In the end, some suffering *is* unavoidable, but to wake up to the possibility of ending the suffering that is needless is a wonderful thing. Even the inevitable is not immutable.

I harbor the hope that others too can come through these gates of liberating reconciliation, to this circle of life—individuals and also groups, tribes, and nations. Glance around at what's happening near and far, and the value of rites of passage and reconciliation becomes obvious. So I'm glad to know that emotional intelligence is a value of growing importance in the curricula of tens of thousands of American schools. Blessed be all the mentors, the facilitators, the medicine-bringers, the healers. Spiritual evolution is possible.

Will somebody say Amen!?

ROBERT GOLLING, JR.

I am a U.S. Navy veteran of the American War in Viet Nam. My tour of duty was from January to June 1969. I am a retired telephone engineer living with my loving wife, Rebecca, and our two sons in the foothills of the Sierra Nevada. I home-school my thirteen-year-old son, Matthew, and watch (mindfully) my sixteen-year-old son, Alex, begin his adult life. My four older sons are grown and have their own families.

I believe it is my duty to live well, to lead a righteous life, and to remember the sacrifice of the soldiers and sailors who came before me. I am currently writing a story about a soldier who comes home from the Korean War, plants roses, and finds enlightenment.

The Body Escort

"Down the street," the mortician said in a voice at once firm and soft. "On the left, here, just a minute," he continued as he turned the car so he could park in front of the house. The trees on either side of the street had grown so large they touched each other to make a canopy over the street. The houses, too, had been there a long time. Tidy places that many families had lived in and loved since the 1920s and 1930s. The Raffertys' house stood farther back on the lot with a well-worn lawn on either side of an unadorned, straight cement walkway leading to the front door. The house was painted dark gray with white window trim. The roof stood tall and sloped steeply toward the street. Looking up, I noticed two dormers indicating upstairs bedrooms.

"This is the family's home," I concluded, half demanding that the last twenty-four hours be over, and half realizing that whatever was going to happen next was going to be harder than anything I had ever done before.

"Oh yes," said the mortician, seeming to understand that I needed reassurance. "Yes, I've been to their house before."

The mortician had picked us up, the casket and me, at Logan International Airport and transported us back to the deceased's hometown, forty-five minutes from Boston. He had verified, much to my relief, the identity of the body in the casket, the body I had been ordered to escort home, the body I had been ordered not to lose. After taking the casket to the mortuary, we were now at the dead boy's home.

I straightened my white hat and started up the walk. Images of a band of kids (boys mostly) playing football and baseball on the front lawn flashed across my mind. Was this the lawn of my youth, or was this the lawn right in front of me? They seemed remarkably the same. At the front step, purple hydrangeas flanked the small porch. The mortician knocked and the door opened slowly, but immediately. I stood split, half of myself playing football on the front lawn without a care in the world, the other half in front of this strange house that seemed so familiar.

"Hello, hello, come in, please," said a smallish man, maybe five feet six inches in height, compact, no extra weight. As he shook my hand, I noticed the muscles and the calluses on his palm. This man, I thought, knows how to work. He was past middle age, maybe the grandfather.

"I'm Michael's father," he said. "Call me Pat."

I removed my white hat as we entered the house. Off the small entry to the right was a parlor with half a dozen people in it. I stood slightly at attention and introduced myself, holding my white hat just in front of my belly, like a shield. In turn the people introduced themselves. Two of Michael's aunts sat on a sofa with crocheted doilies draped protectively across each arm; his oldest uncle was in the recliner; another gentleman and a lady were sitting in folding chairs close to a glass-topped coffee table. Remnants of a buffet-type luncheon littered the table's surface, coffee cups with saucers, plates with sandwich crumbs and potato salad leftovers, and a candy dish with little pastel mints.

Another lady, younger than the others but still older than me, stood in the middle of the room clearing the things from lunch. They looked like my own family, my own aunts wearing their flowered dresses draped over large soft bosoms and smelling of body powder.

I was about to sit down when yet another lady walked into the room. Pat Rafferty introduced his wife, Dorothy. In her late forties, she was large, but next to her husband, she seemed shorter and even stouter, and complemented his leanness. They were obviously a pair. Her dark hair with a soft glow of gray at the temples swept back to a large loose bun in the back. A slight redness only enhanced the brightness of her dark brown eyes.

"Thank you, Bob," she said.

"Ma'am?" I questioned.

"Thank you for bringing my son home," she said as she gave me a hug. It was a hug that lingered in lavender even after she'd sat down across the room.

"Bob, do you like pastries?" she asked.

"Yes, ma'am," I said. Though hungry, I hadn't thought of pastries, but how could I say no?

She was up immediately and into the kitchen, returning with a dinner plate loaded with an Italian whipped-cream pastry.

"Here you are, Bob. Michael so loved these," she said.

We sat, and between mouthfuls of the richest pastry I'd ever eaten, I tried to explain how it was that it was I who had brought their relative home. "Yesterday morning I was cleaning out this barrack at N.T.C. Treasure Island, and the master at arms came by looking for a Roman Catholic. 'I'm Roman Catholic,' I said. Now I'm here." I didn't tell them about the anxiety I'd had about catching the plane, the worry that I'd had about losing the casket, the terror I'd felt about having the wrong body in the casket. We were here; they didn't need to know the rest.

"Michael was a good boy," his mother said. "He was thinking of making the Navy a career. What about you, Bob, is the Navy your career?"

I'd never thought about any career, let alone the Navy. It seemed strange to me that Mrs. Rafferty asked about my career while she was about to bury her son.

"I don't know," I said. "I was in college for a year after high school."

"Michael tried a semester at UConn, but it wasn't really for him. He was so restless," she said.

"Yes, ma'am." I thought I knew what she meant. Things were happening in the world, Viet Nam was happening. "There is the GI Bill. I could go back to college after the Navy." I paused and remembered that her son couldn't take advantage of the GI Bill.

"Yes, Bob," she said wistfully, "Yes." And was quiet.

"Bob," his father said, "have you ever tried fried oysters?"

"No, sir," I said.

"Oh, you've got to try our local oysters and chips."

"Sure," I said, needing a change of scene. "One thing though: I need to find a place to stay."

"He'll stay here, now, won't he, Dot?" he said, speaking to his wife.

"I won't have it any other way. Please stay here with us tonight, Bob." She reached out and put her hand on my arm.

"Yes, ma'am." I smiled.

Leading me upstairs, Pat showed me his son's room. "Put your bag in here, Bob. Have you brought civvies? I'll wait for you downstairs then."

I changed quickly into a sport shirt and khaki slacks. Except for my short hair and spit-shined dress shoes, I looked just like a civilian. On the way out of the room, I looked back. My uniform was folded and neatly placed on the end of the bed, Michael's bed. I closed the door. Meeting Pat at the bottom of the stairs, I followed him out through the parlor. He led me outside and down the front walk. Walking quickly, he said, "Ugh, I'm glad to get out of there. How about you?"

"Oh, I don't know," I said helplessly.

"You're doing fine, Bob, just be yourself. You sure gave us a jolt though, when you came up the walk. You looked so much like Michael coming home. Even the way you walk."

"I, I'm sorry, sir."

"No, no, don't worry about it. It's not your fault. Let's go find those oysters."

We continued walking down the street on a sidewalk that looked as aged as the one in front of my grandmother's house in Oakland, California.

Pat told me all about his family. How he and his wife were older when they married and were able to have only three children: a son, a daughter, and their youngest, Michael. As he said "our youngest, Michael," a kind of a gulp or gasp lurched up his throat; his eyes welled up with tears. He shook his head as if to say, No, no, I'm OK, it'll be all right in a moment, but no other words came out. We walked on. It seemed so strange at the time; Pat had been the gracious host back at the house. He had made sure that I was introduced to everyone, calling on his daughter for more tea and refilling everyone's cup. Warmly, almost cheerfully, he engaged in any conversation that seemed to lag. But here, away from his family, alone with me, a stranger, he was all choked up. Finally he said, "I'll be all right in a minute."

I doubted that he'd be all right in only a minute. After a little while he did regain his voice. Soon, we approached a frayed and worn-looking 1950s red-and-white hamburger stand. No more than half a dozen cars could park in front, so it could barely qualify as a drive-in. One car in the lot looked like it had been parked there since the '50s. Inside, stand-up tables lined the front windows; the order and pickup counter faced front. All was neat and clean with well-ordered bottles of catsup, mustard, vinegar, salt, pepper, and napkins awaiting our attention.

"Bob, you've gotta try the fried oysters."

"Yes, sir, I will," I said, not knowing how I would swallow anything I'd put in my mouth. "I'll have a Coke, sir," I choked out, as Pat ordered for us. I found a couple of stools at the front window counter. Pat joined me a minute later.

We gazed out the window. "You may not believe this, but Michael and I didn't always agree."

"Yes, sir." I did know. My father didn't want me to join the Navy, but I wanted to see the world.

"I always thought he joined to get away from me," Pat said and sipped his coffee. "I think I was too hard on him. I wanted so much for him." Then after a long moment he said, "Now it doesn't matter."

Looking at his face I could see little muscle movements ripple and tighten around his mouth and eyes. His eyes glistened and closed, holding back the tears. Then our order of fried oysters and chips arrived.

Pat loved his fried oysters and was anxious that I too would like them. In all truth, I had to admit, "They're the best I've ever had."

"Ah, Bob, they're the only ones you've ever had."

"Yes, sir. That's true thanks to you, but I do like them." They tasted just like French fries.

We ate looking out of the window. The traffic on the street moved, starting and stopping, with a life of its own. The late-afternoon sun flashed off chrome and glass, dancing across the scene in front of us. The breeze kicked up dust, leaves, and old newspapers. The Frank Sinatra song "September" started to play on the jukebox. Pat and I swallowed in unison though we hadn't been chewing anything at that particular time. Pat was afloat in a sea of sadness, and I was on the shoreline with no lifeline to throw him. We sat without saying anything for a good minute. It seemed like an hour. Then I put my hand on his shoulder, and the corners of his mouth tried to make a smile, well, sort of.

"Ah, Bob, go on with ya," he said with a lilt in his voice. "Finish your oysters."

After we had finished eating, we walked back the way we had come. The evening sun lingered among the clouds and lit up the leaves of early autumn. The air was cooler now and felt good on my skin. Pat took a loud, deep breath. It didn't seem like either of us wanted to go back to the house. We seemed to be in a bubble of mixed feelings. I was not sure what I was supposed to do.

Pat Rafferty knew all too well what was going to happen in the next two days. He surely had buried other people—parents, friends from the war, perhaps a neighbor. He knew the steps to take. These would be the last ones he would take for his little boy this side of the burial. Later, in the years to come, he would go with his wife on the appropriate anniversaries and whenever she wanted to leave flowers and small gifts. But his true memorial to his son would be private. In his remaining years he would keep his son's headstone clean and polished. He would do this on his own, in his own way. He did not know this at the time, nor did I. I did not know this until my own sons came of age to go off to war and not come home alive. It was just there in front of us.

The last of the day's light flickered through the trees surrounding the house. As we approached the walk to his house, Pat stepped back and let me go forward, just as I stepped to the side. We laughed and walked up together, half on, half off the cement walk.

At the front step Pat reached for the front door with his right hand and very naturally reached his left around my shoulder and guided me into his home. Inside, the ladies of the family, Mrs. Rafferty, her sister, and Michael's sister, sat quietly, as at the end of a story. They seemed to be waiting for a new story.

"Bob, tell us about yourself," Michael's aunt requested.

"Well," I sighed, "I have an older sister," looking at Michael's sister, "and four younger brothers. I did have a younger sister, but she only lived a few days. She never came home from the hospital. No, I never learned what caused her death. We just never talked about her. At least I don't remember anything about it."

"You're Catholic, Bob?"

"Yes, ma'am, eight years of Catholic school, and I was even an altar boy."

"So was Michael," Mrs. Rafferty said.

They told me stories of their family and the things their kids had done.

"Michael and the neighbor kids would play football on the front lawn every Saturday afternoon this time of year," his mother recounted.

Then I would tell a story that somewhat matched, and on and on we talked. I didn't want it to end because the next step I had to make loomed so dark and huge in my mind that I couldn't approach it. The clock on the mantel kept ticking. Finally Mr. and Mrs. Rafferty got up.

"Well, we have a lot to do tomorrow," they said simultaneously.

"Bob, I'll show you where the bathroom is."

"Yes, sir, I found it this afternoon."

Boom, just like that my next step was there in front of me, a step on the edge of a cliff. I had to take it to get to the end of my journey.

"Good night, sir, good night, ma'am," I said at the foot of the steps. The stairs were dark. Halfway up Pat remembered, "I'll get the light for you, Bob." Light from the top of the stairs, too bright, lit the hallway and the stairs. Two bedrooms and a bathroom upstairs, I remembered where I'd left my overnight bag and opened the door. Slowly, with a creaking, the door swung in. I turned on the bedroom light. The room before me was much like one I would have liked to have had myself. Old furniture (hand-me-downs?), windows facing the street, bedstead with matching chair in the corner, and a chest of five drawers next to the closet. Bedspread with cowboy motif—horses, hats, and branding iron—smoothly tucked in.

The nightstand with a lamp was next to the lone twin bed. Next to the door on the right as I walked in was an old wooden box with the implements of boyhood carelessly awaiting their master. Baseball glove, tattered baseballs, tennis balls, a football, and a basketball, well used, still full of dirt and dried sweat. Maybe some nephew or niece would borrow them for some future game, but not now, not for a while.

My black overnight bag and uniform sat on the end of the bed. I grabbed my toothbrush and retreated to the bathroom, taking as long as I could. Returning to the bedroom I faced that step again. What was I going to do? The rest of the house was beginning to quiet, but I was perfectly awake. Could I read in bed till I fell asleep? In bed! In Michael's bed! That is the next step. How long had he been gone from this room? He'd been overseas nine or ten months; I think they had said he had been on leave just a short time before that.

It didn't matter. It was still his room. Now I was here walking up his walk, eating his Italian pastries and fried oysters, turning down his crisp, clean, and cool sheets. I took off my civvies and hung them on the back of the chair. Standing there in skivvies, I felt the night coolness press on every square inch of exposed skin. I stood without moving for three or four minutes; it felt like hours. Goose bumps rose all over me and I shivered.

OK, I thought, I can't stand here all night. I turned off the light. The street lamplight jumped in through the window, casting a cold edge on all the objects in the room. I looked around at each and every thing without thinking. Each in turn said nothing but waited for some careless touch of its owner. Atop the chest of drawers, a comb and brush still with hair, his daily missal, Catholic prayer book that looked just like mine, a baseball autographed by Ted Williams, ticket stubs.

Quietly, quickly, a peek in each drawer saw socks, underwear, and cigar boxes of childhood treasures. The bottom drawer held sweaters and a shoebox of baseball cards. To the left was a stack of comics. Should I look deeper beyond *Mad?* Nah, I thought. The *Playboys* would be in the closet, beneath something his mother wouldn't touch. I returned all the drawers to their original positions. I'd only touched with my eyes ever so slightly. A guest will look, will look to find the familiar, he will try to be at home. But still I felt strange. I couldn't put my finger on it. I can barely see it now, thirty-nine years later. It was like seeing a life that was not my life, but was my life. His life cut short, while mine was still in front of me. Michael was at rest, and I must sleep, too. Could I sleep in the chair? No! Slowly, I pulled back the covers further. I turned and sat slowly, very slowly. Trying not to disturb the sheets, I lay back, tucked my legs beneath the sheets. The sheets now cold around me, more goose bumps, alone, cold, I closed my eyes, not moving. I too, lay at rest. Sleep would come sometime.

During the Vietnam War, I worked with the Moratorium in Washington, D.C., helping plan demonstrations. In 1969, I married Barbara Sonneborn, a widow of the war. The indelible mark the war imprinted on her continues to have a dramatic effect on my life. We mourned Jeff's death together for years. Then I became coproducer of Barbara's film, *Regret to Inform,* about Vietnamese and American war widows. The film garnered awards around the world, including an Academy Award nomination, Best Director at the Sundance Film Festival, and a Peabody Award.

I have enjoyed a long legal career. In 2000, after eighteen years on the bench, I retired from the State Superior Court of California. Over the years, I published numerous articles about law and social justice in a variety of media, including *The New York Times Magazine.* Currently I work as a mediator and arbitrator. I've spent the past four years writing a novel about a judge and the basic issue of truth, both in the law and in personal life.

I joined the Vets' Writing Group many years ago. Barbara had been a member, and I was asked to join because my life had been so affected by the war in Vietnam.

Two Husbands in Vietnam

B arbara had a nightmare. I am in a run-down hospital in Vietnam, on a broken-down mattress, green paint peeling from the walls. She bends to touch my face, and I am cold and wet. I am dead.

She was reluctant to tell me her dream because we were leaving for Vietnam in a few weeks to continue filming *Regret to Inform.* I hadn't been there before. In the '60s, I did everything I could to stay away. I demonstrated, circulated petitions, and resisted—as a pacifist and as someone afraid of dying needlessly.

The only person I knew who had gone was Jeff Gurvitz, and I barely knew him. He had been Barbara's boyfriend since they were fourteen. Barbara and I met at the University of Illinois in 1964, after she and Jeff broke up. We laughed and cried and spent all our time together. It was a wonderful friendship and romance. When college was coming to an end, I felt enormous pressure. I was really crazy about her, but I wasn't ready to commit to marriage.

The following year, while I was at law school in Wisconsin, Barbara came to visit. She didn't want me to hear from anyone else that she and Jeff were getting married. I was quite upset. Even though I'd never said it, I believed that Barbara and I would marry.

Later, when I heard that Jeff had been killed in Vietnam, a chill ran through me. I was very worried about Barbara, but I also knew then that she and I would end up together.

So, hearing Barbara's dream and nervous that it might be prophetic, I shuddered, fearing I would become another tragic character in Barbara's life drama: both her husbands dying in Vietnam.

The morning we were leaving, Barbara showed me her hand and said, "I'd like to wear Jeff's wedding ring for this trip. How do you feel about it?"

"I've got lots of feelings about it," I said. "For this trip, it's fine. But I've got lots of feelings."

I never could have taken this journey in the early years of our marriage. Jeff's presence loomed so large in our lives then. But twenty years later when Barbara began her cinematic voyage, our deep love had weathered many seasons. So, with great enthusiasm I joined the project as coproducer. I understood Barbara's motivation, wanting to transform Jeff's death into a powerful statement against war. Now, however, as our moment of departure neared, my emotions were closer to the surface than they'd been in years. As I arrived at Bangkok Airport after eighteen sleepless hours, the sight of a man holding a sign with Barbara's name on it brought me to tears. After plowing through the red tape at the Vietnamese Embassy in Bangkok, we flew to Hanoi, and began the interviews with Vietnamese widows of the war.

We filmed in and around Hanoi for a week. The enormity of the Vietnamese war widows' stories of loss was even greater than we had anticipated, and we struggled to save our tears for each evening's reflections.

After a week of filming, our crew of six prepared for the journey south, anticipating three more weeks of shooting. Each crewmember had a specific job, except me, and I was beginning to feel obsolete. My legal skills had already been tapped—I had negotiated a contract with the Vietnamese government defining the parameters of what we could include in the film—and I had difficulty seeing any future role. So I told Barbara I'd be going home. As she walked with me to the airline office, she began crying and couldn't stop. Suddenly I realized what my role was. Barbara had come to Vietnam as a widow, not as my wife. But I had been providing the glue that held her together. I finally "got it." I decided to stay.

After two more weeks of travel, we entered the village of Que Son, near Danang, in search of the place where Jeff was killed. Barbara interviewed a beautiful, thin woman in her forties, who was dressed in a traditional green Vietnamese tunic and white pants, her long, dark hair tied in a bun. She had been a Viet Cong leader during the war. Barbara asked if she remembered the particular battle during Tet when Jeff was killed, a battle during which Americans troops tried to destroy an underground Viet Cong hospital. The woman told us there had been many battles then, and that her own husband sustained a lifelong injury at that time. She had been captured and brutally tortured by the Americans.

She accompanied us up a steep, rutted road into the mountains. At a mountain pass, probably a few kilometers from the place Jeff was killed, she pointed to higher ground and told us that it had been filled with Viet Cong fighters during the Tet Offensive, the time when Jeff was here. She and Barbara held hands, their eyes reflecting a shared sadness. They lit incense together and said prayers to mark this spot and pay their respects to Jeff and all the others who had been killed in the war.

I wandered down a dusty road, surrounded by scrub forest that had been dwarfed and destroyed by Agent Orange. I thought about a veteran we'd met who had returned to Vietnam to reclaim his life, which had been filled with disaster since the war—broken relationships, lost jobs, drug and alcohol abuse. He wept as he told us about retrieving the body of a dead buddy, whose head rolled off while he carried him.

Too many veterans' lives were derailed in Vietnam forever. And while they were fighting there, I was going on with my life, living with a woman I loved, establishing a legal career that ultimately led to an appointment as a judge, where every day I saw homeless veterans in trouble with the law.

I had been afforded the luxury of exercising my patriotism through protest rather than putting my life on the line. I had avoided a life of physical and mental anguish, haunted by nightmarish images of war.

Our country was at war, one that went on for too many years and required hundreds of thousands of American boys.

Walking along that dusty road in Vietnam, looking up into the surrounding mountains, I tried to imagine what it would have been like to be here in my early twenties, not knowing who I was and why I was here, carrying an eighty-pound pack in this hot, humid weather, waiting to be attacked. Sweating profusely, my heart racing, overwhelmed by fear and sadness, I could begin to touch what had taken place on this mountain road. And I am forever grateful to all the veterans who stood in for me.

SARA HAINES

I was born and raised in Denver and attended the University of Northern Colorado. After graduation, I signed up with the Red Cross to go to Korea. My Supplemental Recreational Activities Overseas (S.R.A.O.) class trained with the first S.R.A.O. class going to Vietnam at the American Red Cross headquarters in Washington, D.C. In class we discussed not using the term *Donut Dollies* or wearing skirts above the knee. There was no mention of body bags, 1,000-yard stares, or incoming. I spent six months in Korea and seven in Vietnam—Da Nang, Phu Loi, and Qui Nhon. The Red Cross transferred us often to avoid attachments. The war seemed surreal, but returning home the day before Tet in 1967 left me feeling even stranger. I continued to work for the Red Cross, first at the hospital at Travis Air Force Base on the psych ward, where the patients seemed like the sane ones. I was overwhelmed with the aftermath of the war when I was transferred to Letterman Hospital at the Presidio in San Francisco. There I worked on the quadriplegic, amputee, and plastic surgery ward. I tried to escape in a marriage that failed, lost a parent, and had many jobs and relationships. Twenty-five years later, I found myself meeting with a group of women in San Luis Obispo who had served in Vietnam. We discovered that none of us had spoken about Vietnam for twenty-five years, and now we couldn't stop talking. I wrote "Dream Catcher" for the wedding of a woman from our group to a Vietnam vet. Deciding to go to the dedication of the Vietnam Women's Memorial with the group inspired me to write "The Wall."

Six years ago, I was diagnosed with Parkinson's. No one else in my family has had this condition, which means it is probably more environmental than hereditary. I suspect that Agent Orange is a contributing factor, as there are a disproportionate number of veterans with P.D. It presents a new challenge, and I try to focus on the small things in daily life that I enjoy. Painting is a big part of my life now. I'm lucky to have a wonderful extended family here in Denver, where I grew up, as well as my second family, the coworkers I've worked with for the past six years. I miss the men and women who live on the edge (California), whose poetry fills these pages. They helped me regain a part of myself and introduce me to the world of poetry. I am honored to be a part of this anthology.

Dream Catcher

Written for Sharon and Larry's wedding 08/11/95

Catch those memories and ghosts that followed us home and pull
    us away
from the joys of the day and peace of the night.
Center us in your eye and focus us on the beauty and ease of the
    present from which all good things in the future flow.
Be a door that allows the simple and ordinary moments of life to
    be enjoyed.
The purr of a cat.
The touch of a loved one.
A breeze, warm and gentle, on a late summer's day.
A baby's smile.
Time to read the Sunday paper.
A great cup of coffee.
Sudden sadness held close in the presence of friends who
    understand.
The bonds from a long ago war that hold us as brothers and sisters
    and give us comfort.
The small details and deeds of daily life that affirm our survival.

The Wall

10/03/93—Written for the dedication of the Vietnam Women's Memorial

I was there to be life-affirming
In an arena that destroyed life
I smiled
I listened
I tried to cheer and console the best I could
My heart encased and held tightly
the tears I never cried
I survived and lived and grew
with a silent, stone cold secret called Vietnam
I was there but I stayed silent

I know there is a stone cold wall that would
melt my heart if I approached it
Twenty-five years of tightly held tears
could not stay silent any more
Another memorial is drawing me near
to approach the wall I fear
I believe in wholeness
The memory of the men who gave their lives
Piece by piece, body part by body part
is a separate part of me
It's strange that the names of those men
written on a wall
could break the silence
and give me back a part of myself that's been
steeled and sealed away
It's right that there are monuments
large like this and
UNDENIABLE.

DONALD L. HANDLEY

I am a sixty-two-year-old Vietnam veteran, and I live in Midland, Texas. I was an Air Force Aircraft Maintenance Officer in Vietnam with the 366th Tactical Fighter Wing at Danang Air Base from July 1968 to July 1969. I recently retired from a local retail store after twenty-two years but still work part-time for a convenience store chain. I am the proud grandfather of three beautiful grandchildren and recently became an equally proud great-grandfather of a beautiful great-granddaughter.

I started writing in 1988 after a visit to the Vietnam Veterans Memorial in Washington, D.C. I was fortunate beyond words to meet a beautiful lady named Lana Spraker, who had been a protester during the war. It was the beginning of a long-delayed healing process. She is my muse, inspiring me to use writing to heal from the psychological trauma of war. I have had some success in getting some poems and short stories published over the years. I have also written two novels not yet published.

Booby Trap

The sudden flash of light,
the loud explosive thump.
He lies there screaming,
legs and torso shredded.
My pistol is out, ready
to end his and my misery.
Then you woke me.

My thrashing hand had hit your throat,
but you wiped the sweat from my face,
and held me against your breast.
The radiance of your body
banished the chill of my nightmare.
I cried and you kissed my eyes,
quietly sending me back to sleep,
peaceful until the mine exploded
AGAIN!

Light Casualties

The man on the six-o'clock news
reported light casualties in the firefight.

He wasn't there to pick up the pieces
and load them into body bags.

He didn't feel my grief and anger
when one of my friends was killed.

He wasn't there to see an enemy soldier
mutilated and dead from a round in my rifle.

He didn't see the death and destruction
from the artillery barrage.

I wonder if he thinks "light casualties"
float away so they can be ignored?

After growing up in New York, I moved to Chicago in time to witness the mayhem that was the Democratic Convention in 1968. After
supporting my husband, Larry Heinemann's, work as a writer, raising two children, volunteering many years within the Chicago public school system, and working at several positions, I turned to my
own writing and discovered how two wars—the war of my father
(World War II) and the war of my husband (Vietnam)—have influ-
enced and defined my life. My journey included obtaining a master's
degree in social science from the University of Chicago and a second
one from the Smith College School of Social Work.

My birth was not only the result of an impassioned moment of
my father's homecoming but also a wish for a new beginning for the
family that had waited out his war tenure. That hope died early as he
practiced medicine for the next ten years while insistently drinking
himself to death. My mother attempted to receive benefits from the
Veterans Administration after his early death but could prove no direct
link and her request was denied. The legacy of being a child of hope
followed and drove me to live out the mission of saving a soldier and
making a family work—one imbued with conflict and paradox. War
and loss have been persistent themes in my life—an emotional legacy
that lives on despite driven efforts to be rid of them. I had to be numb
to be able to type and retype my husband's books *Close Quarters* and
Paco's Story. Those who live with the soldiers who bring the aftermath of war into their homes develop strong barriers around their
hearts. I have spent my life breaking down those barriers. "War in
the House" explores that journey.

War in the House

The last time I saw my father, he was being wheeled out of our
house on an ambulance gurney. He looked calm and peaceful
with the sheet pulled neatly under his chin. His face appeared thin and
translucent beneath the freckles liberally covering his skin. His hair,
still a deep and vivid red, was not orangy and carrot-topped like my
own, but a good rich, thick auburn for his forty-seven, four-days-short-
of-forty-eight years.

I didn't panic as I entered our side yard and stopped, seeing the
ambulance parked in the driveway at the rear of our house. In fact, I

took it to be just another visit to the VA hospital; there had been several in the past year. This warm and sunny summer Saturday I was occupied with wanting some loose change to attend a neighborhood yard fair. I was the baby of the family—no weekly allowance for me, it would limit the rich, out-of-pocket as-you-go cache I was already receiving from daddy. He could rarely say no to me. I stood by the waist-high hedge that bordered the yard of our big, old, rambling, white Long Island shingle house, a grand, respectable house on the outside belying the sparse worn-outness on the inside. I watched as the ambulance attendants gingerly lifted the wheels of the gurney over the curb, snapped the extended accordion-like legs back into the bottom of the stretcher, and gently rolled my dad into the rear of the ambulance. One of the white-coated men stepped into the back of the cab and strapped the gurney in, while the other closed the doors and walked around to the driver's side. I watched the red-and-white cab back out of our driveway and pull past me . . .

My dad didn't come home from the hospital that time. I was ten years old. I never *was* told what he died of, but from overhearing all those hushed, adult conversations in the weeks—months—following his funeral, I was pretty certain it was cirrhosis of the liver (whatever *that* was). He drank a lot—hard liquor—on a daily basis. He practiced medicine in the small village where we lived and, after doing his rounds of house calls in the early afternoon, he would hang out at any one of a half dozen bars within a twenty-mile radius of his territory. He'd come home late, his dinner sitting in the warmer-oven, my mom cautiously placing it on the dining room table with a large glass of milk. He had a glass of milk every night. He was referred to by my mom to her friends over a canasta hand as a "house devil–street angel."

There were a lot of whispers in the house the next day—the day after watching my dad being driven away in that ambulance. My uncle was standing in the kitchen, and the conversation between him and my mom stopped when I came in the back door. He gave me a big hug, asking, "How's the big girl?" his husky voice puzzlingly reassuring. I quickly ran up the kitchen stairs to change into play clothes, having just returned from Sunday mass.

It was late the next morning, Monday, that the news reached me. It had been a typical summer day. I went off to play with my friends; because it was overcast and not a beach day, we hatched a plan to go to the library. I had come home to ask permission. Bounding into the kitchen, screen door slamming behind me, I stopped at the bottom of the stairs. My mom was repeating in an incredulous voice, "This nurse said, 'Your husband has expired!' Can you imagine such a word to use? Expired?" Something in the tone of her voice stopped me from going up those stairs in my usual two-by-two fashion. I heard her hang up the phone, calling me to come up. She sat on the old trunk in the second-floor hallway and told me she had very sad news. "Your daddy died early this morning . . ."

Ah, "expired"! I cried a little, thinking, these tears are not real; I am, in fact, *relieved* that he is out of my life.

I stopped crying and sat a moment, turned slightly from my mom, smelling the faint, but all too familiar whiff of alcohol on her breath. I looked through the spaces between the spindles of the stair railing. I stared at the dust motes reflected in the light from the window in the stairway landing. I didn't turn around but asked quietly, my chin deep in my chest, "Can I go to the library with Rhodie and Peter? They're waiting for me outside."

"No, not today. I need you to stay here with me."

I inhaled deeply, loudly through my nose, nostrils flaring. I got up and walked down the stairs, each footfall a squeak echoing its own burden. On the landing I turned and cried, "But I *want* to *go!*"

"Not now."

I cried. I screamed. I stomped on those creaky, old stairs, and then, obediently, turned and continued down into the kitchen, out to the back porch. I yelled to my two friends sitting on the large, semi-circular wooden bench in our side yard. "I can't go with you." My face was red, my eyes glassy with tears, then, more softly, "My daddy died this morning," that voice drifting, slowly, up through some cavern, a cavern deep within my head. I was holding the porch post with my left arm crooked at the elbow, my right leg straddling the railing. I leaned my cheek against the post and watched them walk out of the yard, around the corner of the hedge, down the sidewalk, out of sight.

He was a doctor, a healer. His eyes, sad and direct, held the troubles of the world in them, but could melt the coldest heart. He was a healer whose reputation was cast far beyond the borders of that small town. Ole Doc Smith . . . People poured into the house all that afternoon and next day, shaking their heads in disbelief, sadness, crying—recounting stories of how he had taken care of their families—"street angel." I was, in my young mind, indisputably his favorite, and spoiled. How could I have felt "relief?" What was that? He had taken a strap to my brother many a time, but had never laid a hand on me. "House devil"—What *was* that? How could the death of a man, with a heart so full of the power to heal, generate relief in his youngest daughter? Crowds thronged the house, the funeral home, all week. Tears were shed by hundreds in that small village. I was met on the street years later with, "Little Smitty, Little Doc, Little Red. I remember your dad *well*. Why, he saved my wife's life. He was the best damn doctor this town ever knew!"

What was this thing called relief?

I was trussed in a navy-blue taffeta skirt, a matching vest lined with blue and white diagonal stripes, patent leather shoes, white socks with ruffled lace borders. At the cemetery my mother took my hand, urging me to walk over to the gravesite. I resisted, pulling my arm away with a fierce tug. I *refused*. I sat back on the edge of the back seat of that long, black hearse and dangled my shiny shoes out the open rear door, watching the backs of bowed heads, beyond which stretched row upon row of white headstones endlessly toward the horizon, when BANG!!!!!! Off went the honor guard rifle salute. KABOOMN!!!! AGAIN . . . and AGAIN. The sharpness of the sound riddled my young body. My dad had been a combat surgeon in World War II, in North Africa and Italy. The letters on that old trunk in our second-floor hallway were stenciled clearly: "Lt. John E.V. Smith, M.D."

Something went cold in the heart of that young girl that day, that brilliant summer day, sun glistening off those thousands of sugar-cube tombstones reaching out to the wooded horizon. Something grabbed her throat, wrapped itself around her heart, and tightened her resolve. That was forty-five years ago. A heart was closed that day, sealed shut by those rifles. A jaw was set, a young life changed. "Relief?" I think not.

The daughter of a World War II veteran . . .

I couldn't believe that I was in love and going to get married. It was a mutual, unspoken thing between Larry and me.

We had met at a dance the day before Labor Day, 1966. I was a junior at Nazareth College, a small, Catholic college just outside Bardstown,

Kentucky, forty-five miles east of Fort Knox. A born storyteller, Larry talked the night away with stories about his grandfather.

"Why, my granddad had this neighborhood kid packing his suitcase and ready to go *three* times—ready to join Pecos Bill on his adventures along the Rio Grande. By the third time, his mother came to our house demanding to know just *when* this trip was going to take place. Told my mother that granddad just better stop making up these stories or she'd just send Joey, *with* his suitcase, down to our house and *he'd* have to contend with him." I laughed and laughed all night, until my sides split.

Six weeks later, sitting on the window ledge at a Jerry's Restaurant in Elizabethtown, Kentucky, waiting for a friend from Fort Knox to return with a car so Larry could drive me back to school, we said our long good-bye.

"It was fun knowing you this past six weeks. It really was fun. Sorry it has to end, but I get my orders this week and expect to be going to Germany. Well, it was really great—thanks. It's too bad it has to end."

But it didn't end. The orders were changed—to "permanent party" he called it; he was to stay at Fort Knox—no Germany and certainly not Vietnam. It was the beginning rather than the end. Our courtship continued with weekly visits—picnics, dances, movies, dinners—or phone calls, and always, *always* letters.

And then, early in December when he came to the Christmas dance, we sat down, trumpets surrounding us with the haunting harmonies of "A Taste of Honey"—he looked at me gravely, and gave me the news that his orders had come . . . for Vietnam. We sat in the folding chairs, at a table off in the corner, suddenly, it seemed, separated from our friends—my hands folded on my lap, dressed in my tweed Villager skirt and matching sweater, he in his finely creased khakis, pin-striped shirt with button-down collar. I looked at Larry sitting next to me; looked up into those crystal blue eyes as he put his arm gently around my shoulder. I let my eyes close, let my head fall on his shoulder. The sounds of giggles, chairs scraping, music—all fell beyond range. A simple numbness overtook me, then, emerging slowly—a sense of inevitability, a tingling of despair, perhaps disappointment and maybe even anger, certainly—familiarity. I was twenty years old, it had been ten years and those brass trumpets rang in my ears like a rifle salute.

We had little time left together. He went home to a suburb outside of Chicago for Christmas; I followed him, for a brief visit, on *my* way home for Christmas vacation. I returned to Kentucky a few days early, immediately after New Year's, to visit with him at Fort Knox before returning to school. Our conversations had begun to include plans of a future together. We fell into the assumption that we would be spending the rest of our lives together. It was a distant future, a dreamy future. Then he returned home to Chicago for his thirty-day leave before shipping out.

I convinced a classmate to visit her family in Chicago for a weekend that cold and snowy January. Larry and I became engaged during that twenty-four-hour visit. We hugged and kissed good-bye. I promised to write, got in the car, and returned to Kentucky. I wrote day after day, pledging my love in as many ways as I could imagine. I would be there when he returned.

. . . *the wife of a Vietnam veteran.*

I was born and raised in Chicago, and grew up in a house where there were no books. Drafted in 1966, I was the most reluctant of conscripts, and was sent to Vietnam as a soldier of the most ordinary kind. I returned home the Spring of 1968, and brought with me a story that simply could not be denied. I guess we could say that I became a writer because of the war, not in spite of it. When I went back to school that fall, my writing teacher gave me a couple of books from his library. He said, "If you want to write about the war, read these," and handed me copies of *The Iliad* and *War and Peace;* those books took a solid year. Nowadays, I look back at my accidental trilogy of novels and memoir about the war, and can see that I have always been trying to cipher out what I saw, what I did, and what it was that I became—the story of any soldier's downward path to wisdom.

"The Geese" is my only piece of work that anyone could call a poem with a straight face. It was first published in Hanoi on March 10, 1997, during a visit there, thirty years to the day after I first set foot in that country. The poem celebrates the completion of my second novel, *Paco's Story,* in 1986.

The Geese

Cold April.
Bodey's Lake,
Indiana.
Passover,
Six A.M.

Takes an hour
to start the fire
and make the coffee.
Hot cup stings
my palms
and fingers.
Shoes soaking
in the grass.
Wear my cardigan sweater
Edie made
of skein-ends;

knitted as her hand
came to them.
Sweater is thick
and heavy,
but warm;
a riot
of colors.

This morning,
I have the lake
to myself.

Across the way;
across the lake,
just over the farmhouse
kitchen garden,
the full moon sets.
Fat and flat,
big as a teacup saucer
held at arm's length;
color of a thick
slice of snowy ice.

Behind me;
back of Bodey's
handbuilt cinderblock cottage,
just over the pasture grove
of hickory and bur oak,
the sun rises.
Huge and yellow
orange,
and warm,
thank God.

Hold my coffee
with both hot hands
and sip deep,
sweet as brass.
Sun and moon,
both large lights,

opposite
and poised
on the horizon.
An amazing moment,
even I know that.
When such a light
touches such a heart,
what happens?

Mated pair
of geese who live
on the pasture pond
fly over the house
and yard,
honking and crying,
loud.
Low enough to hear
the air fiercely
hushing over their
wings and backs;
close enough to hear
the sharp,
hard breathing
as they work.

Cruising side by side,
they ease down;
touch and coast
into the wide
shivery wedge
of moonlight;
make straight
for the shoal reeds.

Long wakes
like arrows;
with feathers,
the patina
of old silver,
clean to the tip.

My earliest childhood memories are filled with laughter, songs, and an extended family so diverse it took me well into early teens to sort out aunts and uncles from close family friends. My father had returned from World War II severely wounded, so he was loved and respected by everyone in his New York City neighborhood. I was the firstborn son of a hero.

In the mid '50s we moved to Long Island. My Catholic school education, guided by aged Dominican nuns, pointed me toward the priesthood. By the time I was twelve, the question was not college or seminary, it was *which* seminary. Two years later, a high school English teacher lent me a copy of Eric Hoffer's *The True Believer*. I read it, and my stars shifted position. I lost the Faith, but not my faith in myself.

I toured with a blue-eyed soul band, built motorcycles and hydroplanes, sang in the New York State Choir, and by the time my draft notice came, didn't have the grades to maintain my college deferment. I'd heard that some draftees were being routed into the Marines, so I joined the Army.

The following story was written with the loving support of Maxine and the Veterans Writing Group. My Vietnam experiences still tear at my soul, but they are much more tolerable when bound to paper.

Now I live in Denver with my patient and loving wife, Laura, and our two heart-song daughters. I have not found a way to avoid my memories when they pull me out of our comfortable life, but I've learned to incorporate the lessons and insights revealed to me into my stories, scripts, songs, and laughter. My advice: *Share your stories.*

Remanded to The Nam

The Makarov semiauto pistol, shoulder-holstered beneath my faded fatigue jacket, made a small bulge that could barely be noticed. It might have been noticed, if the officers and enlisted men on 707 Freedom Flight back to The World weren't drunk or lost in the reverie of landing in Oakland, or wherever their final destinations might be.

I had worn this captured Chinese Communist weapon for most of the past year in The Nam, as we called it, and its heft and oily scent comforted me in a way I cannot compare to any other toy, tool, or person. Nine unlucky somebodies would have to deal with a 9 mm chest hole before getting to me. That would buy me enough time to figure out what to do next. I never bothered to ask myself why somebody would want to "get to me," but I knew I had done something wrong.

Moments before landing, the stewardesses sprayed insecticide over our heads to destroy any stowaway vermin. I smiled. *By rights, all these human cockroaches should be choking now.* But they laughed and smoked and drank their little bottles of airline booze with the promise of sweet American freedom just a few hundred feet below their pimpled asses. One ex-surfer dirtbag described in detail the way he was going to fuck his girl when he got back to Marina del Rey. He snorted like a pig and boasted, "Her snatch tastes like honey." I stared ahead silently with my arms folded across my chest, holding the fabric-covered pistol grip.

Most of the other passengers had been discharged in The Nam and were officially civilians just beyond the reach of military justice. Tired, bedraggled stewardesses fended off every lascivious grope, every drunken pinch with a swift slap or spontaneous punch. The women deftly deflected each lewd proposition with cool words and cool detachment these men hadn't experienced since the last time they chased stateside pussy. There wasn't one man on the plane I respected, least of all myself.

It was just another planeload of nameless, faceless Joes who had "done their duty" and were heading back home to marry some unsuspecting nymph, drink themselves stupid at the neighborhood bar, embellish their war stories over free drinks, dutifully father a litter of damaged kids, weep with the brothers-in-arms at Wednesday night VFW meetings, and die of terminal prosperity.

And so, we mourn the passing of another generation of self-proclaimed war heroes, whose sons will walk the same path, pass the same way. Yet another example of the bullet-headed American cycle of mindless, patriotic, life-tragedy horseshit. I looked around the smoky cabin at the quitters, losers, and insects. I guess I didn't reacclimate well. To me, the guys on that jetliner were part of the problem not the solution to our pigheaded aggression.

When we landed, I terminated my military flight in Oakland and bought a civilian ticket to Long Island, where my family lived. If I continued to travel on military status, the rest of my flight would have been free, but they wanted me to shower, shave, and change into a Class A uniform with badges and ribbons and the works. Fuck it. I was in my camo suit, dusted with Nam dirt and it was just fine for me. Too bad if that upset the civilians. I was upset and they were meat puppets. I had eight rounds in the clip, one chambered, and a pocket full of reloads.

Get yourself a good face-full, shithead. This is what is.

The taxi driver who took me from Kennedy to my parents' house bragged that his cousin was a Marine at the siege of Hue. I listened passively, gulping down a pint bottle of vodka I'd bought at the duty-free store, while the dickless Checker Cab wage slave had a conversation with himself. The cab reeked of old newsprint, cigars, and urine, and I figured it was his personal stink, so I stared through the smoke-smudged windshield, cleared my throat, and spit on the floor to let him know I wasn't interested in a second-hand accounting. The ride became very tense—for him.

Was it the overcast light or the dreary desaturated color of the passing scenery that kept me from feeling that I was back home? Or was it that so little had changed back here. I was struck by the insane realization that I had walked through a twelve-month alcohol and drug delirium, played havoc with devastating weapons, fucked whores who were little more than children, worked the black market, destroyed lives, stacked bodies *and had the time of my life doing it!*

That's right, teen prostitutes are still children. Maybe other vets had explained it away with some "in the context of the war," "given the cultural differences," or "she was very mature for her age" alibi, but I freely admit that it was criminal and I am guilty of being part of the rape of Vietnam.

My mother was overcome with emotion when she saw me standing on the doorstep. If she noticed that I was reeling drunk, it was never mentioned. I stepped across the threshold into the foyer of the tiny Cape Tudor home where I grew up. The green walls and white ceilings I'd painted before leaving to join the Army now looked old and pale. The worn colonial maple furniture and shag rug where baby brother crawled were oddly familiar and off-putting, like a forgotten family album photo recovered from a tornado-torn debris pile.

My father, three brothers, and sister ran to meet me with hugs and promises, plans for a huge celebration. They knew that my tour was up, but I'd never told them my arrival date. Their tears sprang from joyous relief that their long nightmare was over. That relief lasted about thirty minutes.

It was Easter Sunday and the house smelled like garlic, roasting meat, and cigarette smoke. I sat at the dining room table with my father and a bottle of Seagram's Seven. Dad usually kept one hidden under the kitchen sink next to the ammonia and spot remover, but this was a special occasion. He splashed the whiskey into squat glass tumblers and looked for the right words to start. I stared down at the Formica tabletop, marked with oval blooms where countless plates and knives and forks had worn through its woodgrain surface to the dull gray plastic beneath. Time made visible.

When I looked up at my father I saw him as I had never before. He was ruggedly handsome, cerulean blue eyes, carrying his extra weight like an old lion who had bested all his rivals, face set in a brick hodcarrier's grimace—bearing a heavy load, yet determined and unshakable in his capabilities. Had he not been severely wounded while serving with the Tenth Mountain Division in northern Italy, he probably would have been an NFL quarterback in the late 1940s. That was his dream, lost in the snow of Lombardia along with a piece of his right shoulder and several pints of blood.

I'm sure that in the twenty-five years since he was wounded my dad had imagined our present situation at least once or twice: father, son, a wartime homecoming. A Frank Capra Americana Moment. But now, this hawk, who had inexplicably cried when I left for war, was binding up his emotions, gauging his words carefully.

He avoided my eyes. "You guys got a raw deal."

What? Who guys? You mean "we," right Dad? "We got a raw deal. WE. I'm one of you now, aren't I? Wasn't that what this crap was all about, Dad? Now I'm not one of the draft-dodgers you hate so much, am I? Now I'm a veteran with a lifelong grudge just like you, right? Didn't I do what you wanted me to do?

"They never let you fight it like a war. You got the shitty end of the stick."

Jesus Christ! The one person I thought I could confess to was putting me on the other side of the fence with the National Guard stay-homes, the weekend warriors who were "dress-up" soldiers and not World War II heroes like Dad. What a shitty, shitty end of the shitty, shitty stick. Seagram's and sympathy.

"It's like Korea," he said, around a bitter swallow of booze.

It was done. That quick. I was merely an unlucky kid in his eyes, not a man who did his duty, not a soldier who had experienced a different war. Not an adult. Not a man. He looked pathetic, staring down at his hands and sipping his whiskey.

You can die now, Dad. You just flunked Fatherhood 101, and there's no retest, no summer school, no waiver. You coward.

"I don't want this," I said, pushing the whiskey across the table, "I want vodka." I might as well have said those words in Russian for all the good it would do me.

My brothers and sister had no idea what was happening but sensed that it would be a good time to leave us alone. They went back to the living room and chattered about how we'd be having a big party. Their excitement and laughter made me more resolute in my anger.

I unbuttoned my fatigue jacket, drew the pistol, and set it on the table where my glass had been. That changed the mood. Dad had never allowed weapons in the house, not even a BB gun.

"Jesus Christ! Get that out of my house," he sputtered.

I released the ammo clip from its slot in the grip and set it on the table, cleared the chamber by cocking it with a smooth metal click, and slid the pistol in front of him. He stared down at the handgun as I spun the unchambered round on the Formica.

"It's Russian, Dad. It's very reliable."

I offered him the clip.

Go on, tough guy; touch it.

He stood up from the table and walked into his bedroom. My mother, seeing that the man-to-man welcome home had ended, came into the dining room. When she saw the pistol, she panicked.

"I don't want that in my house!" she yelled. For a moment I regretted scaring Mom, in her worn housecoat and slippers. She looked from the gun to the empty chair at the head of the table where my dad had been sitting and back again. I knew she was more afraid of his reaction than any damage the pistol would do.

That's all I remember of that day. I apparently got the vodka I wanted, because I spent the next few days in a walking booze blackout. Friends and relatives who visited me during that time tell me that I was really enjoying myself—an alcoholic's euphemism for being drunk to the point of unconsciousness. I never took the pistol out of its holster.

By Friday I was somewhat sober. That's when I noticed that nothing was happening. Other than watching the strangers who were once my family repeat the same meaningless actions over and over, every

day, nothing seemed important. Nothing seemed to be going anywhere. I waited for something to matter and spent days hovering, no
attachment to the reality ground and no passion wind to fly away on.
More vodka and another week disappeared.

During a subsequent day of sobriety, my friend Jimbo suggested
that we go to an antiwar protest in Washington, D.C. He was the key-
board player in my teen-years rock band. I sang lead and played guitar, and with phony ID cards we played dozens of bars and clubs across
Long Island.

If I were to cast a film about our exploits, I'd be hard-pressed to
find such a dissolute but world-wise sixteen-year-old. Jimbo saw the
protest as a party event and promised reverie and outrageous behavior. I made excuses about not wanting to be part of any antiwar march,
then consciously evaded him to avoid being persuaded by his fun-
loving manner. The next thing I remember was riding in his car, pot
pipe in hand, on my way to the Capitol with Hendrix on the 8-track.

This is what happened on that day and why I decided to send myself
back to Vietnam. Jimbo parked near the Beltway, and we walked with
the massing crowd toward the White House. I saw thousands of people who represented virtually every walk of life in the United States:
pacifists, construction workers, mothers, children, hippies, veterans,
grandmothers, celebrities, Communists, religious leaders, government
officials, and hundreds of others who were united only by their belief
that the war must stop. I breathed it all in and blew it out. This was
something that mattered; this was real.

A dozen or so vets in wheelchairs rolled alongside me as I walked,
and I thought about where their missing arms and legs were now. I
started to cry. A long-haired girl in her twenties walked along carrying a crepe-framed picture of a young soldier in his Class A uniform.
She cried out loud, a wail that tore at me, and I stopped walking, unable
to match my racking sobs to the tiny steps needed to keep in step with
the crowd. I felt arms around me and thought it must be my buddy.

"Let it out, brother," said a black man, whose arms held me steady.
He wore a vest cut from a threadbare fatigue jacket, covered with
military patches and battle ribbons. "Let it out." His body smelled of
sweat and marijuana and alcohol. The Nam.

I lost Jimbo in the crowd but continued on with the people walking toward Pennsylvania Avenue. A group of people I would not have

acknowledged an hour earlier locked arms, and I joined them. We formed a cordon as we approached the center of the protest—an impromptu platform where veterans were speaking over a squealing PA system, and throwing their battle ribbons, uniforms, and medals over the iron spear fence of the White House. I felt strength in our armlock union and the acceptance I needed to feel about being back from Nam.

Service ribbons, Purple Hearts, Good Conduct Medals, tattered Boonie hats tossed in the air; graffiti-covered helmets, flak jackets, boots, and sharpshooter badges, caught in the afternoon light, as they flew over the fence; letters, and baby shoes, and a crepe-framed photograph of a young soldier in his Class A uniform littered the meticulously manicured lawn. Secret Service drones talked into their lapels and hid, frowning behind dark glasses.

A brown-haired boy of three or four sat on his father's shoulders waving a Vietnamese flag. The man and boy were wearing camouflage fatigues, and their faces were greasepainted to look like skulls. I felt a soul shock and washed out into naked vulnerability. "Bring them home!" the boy yelled, and I wanted no more than to come home to a respite from my sadness.

But the men throwing things over the fence were stepping off the platform, smiling, into the outstretched arms of the crowd. I wanted to smile too. So, I stepped up onto the platform, drew my pistol, and held it in the air.

I have never been able to accurately describe the noise that accompanied my action. Everyone in the street saw the handgun, and after a lone pained whimper, there was an abrupt gasp. I heard cries of fear and bellowing outrage, obscenities, and a guy yelling, "Throw it! THROW IT!" I looked back at the Secret Service men, fearing they wouldn't understand my peaceful gesture, fearing that it might become a gun-versus-gun moment.

"THROW IT!" a man screamed, and I tossed the pistol over the fence.

It fell onto the White House lawn and a part of me lay there on the grass with it. A sad part. A forgotten, unloved, angry part. A piece of whatever it was that lived inside of me, ever vigilant to lash out at the most incidental slight, coiled to attack another's innocent inference, poised to destroy the misspoken phrase that made me face the shame I felt.

A crowd commotion started as I stepped back down from the platform, and although I walked away as fast as I could, the people clung to me, laid hands on me, kissed me, and welcomed me home. I cried myself sick, choking and spitting out my hate and fear onto the littered street, while someone held my head the way my mother did when I was a sick child. Another person handed me a canteen, and I took small swallows of warm metallic water, splashed some on my face and then poured some over the top of my head, while staring at the cloud-shot sky. It was the first time I had looked up to the heavens since returning from The Nam.

I recovered, stirred by the thought that I now had thousands of friends and hundreds of relatives who cared about me. They surrounded me, expecting me to add the next word, take the next action that would fire their spirit in the mounting street theater. "I don't know what to do!" I shouted, "and I'm not proud of what I've done."

A skinny girl, a weary girl, her hair streaked with bolts of gray, placed her palm on my chest and her mouth on my ear. Her lips formed soft words that blew into my ear on cinnamon clove breath. "Do something to be proud of."

I broke down. Every emotion I had ignored, every injury I had caused, every trust betrayed welled up and shamed me raw. I had nowhere to hide, no excuse to offer. "What? What can I do now?"

"Tomorrow, then," she said, "tomorrow."

I left the crowd and walked back to Jimbo's car. He was drunk and stoned, asleep in the back seat when I got there. Later he told me that when we split up, he met up with a group of hashish smokers and lay on the grass next to the Washington Monument, watching the throng pass. But he was still pretty stoned, so I drove us back to Long Island, listening to FM rock and thinking through the long night. As I drove, I remembered that children were still being torn into cripples by shrapnel, napalm-scarred into monsters, and sold into sex slavery in The Nam. Their tour of duty is over when they die.

I mean, I wasn't *for* the war. Shit, it was a no-win play on every front and going back was universally seen as the first stage of insanity. But firefighters can return to a burning building without being pro-fire. Christ, there were kids there and I had to go back. I had nothing else.

The Queens Midtown tunnel, lit only by dim fluorescent tubes and my car's headlights, seemed like a headlong dive into the forced perspective of nothingness—a vanishing point that illogically led back to my stateside family. Its tiled walls reverberated my car's roar and hummed a droning note into my ears. The rhythm of my tires thumping the asphalt roadbed's sunken expansion joints lacked only a melodic improvisation to complete the song. So I sobbed as Jimbo snored, feeling sorry for myself—an orphan whose war home was half a world away.

The next morning, sober and upbeat, I had breakfast with my family. After a few good-mornings, I sat in the chair I had always sat in before I went to the war. My mom set a plate of scrambled eggs and sausages in front of me and sat down to her own plate.

"I'm going back to Nam." Confusion, anger, and tears all around.

My father took it as a personal affront, cursing me for the pain I was causing the family. My mother cried at the prospect of another year of sleepless nights and fear-filled newscasts. My youngest brother wailed because everyone else was upset. I was coolly resolute. Their pain, their sadness was just a tiny part of the Vietnam tragedy, fully contained in a lower-middle-class melodrama, meted out in twelve-month episodes. It wasn't my fault.

Meanwhile, there were kids who needed somebody, maybe me. Maybe I could do something to be proud of. Maybe the most heroic act for me would be letting my spent anger resolve into gentleness or being able to be big when someone little needed help, or patiently pouring milk into little cups.

Hell, I might even have the time of my life doing it.

And when I got back to The Nam, I did. I really did.

HO ANH THAI

I was born in 1960 and was evacuated from Hanoi at the age of six because of the American bombing. For the next seven years, I lived in refugee areas in the countryside. After graduating from the College of Diplomacy, I was drafted into the People's Army and served in the 47th Battalion from 1985 to 1987. I was a diplomat in South Asia and am presently a member of the Executive Committee of the National Vietnam Writers Association and Chair of the Hanoi Writers' Association, as well as consulting editor for Curbstone Press' *Voices from Vietnam* series. I've written eighteen novels and short story collections.

In my 1985 novel, *Nguoi dan ba tren dao* (published in the U.S. in 2000 as *The Women on the Island*), I became one of the first writers in Vietnam to bring attention to what had been a forbidden subject: the terrible cost paid by thousands of young women veterans of the Youth Volunteer Battalions of the People's Army of Vietnam. Their main duties during the war were to keep the Ho Chi Minh Trail network open, fill in bomb craters, repair the roads, and defuse or explode unexploded ordnance. After the war, many of the women who survived found there was no place for them in the society they had defended. They were kept together in their old units and sent as labor battalions to underdeveloped parts of the country. Exiled to lives without families or children, having lost the opportunity to get married when they were young, many sought consolation in getting pregnant and having a child out of wedlock.

The following excerpt from *The Women on the Island* depicts a confrontation by a brigade of these women with a callous bureaucrat who brutalizes a pregnant woman to find out who is the father of her unborn child. The women, empowered by the sacrifices of their military service, rebel against his mistreatment.

from *The Women on the Island*

Translated by Ho Anh Thai and Wayne Karlin

When news of Luyen's pregnancy reached the forestry collective's headquarters, the director passed responsibility for dealing with it to his deputy, Mr. Quan. Quan immediately arranged a meeting with the head of the Women's Union, Mrs. Diep, and the Secretary of the Youth Union. But the Secretary, a man in his twenties, blushed every time he had to deal with women's issues, and when he saw Quan barreling toward his office, he fled out the back door. Miss Hao, his deputy secretary, stayed to talk with Quan.

Quan did not conceal his fury. "I'm sure it was Mr. Vien. The camp is in the jungle. Do you think a pilot parachuted in and screwed her? Who else could have done it? Vien is such a womanizer. I'll bet my mother's soul it was him."

But ..." Hao said, hesitating, "... what if Miss Luyen ... was ... with Mr. Cuong?"

Quan's response was quick and vehement. "Cuong has a beautiful wife. Don't you think she's enough for him? Besides, how much damage could that dwarf do? No, we must criticize Miss Luyen at a public meeting so Vien's part in this comes out."

The more Quan said, the more he realized there was no way to speak about this delicately. Miss Hao, who was a bit shocked at first, resolved to do what was necessary to fulfill her duty. And so, the three cadres— Mr. Quan, Miss Hao, and Mrs. Diep—marched through the jungle with fiery determination to go to Viet Hoa and uncover the truth.

The community meeting took place in a makeshift house and began with Luyen reading a self-criticism—required by her superiors—during which she detailed her mistakes, took full responsibility for the matter, and declared her willingness to receive whatever punishment would be given. She had no sooner folded her report and sat down than Quan leaned across the table and shouted, "Who asked you to write that crap? You go on and on about your errors, but you don't address the key point—who got you pregnant?"

Quan's question would have seemed reasonable if it hadn't been a ruse to attack his rival, Vien, the Secretary of the Team 5 Party Cell. Quan was still furious with Vien for questioning Quan's "shoddy recruiting practices," insinuating that he was guilty of nepotism and taking bribes. Quan thought, smugly, Everyone has a scar on his back. It was clear he had taken this case to reveal Vien's sinful back. Look at him now, pretending to be calm. Unbearable!

Suddenly Luyen stood up. "It doesn't matter who got me pregnant!" she said, her voice trembling. "Isn't it enough to humiliate me? Why do you want to know?"

Mrs. Diep felt it was time for her to say something. "Are there any problems here? Is there anything wrong? Tell us so we can help."

The women of Team 5 burst into bitter laughter. "Can you help us find husbands?" one asked loudly.

Disturbed by the impudence, Quan tapped his pen against the table. "That is not why we are here. We are here to criticize the immoral and destructive behavior of Luyen. Now, Luyen, tell us clearly, who is the father of your child?"

Quan glanced covertly at Vien, feeling victory in his heart. He knew that sooner or later he'd get him.

"This is like the opera about the village elder punishing the unmarried, pregnant girl," another girl said loudly.

Quan beat his palm against the table, then whirled around and glared at the woman who said that. "Miss Bao, you are running at the mouth!"

Bao shouted back, "Why should I watch what I say? I'm pregnant, too! Do you want to cross-examine me?" Her anger dissipated as she looked around and saw her colleagues laughing. Then she continued, "Why must you humiliate this poor girl? If you really want to know who 'the culprit' is, ask Luyen in private. We've all known about her pregnancy, and none of us has questioned her."

Sincere words from a sarcastic person can be persuasive. But even these words from Bao could not stop Quan. He was out to get Vien. "You're protecting her because you'd all do the same. Everything here has gone to hell!"

A young woman with a sorrowful but tender face stood up. "Comrade Quan, I demand you keep a decent tongue. You scream, you scold, you criticize, you interrogate, but you don't take the time to find out the reality. We will not tolerate your going overboard this way. Calm yourself, Comrade. We are not as heartless or unforgiving as you toward someone who has made a mistake. If this were a team of single men instead of women and you were one of the men, would you clench your teeth and suffer to overcome your natural desires and the need for love?" The young woman's voice faltered as she sat down.

Quan appeared moved by her words, but he refused to change course. "So, if we want to show compassion for you, we have to bring in a team of men to inseminate you? Even in a herd of goats, only one male is necessary!"

Mien hadn't planned to speak, but Quan's vulgar words brought her to her feet. "Comrade Deputy Director, don't abuse *us* like that! I was born in the Year of the Goat, so I'm forty-two now. During the

American War, I was commander of a Youth Volunteer Platoon, young girls dedicated to defeating the enemy. We dynamited mountains and built roads all over this island. But we always thought that once peace came, we would be able to marry and have children."

Mien looked at Quan. His face was rigid.

"After 1973, our battalion moved to this jungle and built the forestry collective. There is peace now, but marriage never came for us. During the American War, we lived at the edge of death and had no trouble controlling our desires. But now it's no longer possible. My beloved died during the war, and I lost my chance to marry and a child with him. Who did I save myself for? My virginity only brings me loneliness. The collective supports me in many ways, but it cannot bring the joy of raising a child."

Mien sat down, her face filled with sadness. Quan's face had grown redder as she spoke, and now he was more agitated than ever. He punched the table and screamed as though he'd lost his senses completely. The women were frightened but remained quiet, waiting for him to cool down.

"Luyen, I will ask you one more time!" Quan roared. "Who got you pregnant?"

Luyen looked beseechingly to Mien for help. But Mien, exhausted and vulnerable from having revealed so much, remained silent.

"Fine, Miss Luyen!"

"Cuong, where the hell are you?" Quan whirled around, piercing Cuong with a stare that went through him like a bullet. Oh God, he thought. Is he going to blame me for her pregnancy? His little legs twitched nervously. "Cuong!" Quan yelled again. "Take Miss Luyen into the storage house and keep her there until she confesses who is the father of her child. She will be released only on my orders, do you understand? If you don't watch her well, you'll have to deal with me!"

The women leapt to their feet, shocked. Quan had become a brutal dictator. Mrs. Diep, pallid, tugged at his sleeve. "Sir, I don't think we should do this."

Quan whipped his arm away and glared at her as if he were going to eat her alive. "Don't tell me what to do, Mrs. Diep! Who do you think is in charge here? By noon, Luyen will be famished and ready to point the finger at Vien. Then I'll release her." He spun again. "Cuong, you're as slow as a dying rooster."

Cuong, white-faced, scurried over and took Luyen's arm gently, silently begging her to go with him without making a fuss. They walked to the storage shed together, the small man next to the tall woman; both were trembling. Cuong could barely control his fear. What if he were fingered as the father of Luyen's child? He and Vien were the only men in Team 5. Who else could it be? Quan stomped after the two of them, alternately clasping his hands behind him and kneading his buttocks.

At noon, just as Quan was about to take a nap, a timid Cuong approached his bed.

"Sir, the women wish to bring Luyen lunch."

Quan bolted upright. "You will not permit it. She'll go hungry until she makes her statement." He glanced at his watch, grunted a few times in satisfaction, then lay down again, envisioning the moment he would have Vien's fate in his hands. He was sure Luyen would confess by midafternoon. Years ago, when he'd commanded a sapper battalion, there was a soldier suspected of stealing a watch from one of his comrades. Quan ordered his men to tie the man up and put him in a storage shed overnight. By the next morning, the thief had confessed to everything. Luyen was only a woman. Surely it wouldn't take her as long to break down.

But by six in the evening Luyen had not broken her silence. Quan was furious, but his determination remained strong. "Fine," he said to Mrs. Diep and Miss Hao. "Let her stay there overnight. My former soldiers were even more stubborn, and I managed to reeducate them. By tomorrow morning, she will confess and the matter will be over." He tapped his watch confidently and returned to his room.

Cuong spent the night in the room next to the storage shed. He was a weak man, physically and emotionally, and listening to harsh words and loud voices made him dizzy. Although he'd vowed to stay up all night to fulfill his duties as guard, when Miss Bao brought Luyen dinner and threatened Cuong—"If you dare report this to Mr. Quan, we'll destroy your whole rotten lineage, from the roots to the top"—he meekly opened the door and let her in.

Although Luyen was imprisoned, she was sleeping on a proper mat with mosquito netting around it. It was as nice as any guest house.

Quan had been in the military. But the women of Team 5 had been in the Youth Brigade. They'd survived bombs and bullets and risked their lives to build roads in the mountains and jungles. They knew better than to follow a wrongheaded bully.

The next day at noon, as Cuong sat half-asleep in front of the shed, he saw a mob of women marching toward him. He leapt to his feet and leaned against the door of the shed, his hand clutching the keys that were buried in his trouser pocket.

"Let Luyen out!" Bao told him, not bothering with formalities. "One day is enough."

Cuong glanced at Bao's demeanor and felt the urge to run away. Then he pictured Quan's angry face, and he couldn't move. "I can't," he told her nervously.

Bao thrust her finger into his belly like a dagger. "Give me the keys."

His mother had browbeaten him and he was powerless around his wife. His only strength lay in his control of the production team's storage rooms, and he guarded the keys to those rooms with his life. No one had dared touch them before. What could he do? If he refused, these women would tear him to pieces.

"I can't," he said, moaning.

"Do I have to take them by force?" Bao yelled.

Cuong started to run, but he was too slow. After a few steps, the women surrounded him and pulled him to and fro, pecking like chickens fighting over a grain of rice. Bao grabbed his arm and began swinging him in a circle. He tripped over his own feet and fell, and Bao pried open his fingers and took the keys. The exultant women towered over his body, which was curled up on the ground.

"Throw him in the shed!" one of the women yelled.

Cuong rose unsteadily as he watched Luyen walk out of the storage shed. Before he could protest, Bao pushed him inside and slammed the door.

The women took Luyen by her arms and ran across the large yard. A flock of chickens squawked and flapped in terror as they rushed by. The women didn't stop until they were at Quan's door.

"Mr. Quan, it's over!" Bao shouted angrily. "We are no longer sheep for you to pen up and punish according to your mood."

"We will report your abusive behavior to the District Chief and make sure you're punished," another woman cried out.

"Now get out of here!" yelled Bao. Within seconds, the group dispersed, leaving Quan standing alone in the doorway of his room.

HANH HOANG

I grew up in Saigon and left Vietnam in 1974, five months before the war ended. I've worked as a teacher and freelance journalist, earned my Master of Fine Arts in creative writing at Saint Mary's College in Moraga, California, and am working on a Ph.D. in English.

I am finishing a collection of short stories, whose characters are mainly Vietnamese and Vietnamese–Americans. "Field of Heads," which won first prize in the 2005 Writer's Digest Short Short Competition, is about the cultural and social isolation that some of us immigrants suffer in a modern society.

Field of Heads

They brought a new girl to the field today and buried her up to the neck. At least I thought it was a girl: we all had short hair, and they always buried us some distance apart, so it was difficult to tell. But somehow I thought of the new one as a girl; perhaps it was the white translucent skin. Anyway, as soon as they left, she started to wail, just like everyone did the first time. Still, I felt bad for her.

I was the oldest in the group—there were forty-three of us and now forty-four. An unlucky number: four rhymes with death in our language. They weren't concerned about this, however, because they didn't believe in superstitions.

"It's not so bad here," I cried out as loudly as I could. I would have waved to catch her attention but my arms stuck to my torso in the earth, which felt now as hard as the wooden bed we slept on at night, so hard I couldn't even move my fingers now. "In other villages they'd drown us. They'd sell us to be servants. You'll go home soon, so stop weeping, or they'll hear you! You'll see, you'll like it here." But her sobs drowned out my words. Not that she would have understood much had she heard me. "Aah aah gaah aah," that was how I sounded. I tried hard but the words didn't come out right.

The others in our group had watched the girl at first, but now they turned their attention elsewhere. They strained their necks in different directions. It was always during this time—early in the morning right after they left us—that we came alive. As the wind blew, the cloths they had hung above to give us shade flapped, and through the openings we watched birds fly by or squirrels dangle on the ropes of the banyan trees.

The younger ones babbled at everything that moved, trees, breezes, animals. I knew better. I didn't even talk to my favorite squirrel, the one with mange spots on his back, the one who liked to close one eye every time he stared at me. Yet, I was hoping the girl would join the others and talk some. But she kept crying until everyone dozed off, everyone except me and her, that is. As I said, I was the oldest, so I felt responsible for all newcomers, not to mention that my mother had bid me this morning to keep an eye on the very young.

"Aah gooh." *They will harm you. For your own sake, you'd better stop!* I swayed my head back and forth and right and left to make her watch the scenery around us. Couldn't she see how peaceful it was, this field of heads, all bending in the same direction like flowers in the sun? "Eeh geeh aah." *You will soon develop enough neck muscle to bend just so, or to look beyond the sugar canes for your mother.*

But as hard as I tried, the girl didn't understand.

"Eeeh."

She didn't even look at me. Her face was red and all scrunched-up, like a piece of crumpled paper.

Soon the mothers returned. They dampened the soil and showered us with water from watering cans. My mother squatted next to me. "Mama, mama?" I watched blood seep from the cracks of her bare feet.

"Yes, Son," my mother mumbled with her mouth full. "My feet look bad, but they don't hurt, really. Had to work hard today." She leaned over and spat into my open mouth the semolina she had chewed for me.

We smacked our lips, slurped, and swallowed—we were always noisy when we ate—but our mothers were quiet. Of course they listened to the girl, who moaned loudly and monotonously, like a foghorn. I had never been to the ocean, but Mother said that was how foghorns sounded.

Nothing helped. The girl's mother petted her, slapped her, then petted her again, but she wouldn't eat. She just kept wailing. Even I was becoming impatient. Other first-time children would have stopped by now. My head rocked violently back and forth. "Mama! Eeh gaah gooh. Mama!" *Explain to her.*

"She'll calm down," Mother said to the woman, who, embarrassed, nodded and smiled at everyone. She was new to the village, and her hair, like her daughter's, was still silky black. Ours was all dried and browned by the sun. "She'll be hungry," Mother said. "Remember not to let your worries stop you from working, or it will bode ill for your family."

But the girl never calmed down. When her mother left to join other parents to finish the day's work, she shrieked the most piercing shriek I had ever heard, so piercing that my ears rang, and she wouldn't stop.

In the early afternoon her mother came back from the field with the father. I heard the sudden silence: the women in the nearby fields, and the men beyond, stopped chopping the sugar canes. They all stared at the mother, whose feet made a gentle squishing sound on the damp earth.

She dug out her daughter. The girl squealed, flailed her arms in excitement, and smiled the way all very young children do at their mothers, happy, loving, silly, with a wide-opened mouth. The mother unbuttoned her blouse. She placed her right nipple in between the girl's lips. The father leaned against his axe and looked away.

The girl was going home now while the rest of us had to wait until dusk, when our parents finished their days' work.

I was sure the girl wouldn't come back to the field. But what happened to the children who didn't return, Mother would never say.

In 1967, I was in the United States Navy on the Aircraft Carrier USS *America* during the Six-Day War, watching the destruction of a culture by surgical air strikes. The precision of the bombs and the bravado of the carrier crew made a peace warrior out of me. I wrote "Firing Blanks at Moving Targets" to help heal the dreams that haunt me of screaming people in craters full of blood that I still dream in black-and-white 3D images.

I was shell-shocked and caught up in rock 'n' roll when I joined the infamous Philadelphia revolutionary group MOVE in 1971. Then a self-proclaimed child of love, I attempted to bring a wreath of peace into a revolutionary war zone. I labored to explain to MOVE members and anyone who would listen that revolution means total change with an eye on human awareness, not just social structure. It fell on deaf ears as the blind continued to lead the blind into the noise of time. Yet that spirit, that spark of peace and love, lives on as a bullet-proof entity that denies the theater of war respectability. This short story about the MOVE revolution comes from my unpublished novel, *Born under Prophecy,* and my poetics, "War Isn't Peace."

Firing Blanks at Moving Targets

You can't clean up hell. You exist in it and rise out of it, with much effort. This grand statement was spray-painted in big white letters on the doorway of an abandoned apartment. One of many graffiti signs, in revolutionary Powelton Village, Philadelphia, PA. Who would have thunk it—that this off-campus University of Pennsylvania neighborhood, with its hippies and rebels, would become nationally infamous? MOVE, a counterculture organization, put it on the national and world maps.

Daniel Cremel was my name in those days. I was an idealistic poetic activist type wanting more input for my output, so I joined that first wave of people who comprised MOVE, short for "the Movement." In those days I considered myself a peacenik and a rainbow warrior striving for a better, more aware America.

I stumbled into the much talked about MOVE leader, John Africa, at a hippie party, Powelton Village style, with a hearty atmosphere for those who could hang. People reveled in organic produce like apples, grapes, melons, peaches, and rice and carrot cakes complemented with hash brownies. Sandalwood incense burned in every room. The stereo played psychedelic jams, the smell of pungent earthy marijuana scented the air, and semiprivate sexuality oozed from various corners of the house.

John Africa was a medium-built black man with Rastafarian dreads; he wore faded jeans with a rope for a belt, and his neon green T-shirt had white paint stains on it. Don G worked as his right hand and also his shadow; he was a small-built white guy with horn-rimmed glasses and bright baby blues, semibalding on top; he wore torn jeans and a black shirt. He sat off to one corner backslapping and rapping to a small group of women.

Don G studied as a nerdy University of Pennsylvania graduate student and taught sociology at Center City's Philadelphia Community College, where I was a student. I found out via the grapevine that Don's classes encompassed hard-edged political issues and revolutionary tactics. I never took one of Don G's infamous classes, but I went to his lectures, which dealt with revolutionary theory.

Don approached me and announced, "Hey, man, I heard your poetry last week at the warehouse. Far out ... groovy, man."

John Africa approached us, bellowing, "What's up, brothers?" He pushed his big hand toward mine for a friendly shake, beaming a warm, wet smile.

"I've seen you with your walking stick around the neighborhood with your dogs," I told him.

"You're kinda fond of animals, huh?"

While winking and waving to well-wishers and not missing a beat, John exclaimed, "Dogs I can trust; with people you haft to watch your back."

I responded, "I get your drift."

Looking me straight in the eye, unblinking, he continued, "Have you read Eldridge Cleaver's *Soul on Ice* yet? It's a work of social genius."

"No, I haven't. Should I?" I inquired.

John gave me a hard stare, narrowing his black pupils further. He half smiled, half frowned, while slowly yet forcibly uttering, "That book's food for the masses, man."

At that point, as if on cue, Don excused himself and quickly left our conversation to get John and himself some celery stalks, jammed full of peanut butter, and a cup of chai tea. John resumed, "Eldridge tells a story of the struggle from the white man's oppression and the black rage that festers in the urban ghettos gathering steam until it spills into mainstream America like a hot knife in cold butter! *Soul on Ice* is the real deal, a revolutionary work with intellectual insight and balls, brother."

Don G returns loaded down with healthy snacks. "I eat healthy to stay healthy," John asserted. His vegan food lifestyle clashed with my junk food diet, and I felt it was time to go.

"Well, I gotta split, man," I blurted out suddenly.

As I walked away, John reached forward, tapping me on the back. Drawing close to me, he whispered in my ear, "Read that book, now, okay?"

"Sure," I answered. "*Soul on Ice,* that's the title, right?"

"Once you read it, man, you won't forget it, Shit, you can't forget it," he said.

I was halfway to the front door and Don hollered from across the room, "Call me about the vehicle!" He'd promised to lend me a vehicle for a band I was getting together.

Suddenly someone turned the stereo way up and Jimi Hendrix sang the fateful Bob Dylan song, "All Along the Watchtower." The music surged with people partying all around me. I walked past a dancing couple, who passed me a bong. After taking a few hits and exhaling, I walked to the door, opened it, and pronounced, "Later, all." Then I departed into the Powelton Village night.

MOVE had in John Africa a charismatic leader. John utilized provocative revolutionary rhetoric. What interested me was John's mind-blowing manuscript that was considered esoteric. It contained, among other elements, an antitechnological stance intermingled with wisdom from the Book of Revelation. The language was "John Africanism," pure and simple, revamped and polished by Don G. The title was *The Book;* I read the original manuscript and the finished book. John saw the doomsday effect in the western countries' application of the electronic information age. John envisioned a hippie socialistic blending of ideas like moving back to the land and keeping the planet as pristine as possible. John did not believe in the economic system he called money debt certificates with pictures of dead presidents. John Africa had a wide bulbous nose and piercing jet black eyes; his earthy dress and intense manner wasn't like your average Powelton hippie. He was more like a Powelton rebel-hippie, not a peacenik. He was frank and fiery like Fidel Castro, well muscled with big, rough hands. His stature glowed with pride and energy. John would work right beside you sweating and grunting but never quitting until the job was done. He was twenty years older than most of his followers, but you would never know it. John might not have been a Powelton Ivy Leaguer, but he was a man who cared for the people.

MOVE was out front, outspoken, and in your face. Four-letter words intermingled with undisputable facts that peppered the rhetoric they used. The SLA didn't finish their exposé of America's lack of values. The intellectually driven Weathermen couldn't or wouldn't see the full revolutionary enchilada. John Africa's MOVE had a strategy. They would be principal players in the mode of the community-minded Black Panthers.

MOVE's tactics were to take on Mayor Rizzo and the whole Philadelphia establishment. What better place to make an impact than in the home of American Liberty? Mayor Rizzo the ex-police commander was known for ass-kicking and taking names. He was infamous for toting two pearl-handled revolvers even in formal attire. Rizzo, a south Philadelphian, had an ax to grind. MOVE occupied two houses side by side on a corner lot next to a store and dry cleaners in Powelton Village; the houses were provided by Don G. Early MOVE included ten members, swelling sometimes to twenty. Some were college kids, some hippie activists. One was a former Nazi sympathizer. Dotted here and there were ex-Black Panthers and also card-carrying communists.

It seemed in those days that MOVE was part of every demonstration—from animal rights to social and neighborhood issues—that took place in Philadelphia. You name it, MOVE protested it. Soon radio, television, and all the daily newspapers zeroed in on MOVE, preparing us for media scrutiny. John Africa used to give us nightly talks outside on the property under a big tree. He chose close associates; I was one at that time. We sat in a semicircle around him to hear our leader's every word. Don G could always be found going over notes, scripting activities, playing the second in command, and offering you revolutionary theory from the actual *Anarchists' Cookbook*. John Africa would anoint you with the meat and potatoes of social spiritual zeal. His intense rhetoric and graphic descriptions of a society crumbling painted a vivid picture of the social climate of the time. It was a provocative indoctrination in the tradition of the ancient Greek philosophers. Some balked at this approach, so people came and went. The more highly educated argued and left in a huff. The hippies and peaceful types fled after one sitting or two. Only those who had that right mixture of revolutionary intent and social awareness stuck.

The manuscript, now only referred to as *The Book,* wasn't seen anymore. It became sacred lore, like *The Dead Sea Scrolls* and the *Holy Bible,* and was taught at special meetings only to those zealous for its comprehension. Over time, hearsay, bickering, infighting, and word-of-mouth began to run the show. I started having confrontations with Don G; I began to fear he was an infiltrator from a government agency. I sensed that MOVE was changing rapidly from a Powelton social organization to a real revolutionary organization replete with violence.

I began to look at people sideways and examine all rhetoric and written communications. Stories were rampant in the organization and on the street about shakedowns, beatings, and even a killing. Along with others, I suspected by this time that undercover FBI types or CIA infiltrated us, because MOVE was becoming too much like the SLA, Black Panthers, or Weathermen groups.

I was eventually pushed away in a coup masterminded by Don G. My girlfriend, Porsche (who joined MOVE only because of our relationship), was a fighter from the urban ghetto of north Philly. Porsche was small and slender with a beautiful, full bushy afro like Angela Davis. She had a clue and street smarts to boot; this sista was down. Porsche and I were threatened with sticks and stones one night after an intensely vocal meeting at another member's house. As we left the meeting, twenty members followed us to the street yelling that we weren't loyal and throwing stones. We stood back-to-back near a big tree. I found a small iron pipe, and she a big stick, and we started swinging to hold off this angry group of MOVE members on a charged moonless evening. My loyalty to MOVE was never an issue, but Don G saw me as a threat, because my heroics astounded the younger members. After fourteen months of service, that night I left the MOVE organization with a heavy heart yet much wiser. In the coming weeks, I would witness an American tragedy.

I woke on a hot muggy humid day, the air thick, the sun blisteringly bright, set in an azure sky. The radio, loud and annoying, had announced that MOVE in Powelton Village was in a confrontation with the Philadelphia Police and Fire Department, also the mayor's office, at that very moment.

"Well, shit," I proclaimed, as I rose out of my bed and ran a comb through my hair. Porsche was at work, and I was the only one at home besides our many cats. Dodging animals while eating an apple, I put on my jeans with one hand while pulling my shirt on with the other. Then I slipped into my sandals and ran out the door falling and jumping down three flights of steps. I ran the four blocks to MOVE headquarters at full speed, the whole time trying to figure out what this major brouhaha was all about. Could it be the animals? MOVE maintained a stable of animals that angered area residents and violated various health codes. Maybe the gas, water, or electricity companies were finally fed up with the lack of payments. As I turned the last corner, right in front of the blue-and-white barricades, I shouted, "They never paid the last couple of months' rent. That's gotta be it!" A bunch of wilted yellow flowers lay at my feet, and makeshift signs high overhead in a tree in big bold red letters proclaimed:

MOVE IT OR LOSE IT
Y O U R A S S !

People were all over the street gawking and talking loudly to be heard above the din. "MOVE's out on a limb, I guess it's gonna be cut off. The other shoe is about to drop, brother," murmured an aging female Powelton hippie, who was a drooping braless wonder. Walking further down the block toward MOVE's headquarters, my attention was diverted overhead to the police and media helicopters that buzzed the neighborhood. The air reeked with tension. Most of MOVE's neighbors had been evacuated. The buildings stood empty. The rooftops teemed with SWAT members and sharpshooters armed to the teeth. Down at ground level, police cars and trucks swarmed everywhere.

I heard a tall thin white guy holler, "Pigs! Pigs! It sure stinks around here! Pigs wearing black gestapo boots with your guns cocked, get the hell out of Powelton!"

I looked on as I walked toward the barricade in silence as many of the young "oinked" their approval. This lopsided affair wasn't to be a fair fight, I thought. What's new? As I approached the front barricade, a police captain gave me the evil eye, undoubtedly remembering me from surveillance photographs, yet no one stopped me. By then I was an outsider. No one really gave a damn about me; Philly's finest had their target.

I watched, as tears slowly filled my eyes. My former comrades, the voices of the people, were getting ready for the slaughter. Cameramen and reporters poured over the scene, asking bystanders odd questions and looking dumbfounded.

The MOVE headquarters was a fortress. Giant logs hung out to the street from the building, providing a platform for MOVE members to parade, brandishing weapons and screaming into loudspeakers to the local and national audiences. The show of firearms wasn't supposed to happen. MOVE members had spoken of a confrontation scenario, where weapons weren't to see daylight so as not to incur a police assault. Tactics sure had changed since I left the fold five months ago.

I began to reflect on what Powelton was really like and possibly why this was happening, yet I couldn't think clearly. It was summer but in my daydream, a light, falling snow affected my vision. A message was written in that snow in giant letters: "You Can't Kill the Revolution by Firing Blanks at Moving Targets." Next I began to see ugly images of Mantua, the hood three blocks from Powelton. Mantua was run-down, boarded-up, rat-infested tenements. Lots cramped with trash dotted the landscape, where drugs and stolen merchandise were sold openly. There was no love lost between the neighborhoods. Mantua raided us and raped us, yet Powelton was a liberal, flaunting community. The walls that bordered Powelton and Mantua were graffitied with large signs.

GURUS RUN AMUCK!
GHETTOS ARE FUCKED!
WHAT'S UP WITH THAT?

The sun beamed down as I stood transfixed, sweat dripping from my face. I finally looked at my watch. I had been there three hours already. The tension was grave. All eyes glared at the MOVE compound. MOVE sensed that the time was now; everything stopped, including the blaring announcements littered with brazen four-letter words. I always thought MOVE's message was strong and clear, yet the curse words underlined and punctuated their intent. It was a rude awakening for those who slept on liberty's watch. These were fellow human beings inside that compound about to do battle with the industrial military Babylon. Where was John Africa? I wondered. Perhaps giving orders in the basement area with a rifle in hand, while Don G stole away into the backyard with his writing pad and pen planning the next event.

A streaking, pulsating shot rang out loud and clear, seemingly from the SWAT team on the rooftops. Some bystanders pointed toward them. Endless rounds of ammo were fired in rapid succession. Women screamed, "They're going to kill them all, there are children in there!" The crowd surged away from the area, as the police shouted to keep moving and stay low. Through the smoke and the shouting with the smell of gunpowder everywhere, people ran quickly for cover about 300 feet away. The police helicopter hovered high above the scene. The rotating blades were making a loud swishing churning noise. Amid this I could still hear orders being shouted out from the authorities. Now they, too, used four-letter words in rapid succession. More noxious-smelling gunpowder filled the air, and the sound of bullets whistled into the hot day. Huge sections of the MOVE compound were riddled with holes. Surely, Vietnam was just like this, I mused. So was the Revolutionary War, some of which was fought on this very Pennsylvania soil. Then America was the underdog, the rebel, and the terrorist.

Just then rapid gunfire ensued from a side street. "Officer down!" A loud call rang out. "They got one of ours! Those dirty sons of bitches!" screamed a sunburnt police sergeant. These were comments spoken in haste with acid precision. The few of us who remained close by became agitated and antsy. We were in the killing fields now. Anything could happen at any moment. The cops rescued their fallen comrade, dragged him to safety under the watchful eyes of an armed camp. No TV show could hold a candle to this drama. This was the real deal, our boys in blue doing their thing and me with a ringside seat!

A helicopter hovered and buzzed over the MOVE compound's rooftop area. Something was dropped near the compound chimney and disappeared out of sight. All of a sudden, I heard an explosion, and the second story crumbled before my eyes. Fire flashed and smoke billowed everywhere. The building was now a pile of junk. People trapped in the basement hollered, "Oh my God, help us save the children!" Bright-red fire engines and green armored personnel carriers moved into position with hoses at the ready. Swoosh! Boom! Bang! Tear gas was shot into the fallen compound's first floor rubble and the basement area. Almost instantly the water hoses were gushing great torrents of water that shattered basement windows one by one. Water never sounded so harsh, so powerful, as it was being forced into the burning MOVE building. Cops, like storm troopers, entered MOVE's remaining structure with guns drawn, ready to kick ass doing the public's business. The police helicopter swooped low to check out the action. Just then my brain remembered war stories related by returning Vietnam veterans, who told of chopper rescues under heavy fire.

The cops left. The remaining foundation was weak and ready to fall, the water ceased, as bulldozers moved into place for the final phase of the operation. The sun shone big and hot. We could hear sobbing and screams emanating from the compound's basement. A tall African-looking man hollered, "That's a woman, and children calling for help!" Just then someone tried to exit from the side of the compound's basement. Cops rushed to the scene with weapons drawn, poised to kill. All I saw were flailing arms and kicking legs. A second person or persons exited, seemingly a woman and a child. The sounds of children crying rose from the compound's basement. There was loud panicky shouting coming from the gathering where I stood, also from the policemen nearby. "Get the woman and kids out now!" The police officer motioned for us, the viewing public, to vacate the area pronto. As the crowd slowly left the area, a small group of jubilant policemen said the good guys won but that bastard leader escaped somehow.

So John wasn't dead, I thought. MOVE's vision of a more informed mass public had made it to third base via a bloodbath. Who or what was going to steal home?

Walking home in deep thought, I passed the wilted flowers again. This time I smashed the whole bunch with my full sandal until it was one wet spot indistinguishable from the cement. I had just witnessed a military commando-style police action. The wave of things to come had finally arrived. This was like the SLA and Black Panther exterminations.

This couldn't be what the founders meant by life, liberty, and the pursuit of happiness. Finally, in a daze, as if I were a robot, I stopped on an inner command. I looked up. I was home. Once in my apartment, I sought out the fan; next, I slumped into a chair at the kitchen table. Then I reached across the table, turned on the radio; the music filled the room. "Say you want a revolution, yeah we all want to change the world." I stood up and walked to the open window. I stopped and leaned on the window frame peering out at the landscape of hippie Powelton three stories below, as my brain screamed in hot silence.

JOHN PATRICK IGNATIUS

When the Marines stormed the city of Fallujah, I found myself fascinated with the coverage on the *News Hour*. I watched as squads of Marines went from wall to crumbling wall shooting and calling to each other; they even had intermittent interviews with squad leaders and platoon sergeants. These were real people, and I got to recognize them as they continued fighting during the days of that week.

Perhaps my strangest reaction to that week was the feeling like I should have been there with those hard-chargers. I had served in the Marine Reserve from 1987 to 1993 and still felt like a wayward member of this bellicose tribe. My unit was called for the first Gulf War in 1990, but that action fortunately was over so quickly we never made it out of Los Angeles. I have spoken to other former Marines who shared a similar feeling and even know of one vet of the current war who wanted to return after some of the guys in his unit died in Iraq after his tour and contract were up. I still don't know what to clearly make of these seemingly crazy feelings.

A native Southern Californian, I now live with my family in the Diocese of Monterey in the parts of California I love the most. "The Prayer of Saint Francis" takes inspiration from a story I saw on a late-night TV news magazine about a Marine who came home from Iraq to Chicago. I do not recall the name of the Marine in the story, but this "Prayer" is for all Marines.

Now I enjoy chopping wood for our wood-burning stove and looking for sand dollars with my two sons and golden retriever on Grover Beach.

The Prayer of Saint Francis

Bless me, Father, for I have sinned. It's been, uhh, a pretty long time since my last confession and these are my sins."

I could feel the priest's presence behind the screen. The box had that wood-and-water smell that churches have. "Well, I've been drinking a lot, Father, I mean a lot, pretty much every night a half bottle of Beam and a bunch of beer, and I've gotten in a few fights—they're mostly jerks who I fight. Is it bad even if you're the guy that loses? Anyway, I guess being drunk and fighting are both sins. I've got a pretty bad black eye right now if you could see it, but I'm okay. Umm, let's see. I think quite a few perverted thoughts too. You know, about women. Sometimes I think I wanta rail every one of them I see. Young, old, whatever. Except nuns and kids—nothing like that. Oh, I've started smoking again too. Is that a sin? I used to not smoke too much—I was doing the lozenges and all, but I just started smoking again—I guess 'cause I was drinking so much. Oh, back to the women—I've been kind of screwing around too. I mean, I have a girlfriend and all, but I railed a couple of other broads recently too. I'm not sure about the Japanese chick though. I mean, she was kind of passing out, and I was too, so I don't really even know if anything happened. Maybe that wasn't a sin, but I still felt kind of bad, actually pretty bad. I kind of feel like I raped her or something. I basically feel like jumping off a cliff. Am I taking too long?"

Silence like he was thinking about it.

"Maybe, but go on."

"Well I've done worse things too."

"Would you like to confess them?" His voice was soft, almost with a little foreign accent, but I wasn't sure. My knees were starting to hurt, but I tried not to think about it. The pain really wasn't that bad.

"Don't I have to?"

"It would probably be better for you."

I was quiet. Probably? I thought. I tried to make out his shadowy form from behind the screen.

"Well, basically I'm a violent, perverted booze hound, but I think I'm really not a bad guy."

"I'm sure." I thought I understood what he meant.

"Can I come back and continue this?"

"Sure."

"I feel like I'm gonna go get drunk after I leave here. Is that bad?"

"God's interested in the you of right now."

"Well, I didn't really come here to confess all that other stuff, I mean, I'm glad I did and everything, but there's worse stuff than that. Way worse."

"It sounds like most of these are alcohol related."

"No, not the bad thing. I mean the really bad thing—that was sober."

"Would you like to confess it?"

"Well that's why I'm here." I had to say it: *Say it, pussy!*

"I killed a lady. But let me explain, 'cause I've gone over it a million times in my head, a million fucking times, Father. Shit! Sorry I cursed. I do a lot of that too, including the Lord's name in vain. But this woman was walking toward the sandbags; I was the NCOIC. She was carrying a bag, like a fancy paper shopping bag with string handles. Like the kind ladies get at fashion stores. She was one of them, you know, all wrapped in black and stuff. You know, a hajji broad or whatever. Some of the guys were yelling at her to stop, but she kept coming; she just wouldn't fucking stop. I was yelling in my best command voice for her to stop, but she kept coming. One of the guys yelled, 'Ventilate her!' She was reaching into the bag. I had to do something. I just fired five rounds into her chest. Her or my Marines. There were little puffs of smoke on her chest. She fell like in slow motion, Father, and everything was silent. This is the kicker: she had a fucking white flag in the bag. God dammit, why did she keep walking? Oh shit, I'm sorry, I cussed again! I'm fuckin' sorry, dammit! Why did she keep walking?" I felt like I was starting to cry.

The shadowy mass behind the light screen was silent. I felt real shitty that he had to hear about crap like this from jarheads like me, and wondered if I should wait and see if he absolved me or just leave.

ELIJAH IMLAY

I grew up in what was then rural Maryland outside of Washington, D.C., with miles of woodland on either side of a brick home. My father was a paleontologist whose research supported the continental drift theory. He took his family with him summers camping out in mountains and deserts collecting fossils. He and my mother imbued in their children a love of nature and the importance of contributing to the betterment of our planet. My oldest brother, Marc, wrote the proposal for the Endangered Species Act and was the first scientist responsible for listing endangered species. My other older brother, Richard, is a nuclear physicist. I liked science and built a homemade telescope that I spent whole nights using to view objects in the sky. However, my stronger interests were music and literature. I practiced the clarinet a couple of hours a day, which may have saved my life when I was drafted into the army. Like many of my generation, I was opposed to the war in Viet Nam. Three times I evaded the draft, then volunteered to be an army bandsman. I discovered many fine musicians similarly drafted. After the war I worked as a teacher and then a social worker. I studied the teachings and the contemplative sides of spiritual paths, especially Sufis, and became a retreat guide. At the age of forty-eight I decided to write poetry for the first time since college. During a workshop, participants were asked to remember in sensual detail a significant event in their lives, and I was back in Viet Nam. I started writing about the war and located a friend from that time after twenty-six years. At the age of sixty, I discovered that I had completed a manuscript of poetry about the war. Now my interest is in transformation of conscience, individually and collectively, as well as consciousness. My day job is counseling emotionally disturbed adolescents in a school-based program. I live close to the beach in Ventura, California, with my wife, also a poet. We have two grown children who also care about the well-being of our planet.

A Child of God

For Lawrence McKittrick

And I dreamed I saw the bombers
Riding shotgun in the sky
Turning into butterflies
Above our nation
                          —JONI MITCHELL

It could have been me. It could have been
any one of us. It was McKittrick.
He stepped from the chopper, his bent form

a swirl of dust halocd by morning sun.
He wore no-name jungle fatigues, stood
poised for flight like the bird that dropped him off

at Eagle four months late, and like the shell
of a spent round, his gaze was empty
where it fell. When I asked where he'd been

he showed me his bandaged elbow.
A bird colonel came to Camp Evans during
in-country training, and pointing at the first

men he saw, said, *I want you, you, and you,*
not caring that McKittrick enlisted an extra year
to keep out of battle and play trombone. Chosen

for *a special mission for the president,* they flew
to Khe Sanh, still a ghost land from the slaughter
of '68. When a convoy of ARVN soldiers

headed out, someone yelled, *About time they fought*
their own stinkin' war! Every day, first light to last,
McKittrick lifted boxes and crates, hid in a bunker

when he could, saw swarming choppers scurry
to lift off or land or else end up metal husks.
Nowhere was safe. Marines left booby traps

and failed to leave a map. Every day
someone got blown up digging a trench or taking
a piss. Soon there were craters in his mind.

He stumbled into them and stopped his ears
when he could. The silence of woodland mist
beckoned from neighboring hills, unattainable

as the girl from Marysville, Ohio, who left him
for no one else. Two nights ago he saw
artillery flash. By the time he heard the round,

it nicked his elbow and chipped a bone
that bled hard. *Damn lucky,* he said, *so here I am.*
He pointed out vapor trails, bombers headed

for Ha Noi or the Ho Chi Minh Trail
where it passed through Laos: *My mission
was illegal, all records destroyed. The colonel*

*never spoke to me, and if anyone asks, I was here
at Eagle. I never pissed with the dead
or walked on a moonscape that wasn't the moon.*

These images came with him, this trombonist
without his 'bone, from a parade ground
at Khe Sanh, where a band would never play.

Bird Grieves for the Man They Killed

We wore the steel bracelets
of Montagnards—money
for that mountain people,
good fortune for us. I held
my broken glasses together
with safety pins. I wrote
the 23rd Psalm on my helmet's
elastic band. John Jim,
our ammo bearer, gave us
each a Navajo necklace

of turquoise and onyx
with a single white feather
strung by his wife. I took out
earphones every night
and listened to George Harrison
sing *My Sweet Lord.* If only
there were no picture of wife
or girlfriend, found
in the billfold of a Vietnamese
we killed. Easy to say
it wasn't me who shot him,
but I still see his eyes
that never close and should
accuse me, yet don't.
They're looking at her photo.

CHANPIDOR JANKO

In 1968, I was born in Svay Rieng City, Cambodia, near the Vietnamese border. I am a survivor of the Pol Pot regime. I lost my father, my oldest brother, and several aunts and uncles between 1975 and 1979. In Cambodia, I was a teacher at a public high school in Phnom Penh. I married James Janko in 2000. Two years later, we moved to the United States of America. I am now living with my husband in Oakland, California. I have been interested in a medical profession since I was a girl. I will begin nursing school in 2006, and I hope to one day be a nurse-practitioner.

My Father's Photograph

My father, a tall and handsome lawyer, stares straight ahead, his face serious and distinguished. Cambodia's ruler, King Sihanouk, is pinning a medal on my father's dark suit coat. I often stop to look at this image, and sometimes I pretend that I am present, a little girl with her father and the king. I see in my father's eyes great dignity and poise. The king, I am told, awarded him a medal for his work for justice in Svay Rieng Province, a province that borders Viet Nam.

On April 17, 1975, Pol Pot and the Khmer Rouge came to power in Cambodia. On that day, my family, once prosperous, was left with nothing but a bicycle, a little food, and few articles of clothing. Soldiers, dressed in black, fierce looking and loud, ordered us to leave Svay Rieng City.

"Take just enough food and clothing for three days," we were told. "After three days, you will be allowed to return."

We joined a long procession into the countryside. I could not see the beginning of the procession, nor could I see the end. Thousands of us Khmers walked together in the heat of the Southeast Asian sun, the sweat pouring from our bodies. My father, a man admired by a king, balanced me on the seat of a bicycle, and he tied a few supplies to the back of the bike. My mother carried Srey Puv, my youngest sister, who was only three months old. My three older brothers and four sisters carried some food and other necessities for our unknown journey.

Shortly after sunset, we arrived at a small village surrounded by fruit trees. The houses, typical of Cambodia, were made of palm leaves and

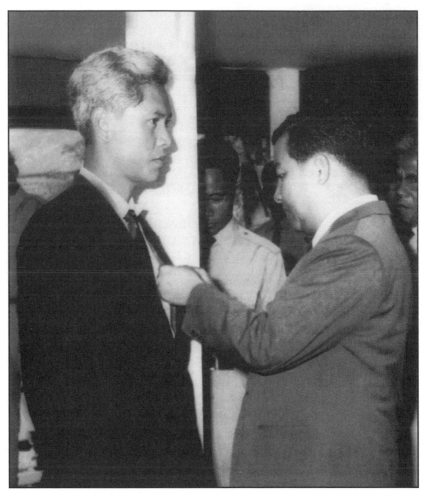

My father receives a medal from King Sihanouk.

bamboo, and were elevated on stilts so that the entrance to each was approximately ten feet off the ground. Livestock—water buffaloes and cows—were normally tethered beneath such houses, but I saw no animals here. Khmer Rouge soldiers ordered my family to stay beneath one of the houses.

Before nightfall, I last saw my living father. Standing as if alone, but standing in a line of men that stretched beyond my vision, he awaited his death. I remember a towel wrapped around his neck, his only possession other than his clothes. I remember soldiers, many soldiers, black shadows with harsh voices. My father and the others were being taken away because Angka, the new government of Pol Pot, supposedly wanted them to study. Later in the war, when families were taken away at night never to return, they were told that Angka needed them to cut trees.

Soldiers barked commands. The line moved; my father vanished in the dusk. It was very easy to die. I believe that my father didn't look at me, his daughter, once more, and that he didn't look at his wife or his eldest son or anyone in our family, because he wanted us to live. At the time, I did not feel grief or sadness. I began to merge with the night, a great darkness filled with nothing. Khmers often refer to 1975 as Year Zero. As a child, I carried its cold, vast nothing in my heart.

Later, as a woman, I heard from my mother my father's last words. She, always a good listener, understood what he said and what he left unsaid.

"Do not cry," he told her. "Do not cry." His tone was soft, but a scream is sometimes soft. My father did not call out, "Please don't cry, they will kill you!" Quiet and dignified, he gave my mother an order. To save herself and her children, she obeyed. Our family shed no tears when my father vanished with the last light of the day. My mother understood the danger of grief. The women and children who wept were told by Khmer Rouge soldiers, "Join your husbands, join your fathers." Those teary-eyed Khmers did not understand, as my mother did, that a different social group, the Khmer Rouge, would abhor their allegiance to family. How could they be good revolutionaries if they loved the men who headed their families more than they loved and honored Pol Pot and his glorious plans for Cambodia? My father's words, *Do not cry,* were the softest and simplest poem called "Survive."

He saved his family, saved everyone but himself, because he spoke and my mother understood.

When the war ended, my family moved to Prekachi, my grandmother's village along the Mekong River. My mother had nothing, not even a photograph of her husband. I, at age eleven, could barely recall my father's face. My youngest sister, Srey Puv, could not remember him at all.

My grandmother was brave. During the Pol Pot years, she hid the photograph of my father and King Sihanouk beneath an old wooden cabinet. If Pol Pot's soldiers had discovered her treachery, they would have killed her. She took a high risk to honor our family.

I gaze at the photograph often. Sometimes I see, in the glass that covers it, my own reflection. My father's photograph tells me who I am. Every time I see his image, and every time I see my living mother, I remember that I come from strength, and that I am born of strength. Sometimes I say to myself, "He's taller than a king, more handsome than a king." I understand that my life must be large enough to fulfill my father's last wish. He wanted, after all, not only that I survive, but also that I flourish, that all of us flourish. He wanted what I want—a dignified peace. Now my mother hangs his photograph on the wall of her home in Phnom Penh, Cambodia, so every child and grandchild can see it. As soon as we open the door, we see his beautiful and distinguished face, and we see his love for us. This photograph is our legacy of bravery, our legacy of hope. My father stands taller than a king.

Stealing Fish

In 1980, one year after the Pol Pot regime lost power, my family lived in a village along the Mekong River, in Kompong Cham Province. Khmers still faced a food shortage. My family had very little to eat, and we had no money. My mother and my older sisters would slice kernels of corn and cook the kernels with the bit of rice we had left. We rarely ate meat or fish. At this time, I was twelve years old. I was a skinny girl. Every day, I dreamed I had a delicious meal with plenty of fish and meat. I could close my eyes and smell fish soup, a steaming bowl with slices of fish and lemon grass and chili and cabbage, and with Cambodia's most traditional flavoring, *prohokti,* a fermented fish sauce that made everything delicious. I would open my eyes and see nothing. Most people at this time had what I had—nothing. We lived on what we could grab with our hands.

The houses along the Mekong River were built on stilts. The pilings were made from the best wood, the wood of the *bayng* tree, which could withstand the raging floods of the monsoon season. The heavy rains were months away, but I remember wanting the strength of great trees, the strength to hold up homes. What could I do with my seventy pounds? What could I lift? How could I help my mother and my siblings to survive?

One bright, shiny morning, I woke with the desire to get fish for my family. I walked through the cornfields to the Mekong River, which was not far from my grandmother's home. As on any morning, villagers gathered on the banks of the Mekong River to wait for the Islamic fishermen. At this time, most fishermen in Cambodia were Islamic; they wore white hats and blue-and-white-striped sarongs. None of the villagers had money, but cups of rice could often be traded for fish. My family had so little rice that we had nothing to trade.

While the people waited for the boats to arrive, I looked at the beautiful view of the hill at the other side of the river. The water breathed softly. I hardly saw waves on the river. Once in a while, a boat passed to the north.

As I attended to the beauty before me, a fisherman's boat approached the bank. All the villagers and one thief rushed to the boat. I suddenly discovered a way to get fish. The barterers gathered beside the boat. I was small and could squeeze my skinny body into the smallest cranny. I lived in shadows, blended with others, and used whoever or whatever came near me as a shield. My eyes stared sharply at a big enough fish; I brought that fish close to me. My hands were very fast. While the fisherman was scaling fish and talking with barterers, I pulled the fish over the side of the boat, waded into the river, and moved away along the shore.

The villagers surrounded the boat. I, the only child, blended with the sandy beach and the bodies that towered above me. Inch by inch, I backed up, and I held the dead fish in the shallow water, hidden from everyone but me. As the villagers continued to trade rice for fish, some of them wading in the water and looking at the fish in the stern of the boat, I turned, swung the fish around in front of me, and walked at a normal pace, my mouth watering, toward home.

My fish weighed about one kilo. He was silver and fat, over a foot long, and lovely. I walked home pressing him to my blouse and to my pants that were held up with a rubber band.

As a girl, my parents taught me to be honest, to respect others, and to be aware that the way I live is a reflection on my family and my ancestors. I was taught to behave in a traditional way, with quiet dignity and humility. I was taught to listen to my parents and my elders. Never, by anyone, was I taught to act on my own.

Hunger is a teacher, as is survival. My mother accepted the fish with surprise and gratitude. My sisters cooked it. We sat together and ate every part of it. We sucked the bones. We felt no remorse.

I stole fish many times. One time a fisherman saw me and said, "Hey!" I was already a great distance from him and his boat. I had nothing against the fisherman, but my family was hungry. I got away with a giant fish.

JAMES JANKO

My novel, *Buffalo Boy and Geronimo,* began at a meditation-and-writing retreat in which children were present. Maxine Hong Kingston, who led the writing part of the retreat, offered a suggestion: "If you write about war, write about it in a way that a child would understand."

I began that day to write about the children and animals of Southeast Asia, and I wrote in detail about the land, the rivers, that which sustains life. I was a platoon medic in the Viet Nam–American War, a war that—in my memory—had been a story about soldiers. But my novel went in a direction that surprised me: The land became a character, and the children and animals became main players. Nguyen Luu Hai (Buffalo Boy) and Antonio Lucio Conchola (Geronimo) are relentless in their search for beauty. They do not compromise. They persevere.

Buffalo Boy

In my next life I will be the sun, I will light the fields.
I will eat java birds, rice birds, before they steal our harvest.
I will be the green of the rice, the yellow of sunlight.
I will have the strength of a bull buffalo, the body of a mountain.
I will carry a rice field and a pretty village girl on my spine.

His boldest song had to be sung in whispers. Nguyen Luu Hai sang to his buffalo and to the sun on planted fields, the light of trees, but he did not sing to his family. At age fourteen, Hai lived with his mother and twin sister in a village near Cu Chi. Had Ma Xuan heard him singing of heavenly light as his light, of buffalo strength as his strength, of a mountain's body as his body, she would have interrupted. "Why waste your time making noise? You think you're special?" She would have reminded him of the danger of pride, the sin that separates an individual from his ancestors, his family, his elders, his village, the ten thousand helpers who guide his life.

So his Sun Song was not for human ears. He whispered it to sky and trees, sunlit fields, and to Great Joy, his bull buffalo, the largest in the village. The animal never complained when Hai rode on his back. After the boy and his family worked in the fields in the morning, Hai would hoist himself on Great Joy and suddenly be taller than most houses in the village. The boy liked to brag to the animal about how tall he had

189

grown. He would scratch the beast's ears and whisper, "Taller than our village, tall as the young bamboo. Tree-tall, sky-tall. Taller than an American soldier. Tall as my bull buffalo and the blowing wind."

He would slap the beast's right flank and sing out, "*Di! Di!*" As Great Joy began his lumbering stride, Hai felt beneath him the power of a moving mountain. The buffalo's curved spine had a mountain shape, and he could carry a boy or ten boys, could drag a plow over ripe earth, could haul a cart heavy with rice from one village to another. He would snort and breathe loudly, and Hai would imitate, snuffle the air into his belly. Nostrils flared, the boy took buffalo breaths, Great Joy breaths. Nose in the wind, eyes shifting, shoulders raised and rounded, he rode across the fields.

He wondered if Great Joy smelled what he smelled. The moisture of a tree near the river. Or a stone in the sun, a ripening field, a white flower, a fish, a muddy shoreline. For Great Joy, did rice grass have a fresh sourness, a smell of longing? Did a fish smell salty and cool? Did a white flower smell of sunlight and rain? Did a river have a night smell, a smell of darkness? Hai wondered if the animal knew more of these intimacies than he would ever know, if the smells—indescribable— were richer and more complicated than those funneled through human nostrils. Once, petting the buffalo along the ridge over its snout, he whispered, "Tell me your secrets, tell me." The buffalo snorted, shook his great head, and licked Hai's fingers. The boy sniffed two hands that smelled of salt and heat and rain.

The animal sheltered him each night. In the sandbagged pen near the family home, Hai curled beside Great Joy, and on nights when the sky roared with wind and fire, his mother and sister also took refuge beside the animal. Sometimes when sleep came, if it came, Luu Hai dreamed of birds that scarred the earth, of green rice fields turned to flames, of trees and huts burned, ravaged, of gaping holes in the ground large enough to bury all the buffalo. But sometimes he dreamed that he and his father rode Great Joy, that his father had returned with powerful arms to swat the birds from the sky, that the buffalo used the fury of hooves to stomp fire into ashes. In dreams, Hai would see his father alive, arms and legs whole, no shrapnel or belly wounds, each part of him in place: eyes, teeth, arms, legs, the wholeness of a body. The boy would wake, reach for his father's arms, and curl into the round warmth of the buffalo. Great Joy took care of him, comforted him, harbored him. And each morning, though often hungry himself, Hai left offerings of food at his father's grave.

Soldiers came and went, came and went, eyes like hammers. They would search the huts of the village, poke their rifles through thatch roofs, pound their eyes in every direction. Their uniforms were identical, their faces nearly the same, except for one who seemed to admire Hai and his buffalo. On the shore of the Sai Gon River, the boy once saw a soldier separate from the others. As his American platoon searched the village, he stood in a small cove and skipped stones in the river. After playing, he squatted, a brown-faced man, his elbows on his knees, his rifle propped against a log, and smiled at Hai and Great Joy. The boy flickered a smile—pure reflex—then scolded himself. This brown-faced demon had a rifle, he too was an invader. He might wish to kill the buffalo, taste its meat, strengthen his body. Hai petted Great Joy and advised him, "Don't trust this man; don't trust his brothers." Most Americans had a frenzied, hungry look as if they could devour every living thing and instantly crave more.

———

One morning in late April, the heat stifling, monsoon clouds on the horizon, the foreigners burned two huts and left. An hour later, stooped between his mother and sister, transplanting *ma* rice—bright green in a watery field, Hai heard a sound overhead, a distant buzzing and then a roar, and then the sun fell from heaven. He had tethered Great Joy to a coconut palm thirty meters away. Hai saw a gold light splinter the palm. He heard the buffalo's cry, the thunder of disbelief. The boy ran forward and saw a hoof not attached to a leg, a length of bone in tall grass. The beast crumpled on his side, eyes vague, head tilted at a crooked angle. Hai heard the cries of his sister, his own cries, but the buffalo had stopped thundering. He touched the animal's throat and whispered, "Wait, hold on. Someone will know what to do. Someone will help you." Hoof, bone, flesh—maybe someone would piece them back together. Blood gushed from the spine and flanks, but the belly was still rounded, still whole. Hai placed a handful of rice grass in the open mouth that wouldn't move, wouldn't chew. Before it was too late, he lowered both hands to the animal's belly and took comfort in the warmth.

In the late afternoon, Hai dug a hole at the edge of the rice field.

Quoc Nam, his cousin, and Qui, his friend, helped him widen it and deepen it, and they harnessed the carcass to Nam's buffalo and Qui's buffalo, and the buffalo survivors dragged Great Joy over the field into his grave.

⸺

The next morning, Hai found fresh meat in the shallows of the Sai Gon River. A great bird, an osprey, had drowned, and clutched in its talons a carp the length of Hai's leg. Newly dead, the yellow-brown eyes of the bird were iridescent. It must have dove fiercely, sunk its claws into flesh, and plummeted in darkness. Hai imagined the thrashing of wings, the desperate plunge of the fish. At first, the carp must have swum toward deep water, and later, as it was dying, it rose in the grip of the bird in an upswell of currents. Hai found the bodies in the cove where Great Joy had often drank and bathed. With effort, he unhooked the claws and separated the fish and bird. He extended one osprey wing, then the other, and marked where the edges of feathers touched earth. Hai could have lain down upon wings, for they were longer than his body. He hid the carp in high grasses and carried home the osprey. He rested, drank a ladle of water, and returned for the fish that lay heavier in his arms.

⸺

Midday. His mother and his sister Nhi were taking strips of salted fish meat and bird meat from a barrel and hanging them on a bamboo rack in the heat of the sun. Hai, squatting beside them, said, "Two gifts. One from the sky and one from water."

"We can give some away," said his mother. "Your Aunt Hoa and Aunt Lan need meat. They need it as much as we do."

Hai hesitated. "Can we give a little to Miss Thien's family? She has no mother or father, only her grandma."

"We'll see."

"Just a few slices," he said, "to dry on her fish rack. She and her grandma would be very happy if we offered them some meat."

⸺

Three days after Great Joy's burial, Hai and Nhi and their mother, Ma Xuan, began the first weeding of the rice field. The task would be less arduous than usual since much of the field had been destroyed by bombing. Several paddy dikes were damaged, and in some places the irrigation water had bled back to the river. Squatting near his mother, Hai glanced at the adjacent field where Miss Thien worked beside her grandma. The girl was his age, fourteen, nearly fifteen, and in Hai's eyes she was lovely. He recalled the morning in the fields when he almost touched her hand in passing. Her breath came fast, her shoulders stiffened, and maybe this meant she liked him. He had called her name, but she turned away and said nothing. She was like most girls of the village: secretive, cautious, too shy to flirt with boys.

Now he swayed as he plucked weeds from the paddy. How did a girl change her body, change the shape of her chest? How did Le Minh Thien spread her hips wider over the earth, and deepen the print of her feet on rice fields and shorelines? Maybe soon the girl would grow wings, lift herself in the air, and soar above the fighter bombers, the *may bay sua rom* that light the earth with fires. He looked up and saw a bird in the far sky, maybe an osprey. As he watched it circling, drifting higher, he asked himself why his own body changed slowly. Luu Hai wished he were wider, stronger, twice the size of an American soldier. At night, often without warning, his middle part thickened and grew hard, but every other part stayed skinny. Now he glanced at the sun and envied its beauty, its bulk. With the help of rain it turned rice stalks bright green in fields cratered by bombs, illuminated the last leaves of skeletal trees, and no matter what happened on the earth that received its warmth, it traveled the sky each morning and afternoon, a force as magnificent and opposite as the new darkness of a girl's body. The sun could not be stopped, nor the stars, nor the darkness of a girl.

Hai plucked another weed and pictured Thien's walk: her hips that swayed, threw shadows; her body as graceful as a moving river. Whether she walked in moist fields, stooped and pulled weeds, or gathered water at dawn, shouldered buckets on a pole, her body remained fluid. *Water girl,* he thought, *rice girl. Girl of the bua ruong, the best soil. Village girl, grass girl. Girl of the changing body.* Hai shaded his eyes and looked toward the Sai Gon River. Something carried the water, formed waves, and it seemed that Thien, in her growing body, was carried by something larger than the currents of a river. *"Cac,"* he whispered, *"dai-duong"* (oceans). Fishlike, Thien could plummet in water, but with sharp eyes, osprey eyes, he could watch her body changing. Maybe she would swallow some darkness, change the shape inside her, and if it were necessary, if she could find no other way to survive, she would grow wings out of water. She would lift herself in the air, fly far above fire, and those on earth would see a dark bird in heaven. Strong wings were better than hands, feet, hooves, claws, fins. The winged ones had to be careful only when they touched down on the earth for food.

The boy ate his lunch, rice balls wrapped in banana leaves. He let the rice moisten on his tongue before he began chewing. Hai thought of how happy he would be if tonight his mother let him bring Thien offerings of fish meat and bird meat. He imagined telling the girl that he caught the carp with a giant worm, that he snared the osprey with a net after it lighted on bushes. But Thien, aware of how much he liked her, would probably know he was telling stories. Maybe the boy would speak truthfully, tell her what he now told his mother and sister who ate beside him: "Great Joy helped me find the food, who else?" He paused, reflected, and said, "And maybe the osprey helped me a little; all my life I've had eyes sharp as a bird's."

Before sundown, when it was still safe to move through the village, he came to Thien's house with strips of salted carp and osprey. He hoped to hand her the white plate that held the offerings, but Ba Ly, Thien's grandma, came to the door, accepted the meat, and thanked him. "Lucky gifts," said the boy. "I found a bird and fish in the river." He stepped forward and smiled. "They were dead," said Hai, "but they clung to each other and washed up near the shoreline." He couldn't see Thien from the doorway, but he imagined her listening and watching from the hut's shadows. "A few minutes after sunrise," he said, "I spotted them floating. I waded in and lifted them in my arms—many kilos." He spread his arms, turned his palms skyward. "Wings wide as a man is long," he said, "or longer." He grimaced. "So I used all my strength to carry them home"—no need to tell them he carried one at a time—"the fat fish and the long bird."

Something sweet, maybe mangos, mixed with the fleshy smell of carp and osprey.

"These strips of meat need to dry more," he said. "They're not ready to eat."

"I know."

"We can be grateful for my buffalo," said Hai, but he was not sure how to elaborate. It occurred to him that those outside his family circle might not understand that a slaughtered animal had guided him to this bounty. "I was lucky," he said, "but I also had some help."

Ba Ly, puzzled, said, "Yes, your mother's a saint, be sure to thank her." She bowed slightly and left Luu Hai standing outside the door.

⸻

Maybe to impress Thien he would need to bring her a live fish from the Sai Gon River. He already had poles, bamboo sticks, hooks fashioned from sewing needles, but he needed to make fishing line from green worms—*sau cuoc*. The next morning, after visiting the graves of his father and his buffalo, he found several worms on a low branch of a *sau* tree. He plucked the fattest ones, each worm about the size of a rich man's thumb, and laid them in a wooden box. His father had once shown him how to peel the flesh with a knife, then use his fingers to unravel the intestines. The inner parts of each *sau cuoc,* approximately three meters in length, could be transformed into fishing line strong as nylon. Hai, his father's knife in one hand, lifted the fattest worm from the box. He glanced behind him at the rice fields, the wedges of green, the bamboo forest north of the village. His father's grave was nearby, and the buffalo's, and the sun would warm their bones, their spirits. Maybe *cha* could somehow witness his son's newfound skill: making fishing line from worms. Hai had to catch fish, not merely to impress Thien, but to compensate for three seasons of poor harvests, ravaged paddies. Head bowed, he peeled the flesh of the worm and imagined his father's approval. "Don't grow soft," *cha* would say, "or the family ends up starving." Hai worked quickly and stripped the flesh of each worm. Now he could unravel the intestines and soak them in vinegar until they had the hardness and suppleness of nylon. Struggling with nausea, the boy did what was required. Come morning, if he was still alive, he could fasten the ends of the intestines, dig up earthworms for bait, and cast a line into the deep waters beyond where he had found the osprey and the carp.

⸻

That night he could not sleep. He tried to pretend he lay near his buffalo, but there was no *bua ruong* smell, no smell of paddy earth, and no belly and hooves that smelled of river mud and fishes. He lay on a mat between rice bins separated from the rest of the hut by a bamboo curtain.

If there was shooting, or if the sky became loud with planes, he would hurry to his mother and sister and guide them into the tunnel he and his father had carved beneath the cookstove. They would huddle there, or he would lead them through a side tunnel and into the now vacant buffalo pen fortified with sandbags. For Hai, nights of silence were often worse. Only shooting or bombs allowed him to join his family, and while he waited for morning there was no buffalo for warmth, no father on a nearby mat, no one in this hut or this village to offer the comfort of their body. He wished he were young enough to share his mother's bed. A few years ago, she and his sister Nhi wouldn't have minded if he lay between them. Now his mother would shoo him away. "Go on," she would whisper. "You have your own place to sleep."

Shortly before dawn, Hai asked himself if his family should look for another home. Since the good rice was mostly gone, since they now ate chicken rice, *tam* rice, maybe they should pack their belongings and search for another village. Although his mother had told him the worst tragedy was to leave one's home, to leave the fields, abandon ancestral graves, Hai could not imagine his family or his village surviving much longer. He wished his elders could advise him, provide direction, but his village was mostly fatherless. The old men, Ong Quan and Ong Truong, made important decisions after consulting with Viet Cong cadre. The young men, the fathers, had vanished into Viet Cong or Republican ranks, or were lost to bombings and shootings, or were taken away by various factions (American, Republican, Viet Cong) to unnamed places their families could not locate. Hai, now among the oldest boys of the village, carried the responsibility of an elder. He sympathized with the Viet Cong, often helped set booby traps and dig tunnels, but he had no desire to live his daylight hours underground, only to emerge at night to harass whatever enemy force camped near the village. Hai knew he would soon have no choice but to be a soldier. He could join the Republicans, support the invaders, or he could live in the tunnels north of the river, a half-buried soldier with the Viet Cong.

He slept briefly and dreamed. He showed Thien his fishing line, told her how he made it from worms, and she followed him along a riverside trail to the cove where he tossed his line toward deep water. The river roiled with fish: carp and cod, a few catfish; one of the carp was the length of the girl's body. Hai tended his line and waited. Nothing happened, no bites. Soon Thien lay on the shore, asleep, but she woke when a great fish took his line and pulled him toward water. The girl stood and shouted, "Let go of the pole! Let go!" Hai, smiling, waded out waist-deep in the river, then chest-deep, and worked the fish until it was too exhausted to fight him. After several minutes of struggle, he dragged his catch to the shore and stopped its frantic flopping with a blow to the skull. For the girl he revealed his sun-strength, his power to pull a great fish from an untamed river. He was happy momentarily, but then he shuddered. The fish, once beautiful, was dead. Thien lay on the shore, asleep again. Hai heard his father's voice: "Catch another one, a bigger one. Stop pitying the world before the world starves you." Hai rebaited his hook, cast toward a deeper hole, and waited. The boy admired the fish darting and circling, the dark waters swelled with currents, the muscles of the river. No bites now, no struggle. Nothing had to die. Again he heard his father's voice: "Watch your line, stay alert." Hai fought the urge to lie down on the shore and curl his stick-shaped body into the gracefulness of Thien.

He woke at first light, dug up earthworms near the river, and went fishing. He fished all morning, caught nothing, and moped his way back to the rice field.

"Be patient," said his mother. "You can't hurry the river. Maybe tomorrow you will catch a fish."

After lunch he began repairing a dike, and it was then that he saw a bird over the river, another osprey. Maybe it was hungry for fish, or maybe it longed for its mate, the drowned osprey. The bird appeared more majestic than sad, however, and Hai envied the wings that gave flight, the keen eyes that could observe the river and earth from here to the horizon. If Americans crossed distant fields, the osprey would see movement and light, the dark silhouettes on bright grasses, the spokes of sun on barrels of rifles. And it would see the bomb-torn paddies, the fringes of forests and hedgerows, and in one glance the over-sized wings that soared toward the sun, or the helicopters that skated low and fast over the Sai Gon River. Hai wished that the osprey could send warnings, or that he too could fly. He imagined himself rising on wings, flying in a swift arc over the village to signal the approach of helicopters or planes. If soldiers came on foot, he would light in a field, gouge his talons in earth, and each family would retreat to a hut or a tunnel, and bring with them any object that might be viewed with suspicion. Butcher knives, tools, even sacks of rice would be placed in difficult-to-find caches. Once the enemy departed, Hai would touch down on the rice paddy nearest the village, fan his wings, strut and cackle. The villagers would emerge from hiding, thank him for his warnings, and prepare a feast from whatever food they could salvage. If their provisions of meat had already been used, Hai would catch fish in the river. Carp and cod, large and small, a variety of fish food. He would watch the river carefully, patiently, and avoid sinking his talons into a fish too great to carry upward through the sky.

The osprey flew away, but another—or maybe the same one—appeared the following morning. Hai set down his shovel, stopped repairing a dike, and stood still as the bird traced a spiral thirty-five meters over the Sai Gon River. He wondered if Thien, from her family's rice field, had spotted the fisherbird. Hai lifted his arms and cackled. The osprey spiraled a long time, and then it seemed to halt momentarily, float effortlessly, before it folded its wings and plummeted toward water. Hai watched it split the light of the river's face, a dark blur that rose with a fish silver and small, bright as jewelry. He heard a soft snapping sound, the breaking apart of fish bones. The osprey soared to a treetop nest a short distance downriver. Hai watched the rise and fall of the beak, the ripples of flesh torn from the fish, most likely a cod. He wondered if Miss Thien liked fresh fish fried in coconut oil and sprinkled with salt.

⚬——⚬

The next morning Hai caught a fish at sunrise. A carp, nearly three kilos, that he dragged through the shallows and onto the muddy shoreline. Flopping and twitching, the fish threw water sparks, drops of light. The boy struck the skull with the knotted edge of a stick. Soon the fish stilled and quieted, mouth agape, body sunlit. "Lord Buddha," Hai prayed, "forgive me." He looped a thin coil of rope through a gill, hoisted the fish, and saw it was nearly the length of his arm.

With his catch, he walked to the paddy where Thien and her grandma were weeding. He lifted the fish in both arms, said, "Lucky day," and they stared at him.

"A nice one," said Ba Ly. "Where'd you catch him?"

Hai motioned with his head. "There," he said, "where I saw an osprey catch a fish." He smiled, straightened his shoulders. *"Khong sau,"* he said. "If you want to know where the fish are, you have to watch the great birds."

He swung the stringer over his right shoulder so that the fish hung down his back, silver and sunlit. He turned away, trusting Thien would watch him as he sauntered toward the village. She would see the ease with which he carried the fish, the surprising strength of his shoulders, the fish scales as bright as the sparks of his body. He glanced over his shoulder, but Thien's face was hidden beneath her sun hat. *One day you'll look up,* he thought, *one day you'll see me.* He walked faster and felt the coolness of the fish down the length of his spine.

In the late morning, he hurried to the jackfruit tree near Thien's house. He looped the stringer on his left wrist, and the fish dangled and swayed as he shinnied up the trunk to a wide limb. Perched, Hai unwound the rope, lay the fish on its side, and waited for Thien. At midday, she ate her lunch in the shade of the jackfruit. Hai's sister Nhi often joined her, and other village girls, but Thien was always first to arrive. Today, before she began eating, Hai would leap from the tree and clutch as with talons the fish he had caught for her. He would approximate the great birds who flew from heaven to thrust their talons into the giants who moved through water. He would make wing sounds, wind sounds, swooping sounds to inspire fear and admiration. Maybe his sky-strength would frighten her more than the changes of her body frightened him. For Miss Thien he would fly, touch down on earth, and display for her this prize fish, this carp the width of his thigh.

As she came toward him in tree shade, he leaned out on his branch, clutched his fish with talons, and plummeted down. He made wing sounds, wind sounds, and cried out in a voice more birdlike than human. Hai fell to the earth beside her, lifted his catch, and heard her say, *"Anh dang lam gi?"* (What are you doing?) He whistled, gripped the fish with his claws, but Thien had no other comment. The girl walked to her family's hut and disappeared through a doorway. He waited for her to come to the side window and wave to him. After a long minute the window remained dark, shaded, so Hai bowed to the hut, her family's nest, and hurried off before his sister and the other girls arrived.

In the early 1960s, when the United States was sending advisors to Vietnam, I was faced with the choice of being drafted or leaving the country. I do not believe in killing people to support the power plays of governments who jump into wars for questionable reasons. So I joined the Air Force Medical Corps and worked in hospital psychiatric wards. During my reserve duty through 1968, I worked in Air Force hospitals in New Jersey and California, helping to treat the increasing number of airmen who came back physically and emotionally wounded from the Vietnam War.

In the 1970s, I taught in community colleges in the San Francisco Bay Area, focusing on outreach to underprivileged individuals and groups. I taught in a reentry program for Vietnam vets returning to college. I also counseled delinquent boys and worked as a juvenile probation officer. I worked as a parent participation coordinator for countywide childcare and development programs and served on the California Governor's Advisory Committee Task Force for Child Development Services.

In recent years, I have returned to teaching—in programs for adults at City College of New York in Harlem and at Children's Aid Society in a community school in Washington Heights. More recently I taught reading, writing, and math skills to youthful offenders at a county correctional facility in western Massachusetts. Currently I am associate director of youth programs for a community center in Great Barrington, Massachusetts.

I also run a poetry and fiction reading series at a local bookstore in the Berkshires and a radio program that features the spoken word and music across cultural boundaries.

Magenta Alert

1

that morning when he tipped the coffee cup and everything went streaming trying to pull from his overcoat pocket the thick black winter gloves so his hands wouldn't freeze when he went back up the stairs ice banks lay like frozen seals on the Union Square sidewalk the gloves caught on his door keys and he jerked but couldn't extract them while with two fingers of the other hand he balanced his briefcase teetering trying to put away his glasses and the copy of the book he had been reading by John Pilger about the new rulers of the world before he got off at the next stop.

—*amazing but not surprising they've been planning this ever since Indonesia 1967 the World Bank the corporations a laboratory for globalization that's why they got rid of Sukarno and put in Suharto to carve it up and parcel out the goods: bauxite, copper, nickel, the tropical forests, mining, light industry, banking and finance*

—*think about it, it was the model for the coup in Chile: Pinochet for Allende and you think it's just the Republicans but it's the Democrats too it's not an anomaly it's the continuum of empire expanding: the imperial America displacing the American republic and now the invasion occupation is going to create democracy in Iraq?—give me a break—it's really about controlling the world's resources but nobody least of all the media wants to talk about that*

2

late that afternoon when he rushed out of the building his knuckle smashed against the heavy steel Wall Street door as it was closing he didn't notice until he was talking with a friend out on the sidewalk and he felt something sticky she said you're bleeding he looked down at the dripping and wrapped a handkerchief around his hand

on the subway home people trying not to look but anxious glancing: one older woman's eyes popped out popped back at the blood running down his hand he didn't like to be stared at so he put on a hard face wanting people to leave him alone trying to control the flow but one young woman pinned him with her eyes he thought he read the words across her forehead: used to just be a bunch of ragged whackos on these trains sermonizing singing or selling shit but now it's some insane terrorist ready to go off with a nuclear bomb strapped to his chest.

I was born in Oakland, California, on January 28, 1947, and raised in San Leandro. I was drafted into the Army in 1966 and arrived in Vietnam on my birthday in 1967. In-country, I served as an infantry soldier in the 9th Infantry Division with Company B 4/47th Infantry and with the 2/60th Infantry. Our area of operation was south of Saigon in the Mekong Delta.

After military service, I worked as a baker. The last bakery position I held was in Alameda County Jail, Santa Rita, where I supervised and worked with inmates. Then I was a supervisor of food services at Highland Hospital in Oakland. My county employment ended in 1995, when I was laid off during a period of downsizing. At first, being out of work brought anxiety; however, I came to realize that it was a gift, which allowed me to pursue education.

I began writing poetry, which has become part of my healing process, while attending Chabot College in Hayward, California. I received a degree in English literature from Holy Names College (now Holy Names University) in Oakland and a master of theological studies degree from the Franciscan School of Theology at the Graduate Theological Union in Berkeley. My master's thesis, which focuses on pastoral ministry to Vietnam veterans, is entitled "God! Where Were You in Vietnam and Where Are You Now: Theological Perspectives and Pastoral Approaches for Veterans Whose War Experience Damaged Their Christian Faith." I hope to publish this thesis. I volunteer as a boxing coach at the University of California, Berkeley. I have one son, David, who at the time of this writing is twenty-nine.

A Rosary

They always broke
or disintegrated in my pocket.
The ones made of string rotted
when they got wet. The ones made with wire chain
kept breaking apart.

Then the reluctant solution, possibly a sacrilege.
I'd break off ten rounds of linked machine gun ammo.
That'd hold together.

I'd pray on them when we broke
in rice paddies, in villages, along dikes,
next to VC bunkers, while on guard, in base camp,
in the field, on night or day patrol, under fire
So that I'd be able to love.
Something in me had begun to give up on everything else.

On Point

He walks
Out of a village gate at night
Past the bunkers, looks
Out on the narrow road
And sees the possibility
Of death. And he doesn't care.
For the past months he hasn't
Slept much and he scarcely feels.
He's getting short, but there's little
At home. He's got few illusions.
"The world": It's hard,
There's little compassion,
And they won't understand. No,
Life is here. On point he can feel.
Fear and the threat of death
Exhilarate him. He's been
Scarred and scared and numb
For months. But on point
He can really feel.
There's people behind him
Who depend on him
And he's good and he cares,
Though he doesn't know
Them well. He guesses it's
Love and walks
Out on that narrow road and
He's alive
For one more night.

Platoon Sgt. Francisco Royas

In Korea at
Seventeen he'd been
A squad leader—a killer:
Royas was tough.
In this next war he'd
Been tough on us too.
Abundant respect's what
Us youngsters gave 'im.

I remember this incident
During a combat operation:
We'd set up, and
Across the perimeter, lookin'
Like an Asian pit bull,
He comes toward me.
With some dread, I'm thinkin',
"What's he want?
Wha'd I do wrong?"
Reachin' me he's got
This excited glow and says,
"Tree! I got this new Ham
And Lima Beans* recipe:
You pour out some of the
Juice, put in some crumble
Crackers and a hot pepper,
Add a can a cheese, and heat it up."
Radiant, almost like a child,
He says, "It's great!"
And I'm thinkin',
"He likes me?"

*A C-ration unit

We Need

We sat at the table
during break, Bill and
I and a woman coworker.
Twenty-five years later
he and I talked
of survival, not battle.
We talked of the monotony,
the lack of sleep, the
heat, the humidity,
the weight we carried,
being continually in water,
and the need for constant
awareness.
Then, while they
talked, I felt my
head slow drop
and my mind go back.
I was in that tidal swamp
Standing in water between
my ankles and knees.
The heat of the midday
sun reflected off the
water's glistening surface.
I didn't know how I'd
go on standing on the
edge of hell in the
Rung Sat. Then Bill hit
the table saying,
   "Come back Bob!"

At his funeral I spoke
saying: "It's good to be
with someone who
understands."

I began my writing and editing career after my return from the Vietnam War; I served as a Marine in I Corps—part of that time as a helicopter gunner. I've published eight books—two memoirs and six novels. Over the last decade and a half, I've been involved in efforts to bring contemporary Vietnamese literature to an American readership, and vice versa, as a form of reconciliation through literature, serving, pro bono, as American editor of Curbstone's *Voices from Vietnam* series. My involvement with that project began when I met Le Minh Khue in 1993, while I was a visiting writer at the William Joiner Center at the University of Massachusetts. Part of the Joiner program was a project to bring together Vietnamese and American writers who were on opposite sides of the war. Khue, one of the leading writers of Vietnam and a chief editor at the largest publishing house in that country, is a veteran of the Volunteer Youth Brigades; she had been one of thousands of teenage girls who had left high school and went to work on the Ho Chi Minh Trails, filling in bomb craters and disarming or exploding unexploded bombs, and while often under heavy attack from our aircraft. Khue and I discovered that we had at one time been in the same area during the war, and I thought about a mission I'd flown on when I'd shot down into that thick jungle canopy that covered the area, and how she could have been under it, an invisible but hated target. That moment of realization was an epiphany for me, and that invisibility and hatred that allow human beings to be reduced to targets or weapons or foci of fear came to stand for me as the exact opposite of what good stories, literature, could do for and to human beings. "The American Reader" is a story which deals directly with that scenario—in it I imagine the young girl on the ground, a reader, as Khue was, of American novels, and that young man in the air and his own reading habits, as the story reveals.

The American Reader

The first time Mai sees Americans they are bathing in a stream about a thousand meters from where she and two of her girl friends lie watching through the foliage. The soldiers' voices don't carry that far, though she can see that they are splashing, probably laughing, their skin occasionally flashing like daylight through the leaves. She wishes she can get closer, but if Ninh, the male section leader, knows they have even gotten this close, they will all be in trouble.

She wants to see them in their flesh. The enemy. Yet still held tightly shut, against the very shattering they would bring her, in the tattered Steinbecks and Hemingways and Londons she carries in her rucksack. Her aunt's treasures, given to Mai when she had joined the Volunteers, gone South to keep open the Trail that knit the Nation. Her aunt a teacher and a good revolutionary and the authors approved for good revolutionaries, but sometimes after a bombing or strafing, the other girls would look at Mai with bitter astonishment. "The American reader," the adjective in that nickname edging into a noun. Yet there is always a wistfulness in their teasing as well. As if what Mai is holding on to is something they can't name but feel sliding out of themselves as well, day by day.

She strains to see the Americans through the screen of leaves. They are still Tom Joad, moving toward a vision of a perfected, kind world, as she, when she remembers, imagines herself doing, moving through the dust of a space she finds unimaginable in the closeness of the jungle—even though they seem now to be trying to turn that jungle, those trees, into that same bowl of dust and emptiness Joad had fled to a greener land. They are Robert Jordan, lying on his stomach, watching the bridge, as she lies on her stomach, watching Jordan's compatriots now, and she is Marie, waiting in the encompassing warmth of his sleeping bag, for the warmth of flesh and connection against the coldness of death. They are a man trying with his hands to build a fire as the circle of howling wolves close in on him, as her own hands, her fingers, work frantically to prevent the fire blossoming from the guts of the bomb that moments before had howled down from them to her; they are the machines that come to kill her and hers; they are the red flashing of tracers through the jungle canopy, the masked, mirroring face hovering above, the sudden light shivering like panic through the branches. They are torn apart in her mind and she needs to knit them together if she is going to knit herself together. They are a weight in her rucksack, the books that anchor her; they give her paths she can follow along the paths she must follow; they give her the courage to face themselves. They are these naked boys in a jungle pond, though they are too far away to really see anything, her friend complains in a whisper, and the other two girls giggle. They are too far away to see anything, she thinks, because they are ghosts, they are lines in a book, they are too many contradictions to be real, to be flesh, to be naked.

———

They are flying over Helicopter Valley, with its cupped wreckage, when DeLeon's scream pierces John's ears, a sound so filled with terror and despair that, filtered through earphone static, he hears it as a wail spiraling up from the broken aircraft below them. The helicopter jerks, up and then down. He traverses the ground with the barrel of the machine gun. He sees no tracers, has heard nothing hit the plane. He risks a glance over at the two prisoners they'd picked up at LZ Crow, drags the flashed afterimage of them quickly back to his stare out of the port. The recon Marine sitting across from them hasn't moved. His M-14 on his lap, his finger on the trigger. The two in olive-green North Vietnamese Army uniforms tattered, muddy and bloody, but not faded. New guys. Sitting motionless also, the base of a triangle, the recon Marine the apex, their eyes dulled, heads leaning toward each other, side by side, as if still fastened together by the wire the Nungs who had captured them had punctured through their cheeks. The Marine—he was a staff sergeant—had cursed and pulled it out when they'd been handed over, the two North Vietnamese jerking like fish as he did it. The holes in their cheeks scabbed over now, but still bleeding red slick snail trails down their swollen cheeks. Tears from strange eyes. The staff sergeant's eyes dulled also, head lilted.

The noise from the cockpit—curses, scuffles—hasn't abated. Sam keys his mike: "Sir, what's happening?"

"A fucking snake," the copilot, Anderson, says, his voice more exasperated than fearful.

A *snake,* he says again, indignantly, and the word, the hot, poisonous sibilance of it, opens into Everything. Into the jagged carpet of smashed helicopters below them. Into the impossible, malevolent, steam bath of tangled, vine-strangled, insect-crawling, breezeless, lightless at midday, hundred-foot-tall triple-canopy jungle they were over again now. Into the men they'd set down in it and taken out, sucked dry like insects caught in a web. Into clouds of hot, red laterite dust sucked into engines at takeoff, the nerve-racking dance of hands and feet on collective and cyclic and pedals, a manic weave on the loom of the very centrifugal

force that wants to tear the thousands of pieces of machinery to pieces;
into landing too hot and too heavy and downwind on slopes picketed
with trees, the heavy wet air pushing down the helicopter loaded with
its weight of flesh and equipment; all the deadly specific numbers: thirteen grunts times eighty pounds each of steel helmets, M-14s, web
belts hung with grenades and loaded magazines and full canteens and
entrenching tools and machetes and flak jackets and field packs, not to
mention the M-60 machine guns or mortars the weapons platoons
carried, not to mention the 150-to-200-pound eighteen-to-twenty-
year-old bodies carrying all of it, not to mention the helicopter's own
machine guns and ammunition and flak-jacketed crew and 2,200 pounds
of fuel, all optimal conditions needed to suck the lift right from under
blades, to wind down, as if it was the clock of your life, the RPM that
kept you in the air; to stop rotor blades like a hand stuck into a fan, to
feel yourself a gracefully floating dandelion suddenly puffed on from
above by a malevolent hot-breathed giant, to be slammed into the terrain below, into other helicopters, into screaming men and suddenly
liberated fifty-foot-long blades slicing through air foliage torsos necks
heads arms and later you come down and see someone still sitting
behind a log as if taking a break and you pick up what turns out to be
only the top half of a sergeant, lighter that way, and yes, a clean-cut
boy, you think. It's all there, in those words, in the utterly appropriate
hissed curse of them: The 12.7 mm North Vietnamese antiaircraft guns
and B-40 rockets and quad-fifty machine guns that send orange and
green fireballs streaking past the ports, and the ship you'd watched go
down yesterday, thick black smoke streaming from the fuel line the
incendiary round had hit, smashing into the ridge, rolling on its back,
bursting into flames, a random pyre autorotating frantically as if to
blow out its own flames before twisting over, breaking its rotored back
on the ground, the sheet of flame moving through the compartment,
the two men jumping out of the back, one too high, to his death, the
other too low, the flaming mass falling on top of him, and the rest all
gone by then, burning bright in that forest of eternal night. And, if
that wasn't enough, there were the prisoners dragged to the rear ramp
like fish flopping on a wire, and the grenade your allies from the Army
of the Republic of Vietnam Itself had left wedged under a red-webbed
seat, and the wounded and dead you'd scooped out of the black

meat-grinding, fire-seared night. And if, just in case, by any chance, as Vietnam would have it, to top it all, if that wasn't enough, then you could still have a fucking snake in your cockpit.

———

She looks at her friends, Suong and Thu Ha, their faces shaded under the floppy green jungle hats, but scratched, smudged, hollow-cheeked with hunger, gums bleeding, teeth loose. If she could see their bodies under the clothes that hung like rags on them, she would see ribs pushing against paper-thin flesh over stomachs bloated with hunger, nets of scars and scratches, insect bites and scabies. They are all like that. She understands what bodies are. She understands the hungers, shares them; they are all young, girls and boys, and they breathe and sleep with death as if they are old, and they want their lives, and they all understand a life can be folded like an endless cloth into ten minutes that you can slowly draw back out and touch and savor all the rest of your life, however long it goes on from that moment. When bodies are laid out on the broken earth they look like part of it. People go South dressed and they come back dead, and that direction itself has come to mean death, and she helps bury them, the dead, though sometimes they are wounded and sometimes she holds them, the way the woman in Steinbeck held the starving man against her breast and gave him suck, and they call her mother, though she's younger than them, and she remembers how, in her village, before she'd gone South, the bombs had struck before the time people knew they needed to build shelters and she'd come back from the school outing to see the bodies huddled under the trees, mothers and fathers with children clutched and melted to their chests. And sometimes they are the other girls or boys from her unit, and often the bombs blast the clothing from their bodies so they go into their deaths as they had come into their births and she had at first, more than death itself, feared that exposure. But she is seventeen now and she knows that death makes everyone sexless. In a line of bodies, what caught your eye was how little difference there was, how easily it could be erased. Her thoughts are scrambled, confused, and mixed now with the dim white figures seen through the screen of leaves, the ghosts that would kill her.

"Where, sir?" John says nervously, keying his mike. He is hearing curses, scrambling noises through the earphones.

"Shit," DeLeon says, his voice high-pitched.

"No joy, no joy," Anderson says. No visual contact.

"It went behind the instrument panel!"

"Are you sure?" Anderson's voice. "I think it's a fucking viper."

"I'm de vindow viper." Punch line of an old joke. John looks down nervously at his feet. Sweat rolls down his neck, under the collar of his flight suit, crawls down his back; he wants to turn, search, raise his legs, dance like a mad bagpiper. He feels his skin contracting under the leg of his flightsuit, his muscles spasming up to his thighs. Snake crawl. "I'm de bamboo viper." He thinks of it sliding behind the HAC and copilot, through the hatch, under the web seats, or along the wiring over his head. Hears, suddenly, the voice of the flight commander, Colonel Watson in his ICS, asking them what the problem is.

The helicopter had reared out of formation—they are flying in a division, four helicopters—when DeLeon let go of the collective. The pilot had pulled out his survival knife and hacked at the snake, which had dropped heavily to the deck, shot like an arrow between Anderson's rubber foot pedals into the tangle of wires behind the instrument panel. Straightened up and slithered off, John hears DeLeon say, with the near-hysterical hilarity which means, John knows, that the incident has already become a war story, will be told everywhere, was humming through the ether even now.

But the snake is still in the aircraft, has not yet crawled into the safety of story. For all he knows it is still coiled around wires behind the panels, cunning, camouflaging itself as part of the technology, using the machinery of the enemy against the enemy. Low crawling, naked and slick, a sapper coming through the wire. Touched my elbow like a kiss, slid along the aluminum ledge under the window, he hears DeLeon say to Anderson, "I'm the vindow viper." Green-brown in complexion, maybe three-foot tall, skinny as a pencil, DeLeon says. He's talking to them now. Fanged and dangerous. Find the fucker. Take no prisoners.

"A fucking snake," Anderson says, and John can feel it, sense the snake, moving under the deck plates, sneaking through the avionics.

Staying just ahead of or just behind them. He glances down, involuntarily. Something to the left of his left foot. Green and brown. He looks at the staff sergeant. He still hasn't moved, and neither have the prisoners. They're each others' stories too, but they don't know the end yet. John slowly picks up the M-1 carbine he'd bought for ten dollars from an ARVN as a backup weapon. What the hell is he going to do, shoot it through the deck? He slowly leans the carbine against the ammo catcher, slides out his K-bar knife. It seems motionless. Playing dead, he thinks. *I'm the vindow viper and I've come to vipe your vindow.* He stares. He should be looking out of his port. It is getting rapidly dark. But the enemy is here. It's too still. Too ... dull. Inanimate. It can't be a snake. He slowly advances the point of the knife, pushes down swiftly. Like a snake striking. The object is solid, unsnakelike. He slowly squats, thinking "grenade." No. A small book. He picks it up, impaled, pulls it off the blade, realizing, too late, it may be a booby trap anyway. No. It doesn't explode.

There's a black-and-white picture of a girl inside, a young couple in front of an iron gate fashioned into a circle of Chinese ideograms. But the writing on the stained pages, cribbed and lined through and smudged and blurring in the waning light, is Vietnamese writing, regular letters tortured top and bottom with little barbed-wire spikes. The written lines broken, as if poetry. Probably belonged to one of the prisoners. He should give it to the sergeant. Snake's diary, he thinks. Viper story. The two prisoners and the sergeant are still staring at each other, motionless as a diorama, as if all three have been wired together. The small book burns his hand, through his flight glove, as if it has dripped venom on him. He straightens up, quickly tosses it out of his port. Follows it with his machine gun barrel, twisting and fluttering in the air, white pages winging against dark sky, the photos flying out like released spirits.

———

It is getting dark, and is darker yet under the thick-knit branches canopied over the creek where she bathes. It is the same pool, a widening of the creek really, where the Americans had bathed. Mai can't see. Knows she can't be seen. Suddenly the noise of rotors beats down on top of the leaves like fists beating on a door, and she freezes until it fades off, leaving only its echoes and then the memory of its echoes.

She thinks, taking herself away from it, how she will make all this into story, mix has-been with could-be; fold the story over herself like a camouflage shelter as the bombs fall closer. This urgency to immerse herself in the same water, she thinks, to take the mystery of them into her skin, she thinks, and her mind tries to flee the thought, but she has trained herself to clutch at those fugitives of her being; they were in the end the whispers that named her. She has a broken sliver of soap from a bar that Thu Ha brought back from Hanoi, a luxury, and she soaps herself, and now she hums the tune of an Italian song all of the girls from Hanoi remember and sing. She has dirt under her nails from the Trail, from the dirt they shoveled back into the craters, smoothing them for the trucks going South, and her fingers stink from the gelignite they packed around the bomb she had embraced earlier in the day, helped lower into a hole, blown up. She scrubs her hands and her body, unable to even see her flesh now, feeling herself seeping away, borders dissolving into the water, the darkness, the insect hum.

Something heavy and cold and reptilian bumps into her lower belly. She stifles a scream. Reaches out tentatively. Her fingers find hair, a head, a nose, a mouth, and the fear suddenly leaves her, bursting like a bubble opening in water; she knows what this is; it isn't the first time a corpse has come floating down this stream to her. She lets her fingers move along the cold skin, feeling the man's flesh, naked to her own nakedness, feeling his wounds open under her fingertips like kisses, this one lover, from all that had gone South, come back to her now in the dark. She knows what this is, but the Americans she has seen that day come to her mind, and the words she feels written on her back, blurred through her rucksack and into her skin by her sweat, and she lets that thought, lets them, float next to her for a moment, and then lets it go; yes, it could be one of them as easily, and perhaps it is, but it doesn't matter, death doesn't only erase sex, and yes, isn't it pretty to think so.

As the book falls, the helicopter formation wheels west, over the mountainous jungle of the cordillera. A place filled with snakes. The darkness is not so much beginning to cover it as it is entering it, like an injected liquid, the top of the jungle canopy configuring into ominous, fluid shapes. Leaf people. Anderson's voice is in his ear again, his words repeated by DeLeon: they want him and Sam to fire into the fleshy mass below. Into the trees. They think *something* is down there. No shit. It's the snake's home. The place of snakes. The home of the snake and the land of the viper. He fires down into it. As he does, he sees an artillery barrage begin, over to the west of their flight path, aircraft diving down, as if called by his fire. A hot shell casing falls on his neck, stings like a snakebite. He fires more, his shoulders shaking, hands vibrating, fires at the ghosts moving under the trees, fires at a girl who bathes with the dead to dream the resurrection of love, who tries to find his face and her own, behind the wind and the fire and the noise and the fragmented light. His rounds curve and streak down and the darkling green absorbs them so quickly it is as if they never existed at all.

I grew up in Israel, where war was a persistent and formative part of my life. Like most Israelis, I identified with the story of a persecuted people defending itself. I saw us as being misunderstood by the world and having only our ingenuity to protect us from annihilation. The Six-Day War took place when I was eleven. By 1973, when the Yom Kippur War broke out, I had begun to see war as a choice and to envision other options for dealing with conflict. I was seventeen, and I decided to leave Israel, unwilling to support the violence being done in my name.

But a few months later, unable to escape the draft, I became a soldier, and by the time I was twenty, I was defeated and numb, my dreams lost. Seven years later, in 1983, I left Israel and have lived in the United States ever since, working steadily to heal the traumas of my life, personal, familial, social, and political.

In 1994, I heard a reading of the Veterans Writing Group at Cody's Books in Berkeley, and I knew I wanted to join the group. I sensed that this would be a place I could dig deep into my fears, longings, and unhealed experiences. Being part of this group has been everything I had hoped for, and more.

The following story, "Esh," gives voice to what I endured in Israel and what I am still struggling with to understand and become whole. For the past ten years, I have dedicated my life to teaching nonviolence in word and spirit, fervently hoping to contribute toward a world in which war is obsolete.

Esh

Would the killing be more tolerable if the sky were not so blue? The weather is perfect, the sun warm and gentle, already past its blazing summer intensity. I have never seen the sky so blue. It's October 1973. War is in full blast 150 miles away. But here in Tel Aviv the air is still, painfully normal.

I turned the radio off long ago, and I refuse to read the papers. I cannot think about it. But I cannot escape the surrealism: just a short distance away, under this same blue sky, people are killing one another. I cannot *not* think about it. I want to shake people: "People are killing one another right now?! What are you going to do about it?" But instead I keep walking, my face blank, watching my sandal–clad feet stepping forward on the pavement.

And what am I myself going to do about it? I can't leave the country; I am of draft age. In only five months I'll be eighteen. I can't get conscientious objector status, because the law in Israel does not recognize it. I can't face being jailed as a deserter. The only way out, I know, is to get married; the law exempts married women. And so I search for a man who is willing to marry me on ideological grounds.

I meet Herzl S., an anti–Zionist foreign student. He is always with Orit, his radical girlfriend, and a group of other history students. Wherever they are I find passion, intense political debates, and cigarette smoke. I am intimidated in their presence. I don't even exactly like him, but he fits the bill. "Hey, Herzl, will you marry me? I want to get out of military service." I ask as if this was not a big deal. He is sitting with Orit and their usual group. Herzl looks at me, a bit incredulous. "Are you serious?" he says. I nod. "Sure," he says. Then he turns to Orit. "I am going to marry Miki," he says, smiling. "She wants to get out of military service." His tone bespeaks amusement, but also some pride. Orit smiles at me, satisfied. "Good for you," she says. I thank her silently.

"I am going to marry Herzl and get out of the army," I say to my parents nonchalantly as I walk into the kitchen. My voice does not expose my terror. Silence descends upon the room. My father looks stern, as always, with his thick, square, black glasses, and perfectly trimmed beard. His mouth is small and tightly closed. *A bad strategy,* I think to myself. My father scrutinizes me from top to bottom, several times, his eyes smaller than usual, contemptuous. *This is going to be bad.*

Say something, I scream inside, trying to steel myself against the impending onslaught. But I cannot speak.

He breaks the silence. "How can you do this to us?" he says. *What was I thinking?* I look away, hoping to sustain my resolve. "Who has been influencing you? Are you out of your mind?" I try to tune him out as he continues, but his words penetrate like poison arrows. "My own daughter evading her duty. How can we face our friends?" *Who cares about your friends,* I wonder silently. *It's my life at stake here, I am too sensitive for the army. How can you not see it?*

I look at my mother to see if she will stand up for me. Sometimes— rarely—she does. But not now. Sitting in her usual spot, she frowns.

She isn't angry; she's worried. My father continues, his voice rising, "Look at me when I talk to you!" I turn back and look straight at him. *You don't need his permission,* a voice inside of me says. *You'll be eighteen soon and can do what you please.*

So why am I dying inside? I swallow the tears about to pour and look away again. He wants to break my spirit. He's been at it since I was two. He thinks it's for my own good. *You don't have to listen to him,* the inner voice comments.

Suddenly my mother joins with the calm voice of reason. "It's dangerous to marry a stranger. I don't trust him. And besides, how will you live in Israel if you've shirked your responsibility?"

"Answer me," my father demands for the fourth time. I stay quiet, shaking inside. "Do you realize what you're doing?" His voice is unyielding, menacing. How can I tell him anything? "I will not let you continue with this disgrace," he concludes without waiting for a response. I stagger out of the room, defeated. I call Herzl and tell him I can't go ahead with the plan.

The remaining weeks until my induction are a blur. I go through the motions of living, breathing, eating, sleeping. I read a lot. I barely talk to anyone. My alienation is silent, invisible. My eighteenth birthday comes and goes. I am officially an adult now, but this does not mean independence.

Finally I travel, one gray March morning, to the induction center. My feet are heavy, my heart numb. "Go home," I say to my parents, who have accompanied me, my voice cold and distant. "I want to be alone now."

The hall is filled with disoriented young women and family members. Suitcases and personal belongings are strewn all over. Some women are tentatively talking with each other, starting to make friends. I sit alone, silent and removed, relieved that no one is trying to talk to me. Every once in a while an officer comes out of a room and reads names in a detached tone. One by one those called are plucked away to stand outside waiting for the buses to remove them from civilian life, adolescence, innocence. "Mikhaela Kashtan." I hear my name. I shudder. They are using my official name, which I loathe. "Call me Miki, please," I say feebly. I step outside, wrapped in a veil of fear.

At last, clunky old buses come to take us away. We stop at the supply base. An officer reads the instructions, and we walk for what seems like hours, picking up clothing and equipment, imperceptibly transitioning from teenage girls into new recruits.

The buses appear again and take us to basic training camp. I cannot escape any more. A tall, stately officer guides us to our barracks. She introduces herself: Second Lieutenant Eel-eel. I am familiar with the name from a poem we read in high school, full of vague longings. But I have never met anyone named Eel-eel before. Her voice, surprisingly calm and gentle, suddenly tears through my fog. I am now in the army.

I spend the next four weeks in a barracks with fifty other young women, two rows of beds with just inches between them. Peculiar, impersonal intimacy is forced on us. I lie awake at night. Someone has a radio blasting. "Can you turn it down?" I ask sheepishly. "I can't fall asleep." Someone repeats my words, with a mocking lilt. I shudder; I should have known better, I have seen them taunt others. They talk to one another now as if I am not there. I have become an outcast, a target. Eel-eel is my only shelter. I ask several times to meet with her. Each time we talk, I gain a bit of my dignity back, but not for long.

The days offer a relief from the nightly taunting, but are filled instead with army tedium—inspections, lectures about things I don't want to know, and pep talks about how important it is for us to be in the army.

In the Israeli Army women don't go into combat. But we are trained in shooting—a symbolic gesture to remind us we are in the army. We are given heavy, World War II Czech rifles to carry. Eel-eel shows us how to shoot, explaining the mechanics, and then we practice without ammunition. After three weeks of training, we march to the range and practice with live ammunition on cardboard dummies.

At the range, rows of women are lying on their stomachs, rifles under their shoulders, awaiting the command. I lie down on the woolen blanket, arrange the rifle on the sandbags, and aim. The instructions are methodical, and years later I will still remember them. When the command is given, I pull the trigger and shoot the first bullet. I feel the weight of the rifle kicking me back. I feel invigorated and am surprised by how much fun shooting is. I load the rifle again, the command to fire comes again, and another bullet springs forth and tears a tiny hole in the cardboard. And again, taking a breath, unloading the empty chamber, putting another bullet in—command—and firing. My bullets cluster beautifully, less than an inch from each other, right near the dummy's left eyebrow. I feel proud of my accomplishments. I have the best cluster in the group. It would have killed a human being. Some time ago, these same rifles shot at living people.

A week later, with four weeks of basic training about to end, we are assigned to permanent units. Some will be clerks, some code breakers; others will offer social services to soldiers from difficult neighborhoods. Our job is to relieve the men from noncombat duty. We have little say in the matter, but we can express preferences. Some of the women are selected for training as basic trainers. No one wants the job, in a women-only base, of repeatedly instructing recruits in shooting and conveying the principles of army life.

But somehow my exhausted brain latches on to this idea, and, at the last moment, I ask to be part of this training. Why am I choosing to represent this army I so abhor? Out of defiance? To be accepted? To stay close to Eel-eel?

I am examined thoroughly. "You are not well liked," the interviewer tells me. "How will you command the respect of young women?"

"I know," I say, my voice breaking as I fight back the tears. Suddenly this is as important to me as life itself. "Please give me a chance. I want to try. I think I can do it." I don't recognize my own voice. It sounds metallic and foreign. The more she doubts me, the more I want in, until she relents, signs the papers, and summons the next person in line. Thirty-nine of us are chosen for a three-month course to become basic trainers.

In one role-play exercise during the course, a fellow student is assigned to play a pacifist who refuses to shoot. The rest of us, one after the other, play the role of commander, trying to get her to shoot. "Shooting in a range is not going to kill anyone," says one. "You owe it to your country to know how to shoot," says another. "You must do this." They are so sure of themselves. "There is no way I will do it," she insists calmly. I look at her, amazed by her dignity. She is standing proud, defiant, and peaceful amid the attacks. "It is against my deepest values. I will not touch a weapon under any circumstances." I listen to her closely, gradually realizing she is not playing a role, but expressing her true beliefs. Does anyone else know? I have never heard a pacifist before. I breathe in relief when the exercise ends before my turn to play the commander. I didn't know what to say to her. All I can think of are the little holes torn in the cardboard. Are the others as shaken by this exercise as I am? Did they notice that she is real?

Toward the end of our three-month, intensive course, we walk again to the shooting range. Instead of hundreds of young women, this time we are thirty-six women; three have been thrown out, I assume to their relief. The blankets are spread on the ground, with the sand-bags and the rifles lying peacefully on them. All is very familiar, but I am frozen, can barely move my muscles. I can't bring myself to shoot again. I am supposed to instruct others in doing this, but I can't even do it myself. I lie down, take my rifle, place it on the sandbag, tuck it in its familiar place under my shoulder, and look at the dummy, its silly little head with a target tacked on. I try to aim. I know how to do it so well. But I shake with every move and can't focus. I hear our officer give the command. I burst out crying and put my rifle down. Every-one else has already shot her first bullet. They look at me nervously, and I am unable to stop crying. I can't even touch the rifle. Someone approaches me, tries to calm me down, but I keep on crying. Anytime I look at the dummy or the rifle, a new wave of sobbing seizes me. *I will never again do this,* I think, as I cry. *I don't care what I have to teach the new recruits, I will not do this.* I am out of control, just like the new recruits I am supposed to handle.

In the end, I must have shot, although I can't remember it. How else would I have become a trainer?

There's a special tone to the firing command. "Fire," in Hebrew, is one short syllable: *"Esh."* When you say it correctly, it inspires con-fidence and trust. It has to be short, self-assured, firm but not harsh. *"Esh,"* I say. Too hesitant. *"Esh."* Too long. *"Esh."* Too loud. If you don't get it right, the recruits could get nervous and even turn around with their loaded rifles. There have been fatal accidents. *"Esh."* Yes! That's it. *"Esh."* Thirty new recruits fire their bullets and thirty dum-mies are killed. *"Esh."* Thirty tiny holes in my soul are torn open. *"Esh."* Thirty new women fire. *"Esh."* How many dummies am I responsible for? *"Esh."* How did my resistance get muted? *"Esh."* What did I shoot inside to get to this point? *"Esh."* How did I come to tell others to shoot faceless dummies? *"Esh."* Will the holes in my soul ever heal?

Growing up, I had tears of pride in my eyes as the flag passed by. My heart beat more quickly as they played the national anthem. My father served (was drafted) into the Marine Corps in World War II. He was called up to serve again, in Korea, and served at the Chosin Reservoir. He served further as commander of his VFW post in South Denver, where I grew up. I wrote the newsletter, sold poppies, and listened to the vets' stories.

I was raised to believe in the good things our Constitution and our country stand for. I believed, and still do, that everyone should give service of some kind for two years. I was raised to take the responsibilities of citizenship seriously. Trying to put myself through college was tough, as women weren't paid much for their work. At the age of twenty-one, ripe for service, I was very thoroughly recruited by a family friend; I believed that I would finish college, become an officer, and serve my twenty or more years to retirement. And, yes, that I would be treated equally with the men. I proudly donned the USAF uniform. I enlisted in 1969 during the Vietnam War.

Today I work for peace. As the vice-president of Veterans for Peace, I strive to maximize the voices of veterans to end war and the militarization of our youth. I work to make visible the misogyny and treatment of women in the military. I struggle daily with the seeming ambivalence of so many of my fellow citizens to taking direct action to stop the Iraq War.

The Silent Scream

I feel it! Do you feel it? The soul pain?
Sometimes I just want to scream.
Do you ever want to scream?
Do you? Ever scream?
Not silently, into a pillow . . . so as not to disturb anyone.
Not locked safely in the car on a deserted street.
Not riding on an amusement park roller coaster.

Sometimes I just want to scream.
Scream from my guts.
Scream from my heart.
Scream from my very soul.

I can never again pretend I don't see,
Pretend I don't know,
Pretend I don't feel the shame, the betrayal, the pain—
    of our country's collective karma.
You see, I took the red pill.

Sometimes I just want to
Stand up in the middle of the street and scream . . . Wake up!
Stand up in the middle of the shopping center and scream . . .
    Wake up!
Stand up in church in the middle of the service and scream . . .
    Wake up!
Stand up in the middle of Wall Street and scream . . . Wake up!
Stand up in the middle of the Congress and scream . . . Wake up!
Stand up on *Oprah* and scream . . . Wake up!

I feel it! Do you feel it? The soul pain?
Sometimes I just want to scream.
Meanwhile in Baghdad . . .

Sometimes I just want to scream.
I want to scream to the father of my friend . . .
    who voted for Bush, both times.
I want to scream to the Republican husband of my friend . . .
    who voted for Bush, both times.
I want to scream to the elderly black woman veteran
    I met at the VA . . . who voted for Bush, both times
    "because he does so much for us veterans."

I want to scream to the brother of my friend . . .
    who patted me on the knee and said it was
    "okay to torture those people" to save "American Lives."
I want to scream to the mother of my friend . . .
    who said "Our president is such a godly man."
I want to scream to the veteran who says we must follow
    the president . . . like he's God.

I want to scream to a reporter . . . do we have any left?
I want to scream to the man on the nightly news who says what
    he should to keep his job.

I want to scream to God . . . you know that "Christian God that
    Bush prays to."

I want to scream to the people of Iraq . . . "Please, forgive us,
    for some of us know not what we do."
I want to scream to the rest of the world . . . "We're sorry they
    won't wake up."
I want to scream to the universe . . . "Somehow, please stop us."

Instead . . . at 3 A.M. . . . I send silent screams on the Internet to
    president@whitehouse.gov.

Holiday Madness

I'm lying on the futon on the floor. There's no heater in this room.
California houses aren't built for winter. The lady doesn't heat her
house. I'm wrapped up in all my clothes. Cold. I'm so cold. Can't get
warm. So cold I'm shaking. My whole body is shaking. My skin hurts.
Everything hurts.

Is it the cold or is it the pain. I'm so tired of the pain. Three car
crashes this last year. Why did they run into my car? It's like I had a
bull's-eye or magnet or something. Hit from behind on my way to
teach. Hit from the side on my way to the airport. Not even safe at a
stop sign. Crash. But that's not all the pain.

I can barely breathe. It hurts to even try to take a breath. My chest
hurts. My heart hurts. Is this what they call angina? I can barely move.
Just shake. I can't stop shaking. Will nothing stop this pain? God, make
it stop. Is there something wrong with my heart? Is it something else?

So alone. Holidays alone again—since my divorce, since my Mom
died and my Dad went weird again. But it's different this year. No
home. No family. My best friend moved away. Can't work. No money.
Lost my health insurance when I couldn't pay the premiums. Car insurance won't pay for what I need. No hope left. Nowhere to go. I have
a car and nice clothes so everyone thinks I'm okay. I'm thin and blond
and some say I'm beautiful. I have a college degree. I used to have a
profession. You're supposed to be okay at our church. Just get the
prayers and your mind right. You're supposed to be abundant and
prosperous.

Timing. I have to get the timing right. I don't want her cats to go hungry. If I put out enough food—they'll be okay for three days won't they? Dogs wouldn't be, but cats will. Tomorrow morning I'll clean the cat boxes and vacuum. I'll bring in her mail. Put my things in the car. Leave food and water for the cats. The lady will be here in three days. I know I promised to housesit till after Christmas. Promised to care for her cats. Tomorrow is Christmas Eve. I can't wait. I won't. Enough!

Tomorrow I get to leave. I know just the place on Route 1. Yes. I know the place. It's beautiful. There's no guardrail. I should be there before noon. Then the pain will be gone. Tomorrow I find peace. Good plan. Tomorrow it's finished. There's a weird kind of peace now that I've made a choice. I turn out the bedroom light.

Who's there? Who turned on the light? It's 3 A.M.—how did you get in here? Who are you? Why is the light so bright? What are you saying? What are you showing me? Why are you doing this?

No! I don't want to look. No! Don't tell me I have to stay. They always make me come back. Not fair. Not fair. Not fair. I don't want to be here anymore. I don't want to do this. I Won't. You can't make me stay. It's too hard. I'm not that person. How can I be that person? If you think you can get me to do that—well, good luck. I can't even imagine it. All those people. What could I possibly say to them? Who am I to say anything? Don't you hear me? Make it stop.

"Go away!" I shout, pulling the pillow over my head, hoping to retreat into the oblivion of sleep.

The cats are making a racket and banging on the door. There's daylight streaming in the window. Was that a dream? No. I was awake. I know I was awake. Oh! God! I can't leave. Now I'm really pissed. There's a knock on the door. A package. The lady has a package. No. It's for me. Only one person knows I'm here so who could have sent it. I recognize the handwriting. I tear open the wrapping. It's a book. Hardback. My favorite author of the moment, Richard Bach, *One*. In between each page is a crisp dollar bill. Hundreds of them.

Better figure out why I'm here. What's so damned important that I have to stay?

JOE LAMB

I served as a hospital corpsman in the United States Navy from 1968 through 1971, during which time I worked on intensive care and psychiatric wards. My jobs after the military have included building solar homes, teaching ecology, and organizing against nuclear weapons. In 1990, I founded the Borneo Project, a nongovernmental organization that promotes rainforest preservation and indigenous rights. I am co-owner of Brende&Lamb, a company that cares for trees. I live in Berkeley, California, with my wife, Anna; my four-year-old daughter, Carson Lamb; and our dog Xtra.

Reuniting Gondwanaland

Sudan is found
in my television set,
on a map in my study,
and in articles from newspapers
that fail to scream or bleed,
and that, once read, are neatly folded
and placed in blue plastic boxes for recycling

Sudan is found
on the drifting continent
behind our eyes
where the Gulf of Guinea
reaches for Brazil's shoulder
and the mouth of the Amazon
murmurs to the Ivory Coast
of the reunion of Gondwanaland
and of the mysteries of Eden
that are not lost
once only

What is out there
is strangely in here—
and perhaps the old man was right
that the earthly paradise could be seen
if only the Africa of the heart reunited
with the Antarctica of the mind

Perdition

In the summer of my thirteenth year, Floyd's Pool Hall seemed as exotic as the drawings of perdition in my grandmother's Bible. When Grandma was out feeding the chickens, my cousins and I would study the color plates of the destruction of Sodom. Rays of light through black billowing clouds lit up the startled faces of the doomed. It was Joe Bob who first found the bare-breasted woman among the writhing throng.

Like those drawings, Floyd's place was a study in light and darkness. Its two small windows faced Main Street, and the light they gave struggled halfway to the back before succumbing to a haze of cigar smoke and shadow. The first two pool tables were the only ones in direct light, and their yellowing velvet marked the insistent passage of the sun. In the back room, where men played dominoes for money, only a single bulb dangling from the ceiling was lit. In the shade near the minnow tank Floyd kept his only billiard table, and it was, though very old, still moss green. It had the feel of something a beautiful woman would wear. The constant rumble and hum from the swamp cooler blended with the bubbling from the minnow tank to yield a liquid, dreamlike accompaniment to the Hank Williams songs whispering out of Floyd's radio.

When there were no paying customers, which was most of the time, Floyd let my cousins, Joe Bob and Billy, shoot pool for free. Floyd was the kind of man who treated kids as if they knew something adults had forgotten. When he talked with us about fishing or horses, he would listen more than he would talk, and his voice never had the teasing quality so common when adults talk to children. Floyd showed us how much to chalk the pool cues, taught us to hit low on the cue ball if you want it to come back toward you, told us always to shoot with the next two shots in mind. My first day we played eight ball over and over and over until finally Billy got bored and suggested we go next door to buy comic books.

There were only two people in Antelope Grocery, a large drowsy clerk behind the counter and an old woman wearing a floral print dress. A thin layer of sawdust covered the wood plank floor. The air smelled of bologna and turpentine. A roll of flypaper peppered with tiny carcasses hung just behind the counter. The old woman talked to the clerk about the chance of rain, then bought a bag of flour and left.

When the screen door creaked shut, the clerk seemed to wake up. He asked us if we were going to go swimming down at the creek and warned us to watch out for snapping turtles. "If you're not careful they'll bite off your johnson," he said, winking maliciously. "Susie Trout wouldn't like that."

The little bell above the door rang. Two Indian men, one in his early fifties and one about nineteen, walked up to the counter. They looked like they wanted to ask for something. The clerk started joking with them, asking them about their squaws. They looked embarrassed, but laughed a little.

"Mr. Butz. How about a couple of bottles of green?" the older man asked.

The clerk replied, "Earl, your tab is up to twenty bucks. No money, no green."

Earl reached into a gunnysack he was carrying. He pulled from it a ceremonial headdress.

"Ray Blackhorse's war bonnet. Very old."

He handed it to the clerk and looked at the floor. The clerk turned the bonnet over in his hands. He smoothed out the white edges of the eagle feathers, and ran his fingers over the beadwork. Like a blind man reading hieroglyphics, he traced the circles, the lightning bolts, the dancing figures, the animal shapes sewn in red and white beads.

"Is it cowhide?" he asked.

"Antelope," the younger man replied. "Very old."

"Shit, Frank, there ain't been an antelope around here in over a hundred years."

"Antelope," the younger man repeated. "Very old."

The clerk winked at us. "OK. I'll erase your bill and give you two bottles of green. Deal?"

Earl nodded. The clerk went to the refrigerator, moved a case of milk to one side, and revealed a row of green bottles of AquaVelva aftershave. He set two of the bottles on the floor and replaced the case of milk. The warm, humid air condensed on the bottles, frosting the glass.

"Nice and cold," he said as he gave one bottle to each man. "Next time, no money, no green."

Joe Bob nudged me with his elbow and motioned toward the door. I followed him around back to a little alley where the town's water tower rose up from a field of tumbleweeds.

"Come on," Joe Bob said, "Nobody's looking. Let's go to the top."

We climbed up the galvanized steel rungs to a little ledge about seventy feet up. We could see beyond the town to the wheat fields stretching toward the horizon in every direction. An old pickup rattling down Main Street trailed a plume of red dust. I sat and admired the shine on my new boots as they dangled so far above the ground.

Billy tapped my shoulder and motioned for me to look down. Frank and Earl came out of the store and into the alley. They walked behind the pool hall and sat with their backs to the wall. Earl took a drink of something and handed it to Frank.

"What are they doing?" I asked.

"Drinking the aftershave," Joe Bob whispered into my ear. "It makes them go blind."

I rubbed my eyes and looked at the sky. Big rain clouds were building in the west and darkening the line of trees along the river. I looked for a shaft of light like the drawing in the Bible but only saw one large bird circling slowly in the distance. Joe Bob followed my gaze and said, "Vulture."

Little Fool

The back of the hand
was seldom necessary.
Nor was the belt,
nor even the belt's nickname.
A glance would do.

At first it took a stare, later
just an eyebrow lifting
over the top of the horn-rims.
After years of practice
no visible signal was needed.

And yes, of course, there's a lot
to be learned the hard way:
like how a king is not a king
unless he has a fool;
and why all fools need
to practice, practice, practice
the art of falling down.

With enough practice
you can almost imagine
twelve-year-old boys
asking to be sent into battle
armed only with rake handles.

With enough practice
you can almost see them
searching the ground
for the land mines
so that their fathers can swim
through the blood and smoke
with rifles blazing,
their voices lifted in song.

The Measure of the Man

The only symptom Will complained about was the itching of his toes. He could wall off the dull throbbing in his knees and wait out the phantom pains that ripped his calves—these had an end. But the itching was constant; it chewed through his defenses and gnawed at his core. Will couldn't understand how something that no longer existed could torture him with such specificity. His big toes itched in the hairs just above the nail, he'd reach to scratch, there would be nothing there. On my morning rounds, I'd wash the men's stubs, change their bandages, empty their urinals, and hand out their sedatives. In the afternoon, when the ward quieted down, Will and the other members of the betrayed generation killed time playing cards. We drank coffee and smoked Kools; we talked about girls, movies, Jimi Hendrix, but never about Vietnam.

While waiting for the Marines to discharge him and ship him back to Watts, Will grew an Afro—a big, bushy, black Afro. Captain McQuithy, the lifer nurse who ran the ward, ordered him to cut it. When Will refused, she wrote him up for insubordination. I tucked Will's robe around his knees, lifted him into his wheelchair, and pushed him down the gray linoleum ramp to the French doors that read "Security." A potbellied man with gold hash marks on his sleeve took the nurse's report and began filling out the forms for the court-martial. He asked Will the usual questions: name, rank, place of birth, race, height. Will replied in a flat voice, "William Counts, private, Los Angeles, Negro, four feet three inches." The petty officer stopped typing and repeated the question about his height. Will repeated, "Four feet three inches." Leaning out the door, the petty officer looked at Will for the first time, his skin turning a faint pink as he mumbled that he meant his height before. Will pulled himself up in his wheelchair and yelled, "Measure me, you motherfucker, measure me."

One Small Exception

I apologize to big questions for small answers.
—WISLAWA SZYMBORSKA

My time in the military was spent changing bandages, drawing blood, and taking care of soldiers on the psych wards. Their wounds were harder to heal than those caused by metal ripping flesh. Counseling men—some of whom were severely psychotic—was an unsettling experience for a nineteen-year-old. I was uncertain what I had to offer other than a willingness to hear whatever they wanted to say. Most were grateful that someone was listening. Being listened to was not a common experience for most of them.

The inhabitants of the psych ward wore blue-and-white-striped robes that hung to their ankles. Pacing around on the gray linoleum, they looked like lost Bedouin tribesmen trying to find their way to an uncharted oasis. Many had recently returned from Vietnam, but their experiences in the war were not discussed much, even in group therapy. In 1969, PTSD had yet to be identified, and back then there was a stigma attached to admitting mental problems resulting from combat.

The prevailing attitude was summed up in *Patton,* a 1970 film about the World War II general. On a visit to a hospital ward, Patton encounters a soldier who says he is suffering from "shell shock." This admission enrages Patton; he calls the man a coward and beats him with his riding crop. Patton's attitude toward shell shock was commonplace. Soldiers were expected to kill other human beings and to witness the death of their close friends without that violence damaging their minds and spirits.

The psych ward, it seems to me now, was a great place to gain perspective on the late sixties and early seventies. Handing out Thorazine on the T-ramp, it looked to me like the Vietnam War had driven the entire country crazy. At the time, it was not where I would have chosen to spend the end of my youth. While scrubbing bedpans on the graveyard shift, I would imagine my friends in college smoking pot and making love. That envy was one of many reasons I did not fit well into my uniform. My shirt was always a little wrinkled, my hat slightly askew. I cultivated my unkempt appearance as an act of childish defiance against an authority that seemed confused and hypocritical. My rebellion against form extended to the manner in which I interacted with the psych patients. Because the Freudian theory, given us in our neuropsychiatric technician class, did not match the experience of the ward—fear of the phallus didn't seem a reasonable explanation for the paranoia experienced by men who had recently returned from combat—another corpsman and I invented our own brand of therapy. It consisted of three simple techniques: Listen even when you don't want to; treat everyone with respect; and tell what you believe to be the truth unless doing so would be an act of cruelty. We called our program Kindness Therapy. I believe that it got good results.

Like many others in the military, I thought the Vietnam War was a bad idea. It wasn't that I thought that America itself was some kind of evil monster. I had then, and have now, great affection for the giant, imperfect, evolving, and indefinable being that is America, a being best symbolized to me by Hank Williams, Martin Luther King, Jr., and Huckleberry Finn. America, above all, was the people I knew, and I liked most of the people I knew. Nor was my opposition to the war because of some antipathy toward the military itself. Like many boys born in the wake of World War II, I grew up idealizing the warriors who had defeated fascism. For much of my childhood, we played war whenever we had the chance. Crawling around in the arroyos near our grade school, my friends and I shot at each other with BB guns. We practiced stealth, drawing a clean bead, and the art of the dramatic death. At the time, I did not understand why World War II veterans were not happy when their children played those war games.

The reason I opposed the war was very simple: I had an undeniable feeling that those leading us into Vietnam did not know what they were doing; that they were suffering a fundamental disconnect from reality; that, if you stripped away the pomp and ceremony, they were as lost and uncertain as the guys in the blue-and-white-striped robes. What I saw on TV seemed too much like what I was seeing on the ward. The grandiosity, the paranoia, the belief in global conspiracies, all this was uncomfortably similar to the delusions of the guy on Stelazine who thought he was controlling Neil Armstrong by beaming radio waves directly to the moon from his head. Whenever you asked him to explain how that was possible, he would get angry and tell you that you were crazy if you didn't understand. When politicians responded to questions about the war in the same way, I felt like someone was tying my intestines into knots. From where I stood, the bravado, evasiveness, and anger displayed by those leading us into war were a sure sign that hidden underneath was an ocean of uncertainty, ignorance, and fear.

I was fully aware that my right to such a strong opinion was suspect. A high school dropout forced into the military by his parents because he was running wild was in no position to challenge the whiz kids running the show. And, like everyone in the military under twenty-one, I didn't even have the right to vote. Where did a nineteen-year-old get off thinking his leaders had lost their minds? I knew that I knew very little about Asian culture and history. To the lasting harm of many in my generation, those who sent us to war shared my ignorance, but not my humility.

I felt guilty being in the military during the Vietnam War, and at the same time I felt guilty opposing the war. In that regard I was a little schizophrenic, like America itself during those times. To my surprise, this internal conflict had an upside: It helped me empathize with the patients, and it helped me keep an open mind while feeling my way through the broken psyche of my country. Decades after the fact,

I realize that I was blessed to be working on the psych ward, to be with those men and women, in that place, during that time.

Chief among my considerable blessings was that I did not get killed or suffer irredeemable psychological harm. Most of the Navy corpsmen who, like me, went through field medical school, were sent to Vietnam as field medics with the Marines. Through luck or fate I was sent instead to neuropsychiatric school. I doubt I would have been strong enough, if strong is the right word, to keep mind and body whole after experiencing combat. If I had killed anyone or had seen any of my friends killed, the experience would have blown my spirit so far out of my skin that I might never have been able to settle fully into my body again. Many guys wearing the blue-and-white robes were searching the linoleum for passageways leading back home.

Like many in the military, I marched in peace demonstrations and tried to organize some kind of resistance to the war within the ranks. I did so thinking that the military was all-seeing, and that, when discovered, my antiwar actions would get me in deep trouble. However, "Don't ask, don't tell, and don't see" must have been the unstated rule toward antiwar attitudes within the ranks. I think that those officers aware of my protests felt more compassion toward me than anger. The chaplain at the Naval Hospital in Philadelphia met my arguments against the war with an indulgence that almost expressed genuine interest, and only occasionally blurred into condescension.

I was stationed in Corpus Christi, Texas, when, after a private screening of *Patton,* President Nixon ordered the invasion of Cambodia. The manner in which our president wrapped himself in the flag so outraged me that I was moved to wear a black armband to an inspection in which everyone on the base wore dress-white uniforms. I wish I could report that my gesture was an act of bravery, but I was scared to the bone. Having worked myself into a frenzy, and fully expecting to be sent to the brig, I stole a Thorazine from the ward and took it before the inspection in the hope that it would calm me down. (It had no effect other than to blur my vision.) To my surprise and grateful relief, the inspecting admiral did not send me to jail, bite off my head, or even give me a dressing-down. He just glanced at me, and at my armband, and then kindly ignored me. I think he was mildly embarrassed, but he might have been amused. His only comment in the speech given to assembled troops was that our inspection was perfect, with one small exception.

The unexpected kindness and tolerance that I often encountered in the military were sometimes jarringly absent in my interactions with the civilian peace movement. It was an unpleasant and recurring surprise to find that many peace activists expressed an arrogant self-righteousness toward soldiers. In this regard they demonstrated a disdain toward military people that was widespread in the culture at large. Part of the pathology of the Vietnam-era, shared psychosis was that the culture blamed the war, and later its loss, on the soldiers that it sent to fight that war. This perfidious attitude was one of the ways the culture betrayed the Vietnam vet. A bizarre myth popular back then held that the reason war exists is because young men, by their nature, want to kill and die. Many people acted as if the conscripts fighting the war had somehow created the war. It was a crazy idea and another indicator that the culture itself was in need of therapy. Young servicemen and women do not make foreign policy, and they don't choose to be wounded, to die, or to witness the deaths of their friends. This myth dismisses the soldier's sacrifice at the same time that it becomes a kind of perverse justification for sending him into almost certain suffering, a kind of "that's what they wanted anyway" attitude. And while this tendency to blame soldiers for the war isn't the only reason that the trauma of Vietnam didn't end when the soldiers returned stateside, it is part of the reason why hundreds of thousands of veterans continue to have trouble putting their lives back together.

There was, of course, a far greater betrayal of the soldier than blaming him for the war. Listen to the White House tapes of Lyndon Johnson, or to the reminiscences of Robert McNamara, and it becomes clear that those who sent our young men and women into harm's way did so without understanding who the enemy was, what the enemy was capable of, or what the enemy was fighting for. It was with more sorrow than anger that I watched McNamara confirm what I felt in my gut as a young man. In the documentary *The Fog of War,* he admits that the Domino Theory—the rationale for the Vietnam War—was built more on fear than on fact. Those in power told us that we had to fight the communists in Vietnam to prevent "Red China" from forming an alliance with Vietnam to take over all of Asia, that the safety of America itself was at risk. The theory was presented as a rock-hard certainty, worth fighting and dying for. It was far from certain, as our leaders should have known. They should not have been surprised to learn that Vietnam has fought against Chinese domination for nineteen centuries; they should not have been surprised that after America left Vietnam, instead of joining forces, Vietnam and China went to war with each other, taking twenty thousand more lives. If our leaders had done their homework, they would have known that "Fight them in Vietnam or we will have to fight them in California" was a paranoid delusion. And if we, the people, had done our duty we would have made sure that our leaders knew what they were doing.

Understanding and forgiveness are not identical emotions; each has its own rigors, its own limitations. We often confuse the two, thinking "I understand" also means "I forgive." This confusion creates barriers to understanding those things that we cannot find it in our hearts to forgive. In the age of nuclear terrorism this confusion carries great danger: our survival may depend on a deep and ongoing attempt to understand many unforgivable things. It is not my place to speak for those who have died or for those veterans sleeping under bridges. But it is my place, my duty even, to speak the truth of my own experiences. For my very small part, I forgive those who acted less than kindly toward those of us in uniform. There were many in the peace movement who, like Grace Paley and Maxine Hong Kingston, understood that the soldiers were among the victims of war. There were many Quakers and Quaker-like souls who protected soldiers and provided vets with psychic wounds a place to heal. People who practice peace as well as preach it, both within the military and outside it, have my respect and admiration.

A few of those who led us into Vietnam have, many decades after the fact, found the courage to admit their mistakes and acknowledge that those mistakes caused others great suffering. Such admissions cannot bring back the dead. Perhaps they could reduce the suffering of our children's children by helping us avoid repeating past failures. As much as it is my place to do so, I forgive those leaders, like Robert McNamara, who have had the courage to take responsibility for their errors. The courage to admit mistakes is much needed; it is in short supply. McNamara, at least, is trying to help the country avoid repeating his mistake of failing to understand the people he designated as the enemy, of letting his pride hide his ignorance. The ancient Greeks could have warned him against hubris, the classic flaw in most tragedies.

Every crusade has had such blind and naïve arrogance at its core. I can understand, as well as I am able, that those who were swept up into the global insanity of World War II—who witnessed the birth of nuclear terror in Alamogordo, who knew intimate details about the fire bombing of Dresden, the Rape of Nanking, the ovens at Auschwitz, and the starvation in the Gulag—had good reason to fear humanity's ability for self-destruction. Within a few decades after World War II, we had, for the first time in history, the ability to exterminate our entire species. I understand how this fear might guide men into a war they did not understand. In their place, I might have succumbed to the same fear.

One betrayal of the soldier, however, I cannot forgive. During the Vietnam War, those in power would sometimes hide their mistakes and misjudgments behind the flag, and even more cynically behind those they had sent into combat. They would say that those who questioned the war were guilty of betraying the soldier, and that protesting the war was unpatriotic and anti-American. It was not and it is not. A lie does not become a truth when wrapped in the flag. I cannot forgive this betrayal because it is ongoing, and I don't know how to forgive an abuse that doesn't stop.

Because soldiers don't send themselves to war, it is our duty as citizens to examine the reasons for fighting as though our own lives were at risk. We have to find and tell the truth, to call a lie a lie, even when those in power paint that lie red, white, and blue. The importance of holding our leaders accountable does not stop when the shooting starts. In fact, it increases. Although it is unpopular to challenge a war after many have died, we owe it to those who have died as well as to those still fighting to test the reality underlying the theory for war. More than 20,000 Americans lost their lives in the last three years of the Vietnam War. If the theory proves false, you do not honor the dead by sending more to die. Increasing the body count does not transform theory into truth.

———

I wish I could say that in the thirty-five years since I left the psych ward, the world has become a saner place. We have abandoned Mutually Assured Destruction—MAD—the nuclear deterrence policy that called for the total annihilation of the U.S. and the U.S.S.R. I hoped that when the Berlin Wall came down the world would become a little less schizophrenic, that there would be a massive peace dividend spent on a global effort to eradicate poverty, and that we would eliminate nuclear weapons. I little expected that humanity would want another Middle Ages, complete with ethnic cleansing, state torture, and calls from religious and political leaders for Crusade and Jihad. The nineteen-year-old boy who believed in Kindness Therapy would argue that fear is not the best guide out of our current darkness. He would say we are still letting people die without making sure our leaders know what they are doing. Something in my gut tells me he's right.

ROBERT LANDMAN

In 1969, I was in the infantry on the front lines in Viet Nam.
After nine months, I had a unique encounter on a mountainside
with a North Vietnamese soldier that changed my life.
"The True Geography of Meeting" is the story of that encounter
and all that followed.

Currently, I live on a mountainside in Occidental, California,
called "The Place of Peace" by the Pomo Indians, the first people
who lived here. It is a good place to "be in the silence" to better
hear the voice of Spirit. This is where "In the Silence" came to
be written, although about a silence of a different kind.

Since the beginning of the Veteran Writers' Group, I have
worked with many forms of storytelling and writing. I discovered
that screenplay writing is a powerful way to shine light on the great
mysteries of life and a profound way to express the deeper truths
as they are revealed. A good story can become a great movie
that can transform people's lives and the world.

Over many years, Maxine Hong Kingston, Earll Kingston, and
many other members of the Veteran's Writer's Group and I
have been working on a story for a movie. It is based on the writings
of Maxine Hong Kingston and original ideas from our meetings.
Called *The Way of Peace,* it begins in ancient China, where the lives
of a young girl and boy interweave over three lifetimes. With a charge
from their ancestors, each searches for the lost *Book of Peace.*
In an unfortunate incident and loss of innocence, they enter into
an escalating cycle of violence that spans
continents and centuries. Ultimately, they find the *Book of Peace.*
As they read the *Book of Peace*, the fragile,
ancient text disintegrates in their hands. What they learn is enough
to begin a new path, but
with a catch . . . Their story is our story,
for our time and our world.

Over a lifetime of reflection, I have come to believe that everyone
has a gift. Finding, developing, and sharing our gift is our true work.
The fruit of our work is our gift to Spirit and to each other.
Our gifts grow best in peace. The greatest gifts foster peace.
My greatest prayer: May everyone find and share their gift.
May everyone live in peace.

The True Geography of Meeting

East Meets West

September 1969. Viet Nam. In the mountains near the border
with Laos and Cambodia, a North Vietnamese Army (NVA)
soldier was captured and being interrogated by the Captain of
the infantry company I was assigned to nine long months before.
Our company had an attached South Vietnamese Army
Interpreter to translate in just such a rare opportunity with
a live enemy soldier.

The Captain was hard and unrelenting in his style of interrogation.
I could not hear what was said, but the angry, wild gestures
with his arms and the grimace on his face spoke volumes.
I witnessed the silhouette of the NVA soldier sitting on the ground
slowly and progressively crumple up like a piece of paper,
ready to be thrown away. Even the interpreter looked pained
and smaller. Satisfied with his harsh performance,
the Captain concluded the interrogation with a gesture
of arrogant dismissal, then nonchalantly walked away.

Now, under minimal guard, the NVA soldier looked dejected
as I continued to watch him. I wondered about him . . .
As we were many miles from the nearest U.S. military base,
it would be more than an hour before the NVA soldier would be
picked up by helicopter and taken back for further questioning.

I wondered . . . how had he come to be here . . . ?
What was life like for him before the war . . . ?
After the war, what would he do . . . ?

North Meets South

As the South Vietnamese Army interpreter and I, over long
months, had become friends, I asked him if I could talk to
the NVA soldier. Relieved, the interpreter perked up and said,
"Sure, what do you want to talk to him about . . . ?"
As we approached, the NVA soldier looked up and appeared
very apprehensive.

Through the interpreter, I asked him his name. The interpreter smiled when I replied with my name. Continuing in this triangulated conversation, I asked, "Where do you live?" He said, "Hanoi." I said, "I live in San Francisco."

"How did you come to be here?" He was drafted out of school into the army. I said, "Me too!" "How old are you?" "Nineteen." "I'm nineteen also ..."

"Do you have a girlfriend or a wife?" He said, "Yes ..." He pulled something from his shirt pocket, momentarily looked at it tenderly, then showed it to me. It was a black-and-white picture of his wife. He looked up and asked me if there was someone special in my life.

Painfully, I looked down at the ground, stumbling over my words, trying to find a way to express that I really didn't, as I'd received a Dear John letter some weeks before, but the interpreter quickly interceded and said, "Yes ..." and was nodding in amusement over how well the "interview" was going. The interpreter asked me for my wallet, which he opened to the colorful pictures inside, one of an attractive woman and another of a happy family, pictures that come with a new wallet that for some reason I hadn't taken out yet. With a big grin, the interpreter pointed to the picture of the woman, saying, "She's number one!" as the NVA soldier inflated some, smiled, and nodded in agreement. I did not have the heart to tell him that she was not my number one ... and I did not want to rob him of enjoying the moment and my seeming good fortune.

After an awkward silence, I asked if he was hungry. I didn't need the interpreter to tell me that he was. I opened up a can of food and gave it to him. He ate some, then offered some back to me. I gestured no, that it was for him, and he ate the rest of the food. When he finished, he looked at me. I mean, he really looked at me, deep into my eyes, perhaps into my soul. I looked back, trying to see in him what he might be seeing in me.

It was a long moment . . . one of those rare moments outside of normal time and space, where the ways of the world cease to apply. It was as if I was looking into a mirror and the reflection looking back was another face . . .

It was the experience of really being seen, and in that moment I really saw him . . . not as a prisoner . . . or even a soldier . . . but, as who he really was . . . a human being caught up in a war that he and I would never have wanted to happen, did not want to be part of, and wanted to end as soon as possible without any more loss of life.

Meeting

In that moment, a silence came over that side of the mountain. In this moment, looking back over my life, I have learned there are many different kinds of silence. Remembering that moment in my life, it was the silence of peace . . . beyond all understanding . . . lasting only a moment. As unforeseen and quickly as it had come, the moment began to evaporate.

The noisy approach of a helicopter grew louder, assaulting this moment of silence. Those in charge were coming back for the prisoner. The machinery of war and accompanying chorus of chaos escalated, finally overwhelming this moment in time, this small geography of peace on the mountainside.
The helicopter arrived and hovered above the treetops.
A rope with a seat quickly lowered to lift him aboard.
I wanted to say something to him, but did not know what to say.
We were in regular time now, and there would be no time
to say anything.

Then it came to me. No words need be spoken, or followed.
I had a black scarf around my neck. I found myself taking it off.
I offered it to him, and he put the scarf around his neck.
Watching this, the Captain nodded in approval, but for reasons,
I think, very different from my own.

As the NVA prisoner was lifted up to the helicopter overhead, we looked at each other one last time. I gestured to him that I wished him well. I think he understood. He smiled back at me as he was pulled inside the helicopter. As quickly and noisily as the helicopter arrived, it abruptly turned and flew away. Then, a silence of a different kind followed . . .
He was gone, but something of our moments together remained, something unexplainable, something transformational.

In the Truth

I realized that he was not the enemy . . . and . . . I could no longer be a soldier. From that moment on, I did not want to be in a position to bring harm to anyone. I immediately went to find the Captain and the Top Sergeant. When I did, I told them the war was over . . . for me. I was immediately threatened with a court-martial and being sent to the military prison at Leavenworth, but still experiencing a profound peace, I was not worried about what would happen to me. I was not afraid or intimidated and responded, "What's the worst that can happen . . . send me to Viet Nam?"

They did not know whether to laugh or cry, but what they did get with certainty was, that for me, the war was over. I told them I would keep my word to honor and serve my remaining time in Viet Nam, but not in a capacity of taking life. I did not know how, but I would do all I could to help protect and save lives, on both sides. I would continue to carry a twenty-five-pound radio, but with my rifle hung upside down on my back. They let me be . . .

The next three months were long and hard, and I prayed longer and harder for help. My prayers were somehow answered. During that time, there were no casualties . . . on either side. This does not happen in war. Help and protection came from somewhere else, I believe from the same ever-present, unseen realm paralleling our own that had opened to and welcomed two men on a mountainside three months before.

Makes All the Difference

After serving my time, I went home. In the years that followed,
I had more time to think about what occurred. From that moment
to this, I will be eternally grateful for that unexpected encounter
on a mountainside in Viet Nam. In the middle of a war,
in a Buddhist country, 10,000 miles from home,
I was reawakened to the central teaching of Christianity,
to treat others as we wish to be treated, and discovered the
deep wisdom of Buddhism, to do no harm to any living being,
are different expressions of the same truth . . . how we can meet . . .
and . . . where we can meet . . . in peace.

In the Silence

Easter Sunday many American families travel long distances to
gather together in remembrance of the day and for a family meal.
In 1969, in more than 400,000 households, there was an
empty chair that would have a great deal of attention upon it,
spoken and silent. The missing occupant was a son or daughter,
10,000 miles away in distant Viet Nam.

That year in a San Francisco household, the chair that
nineteen-year-old Robert Landman would have sat on was empty.
The infantry company he was assigned to was undermanned, and
he was a welcome replacement for someone who was killed
just a few weeks before his arrival.

Easter morning halfway around the world, his company was
airlifted by helicopter to search a massive bunker complex in
the mountains near the Cambodian border that was discovered
and photographed by aerial surveillance the previous day.
It was a stopping point en route for North Vietnamese Army
soldiers and equipment heading south. The photographs
also showed the presence of many NVA soldiers.

That afternoon the company reached the bottom of the mountain where the bunker complex had been seen. A squad of four men was selected to go into the bunker complex. If the four walked into an ambush, it would be the fewest casualties considered by the Commanding Officer (CO) to be an acceptable risk and loss to the company. The little squad was ordered to prepare to go up the mountain trail.

At the time of briefing the squad leader, the CO's face was distorted with fear. The squad leader's face took on the same look as he listened. The CO's nearly inaudible last words were, "Good luck . . ." as he looked away in shame. The squad leader looked into the faces of three men: "Get ready to recon the area." Then he looked at me and said, "Robert . . . you're on point."

The four of us started along a well-worn trail up the mountainside that led to the bunker complex. Raised in the city, I was unfamiliar with the messages in the sounds of nature. When the animals and insects go silent, it is a warning of immediate danger and, if unheeded, something terrible inevitably follows. Even if I had been born in the country, there is no amount of experience that could prepare one for this. I did not see the cutout window opening of the first underground bunker until I walked right in front of it, where an AK-47 would usually be aimed right at you and the first sound that breaks the unnerving silence is the "crack" of automatic rifle fire that shoots you dead, and all of the other soldiers following in terror behind you . . .

At that moment I stopped in shock three or four feet in front of the bunker. Staring into that bunker window, I saw no AK-47 pointing outward nor were there any NVA soldiers manning the three other bunkers evenly spaced on the sides on the trail now visible just ahead. The squad leader came up to investigate and had a muffled conversation on the radio. The CO's new orders were predictable, and not what we wanted to hear, "Check out the rest of the bunker complex . . ."

As we walked singlefile deeper into the complex, each step seemed slower, weighted down with the gravity of fear pulling in the opposite direction. There was all kinds of evidence that many soldiers had been here, seemingly only hours before: discarded trash of an army on the move, open red mackerel cans, plastic wrappings for rice, warm embers of recent cooking fires.

More than an hour later we reached the end of the complex on the other side of the mountain. The bunker complex was not just on the mountain; it *was* the mountain. It was a relief that it was empty. We stopped to make a radio report to the CO. Upon coming to a small stream, I signaled for the squad leader to come forward. In the muddy sand were the imprints of many sandals. As we watched in horror, the sandal imprints started to fill up with water.

We were only seconds behind the departing NVA soldiers. The squad leader radioed another situation report to the CO. Although we could not hear the CO's new order, we knew it would not be good. He told us, "Recon the area on the other side of the stream . . ." Before we crossed the stream, the squad leader relieved me of being point man and asked me in turn to relieve the Radio Telegraph Operator (RTO) by carrying his 25-lb. radio.

It took only a few steps to cross to the other side of the stream into a large open area. We were all in the open and moving as quickly as possible toward safety and cover of the brush and tree line in front of us when there was a lot of movement in the brush, like many startled animals. Several AK-47s opened up on us. Even with the radio's twenty-five lbs. of extra weight, diving to the ground did not seem fast enough, as I could see three rounds streak toward the other members of the squad beside me and three more rounds streak over my head as I hit the ground.

After three or four seconds of the longest silence I have ever experienced, three more rounds mowed down some blades of grass in front of me. More movement in the tree line, and for some unknown reason none of us returned fire. Then silence. Just as suddenly as everything had happened, an unexplainable and most amazing thing occurred. A voice said, "We mean you no harm. . . ." I do not remember if it was my voice, or their voice, or whose voice it was. I could not even tell what direction the voice was

coming from. I do not believe I heard it with my ears.
What I do remember is hearing the voice in the center of my head.

Immediately and simultaneously the movement stopped.
The automatic rifle fire shooting at us stopped. Everything stopped.
The sounds of war ceased. Silence came over the entire landscape.
Then, the animal and insect sounds resumed. The heavy weight
of fear lifted.

After a minute or so of waiting and wondering, what followed
was strange. Without discussion, in unison, we simply stood up
and quickly walked back across the stream, back through the
bunker complex, back to rejoin the company, but they did not
know what direction we were coming from and they opened up
with automatic rifle and machine gun fire on us. We could see
the horror on their faces when they realized it was us. Again,
we were unharmed. A moment of grace . . . ? I do not know.

As we were debriefed, the CO was visibly shaken. What had
transpired did not fit his reality or he simply did not believe
our account of being in the bunker complex. He decided to send
another squad back into the bunker complex.

Within minutes there was a burst of three rounds. The point man
was hit and the rest of his squad could not get to him, as they were
pinned down. It was a long time before the other members of his
squad were able to reach him. When they did, it was too late.
The point man bled to death.

I remember the four members of my squad standing
in respectful and stunned silence as his body was carried
past us. We could barely look at his lifeless body, barely look
at each other. My eyes lower to the ground before my feet.

In disbelief, a voice says, "He has been in-country for only
two weeks!" Another voice says, "That could have been you . . ."
An inner voice of despair says, "You have eight months to go."
The inner voice of eternal guilt accuses, "It should have been you."

I say nothing. In the silence, thoughts and feelings scream
inside that cannot be expressed outwardly. I start to shake

all over. Something detonates inside. I go numb. That day,
some part of me dies and is carried away in his body bag.
Over the years, a voice still whispers, "It should have been you . . ."

With every day that passes and every Easter Sunday,
there is a silence around the family table, as his chair
will always remain empty.

In every year that comes another silence continues.
I too, am among the many missing in action, when invited
to sit at the banquet table of life.

In the space between all words . . . other voices speak.
In the time between all moments . . . other stories unfold.
In the silence between all things . . . is the eternal call to listen.

The road to hell, they say, is paved with good intentions. So was the path most of us took to Vietnam. In my case, this involved my father, Earnie Larsen, a warm, rough sports-obsessed man of Viking heritage who valued physical prowess to an extreme degree. Unfortunately, I took after my maternal grandfather, a small artistic fellow whose only obsession was his clarinet. Never doubting my father's love, I was nonetheless unable to excel on the athletic fields that so captivated his attention.

But I did find a way, and that was the war in Southeast Asia.

Much later, I discovered that healing combat trauma often demands resolving the initial motivation that led to the battlefield, as well as what happened on it. Men go to war for many reasons. The most common, I believe, is blind obedience and the surrender of our moral authority. My father loved me dearly, but carried into adulthood wounds of violence and self-doubt that compromised his ability to parent wisely.

In the way of fathers and sons, his doubt became my doubt.

On the day I was wounded, I realized I had crawled into battle as much to win Dad's approval as to help wounded grunts. If Vietnam taught me any one thing, it is that I alone am responsible for my choices. This is a lesson I have tried to represent in my personal life and psychotherapeutic work with combat vets and others.

The "New Vietnam"

I never planned on going back to Vietnam. Hell, I didn't *plan* to go there in the first place. In my life, Vietnam doesn't seem to work that way, and the decision to return (on Leap Year morning of 1996) was as unexpected as it was necessary.

It had taken a long time to clear out the ghosts that followed me home from the war. Three gunshot wounds cut that trip mercifully short, but a nine-month hospitalization did absolutely nothing to dampen the memories of too many friends exploded into human mush. After I was discharged, my life tumbled into a self-destructive spiral nearly getting me nabbed in a Mexican heroin bust. And *that* was the eye-opener that finally caused me to seek help.

Years of treatment led to graduate school and, eventually, state licensure as a psychotherapist. Throughout the mid-'70s, I worked at a clinic, saw private clients, and taught part-time at the university where I earned my master's degree. Life was good again, and in 1978 my wife and I moved to a small Northern Californian town in the Sierra foothills to start a family and open a private practice. After wrestling so long with my own demons, treating the combat trauma of others was the last thing I would have expected, but in 1980, the official recognition of Post-Traumatic Stress Disorder initiated a nationwide flood of veterans seeking treatment. In our mountain community, my history made me the one they usually turned to. Before long, I had a full caseload of traumatized vets, with new calls coming in each week. I hired another therapist, then another. But the calls kept coming, and little by little, year after year, I found myself struggling just to keep up.

The therapy group met in the basement of the county veterans' building, a long narrow dining hall topped by an eight-foot ceiling, giving it a claustrophobic, bunker-like effect that tended to stimulate the vets' anxiety, mine included. Our little band—dressed mainly in baseball caps and T-shirts, Levis, or baggy shorts—formed a tiny circle in one corner, near the only door leading outside (an "exit strategy" insisted on by the vets at the first meeting). After each man checked in that night, I reminded the guys I'd be in Southeast Asia for the next three weeks, so another therapist would be subbing. Then, as always, I asked if anyone had unfinished business from last group.

Big Harold immediately started in, rekindling an unresolved issue that clearly had the interest of the ten men suddenly leaning in around the circle. "I still don't get it," he drawled, shifting his bulbous torso so slowly it seemed to move in waves, the hairy eye of his navel peering out beneath a ragged black T-shirt. Pausing, Harold regarded me dubiously as his ham-hock fingers thoughtfully stroked the wispy blond hairs decorating a triple-fleshed chin. He seemed to be considering his words carefully.

"*We* supposed to be the crazy ones, Doc," he finally said, motioning to the haggard middle-aged faces around the circle. "And here, *you* the fruitcake, nutty enough to be going back to Vietnam." The last word lingered in the air like spent smoke, releasing vapor trails of memory linking all the vets present. Harold leaned forward, staring at me through puffy, squinted eyes. "Why is that, I wonder?"

He hadn't been south of the Mason-Dixon Line in twenty years, yet Harold still spoke in a fluid, lilting cadence soft as a Georgia peach. But his tone was challenging.

It was a difficult question to answer because I wasn't sure myself. I tried telling him I had never really met the Vietnamese. My combat tour had been spent fighting the North Vietnamese Army in the vast Tay Ninh jungle, far from any settlements. For that reason, something always seemed missing from my war experience. Vietnam had turned my life inside out, I said, and after so many years of processing the combat trauma of American vets, I needed to meet the people of that country to feel complete.

The skeptical look in his eyes told me he wasn't buying. Harold had logged two tours slogging through the hamlets of the Mekong Delta. Sporting scars on both his body and mind, he *had* met the Vietnamese, and he considered himself no richer for the privilege.

Hemming and hawing, I tried another approach. I told the group I wanted to test all the years of therapy and verify the emotional healing I needed to believe was real and not just a smoke screen masking hidden fault lines that had disrupted my life in the past. This sounded good, I thought, perhaps even inspirational. But the incredulous stares of the group made it clear that *nobody* was buying this one.

"Hell, go to LA," called out Roger, a commercial logger, who always dressed in razor-crisp khakis and was the only Republican in the group. "It's just as weird and you save the expense."

I then did something that's not always the wisest move for a shrink. I told the truth. "What can I say, guys?" I asked them. "My shit's weaker than a dead puppy, and I really don't know what to do about it. Call it a midlife crisis, but the fact is I'm losing the battle with my chronic pain, and the VA just gave me a 30 percent disability rating for vision loss. I'm scared, guys, and to be honest, I'm fucking pissed. And if you want me to be *really* honest, I'm blowing it at home and have created a goddamn crisis in my marriage." The faces looking back at me were stunned, and I felt a stab of guilt for having obliterated even the appearance of a professional boundary.

"Hey, not to worry," I assured them. "All I'm telling you is that I need a change of scenery to get away and work things out in my head."

The group remained perfectly quiet after I spoke. Such silence was a rare, usually uncomfortable experience for this group of traumatized men, and I thought that maybe I had reached them at a deep level. But then I saw Big Harold jerking in disbelief, his meaty whiskered lips slapping against themselves as he tried to voice a realization so horrible it was screaming through his eyes. "I . . . do . . . not . . . fuckin' . . . believe . . . this," he finally whispered through gritted teeth. "People!" Harold cried out, flinging a fleshy arm toward his fellow vets, "Don't ya see? Doc's goin' to Nam for 'R & R.'"

My decision to return had been made abruptly. Nine years into combat therapy work, I was sick to death of the daily war stories recounting atrocities of every sort imaginable; stories describing unbearable afflictions perpetrated on—and by—the vets I was treating. Stories all too like my own. I thought I had resolved my Vietnam issues, but the continuous inrush of combat vets made the war—and the land in which it was fought—as much a part of my life as it had ever been. A medic in Nam, I obviously still had a need to save wounded grunts, and within a year the intensity of this effort began eclipsing everything else in my life. My own PTSD issues had clearly gotten triggered, and this fact, along with the ongoing stress of running the therapy program, gradually turned me into a snarling recluse at home. Several years of this had done as much damage to our family as an enemy incursion. And I was too caught up in my mission to see any way out.

Then, in the mid-'90s, after President Clinton lifted the trade embargo against our old enemy, the news media began crackling with reports of a "New Vietnam." Our former nemesis, they said, had become a land of civil reform and rising economic opportunity, whose people had overcome the shackles of the past to embrace a future based not on armed conflict, but prosperity and peace. Caught up in the multifaceted crisis of my life, this message of hope was just what I needed to hear. Like many vets before and since, I decided to see for myself.

Ten days into the trip, I was duly impressed. I spent a few days floundering around the overcrowded commercialism of Ho Chi Minh City. Negotiating the teeming crowds of this former capital quickly became overwhelming, however, so I caught a flight north to Danang, and then rode a bus south to the ancient—and, by Vietnamese standards, wealthy—port city of Hoi An, in coastal Quang Nam Province.

Here I found the Vietnam I had been seeking. It was a dream come true, for, Big Harold's skepticism notwithstanding, I really did need to meet the people the war had estranged me from twenty-seven years earlier. And Hoi An was the perfect venue for this long overdue introduction. For a week, I wandered along rustic, clean-swept streets talking to friendly shop owners and admiring fine regional artwork; exploring the architectural wonders left centuries earlier by Portuguese, Dutch, and Japanese traders; relaxing for hours at the pristine beach before enjoying sumptuous two-dollar dinners at the cafés nestled along the Thu Bon River. It was an idyllic setting, one that represented the "New Vietnam" very well, I thought. Clearly, the news reports had been correct.

One day, however, while resting at a roadside Buddhist shrine, I met a saffron-robed monk who inquired about my impressions of his country. We had taken tea and been stumbling contentedly through our language barrier for nearly a half hour, but on hearing my effusive praise of Vietnam's unfettered progress, this previously sedate monk's English became so broken I could not ascertain the cause of his agitation. I finally understood that he wanted me to visit Peace Village, a rural medical clinic just south of Danang. His intention seemed to be helpful, so I quickly agreed.

To arrange transportation, I sought out my Vietnamese friend and guide, Sergeant Loc, and we agreed to meet me after lunch the following day. Loc is a former South Vietnamese soldier who spent four years in a jungle "reeducation camp" for aiding the Americans during the war. We met on my first afternoon in Hoi An, as I left the mock-colonial grounds of the state-run Hoi An Hotel, where Loc was trolling for tourists. As I strolled onto the sidewalk, a chubby little Buddha guy rose from where he squatted beside his motorcycle. He smiled and greeted me, explaining that he had worked with the Americans and spoke "much good English," so would I please hire him to show me the city? We got on immediately, and from that moment on, he became my daily companion and interpreter, steering me through the crowded blur of Vietnam on his motorcycle, explaining Vietnamese customs and mediating my frequent interchanges with the local community.

On the day after I met the monk, Loc and I set out in the mid-afternoon. Even in Hoi An, crowds are ubiquitous, rolling in and out of the countryside like the tide of a great sea; and on that hot afternoon the bustling two-lane roadway was busy with travelers—some in cars, many on foot, but most on motorcycles like ours. Soon we were whizzing through an interwoven scene of shops and small family homes interspersed with rice paddies, ponds, the rare industrial unit, and many side roads leading to rural hamlets. Leaning back, I took it all in, noting how congested the road grew as we approached Danang.

The bike's engine noise had lulled me into a dreamy stupor, so I gasped in surprise when we suddenly veered right through twin iron gates and were greeted by a spacious green hillside, topped by a modest white building. The contrast with the crowded highway could not have been more dramatic. Loc downshifted, and we cruised up the long winding driveway.

———

Peace Village turned out to be a small, single-story building the size of an American ranch house. On a plaque beside the front door, we read that the clinic had been founded by Le Ly Hayslip, the Vietnamese peasant whose story was told by Oliver Stone in the movie *Heaven and Earth*. Le Ly's rural village had been decimated in the fighting that enveloped the countryside around Danang, and she eventually married an American engineer and came to the U.S. before the war ended. Recognizing her good fortune, she returned a few years later to bring healing to her battered land.

Entering the building, we found ourselves in a small foyer with an open doorway off to one side. I peeked in, and an elderly gentleman leaped up from behind a small wooden desk, knocking over his chair. He had obviously been dozing. Rushing out to greet us, he swooped in on me as if meeting an old friend. Gripping my hand in both of his, he spoke through Loc, explaining to me in rapid-fire Vietnamese that he was director of the clinic. An English-speaking doctor would be back soon, he said. After several more handshakes and bows, the director went back to his desk, and I was invited to explore on my own while Loc visited relatives in Danang.

It had been a relaxing day, and my mood was as light as the sunshine filtering into the empty halls. Despite its impressive architecture and museums, the smoggy overcrowdedness of Ho Chi Minh City had repelled me. Hoi An's rural tranquility provided an oasis of relief, and the discovery of a "Peace Village" now warmed my heart beyond measure. I marveled again at the "New Vietnam" as I strolled past a room full of sewing machines used to train women for gainful employment; turned one corner and discovered a locked medicine cabinet crammed with western pharmaceuticals; turned another and found a second cabinet filled with indigenous herbs and native remedies.

Reaching a back hall, I wandered past a washroom and kitchen area, then came to the only closed door I had found. The director had said I could look anywhere, and since every other door in the clinic was open, my curiosity was aroused. Turning the knob, I peered in. The room was clouded in late afternoon shadow. One small rectangular window cast a frail light over the cluttered contents: two large metal fans, scattered boxes of medical supplies, a dusty wooden desk. As my eyes adjusted to the dimness, I also noticed an irregularly shaped pile of . . . something . . . at the rear of the room.

Sliding my hand along the wall, I switched on the overhead light and was startled to discover a large pile of artificial legs stacked like firewood along the back wall.

Breathlessly, I entered the room. The pile of legs was about three-feet high, toes stretched outward, each limb milky white and made of a thin plastic that marked it as decidedly inferior to the sturdy high-tech prostheses used by some of my vets back home. I did a quick tally, and counted nearly a hundred legs. All had Vietnamese lettering scribbled along the shin. My eyes tore into the foreign scrawl, trying, irrationally, to unlock the mystery, but the writing, like the legs themselves, was inexplicable. For some time, I simply stood there, numb and perplexed, fondling the bizarre artifacts and wondering why they were there.

I finally backed out of the room in search of someone to explain. At the front office, I encountered the English-speaking doctor the director had mentioned. He was a young Vietnamese with a shy demeanor. Dressed in a blue smock and wearing black-rimmed eyeglasses, the young man was thin, tight-lipped, and clearly embarrassed by the abrupt intensity of my question. Grasping my right elbow, he quickly ushered me into a small conference room, closed the door, and hurried to the far side of the rectangular table set beneath the room's one small window. He took a seat and, with an elaborate hand gesture, motioned for me to sit across from him.

"Mines," he stated flatly, answering the question I had put to him in the hall. The legs were going to villagers who had lost legs to land mines.

"What?" I exclaimed, somehow not grasping the implication. "Where? How?"

A flicker of annoyance twisted the doctor's face. His eyes darted away, dropping to watch his fingers pick a speck of lint from the blue smock. "Mines left from war," he said casually. "All over countryside. Farmers grow food, children run play—boom. Lose leg."

"My God," I whispered, staggered at the thought of this continued maiming twenty-one years after the war ended. "How many people has this happened to?"

Slowly, his eyes rose to mine. "So many," he whispered, the corners of his sharp young face collapsing to betray its underlying fatigue. "U-nited Na-tions come look," he continued, "find so many people lose legs."

His scribbled in the air with his left index finger, trying to compute the problem I had given him. But here the young man's English failed him. For several moments he struggled to convert his reality to the appropriate English numeral. "No, wait." Reaching down the table, he slid back a pen and sheaf of paper, and wrote very deliberately. "Here, this many."

The paper was a sheet of Vietnamese stationery, thin, roughly textured, and colorless. On it he had printed: "dead–1,100   injure–1,800"

"That many?" I asked incredulously. "Nearly 3,000 have been killed or wounded since the war?"

"No, no!" he barked, shaking his head emphatically. "Not since war. Now! Viet Nam!"

Snatching back the note, he hunched his entire body over it, laboriously spelling out the word y-e-a-r. Peering intensely at his effort, he nodded once, dropped the pen on the table, and jabbed the paper so forcefully it flew in my direction.

"Each year? Three thousand Vietnamese are killed or maimed by mines each year?"

"Yes, yes," the doctor nodded vigorously, snatching the paper again to write: "world–25,000."

His smile was a thin grimace as he arched his left arm slowly upward. "Whole world," he breathed incredulously, gripping me with soft tired eyes as he pointed to the figure. "That many lose legs," jabbing again at the word above.

"Every year?" I asked again, drawing out the sound in disbelief. "Twenty-five thousand people in the world are maimed by land mines each year?"

"Yes!" Satisfied he had been understood, the young doctor's face softened, and his hands came to rest on the table between us. The afternoon light coming in through the screened window had faded, leaving a web of flickering shadows on the wall behind him.

I was stunned, and what came out of my mouth next was a question I have come to regret. "But what, I mean who . . . ?"

He scowled again, but this time his eyes stayed fixed on mine. Slowly, his hands rose to form a loose-fingered bridge below the tightly drawn lips, and he regarded me somberly for several moments. Then he leaned into the space separating us, spreading his palms outward as if releasing the only relevant answer to what I had asked.

"Child not care who. Farmer not care who."

The late afternoon shadows deepened as we lapsed into a meditative silence. But the quietness only intensified the question in my eyes. Finally the doctor spoke again, in a tone devoid of the slightest inflection. "Soldiers put mines," he said. "Soldiers all sides." Gesturing toward the window, "All over countryside."

"Does anyone know how many?"

"Yes, yes." Head bobbing, he reached again for the paper and pen, furiously scratching out his first attempt before completing the figure he held up for me to see: 3,500,000.

"Three and a half million?" I gasped. "There are still three and a half million land mines buried in the Vietnamese countryside?"

"Yes!"

Oddly, the serious young man beamed, then flicked the end of his pen toward me as if rewarding a plodding student. Enunciating very carefully, he dotted the air between us with the pen, "U-nited Na-tions say."

A wave of dank realization suddenly swept over me, and I found myself struggling to grasp the implication of what I had just heard. "But then . . . the war. It . . . it isn't over," I stammered. "The war is still going on."

"Of course," he sighed, shrugging his shoulders in the resigned manner I had come to recognize as being very Vietnamese. The doctor reached again for the paper, shaking his head as he studied the numbers. Crumpling the note, he tossed it into a waste can near the door. "War always go on." Then the young doctor pushed back his chair, rose, and met my eyes one last time. "So many more to lose."

On May 10, 1968, my husband, Sgt. Howard E. Querry, was killed in the jungles of Vietnam. I was twenty-two years old and seven months pregnant.

For the following twenty-five years, I suffered from nightmares, depression, and unresolved grief. In 1990 after a significant loss, I fell into a major depressive episode. For the first time in my life, I lost my will to live.

Because I had a daughter still dependent upon me, I chose to investigate the loss rather than commit suicide. I started therapy, began 12-Step Recovery work for my addictions, and most importantly, started writing.

Writing was the container that could hold my grief. The blank page wanted to hear every last detail.

Since publishing my memoir, *Grief Denied: A Vietnam Widow's Story,* I have been helping others explore their unresolved issues through my work as a Life Coach, an Inspirational Speaker, and a Workshop Leader.

For more information visit:

www.griefdenied.com and www.gutsycoaching.com

Shattered Dream

It's a beautiful Sunday afternoon—Mother's Day, 1968. Spring in the Midwest is sprouting with life and possibility. The peonies are shooting stalks through the rich, black soil in the flowerbeds. After morning mass at St. Joseph's, I am sitting in the shade of the big sycamore in Mom's backyard.

My husband, Howard, has been in Vietnam since March. He thought it would be best for me to stay with my parents while he was gone. Princess, our black German shepherd, is my constant companion. She lies at my feet as I glance through the Sunday paper. I notice wedding announcements, sales, ads, and upcoming movies.

Nestled in the back pages of a remote section of the paper, I spot an article about a battle in Vietnam. I avoid reading about the war, but this article found me. The action described in the article involved Howard's unit—3rd Battalion, 39th Regiment, 9th Infantry Division.

War Refugees Are Flooding into Saigon

... The Command Post is in a Buddhist pagoda, 20 yards
from a tiny Catholic church which serves as the medical
aid station. "They hit us hard all last night with mortars
and rockets," said Maj. Boone. "Two soldiers from Alpha
Company held out during a three-hour attack on a little
bridge across a feeder canal. I don't even know their
names but they are up for the Silver Star. We've been
lucky so far—only four killed and fourteen wounded in
the battalion."

Howard is dead. I know it. I don't know how I know, I just know.
I can't breathe. Tears are coming. I'm trembling inside and out. Mom
comes out into the yard and asks, "What's wrong?"

I show her the article and whisper, "Howard is dead."

———

Three Days Later—May 15, 1968

The potatoes fry in their usual pool of lard, lard rendered from the
hogs my uncles and brothers slaughter every January. Mom stands over
the stove, stirring the potatoes and turning the blood sausage frying in
an adjacent skillet.

Princess greets me after I return from my job at Scott Air Force
Base. My father sits in his favorite chair, watching the evening news
and waiting for dinner to be served.

Something draws me to the front windows. An ugly green sedan
with the words "U.S. Army" printed on the side is parked in front of
the house. Two men in uniform sit inside the car, looking down at
paperwork on their laps.

The room starts spinning, my hearing becomes muffled, reality is
slipping away from me. Princess barks as Mom walks to the front window to see what's causing the commotion.

They're coming to tell me he is dead.

"Please, God, let him be wounded, not dead," I say.

The men continue to sit in the car. Hours seem to pass before they
get out, straighten their uniforms, and head toward my door. I put
Princess in the basement—she doesn't welcome strangers. I come back

to open the door and see the two men standing before me with the same terror in their eyes that I'm feeling inside of me.

"Good evening," they say, as they remove their hats. "We're looking for Pauline Querry."

"That's me."

They look at my protruding abdomen that holds my unborn child and then look at each other in silence that lingers too long.

"Was he wounded or killed? How bad is it?"

More silence. Finally they begin.

"We regret to inform you that your husband, Sergeant Howard E. Querry, was fatally wounded on the afternoon of May 10 by a penetrating missile wound to his right shoulder."

I'm dizzy. I can't think straight.

"Dead? Is he dead?"

They don't answer. They just reread their script as if practicing their lines for a performance they'll give someday.

"We regret to inform you . . ."

The room is spinning. I can't think, I can't hear anything. I'm going to faint. Alone . . . I must be alone to sort this out. Leave me alone.

Instead, I sit politely as they inform me of the details . . . funeral . . . remains . . . escort . . . military cemetery . . . medals.

Finally they gather their papers and leave. I politely show them to the door. My parents are hysterical. My dad weeps, my mom trembles. No sound is coming out —her whole body is shaking in upheaval.

After retrieving the dog, I stagger to my room and shut the door. I throw myself on the bed, gasping for air. My heart races and pounds. My unborn baby starts kicking and squirming. I hold my dog with one hand, my baby with the other, and I sob. I'm shattered, blown to pieces. It can't be true!

No medics come, no helicopters fly me away to an emergency room. I struggle to save myself but I cannot. I die.

Half an hour later, a ghost of my former self gets up off the bed and begins planning Howard's funeral.

Mom calls relatives. People come over to console me. I just want to be alone. I just want to be alone.

LE MINH KHUE

During the American War, I served in the Youth Volunteer Brigades working on the Ho Chi Minh Trails. Later I became a war correspondent. I was in the war from 1966 until its end in 1975, serving on some of the most dangerous battlefields. I've written eleven short story collections and novels, and I'm currently chief fiction editor of the Vietnam Writers Association Publishing House, and a consulting editor of Curbstone's *Voices from Vietnam* series. Many of my stories and books are concerned with culture, environmental degradation, and human kindness, and in "Fragile as a Sunray" the dream of healing some of the wounds war left in my country.

Fragile as a Sunray

Translated by Bac Hoai Tran and Dana Sachs

For years, I didn't understand why, at certain moments of leisure, my mother seems sad. Our family is rather well-off. My parents run a private clinic that has plenty of patients. I am studying medicine and sometimes go home to help them in the clinic with diagnosis and treatment. My younger brother and I are devoted to our parents. My brother has even won some prizes at the math competitions for high school students.

But why is my mother still so sad?

She is just over forty and very beautiful, but her eyes are filled with sadness. She mixes with many people every day. Occasionally, she gets angry. If she is cheated out of a bit of money, she'll cry. And she also argues with the neighbors. She's no different from anyone else. But I still didn't understand what makes her so sad. I tried to find out and one day I did. And then I learned that even ordinary people have secrets. The heart is never at peace.

———

Late one afternoon, a military ambulance pulled off the road onto a footpath, preparing to wait until dusk to cross the pass. The doctor and two male nurses strung their hammocks alongside those of a unit headed south and fell asleep immediately. The woman with them, who looked like any other well-educated female soldier, enjoyed roaming a bit and so she went down to a shallow section of the stream, where one could wade through water that came up only to the ankles. On this side of the stream a few soldiers were washing up. On the other side a scene appeared to her that seemed extraordinary to a female soldier making her first visit to the front. Truly extraordinary. Blood rushed to her head. On the patch of pebble-covered shore sat about a dozen men wearing camouflage fatigues, each eating from a ration box.

"These are the prisoners from the battle of Route Nine," the soldier standing next to her explained.

She sat down on a rock on this side of the stream, and pulled out a towel and slowly washed it. The most extraordinary thing about this moment, the first moment she had ever seen the enemy, was that the only emotion she felt was curiosity. Most of the prisoners were busy eating and there was nothing extraordinary about those faces. Except for one. He was still very young, not much older than twenty. He had a strong build, but not the kind that comes from working in the fields. He looked more like an athlete. All of his features were symmetrical and harmonious. He was holding his ration box in his hand without eating and staring sadly into space. She'd never seen a face like that in her life. That was the face she imagined when she read novels. While still at home, she would linger in bed under the mosquito net in the mornings, listening to the sounds outside and daydreaming until her mother called her. During those moments, she often imagined a face like that one. It was impossible to separate the features on that face to describe it, impossible to talk about it, but she had dreamed of spending her life with a man with a face like that.

Her heart pounded in her chest and her arms and legs suddenly went icy. While her hands kept washing the towel, her eyes were fixed on the scene across the narrow stream. The enemy soldier abandoned his despondent stare, looked down at the ration box, then, looking up again, suddenly noticed her. Two pairs of eyes met. During that brief moment, a terrible lightning struck her "wanderer's" soul. *Wanderer* was the word her worried mother always used to describe her.

"You won't be lucky in life," her mother used to say.

Startled and guilty, she jumped up. On the other side of the stream, the enemy soldier did the same thing, as if he, too, were shocked. The gesture caused one of the guards to abandon the conversation he and the other guards were having and to point the barrel of his gun at the prisoner's temple, forcing him to sit down. But his gaze still burned her. She walked dazed and unsteady back to the ambulance, pulled out her hammock, strung it between the trees, and climbed into it. Her heart rebelled, but fear overwhelmed her. How could she allow herself to think such thoughts? He was the enemy.

She lay in the hammock for most of the afternoon. Finally, the senior doctor got up and hurried them along, saying, "Eat and finish your washing; at dusk we'll get going."

But she continued to drift along in indescribable sadness. Like that. Like that. The sounds of conversation penetrated her sorrow. The voice of a stranger asked, "Are you a doctor, comrade?"

"Yes, I am," she heard the doctor reply.

"Can you please help us? A soldier is running a fever from a swollen wound and tonight we have to march. Can you help him so that he can walk?"

"Is he a prisoner?"

"Yes, just captured."

"Okay, I'll come right over."

She sat up immediately, her gaze fixed on the doctor. He looked at her. "Ah yes, please come with me and bring the medical kit," he said.

It was him. His eyes were clear and innocent, and his face was peaceful. It was a face that existed outside the war. Her fear of herself increased when she dared to look into the face of this enemy officer, but she did so anyway, unable to turn away. With the afternoon sunlight piercing the branches of the trees, and the guns momentarily silenced, the war seemed more cruel, embodied in the contrast between the cold features of the guard and the hopeless face of the prisoner. She watched carefully as the doctor examined the wound in the prisoner's thigh. He frowned when he saw the infection.

She washed the wound with alcohol and cotton wool. She could hear the prisoner clenching his teeth, but he didn't cry out. When the doctor turned away to let the guard light his cigarette, she spoke softly to the prisoner.

"Try to bear it!"

"Do you know where they will take us?"

"No. I wish I did."

"I'm a doctor also," he told her.

"Really? How did you end up here?"

"War knocks on every door. I tried to avoid it but I couldn't."

"I know."

"Can you help me?"

The doctor and the guard turned back around.

"Are you done yet?" the doctor asked.

"Yes. I gave him an injection," she said, trying to avoid the burning gaze of the prisoner. It wasn't a gaze of fear. Absolutely not. And it wasn't a gaze of pain or begging. It was a clear gaze of amazement that in this life he had discovered a person who could have belonged to him, who could have understood him, who could have spent her life with him. And that there should be no chasm, no division between people.

With compassion, the doctor asked the prisoner, "Are you able to walk?"

As if a certain hidden strength suddenly woke and pushed against his back, the prisoner stood up, his face white with the pain and determination.

She knew that it was thanks to her presence. War could not cut the loving thread that linked the hearts of two people. But how would fate treat him, with his wounded leg and his resolution? Carrying the medical kit, she followed the old doctor back across the stream. The group of prisoners was preparing to set off and the steely voices of the guards rose around them. Surreptitiously, the prisoner raised a hand toward her. His face was full of sorrow and despair and a hope that there would be something for them in the future.

Now, twenty years have passed and many barriers have been torn down. And yet her hope has never been fulfilled. If only they could meet again, even for a minute.

———

During those moments when my mother isn't busy earning a living, she is sad. Everybody has a secret, a sorrow, a memory.

I believe that my mother has been able to live until now because of such a secret, such a sorrow, such a desire.

JADE LEE

From my earliest memory, I was told what my duties and responsibilities to my family and my race were as a first-generation Chinese girl learning English in 1940s San Francisco Chinatown. The concepts of responsibility and duty were difficult for me to understand, though I did get that they were important and something I had to do, though I wasn't sure why. As I was growing up, I faced sexual abuse, battering, and cultural and religious conflicts. I was usually told that the sexual abuse and beatings were my fault for something that was intrinsically wrong or "bad" about me, so I focused on myself to avoid being "bad."

The events described in "Beating" marked a major change in my thinking and perception of my place in the world. When I saw the blood on the back of my grandmother's bathrobe, I felt responsible for her pain, and from that time took on the responsibility for the well-being of the people I loved and, for many years later on, for the world.

It took several years of counseling, support groups, and "talk story" for me to be able to come to terms with the pain of my childhood. As a counselor and an activist I became comfortable speaking of the abuses in my childhood without shame or fear. A close comrade took me to the Veteran's Writers' group, led by Maxine Hong Kingston. "Beating" was the second thing I attempted to write after joining the group. After reading it and getting feedback from the group, I was able to see myself as a veteran of domestic wars.

Movie Song

First verse:

We must hate and never walk together
We must not share a cup of tea
We must be angry at each other
I must hate him, he must hate me
Said his father and my mother
It's our family's history

Chorus:

This tradition of bitterness and hate
Must it be our fate?
This dance of fear and violence
No longer makes much sense
Can we change this dance?
Can we take the chance?

Second verse:

Throughout our generations
We kept creating wars
Can peace be our creation?
Can we find it in our cores?
We're another generation
Together we must soar

Chorus:

This tradition of bitterness and hate
Must not be our fate
This dance of fear and violence
No longer makes much sense
We must change this dance
We must take the chance

Movie Song II

We met in battle forever ago
Families on different sides
You and I, throughout time's flow
Blindly fighting through time's tides
I saw myself reflected in your eyes
Senseless anger, fury, hate
We'd fought so long that we forgot the whys
How did we create this fate?
Are we not more than senseless violence?

Can we choose to stop this fight?
Can we lift this fog, so fiery and dense?
Aren't we more than angry might?

Come, let us have a cup of tea
Let us share a bowl of rice
Look in my eyes and see just me
Let me see in you what's nice
Past the anger and past the hate
Beyond the past, through the fog
Let us find a different fate
We'll create our epilogue
Let me touch you, feel your heartbeat

Beating

The moon was early and almost full. My step-grandmother, with her calf-length hair braided into a crown on her head, looked like a tall figure in an ancient painting. She stood in her turquoise chenille bathrobe, watering the strawberry patch. "Are you ready for bed?" she asked.

"Yes, Ngin Ma, and I remembered to wash the back of my neck, too. I'm going to say 'night to Grandpa Jack," I said, trying to sound normal. She smiled and turned her attention back to the strawberry patch. I stopped calling him Ngin Pa almost two years before. She had made several attempts to find out why, but let it go when I refused to explain my reasons.

As I walked the fifty yards from the house to the trailer, everything seemed normal. There was the sound of crickets, an occasional frog, the wonderful clean fragrance of the earth, and the faint thin strip of dusk light on the horizon. I imagined myself wrapped in moonlight, and repeated over and over a mantra, "Moon Lady, please keep me strong, Moon Lady, please keep me strong." A few steps away from the trailer I stopped. I made the Catholic sign of the cross, bowed to the Christian God and his Concubine, bowed to their Son, bowed to Confucius, Buddha, Kwan Yin, the Eight Immortals, Shiva, Kali, Thor, and the Moon Lady. I took a deep breath, squared my shoulders, walked to the door, knocked, and called out, "Grandpa Jack, may I please come in?"

When he answered, I gathered up all my courage and opened the door. There was a dim overhead light, making the single eight-by-fourteen-foot room look dingy and worn. At the end of the trailer to my left was an unmade built-in bed with a white enameled chamber pot on the floor beside it. To the right of the bed, facing me was a short counter with a water pail, washbasin, kerosene stove, and an open bottle of red wine on it. Directly in front of me was a maroon padded storage bench where Grandpa Jack was sitting, removing his shoes. "Came to kiss me goodnight?" he asked, opening his arms.

I stood with my hand on the door handle and said, my breath and my words rushing out, "No, Grandpa Jack. I came to say 'night and to tell you I don't want you to do that stuff to me anymore."

He leaned back, folded his arms, crossed his legs, and asked in a quiet yet threatening way, "What stuff?" I was startled. I knew he knew what I was talking about, and that he was playing some kind of game I didn't understand. It confused me. I wanted to look away from him to figure out what to do. But I forced myself to look directly into his eyes and to stand very straight and still.

"You know what I'm talking about. I don't want you to put your hand on my 'shee-shee' and I want you to quit trying to put your thing in my mouth." I could feel my face warming and my hand on the door began to tremble. I tried not to look defiant, tried to keep my face expressionless.

He tilted his head and leaned forward, stretching his arms out to me as if he were pleading. I could tell it was a pose and some of my fear dissipated as I began to get angry. Not wanting to get in trouble for being angry, I tried to control my anger, but it kept on growing as he said in a whining voice, "But you like it, Baby Doll. I only do it for *you,* because I love you."

"I already told you I don't like it. I hate it. I'm not a doll and I'm not a baby. I'm six years old," I said, stamping my foot. "I want you to stop. Leave me alone!"

"Don't say that, you don't mean it. You don't really want me to stop. You always tell me you like it."

"'Cuz you beat me up if I don't say it." I was crying, knowing that he wasn't going to leave me alone, and getting angrier. I was confused.

My plan to be very grown up and tell him simply and calmly what I wanted and to get him to agree wasn't working. I was reduced to a helpless little girl again. Through my tears and runny nose I shouted, "I want you to stop. Leave me alone. If you don't, I'll tell on you, I'll tell on you, I'll tell Ngin Ma," and opened the door to leave.

Before I could get out the door, he grabbed my sleeve and said in a menacing voice, "You'll do no such thing, Baby Doll. First of all, she won't believe you. I'm her husband, and she'll believe me. Second, if you say a word to her, I'll beat you within an inch of your life. You'll hurt so bad you'll wish you were dead!"

"You already did that last year, Grandpa Jack. Why would she believe you? You're not even Chinese. You're just an ignorant white barbarian!" I was so frightened and angry that I was just reacting, the words coming from some deep raging place hidden inside me. "You're so ignorant all you can do is hurt little girls, you ignorant barbarian!" I jeered, scared, knowing it was dangerous but unable to stop. "You're so ignorant you're just using Ngin Ma for a meal ticket." I didn't know what a meal ticket was. I had heard other family members say it. "You're so ignorant that we live in the house and you have to stay in the trailer, just like a doghouse, out here with all the ducks and the chickens. Even the dog gets to live in the house with us!"

"You goddamned little bitch, I'll kill you!"

"You said you love me, how can you kill me?" I screamed, jerking my arm free and running out the door.

"I'll show you how, you smart-assed little bitch!" he yelled, taking his belt off.

Running as fast as I could, I was sobbing and crying out, "Help me, Moon Lady, he's mad and he's going to whip me again. Moon Lady, please, Moon Lady, please help me!" I ran on and on and began to think I might get away when I was halfway to the house. Then I felt the first lash of his belt on my right shoulder, propelling me forward faster than my legs could carry me. I stumbled, caught my balance and heard the next strike, thwack! Then the next, thwack! The sudden fiery pain of the lashes surprised me and my place of rage screamed out, "Kali! Thor! Get him! Get the *fon gwei,* get the *fon gwei!*"

Nearing the end of the strawberry patch, I saw my grandmother with her robe hiked up almost to her knees, running through the strawberries toward me. I ran through the patch, still sobbing, screaming my rage and my commands to Kali and Thor until I reached her, throwing my arms around her. She jerked my arms away, spun me around so my back was to her, shoved me down into a crouch and covered me with her body. She made comforting noises, holding me tightly, and once again I was a helpless little girl without the power of my anger to command the deities. In its place was incoherent, overwhelming fear and terror.

I could hear the thwack! thwack! as Grandpa Jack whipped us, and his voice, filled with fury, "I'll kill you, kill you, smart-assed little bitch! Kill you, kill you, kill you, kill you!" Some of the blows made my grandmother grunt, and shoved her body into mine. It was as if he were trying to cut through her to get at me. When I realized that, a small part of my mind seemed to clear, and I became afraid for her.

I struggled, trying to get away, screaming, "Lemme go, lemme go, Ngin Ma. He'll kill you. He wants to kill me, not you. Let me go. He'll leave you alone, lemme go!" She just held me tighter, until a long time later, the blows stopped. We stood up. Grandpa Jack, with one shoe on, was calmly walking back to the trailer, the belt hanging from his hand. We watched him and I began to get angry again. "Ignorant white—"

My grandmother's hand was instantly over my mouth as she hissed at me, "Enough!" Then she slowly walked to the tap to turn off the water, and in the moonlight I saw the dark, irregular lines of blood on her bathrobe. I stood among the crushed and torn strawberry plants that she had lovingly tended, staring at her.

Belief that my actions caused that blood, guilt, shame, and horror filled my entire six-year-old being. I had tried to be very grown up to get what I wanted, and now someone I loved was injured and bleeding. I thought then that I understood, truly understood for the first time how my actions could cause pain for someone else. Devastated and with great regret, I accepted another harsh lesson in life as Ngin Ma took my hand and we walked to the house to tend our wounds.

In the kitchen, I sat on a stool as Ngin Ma gently rubbed salve on my back, saying nothing to me. I tried to be brave but wasn't able to keep some cries of pain and sobs from escaping. She was silent until she was done, then handed me the fragrant Chinese container. I set it on the old wooden table and got up and slipped on the clean shirt she handed me. She took off her robe and placed it, along with the dress I had worn, into the kitchen sink that was filled with cold water.

She sat on the stool, forearms resting on her thighs, staring at the gray concrete floor, waiting for me to rub salve on her wounds. I dipped two fingers into the red-and-yellow tin and stood staring at her back, afraid to touch her. There were many swollen and red welts, two to five inches long, all over her back. Most of them were near her shoulders and some were still bleeding. "*Fi nay uh,* get started," she said. I forced myself to start, trying to be gentle, barely touching her. She said nothing, continuing to stare at the floor. Sometimes she flinched. Sometimes I could hear a sharp, indrawn hiss with the flinch. Silent tears ran down my face. When I was finished, she said, "Tomorrow we'll wash our backs and do this again."

After washing our hands and faces in the bathroom, we sat at the table in the kitchen. We sipped hot green tea, with some herbs she added to it, in silence. After a while she asked me, "Mon Lai, why was he so mad?" I was too ashamed to tell her. I had made only one attempt to tell someone when I was almost five years old. My parents got angry, my stepfather said I had a wild imagination, and my mother asked how I could say such awful things about someone in our family. I didn't know what an imagination was, but thought it must be something awful if it was wild.

I was afraid to tell Ngin Ma, so I said, "Maybe because he was drinking?" He drank whiskey or wine often and frequently became angry while drinking. I didn't want to lie to her, but was more fearful of telling her the truth. "I'm sorry, Ngin Ma. I didn't know he'd get so mad that he'd whip you, too. I didn't even think you'd get hurt. I thought he was just mad at me and wanted to kill me. Oh, Ngin Ma, I won't let him whip you again. The next time he gets mad I won't run away from him. I'll try to stay away from him if I'm alone, if I know he's been drinking. I'm so sorry, I don't want him to ever hurt you . . ."

"Ah Lai, Ah Lai, stop crying. You don't have to protect me." She wiped my tears, moved me to the stool next to her, and gently put her arms around me. "He won't whip you again. I can't watch him all the time, so I'm going to send you back to your Mama. You will stay close to me until our backs are healed, then I'll have the neighbors take you

to the bus. We'll go into town in a couple days so I can call your Mama."
I was still crying. She lifted my chin and looked into my eyes for a long
time. She sighed and said, "Ah Lai, you are such a little girl to have
such big secrets. You wouldn't tell me what happened last year when
he whipped you so badly. You even tried to pretend that you weren't
hurt, and I know you're not telling me what really happened tonight.
I know you won't tell me, no matter what I say. I want to help you,
but I can't if I don't know what's going on." She sighed again and let
go of my chin.

I knew she meant what she said, and I almost told her what had happened, but I couldn't. I was still too ashamed and afraid and didn't
believe that anyone could really help me. I was torn between wanting
to confide in her and my fear and shame. I cried harder. She said, "Don't
worry, Ah Lai, I won't try to force you to tell me." She rocked me and
kept saying so softly that I almost couldn't hear her, "Ah Lai Ah, *mo
lok sui, mo lok sui.*" Ngin Ma continued to rock me, comforting me
and softly telling me not to cry, as I sobbed and was once again just a
little girl.

MICHAEL LITLE

Two American wars bookend the middle passage of my life and the lives of the writers alongside me in the pages of this book. While my father was leading a battalion of helicopters in Viet Nam, I quit military service for good reason.

Let me begin at the beginning. In the spring of 1944, I crouched in my mother's belly. At twenty-one years, my father was the trainer of bomber pilots until the U.S. Army Air Force put him on the short list of pilots to drop the atom bomb. I thank the infinite wisdom of the Pentagon that he was passed over as too young for the job.

I was born just as World War II ended. Civilian life didn't suit my folks, so they reenlisted in the new aviation branch of the Army and got sent to Austria in 1949. During the fifties and sixties, I traveled as one of three dependents from Austria to Fort Bragg, Japan to Fort Rucker, France to Fort Leavenworth. My father is credited for his role in creating the helicopter-mounted machine gun. In 1965 to 1966, when my father joined the 1st Air Cav as a helicopter battalion commander, I joined ROTC at Dartmouth College. I twice refused military service: once with courage, once with cunning. After the birth of two sons, I began teaching college and making movies. In 2003, I went home to Fort Hood. Texas, to take care of my father in his last round with Parkinson's disease just as the liberation of Iraq turned sour. While on errands, I began to interview the families of soldiers. (Readers can use Google to find the community blog HomefrontBulletin and watch these interviews.)

Over forty years, shame and guilt have circled over my manhood like birds of prey. Shame that I betrayed my father, guilt that good men went to war in my place. This is the account of how, watching over my father's dying while the American War in Iraq turns sour, I redeem myself.

Gatesville

War is a matter of vital importance to the state;
the province of life or death; the road
to survival or ruin ... appraise it in terms
of the five fundamental factors ...
the first of these is moral influence ...
that which causes the people to be in harmony
with their leaders, so that they will accompany
them in life and unto death.

—SUN TZU

My father apologizes for the diminished volume of his voice and raises his glass to the family whose airfares he has paid to gather round him. He waits until all of us have our glasses aloft and says, "I have Parkinson's disease." Sitting at his left side I see the tremors rippling the dark wine. "I can expect another dozen good years."

Ten years pass. He handles the long descent like a mail pilot with a pinhole leak in his tank. Soar the uplifts, dive through the downdrafts, cross the mountains at the pass.

I visit during opening of the Iraq war. We watch the statue of Saddam Hussein being pulled down. With the remote, Dad turns off the TV and hands me a book to read from the Hemlock Society. An assisted suicide is not that difficult. You just take the plastic bag off the beloved's head before the coroner shows up. "An option," he says without winking. He wipes ice cream from his lips and pops an Oreo cookie.

I can't tell how serious he is about this option. The coordination of the muscles in the face, as well as in the body, is disrupted—more or less at random—by the neurological disease.

Thirteen months of the Iraq war pass before my mother calls me. "You have to come home. I can't handle your father."

The count of the American dead has reached 850. Enemy casualties are estimated at 35,000. After the initial victory, a captured munitions dump, left unguarded, was raided by the insurgents.

As I fly from California to Texas, childhood memories float through my mind. The earliest is of my mother squeezing me tight inside an open cockpit as her hair whips my face and the engine roars ... aboard a military transport ship on our way to Austria, I smell our hunting dog's urine on the gray marine paint . . . driving along a narrow road in the Alps, sheep block the road, a boy in lederhosen glares at me over the convertible's chrome and canvas.

Mom leads me to their bedroom where Dad sleeps, his hands darting under the sheet like mice. The strong nose rises from his face, a mountain peak over a wrinkled desert. I remember him clipping my toenails.

His eyes open, "Hello, son." He smiles the full smile of waking from a good dream.

I see that unlike on the last visit, his facial muscles are operational. He drags his skinny legs over the side of the bed and indicates for me to fetch a cane. I pick the wooden one. He levers himself up on his own. He says, "This is my Kentucky cane." His spunk is back. My fears fly away, buzzards off a road kill.

Dad hasn't been in the pool since last summer. Thirty feet of rough stonework has become a barrier. He refuses a walker, but he'll consider the wheelchair. I see a way to make myself useful; I'll make a ramp. At the lumberyard, I spot a white-haired woman in cowboy boots loading a church van. I put on my father's hunting cap, and ask what they're up to.

"Care packages."

"For the troops?"

"Yep."

The van is crammed with boxes from the hardware store.

"I'm interviewing people about the war. Can I ask you some questions?"

She and the hardware store owner look at one another. I think they smell a liberal.

"Some of the interviews air on the satellite."

"What channel?" the guy asks.

"Free Speech TV, 9415."

"Never heard of it," the gal says, "and we're too busy."

I set up the power saw so he can watch me work through the patio door. A long diagonal rip turns an eight-foot two-by-six into a pair of stringers for a ramp.

"Dad, are you willing to try the new chair? Maybe go for a swim?"

He shoots a baleful glance at the hated wheelchair. "Not today."

"He gets cold easily," Mom says, softening the blow to my exuberance. "We'll leave the pool heater on overnight and try tomorrow."

After breakfast the next day the central Texas sun is already hot. I approach his reclining chair. "Your cane, Sir. We're going swimming."

A faint smile passes over his lips. "Why not?"

With long windup then a sudden lift, he rises like a helicopter. We get to the door with a cane. He agrees to transfer into the chair. The first ramp works fine, but the next is narrow, and I skid off onto the lawn, nearly dumping him. "Watch it!"

The scolding makes me smile. Soon we arrive at the edge of the pool right under the perch of a mockingbird. With a skinny white foot, he tests the bathtub-warm, blue-green water. Suddenly he's eager to get in. He forgets he's wearing a full-length leisure suit. It billows up around him. The wooden cane floats sideways. He dances on his toes. His eyes open wide, his cheeks pull back in a madman's grin. I push the yellow floating ball toward him. Whack! He swings the cane. Swat! I scoot the ball back. His eyes narrow, his lips purse. Whack! The ball rolls over the water toward me. His hits are wild, my pitches are careful. He's the son, I'm the father.

My mother joins us. Her swimsuit is black and her hair is silver. I cannot remember her so radiant. She swims around the two of us. She circles her revived husband and her son. I remember a sedge-cut photo of me at five crying in my father's arms, learning to swim in an alpine lake.

———

Mom wakes me. "Your father's packed again."

I've never seen her out of control like this, weeping. "He says he's going somewhere. He put his socks and toothbrush into his briefcase."

Dad sits at the bed's edge, hair wild, shoulders pinned back, one hand gripping a leather briefcase. He looks at my mother, then at me. "Keep that woman away."

I sit down close. "Where we headed?"

"Don't know. Just going."

"OK then. I'll carry the briefcase."

I help him up. Out the bedroom door, our first choice: hallway left or hallway right. He nods left and off we shuffle. His breath is fast, exhausted from the packing. It's a dark corridor. We reach the guest room, where he collapses into the spare bed.

The next day he has his wits back.

"You're going to interview a civilian about this war, and your mother's going to the PX. Two of us will be gone. How many are left? Your brother and the two dogs?"

"That's right," I say.

"Well, I'll be sure not to put any responsibility on the four-legged critters."

———

I pass a guy digging a trench alongside a bank who agrees to be interviewed if he can sit in the boss's truck with its red, white, and blue sign: "Patriot Pest Control."

"Have you decided how you'll vote?"

"I'm not voting for Bush. Maybe Kerry."

He tells me he's out a year and a half now, but some of his buddies are in Iraq.

"What do you think about the war?"

"They're killing us left and right."

His cell phone rings and he tells me he's got to answer this, it's his girlfriend.

"I'm busy right now . . . I can't talk now . . . I'm doing an interview."

I hear excited squawking.

He says, "Free Speech TV."

More squawking.

"Babe, I didn't expect to be doing an interview just now. I'll call you back."

He slaps the phone shut and repeats, "That's my girlfriend. Her dad was killed last month."

"Oh, no."

"Yes. Yes. Every time Bush comes on the TV, I have to calm her down. I can't afford another TV."

The pest controller returns to his views on the war.

"We got Saddam. There were no weapons of mass destruction. They're killing us left and right. They don't want us there no more. Ain't gonna be no peace so long as we're there."

———

Next day, Dad is ready to swim again. Dog-paddling the pool perimeter, he studies each tile as if he's reading the news. I flutter nearby when he's in the deep end. It takes a few minutes to get him out. He rests, wet trunks on the hot leatherette of the wheelchair, eyebrows soggy. His chest is concave, belly pumping for air. He looks up at me. "The devil may care." He indicates to take his elbow. We begin lurching over the rough stones. Soon we're both in a sweat, me cupping each elbow in one hand, behind him like a tailgating cyclist. It takes about ten minutes to make the thirty feet into the shade, where he collapses into a porch chair. I go to the bar and pour two glasses of scotch-on-the-rocks. He sips cautiously. The mockingbird sings.

"You find the elevator, then take care of the cars. I will stay here and do my best to assure that the meeting comes to a proper conclusion, though I have my doubts."

I'm happy to be included in his delusion.

———

This morning I am shaving him. He says, "Do you see the knot in the beam up there?"

I look up at the ceiling. "Yes."

"Some would say that is a unique knot, but I have discovered something quite unusual about that knot."

"What's that?"

"There is a beam with that exact knot in another house."

"Really."

I get up to refresh the bowl of hot water and ask, "Where is the other house?"

"Gatesville."

"Who lives in the other house?"

"Your mother and I."

I lather the patch under his lip. "Why are you over here in this house, then?"

"I haven't figured that out yet. Your mother thinks I'm crazy."

"You make sense to me. Compress your lips."

He makes his lips a thin line so I can shave the area hipsters call the soul patch.

"I really don't belong here."

"Then who is the woman out in the kitchen?"

He turns cagey, "She'd have to be your mother, wouldn't she?"

Dad directs me to turn on a road I have never been on before.

"Where are we going?" I ask.

"Home," he says.

We drive for a couple miles. I see a sign that reads, "Gatesville: 10 miles." I am surprised. "So Gatesville is a real place?"

In the tone of a teacher working with a slow student, he says, "That's right. The town of Gatesville is down this road."

"But this is not the way home, Dad."

He gestures to proceed.

"Mom will worry if we don't get back soon."

"She's in Gatesville."

"We just left her back in your house on Ash Street. She's probably making us lunch."

He points straight ahead, ordering now, "Go this way."

I pull over. "Dad, do you want to go home?"

"This is the road home."

I begin to make a U-turn.

"What the hell do you think you're doing?"

"Going to where Mom is."

"We don't live there anymore."

"I'm pretty sure you do."

He reaches out to wrestle the wheel away, but the seat belt restrains him. He looks for his cane to whack me, but it's in the back.

"We can always come back to Gatesville later. OK?"

"There's nothing I can do about it, is there?"

He fumes in silence for fifteen minutes. Instead of pushing the button to open the garage, I pull up as if we are here for a visit, and open his door. He doesn't budge. I walk to the front door and knock. The dog spots his master and charges. I tell my mother about this Gatesville thing. It is not new to her.

We go to the car where the dog is licking my father's astonished face. She caresses his cheek, helps him down. Soon she is feeding him turkey and mayonnaise at her table.

It is spring in New England, and I am marching around the college green in a uniform left over from the Korean War. A bearded friend of mine walks alongside the squad, telling us of the Buddhist monk in Saigon who sat cross-legged while burning himself to death to protest the violence of the regime against Buddhists.

"Why would someone burn himself to death as a protest," my friend asks, "if the South Viet Nam regime deserved our support?"

Our sergeant tells us to ignore the "friggin' raghead."

My antiwar friend talks me into going to Detroit for the summer. His older brother runs an artist's workshop between the African–American ghetto and Wayne State University. It has become a center for radicals. I am welcomed by a lovely poet who takes me to bed. To make myself useful, I scrub a neglected bathroom spotless. The next day Allen Ginsberg uses the bathroom. For money, I unload freight cars on the graveyard shift. I meet a saxophone player, Joseph Jarman, who reveres John Coltrane, and a trumpet player who shares my new girlfriend. I meet a guy who eats macrobiotic food and drives his Avanti all night from Montreal to Detroit to smuggle hash.

The sax player was in Viet Nam early. His first year back, he did not speak a word. Instead, he learned his instrument and formed the Chicago Art Quintet. Decades later, Joseph would found a Buddhist sangha in Brooklyn.

One of our actions is to put on the Motor City's first "Be-In." In exchange for LSD, the Hell's Angels agree to control the crowd. Several thousand people show up for the Be-In, planned as a peaceful afternoon of music and face-painting. No one notices the troop of mounted police at the other end of the island. I melt into various shapes while lying in the sunshine and listening to the jazz. No one is drinking, but the smell of marijuana is everywhere. All is copasetic.

The bandstand clears, and the MC5 rip into their earsplitting anthem, "Kick Out the Jams." A biker is inspired to rev his engine as accompaniment. The police line begins to move. As the horses break into a trot, people scatter. Men in helmets and leather swing batons at fleeing hippies. Most of the crowd gets away unhurt. A few whites and a number of blacks are bleeding. It's a defining moment; the rest of the summer, patrol cars cruise by the workshop every hour.

⁓

Dad sits watching the colony of young martins practicing their flying skills. They will head south to Central America soon. I'm reading one of his books on Parkinson's. "This book says you may be having hallucinations."

He looks at me. He's read the chapter on delusion and hallucination several times already. He points to a corner of the room. "So I don't need to worry about what those three Japanese fellows are saying?" His tone says he's kidding me.

"Really?"

"I see them out of the corner of my eye. But I know they're not there."

"Yesterday how did you feel after I turned back from Gatesville?"

"I was annoyed. Really annoyed. But when we got back to this place, my jaw dropped."

We can count on him hitting the floor three to five times a day. His body crumples, a marionette abandoned by the puppeteer. Each fall scares Mom. She can't pick him up alone. Her back damaged from skiing accidents might go out if she tries to get him up from his spread-eagled-on-the-floor position. His collarbone snaps in a fall. The stub of broken bone stretches the skin. The medic says there's nothing to do.

After a drooling collapse, he says, "Whether I'm smart or dumb or funny or whatever the hell I am, I need to see a doctor. Soon."

"I'll make an appointment to see Dr. Abrams tomorrow."

"Who?"

"Dr. Abrams."

"He's a good man."

We wedge him into the non-electric wheelchair.

"I don't know if he can see you tomorrow. I think he's in Fort Hood. But if not, then Monday."

"Whatever, I can see him Monday or Tuesday or Wednesday. My calendar is open. Well, both of you have done a remarkable job getting me here." He points to a flap of oozing scab. "But would you avoid this spot next time?"

The neurologist says all that's wrong with him is that he's not eating. The top specialist, he has seen thousands in late-stage Parkinson's. My mother is too polite to swear at the doctor. It's her food he refuses. On the way home, he gets a yen for some Texas barbecue. He collapses in the restaurant doorway. A couple of kind Texans help gather him up.

I set my mind on getting an electric wheelchair for Dad to motor out to the garden. When I leave, he can watch the birds up close. We drive up to the military hospital to learn how to run the chair.

"We're concerned your father might drive the chair through a glass door."

"He's been a pilot all his life."

Dad proves he can run the controls following his coach through the maze of hospital corridors. However, Medicare won't pay so long as a person is able to hobble around on his own.

———

After a nap, he looks accusingly at me and says, "Where have *you* been?"

"I've been around."

"Tell me what we did today."

"We went to the hospital and you chased a pretty woman in your electric chair."

Mom adds, "You even turned it around inside a telephone booth."

"Then you went across the street and back," I tell him.

He says, "I remember . . . vaguely." He gets the handkerchief he always keeps handy for drool.

I go on, "When we got home, you knocked yourself out in the shower. The male nurse called rehab. Since you are now officially a danger to yourself upright, you can get the chair."

"It's been a pretty good day then."

The motorized chair comes in through the back gate. Dad drives it smack into a wall. The chair goes back.

———

I'm reading out loud from a book by Antoine de Saint Exupéry. Caught flying through a cyclone in the Andes, the hero literally wrestles the wind as he hangs on to the wheel of his airplane.

"Does this describe how it is when you freeze up and have to fight for control of your body?"

He gestures with his long fingers, as if holding a joystick. He banks to the left, then the right.

"Can't be sure how far to move the stick. Just when I about get it right it's time for bed."

———

I am twelve. I have just refused to say prayer at dinner. Reading sci-fi novels has toppled the Presbyterian God.

"Go to your room," comes the command.

"God was made up by people. He's an anthropomorphic fiction," I quote proudly, and head upstairs without dinner.

The next night my brother takes over prayer duty. Dad buys me a large coffee-table book about the world's great religions.

———

"What time is it?"

"Seven o'clock."

"Show me."

She shows him the clock. "Seven-o-five to be exact." Pause.

"In the morning or evening?"

She laughs. "It's dinnertime." She goes to cook. I sit down.

"I'd like to take a walk around outside this house. I have no idea what it looks like."

"Really?" I say.

"I often wake up and don't know what day of the week it is."

"I do that too."

"Or who your mother is."

"Is that scary?"

I look at his eyes. He looks back.

Since that rebellion at age twelve, I have never talked to him about the afterlife. It seems indelicate to ask directly, so I approach the subject from the side. "This must be depressing," I say.

He nods a few millimeters.

"Does it make you angry?"

He tilts his head.

"Is it scary?"

He clears his throat. "What's to be scared of?"

This will be the extent of our talk about the afterlife.

———

I'm looking forward to borrowing the family car and getting away to

Austin for a day. I come into the kitchen, turn down the Rush Lim-
baugh radio show. "Mom, a person I know in Austin arranged for me
to interview a guy who went to high school with George Bush."

She's furious that I would consider leaving at this time. "Your father
needs you."

"Mom, it's only two hours away."

She walks away. I taste again the deep suffering from Viet Nam.
"OK, OK. I won't go."

It's snowing on the old cemetery next to the ROTC building. I take
my cue from a gravestone inscribed "John Shortliffe" and go in to see
the commandant.

"Colonel, I don't think I can continue in good faith."

"What do you mean?"

"I have to quit ROTC, sir."

"It's too late for that, Cadet. You signed up. You're on Uncle Sam's
payroll."

I grab in my bag of confusion. "Sir, this summer I worked with a
subversive organization."

"Say again, son?"

"A subversive organization, Sir. The Detroit Artist Workshop advo-
cates radical changes in our government."

The colonel blinks and opens a drawer. He pulls out a list of subversive organizations published by the Nixon administration.

"There's no artist workshop here."

"Sir, I am convinced the war in Viet Nam is a mistake. And wrong."

He tells me what can happen if I refuse. I can lose my student deferment and become draft bait. "Think about it."

I go back and forth with my mother. The colonel and his wife come
for dinner to help my mother. She feels I am betraying my father, who
is at that moment in harm's way. I argue morality: President Dwight
Eisenhower had agreed at the Geneva Accords to allow Ho Chi Minh
a free election two years after his defeat of the French. Why did the
U.S. break the promise of a democratic election? I send an agonized
letter to my father, saying I support him, but I cannot support the war.

The spare bed's been moved downstairs to Dad's library. A portable toilet sits under the big alpine bird my mother shot fifty-five years ago during the Allied occupation of Austria. I show him a new book of photos taken looking straight down from a helicopter a few hundred feet up. We see a market of melons, the crevasses of a glacier, faces upturned around a well. He repeats what I read from the captions like a child. He sees a raccoon down in a forest. I turn the page to a patchwork of fields. He sees a bear. He falls asleep.

———

"Dad, let's use the bedside commode, OK?"
    No response.
    "If you just have to pee, we won't have to climb the stairs."
    "OK."
    "I'll grab you by the hands and we'll swing left. Mom will drop your pants, and I'll drop you in position."
    Unexpected grin.
    "Ready, Mom?"
    Dad reaches out and grabs my forearms in a trapeze hold.
    "Here we go . . ."

———

Big smile as I come 'round the corner. "I didn't expect to see you. Who's here?"
    "Just me and your wife and your dog."
    "Just one dog?"
    The other two dogs died some time ago. He sees my mother through the window, watering the plants under the window. To change the subject I say, "Linda just peeped in at us."
    "Don't call her Linda. She's your mother." He yawns.

———

I look at my father's snapshots of a patrol from '65 or '66. A grinning young man carries a machine gun on his back. Five shirtless men dig foxholes at the edge of a bamboo grove, black skin glistening. A few Hueys hang, wasps over a rice paddy. A dozen soldiers file across a shallow stream, the forest canopy completely defoliated. Peasants with folded arms stand in front of their homes. One soldier lights another's cigarette.

Back from his tour, my father is at the War College in Pennsylvania studying to be a general. A widespread offensive by the Viet Cong inside territory assumed to be under our control starts January 31, of 1968. In the first six months, American deaths nearly double. The photo of a Saigon officer shooting a suspected Viet Cong through the head is published. Walter Cronkite visits and comes back to report that the war is going badly, despite General Westmoreland's claim that we have driven them back. President Johnson's polls are at their lowest; key civilian advisors are pessimistic. There have been 9,592 American soldiers killed in the first half of '68, making a total of 53,700. In the public mind, a classic fallacy prevails—we must honor the dead by continuing to die. In April, a week after the assassination of Martin Luther King, Mom and Dad come to my hippie wedding by the Shenandoah River in Virginia. Forgoing his dress uniform, in a polo shirt he looks out of place among the young people in their hippie finery.

My father is having a clear day. "Dad, what is this?" I pick up a twig with thorns the size of an eagle's claw that has been mounted on a block of polished wood.

"That's a piece of the briar patch we cut to make the golf course."

The "golf course" was the first large clearing made for the helicopters. He stares at his library, floor-to-ceiling books on war. "If you were to read the greater part of those books, like I did, it would take you a long time. Common sense would save you the effort."

"Dad, I think you already know this, but I want to put it on the record. I'm proud of your service in Viet Nam." He pretends not to hear me. On this topic he's been mute for nearly forty years. I plod on, "You thought you were doing the right thing."

"I'd like a glass of water."

I come back with the water. "And I thought I was doing the right thing."

He drinks the water. "That's a long time ago."

The summer of 1968, whole city blocks are burned down all over America. The draft scours the roster of recent college graduates. At our draft physicals, my friends and I are armed with youthful arrogance, ready to resist the war by any means necessary. One insists on seeing the man in charge; then refusing to leave, he exhausts the officer with an argument on the illegality of the draft. Another passes out copies of his rant against the war, saying he is actually on Ho Chi Minh's side. I tell the civilian shrink that weekly doses of LSD have merged my wife and me into a single being: "I" have become a "We"—and "We" are entirely unsuited for combat. My friends and I are disqualified from service.

———

I'm shaving him. "Dad, look at me." His eyes open, the first of the last dozen looks between us. I make a reverse pucker with my lips. He imitates.

———

The American war in Viet Nam actually lasted twenty-five years, according to General Bruce Palmer, who authored one of the better books on it. Dividing the roughly 58,000 American soldiers killed in Viet Nam into the 3.5 million Asians killed during the twelve years of the most intense conflict gives a kill-ratio of one American to sixty Vietnamese.

If roughly 35,000 Iraqis have been killed since the invasion in April 2003 as the Pentagon estimates, then dividing by 2,200 Americans as of this writing makes the following kill ratio: one of us to sixteen of them.

I interview a Navy veteran of Gulf War I. "I ran the computer that targeted the big guns of a battleship. The target lights up when there are warm bodies moving inside. You know you have a hit when the little light goes out."

If you go back to the first Gulf War and include those who died as a result of disease and malnutrition, you get a kill ratio of one of us to about 750 Iraqis. For every person killed, there are parents, siblings, and children who remember.

———

I'm reading a book from my father's library, Griffith's 1963 translation of *The Art of War,* mostly quotes from a brilliant general named Sun Tzu who lived in the fifth and fourth centuries before Christ.

When the army engages in protracted campaigns the resources of the state will not suffice ... While we have heard of blundering swiftness in war, we have not seen a clever operation that was prolonged ...

The best policy is to take a state intact; to ruin it is inferior to this ... Do not put a premium on killing ... To capture the enemy's army is better than to destroy it ... The worst policy is to attack cities ...

When the army encamps you must not cut down trees, destroy dwellings, take away crops, slaughter the domestic animals, or burn the granaries. Thus you demonstrate to the people that you have no desire to oppress them.

War is like unto fire; those who will not put aside weapons are themselves consumed by them ... All the soldiers taken must be cared for with magnanimity and sincerity so that they may be used by us.

———

The Abu Ghraib story comes out on the *News Hour* and Dad mutters, "What a mess," and uses the remote to turn the TV off. He sits forward ready to go.

"Where are we going?" I ask.

"I want you to show me that ice machine."

"Ice machine?"

He grimaces, exasperated that I don't get the urgency.

"The ice machine," he repeats and clamps his mouth.

"Are you unhappy, Dad?" This is an intimate question.

After a brief hesitation, he answers, "Yes."

"I got an idea: let's walk. Just a little circle right here."

We shuffle a semicircle. When he has no steam left, he grabs the back of his office chair.

"Impressive," I say. "Shall we head back to the bed?"

We shuffle over a few feet. He sits back down. "You still unhappy?" He nods. "I can see how hard this is." He hangs his head. "This suffering is going to end." That he does not want to hear. He rolls his eyes.

"Get me a pillow."

I grab a pillow.

"Not the soft one."

I get another.

"No. The hard one."

He folds over like a comma, glances sideways up at me. "It's time for you to take me to Gatesville."

"How am I supposed to do that?"

He glares. "Just too tired, huh?"

I spread my hands. "Mom's out with the car."

He struggles to zip his running jacket. I zip it for him. He folds his long legs up like landing gear and turns so he's sitting up.

"Do you think you're strong enough to get to the car?"

"I plan to fly," he says and pulls at the thin blanket, using his fingers like chopsticks. I get what he's doing. On the imaginary instrument panel under the cotton blanket, he toggles an ignition switch. I hear a satisfied "Hmmm."

"Contact?" I say.

He replies by circling his hand, a last check to see that the elevator and ailerons are free. He clears his throat. "All clear!"

"Tell me about it when you get back. OK?"

He nods. "Affirmative."

Dad opens his eyes, pushes the sheet away. Scabs cover his forearms, craters within craters, from the falls. I put a book down, and get up to copilot. "Where we headed?"

He thrusts his head toward the exit. "North."

We head out, me backwards right hand on his hip, my left forearm in a trapeze grip. He shuffles a yard or so, then begins to walk, small steps but actual walking. Soon we're doing a fox-trot, him leading.

"Where are we going?" I ask.

"We'll find out when we get there."

The burst of energy sweeps us across the room, up the short flight of stairs, down the hall. We sortie into the kitchen, bare feet on the terrazzo. I'm his consort, a giddy war bride.

"Take me to the bathroom."

He's been condemned to the plastic potty. I get him to the bathroom, where he drops his own trousers and pees standing up. Then we taxi down the hall, still in the fox-trot. This level of trust between us disappeared forty years ago.

"I haven't had a chance to tell you about my theory of weights and measures."

"How's it go?" I ask.

"Well, first, you can be not losing and yet still not winning."

"Like in Viet Nam?"

He gives me an annoyed, sideways look. "I was referring to being here instead of Gatesville."

The back door bangs, and the dog barks. Mom has returned from shopping. I hope she takes her time unpacking but instead she enters immediately, breaking our conversation.

"Dad's having a great day."

Mom touches his face.

He says to her, "Been too busy keeping from drowning to talk."

"Can I get you anything?"

"I'd like some ice water."

His gust of life force fades. I feel mournful as a hound yanked from the hunt.

—

It's dark outside. I have only a few days left before I must return to teaching. Mom's watching the last scene of a favorite movie, *The Third Man*. She attended the 1950 premiere in occupied Vienna. Dad lies on his back in the bed, asleep, half-naked. Skin gullies between the ridges of his bones. I draw the blanket over him, and begin to putty over the finish nails on the bathroom opening I widened to let the wheelchair pass.

"This is a very unusual home. Very unusual," my father says.

I watch my putty knife smooth the dimple of a hammer mark. "You can get through the door with the wheelchair now."

"Will you sleep here tonight?" he asks.

The question startles me.

"I'd rather not be alone."

I am terrified. I get out of the room to think. By the time I get back, my mother has got into bed with him. My answer becomes moot.

—

I ask a former superintendent of West Point, author of several military histories, to compare Iraq and Viet Nam.

"This is a resource war, Viet Nam was not. But there are two important similarities. We are on the enemy's soil and our domestic politics weigh heavily. A democracy cannot fight a war much longer than one president's term; the people grow tired of it."

I ask what the enemy wants in practical terms. He says that no one knows, but one short-term goal is clear. "They want us out of their part of the world."

I call another number my mother has given me, a retired military couple she is fond of. Once a four-star general, the husband is well liked by the community. He spends his free time at a local high school. His wife asks about my father's health. Can I interview her and her husband about the current war?

"I do not know of a single general officer who thinks this new war is a good idea," she says.

When the camera rolls, he won't discuss the war. After I gain trust talking about less volatile subjects, he tells me that three teenagers at the local high school lost their parents this semester.

"The whole community came out and put on a moving show of support."

In his den under the animal heads from Austria, beside the books on war, he sleeps while I keep watch, ready to write down whatever he says. He opens his eyes and looks right at me to say clearly, "We are alone." He goes back to sleep. I know exactly what he means.

Dad is buttoning his shirt while riffing orders like a jazz musician. "If you want to scout the terrain, that'd be all right but partner up ... If you find a bottle of rum, I'd like you to bring it back and open it up ... One thing we're sure of, here is where the bed lies ... I'd like to have everybody in here and not scattered ... And here is where we are right now ... But where is the kitchen for instance? ... Your mother is a very important part of the team ... She can cook ... Look at that, I managed to button my own shirt."

I come out of the bathroom to find him folded sideways on the thick carpet. I throw a quilt over him and let him sleep. Mom arrives from shopping, looks at me accusingly. She begins to tug at him.

"Mom, stop. Let him rest."

"It's just not right to let him lie on the floor like that."

"That's your problem, not his."

Dad opens his eyes, looks out along the floor at her feet. "I'm all right down here, but not for too long."

———

My mother wakes me from a dream, desperate. "Your father fell again. He's all jammed up in the shower. He's been there I don't know how long." She warms him with the hand sprayer while I get him unfolded. We all three get soaked.

———

A potbellied guy from hospice has spread out paperwork on the table. He's been telling us about the options. I wait until my mother leaves the room. "He's going downhill fast," I say. "I think he has just a few days."

"Could be."

"My mother thinks he has weeks."

"That's normal. No harm letting her think that."

———

His head hangs forward from his spine, chin near the chest. He points out odd-shaped rocks and gives them the names of animals. I push his chair toward the pool too fast, to get a rise out of him.

"Slow down!"

The reprimand echoes down the canyons of a lifetime.

I roll my cuffs up and step down into the water. I balance his ninety pounds on my knees so his feet touch the water.

———

The hospice man comes back the next day for a check-in. "How you doing, Colonel?"

"Fine."

"Who's the president?"

He looks at me for a clue.

"What's-his-name," Dad says, "Ronald Reagan."

"What year is it?"

"1988."

"Who is this fellow?" he says, pointing to me.

"This guy?"

"Yes."

"That's my younger son."

Dad has mistaken me for my brother who is coming tomorrow with my cousin from New Jersey.

———

It's time for me to go. The fall term begins in a few days. Dad's by the wall of family photos, the place in the house where good-byes begin. I don't know what to say. He leans forward. I tilt my face down to hear. He pats me twice on my left cheek and says his last words to me, "Don't try so hard."

"Don't try so hard" is what my father often said while teaching how to fly. Tensing one's hand on the stick of a small plane prevents the pilot from sensing the air as it rushes over the elevator and the ailerons. A well-trimmed plane flies itself, even through a cloud. If the pilot is tense, the ride is rough.

———

I ask the cabbie as the car passes the gate to Fort Hood, "Many troops at the airport today?"

"I gave a ride to two on rotation."

"Which way?"

"They were coming home."

"How were they?"

"I'd say they were jumpy. But glad to be home."

———

Three days after I'm back on the West Coast, my mother, brother, and a cousin are with him. He says, "Glad to see you all, but I'm sorry about the circumstance." They report that he shook like an airplane coming apart in midair.

I was born in Fairbanks, Alaska, of an Armenian father whose family escaped the 1911 genocide by the Turks, and I grew up under the shadow of the DEW line—the Distant Early Warning system that was supposed to alert the United States when the Russians attacked. My dad was a civil defense director, and it was his job to ensure that citizens stocked up on emergency supplies in the event of nuclear war. I worried because permafrost prevented anyone from digging a bomb shelter. But the things we worry about are seldom the things that destroy us.

Vietnam was at the other end of the world from my isolated life in Alaska. But it was a different enemy that took me prisoner a quarter of a century later. After eight years, I am still caught in the crossfire of the so-called War on Drugs, a war that blames its victims, criminalizes its wounded, and enriches its enemies. Like Vietnam, this U.S-backed war is a losing battle, and America has once again turned its back on those forced to fight on the front lines.

A Place Called Home

Before I knew anything else of the world, I knew about cold. As a child—bundled in ski pants, mukluks, parka, and mittens—I walked home from school in snow that seemed lavender in the already darkening sky of midafternoon. During the few hours of winter daylight, when the sun melted patches on rooftops, the water dripped to the eaves, where it froze into jagged swords. Beneath the icicles, windows glowed yellow and beckoned to the warmth inside. Home to me is squares of tallow light reflected on lilac snow—a sanctuary against the cold. This was the kind of home I tried to make for my own family.

Like the brand-new, cedar-sided house in Fairbanks, where we lived when my son, Benson, was a toddler. In the summer, he rode in the carrier on my bicycle as we peddled round and round the neighborhood so he could point at all the "digger-machines." One night, he woke up screaming when the jungle animals leapt out of the mural on his wall. Because I could not coax him from his dream, he slept the rest of the night safely in my bed. That was the house we lived in when I got so sick during the meningitis epidemic. My husband being out of town on business, as always, I turned my son over to his teenage babysitter and her mother, not knowing if I would ever see him again.

Soon after I returned home from the hospital, we sold this house and moved back to Anchorage, into an apartment where Benson announced, after reading *The Cat in the Hat,* that he wanted a sister named Sally. He could have a sister, I agreed, but she had already told me her name, and it wasn't Sally.

By the time Marissa was born, work had so consumed my husband that the children and I were on our own. We lived in a duplex on Government Hill when Benson first started school, when he lost his first baby teeth, and when one sunless December afternoon not long after his fourth birthday, we sat at the kitchen table and he first began telling me the stories that would one day blossom into a life of imagination. In one story, which I dutifully wrote to his dictation as he drew accompanying illustrations, imaginary creatures engaged in a war of mythological proportions. In the end, everything worked out and they all went home. He drew a picture of their home, with a mother, a boy and his sister—and a father who came home after battle.

It was in this house that I read about Dolores Johnson. An Eskimo from Pope'vannoy, she was taking the family in their fishing boat to its winter home on Lake Iliamna when they became trapped in the ice. She left the motor running to keep her children warm and took the skiff out to clear a path to open water. Though the children didn't understand what she was doing, they were comforted by her nearness. They could hear her chipping away at the ice that kept their boat imprisoned.

Cold has an insidious power. It comes at you from all sides. You breathe it in and it freezes you from the inside out. More dangerous than cold, though, is the illusion of warmth. Before long, Dolores began to perspire. She would have liked to stop, but already the water she worked so hard to uncover had begun to film over. She paused to take off her snowsuit, then picked up her oar and chipped at the ice again and again until she felt light-headed.

Perhaps there was a piece of especially thick ice. Probably her children were crying because they were cold and hungry and she had already been gone too long. Night was now edging the sky. She needed to hurry, for unless she beat the darkness, her path would be gone; she would have to do the whole thing over tomorrow. And the ice would be one night thicker. Racing, and exhausted from laboring without food or rest, she pounded the ice with her oar. It was heavier now, and each plunge into the open water added a thin layer of ice crystals. Even so, she lifted the oar high, and let it down with a hard slap.

Then, a slight slip of the oar, an unexpected break through the ice, and she was pitched into the cold, black water. Quickly, she fought to the surface and swam to the edge. She hauled herself up and rolled onto the ice, clumsy with chill. The cold confused her; she didn't know where her children were, her eyelashes froze shut when she blinked. She wandered, stumbled through the snow until the cold reached her heart and she fell one last time. In the distance, although she could not hear, her children called her name.

Dolores's children were found alive two days later. Reading the story, it occurred to me how those children must have felt, ice-bound, watching their mother struggle. In their memories, she will always be trying to get home.

———

The same year Dolores died, I left my husband and Alaska, the only place I had ever called home. My children and I moved to California, where we lived in a series of houses. Our first was a Victorian carriage house that my dad's aunt bought in 1933 because of the view and the great soil, which produced apricots, persimmons, olives, chiles, flowers, and bamboo. Marissa learned to ride a bicycle on its wide expanse of land, and Benson practiced pitching a baseball until he could hit the bull's-eye painted on the front door with frightening accuracy. When I told my father I was going back to school and asked if we could stay in the house for the two years until I finished, he immediately sold it.

Eventually, I bought a house with my new fiancé. We dug up the yards—tore out the rotted apple trees; shoveled out the hardpack clay, replaced it with rich black soil; pulled down the ivy and the shabby grape arbor; and planted roses, lilies, and sage, butterfly bushes, alyssum, narcissus, and tulips. This was the house that was most traditional: four bedrooms, two baths, and an oversized garage. It was a house of expectations.

I thought if I could give my children a big house with the father they always wanted, it would be like eternal summer. But all things have their season. Sometimes a lake freezes slowly with gradual winter;

sometimes it stays liquid-soft; and sometimes a sudden cold snap shocks it from one state to another. In our case, crystal meth descended like a blizzard. We moved out of the house with its ever-fragrant garden, using the money instead to send Benson to treatment programs.

———

One night years later, while the cats napped languidly across the foot of the bed where I lay hunched in sleep, the phone rang. The cats streaked for cover and I fumbled for the receiver, my mind racing through possibilities: *the hospital the sheriff or dear-God-no-not the coroner.* But caller ID showed a pay phone number in San Francisco, where my son, now twenty-three, had last been seen. I lifted the receiver.

"Mom?"

When I picked him up from the sidewalk at 16th and Mission, Benson lay slumped against the Plexiglas in the bus stop, a cigarette lodged behind his right ear. The neon light from the BART station cast slices of shadow across the crevasses of his face, deepening the lines that made him look careworn. He stumbled into the car and I scrunched my nose at the smell. He cringed at this rejection and looked away.

In silence, we drove through dimly lit streets strewn with overburdened shopping carts alongside uncertain lumps in doorways. I tried not to stare and focused instead on beating the red light at Van Ness.

"Mom?"

He was shivering, so I turned on the heater and a blast of warm air slapped us in the face.

"Mom?" he asked again. "Do you ever wish I'd never been born?"

"Not for a moment," I answered without hesitation.

He must have sensed the honesty in my voice, this streetwise, charming drug addict with an animal's instinct for where to find free food, whom to approach for spare change, which cardboard tent to share on cold nights. He leaned his head against my shoulder and in the warm shelter of the car, fell fast asleep.

His breathing sounded light in my ear: little puffs like baby's breath. I drove with one hand so as not to disturb his sleep. Around us, city lights blurred in the mist. Here and there, the fog closed in, blending with the steam from manhole covers like ghosts playing in the empty streets. The soft vibration of the engine resonated through my thoughts and I took a deep breath, then sighed. We crossed the bridge, drenched in clouds, and climbed the hill on the other side and into the tunnel, unable to see because of the fog, yet confident in our destination—home.

———

Early one wintry morning my daughter and I walked across the mud-flats of the marsh before the joggers and mountain bikers crowded the path. A hazy sunrise dusted the eastern sky. We stepped single file through the anise bushes that loosened their scent on the breeze when we passed. The mud had hardened overnight, and we kept our eyes down, watching the ruts where we walked. The remains of the night air cooled our cheeks.

We strolled along, comfortable with the silence between us as only two people whose hearts are connected by shared pain can be. After a while, we started talking. I don't remember what prompted the turn in conversation—maybe that vague homesickness all wanderers feel—but we started talking about moving to the country, where we could have a garden and grow real vegetables—ones with that rich, musky smell of black topsoil and the sweet, sweet taste of sunshine. We talked about the animals we'd have—a cow for milk, a pig for bacon, chickens and ducks for eggs. And a horse, just for the beauty of it. I had no words to name the yearning I felt, after all the years of struggling for a place where we could unpack our books, hang pictures, have a puppy, a garden, perhaps a pond. Marissa wanted a steady address just so her friends would remember where she lived. At least that's what she said.

Not long after our walk, I was searching through the boxes stored in our apartment and came across an old copy of *Victoria* magazine. Leaning back against the wall, my legs crossed, I slowly flipped through its pages, savoring the colors, designs, and elegance of the homes and gardens—places I had once dreamed of making my own. Those dreams had evaporated, along with the plan for a second marriage. Once again my children and I were on our own. We moved out of the house with its ever-fragrant garden now masking the smell of crack cocaine, and I continued chipping away at the ice. Since then, we've lived in other places, but owning a house has never been important compared to keeping our family intact—we three intrepid survivors against oblivion.

We've recently added a fourth, my son-in-law, a man who likes the solidness of a home-cooked meal; a political refugee who also dreams of home.

Sitting on the floor, I blinked away the memories and flipped through the pages of the magazine again until I came across an article where I had once underlined some text and added a series of exclamation points in the margin. Curious, I reread it: A short anecdote by Susan Cheever about her dad, the great writer John Cheever. Her writing was evocative and comforting, like visiting a friend for tea. She told the story of her brother walking through the snow with their father at twilight one winter evening, headed back to the warmth of their house.

"I want to go home," he told his father.

"We are going home," Cheever replied.

"No, not that home."

I think now I understand what he meant, that longing to be peaceful, finally.

I slapped the magazine shut and threw it back in the box. I wouldn't think about that, nor about my prodigal son, who had left again to wander the streets in search of eternal painlessness.

Instead, I will think of open water. Of finding that place in the country. Of making it home. And after we have lived there for a while and it begins to feel like it will always be home, perhaps there will come a time when my son no longer feels the need to ask if I wish he had never been born. Perhaps then I will tell him of those nights in the darkness when I lay hunched in sleep against the next phone call, when wild things haunted my days, when I thought I would drown. Perhaps then he will understand—and Marissa, too—the peace of tallow light against a lilac snow.

FRED MARCHANT

I was born in Providence, Rhode Island, and enlisted in the United States Marine Corps in 1968 so that I could go to Viet Nam and be, as I imagined it, a writerly witness to that war. I was a young poet, just out of college, and thought it was my special fate and duty to do this. Underneath my conscious understanding of what I was doing were all sorts of tangled motives, including the desire to get out of Providence, the desire not to "miss" the war of my generation, especially given its by then apparent moral emptiness. I have to admit also that I was out to prove I had a certain version of "manhood," and perhaps even had the desire to pull a trigger.

Two years later, while I was serving on Okinawa and within a few weeks of rotating into Viet Nam, I formally declared my conscientious objection to the war in Viet Nam and to all wars. Six months later I was honorably discharged as a conscientious objector, one of the first Marine officers ever to be so discharged. The months preceding and following that decision were in effect the crucible out of which I claimed and began to forge my own being. It also took me twenty years of writing before I ever wrote anything worth reading about that experience.

C.O.

In memoriam: Robert Lowell

Cold scrambled eggs. Burnt bacon curling
under his slightly cockeyed glasses.
Opera on the stereo, the bay ice-flat
and gray as a naval deck. The shore
rimey and swirling with snow, gusts
rising up to us, a window rattling
behind his "I can breathe out here."

A Sunday in November 1969,
the morning after Trinity Square
mounted his Old Glory trilogy.
Bloody Mary toasts, with celery-stick
swizzles, Worcestershire, horseradish,

and fiery talk about the Narragansetts,
and the colonials who were slavers.

To the sunporch beaming with poets
I carry with me a shadowy prosaic:
orders to Viet Nam. A green lieutenant,
shave-headed as a monk, I leave tomorrow
and can't fathom Lowell's question about
the Green Bah-rehs, his breath chopping
the word into hardly intelligible halves.

He takes over and pictures the pajama'd
guerrilla flying out the rear hatch
of the helicopter. He asks me
if I have seen this, and he assumes
I know more than I am saying, me
now the dim, lumpen, and enemy soldier
pleading innocence, ignorance, dismay.

It is as if a vacuum has sucked up
the stray talk, and under his affronted
glare I feel like Hawthorne's young Robin
Molineux bewildered by Boston's
mocking, checker-faced hostility.
I too am blistered by the moment,
and can't believe this is happening.

The china clinks, and talk slowly
resumes while I come to, blinking
like a hammered calf. I hardly know
the abbreviation C.O., but a conscience
must be at work when he leans over
and whispers, "Come back. Intact,"
rhyme nearly full, orders fully meant.

Elephants Walking

i.

Curled in a window seat, level with wind-swayed oak,
    aching on a green vinyl pad,
I think of the fortunes spent on the hardwood, wainscot
    study, and the slates fitted
for the arbor walkways, the labor it took to lug bricks out
    to each overly articulated
corner, in which nook a child of fortune, cushion-tassel
    between his fingers, might
look up from his reading to see in heat waves rising
    over the pale, shimmering
delphinium, a plot miracle perhaps, the sudden death
    by spontaneous combustion
and the child wondering how, why, and could it have been?

ii.

My childhood bedroom, summer night, one hand marking
    the book, the other's palm
and fingers printing moist, disappearing shadows on the wall.
    Then the college library,
Harkness Hall, and aged, white-cowled Father Benilde
    smelling of coffee, muscatel,
and Old Spice as he opened the doors at 7:30. First in line,
    I was all business, heading
straight to my end of a long, immovable table, to my first
    reading of Dante, a paperback
copy of Ciardi, with its cover of red, grinning, cartoon
    devils, which I in a fit
of verisimilitude (which word I had just learned)
    had charred with a lighter.

iii.

My first lines that year: "Butt, butt, base, bale beast.
    I fear your horns not
in the least!" The intended tone was courtly love,
    but the words were

apostrophe to a buffalo in Roger Williams Park,
    one that had leaned
hard into a sagging hurricane fence near my date.
    The lines came to me
as I woke after a nap in the library. I still love
    to sleep in libraries
whenever I can. I fix my head sideways over
    my folded hands,
and make room for the little puddle of drool
    I'll quickly wipe away.
I wake into a barely believable clarity
    throughout my body.
I'm ready to grapple with fate, love, sex,
    the stirrings within.
Over readers and sleepers alike hovers a mist
    or a pollen, and in it
I see words shuttling back and forth like birds.
    In the darkness or dream
something hugely important had been freed,
    to roam. Grateful,
I say to myself, "Elephants have been walking."

iv.

"Son, we must give this country great poetry!"
    decreed the older poet
to my nodding head, as he shook my hand after
    the Crystal Room reading.
Later, as I walked back to my dormitory, sleet
    failing to cool me
I turned his pronoun over and over, thinking,
    yes, we do, we do.
On the news there was the familiar footage:
    a Phantom run
ending in a hypnotic burst of a lit yellow napalm.
    I knew the war
was wrong, but that was why, I claimed, I should go,
    to sing the song

of high lament, to get it into the books. Like Ishmael
    I would sign on
for a three-year voyage under a madman captain.
    Frissons to be had
instantly: a pity-the-youth-soon-dying look in the eyes.
    "Are you crazy?"
said my girlfriend. But I was filled with vibrant life
    and felt neither suicidal
nor confused when I dialed the Marine recruiter: "Yes,
    I look forward to reporting."
Phone in my lap, I sat sideways, my legs dangling
    over the arms of my red
leather reading chair. A warm spring wind was
    melting the snow
down to bright medallions of ice. I felt clear-headed
    and refreshed.
I just hoped the war would last until I got there.
    Elephants were walking.

Hue, in Darkness

At Nam Giao Altar

I think sometimes Hue is the center of the universe,
    that thousands of eyes have turned toward us here.
The reticent eye of the full moon with clouds.
The burning eye of the lit bundle of incense
    wedged into stone.
The magnified eye of the imperial courtyard,
    its marble sounding board.
The skeptical eye
    of the woman praying on the shadowy steps.
The blinding eyes of the van's headlights.
    And the soft pinpoints of candles cradled on the river.
The eyes of the many no longer here.
    And the living eyes of friends who are.

Occasional Verses at Con Son, after the War

Cotranslated by Fred Marchant and Nguyen Ba Chung

Nguyen Trai *(1380–1422)*

(Nguyen Trai was both a general and a poet, one who preferred writing poetry to making war. Con Son was his mountain writing retreat, where his ashes were scattered after his death by assassination.)

Ten years away from what I knew and loved as home,
I return to pine and chrysanthemum grown rampant,
to patient streams and trees wondering where I've been.

I am covered in dust.
There was nothing else I could do.

Now that I am home, my life seems nothing but a dream.
The war may be over, I may be alive, but I want nothing
more than a cloud-tipped mountain, good tea, a stone pillow.

ROMAN A. "HOPPER" MARTINEZ

I enlisted in the Army in January 1969 to be a chaplain's assistant. I was an altar boy and a choirboy and believed in "Thou shall not kill." So I joined the Army to do my service to my country in the shortest possible time, which would be a two-year enlistment. Unfortunately, my enlistment officer didn't tell me that he put me in for infantry rather than as a chaplain's assistant. So after four months of training, I ended up in Vietnam in June 1969. I informed my officers that I was a conscientious objector and that I had enlisted to be a chaplain's assistant, so they volunteered me for a recon platoon, which was totally contradictory to my beliefs.

The time that really got me ... I was very new in-country and new in the recon platoon. We met the enemy. He fired on us and we fired back. There was a saying, *"cho hoi,"* which means, "Open arms—I surrender." We hollered out to them *"cho hoi,"* and when they surrendered we killed them. That was my first experience of how things were done.

I had a burial ceremony for myself. I actually got an M-16 and a bayonet, and I had a funeral for Roman Martinez. I buried him and my God, so that the altar boy and God could not see what I was doing.

My alter ego, the one who was stronger than the altar boy, took over and Hopper came out. That was what they called me in Vietnam. He took over the responsibility for the carnage that was going to happen. Death and having to die were all taken care of by my alter ego.

All the memories of the horrors of war were buried when I came home. I didn't think about them. I grew my hair long and put on hippie beads and pretended like I never went. After the time went by, things started to happen. The old time bomb of the Vietnam vet.

Hopper's Last BBQ

I was pointman for my Air Rifle team (2/17th Cavalry with the 101st Airborne). We had been awakened early by the scramble horn, to go out to rescue the crew of a downed helicopter from our unit. It was very early, and we didn't get breakfast. We were dropped at the bottom of the hill, and hiked up. The chopper had crashed in a really rough spot, and they couldn't get an air ship in for the "rescue mission." I led the platoon at a fast march, thinking we were picking up survivors;

but still, it took us hours. Just before I found the crash site, I started smelling something cooking. The smells started making me hungry, reminding me that I hadn't eaten breakfast, and it was nearing lunchtime.

I was the first person to find our downed LOCH helicopter, in a clearing it had made when it crashed and burned. I was overwhelmed to find out that the smells that had me salivating were coming from my cooked buddies. I was disgusted that I was salivating. There was a pile of ashes with three "lumps" in it, the lumps being the aircrew. I had partied with the enlisted men just the night before. Of the three comrades, two were my friends, and they were cooked just right, roasted in a magnesium fire.

Of the entire unit at the crash site, only a black sergeant and myself had the intestinal fortitude to put our buddies into the body bags, for the trip back Home. While the rest of my squad was puking their guts out on perimeter security, the sergeant and I bagged our aircrew. I held back my tears, even while I had boots and other body parts come off in my hands; like pulling a drumstick off a roasted turkey.

After bagging the men, I fell in as one of the perimeter guards. While looking through my tears, I had a chickenshit sergeant order me to help carry the body bags down the hill. I told him that if he didn't have the balls to bag our men, then he didn't have enough to do anything. He tried to order me to carry them, so I flipped my "16" onto auto, and I invited him to join the others in the body bags. Luckily, our lieutenant came up to us and told the sergeant that he should not push his luck.

Thinking back on the experience, I had no qualms about personally sending that sergeant to God. If he had not backed off, I would have blown him away and bagged his remaining body parts.

The remembrance of this occasion brings on a depression, and sometimes a rage. The smell of hot metal (such as a hot skillet) or the smell of burned barbecue meat, brings back all the emotions of disgust, sorrow, and rage, and I can be terrifying to those around me, mainly my family. "Why is Daddy so mad and hollering at us and acting like he's going to *kill?*" Needless to say, we don't have Memorial Day barbecues anymore.

"God knows where we are," July 1969. LTC Maurice J. Errico saying Mass around a mortar pit, with the altar made out of mortar-round boxes.

KEITH MATHER

My life began on November 30, 1946, in San Mateo, California. A year later my family moved to Sterling, Colorado. I was raised on the prairies near the Kansas–Colorado border in a working-class town. We had good schools; it was a safe place to grow up. We all walked to school by ourselves, even at five years old. The winters were hard on my father; he was a plumber and he was frostbit the winter prior to our leaving to return to California.

We arrived in 1957 and lived in Brisbane, just outside San Francisco. We moved to San Bruno after a year, where I attended school and had the California life. As a teenager, I had a difficult and wonderful time, a few problems with the law and at school, but somehow the '60s worked for me. With my rebellious nature, the music, dancing, and progressive thought moved me to happy and meaningful times and places. I danced at the Avalon Ballroom to Moby Grape and the Dead, Quicksilver, Country Joe and the Fish, the Airplane, and Janis Joplin with Big Brother. We all had a good time.

Then came the draft. I was inducted into the Army on the 17th of September, 1967. After basic, at Christmas, I got a two-week leave. I got back in with family and friends, and during that time I decided to resist the war. In July, I was a member of the Nine for Peace— nine AWOLs representing all four branches of the military. We held a press conference and resigned from the service and said, "Come and get us!"

Three days later, they did. I was put in the Presidio stockade. On October 11 a fellow prisoner, while on a work detail, was shot to death by a guard. Twenty-seven of the prison population demonstrated nonviolently, and we were charged with mutiny, punishable in wartime by death. Shortly after the mutiny, I was convicted and sentenced to four years at Leavenworth. Awaiting a second court-martial for mutiny, I chose to forgo decades in prison. Along with a friend, I escaped on December 24, 1968, and went north to Canada, where I lived for twelve years, finding other deserters and draft resisters. I lived, played music, and worked. I returned in 1980 with my two young children and, in 1984, served four months in a military prison and then received a dishonorable discharge.

The Hunt

In the summer of 1969, I traveled to the Upper Hat Creek, near Ashcroft, British Columbia, to live on a commune. Six miles up a dirt road sat the PX Ranch—120 acres of meadows and cottonwoods, with mountains to the southwest and northeast. A good creek flowed past the main cabin. It was breached by a decrepit bridge. More than one soul fell through that windswept log and plank, at least up to the knees. One felt blessed upon arriving at the other side and always thanked the Spirit of the Bridge for safe passage. The bridge felt like a place one could pass over the problems in life. It rested on the earth on each side. It was high off the creekbed at its middle, and a view was presented in all directions with trees and pasture all around. If you walked it alone you felt that oneness we all longed for those days.

The Spirit of the Bridge, according to the story told to us, was a young Indian woman who was thrown and drowned while riding her pony in the creek near where the bridge was later built. Two local Indians, Papa and his son Maynard, who lived up the road, told the story between long pulls from a quart of gin. I was never quite sure whether it was the sprit in the bottle or our friends from the reservation who were telling the story.

One afternoon while I was crossing the creek, a large branch fell from the top of a tall cottonwood tree and narrowly missed me. Several bridge planks snapped under its force, and I nearly fell into the creek. Only by kneeling on one knee did I manage to stay dry. The next day, after two of us fell through the bridge, we gathered at the river, sat in a circle under the bridge, and told the Spirit we were her friends. We placed wildflowers at each end of the bridge and replaced all the rotten planks. This seemed to calm the Spirit of the Bridge. We were peacemakers.

The population of our commune varied from eight or ten in the winter to thirty souls during the prime days of summer, long sunny wild windy flowing happy days of acid trips, swimming, and exploring our times and lives. We were young, sixteen to twenty-six years old. We were artists, runaways, deserters, draft dodgers, Yanks and Canadians, dreamers all. We were mostly vegetarian and peaceful and hungry for calm.

I sat gazing out at the beauty, worked, and ate. We rode the branches of the cottonwoods as they swayed in the breeze. We took our own tree in the ring of tall ones that surrounded the thirty-acre meadow at the back of the PX Ranch. Out of sight. We lived in barns and log cabins with wood stoves, and there was a main house next to the garden where sunflowers and potatoes grew alongside a low fence and a scarecrow. Oh yes, we had seven dogs and one chicken.

I lived with my girlfriend, Nancy La'plante, and our dog, Jester, in a one-room cabin on the meadow. Home, sweet home. There were children with their parents, and we all took an interest in their welfare. Nancy was going to have a baby in September: six months and counting. We had little or no money. I was in exile, an illegal immigrant, an American Army deserter from San Francisco. Nancy and I had met a few months before we moved to the PX Ranch, and, together, we made a family. I had left mine in California and Nancy had left hers in Montreal when she started to show. We rescued each other and told each other our troubles. But we all needed a better diet, and I thought of Nancy and her child, who needed protein. Peanut butter wasn't cutting it. We were hard pressed to get a balance of protein and legumes.

I borrowed Clay's Winchester .30-30 carbine and four rounds, 150-grain soft tips. This would take down any deer. I thought that I could do it: kill. Something my government spent $100,000 training me to do during my six months of basic and advanced infantry training. I had qualified on everything they had. The M-16, M-14, the M-60 .30-caliber machine gun, the .50-caliber machine gun, the M-79 grenade launcher, the L.A.W. and the Colt .45. Christ, they even trained us in the quick-kill method by teaching us to hit a quarter-sized slug with a BB gun. You had to throw it in the air eight feet and hit it ten out of ten times without aiming, just point and shoot, before they would allow you to fire a rifle with live rounds. A .30-30 carbine. Big fucking deal.

I went with Charlie, a fellow I'd met in Vancouver, who also traveled to the ranch for some R & R after going AWOL and coming up north. We were both American Army deserters and agreed there was no way either one of us was going to fight in Viet Nam. The odds were really shitty that we would survive. Infantry line troops had a life expectancy in combat of 3.2 seconds in 1969.

But this was a different situation. We needed food! Meat. Fresh meat. We walked. Yet it felt weird carrying a gun. I had always thought about what the killing would do. How would it change me? Charlie carried a skinning knife, so between us we were prepared to hunt game.

We walked for thirty minutes or so; the dirt road was like a frying pan in that late morning in early July, with shade in the bush on either side. Our boots kicked up dust that rose above our boot tops. Bees buzzed. A crow cawed.

As we stood there, I looked slightly upward, and to my right I saw a black bear standing upright on its hind legs, large paws high in the air! No more bees.

"Shoot! Shoot!" Charlie pleaded. We stood in the dirt less than twenty feet from an eight-foot-tall, angry bear. In awe, I turned and fired. It hit his center chest point blank, we were so close. The bear spun and ran into the bush. Then I got afraid, really afraid. We could hear the crashing of the wounded bear and bellowing, almost like a scream. The bush was alive with combat, the killing had begun. I knew that a wounded bear was not something I could walk away from. I had to go into the bush; it had to be now. We followed the blood trail and trampled brush. Charlie followed close to me at the rear saying, "Watch out I think he's close by. Do you see anything?" As I passed a crushed sapling I saw a large black head rise up fast! I aimed and fired from ten feet. The head fell. We took slow steps. I began to relax as we got closer. The hunters and the hunted got close in the thick brush. We stood before two black bears, lying side by side, a large full-grown mother and her yearling, about half her size. The mother was still breathing, lying next to her very still cub. I raised the rifle and fired at the mother's head. Her breathing ceased.

My heart sank. What had I done? Charlie and I spoke in whispers as if we were still hunting, yet now it was over. I knelt at the bodies of those beautiful bears. Once again we heard a loud crashing from the bush, fast and closing. Followed by the sound of crushing bushes and more bellowing: Another bear! Startled, I turned and, as I did, I squeezed off the last round into the beautiful blue sky over our heads. In disbelief Charlie said, "Why did you do that?" Fuck! He fell into a dead run, I ran past him carrying an empty .30-30 carbine in both hands. The crashing came closer and we ran faster. Now we were the hunted. We ran the two miles back to the ranch, not only to escape the wrath of a third bear, but so we could return and save the meat from going to waste. We needed to bleed those bears and remove their organs, and transport them back to the ranch where I could make a smoker out of a fifty-gallon drum. I desperately knew I had to save the meat. I found Clay and Frenchy down by the creek. We all climbed into Clay's blue VW bus and quickly made it back to the spot where Charlie first saw the bear. As we got out I held my finger to my lips and tried to listen. As we started into the bush, I heard the bear. Clay pulled out his 270 Remington from behind the seat and loaded it with five rounds. I saw a yearling cub standing over the bodies of his dead family, making noises like an angry child. I had fucked up. But I couldn't let it be for nothing. I had to save the meat.

Clay stood next to me and asked if I wanted him to shoot this third bear. I threw rocks and yelled at this bear to chase him off, so we could get to the others to save the meat. No way; it was a sibling of the other cub and was not going to leave his family. This mother against great odds had raised two cubs that would be on their own after another winter. I took the rifle from Clay's hands and walked away from my friends to within ten feet of the cub and fired. Now all three lay still. I needed a knife and some help. I had to put their heads downhill and bleed their bodies. I pleaded for help, and my American friends' hands moved. The last bear was now at the road. We worked fast; the cleaning was done within an hour. Loading the bears into the van, we all held on with the side door open. We painfully wheeled into the ranch, to be greeted with disdain, anger, insults, tears, and some words I'll never forget from the father of a ten-year-old boy, "You should get a medal for what you have done." It hurt to hear what he had to say; I still don't agree. His son needed better nutrition. Nancy and I worried about him, and we would sneak eggs into his pancakes because his parents would not allow him to have any animal products and there was little else as a protein source. Not everyone was unhappy. Some welcomed the meat, yet this killing divided the commune and a split was in the air.

I had refused to kill. I had left my country and was in exile because of my refusal, yet I had killed.

PHYLLIS MESHULAM

Like everyone of my generation, the Vietnam War made its mark on me, savaging my college-aged sensibilities with its insanity. However, I was not affected directly as so many in our writing group were. By the mid-'70s, I had put it out of my mind and gone on trying to address my own issues of how I fit into this world and what I was going to do in it. I taught, raised a family, and took many, many years to acknowledge my interest in writing. This I finally did in the late '90s, going back to school and getting my MFA in both poetry and fiction. In late August of 2001, I sent my older daughter off to Pomona College, my own alma mater. When the attacks of September 11 occurred, it became obvious that our country was going to go to war again and the feeling of déjà vu was overwhelming. I was overcome by a huge sense of responsibility for not having attended to war and peace issues during the intervening decades. I became a peace and political activist and still struggle to find ways to use my skills as a writer in the service of nonviolence. Learning our own ecosystems, eating locally grown organic food, entertaining one another with our own words and music—these are indeed recipes for more harmonious, vibrant living, free from corporation-dictated excesses.

Hope, the Thing with Feathers

> The earth promises to be more
> than a battlefield or hunting ground;
> we dream of the time when it shall
> house one great family of co-operative beings.
> —ANSEL ADAMS

Alone, I watch the knobcone pines
spread their peacock fans
in front of this small amount of ocean
in the earth's cupped hands
. . . a bass line from frogs,
a few unkempt clouds,
an extravagance of stars . . .
I thought it had all been sold
for insignificant sums of silver.

Nearby, a new tribe poised to convene.
    a vine of heart
    a light of mind
Even apart, I imagine us all a part.

On the shore of the day,
my hair drinks in the fog
as do the weeds,
the buxom hills,
green inkblot of trees.
A bird pours a shimmer of song down
from its branch.
Another, brave soul,
wings its way through fog,
no path to follow.

The pull of this tribe
    a vine of heart
    a light of mind
like a submerged moon.

In its compass,
against the bloody canvas of these times,
the tattered newsprint of our fragile peace designs,
we make many small offerings:
an arpeggio,
a fiddle string,
a drop of salt water,
a catch in the voice.

And then,
a contagion of wonder, a fledging of heart.

Weaving Peace

I ask to be a loom in the service of peace.
Let voices weave through me,
whether barbed with the burrs and seeds of pain,
or carefully carded and spun with light.

Let me bring forth
a tapestry, blanket,
kafiyah, tallit.
Where there is unraveling,
let me remember to knit.
If I meet the flash and stab of fire,
let me be rebuilt from fresh wood.
In a state of green,
let me remember the cinder.
In a state of rubble, let me remember the weave.

Recipes for Independence Day,
Labor Day, Harvest, Interdependence Day

Organic garden opens its chicken
wire fences, offers a community meal
Long tables, plates mounded with yellow
watermelon flesh   Spicy couscous,
cooled with bits of fig
Salad, flexing its freshness,
zapping the eyes with mustard
greens, cherry
tomatoes, orange nasturtiums
Stinging garlic bread
Savory squash pie, brown
as Brazil nuts, orange
as Mars   Tiger tomatoes meet lemon
cucumbers
Hay-strewn paths
below, grape arbor above
Paint your face, carve your pumpkin
Hay-bale castle, tunnels,
dungeons   Beehive oven
invoking the sun with a clay medallion
Guitar duo recommends:
"Give Yourself to Love"

Voices hover like fireflies
Cinematic sky. Glance at your plate
of peaches and raspberries;
glance back at a sky of the same.
Glance again. Faster than you can shut the door on Oz,
Technicolor fizzes into black and white.
The firewood is piled up then,
Isadora Duncan released in a blaze.
Poem pigeons are lofted
        first person pluralized in a collective breath
windward

CLARE MORRIS

I am a veteran of the peace movement, in which I have been involved since 1968. In 1971, I helped found the Ecumenical Peace Institute of Northern California, a chapter of Clergy and Laity Concerned About the War in Vietnam. After working full-time with the institute, I experienced the need activists have for deepening their contemplative life and, in 1974, helped to organize the Angela Center in Santa Rosa, California. Its programs integrated social responsibility, spirituality, psychology, and the arts. In 1983, I left Angela Center, earned a Ph.D. in psychology, and became a licensed psychotherapist. At the same time, I was trained by the Guild for Psychological Studies in San Francisco to lead seminars in spirituality, myth, and depth psychology.

I have participated in the Veterans Writing Group since 2001. The privilege of hearing poems, stories, and reflections written by people with a wide variety of military experience has deepened my understanding of war and its imprint on the Web of Being.

Regulations

1 California,
Riding through Chinatown

At the Powell stop, doors bump open.
Thirty people waiting to squeeze inside.
An Asian woman climbs on first,
carrying groceries and a live chicken.
"Lady, you can't bring that bird on the bus."
"My dinner."
"Fine, but you can't get on with that chicken."
"My dinner."
"You have to get off—now."
He stands up.
She backs down the stairs.
She swings the chicken at a lamp post.
She's still first in line.
She climbs on again,
chicken limp over one arm.
"OK now?"

Slightly Damaged Buddhas—20% Off

In silence, shopworn Siddhartha sits
on a shelf, eyes downcast, lips turning toward
a smile, revealing how time and experience
can etch and scar wisdom's markings into
bronze or clay or human flesh.

From Strength to Strength
A Story of Mothers and Daughters

Our wrists are so alike, Mother's and mine: flesh of her flesh, bone of her bone. A single pair of handcuffs encircles them—a new umbilical cord. My childhood dependence has become adult inter-dependence.

We ride facing the rear window of a police wagon, wondering if someone could be following us on the freeway. Someone we know? We laugh as we think of my attorney father, now dead three years. What would he say about our arrest and jailing? He viewed law as process, meant to serve humane values; he respected protest and the right to live from conscience. If he were still alive, he too would have found a way to cry out against the habit of war.

Our transport deputy switches on the radio, settles the dial at a rock station. I try to escape its beat by sweeping over the past five days. Riding backwards, I find it easy to think backwards, from Tuesday to Monday to Friday.

Early Friday morning, we arrived at Lockheed Martin Missiles and Space Division in Sunnyvale, where the Trident submarine and its missiles are designed, where the ground between us and the nuclear edge is eaten away. We were six and looking small in the face of the military-industrial complex. Noting our small numbers, Edith, my mother, remarked, "Can 'what is enough' be measured in mere quantity?"

Besides Edith, into her seventies, and me, an Ursuline nun, there were six in our circle: Claire Feder, a local activist; her mother, Elizabeth Bradley, who was blind and nearly eighty; Larry Purcell, founder of a Catholic Worker House for homeless teenagers; and Dan Delaney, founder of a Catholic Worker House for prisoners' families.

As planned, Larry and Dan went immediately to the flagpole beside the main entrance of the Lockheed Navy building. The two men took down and folded a submarine flag. Next they lowered the American flag, turned it upside down, and raised it to half-mast, the international signal for distress. Two United Nations flags were then unfurled by Edith, Claire, and two helpful, though unsuspecting, Lockheed workers. The flags were placed on either side of the front steps. They had been given to us by a San Francisco city bus driver, who was passionate about the dangers of nuclear weapons.

With the flags in place, the Navy building's exterior was now transformed, expressing our hope for inner transformation. As Daniel Berrigan once said, "An act of civil disobedience is an act of contemplation."

The new flag arrangement might have remained outside the Navy building all day without notice had we not begun to distribute a flyer we had prepared comparing the ash fallout from the recent eruption of Mt. St. Helens to the nuclear fallout from a one-megaton hydrogen bomb.

When Lockheed's head of security, Peter McGivern, arrived, he held his gray head and exclaimed, "You people! You're really aging me!" Then he caught sight of blind Elizabeth, standing by the front door, her fragile body bending toward morning sun, her white cane planted firmly on U.S. Navy property. "Oh no!" he moaned, "Now you've gone too far—You're really pushing it this time! Look, if you'll just leave, no charges will be brought against you. All you have to do is to walk away, and you'll be free." Free? Of conscience and its burden? Elizabeth Bradley settled the matter. "I know what I want. I'm going to stay right here."

There was nothing to do but arrest us. As a cadre of Sunnyvale police approached, I turned to Edith and said, "Besides the gift of life itself, you have given me nothing of greater value than this moment."

After preliminary booking procedures, the four of us women were taken to a squad car. Elizabeth sat in front, behind the riot gun, with a bushel of bullets at her feet. When our driver had safely deposited us at the Elmwood Detention Facility for Women, in Milpitas, he turned to me, waved, and said, "I'll see you again, I'm sure—Bye!"

During the next five hours, we were stripped, searched, disinfected, dressed in pj's, fingerprinted, and photographed. Since I had been here last October, this experience with Elmwood's rite of devaluation, known as inmate processing, was now much easier. It had lost its power.

Sometime midafternoon, as Edith was soothing herself by reciting George Santayana sonnets, the ones she used in the dentist's chair, I was summoned from our hamster-cage holding cell. A male guard led me to a series of tiny cubicles, where inmates met with their clergy-persons and psychiatrists. A female officer waited for me inside one of these cubbyholes. As soon as the door was shut and locked, she threw her arms around me, crying, "Angel—Do you remember me?" I looked again. I remembered. "Nancy!" In the second year of my novitiate training as a nun, Nancy had been a first-year. I had been her "angel" or "big sister." She said, "I'm so embarrassed. Here I am, a fuzz, and there you are—a—a . . . " "Anything but an angel," I said, smiling.

Nancy moved quickly to the real reason why she wanted to talk with me, and asked, "Why in the world are you subjecting your moth-ers to this?" I laughed. "You don't know our mothers! They're here because they want to be. Why should their age take this privilege from them?"

She shrugged, then looked at a clipboard in her hands. "But you have a record, an FBI file." I pointed to Mother's picture on the page. "She does too." "Is that what you want?" "Yes, Nancy. Let it be recorded that on this date Edith Johnson Morris and Clare . . . " "Stop!" she said. "I mean, having a record is shameful!" "Could you frame them both?" I asked. "We'll hang them next to the painting of my great-grandmother, whose farm was a station on the underground rail-road." Shaking her head, Nancy pronounced her verdict: "You always were unpredictable. You always will be." Our interview was over.

Through the days that followed, the four of us felt increasingly at home among Elmwood's residents. Questions in the first twenty-four hours were typically, "What's a straight woman like you doing in a place like this?" and "If there's a juvenile hall, why isn't there a geriatric hall?" We had many openings for talking about why we were there, about the futility of war in a nuclear age, about the moral imperative to call the insanity of militarism what it is. The inmates' support was immediate and strong. As far as they were concerned, reasons for war were to inflate the economy and decrease population. The guards, however, expressed fears of vulnerability to the USSR. At the same time, they separated protesters from "criminal types" who had "done wrong."

Edith and I attended a church service during the five days we were there. The sermon was focused on asking "repentance for grave sin." The inmate congregation was spoken of as "you who have committed many sins, you who are risking God's displeasure, you who are in danger of everlasting exile." Here, protesters were not distinguished from "criminal types." We were all flawed humans. I liked that.

Despite the cigarette smoke, blaring pop music, and bright florescent lights of Elmwood's eighteen-hour days, in the midst of forced labor, drugged day sleepers, and raging conflicts, I discovered lotus blooms in the mud of this county jail. Newcomers arrived and old-timers helped them get settled. Sore backs were noticed and massaged. The need to tell one's story was given time and a hearing.

One of these lotus flowers was named Indian Power. About three o'clock one morning, Pearl staggered in, still drying out. Exhausted and sick, she flopped on her thin, plastic-covered mattress, unable to cope with sheets and blankets. During one of her frequent trips to the bathroom, Indian Power, who slept on a top bunk, climbed down, made Pearl's bed, and quickly returned to her own.

Another time, as I was reading a Hermann Hesse novel (chosen from such library selections as *Voodoo, Fathers of the Desert, Nietzsche, Shakespeare's Sonnets, Witchcraft,* and *The Practice of the Presence of God*) I overheard a group of prostitutes talking shop. "You use 'Handy Wipes' too? Gotta' take care of that 'Glory Hole,' yeah?" Brenda, who had made that remark, realized I was nearby, though evidently reading. She came to me, saying, "Hope you don't mind our girly-talk. We don't know nothin' else." I said, "I figure it's a good thing to find people you can talk to." She returned to her cluster of friends and asked them, "Do you think she's really a nun?" The prostitutes I met at Elmwood were my favorites among the residents. Though hardened by their work, they expressed a vulnerability that let us glimpse their pain.

Brenda was older than Lisa, one of several eighteen-year-old prostitutes in our dorm. One morning, Edith said to Lisa, "I love to watch you sleep. You are so beautiful, like a very young girl on the verge of womanhood." After a pause, Lisa said wistfully, "I wish I was." The older prostitutes told Edith and me that Lisa might not live very long, though there were elderly "hos," little old ladies in tennies and mini skirts. If Lisa "broke out of her ring," Brenda said, she would be "beaten and killed or a slave of her 'old man,' who would take her pay, and tell her to boost [steal] her clothes."

Being able to go straight didn't occur to anyone with whom we spoke, including Katie, the unofficial dorm leader. She was full of stories about how to use children for "jobs," what to do to avoid detection when stealing in a department store or supermarket, and how to avoid sexually transmitted diseases. Katie was a big-boned, rough-tough redhead, a horse trainer as well as a "mom" to all of us "dorm children."

Katie was also "Keeper of the Cobbler's Shoe" at Elmwood. A single crocheted slipper was passed from inmate to inmate, carrying with it the authority of a royal scepter. The Keeper must be able to crochet copies of this bootie for anyone who asked and was willing to pay for it. "If you got one of these pinned to you," Katie told us, "wherever you go in the world, people will know where you've been." Inside the Keeper's shoe, she kept a contraband quarter. This coin was given to chosen individuals when they went to the courthouse for sentencing.

Another duty of the Keeper was to crochet small white flowers for anyone whom she thought was ready to be released. Katie said these flowers, worn to a sentencing hearing, were a message to the court from the Keeper of the Cobbler's Shoe: "The wearer has been judged already. Let her be freed." Edith and I found a white flower on each of our pillows the day we were to be released, and Katie pressed a crocheted bootie into our hands as we hugged everyone goodbye.

One evening Katie warned, "You protesters had better watch out. Two misdemeanors make a felony." Edith said quietly, "That wouldn't matter." Katie shook her head and groaned. Then Edith changed the subject. "Do you all think I should cornrow my hair?" The women laughed, and some offered to undo her chignon and begin to braid. She surprised them by agreeing. For the next several hours, four residents brushed, measured, and wove Edith's graying, waist-length hair. The result resembled a Native American grandmother, ready to move on to her next seasonal village. We then had the dilemma of whether or not she should wear her many braids to court.

Then someone found out that Edith had secretly celebrated her seventy-fifth birthday at Elmwood. One of the residents donated a shoebox, covered it with bright paper, and filled it with treasures: a new tube of toothpaste, a candy bar, a small pad of paper, poems and songs they had written, pictures they had drawn with the pencil stubs they were allowed to have. "I never imagined that my seventy-fifth birthday would be so deeply honored. Now I will think of it as my favorite."

Here we are, a motley four, riding backwards to court. As we bump along to rock music on the radio, I smile at Katie's reprimand: "Listen! These dorms are crowded, people sleeping on the floor. Next time you guys want to protest, call first." Next time I'm at Elmwood, Katie, I hope you're not there. I hope you never return. It's different for us. We choose to be there.

DON EDWARD MORRIS

What do you do when you are sixty-two and permanently disabled by multiple sclerosis? The world gets much smaller when you can no longer go out into it easily. Time gets harder to fill without the use of hands and with increasingly limited endurance. Two problems arise, how to meet the needs for community and creativity. It helps to have a bit of serendipity. A year ago, I happened upon an article in the local newspaper about a writing group started by Maxine Hong Kingston that was still meeting after ten years. While the group's original purpose was to heal the wounds of Vietnam veterans through writing and an encouraging community, it had grown to include people from a number of backgrounds. Best of all, from my point of view, the group met only fifteen miles from my house. I had found my community.

A few years earlier, I had discovered that writing poetry was just the right medium for me. Poetry gets right to the point. You get in and you get out. It is a sprint not a marathon. A poem can be written easily on the computer with speech-recognition software. Most importantly, the poem, which originates in a chaos of images, impulses, and emotions, settles into a form in language which reveals a certain meaning. I believe, however, that even such a solitary pursuit as writing poetry eventually needs community for criticism, support and inspiration. In time, out of the community come individual friendships and teachers.

I wrote these poems in the early days of the Iraq invasion. They betray my "youth" as a poet. I am proud, however, to have them included with the writings of others who have lived through disabilities and dark times.

Shipping Away

Is there a space
for one more breath
in the farthest darkness
of a moonless night
in solitude and quietude
when life comes in
when life goes out

and a decision is made
to awake or stay dead
asleep?

The telephone . . .
the telephone . . .
the telephone . . .

Reality's ice cuts me awake
through so many layers of sleep,
where I was safe from what is,
where I was held in tepid timeless
unconcern . . . the telephone . . .
          I jump up,
without knowing where I reach out
        and grab . . . the telephone.

I can't think of anything warm
or polite to say,
I stand angry and dumb.
I hear a voice distant,
yet familiar, like home,
my beautiful son speaking:
dad, we're shipping out today.
I only have a minute left
and I wanted to say goodbye.
Goodbye dad. I love you.

I think I said
I love you too, son. Take care.

Nothing left but to crawl
back into sleep and sometime
closer to morning fall
into a dream.

A strange desert.
Wind driven by centuries
of last sighs
drove the sands
into shrouds

infused with
moonlike peace
welcoming
1,000 last breaths
to enter.
One turned
around
and waved
goodbye.

Letters from Lindsey to her Dad on Active Duty Somewhere in the Middle East

The Allison Family:

David, 35, Electronics technician, SSgt. Army Reserve
Jennifer, 32, Customer Service Representative
Ryan, 13, 8th grade
Lindsey, 10, 5th grade
Bucky, 3

Dear Daddy,

Mommy said I could write anytime I wanted so here
goes. Yesterday when you went into the airplane
Mommy started crying then I did then Bucky. Even
Ryan started. Then Mommy said lets go to McDonald's.
Bucky started shouting "go have pig yak" until Ryan told
him to stuff a sock in it. We all laughed.

Love,
Lindsey

Dear Daddy,

How are you? Have you got there yet? Where are you
going to be stationed? The Army won't tell us. We really
miss you already. You know Bucky's favorite animal book

that he only let you read to him? Now he only wants
Ryan to read it to him. Yesterday when Ryan was playing
video games Bucky just went over and sat down on his
lap and said read. Ryan got all mad but read it to him anyway.

Love,
Lindsey

Dear Daddy,

Today at school Stephen T. said you were just going over
to kill a bunch of people. He said you would be a
murderer. I felt like killing him. But Mrs. Hammond told
us to sit down. Later I told him you would never kill
anyone. Would you? Please write and tell me.

Love,
Lindsey

Dear Daddy,

You haven't written to us yet, are you ok? I asked
Mommy where you were and she said the Army can't say
that it's a secret. Amanda's mother got called up too. She
is a nurse. It's going to be real hard for her dad because he
got laid off from his job. Amanda has three sisters and one
brother.

Love,
Lindsey

Dear Daddy,

I'm really worried about Mommy. She cries a lot and
doesn't get up in the morning until late. Kimmi's mom
has been coming over in the morning to give us breakfast
and get us ready for school. When we come home mom
is still in her bathrobe. Uncle Dennis is coming over
tonight to talk to her. I think she misses you a lot.

Love,
Lindsey

Dear Daddy,

Mommy had to go to the hospital for a few days. We stayed with Uncle Dennis and Aunt Sally. Now Mommy has to take some pills but she is feeling better. But she still wishes you were here. So do I.

Love,
Lindsey

Dear Daddy,

Are you ok? We get no letters from you. Yesterday Ryan got suspended from school for fighting. He has been getting bad grades since you left. He and mom fight all the time. I wish you could come home so our family could be happy again.

Love,
Lindsey

Dear Daddy,

Grandma and Grandpa Allison came over Saturday. They brought me the newest Harry Potter book! They were going to a big antiwar march in San Francisco. They wanted mom to know that they love you and pray for you every day but they think what the government is doing is wrong. They had a big sign with your picture on it.

Love,
Lindsey

Dear Daddy,

The news keeps saying there's lots of fighting still. Are you okay? Bucky is really mad because mom won't let him watch his cartoons on TV. Mom just wants to watch the news. They talk about the war all the time but they don't say much. I hope you are safe. Have you killed anyone yet? Mrs. Hammond had to stop class yesterday because so many kids were crying. We are going to have an assembly today.

Love,
Lindsey

Dear Daddy,

When is this stupid war going to be over? When are you going come home? Mommy is starting to cry again. Ryan was caught with some marawana at school and was suspended again. Mommy is worried about losing her job. We got a new puppy to make us feel better.

Love,
Lindsey

Dear Dad,

Please come home now. Things are getting really bad for Mommy and Ryan. We need you here at home. Bucky gave me this picture for you. He says it's him and you painting the house. I love you. COME HOME SOON.

Love,
Lindsey

I entered college in the Fall of 1966, not long after "The Ballad of the Green Berets" hit number one on the charts. It was early in the Vietnam War, and I was a strong supporter of the war. I majored in political science, with dreams of a glamorous, globetrotting life in the diplomatic service.

By the spring of 1969, the war was tearing America apart. I took a course in international relations, and for my term paper I determined to prove our involvement in Vietnam was legal under international law and in our national interest. After weeks in the library trying to prove us "right," facts forced me to opposite conclusions, and I became a vocal opponent of the war.

"Draft Night" is a story of events triggered by Richard Nixon's draft lottery. Like several characters in the story, I pulled a bad number that night. I had no intention of fighting in a war I knew to be wrong, and considered Canada. But as bad as Vietnam was, Soviet divisions were poised to strike across the Iron Curtain. Rather than submit to the draft, or evade it, I conflated my crisscrossed beliefs and became what the U.S. Army called a D.I.E., a "draft-induced enlistment," and did my time as an MP in Germany.

"Draft Night" was originally to be part of a novel about the damage done to American society by the war in Vietnam. Eventually, I decided the best way convey how Vietnam warped our history was to create a world in which there had been no Vietnam War. The result is my first novel, *The Energy Caper,* in which a "good" Richard Nixon, with no Vietnam or Watergate to slow him down, fights the Arab oil embargo and unwittingly saves the planet from the catastrophe of global warming. Somewhere, in a parallel universe or an alternate reality, it could even be true.

Draft Night

On the evening of Monday, December 1, 1969, President Richard Milhous Nixon held a prime-time lottery that riveted America to its television sets. The drawing was not your usual get-rich-quick, jackpot type of lottery, but a roll of the dice to determine which young men would be conscripted to fight, and maybe to die, in the faraway jungles of Vietnam.

I was only eighteen, a lowly freshman pledge in my second day of Hell Week. If I made it through, I would be brotherized, becoming a full-fledged member of Tau Kappa Omega, TKO—a Toke. I was also at the start of a four-year student deferment, so I wasn't too worried what draft number I pulled, but for guys whose four years were almost up, their numbers could be a matter of life or death.

I was on bar duty making the rounds, refilling beer cups from a pitcher from the newly tapped keg. It was rare to tap a keg on a weeknight, even at a hard-core party house like TKO's, but this was a night unlike any other. There must have been a hundred people in the house. About a third were women—in those days everybody called them "chicks"—the dates and pin-mates of various brothers and their guests, as well as TKO's "Little Sisters," honorary Tokes who were hands-off to all brothers.

Our pledgemaster, Kellner, blew his whistle and ordered everybody out of the living room so we could set up like we did for watching away football games. Everyone moved into the foyer and the card and dining rooms, everyone but Looney Larry. At twenty-four he was the oldest guy in the house, a super-senior who should have graduated but had gamed the system into extending his deferment. He just sat and grinned, forcing six of us to pick up his chair and move it with him on it while he blew smoke rings like the lunatic he was. He should have been deferred by reason of insanity.

We arranged the couches and chairs into a wide horseshoe around the color TV, ran the big vacuum, emptied ashtrays, sponged off tables, brought in logs, and stoked the fire until it roared. It was my turn to feed our St. Bernard mascot, Aphie, so I went to the service kitchen for dog chow and the bones and scraps the cook always sent up the dumbwaiter. I filled her bowl and water dish, took them to the side porch, and called "Aphie!" She came right over and let me towel the snow off her thick coat and snap on her chain. She would be content gnawing on her bones until we let her in later to sleep by the fire. Unlike the rest of us, Aphie was not concerned who won or lost Nixon's lottery.

The Little Sisters, all of them in TKΩ Penn State sweatshirts, had been busy making twelve narrow posters, one for each month, using magic markers and sheets of butcher paper from the kitchen. The posters had the days in a column on the left, and on the right were two blank columns with room for a name and a number. We put them up on the living room walls with masking tape, January through December. "Makes the place look like a bookie joint," somebody said.

When the room was ready, Kellner blew his whistle and yelled, "Listen up! Anybody who's not in the pool yet, see pledge Rhinebecker. Okay. Ready, set," and he blew his whistle, setting off a stampede as brothers vaulted over the backs of couches and elbowed each other out of the way in a race to get the best seats.

Everybody was on edge, but the seniors were really sweating, including my "big brother," McGill, who everybody called "Stick" because he was so skinny. I'd picked him as my big brother partly because he played guitar, but mostly because we were both from Milltowne and he had his own car. He was a political science major and planned to go to law school, but he would be graduating into the teeth of Nixon's new system. A Little Sister went up to him and asked, "Did you send off your applications yet, Stick?"

"No, but they're all filled out. If I pull a decent number, I'll write the checks and send them first thing tomorrow. If I'm screwed, I'll bag it and use the money to go to the Orange Bowl."

His plan made sense to me. We'd been undefeated for two years in a row, were ranked number two in the polls, and set to play number five Missouri in the Orange Bowl on New Year's Day. If I knew I was going to die in Vietnam, there's no way I'd have blown good money on law school applications if I could have used it to party in Florida and see us win a national championship.

A girl in a flowery *Make Love Not War* sweatshirt asked McGill, "Can't you just get a note from a doctor if you get a bad number?" Tens of thousands of guys had been getting phony medical "outs" to beat the draft. Trick knees were a favorite because they were hard to disprove. You could also get out for minor defects like flat feet and curvature of the spine. Doctors for many famous athletes swore their patients' knees or shoulders or backs prevented them from serving in the military, but were not serious enough to keep them from playing professional baseball or football.

For healthy guys who weren't sports stars and didn't have a doctor willing to lie for them, there were various self-inflicted outs, like blowing off your little toe with a shotgun, inducing high blood pressure with drugs, pigging out to become overweight, and for the really desperate, claiming to be sexually perverted. McGill was skinny and klutzy, but neither condition rated an out. He just shrugged and told her, "Nah, I'm healthy as a horse."

She tried to be upbeat. "Well maybe when you take your physical they'll find something you don't know you have?"

"Ha, now that's a laugh," said McGill's old buddy, Frankie Dombrowski. Frankie was on leave from the Army, and had hitchhiked up with his guitar for a final fling before shipping out to Vietnam. They'd been in a rock 'n' roll band in high school, Frankie and the Dynamos. I'd seen them play once, four years before, at my junior high prom. The girls called Frankie "the Polish Elvis" because of his chiseled good looks and wavy black hair. He'd gone to college at Pitt and, like McGill, would have been a senior, but last spring he'd flunked French, his average dropped below 2.0, and the draft board nailed him. With his buzz-cut GI haircut and olive-drab Army field jacket, he didn't look much like Elvis any more.

"Let me tell you what my physical was like," Frankie said. "They made us take our clothes off and stand bare-assed with our toes on a yellow line. Then two guys in white coats came along. One said open your mouth and say aahh, and the other said bend over and spread your cheeks. Then the first one shined a flashlight down your throat, and the second one shined a light up your asshole. If they didn't see each other, you passed."

We all cracked up, and Frankie said to McGill, "I'm supposed to pick that Annie chick up at her dorm pretty soon. You were going to make me a map to that parking spot in case I get lucky."

How Frankie had finagled a date with Annie Chambers, president of Chi Omega sorority and this year's Homecoming Queen, God only knows. He'd just met her that afternoon down at the Lions Den. I couldn't imagine a girl like that going parking on a first date.

It was a strict university rule that women were not permitted above the first floor of frat houses after nine, so McGill drew a map to the duck pond, where they could park without being hassled by cops. "There's blankets in the trunk," McGill said as he gave Frankie his keys. "And don't forget, Ladies Curfew's at midnight."

"Thanks, Stick," Frankie said, and as he headed out the door he flashed a peace sign and yelled to everybody, "Good luck you guys."

Kellner's pin-mate, Darlene, a Tri-Delt, who were arch-rivals of the Chi-O's for best sorority, went over to McGill and asked, "Does your friend really have a date with Chambers?"

"Yeah, why?"

She gave him a sly smile. "Well, you know what they say about Chi-O's and Vietnam, don't you?"

"No, what?"

She was delighted to spread the rumor. "They're into a Florence Nightingale thing. If your friend is on his way to Vietnam, he'll get a Chi-O mercy fuck."

McGill broke into a laugh. "He might get laid, but it won't be out of mercy. Chicks cream their jeans for Dombrowski."

Like most eighteen-year-olds in those more innocent days, I was still a virgin, so it was hard for me to imagine what a Chi-O mercy fuck with a Homecoming Queen might be like. Would the other Chi-O's do a sorority cheer and wave pom-poms?

Rhinebecker was walking around with a flip-over calendar and a cigar box full of cash for the house pool, calling out, "Anybody not in yet better sign up. Only a few minutes to go."

I already had my money in, but McGill waved Rhinebecker over and said, "How's it work?"

"Everybody puts in a buck," Rhinebecker said. "Third place gets five, second gets ten, the winner gets the jackpot. Ties split."

"Oh, how exciting," Darlene said. "Can I get in too?"

"Sorry, no chicks allowed," Rhinebecker said with a firm shake of his head.

Her lips turned down in a pout. "Guys have all the fun."

"Oh yeah," McGill said as he handed Rhinebecker a five. "Waiting to see if your life is going down the tubes sure is fun all right."

"When's your birthday, Brother McGill?" Rhinebecker asked as he counted out change.

"March seventeenth."

"Hey, St. Patrick's Day," Rhinebecker said as he flipped the calendar to March and wrote McGill's name in the 17 square. "Luck of the Irish to you, Brother McGill, sir."

McGill gave him a dollar back. "Put this in for Dombrowski. November third."

Rhinebecker furrowed his brow. "But he's already in the Army."

"So?"

Rhinebecker seemed confused. "But the lottery won't affect him."

"Are you arguing with me, pledge?"

Rhinebecker shouted, "No *sir,* Brother McGill, *sir!*" He took the dollar and hurriedly flipped to November and wrote in Frankie's name before McGill dropped him for push-ups.

The room was crackling with excitement as Nixon's big show began. Not even during the frenzy over Walt Disney's *Davy Crockett* had so many war babies (we were not yet dubbed "boomers") been glued to the tube at the same time. To one degree or another, the results would affect the majority of healthy guys born between 1944 and 1952. About the only guys who would not be affected were those who were currently serving in uniform, those who had already served in uniform, and the 30,000 or so who had already died in uniform.

The rules for who had to fight and who did not had changed over the years as the war dragged on. Between 1964 and 1967, President Lyndon Johnson eliminated, one by one, deferments for marriage, children, and graduate school (except for medical and divinity students). Only the four-year deferment for college undergraduates remained. For the past several years, all males between eighteen and twenty-six who were not full-time students with a grade-point average of 2.0 or higher were "draft bait," with the oldest taken first. It was a system that put guys at risk for eight long years. Many said it was a major factor fueling the antiwar protests, and there was widespread criticism from all quarters of its fairness.

Nixon was changing the system so that all the American males in the draft pool would be assigned random numbers based on their birthdays. Barring a national emergency, males in this pool would be at risk only for the next year—one year instead of eight. New lotteries would be held in succeeding years for boys who had come of draft age, and future quotas would be filled by the boys of those cohorts who did not receive college deferments. Critics said the lottery was a devious Nixonian ploy to take the steam out of the antiwar movement. By limiting the risk of being drafted to an unlucky few, and placing the burden of future drafts on younger boys not yet old enough to drive, much less vote, there would be fewer angry males willing to take to the streets to protest. I wasn't sure about Nixon's motivation, as I was only six months out of high school and didn't know much about political ploys, but I knew he wasn't called "Tricky Dick" for nothing.

Before the drawing, the Pentagon had been publicizing the Army's anticipated manpower needs for the coming year so everybody knew what to expect. The official estimate was that males in the highest third, with lottery numbers from about 240 and up, were relatively safe and could get on with their lives, those in the middle third, from "about" 125 to 240, would "probably" not be drafted, and all healthy males in the lowest third who had no deferment were goners.

I thought the new system was good for me. As a freshman starting a four-year deferment, if I kept a gentleman's C for the next year, I wouldn't have to worry unless things got so bad Viet Cong war canoes came paddling up the Ohio River and attacked Milltowne.

When Nixon's show began, the carpet in front of the TV was packed tight with guys sitting cross-legged, like at a rock concert. The crowd behind the horseshoe of couches and chairs stood four and five deep, with guys in the back standing on radiators and tables and chairs brought in from the dining room to get a view of the tube.

The soothing voice of Walter Cronkite, America's most trusted journalist, explained how the drawing would work. The camera focused on a clear, cylindrical jar, about two feet high, the same exact one used in the lotteries of 1917 and 1940. At the bottom of the jar were 366 blue plastic capsules, about an inch long, each containing a piece of paper with a different day of the year on it. Cronkite held up a sample, and somebody in back yelled, "What's it look like?"

"Like a fucking horse pill," came an answer.

The capsules would be picked at random, and the order in which your birthday came up was your very own draft number. Unlike most lotteries, the sooner your number came up, the bigger you lost.

When Nixon's face appeared on the screen, the house rocked to a cacophony of hisses and boos and shouts of "asshole!" and "motherfucker!" Just then I saw that Rotsee Ross had come in, carrying his white saucer hat in one hand and brushing snow off the shoulders of his navy-blue ROTC overcoat with the other. He grabbed a chair from the dining room and climbed up. When he saw Nixon, he began shaking his hat at the TV and motherfuckering louder than anybody. I could hardly believe it. What did it say about the war if a future officer in the United States Navy hated Nixon that much?

The event began when a dour Republican congressman nobody had ever heard of stepped up to the jar to pick the first number. The banter stopped, and the house became eerily silent. It must have been like that all across America as millions of guys and their friends and families gulped and held their collective breath. The congressman seemed to be enjoying himself as he bent over and shoved his arm deep into the jar, right to the bottom. He fished around for a few seconds, then pulled out a capsule and handed it to an official seated at a table. The official opened the capsule, removed the paper, read it, showed it to other officials sitting around him, held it up, and said, "September fourteenth."

"September fourteenth," Cronkite repeated in his most stentorian anchorman tone. "September fourteenth is number one."

Everybody looked around to see who would claim the first-place money, but no one did. Rhinebecker checked the calendar in case the winner wasn't present, shook his head, and said, "Nobody's got it."

A Little Sister wrote "1" next to 14 on the September poster with a black marker and put a line through the space where a name would have gone.

After the first pick, instead of an official doing the picking, the remaining numbers were chosen by 365 young men of draft age from every state in the union, who had been flown in to do the dirty work. A cheery-faced guy no older than me stuck his arm in the jar, picked a capsule, and handed it to the official. Soon Cronkite intoned, "April twenty-fourth. Number two is April twenty-fourth."

"Hey that's me!" said somebody's date, but she didn't count, and nobody else said anything.

Rhinebecker checked and said, "Nobody's got it." A Little Sister with a black marker wrote "2" next to 24 on the April poster, and another used a pink marker to write in the nonwinner's name.

On the third pull Cronkite said, "December thirtieth—"

A plaintive *"NOOO!"* wailed out, and up from a couch jumped Baker, a ladies' man who always seemed to have a different girl on his arm, just about the last guy you'd expect to see carrying a rifle. Like McGill, Baker was a senior and out of options. He hopped around, shaking his head, tugging at his blond, Beatlesque hair and screaming, "NOOO! FUCKING *NOOOOO!*"

The brotherhood offered him its sincerest condolences:

"Die, Baker, *die!"*

"Your ass is grass, Baker!"

"Dead meat, Baker!"

Somebody sang out, "Bake, Bake, Baker man, go to Nam, fast as you can," and everybody joined in, chanting, "Bake, Bake, Baker man, go to Nam, fast as you can!"

A Little Sister using a red marker put a "3" next to 30 on the December poster, wrote in Baker's name, drew a fat circle around it, and put a big red star next to it.

Rhinebecker took out a ten and a five to cover second and third place and handed Baker the cigar box stuffed with cash. "Congratulations, Brother Baker, sir!"

Baker opened the lid, peered in, then shaking his head in disbelief, slumped down in his seat on the couch and made a goofy show out of counting his winnings, one bill at a time, but his wide-eyed, shit-eating grin betrayed his utter despair.

With the big money out of the way, everybody relaxed, and the race was on for second. For a while it seemed nobody would take it until Cronkite said, "Number eighteen is September twenty-sixth—"

"Holy shit!"

It was a guy in my pledge class, Sharrock, a freshman like me.

"Pledge Sharrock takes second," Rhinebecker announced, and handed him the ten-dollar prize. It seemed unfair for a freshman to be in the money, since if he kept a C average for a year he would be safe unless Nixon changed the rules again.

On the twenty-seventh pick Cronkite said, "July twenty-first."

"Jesus fucking tits!"

It was Zovis, a junior, whose GPA hovered dangerously close to 2.0. Already overweight from his job as a fry cook at the Char-Pit, he often joked about eating his way into a deferment. He wasted no time, taking his five-dollar prize and yelling, "Sharrock, go call Marino's and order me a large pepperoni with mushrooms and extra cheese."

Next up was fourth place, just out of the money, the biggest loser of all—the douchebag of the day. A few numbers went by and Cronkite said, "March seventeenth is number thirty-three. Saint Patrick's Day is number thirty-three."

McGill was standing in the back, a cigarette in one hand, a beer in the other. A dazed, ashen look came over his face as Rhinebecker yelled, "That's Brother McGill!" and everybody began hooting, "DOOOOSSHH! DOOOOSSHH! DOOOOSSHH!"

The numbers rolled on, with guys going down, boom-boom-boom. At sixty-seven they nailed Stugall, a super-senior who had an apartment in town. "Fuck this shit!" he yelled, held his cup up high, and cried, "Tales!"

An echoing roar of "Tales!" went up, and the guys with bad numbers charged downstairs for what would become an historic session of every fraternity's favorite drinking game—Wales Tales.

Twenty minutes later, I pulled ninety-three, and felt a little guilty for not being worried. All I needed was a C average for a year, and after that I could drop out, flunk out, or do any damn thing I wanted and not have to worry about dying in the jungles.

When the numbers hit 125, Kellner surprised us pledges by giving the four of us with bad numbers the rest of the night off, suspending our Hell Week, while the lucky pledges who had yet to pull numbers painted the third-floor hallway.

Man, were they ever pissed, but I felt no guilt and headed right down to the action in the Red Room, TKO's party haven for over fifty years. You could smell the Red Room when you opened the door at the top of the basement stairs as the sour aroma of five decades of beer parties wafted up and punched you in the nose. It was about forty feet long by twenty feet wide, and had a masculine, hunting-lodge-meets-rathskeller ambiance. Built into the walls around the room were bench seats of cushioned red vinyl, and it was furnished with six highly varnished oak picnic tables and benches. The walls were dark maroon, with oak trim, with a pair of Old West–style saloon doors leading to the dance room. It was the heart and soul of a party house like TKO, and pledges waxed and buffed its hardwood floors to a glistening shine after every event.

When the drawing hit 125, the Pentagon's projected cutoff of those who were "likely" to be drafted from those who "might" be drafted, guys whose numbers hadn't come up yet got to feeling better about their futures and came trickling to the Red Room to get into games.

When anybody's birthday was drawn, Rhinebecker would announce it. When he came down and yelled, "Brother Nichols is two-forty-eight," Nichols stood up and shouted, "Here's to Richard Nixon! I'm fucking *out!*"

McGill gave him the finger. "Fuck you, asshole."

The keg kicked about midnight, but the losers insisted on tapping the spare keg to keep things going. About twelve thirty Frankie showed up to the roaring din of six simultaneous Tales games. He came over to our table and asked McGill, "How'd you do?"

"Thirty fucking three."

Frankie shook his head. "Damn, Stick, that's a bummer."

"Know what you'd have been, asshole?"

Frankie grinned a wide, satisfied smile. "Nah, I was getting to know Annie. She's a very friendly girl."

"Three-forty-eight. You'd be home free if you hadn't flunked French, and now you're gonna get your ass blown away for nothing. Fucking nothing. You really piss me off, Dombrowski."

Draft Night voided all the rules. For the losers like Baker and McGill, it was a night out of the *Rubaiyat,* a night to forget how screwed you were—*eat, drink, and be merry, for tomorrow we may die!* For the winners with safe numbers like Nichols, it was a night to celebrate the biggest victory of their lives. For the guys in the middle, it was a night not to be missed, the most emotional, fuck-it-all bull session in modern American history. Guys argued all sides of everything, for and against the war, the winners ragging the losers and everybody wondering just what they were going to do with the rest of their lives.

For the first time in TKO memory, the heads rolled joints right out in the open and passed them around like it was Woodstock. Even the most tight-assed straights kept their mouths shut, and several even turned on for the first time. And if you started feeling sick from too much beer, you went outside, stuck your finger down your throat, blew lunch in a snowbank, and came back for more.

We took occasional breaks from the games and got into the bawdy drinking songs the alumni always sang when they came back for Homecoming. One verse in particular summed up the lifestyle:

> We toast the girls who do
> We toast the girls who don't
> We toast the girls who say they will
> And then they say they won't
> But the girls we toast
> From the break o' day
> Until the late o' night
> Are the girls who say they never have
> But just for you they might.

Say I-I-I think
We need another drink
Say I-I-I think
We need another drink
Say I-I-I think
We need another drink
To the brotherhood
Of Tee-Kay-OOOhh.

Frankie sat at our table and joined the game, and at one point some-body asked him, "How'd they get you? You went to Pitt, right?"

A sheepish look came over Frankie's face. "I was in a new band and gigging a lot, and I didn't put much time into French, so—"

"Oh, bullshit, Dombrowski," McGill said and belched a long, beery buurrrppp. "You got your ass drafted because you think you're fuck-ing Elvis. But they drafted Elvis, douchebag, like in *Bye-Bye Birdie*. So now it's bye-bye Frankie, and you're gonna get your ass blown away for nothing. Fucking nothing. What an asshole you are."

"That's how they got Johnny Zimmer," somebody said. "He flunks chemistry, and the next thing you know he's beating the bush in some place called Phu Bai."

"Have you thought about going to Canada?" somebody asked.

"I hear Toronto's okay," Frankie said, "but I don't —"

"Screw Toronto, Dombrowski!" McGill shouted. "Haul your dumb ass up to Montreal where you can *parley-vous* some French and maybe get your fucking grades up."

Frankie smiled and gave McGill the finger. Then he reached for his wallet and pulled out a piece of paper and began unfolding it. "Talk-ing about being drafted, ever see one of these?"

"What is it?" somebody asked.

"A greeting from Uncle Sam," and he passed his induction notice around for everyone to see. When it got to McGill, he held it up and read it out loud:

SELECTIVE SERVICE SYSTEM ORDER TO
REPORT FOR INDUCTION

From: The President of the United States

To: Francis James Dombrowski
184 West Seneca Street
Milltowne, Pennsylvania

GREETINGS:

You are hereby ordered for induction into the Armed
Forces of the United States, and to report at the Federal
Office Building, 1000 Liberty Avenue, Pittsburgh,
Pennsylvania, on 12 July 1969 at 6:45 a.m. for forwarding
to an Armed Forces Induction Station.

Signed Edward T. Braatz
Clerk of local board #758
For Brig. General John S. Hershey
Commander, Selective Service System

McGill folded it up and started to put it in his own wallet.
"Hey, what do you think you're doing?" Frankie said.
"I'll hang on to it so you don't lose it in a rice paddy. When you get
back, I'll buy you a beer and we'll burn the sucker."
Frankie grinned. "You're on."
I crashed out on a couch at about three, but McGill and Frankie
and the other losers stayed up till the keg kicked. In the morning, I
went back to Hell Week, and I didn't see McGill or Frankie until after
dinner, when it was my turn for door-duty. They were in the living
room, which still had the feel of a bookie joint with the lottery-result
posters hanging on the walls. There was a fifth of Jack Daniels on the
coffee table, and they were laughing and folding the pages of McGill's
law school applications into paper airplanes and sailing them into the
fireplace.
I took my station by the front door, and when the pay phone in the
coat closet rang, I answered, "Tau Kappa Omega, Pledge Dawkins
speaking. How may I help you?"
"Can I speak with Frankie Dombrowski?" asked a female voice.
"May I ask who's calling?"
"Annie Chambers."
I called Frankie to the phone. He closed the closet door, and a minute
later came out and told us Annie was going to sneak out of the dorm
and asked McGill if he could borrow his car and some money for a
motel room.
She was taking a big risk and could be expelled for violating the
strict *in loco parentis* rules. McGill gave Frankie his keys and his last

twenty and ordered me to call the Holiday Inn and book a room for Mr. and Mrs. Dombrowski.

Around eleven the next day Frankie brought Annie to the house and introduced us. Her silky blond hair was in a ponytail, and her complexion so perfect she could have stepped off a magazine cover, but her eyes were puffy, like she'd been crying.

We loaded Frankie's duffel bag and guitar case into the trunk. I rode shotgun, McGill drove, and Annie clung to Frankie in the back seat as we took her to the dorm. I tried not to listen as she sobbed like a kindergartner and Frankie promised over and over he'd be careful and would write as soon as he could. He gave her a long kiss in the parking lot, and as we pulled away I watched the most beautiful girl I'd ever met standing in the snow, wiping tears from her eyes, and looking like she was the one who needed mercy.

"Man," Frankie said, "chicks are so strange."

On the way to the hitchhiking spot McGill offered to take Frankie to Canada. "Niagara Falls isn't that far, and if we leave right now we can have you across the border before dark. And I've got a couple hundred from those law school applications I won't be needing you can have to get started."

Frankie shook his head. "Thanks, Stick, but I'm no deserter. So what are you gonna do now that you know your number?"

"Damned if I know," McGill said. "I've got a few months to figure something out."

Nowadays old friends would hug at a big good-bye like that, but back then guys wouldn't be caught dead hugging each other. No way. I took Frankie's stuff out of the trunk as he and McGill shook hands, strong, John Wayne handshakes, followed by a long hippie peace clasp— thumbs interlocked, fingers wrapping around the back of the other's hand—and gave each other hearty slaps on the back.

"Nice knowing you, Bob," Frankie said, giving me a handshake and a peace clasp. I can still see him standing there in the snow, wearing jeans, combat boots, his Army field jacket, and a Steelers stocking cap and holding the cardboard sign I'd made for him with PITT on one side and MILLTOWNE on the other. Right away a VW bus with a Peace Now bumper sticker stopped. The side door rolled open, and Frankie handed in his guitar and duffel bag. Then he turned to us, grinned, and flashed a peace sign as he climbed into the van for the first leg of his journey to Vietnam.

After Draft Night, things got back to normal for everybody except the big losers whose deferments would soon be up. I made it through finals and Hell Week and got brotherized, but McGill didn't even bother studying. With a healthy body, a bad draft number, and an expiring deferment, grades didn't matter any more. Instead, he read *The Hobbit* and all three volumes of *Lord of the Rings* and organized the TKO expedition to the Orange Bowl.

The plan was for a dozen of us to go down in three cars, meeting up at the Miami TKO house. McGill picked me up at my parents' house in Milltowne at 5 A.M. the day after Christmas. We took the turnpike to Philadelphia, where we picked up Baker and Nichols, then headed south. The Miami house was not locked, and the only guys there were some Tokes from Missouri who had the same ideas about fraternal visitation privileges that we did. It was as if the Miami Tokes purposely left the house open for us. We moved right in, and didn't do any damage I knew of, though I'm sure they weren't too happy when they came back and found the mess we left.

Our defense dominated the game and we won easily, but the team ranked ahead of us in the polls, Texas, won its game in the Cotton Bowl. We had played the better team, and had been undefeated for two straight years. We were hopeful that if the sports writers voted for the best team, we would be number one.

But Richard Nixon, in keeping with his "Southern strategy," killed any chance we had by calling the Texas coach and proclaiming them the national champions. He didn't even have the decency to mention our claim to the title, which should tell you all you need to know about the character of Richard Milhous Nixon.

We slept in late, then headed north, stopping in Daytona Beach for the night to check out the action. We laid around on the beach the next day, and about eight that evening we climbed in the car and took turns driving straight through. We dropped Baker and Nichols off in Philly about ten the next morning just as a freezing rain began to fall. McGill and I got on the turnpike and pulled into a Howard Johnson's service plaza to clean up and eat breakfast before the final push across Pennsylvania to Milltowne.

We gassed up first, and then used the men's room. McGill stayed to brush his teeth and shave while I went to wait in line for a booth in the crowded restaurant, figuring to clean up after we ate. I bought a *Pittsburgh Post-Gazette* in the gift shop, got a table, and ordered two coffees. I was leafing through the paper when a headline caught my eye: "Services Today For Local Singer." An icy despair shuddered through me when I looked at the photo under the headline and saw Frankie's face looking back at me.

The article said: "U.S. Army Private First Class Francis James Dombrowski, twenty-one years old, a popular singer from Milltowne, was killed by multiple fragmentation wounds the day after Christmas while on patrol in Phuoc Long province. He had been in Vietnam for only eight days when he died. Services will be held this afternoon at Stigwood's Funeral Home in Milltowne."

McGill slid into the booth and said, "What's new?"

It was all I could do to just push the paper across the table.

I sat in the bright orange vinyl booth and watched McGill read about Frankie. I was totally numb, hardly able to breath. He looked up at me in wide-eyed disbelief. Tears were streaming down his face as he read it for a second time. And a third. Then he calmly folded the paper and said, "We gotta go."

It was not until many years later, after I became a psychologist and started working with combat vets, that I came to understand what might have happened. I told a few of the vets I work with about Frankie and asked what they thought, and they all came up with similar scenarios: Frankie was the "FNG"—the fucking-new guy— and FNGs were always screwing up and getting killed. Maybe his platoon came across a village of "doubtfuls," grunt slang for peasants whose loyalty was impossible to determine. His sergeant might have ordered him to check out a hooch for signs of Charlie, and in his inexperience, he tripped a booby trap. Chances were high he never knew what hit him.

We raced along the sleet-covered turnpike, through the tunnels and past mountain after dismal mountain of naked black trees in the dead January landscape. McGill kept his foot to the floor, ninety, ninety-five, a hundred-and-five, weaving in and out of traffic, chain-smoking cigarettes, blaring the horn and flashing the lights and yelling, "Get the fuck out of the way!" We somehow made it to the funeral home alive before the procession left for the cemetery. I'd only known Frankie for a few days, and wasn't sure I even deserved to be there. There were hundreds of somber people, heads hung low, all in their Sunday best. I felt like a Slobovian jerk in jeans and a sweatshirt, with two days of stubble on my face. I hadn't even brushed my teeth. It was also my very first time in a funeral home, and I had no idea what to do or what to expect. After all these years, I still think of Frankie every time I walk into one. They say the sense of smell evokes the strongest memories, and the gooey-sweet smell of funeral homes always brings him to mind. An organist was playing music that made it seem ten times worse.

A group of old friends saw McGill and came over, the girls crying and hugging, the guys speaking in whispers. Frankie's two little brothers, about eight and ten years old, saw him and raced up yelling, "Mom, Dad, Stick's here, Stick's here!"

He bent down and wrapped them in his arms, and I followed them over to where Frankie's mom and dad were accepting condolences. His dad was wearing medals on his suitcoat, showing that he too had served his country. The only jewelry Frankie's mom wore was a single Gold Star, pinned on her black dress. It was only later that I learned Gold Stars were given to mothers whose sons were killed in the line of duty.

The casket was closed, so Frankie must have been torn up pretty bad. Flowers were everywhere, and there were pictures of Frankie on tables around the room: at four, in a cowboy hat shooting a cap gun; at seven, in a Superman cape, arms extended, pretending to fly; at ten, in a Little League uniform with a baseball bat over his shoulder; at twelve, with his first guitar; at sixteen, in a tuxedo for the junior prom; at eighteen, with his Stratocaster slung low to his waist and belting out a song under a *Frankie and the Dynamos* banner. It occurred to me that Annie Chambers probably didn't know what had happened, and I had a pang of guilt for being thankful it was McGill, and not me, who would be the one to tell her.

He talked to Frankie's mom and dad for a few minutes, then he introduced me. "This is Bob Dawkins. He met Frankie when he came up to see me."

I had no idea what to say to the parents of a guy I barely knew who had just been killed in the war. "I . . . I only knew Frankie for a few days, but I really liked him."

His dad seemed to understand how awkward it was for me, curling the corners of his mouth up in a sad smile. "That's how Frankie was, son. Everybody liked him."

Others were waiting in line to offer condolences, and as we moved away McGill said, "I need to go have a talk with Frankie."

As he approached the casket he noticed Frankie's Stratocaster, with its flaming-orange sunburst finish, on a guitar stand, a musical island in the sea of flowers. It was as if Frankie was between sets, just taking a break, and would stroll up any minute, strap on his Strat, and launch into his gritty version of "Susie Q." McGill picked up the guitar, knelt down, put it over his knee, and strummed a chord. It was off, so he meticulously tuned each string. When he got it just right, he played a few chords, and carefully placed it back on the stand.

The casket was draped in an American flag and guarded by two U.S. Army soldiers with ceremonial rifles. A big photo of Frankie, with his wavy black hair and his Elvis Presley good looks, smiled out from a gold frame at the head of the casket. McGill put his hands on top of the flag on the casket, and just like he always did, said, "Hey, Frankie, what's happening?"

He was silent for a long minute. Then he picked up Frankie's photo and began talking at it and shaking his fist as he reamed Frankie out for flunking French and getting his ass blown away for nothing.

After a while he put it down, thumped his fist on the casket with a dramatic WHAM! and shouted, "*Attention!* I need your attention. First of all, cut the organ. Frankie hated that crap."

The music stopped instantly as everyone froze, their eyes fixated on McGill. There wasn't a sound as he took out his wallet, removed a piece of paper, carefully unfolded it, and held it above his head. "Frankie came up to see me last month, right before he shipped out, and he gave me this for safekeeping. It's his induction notice. I promised I'd buy him a beer and we'd burn it together as soon as he got back."

McGill held the "Greeting" in front of Frankie's photo, making sure Frankie could watch. He sparked his Zippo, touching the fire to the lowest corner. The crinkled paper burned slowly at first, then flamed up in a bright orange *WHOOSH* before dying out in a puff of white smoke and a flutter of gray ashes, which came peacefully to rest on the Stars and Stripes covering Frankie's coffin.

B. COLE MORTON

I was born Bruce Cole Morton, in Pittsfield, Massachusetts, on June 27, 1941. The first thing I remember is the whooping cough: Cheerios floating in the toilet. My oldest brother is eighty-four and just remarried. My dad, born 1897, was in the Navy during World War I, many uncles and aunts in World War II, another brother in Korea, so plenty of patriotic upbringing: church, school, Boy Scouts, and more church after my dad died young and my mom relied on religion to carry us through. I was ten and tried very hard to believe. On and on. U Mass Amherst; Teachers College, Columbia University; USMC Infantry Officer School, Quantico, Virginia. Then Vietnamese Language School, Monterey, California, before Danang, An Hoa, Phu Loc 6, and Hue City, Tet '68. Distrustful of authority. Abused alcohol and drugs. Never worked for anyone else since Marine Corps. I have been knocked out and temporarily blinded by lightning, attacked by a big shark, drowned and resuscitated, survived drunk and passed out in the backseat of a car driven by my second wife off a cliff in northern New Mexico, eighty feet through the air. Lost a couple of inches off my right leg in that one. Owner/operator rubbish removal company on Cape Cod. Sold used cars in Santa Fe, New Mexico. Played poker. Smuggled drugs. Two daughters, two sons (one deceased). Three marriages, third one thriving. Living on Cape Cod, thinking of moving to Vermont. Maybe it's quieter and safer there.

August 10, 2005

In the big corner of your mother's garden,
Five years and the lilies are blooming again.
Every year at this time.
Every year. Every year.
Last year on August 10, they bloomed gloriously:
Two years' dry season, they were stunted but exploded with
    blossoms.
But five years ago when you were killed, the lilies were eight feet
    tall and blinding white
Like angels' trumpets. Raiment as lightning!
They called us and told us you were dead.
And you were gone.

Every year when the lilies bloom, you are gone,
And we miss you again.
Just like, "What happened? Zac is dead?"
It can't really be true.
Your shining smile,
Your giggly/crazy laugh.
Gone forever.

If you brush too closely to the lilies. (Don't get too close.)
You'll be indelibly stained by the big brown stamens.
That sepia brown absolutely will not wash out.

The Brown Sadness in my soul.
Still here undiminished
When the lilies bloom again, in your mother's garden.

I dread those lilies every year.
We ought to chop them down. But we can't.
They are too gorgeous, too dazzling, too beautiful, too joyful.
How could you chop down a beautiful life?
How can you chop down something you love?

Sitting in My Yard by the Salt Marsh Yesterday Untangling String

Untangling string Crows
calling Untangling string
Mockingbirds sing
Untangling string I'm all
alone Untangling string the
Neighbors gone
Untangling string No wind,
gray sky Untangling string
Clothes hung to dry

Untangling string in the warm wet air
Untangling string in my underwear
Untangling string nobody home Untangling
string I'm almost done

Sometimes
I think
My life
Is like ... You guessed It:
Untangling string.

ODD DAY
WARM AND GRAY
AND ME UNTANGLING STRING

TANGLED KNOTS
FROM TIME FORGOT
AND UNREMEMBERED THINGS

ALL GONE TOO FAST
MY WHOLE LIFE PAST
THE FLOWERS BLOOM, THE BIRDS ALL SING

YET STILL BEREFT
AND ALL I'VE LEFT
ARE THE KNOTS IN THIS GOD-DAMN STRING.

PFC Porter Cleveland Bumpus USMC

One of his hands has just fallen right off, burned off. Now his
charred wrist bones are sticking out from under the ponchos we
wrapped him in to drag him up here to our night position. We had to
use a second poncho to cover where the first one had melted because
he was burned so hot.

PFC Porter C. Bumpus died today in Viet Nam, January 11, 1968,
burned to death in the service of his country. A blond, fair-faced kid
we all loved. Didn't even shave yet. Didn't even shave! The other men
would tease him, "Hey Bumps! How about lettin' me borrow your
razor!"

Every man loved him the best. Sweet smile. Happy laugh. Sometimes he would talk to me about how he imagined his father, sitting
in his easy chair at home. How he could almost see him, reading a
book by lamplight. Peaceful and warm. How he missed his dad. No

memories now. No smiles. No laugh. Just a blackened body with bones sticking out.

I'm his platoon commander. I gave the orders. He just went too far—only about a hundred meters past the bridge. I was clear, "Don't proceed beyond the bridge. That's our objective. Secure the bridge." Huge explosion, like a blast from the underground fires of hell. Command-detonated mine.

Don't go past the bridge.

But he was like that, always wanting to do more, always wanting to excel, like most of the other Marines in my platoon. My job is to control them, control their movements, control their fire, control their blood passion.

Don't go past the bridge.

A simple clear order forgotten in the bloodlust of combat.

And now as I sit here, everything is completely still. Sunset. Orange sky. Red clouds. Water buffalo knee-deep in the pink-orange water, grazing on tender-green marsh grass along the shore. Fishermen's sampans anchored out in the lagoon. Fish cooking. Smoke rising straight up. No wind. No breeze. Everything very quiet. So serene! How do they go on living day to day like this with a war going on all around? Guess you've just got to keep going on. Hope for the best.

Now starts the birds' songs and jungle cries all around. Evening symphony. Dark green mountain forest reflecting in the pink mirror lagoon.

PFC Bumpus's cooked body is cooling off. The sick-sweet smell is going away.

It was too late to fly his body out. His charred, twisted body lying here next to me. He's a ROUTINE MEDEVAC. The wounded go out first. Of course they get higher priority. The grim efficiency of war. Too many wounded today. His body stays with me tonight. Burned black! Jesus! Cooked meat.

Now the fishermen's fires seem brighter. The sun has gone. The birds stopped singing. Darkness comes.

SHOOSH!

CRACK!

Shouts of "INCOMING!"

FUCK! ROCKETS FROM UPHILL!

Blinding flashes like bright orange fireworks.
Shrapnel cracking into the trees all around us!
Men screaming: "DOC!" . . . "DOC!"
"WHERE THE FUCK'S THE DOC!"
The first rocket hit his position!
CRACK!
CRACK!
Now we can hear mortar tubes thumping out there.
ROCKETS *AND* MORTARS! Can't do a fuckin' thing but lie
here.

Face down. Caught in the open for watching the sunset. More shrapnel cracking into trees. Now the smell of broken trees.

Each explosion comes closer. Fuck! They're walking mortars across
our position. Each one closer. Each one louder. The ground jumps
higher under me, bruising my bones. Dirt and rocks fall on my head.
Hot shrapnel! It burns my hair. No helmet! Shit! The next one's coming right up my ass. Jesus Christ I'll kill those fuckers! Just let the next
round land past me . . .

Come on . . . Come on . . . Come on . . . CRRACK! They missed
me. I breathe this most delicious smoke and dust.

I am lying with the top of my head in PFC Bumpus's armpit! The
meat is falling off his bones. It's stuck in my hair. FUCK! FUCK!
FUCK!

I wonder if his body took any shrapnel for me. I don't want to know.
I scramble to cover him up.

A man crying for his mother. Gurgled coughing. "Help me. Why
can't you help me?"

"You're gonna make it."

"You're gonna be okay."

Muffled sobbing.

All in this new, total quiet darkness of the night. Only moaning,
whispering, scuffling. And waiting. Waiting. Waiting.

I come to my senses: Too quiet. Assault coming soon. Sure as shit.
I can feel it. I *know* it. Too quiet. Got to get our shit together. Perimeter defense. Redistribute ammunition.

And now, Where am I? I never again wanted to remember that
cooked flesh stuck in my hair. I never wanted to. I made myself forget.
I shut it down. Too painful. Too horrifying. But now here I am, six

days into this meditation retreat. Seeking peace for myself. No drugs, no alcohol, no busyness to keep my mind occupied. Yes. I am sitting in this beautiful spring garden, listening to the birds and breathing the flavor of the flowers. And sobbing. And feeling like vomiting, as all of a sudden I remember, now, twenty-six years later, that . . . that . . . *I shaved my head!* Over and over and over again for *months*. My head was shaved when I arrived home from Viet Nam. Just became habit.

It is incredible to me that I have blocked these memories for so many years. Totally gone for so long. And now that day and many days, weeks, and months all run together in my mind with no logical sequence. Still half-forgotten or totally fogged out. Very clear, vivid, ferocious, bloody dreams, that when I am awake I cannot remember. But now they are coming back and I am scared and I curse God.

But this horror and grief is also bringing me to life once more. More alive to my senses. The sky seems a brighter blue. The clouds whiter. The trees greener. And I am thankful.

I wonder if this makes sense to anyone. Now I'd be ashamed ever to forget again. I want to remember more. I know there is much more holding me back from living. Now I WANT TO REMEMBER EVERYTHING. I have not really been alive since that day. Like living inside a gauze cocoon, partly wrapped up by the spider of death. I want to rise up, break out into the fresh air and sunlight like these trees blooming with life and caressed by the warm breezes after sleeping all winter. Yes, maybe now I can do that too.

Can I ever completely wake up again? Maybe not; but today I am more alive than I have been for a very long time and it is horrifying and magnificent at the same time.

CHARLIE SHERDYL MOTZ

September 11, 1942–May 7, 2005

From Sherdyl's memorial ceremony

Charlie Sherdyl Motz, Sufi and Peet's habitué, was a bit of a public figure around Berkeley. After growing up in an Army family, moving around constantly and living in other countries, losing his mother at the age of thirteen, serving in Vietnam and becoming disillusioned, getting a degree and doing some graduate work at the University of Arizona, Charlie moved to Berkeley, where he really fit in, loving the street scene and helping many people.

A disabled vet, he gradually worked off his extreme trauma syndrome through forgiveness and kindness. Sherdyl had taken the Bodhisattva Vow and Green Tara Empowerment and practiced the identification with that aspect of the Love of the One for more than a decade. When he was without sufficient oxygen and couldn't manage his equipment or move from his bed, he turned to the image that he used for daily practice and was found later by friends with his arm outstretched toward the image of Green Tara, in a beautiful and angelic repose position, having made his transition already.

He kept close to the Quaker and the Buddhist communities he had practiced with as part of his eclectic Sufi tradition. Thich Nhat Hanh was special to him because Sherdyl was a Viet Nam vet. His Sufi name, Sherdyl, given to him by Pir Vilayat at his Sufi initiation twenty-five years ago, means "Lion Hearted," and he truly had miles and miles of heart. Many people treasured his listening ear and his humor.

Dragon River

The Vietnamese river lay in wait
for me, like an unchained dragon stoned
on opium. When awakened, it was
cranky and wrathful and spit fire.
Every night our puny plastic patrol boats
plied the serpentine folds of the Mekong
Delta, intruders in the darkling lair.

Simple fishing folk sailed those waters
too, their lights marking the murky
shore. The Southern Cross looked
on as sampans sliced the smelly, swampy
river, their eyes searching for shadowy
demons. Often they found us
and gunfire ripped the gloom.

Then we cruised a night cave lit
by tracers; buzzing close
in whistling fury—
ours red, theirs yellow.

When bushwhacked, we called a mighty
wrath upon their heads—shells
and bombs bursting by the napalm's
red glare. A plane called "Puff the Magic
Dragon" poured bullets thick as
monsoon rain into the beleaguered jungle.

I survived that fiery year; then slipped
thru a wormhole to the present, but
the memories still lurk and smolder.
Some nights I awaken
—sweating oceans
—still on patrol.
—And the dragon's still there.

The four stories that follow are excerpted from my Vietnam Memoirs *(unpublished). By this point in the stories, you would already know that I was a part of a four-man, river-patrol-boat crew. The other crew members were our boat captain, Gunner (Jim Cooper); a young, brash seaman named Jim Sims; and our engineer. "PBR" stands for Patrol Boat, Rigid (sometimes River or Riverine), a rigid-hulled patrol boat deployed in the Vietnam War to stop and search traffic in areas such as the Mekong Delta in an attempt to disrupt weapons shipments. An "LSD" is a dock landing ship, designed to support amphibious operations. "Taking" or "manning" or "having" the "conn" means to take the wheel of the boat. A "click" is jargon for a kilometer. A "Huey" is a helicopter gunship. "VC" means Viet Cong—the enemy.*

My First PBR Patrol

After a few weeks on a ship (an LSD) anchored in Vung Tau Bay, I was transferred to the base of Vung Tau itself, to the PBR support staff. I wasn't doing much on that ship except playing poker. As support person on the base, I was supposed to fix the radar sets and radio equipment, but it was soon apparent that I was not just unenthusiastic, I really didn't have the electrical skills to do the job. After a few weeks of bitching and moaning, I was transferred to the PBR boat crews, which was what I wanted in the first place.

I will never forget my first patrol. We covered a part of the Long Tau River for twenty-five clicks from Vung Tau Bay to a third of the way to Saigon. I had little idea what to expect. We arrived on station a little before sunset and it quite rapidly became very dark. The moon was a no-show, and the stars of the Southern Cross shined dimly. In later patrols, the stars would become my good friends; I spent many long hours watching the beauty and magnitude of the constellations.

The Long Tau River was the main shipping channel into Saigon— the route that freighters took to carry war materiel into the fray. VC were always trying to sink those freighters in the middle of the channel with command-detonated mines. The river was, for the most part, about a half-mile wide, which seemed claustrophobic to me. Dense foliate lined the river. Viewing this lushness during later-day patrols, I was amazed and delighted with the richness of the jungle and its riotous varieties of the color green. But for now, all I could think about was how perfect it was for VC ambushers to hide in. I was paranoid and kept wanting to pee real bad.

For most of the patrol, I was stationed in the forward gun tub with its twin .50-caliber machine guns, large, solid, threatening-looking, and, for me, reassuring. My main job was to scan the river and shoreline ahead of us with binoculars. After a while, paranoia and boredom played tricks on me. A fish jumping out of the water became an enemy sampan; a duck, a floating mine or a VC frogman. There were many false alarms.

At about 2 A.M., the bosun's gruff voice pierced me from the conn: "Radar contact! Dead ahead! What do you see?"

The crew became tense, our senses sharpened, adrenaline flowing rapidly. The radio crackled to life, as the bosun notified our cover boat of possible contact. I strained my eyes to see through the gloom and, finally, I saw a sort of black blob with a white mustache a bow wave ahead.

"Contact is a boat. Can't tell whose," I whispered tersely.

"General quarters!" shouted the bosun as he shoved the throttles to the max. The boat leapt forward as its twin diesels roared to life with their throaty growl. "Be alert," he said, unnecessarily. "Lock and load!"

I jacked a live round into each machine gun and put a death grip on the handles. My thumbs caressed the twin triggers. We were closing fast. Now we could see the outline of the unknown boat riding its white bow wave, moving pretty fast. Was it a sampan full of VC? Would they open fire? I was in the bow and suddenly felt very exposed. Was I a candidate for a body bag? Suddenly, I lost my enthusiasm for war. I didn't want to die yet. And the urge to pee was overwhelming.

I gripped the handles even more tightly and prepared to unleash a twin stream of death into the night. Why didn't that damn bosun give the order to fire? What was he waiting for? We were the only ones supposed to be on the river. There was a dusk-to-dawn curfew, and it was a free-fire zone. Slowly, I started squeezing the triggers. The other boat was very close now.

"Don't shoot! It's another PBR!" came the voice of the engineer, who was squinting through his binoculars. Slowly, I relaxed my grip on the triggers. My hands and fingers had been glued to the guns and ached from the tension. I'd almost fired on a friendly boat and felt very foolish and ashamed. A bullet is a totally irrevocable and unforgiving thing. I unloaded the machine guns, more aware than ever of my own mortality. All the bravado and patriotic bullshit of training camp and the macho barroom bragging faded into foolishness, and I was aware of the power we had to cause great harm to these simple Vietnamese fishing folks, and ourselves. I was still high on adrenaline coursing through my veins. Slowly we relaxed. The rest of the patrol was uneventful, even boring. I'd become a patrol veteran.

The VC Palm Tree

It was dark. The diffused light from Saigon twenty-one clicks away reflected on the sparse clouds. There was no moon yet, and only a few stars twinkled in the sky. The air had recently been scrubbed with monsoon rain, but the swampy smell of the river persisted. Our patrol station was Point Yale Alpha on the Soirap River, which has a long, lazy, figure-S meander to it. It was a known hot spot where VC frequently tried to cross. We didn't much like this particular stretch of the river. On Christmas Eve, we would like it even less.

The airborne legions of fruit bats had finished their nightly flight across the river and were roosting in the treetops. We made a lot of jokes about vampire bats, but actually, fruit bats are harmless. But they were huge, an eerie and awe-inspiring sight flying by the thousands close above us across the river at dawn and then back again at dusk. The spraying of Agent Orange (Dioxin) killed millions of the helpless creatures.

I had the conn, and we were going upriver toward the top of the figure-S meander. A large blip appeared on the radar screen. "Contact!" I cried. "Dead ahead, range . . . about half a mile, close to shore."

The crew was instantly alert. The engineer, still foggy with sleep, manned the after .50-caliber machine gun. A heavy "thunk, thunk" issued from his weapon as he jacked a round into the chamber. In a flash, Gunner was beside me, staring intently at the radar screen as the blip crawled toward us. "Sims," Gunner called to Jim in the forward gun tub. "What do you see?"

Jim strained to pierce the gloom with his binoculars and after a few minutes, whispered, "It's just another fucking palm tree." It was monsoon season and when the river overflowed its banks, uprooted whole trees ended up floating down the river. It made the same strong blip on the radar screen as a sampan or a junk. We approached cautiously with our cover boat close behind us. We were keyed up, adrenaline savagely pounding through our veins.

We got to within a hundred meters of the tree, fired a few M-16 rounds into it, and were satisfied that it was, in fact, a palm tree. The engineer went back to sleep, and Gunner relaxed amidships, as much as he ever relaxed. After getting his first PBR shot out from under him, Gunner was a little shaky. At first, we thought he was chickenshit and made a lot of jokes at his expense. Later on, after being in a few hot firefights, the rest of us got a little more cautious, too. There's something about the nasty, waspish sound a bullet makes when passing close to your head that is very sobering.

I watched the tree's progress on the radar scope. It was approaching the bottom of the S. I knew from experience that it would get caught in the whirlpool current there, go around a few times and then move off downriver toward Vung Tau. We were a little more relaxed now after this false alarm. But in the combat zone, we were never truly relaxed.

The engineer had just started to snore again, and when I glanced at the radar screen, lo and behold, the tree wasn't going around and around in the whirlpool. It was moving straight *across* the river against an 11-knot monsoon current, and moving out right smartly, too.

"General quarters!" I shouted, reversing course and ramming the throttles to flank speed. Our twin Chrysler engines roared as we sped off downriver. Gunner took the conn, and I grabbed the radio mike. "Porpoise 24, this is Porpoise 26. Follow us! Flank speed? That goddamn tree is crossing at Point Yale Alpha."

"Roger, Porpoise 26! Say, whadda you guys been drinking?" It was the gruff voice of the bosun who commanded our cover boat. We got to within 200 meters of the tree, and all of a sudden the damn thing opened fire on us! Automatic weapons, too, several of them. Were we ever surprised. We slowed down to let our cover boat catch up, and we both began returning fire, shooting as their muzzle flashed with our wicked .50-caliber machine guns.

The palm tree had been a camouflage on top of a VC sampan; it scurried into a little side canal and disappeared. We were so mad we fired into the canal for half an hour and used up most of our ammunition. We called in a Huey and they fired rockets and machine guns into the area. They searched for hours with their searchlight and flares, but found nothing. It had just disappeared.

The Vietnamese army searched the area right after daylight, and they didn't find anything, either. Several boat crews on station that night overheard our radio chatter, and we were the butt of lots of jokes about "hallucinations" and "VC palm trees."

After that, we treated every tree we encountered in the river to a liberal dose of grenades and small-arms fire. It took me a long time to trust a tree again. The world had become a sadder place.

The Zen Junk—Soirap River Day Patrol

A nother busy day patrol. We were doing the standard drill, boarding and searching junks that looked suspicious. The ones that hugged the side of the river were particularly suspect, as were the ones that tried to steer a course to avoid us. It was probably a mostly futile gesture, though, because for every sampan or junk we boarded and searched, hundreds went by unmolested. There must have been hundreds of thousands of junks and sampans in the Mekong Delta. We couldn't check but a small fraction of them.

One of our favorite pastimes on day patrol was watching the fishermen in their small sampans. We knew a lot of them, because we had searched them several times. They would throw out their nets, stand around awhile, and then haul the nets in. It must have been pretty boring but that was their life. Sometimes, as they waited for the right time to pull their nets in, they would have sex with a woman on board. We would see a sampan bobbing up and down with no one showing and then we'd see the man's butt appearing rhythmically over the top of the hull and know they were doing it.

We would holler with glee, ram the throttles to full, and swoop down on them and search them. It was a pretty rotten thing to do. They would be hastily putting on their clothes and glaring at us as we came alongside. We'd make a perfunctory search and then go on, satisfied and smug that we had interrupted their connubial bliss. We caught a lot of them humping in their boats. It probably did our reputation a lot of good. They considered us uncaring, trained killers and barbarians, and it was all right with us if that's what the VC thought, too. Later we would find out how much they feared us.

We cruised our ten-mile patrol area on the hot sultry Soirap. It wasn't quite monsoon yet, it was muggy and hot, and we were irritated. Besides that, a sniper had taken a shot at us as we came on station, and we were pissed and looking for trouble.

The water slapped rhythmically against the hull as we slowly cruised back and forth. There were millions of ducks now, carpeting the river for miles. It was like their winter resort area. They made for some good eating for us and our interpreter and his family.

Downriver something very big slowly nosed out of a tributary. I was on watch in the forward gun tub and trained my binoculars on it. "What in the hell is that?" I shouted. It was huge.

Cooper had the conn and responded, "It's a floating barn!!"

It was in the main river channel now and turned toward us, pointing upriver toward Saigon. "Sheeit!" the engineer exclaimed. "That's the biggest fucking junk I've ever seen."

Jim quipped, "It's bigger than Noah's ark!"

Gunner goosed the throttles and we approached, fingering and checking our weapons. Indeed, it was bigger than a house. In fact, it was bigger than a barn. At first it seemed as big as a battleship, but it wasn't, really. It was made of dirty-brown planked wood. The bow, like all its smaller brethren, was painted bright red with white trim and had two eyes painted on it. Every sampan or junk had the same design on its bow. We asked the fishermen about it, and they claimed it was to keep them from getting lost at night. They also allowed that it let the boat itself see night demons so they could steer around them. The Vietnamese, especially the fishermen, were big on demons.

We were pretty paranoid as we approached at flank speed. There was room enough in the damn thing for a whole regiment of heavily armed Viet Cong. I imagined hundreds of VC suddenly jumping up with machine guns and decimating us. I always felt naked in the unarmored forward gun tub, despite the reassuring presence of the twin .50-caliber machine guns.

But nothing happened. First we circled and hailed them through the megaphone. Then we got pissed and lobbed a few grenades across her bow. She still ignored us. No one even peered over the railing at us. We were getting really mad and both our PBRs circled around and around the thing, shouting and firing rounds in the air. But it was like two mosquitoes threatening a bull elephant. We must have wasted a coupla hundred rounds trying to attract their attention so we could board and search her.

It was thirty feet high and a hundred feet long. There were no ladders or ropes trailing over its side, so we couldn't even get on board. No matter what we did, it just chugged serenely on at a whopping six knots. We were frustrated, mad, and scared all at the same time. We were really working ourselves up into a lather.

We called Porpoise Control on the radio and asked for instructions. After ten minutes, the radio crackled to life, "Porpoise 26, this is

Porpoise Control. If the junk doesn't fire at you, just leave it alone. We'll call in a large cutter from the Vietnamese navy to board and search it. Acknowledge, over."

Gunner acknowledged, not that it mattered. We could have emptied every round we had into it and every grenade, too, and not harmed it in the least. So after all our anger and antics and firing into the water around it, it just sailed calmly off up the river, as if we weren't even there. It truly was a Zen junk.

The Floater—Soirap River Night Patrol

Another quiet night patrol. We were patrolling around Point Yale Alpha, drifting with our engines off, hoping to catch a VC sampan crossing with our silent approach. There was no moon or clouds, but plenty of stars. The chief was on board as patrol leader and also Vinh, our interpreter. The stars had become my good friends. They kept me from going bonkers on these fourteen-hour patrols. I could contemplate the heavens and feel not quite so alone.

The whiny, droning sound of the radar antenna going around and the waves caressing the hull were somehow reassuring. The bow of the boat showed dimly through the gloom. I strained to see through the binoculars, but nothing stirred. The river reeked its usual fetid, swampy smell. A cluster of lights showed on the shoreline as we drifted past a small Vietnamese fishing village fast asleep at 3 A.M. I wondered how many VC were creeping through that village, or whether it was a VC headquarters.

My meditation on the stars was interrupted by a sickening smell. It was our second pass by that particular village, and there it was again. I knew it was a floater, but I didn't say anything. I didn't want to have to deal with it.

Three nights ago, we had caught a sampan right in the middle of the river. We had launched a handheld flare over it, and they opened fire on us. We returned their fire. It was no contest, their few, puny rifles against our .50-caliber machine guns. One man with a big pack had been caught square in the chest by a .50-caliber slug and flung like a sprawling rag doll twenty feet from his sampan into the river. He sank like a stone. It had been over in a few minutes.

Bodies would lie on the river bottom for a few days, decaying in the warm water. Then the grasses would seal the bullet holes and they would float up to the surface, bloated and smelling god-awful. Once you've smelled a rotting corpse, you can never forget it. We called them "floaters." This must have been the floater from our engagement three nights before.

The light breeze changed direction, bringing the smell our way. Gunner, who had the conn, smelled it, too. "Looks like we got a floater out there, boys. Let's go get it."

"Let's not and say we did," I grumbled. Gunner must have been really bored. We searched the area for a few minutes and there it was. His body was bloated to twice its original size, bursting out of its uniform. The smell was vile. There's no smell as gross as a rotting human body. My stomach grew very uneasy.

"Charlie," barked Gunner. "Jump into the water and secure a line to that floater."

"No way, Gunner," I said. "I'm not going for a swim with the fucking maggots."

"Jim, how about you. Charlie's chicken."

"No chance, Gunner," Jim said.

"All right," Gunner said. "I'll do it. You guys are sure a bunch of chickenshits! Jim, you take the conn."

So Jim took the conn and Gunner stripped to his shorts, took a line between his teeth, and jumped into the river. He swam out to the floater and secured a line to it, then wrestled the pack off its back and swam back and climbed back aboard. Even the pack smelled like a charnel house. I could taste bile rising in my throat. I wanted to puke. I was glad when we got under way again so the breeze of our movement kept the smell of the floater and his pack behind me. The chief and Gunner and Vinh went through the captured pack. "We make good catch," Vinh said. "This man VC paymaster." He waved a fat wad of Cambodian bank notes at us. There were several pages of pay records in the pack as well. In one pocket there was a faded picture of a woman with four kids. My heart went out to them.

The chief called in on the radio. "Porpoise Control, this is Porpoise 26. We got a floater in tow here. It's probably one of the VC we shot off that sampan three nights back. He's got a pack of Cambod money and what our interpreter says is pay records. Whadda you want us to do with the body? Over."

Some comedian got on the radio and quipped, "If you all are hungry, Porpoise 26, why doncha eat it raw?"

A voice came over the radio interrupting him, "Uh, Porpoise 26, this is Porpoise Control. Bring it on in. Over."

The comedian came back: "Looks like the brass is hungry, too."

As we towed the body back to Nha Be at a piddling five knots, we were pissed off. At this slow speed, we were a sitting duck. What did those jerks at headquarters want the body for now? In the morning, when we came off patrol, would have served just as well. Maybe the comedian was right.

"I wonder why they tried to cross here?" the engineer asked.

"Guess he was trying to float a loan," replied Jim.

Fortunately for us, the VC snipers must have all been asleep. We arrived back at Nha Be without incident, off-loaded the body, and returned to our patrol station. Later that week, with the typical military thinking that defies all logic, we all got a commendation in our service records for this exceptionally brave deed. We called the incident the Floater National Bank.

JOHN MULLIGAN
June 2, 1950–October 12, 2005

John Mulligan was born into a family of ten children in Kirkintil-
loch, Scotland. After emigrating to the United States with his family, at the age of nineteen, he was drafted, and served a year's tour of
duty in Vietnam, mostly in heavy combat. Although physically unin-
jured, Mulligan suffered Post-Traumatic Stress Disorder, which eventually resulted in total and permanent disability. After the war, he
fought increasing illness and alcoholism. Though he struggled for a
normal life, he spent ten years on the streets of San Francisco, where
Café Trieste, "the living room" of writers and poets, provided a place
of stability. In 1996, while still on the streets, he was invited to join
a writing group for homeless veterans, started by Maxine Hong
Kingston. In this group, Mulligan's natural talent found expression
in his seminal novel, *Shopping Cart Soldiers*. Writing at the café, or out
of the rain under the steps of the Basque Hotel, the novel flowed,
resulting in a powerful story that blended Celtic and Asian mythology and embodied one soul's destruction by war.

Published by Curbstone Press, the novel won a PEN Award for
excellence in literature. Studied today in universities, *Shopping Cart
Soldiers* was called one of the top three novels in literature of the Vietnam War. Mulligan spoke in front of Congress on behalf of homeless veterans, and worked with groups such as the National Coalition
for Homeless Veterans.

John Mulligan continued to write brilliantly and to devote himself to helping his brother and sister veterans. Tragically, on October
12, 2005, he was killed in a car accident. He is survived by three children and a granddaughter, all beloved.

from *Shopping Cart Soldiers*

*O*n some level he knows me. He wonders who I am it's true, yet it's all so
simple. I am a woman. A simple enough statement to be sure, but laden
with complications at the same time. At least as far as Finn and I are concerned,
now that he's begun to know me, now that he's begun to feel me. He thinks my
name is Madman. That's what he calls me anyway. Madman! But what does
he know?

In spite of acknowledging me to some degree, he won't take me back, won't *let me back in. And therein lies the problem. For twenty-five years or so I've been trying to get him to open up, but he doesn't even see me; nor does he listen to me. He can feel me though. I know he can feel me, the blackhaired, blueeyed, paleskinned, selfnegating bastard, yet he won't let me in. I don't often talk about him that way, I don't enjoy talking about him like that, not really. But he does anger me. Perhaps he won't take me back because I'm a woman. That's a hard pill for him to swallow. He feels me though, senses my femaleness, and locks me out. Perhaps he won't take me back because my beauty intimidates him.*

I am a beautiful woman. My hair is short and black, as black and shiny as newcut coal, trimmed in the style of a bonnie wee schoolboy. That's another thing! I talk in a strange dialect just as he does. But he's an Albanach remember, so I talk just like him.

I must excuse myself; sometimes I forget. Alba is the ancient name for an ancient country filled with an ancient race of Keltic people. It's been Finn's delving and diving into his distant past that has compelled him to employ such an archaic term. But he likes it; it makes him feel closer to his ancestors, and I like that! Knowing from whom he descends might save him. Alba, you know, predates even Roman civilization and probably the Greek too. Some say the Kelts came from a place Northwest of the Alps and that they were like both the Scythians and the Persians who lived and flourished in the millennium before the time of Christ.

Finn first saw the word *Alba* as a child growing up in Scotland. He saw it in an ancient manuscript handed down through the years by father after father of the Donald Clan, his ancestors. Finn's father knew it as *The Red Book of Seeing and Believing*. His father told him that Alba is the ancient Gaelic name for Scotland, the land of his birth. But he forgot all about the book and its lessons until one night in the jungle many years later.

He is sitting in a bunker with Romeo Robinson, waiting out another tense night of guard duty. The monsoon season has finally decided to assert itself, and the night is black, heavy, and still.

"Hey, man, where you from?" asks Romeo, sitting back, leaning against the sandbags of the bunker. Romeo's holding a roach between his thumb and index finger and, after taking a long toke, passes it to Finn. Finn takes the joint, thinks for a minute, then laughs.

"Nowhere," he says. "I come from nowhere!"

"I can dig that, man, but ya gotta be from somewhere."

For a long time Finn is quiet, lost in his thoughts of Alba and of his family.

The whole MacDonald clan is gathered around the kitchen table listening to the da espousing the wonders and benefits of living in America. The da of course sits there sternfaced and grave; the ma has a worried expression on her face, as if the subject is one she'd rather not even think about let alone consider with any objectivity or seriousness. The da notices her confusion, her consternation. He rises to his feet and paces around the table.

"We haftae leave," says the da. "There's no point in livin' here without work when I've been offered a job in America." He is adamant; he has made up his mind. "Christ, Kate," he continues, "ah've been outa work for nearly a year now. Me! One-a the best machinists in the westa Scotland. An' why? Because ah'm a Catholic, an' a staunch trade unionist! Aye, that's right, a bitter combination in this tinyminded, dour wee country." The da is revving up now. "Ah'm sick of it, Kate. Ah'm sicka the bigots, an' ah'm sicka the bluidy weather. Clouds in the sky every day, rain, rain, rain! Ah've had it." The da sits down again in his chair. "Ah want these weans of ours to have a better life than we did, give them a fightin' chance at least!"

Finn, the oldest of the children, is beaming, obviously happy at the prospect.

"Where would we be going?" he asks the da. "What part of America?"

"Detroit," says the da, rather grimly.

"Magic!" says Finn. "Motown! I can go an' see the Four Tops anytime I feel like it. The Temptations, Joe Tex, the Supremes! It'll be great, da!"

The da just rolls his eyes heavenward; the ma looks worried. The younger children shout and laugh, oblivious to the huge and impending changes under discussion at the table around which they play. It's a tense time at the MacDonald's dinner table.

"What about the war, Joe, what about Vietnam for God's sake?" the ma asks of her husband in a whisper she would usually save for church or the library. "He'll be eighteen soon," she reminds him, pointing to Finn who isn't smiling any more.

"Aye, that's right, da," says Finn. "Ah forgot all about that. Ah'll get drafted!"

"No yae won't, son. It's a government contract. We'll be makin' helicopter gears, helpin' wi' the war effort. There's as much chance they'll draft me as they will you." The lame joke backfires.

"They wouldnae do that would they?" asks the ma, now absolutely terrified.

"Don't be daft, Kate, don't be so bluidy daft!" says the da, who is fast becoming exasperated.

"Are yae sure ah'll get a job, da?" asks Finn.

"Aye ah'm sure. Ah made them put it in my contract. As soon as yae turn eighteen they'll hire yae on as a machinist. Ah told them yae had three years experience already. They'll be glad to have yae they said!"

"Let me see it," says the ma. "Let me see the contract!"

But Finn hated the job making helicopter gears. They stuck him on nightshift six nights a week. In no time at all he was fired for sleeping on the job. In even less time he was classified 1A and was drafted shortly afterward. Now he is sitting in a sandbagged bunker smoking a big fat doobie with his pal, Romeo.

"It's funny, Romeo, but I don't feel like I come from anywhere. I was born in Scotland, but after all this war bullshit I wonder if I have a home any more. I can't go back, an' I sure as hell don't know where I'll be tomorrow."

"I know what you mean," said Romeo, lost in his own thoughts. "But how d'ya get here in the first place?"

"Same as you. I got drafted!"

Romeo burst out laughing.

"Drafted?" he says. "What d'ya mean drafted? You're a goddamn foreigner, a Scotsman. How can they draft a Scotsman?"

"You live in America, you register with the draft; that's the law. The price you pay. You don't get nothin' for nothin', Romeo! An' don't call me a Scotsman again. Scotland doesn't exist any more! In the olden days it was called Alba, so I come from Alba now."

"I hear that, Alba man. I hear that! Ain't no Chicago neither."

"Anyhow, when I got drafted the whole family went back to Alba. I think the actual shock of me being drafted was too much for them."

I thank God regularly for keeping Finn alive and somewhat hopeful during these past years of difficulty, all twenty-five or so of them. But he's shown signs of late that he might have found an exit to the twisting maze he's been wandering around in for so long. I'm relieved about his new clarity, because I came out of him; I need him well and healthy. All that stops him from accepting me is his pitifully closed mind. But it's begun to open up somewhat these past two or three years. Not much, mind you, but I am hopeful.

My eyes are green like the North Sea is green, and even though it's common to say so, they are shaped like almonds. How that particular oddity came about has always been a source of mystery, if not consternation and complete confusion to me, ever since The Leaving at least. After all, if I came from Finn, a Kelt, how can I possibly have almond eyes? It's easy! I figured it all out. It is so easy I laugh, because the part of Finn that I am is Asian. That's all there is to it!

Perhaps we're from a land farther east than has been imagined. One of the Asia Minor tribes perhaps. A long time passes before I can comprehend that myself, so I can easily understand why he's having such a difficult time with it. That I'm a woman goes quite against his grain to be sure; that I'm an Asian woman really does confuse him. It isn't as bad as it used to be, because for the last two or three years he has begun, finally, to learn more about his heritage. He's discovered that Keltic people and Asian people aren't so far apart, not in a mythological sense certainly and probably not, as I mentioned, in an anthropological sense either—a few thousand years perhaps, not much more.

My almond eyes became easier to understand after I began to know, through Finn's delving and diving, our Keltic heritage. Thanks, again, to Romeo Robinson and his quiet questions that dark night in the still jungle. They began a process that might, in retrospect, have saved Finn's life.

I am tiny, petite if you will, and my skin is pale like goat's milk. By contrast, I wear a flowing, bloodred robe fastened at the waist with a long, silver umbilical cord. After quarter of a century it continues to drip dark, thick blood. I alone can see the cord, though sometimes even I can't see it, but I know it's there. Somehow it's just there! And whether truly there or not isn't important; I need to think it's there, because that's all that keeps Finn and me together in some small way.

Finn and I separated when the Great White water buffalo, the bull, is murdered during The Leaving. Until then we are happy together, as one.

July nineteen-seventy, is a bad month. All five of us are flying in a helicopter gunship, armed to the teeth, somewhere above Vietnam. We're out during the monsoon rains searching for the downed cargo plane; it has smacked into a mountainside. The plane carries twenty-six passengers, all soldiers, homeward-bound after a long, hard year of jungle-rot, growing pains, and broken, bloody bodies. Ivy League, our friend, is one of the twenty-six, one of the dead twenty-six, a *waste no matter how one looks at it. It is the waste more than anything else I can't come to terms with. All that violent waste, the pitiful pouring away of precious life into the already red Asian soil. Finn, at the time, doesn't understand why part of him thinks, no, feels the way it does. More like a woman, that is. I think he feels there is something wrong with being sensitive to the madness going on all around him every day. It isn't manly to be sensitive. Who knows! But we split apart that night and he chases me away. A hundred years ago it seems, perhaps longer.*

I've been following him around ever since, plodding relentlessly after him, like the Hound of Heaven, watching the years tumble along one after the other, wondering always who is the shadow, wondering always who casts the shadow. In all fairness you'd have to say we had an equal right to dwell inside that physical shell everyone knew as Finn MacDonald. But he cast me out, doesn't want to share himself with me, doesn't want to believe that I come along with the package, that I am part of the package, though it's not as simple as you might think, this twoness.

Finn wants to be a man, a soldier, a hero! There are times I can't help but laugh when I think of it; it's all so insane. There are times too when I can forgive him; there are times when I can't.

He's a grunt, an infantryman, just like the rest of his pals. He's up in the control tower visiting a friend when they finally give Captain Peterson permission to take off. The weather has cleared. Too soon into the rain perhaps. God only knows, too soon. The plane crashes into the mountain when the weather unexpectedly closes in again.

Finn and four of our friends go to look for the plane. I know; I am there with them! We jump into the gunship laden with bullets, and go to look for our pals. A mission, a mission of mercy to save our comrades. I remember Finn telling Frankie Chen he's scared shitless; he's never been on such a dangerous adventure. Frankie tells Finn he's scared shitless too.

The weather's clear again. But we've been smoking dope ever since we first heard of the crash. It might as well be raining still we're all so stoned. It's that sort of place, the war zone. Crazy! Topsyturvy! For the first hour or so we can't find the lost plane, though we're hungry for some sort of action. When we don't find any we invent our own, such being our need, such being the depth of our rage. We have to, we need to, for we are filled with anger. We have to hit back, and we have to hit back hard! The enemy's elusive! They like to set their booby-

traps or ambush us, then scarper down the holes of their tunnels leaving us frustrated with nothing to shoot back at, filled with teethclenching, bloodred rage.

The moon is big behind a break in the clouds and we can see quite clearly. We happen to pass over a fenced-in pasture and see a huge water buffalo, a bull. I can't believe how big he is, how huge. At least ten feet long and six feet high. Romeo Robinson can't believe it either. Romeo, when he isn't pulling guard duty, is our door gunner; he is itching for relief, itching to do the job he's been so well trained to do. I don't think he cares much any more. He's been out on so many missions, flying above the jungle so often, he lives on borrowed time anyway. What amazes me more than anything else as I sit there in the chopper, cradling my rifle in my arms, is how young we all are.

Ivy League was the oldest in our group. He was twenty-three and an old man already. We looked up to him. He knew a lot about things we'd barely heard of. When he played his saxophone underneath the sultry Asian sky my skin would tingle. Ivy League came from the east coast and had gone to a posh university. He volunteered for combat, same as Finn. I think that's why they liked each other so much. Ivy League was aboard the lost plane. We had to go look for him. He was what we all wanted to be when we grew up. Tough soldiers all, we would never have admitted how much we loved him, how much we looked up to him, as we might an older brother.

The bull charges around the pasture. Romeo screams with delight as he maneuvers the gunship's big doorgun into a better firing position. He lets go a burst of bullets and catches the bull right on the arse. It bellows and rages. Oh, how it bellows and rages against the night. Careening around the field, the White One searches for his tormentor, his pain-spitting persecutor.

I feel as if I've taken acid, because I sense things much more intensely. I'm hot and flushed and my skin tingles and prickles as if I'm wearing a hair shirt or hearing again Ivy League's saxophone. In the distance, lightning bolts jolt and shatter the sky, but I'm enjoying myself listening to the rotor blades throbbing, making mincemeat of the surrounding air. They sound out a hard-driving dancebeat, and we are dancing all right! Dancing high above the bloodwet earth we hate so much, freed for a time, disengaged, disentangled, divorced, away from it! Every so often Romeo fires a burst and we watch the tracers make their way down to earth. Our pilot, Tommy-up-front we call him, makes a sharp hundred eighty degree turn and flies back over the pasture. The White One careens around the field lost in his madness. I wonder if he's enraged that something so evil, so malevolent, could invade his domain so completely, so definitely. We fly just a few feet above him, following him like a shadow. Tommy-up-front is good. He sticks to the bull as if he were a part of him, as if he were a hawk in pursuit of a sparrow. Romeo puts a bullet into the White One's balls and everybody laughs. I begin to know then that something isn't quite right between Finn and me.

When the bull is shot, as we turn and cross behind his charging form, his balls explode, and I watch that two thousand pound creature jump ten feet off the ground. Does he know Death is close at hand, that Death stalks him? How does he feel when his peaceful night is disturbed by the huge and noisy monster following so fast, so close, behind him? The bull's red fury becomes almost perceptible, almost as red as the tracers blasting into him. He charges toward the barbed-wire fence surrounding the pasture, intent only on escaping the unseen thing that has rent his world asunder, split apart his quiet, fucking life. He jumps but, alas, catches his forelegs on the topmost wire and, caught in the barbs, he rages at the injustice of it all, his big brown eyes like deep water, mirroring the puzzled fear in his soul. We turn and come back around the pasture. I look over at Romeo. He smiles gleefully, almost greedily, and I know the bull is big in his gunsights. The whole world becomes quiet then. I hear not a sound, but my eyes are full, full of the color of blood as each of a long line of bullets blast their way through the neck of the bull.

We circle the pasture, we fly back and forth across the path of the bull, we watch him in his death throes. We see the beautiful horned head fall forward over the other side of the fence, attached only by a thin piece of skin and ligament, followed at once by a gush, a fountain, of thick red buffalo blood. Red, red, red! A river of blood as red as my robe. And as the white bull lies twitching on the wires, I watch his soul escaping, drifting out through the gaping hole in his neck. The whole world turns red as we fly through our sea of blood. Tommy's circles above the pasture become tighter and tighter as we rise higher and higher into the dark night sky. I feel myself leaving Finn then, coming out of his body, though I can't leave him completely. Like the head of the bull I, too, seem to be attached by a sliver of skin and ligament. Part of me remains attached to him, and all the world is bloody. The soul of the White One hovers above the quiet pasture and Finn, as if coming to, screams and kicks like a man gone mad.

I feel in that instant a terrific force pushing me out of his body, out of the whirling, vibrating aircraft, out into the cold, rushing air. I hear Finn scream as I, covered in blood, topple toward the bewildered soul of the dead white bull.

During my descent I feel a chill of such bonepenetrating coldness it defies def-

inition, though it goes through me like a spear of ice, then swims around me, filling me with dread and foreboding. Then it is gone!

The bull and I swirl around and around, caught in the turbulence generated by the gunship's rotor blades, clinging to each other, wondering what has happened, wondering what could have put us outside of our bodies. The body of the bull is dead; I can see it still, hanging across the barbed-wire fence. The bull can see it too, his big eyes wide, filled with fear. But my body lives. Finn lives. His arse is numb from sitting on top of his steel helmet. What's ironic is that we sit on top of our steel helmets to protect our own balls from those nasty bullets coming through the floor of the aircraft.

As I dance about the sky, riding the bull, I wonder what has compelled us to kill him so senselessly. What have we become after all? I take great pity on the bull after we shoot his balls off, after Finn casts me out of his body. And as the soul of the bull and I drift above the jungle, I cling to him tightly as we follow the gunship until, at last, we find the downed aircraft. I've been riding the bull ever since, riding the confused white bull, in one form or another, through the maze of our bloody madness for quarter of a century.

The gunship drops the boys off in a clearing nearby. The rain has stopped, but the trees are dripping as if it is still raining. Drip, drip, drip they go, monotonous and annoying. We walk, all five of us, single file, along the jungle floor, doing our best to dodge tripwire boobytraps, snakes, and tiger shit. The bull is drifting above the treetops. Finn walks in the middle of the file; he is less experienced than the other grunts at jungle games. I walk ten feet behind him, but I've tied the umbilical cord around his waist; I don't want to lose him. Without that cord, or the idea of it, I would surely have lost him long ago and, just as I am new at this particular way of living, Finn isn't yet aware that he's lost his soul, that he's kicked me out of his body. What becomes immediately apparent to me is that at the very moment before my expulsion from his body I have only the same abilities as he. I am humanly limited; yet, when he kicks me out, I go immediately back to what I truly am: a pure spirit, an Invisibility, as some folk call me. I have all the accompanying attributes of a spirit: I can see things and hear things no mortal could ever hope to see or hear. No ordinary mortal, that is. A visionary, perhaps, might see many of the things I do. Finn doesn't yet know that unless he embraces me once more, takes me back into himself, he will never be complete. He will always be an Empty.

We smell the downed aircraft before we see it. Among all the other odors associated with a burned-out aircraft, we smell the horrifying and unforgettable stench of roasted human flesh. The plane has burned almost completely, though it still smolders in spite of the heaviness of the recent rains. Many of the bodies remain strapped into their seats; others are scattered and strewn about the jungle floor all around us. We stand motionless, staring with horror at our barbecued pals. Some of the bodies are still intact and of those, most have been stripped of any valuables, including wallets, rings, watches, and the like and, naturally, their weapons. We find Ivy League tied to a tree, his face beaten to a pulp and what seems to be a bullet hole in his forehead.

"Jeezus god," Finn blurts out before dropping to his knees and throwing up all over the ground before him. When he recovers he gets up and, with an angry jerk, pulls the dogtag from Ivy League's mutilated body. He wonders why the other whole bodies haven't been mutilated and why they haven't all been robbed of their personal belongings. Then, a moment later, he knows.

The explosions rip apart the drip, drip, dripping night and Frankie Chen falls dead to the ground.

I think Frankie died of a heart attack; he was such a frail wee sparrow of a man. Finn goes down too, but fear buckles his legs rather than bullets or shrapnel. He pisses himself, and his long black rifle falls by his side. Before he can pick it up a tiny young girl, no more than sixteen, dressed in black, silk pajamas, whose eyes are shaped like mine, comes charging out of the undergrowth and stands, smiling, over my sprawled-out Finn, her long black rifle pointed menacingly at his head.

Before she can pull the rigger, Romeo Robinson's machete comes swinging out of the darkness we have landed in and sweeps cleanly through the young girl's neck. The machete is Romeo's favorite weapon. He likes the closeness of it, the personal touch. Finn does too. Romeo told Finn he liked feeling death creep up along the blade and through the hilt into his arm. He said he liked the power it gave him.

The pretty head falls beside Finn. He looks straight into the eyes of the dead soldiergirl and he swears on his very soul he sees life there before the head lolls to one side, now finally dead. Had circumstances been different, he might have enjoyed sleeping with this girl with the almondshaped eyes. When Finn looks at the decapitated head, its eyes still open, lying there as still as stone, he snaps.

"Ya fuckin' bitch," he screams. "Why'd yae have to go an' do that? I don't even know yae."

Romeo Robinson laughs and, in a voice filled with disdain says, "Welcome to the war, Alba man!"

"For chrissake," Finn said many years later, "that coulda been my Mary lyin' there!"

The ambush ended almost as abruptly as it began. We are well-versed in counter-ambush tactics, because we've trained well, and we've lived through ambushes before. In spite of Finn's panic-induced pissings, we rip the enemy to shreds. There's nothing like fear to make the adrenaline flow, or to make a man a heroic warrior. After it's all over, the smoky smell of cordite hangs thick and heavy beneath the canopy of leaves and the jungle goes back to its drip, drip, dripping monotony.

We hear then a soft whimper nearby and when we look around we see Johnny Quinn's broken body lying a few feet away. Finn lets out a loud, piercing scream; Johnny, after all, is his best friend, Mary's brother. And Johnny is a poet. On many a warm southeast Asian night he would read to us from a big fat book of poems he kept by his bed.

The dead white water buffalo, bellowing madly, comes crashing through the leafy canopy, his legs flailing wildly. He doesn't understand why he'll never get back into his body, broken as it might be or why, with the same suddenness, he can now fly like the birds who once perched, picking and pecking, upon his haunches.

"Help me, Finn, help me," begs smiling Johnny as if his mouth is filled with toffee and marbles.

Johnny has blond, curly hair which he's always trying to straighten. I never could understand why he didn't like his curls; they matched just so his perfect smile they were so beautiful. Johnny's legs are severed just above the knees and half of his face is shot away.

"Goddamit, Finn," the young Johnny pleads. "For the love of the good God in heaven, kill me!"

Johnny tries to push himself up onto his elbow, but the strain overwhelms him. He falls back onto the grass and looks up at Finn, his eyes imploring, beseeching, begging.

"I can't, Johnny," says Finn. "Don't ask me to do that, please don't ask me to do that!"

Johnny sticks out his hand and grabs Finn's ankle tightly. "YOU PROMISED!" he screams, as best he can, blood and bits of broken teeth flying everywhere. "Don't send me back to my ma like this." He knows he's a goner. Both he and Finn have talked about the possibility many times over.

Finn stands, picks up his rifle and looks down at his fallen brother. He kneels beside Johnny and kisses him full on the bloody red lips. "Sssh, Johnny," he says. Then he stands over Johnny once more. When the shot rings out, echoing through the trees, the smile leaves Finn's face forever.

He drops to his knees, crying like a baby, as Johnny Quinn's spirit comes out of his body. Confused, it hovers above us.

I crouch beside Finn. He is still alive and, though I can no longer rest inside him, inside our body, I can no more leave him than the day can leave the night. Having no place else to go, moving on instinct alone, Johnny straddles the back of the great white bull, and I remember hoping then they might comfort one another as they ride away together to the Place of Truly Dead Souls.

Finn the Albanach, newly turned twenty, kneels down upon the wet leaves of grass, at the very moment of Johnny's death, and cries.

I realize that when he killed Johnny, Finn also killed something inside himself.

He rushes over to Romeo Robinson and grabs the machete from the startled gunner's hand. "Gimme that fuckin' thing," he snarls, then begins hacking wildly at the bodies of the dead Asian soldiers, aiming for their genitals. And seeing themselves so mutilated, their spirits scream and dance wildly among the treetops.

Finn becomes a cold, insensitive killer that night; life means nothing henceforth, and the realization that death really is his business becomes clearer than any textbook, story, or drill instructor might ever hope to tell.

Though Finn has no way of knowing it, the chopping in two of the White One and the hack, hack, hacky beheading of the smiling Asian soldiergirl have forever put their numbing mark on him, and the bullet now resting inside the brain of Johnny Quinn will forever have Finn's name etched upon it. Nonchalance and apathy become an integral part of him that night, more so perhaps than even the blood running through his veins. They are now as much a part of him as are his eyes or his hands or the color of his hair.

His emptiness is now complete; he did become an Empty that night, doomed to traipse around the earth without me, without his Madman, without his spirit. I remember falling to my knees as I watch him, then beg him, for the first time, to take me back.

"Please, Finn," I beg. "Take me back. I am your spirit, I am your passion, I am all the love, all the creativity you could ever hope to muster. Anything you want to love," I tell him, "I am that which will enable you to do so."

He doesn't hear a word of it, and the deep, red blood of the rainfilled night strikes my Finn, my blackhaired warrior, deaf, dumb, and blind.

Tommy-up-front is as nervous as hell, though he's the most fearless gunship pilot I've ever seen. He doesn't fly his aircraft. He rides it like a wild bronco. I think he could have stood and flown it, still managing somehow to operate both the foot-pedals and the hand-controls simultaneously. But he's jittery; we've left the gunship, his baby, unprotected and, in spite of the monsoon rains, the area seems to be infested with Viet Cong. What's worse, though, is that we're illegal. We don't have any orders to go on this mission. We've simply taken it upon ourselves to go look for our friends. The implications, since we're returning with dead comrades, could be terrible.

"Let's get the hell outa here," says Tommy, as he grabs the body of Frankie Chen and throws it over his shoulder. "Now!" he demands.

"Bullshit, man," says Romeo. "The gunship's just up the way! Go get it an' pick up these bodies."

"You're crazy, man! I don't give a rat's ass if Jesus H. Christ's just up the way; we're gettin' the fuck outa here. Let's go, move it!"

"I ain't goin' nowhere, asshole. Ivy League's tied to a fuckin' tree back there," says Romeo, clenching his bloody machete more tightly than ever.

Tommy-up-front spins quickly around, pulling out and cocking his sidearm as he spins and, grabbing Romeo by the shirtfront, sticks his pistol into Romeo's temple.

"You disobeying a direct order, lover boy?"

They each stand their ground, staring one another down for a very long and tense moment.

"Shit," says Romeo, and spins away. "Watch your fuckin' back, asshole," he mutters through clenched teeth.

"Huh? Watch my back? I'll mess you up real bad if I hear that kinda shit again," says Tommy-up-front. Then he chuckles. "Don't you have no respect for your elders, Romeo?" he says. The tension evaporates. Even Romeo smiles.

"Awright, you guys. Grab Johnny an' the rest of 'em an' let's get the hell outa here. We'll take the bodies to Triage; the nurses can beg 'em up!"

The flight back to base camp is uneventful and quiet. All except for the dull, boneshaking throb of the mincement-making rotorblades. All of us are lost in our own thoughts as we watch the pools of blood gathering under the bodies of our dead pals.

———

"I want that bullet," says Finn.

The nurse, who is in her early twenties, looks at him and chuckles sardonically. She leans over the body of Johnny Quinn, then stares straight into Finn's eyes.

"And which bullet might that be?" she asks. "There's half a dozen in him."

"I want the one stuck in his head. That's the one that done him in."

"How do you know that?"

"I know it because I fuckin' well know it! Is that no' enough?"

The nurse looks at him and shrugs her shoulders. She is haggard and tired, exhausted. A dark brown curl hangs over her forehead.

"I don't have time for that kinda crap," says she. "I'm too busy patching up the living."

"Nurse, I want that goddamned bullet."

She runs her tired eyes over the grim figure of Finn.

"Then get it yourself, soldier," she says, and hands him a long-nosed tweezer-like instrument.

He stands there for a moment gawking at the nurse, not quite sure if he heard her properly. Romeo bursts out laughing. Tommy's purple with rage.

"You're one cold-hearted motherfucker," he says.

There's a smile on the nurse's face.

"Man, you ain't really gonna do that, are ya?" asks Romeo.

Finn steps up to the gurney. He probes the bullet hole in Johnny's forehead. He hits soft stuff at first. He feels sick. Then solid stuff. Maybe he got lucky right away. Is it the bullet? Forget it, man! It's just bone. Skull. He's nauseous. There's a hole in the solid stuff. The path of the bullet? Get through the hole, through the forehead. Oh, christ, it's soft, soft and mushy! The brain, he's reached the brain. Wait a minute! Is there a hole in the back? He reaches under Johnny's head. Feels. Should be a hole as big as a baseball. There ain't no fuckin' hole in the back. Where's the bullet then? Must still be inside. Was it bouncin' off bone, ricocheting from bone to bone? Where did it rest? Could be anywhere. Don't talk to me now, Johnny, please don't talk to me now. His hands are covered in blood. My hands are covered in your blood, Johnny. He gropes, twists, scratches the skull. Sounds like a hundred fingernails screeching down a blackboard. Bloodcurdling. He heaves. He purses his lips, expands his cheeks. Heave. He holds it back. Reactionary forces are at work now, they've taken over and conquered his will. Heave. He's lightheaded, ready to swoon. He wishes he could. Heave. Can't back off now. Save face. He's a dangerous warrior now. A hero. Why am I doing this, he wonders. What the fuck am I doing here inside my buddy's brain? Evidence? Take the evidence and hide it in a deep, deep hole somewhere so that it will never, ever, ever be found? The vomit rises. Heave, Finn, heave! With all his will he swallows hard, forcing it back. Romeo pukes for him, sickened. The tweezers strike something solid in the middle of Johnny's mush. He grabs at it and pulls, pulls out the killer part of an M-16 bullet. He stares at the nurse, his eyes blazing with fear and hatred. Why'd she have to make me do that? He sticks the bullet into the top left pocket of his jungle fatigues as it it were a pack of cigarettes, then heaves once more.

He rushes off towards the door of the Triage tent, holding his bloodied hand to his mouth. The nurse stares after him, a look of abject disgust creasing her face.

"Body bag!" she shouts to a medic, tears of exasperation and pity welling up in her eyes. "Bring me another goddamnfuckin' body bag!"

Before Finn reaches the door he hears the whistle, the sickening whistle of an incoming rocket, followed by the dull thud of the impact before the explosion. He hits the deck, smiling, and holds his rifle tightly.

"Missed, motherfuckers," he says.

Then the second whistling noise disturbs the night, wiping the smile from his face. It smashes through the flimsiness of the Triage tent, thuds into the floor underneath the table where Johnny's being bagged and blows Johnny's remains and the body of the brown-haired nurse to smithereens. Finn, shocked into inertia, is splattered with bodybits and blood. His numbness is immediate and so complete he can't speak, and from that moment on he is unable to smile. For the second time that night he throws up, and throws up, and throws up.

In whispers, the doctors mumble, "Battle fatigue!" A numbness has taken him over, and he has a vacant stare in his eyes, as if he isn't really there at all. A month or so later, his commander, with as little fanfare as possible, relieves him of his immediate duties and shoves him into a quiet occupation for the remainder of his time in-country. He shuffles papers from morning until night. He cries a lot. Quietly and softly. He goes back to his hooch after his duty day is done, plays hard rock music loudly through his headphones, and loses himself in the dreamscapes, the fantasy world, of his heroin-prompted wanderings, his only comfort.

———

I stick with him every moment of every day until at last his war is over, all three-hundred-sixty-five days day of it. I send him messages, I niggle him and pester him. I'm thankful he's still intact. In body at least. He's glad to be away from it all as he stands there next to the huge air terminal in Saigon. He'll be twenty-one soon. He's looking forward to his first legal drink when he arrives in San Francisco. Finally an adult in the eyes of the world.

The air terminal buzzes with activity, with the movement of people. As he stands there, he thinks how strange it is to be in a war zone one minute and out of it the next, back at last in mufti. He's just returned from a walk around the teeming streets of Saigon city. It really is like San Francisco, he thinks: beautiful, sultry, sexy! But like the city by the bay, Saigon also entices like a whore, a shameless goddamn whore.

Saigon city in the Maygone month of June is a magical place too, spiritthick and colorful, teeming and pulsing with a mysteriousness that transcends even bombs and bloodhungry bullets. I can feel the mystery myself, can almost see it in the heat-rippled light of the hot summer day, standing there at the airport with Finn, wearing my long crimson robe, waiting to go home, filled with regret. It could have been so beautiful, he feels. If only.

If only this, if only that! His post-Vietnam list of if-onlys has tripled, perhaps even quadrupled, compared to the days before Vietnam. "If only! The words of a dreamer," he says. What a waste. If only I'd stayed at home, if only I'd stayed in Alba. Now there's a thought for you. Alba, what a strange word it is right enough. These days at least. So ripe with emotion, bursting so with such a profusion of moods and feelings. His head pounds with memories as he stands at the terminal gate in his new silk suit, Hong Kong cut for a few lousy bucks. He had it tailored to fit to perfection some months before; but the suit now hangs miserably over his heroin-mangled frame. Home, he's sure, is where the blood is. Aye, that's it all right. Where the blood is!

When the White One's soul leaves his body, on the night Finn kicks me out, I feel sure it'll be easy to get back inside him, but he's so confused himself he doesn't have the slightest idea how empty he is. He doesn't even know he's an Empty. I feel certain it'll be easy to somehow communicate with him; even as a child his openness to mystical considerations is mature beyond both his years and the strictures of the ordinary, workaday world; that's why I'm so surprised he doesn't yet know he's now an Empty himself.

He always loved Alban winters, particularly during those long nights when thick fog descends over the fields in which he plays. He could feel the mystery then too, and knows intuitively that spirits and other Invisibilities roam around on such subdued nights. The wispiness of spirits, after all, blends well with fog. Proofs and the like are of no consequence. He just knows! He feels the presence of Invisibilities much too strongly. He is open to the feel of them!

I have always been inside Finn, though quietly. It's only since I've been outside him that I have to niggle and annoy him. When inside him, I am simply a part of him. I remember one particularly foggy night when he awoke disturbed from a fitful sleep.

He is around twelve years of age at the time and has awakened to the sad and plaintive moaning of the bagpipes. They beckon him, invite him to seek the source of the sound. He jumps out of bed and dresses hurriedly, not daring to awaken his family. He slips out the door into the night like an Invisibility himself and walks off into the darkness. All is quiet but for the sound of the pipes coming to him wrapped in the droplets of water forming the earth-embracing clouds. So enshrouded in music and clouds, he feels the pull of his heritage, the inexplicable pull of some ancient mystery, as if he's become one with the trees and the grass and other things beyond the usual ken of man.

And so pulled, he passes the homes of all his friends and loved ones, into the fields, through faerie rings and thistles, until he feels as scratched as the suffering Christ himself. He stops, half dead, and drops before a high hill where the music began. On top of the hill stands the piper, dressed in an ancient kilted plaid. The sad and plaintive dirge plays on, crying to him. For the first time in his life, he feels a great heart-heavy pain. The prostrate Finn looks up and the piper turns, his eyes filled with tears. "Mo thruaige ort!" says the piper in the language of the ancients. "Woe to thee!"

Oh why, Saigon? Oh, why those scratches of Christ from the mists of Alba to the teeming, pulsing mystery of Saigon city? Alba, light years away, is real only at a gut level and in memories. Finn's last memory of Alba is of getting drunk, sitting around a fire with his friends in Fingal's Park, a few hours before being poured onto the plane for America, land of the free, home of the bygod brave.

And America, what of America? He lived there just a few short months before being drafted, but he's learned so much about being American as he plods through jungle and guts with his fellow warriors who are all as young and as innocent as he. He knows even then he will never be an American, that he never can be an American. Nor is he a Scotsman any more. The many thousands of miles of separation and the many rounds of spent ammunition and the blood and the guts and the heroin overdoses have seen to that, have made him a stranger, a loner.

He stands at the air terminal in Saigon city in the Maygone month of June feeling like the Steppenwolf. And he weeps.

He's sure it's the killing of Johnny that makes him a loner when, in fact, it is the killing of the bull that makes him so. I've often wondered what they were thinking, those young men, when they took the life of the bull, when they killed the bull so certainly, so irrevocably. Were they killing themselves? Did the bull represent manhood, virility, propagation of the species? Or was it something more basic, more primordial even than that? Isn't Zeus, the father of all the gods, represented by the bull in classical mythology? Were they, killing God? Perhaps that's why, since then, Finn has felt that he belongs nowhere, but that he belongs everywhere too!

He feels the mystery of Saigon, though he doesn't know exactly what it is he feels; nor can he possibly know how to describe it, yet there we both stand at the airport feeling it. I've learned by now that Finn won't let me back into him without a tremendous struggle. Had I known then how long the struggle would be, I might have given up and let him do as he would, with or without me. But I know what we are, what our existence means, because I come from the Land of the Truly Alive which he knows so little of. I am the spirit; he, the body and the mind. He calls it toughness, will, one-and-one-equals-two pragmatism. I know better. I know it to be ignorance. No more, no less. Ignorance and pride!

But I won't let him go. No matter what, no matter whatever happens to him, I'll keep the blood-dripping umbilical cord wrapped safely around his waist, and I'll continue to plod along by his side until he takes me back or until he kills himself. Perhaps I'll hang him with the cord myself; it might be better than suicide.

He's been trying to kill himself ever since he put the bullet into Johnny Quinn's brain. Not so much by suicide, but through careless bravado at first and, now, through the extravagant use of heroin, pure China White.

He is loaded to the gills now as he stands here waiting for the plane to take us to San Francisco, where he plans to live after a short visit to Alba, as he will always call it. He has a vial of herion in his pocket. He's going to stick it up his arse and smuggle it into America. It will last him a long, long time and will enable him, he's sure, to withdraw completely from the awful stuff. But he's afraid. When his flight is announced, he runs into the bathroom and snorts enough of it up his nose to choke a horse. Though he's become emaciated through guilt and the consequent heavy use of dope and is thirty pounds underweight, his tolerance is high. As a junkie, he is at his peak. He feels somewhat normal as he stuffs some more of the heroin into the end of a cigarette. If nobody bothers him, he'll smoke it on the other side of the Pacific; if it doesn't go so well, he'll simply drop it on the ground and hope for the best, withdrawals be damned!

And so it all is, over and done with—history. A year, every minute of it spent counting down the days, accompanied by the agents of madness as they do their best to mold him and make him what he will become for the rest of his mortal life.

I hope that a visit to Alba after the war and a life in San Francisco will bring him around. But it doesn't! We grow farther and farther apart as the years fly by, as the years tumble headlong, one into the other.

MAUREEN E. NERLI

A native San Franciscan, I attended University of San Francisco, Stanford (postgraduate work in broadcasting), San Francisco State, the Maine Film Directors Workshop, and recently the Hollywood Film School.

I left a fulfilling job as musical director of KFRC-AM, a leading San Francisco radio station, for the job of a lifetime—associate director of the Tan Son Nhut USO Club in Saigon, which lasted eighteen months. After Vietnam, I country-jumped to the USO Club at Utapao, Thailand, and from there I was lured and hired as a Department of the Army Civilian with U.S. Army Special Services, serving in South Korea and Fort Ord, California.

With the Vietnam experience behind me, I set out to right a wrong. I became an activist for the civilian women who served in the Vietnam conflict. I've told my story (and their stories as well!) in the following books: *A Piece of My Heart: Stories of 26 American Women Who Served in Vietnam; Reflections Between the Lines; Visions of War, Dreams of Peace; and Valiant Women of the Vietnam War.* I consulted in the theatrical production of *A Piece of My Heart* and was featured in *Diversion: Vietnam,* an award-winning documentary short about USO and American Red Cross volunteers in Vietnam. I also consulted on the ABC-TV series *China Beach,* which was based in part on *A Piece of My Heart.* I was also asked by Diane Evans, Director of the Vietnam Women's Memorial, to write a story about the USO for the Vietnam Women's Memorial Dedication book. And I served a four-year hitch as president of the San Francisco Unit of Women's Overseas Service League.

I am founder of the first memorial in the nation to honor the civilian women: The Civilian Women Volunteers All Wars Memorial Highway, in San Mateo, California. I realized this dream after three years of hard work, speaking to the California State Assembly and Senate for approval and raising the private money for this non-government project, and I received a commendation for my work on this from Congressman Tom Lantos.

I believe that once a broadcaster, always a broadcaster. So I was deeply honored to be nominated and accepted into the San Francisco Bay Area Broadcast Legends organization.

I still feel obligated to continue my activism for the civilian women who served in Vietnam. Whatever that course may be, I'm ready.

Sister Ambrose, the Flying Nun

I celebrated my birthday on April 13, 1970, by visiting St. Anne's Catholic Orphanage in a charming residential section of Saigon. There were sweeping reminders of the French occupation—tree-lined streets, two-story elegant homes with entryway balustrades, well-manicured lawns, and pots of blooming flowers. The American ambassador lived just a few blocks away.

Our USO visits to orphanages were generally to distribute ice cream and cake. But this time was different. Mary Beth Breen, the associate director of the Di An USO, invited me to visit at the request of Sister Ambrose. Mary Beth had heard about the good sister from a pilot friend, who praised her dedicated works of mercy rescuing and caring for the homeless children of Vietnam.

Mary Beth drove her pink jeep, on loan from the motor pool. Pink was the only paint color left in the motor pool that week, and Mary Beth and her jeep were a common sight in Saigon. She drove like a race car driver. After a few wrong turns on Tu Do Street, we finally found St. Anne's. Tu Do Street was a beehive of activity—tea bars coexisting with French, Italian, Spanish, Chinese, Greek, and American-style restaurants, Max's night club, the International House, and the Saigon USO on Nguyen Hue. The French, Italian, Spanish, Chinese, and Greek restaurants had nothing to fear from the menu at the Saigon USO; the fries, burgers, chili, and freezes were all-American, and cheap.

St. Anne's Orphanage shone at us with welcome. It was a two-story, French-style villa, painted in a fading soft coral with forest-green shutters and front door. The gravel circular driveway caressed a flourishing green lawn bordering the street. The foliage surrounding the villa was a treat for these battle-sore eyes; magnificent red and yellow roses *(hoa hong)* stood proud in Kelly green planter boxes hanging from the first- and second-story windows. Stark green ivy gracefully made its climb to the roof and covered the right side of the villa façade. Along-side the front door were two coral planter boxes showing off yellow chrysanthemums. A magnificent sweet-smelling magnolia tree found its role in life as cover for the visitors' parking lot.

Mary Beth parked the jeep under the magnolia tree, and we walked to the villa's entrance. Suddenly we were stopped in our tracks by the most beautiful operatic voice, coming from an open first-floor window: *"Laudate Dominum, laudate Dominum, omnes gentes, alleluia."* As Catholic school graduates, we knew the words: "Praise God, praise God, everyone, alleluia." The voice was heavenly. It compelled you to listen and experience its power, joy, and love.

A young Vietnamese sister welcomed us at the door, her face barely visible through the white habit.

C'iao. May I help you?" the little sister asked, beaming an angelic smile.

"We are here to see Sister Ambrose, Sister," answered Mary Beth.

"Of course. I will tell her you are here," she said in perfect English. "Sister is singing. She sings every day at this time. We love to hear her. Such a beautiful voice."

The sister led us to a sitting room near the foyer and motioned for us to sit down. The room was sparse, to say the least—two straight-back wooden chairs, a well-polished round table, and a large glass vase with one yellow and two red roses. Asians never place two flowers in a vase. Even numbers are considered back luck; odd numbers good luck.

The singing came to a thunderous end, and there she was, Sister Ambrose McDermott. We both stood up. "Sorry to keep you waitin', ladies. I practice my singing every day at this time. I'm Sister Ambrose. 'Tis a grand day for you two to be visitin' St. Anne's, is it not?" She extended her right hand to Mary Beth, then to me, the handshake of a strong, fearless woman, a woman in charge.

We introduced ourselves. "I'm Maureen Nerli. I work at the Tan Son Nhut USO Club, Sister."

"I'm Mary Beth Breen, Sister. We spoke on the phone yesterday. Thank you for inviting us to St. Anne's."

"Welcome, ladies. So glad you could visit."

Every movement of Sister's was purposeful. She was the Westmoreland of her command. Even on this blistering hot day, she looked cool in her layers of white cotton. The long, full skirt and apron were cinched by a large brown wooden rosary that hung softly from her small waist. Her arms were covered with long balloon sleeves, held up by an elastic band around her wrist. The white collar and hood framed her beautiful face. She looked very young, perhaps thirty. Her glowing, freckled face, pink cheeks, sparkling white teeth, thick black eyebrows, full rosy lips, and sparkling blue eyes, the look that Irish ballads are written about, made a startling first impression. And her Irish brogue was thick and rich, with the Irish propensity for ending each sentence with a question.

Mary Beth had told me that Sister Ambrose was from Galway. She was a Sister of Mercy. The foundress of the order, Mother Catherine McCauley, a missionary herself, instilled the virtue of reaching the multitudes in the name of Jesus Christ. Sister Ambrose was a living example of that principle.

"Let me show you the orphanage. You'll be followin' me now, won't you?"

As soon as Sister Ambrose showed us into the nursery, we entered another world. It was a gigantic room, perhaps a ballroom in its former life, with high ceiling, ornate wall lights, and hardwood floor. In the heat of Saigon, this room was cool. Not a speck of dust anywhere. Even the afternoon Saigon sun beamed its approval through the large shuttered windows blanketing one side of the room. Children were leaning out of rusting cribs, some were laughing, some reaching their tiny hands through the crib bars to touch us. We reached out to touch these little ones in return. A few giggled. One started to cry. A sense of curiosity filled the room—on both sides.

There were twenty children and four nuns. Four of the children were sitting at a small table in the middle of the room, singing a Vietnamese song led by an enthusiastic sister. Several other children were in pursuit of a small red ball thrown in their direction by a bespectacled sister. A crying baby was being rocked to sleep by a young and loving sister in her early twenties. Another sister was lovingly changing a diaper. This nursery was the heart of St. Anne's. The sisters, happy and content, acknowledged us with warm smiles. There was a sense of tranquility in the nursery despite the war, the future, the pain and loss.

"As God is my judge," Sister Ambrose said, "The sisters work from dawn to dusk caring for these children. Many of the children are all alone in the world. Weren't their parents killed by the Viet Cong during raids on their villages? Entire families destroyed by the rattle of a gun, the drop of a bomb. There is no one left to take care of them.

That's our job, isn't it now? God willin', we will be here at St. Anne's as long as we can." Sister Ambrose ended her sentence with a serious tone in her mellifluous voice and tears in her Irish blue eyes.

Mary Beth nudged me to look at the most beautiful little girl standing in the corner of the day room. Her long black hair cascaded to her waist. She wore a red dress that tied in the back into a big bow. She turned to look at us and then grabbed her hair with her left hand and her dress with the right hand and pulled and yanked in anger, fear, and pain. Mary Beth walked toward her, arms outstretched, but Sister Ambrose put a hand out to stop her. The child started to scream—a wail that shook the nursery. She couldn't and wouldn't be soothed by the sister who came to her rescue. The wail dragged on, finally tapering off amid sobs and tears.

"Isn't she a beautiful child, Mary Beth?" Sister asked.

"Sister, did I do something to frighten her?" asked Mary Beth.

"Is she ill, Sister?" I asked.

"'Tis a sad story indeed, indeed. Mai is only three years old. Herself already tastin' the bitterness of life. In the months Mai has been here, I've grown to understand her pain. She just stands in the corner all day, tuggin' at her hair and dress. No one can get near her. We were told by the good men from the rescue unit that she witnessed her parents being decapitated by the Viet Cong. Sad it is that she will never be able to lead a normal life. I have hopes that she will grow out of this pain with love and counseling, but it doesn't look good. Even the doctor that treats the children told us that Mai is scarred for life. It's love we give her now, and God will have to handle the rest. Poor little thing."

Sister Ambrose was interrupted by the force of a stocky little boy running playfully over her sandaled feet. He was one of thousands of Amerasian children who would be the outcasts of the Vietnamese society in a few years. But for now, this blond-haired Black/Vietnamese child was savoring the fun of the moment and playing toward exhaustion. His smile warmed my heart. His teeth, white and even, sparkled in the glow of the afternoon Saigon sun as it beamed through the windows of the nursery. He was neatly dressed in a pair of blue shorts, a red-and-white cotton T-shirt, and transparent plastic sandals. His muscular legs enjoyed the exchange with Sister Ambrose's feet and he giggled. What a happy child. She reached down to grab the tyke. Once in her arms, he reached around her covered neck, wrinkling her hood and collar, and planted a big kiss on her rosy cheek. She returned the affection by placing a soft kiss on his bronze brow. He knew unequivocal love when he saw it. She then placed him on his feet. He looked up at her and smiled as he ran off to join his pals.

"Do you have a difficult time raising funds for St. Anne's, Sister?" Mary Beth asked.

"We live on a meager income, Mary Beth. Our support comes from the donations given to the Sisters of Mercy Missionary Fund in Ireland and America. Also, the bishop here in Saigon gives us a helping hand. In fact, he found this building for us. We thank God for all the generous gifts. Can we not forget the American military here in Vietnam? Fine lot they are too, getting us clothes from America and sometimes food from the mess halls. Grand lot."

We waved to the children and sisters and took one last look at Mai. "May God be with her," I thought.

The nursery tour came to an end. Sister Ambrose invited us to make a visit to the chapel down the hallway. We followed her there, blessed ourselves with holy water in a bowl at the door entrance, and found a kneeler. The altar was covered with the customary white altar cloth. The tabernacle was resting on a small platform on top of the altar. Ten chairs, in two sections of five each, faced the altar. It was a tranquil place of worship amid the sounds of children at play, the noise of war, and Saigon traffic.

I prayed for my family and friends in California, for my friends here in Vietnam, for an end to the war, and for the children and sisters of St. Anne's. I thanked God for all the gifts he has given me. I was grateful to be here in Vietnam to do some good. I knew way back in 1968 that I was being called to serve in Vietnam. It was something I had to do. Now I'm here and making the best out of each day.

I thanked God above for allowing this wonderful lady from Ireland to be of such service to the children of St. Anne's. My few moments in the chapel felt like a weeklong retreat. A respite from the fast-moving world of Saigon was so welcome. God reads our thoughts, so I knew he heard Mary Beth and Sister's prayers too.

We got up at the same time, made the sign of the cross, and walked silently toward the chapel door, dipped our fingers in the holy water, blessed ourselves, and walked into the hallway.

"Sister, does a priest say Mass here each day?" I asked.

"We are blessed, Maureen, to have gracious chaplains from Tan Son Nhut Air Base. They come here and share the Eucharist with us each day. We are grateful to God for their time.

"Ladies, would you be wantin' a cool drink of lemonade?"

"We don't want to take too much of your time, Sister, but your offer sounds too good to turn down," said Mary Beth.

"I'd love a glass, Sister. Thanks," I said.

Sister invited us into her office next door to the chapel. Her office was sparsely furnished, as all rooms at St. Anne's seemed to be: a desk, a telephone, two chairs facing her desk, a single yellow rose in a cobalt blue vase sitting proudly on the bookshelf under the bare windowsill.

There was a gentle knock, and the sister who had led us into the orphanage half an hour ago entered carrying a black lacquer tray with a pitcher of lemonade and three tall glasses filled with ice. She placed the tray on the desk, smiled warmly at us, and bowed as she left the room.

"Thank you, Sister Phu," Sister Ambrose said sweetly.

Who would refuse lemonade? The ice cubes rattled with gusto as Sister Ambrose poured it. At the moment, lemonade beat the joys of even a chocolate shake at the nearest USO club.

As I nursed my lemonade, I glanced around the room and saw a three-peg wooden coatrack near the door. Hanging on the first two pegs were a flight jacket and a helmet. The name on the jacket read "The Flying Nun, Sister Ambrose, Commander of St. Anne's Orphanage." The insignia on the helmet simply read "Flying Nun."

"Are those yours, Sister?"

"'Tis a fact, Maureen, indeed they are. The men from the Thirty-fourth Support Group Helicopter Squadron and their commander, Major Woodard, gave them to me as a gift. Dear ones, all of them."

"You fly out to the fields and firebases?" I asked.

"The men notify me when a village has been destroyed and children have been spared. I'm always ready to go. We pick up the cryin', frightened little ones and fly them back to Saigon and the safety of St. Anne's. The men are so caring. Isn't it a great service to help St. Anne's? Major Woodard told me my nun garb is not appropriate for flying in a helicopter. He said too many layers of white. I'm a target." She laughed.

Sister Ambrose poured some more lemonade.

"After me first ride in that helicopter, I agreed. He gave me a set of fatigues, the helmet, and the vest to look more military. I fit the bill now, don't you think?"

I could imagine Sister jumping out of a chopper, running toward the children, grabbing them, running back to the chopper, holding them in her arms, drying their tears, soothing their fears. This was a brave woman. Bullets be damned! She knew the risks, as all of us did when we volunteered for Vietnam duty. But somehow, we just knew we'd be safe from harm. It was an unspoken truth that we'd be safe. And we were. One could only imagine how many flights she'd taken into the war zone.

Now she began asking us questions. "What brought you two ladies to Vietnam. 'Tis a great risk you took?"

"Guess the patriotic streak in me, Sister," Mary Beth answered.

"I got tired of hearing the negative aspects of the war, Sister. I needed to get over here and see what was happening firsthand. I needed to do my part. I haven't regretted one day so far," I replied, and I meant it.

"What made you come to Vietnam, Sister? The Sisters of Mercy have many missionary destinations, why Vietnam?" I questioned.

"Ah, the Lord has plans for us all, ladies. I was studying to be an opera singer at the University of County Galway, renowned for its outstanding theater arts and traditional music study. Had me sights on the London stage, I did."

"I know the feeling, Sister. Those of us at the USO all have theatrical experience, too. You should see and hear us at firebases, singing folk songs like there's no tomorrow," I added.

Sister Ambrose smiled. She knew the story. She was living it herself. "But what can you do when He taps you on the shoulder and tells you *you* are going to become a missionary."

"We know what you mean, Sister. That's why we are here in Vietnam," Mary Beth answered.

"Sometimes I think we, too, are missionaries, Sister," I said.

Sister Ambrose started to laugh. "One can't fight the Big Three, now, can we? As for Jesus, He's got me now."

She raised her left hand and wiggled her ring finger, looking at the silver ring signifying her marriage to Christ. "I don't regret the choice

I made. As far as me singin' is concerned, I must be doing somethin' right. You know, it's not that big a jump from the theater to running an orphanage. You see, on stage you're in control of yourself. At St. Anne's, I'm in charge of everything. Not that big a jump, aye, not that big a jump indeed. In Ireland, there's a saying: If you're Irish you have no trouble standin' alone. I think that's brill'.'"

Sister informed us that in addition to her singing, she'd written many songs for Catholic worship. She told us to watch out for them when we go to Mass back home. "Just look for me name," she said with a big Irish smile.

There wasn't time for us to hear her songs that afternoon. Nor was there to be a next time. Sister walked us to the front door, shook our hands, and told us she would pray for us. I felt like crying. I don't know why, but I did.

We walked silently to the "pink wonder." Backing out of the gravel driveway, I took one last look at St. Anne's and thought there was some good in Vietnam after all.

In the course of stories about Vietnam, what is often left out is the likes of Sister Ambrose and what she and her order did in Vietnam. In every situation there's a balance. Sister Ambrose, the Irish nun who just happened to be an aspiring opera singer, made me see that balance in my own life. I still think of her. Life is full of memories, and Vietnam left me with more than my share, bad and good. I'm not complaining, believe me. I need those memories to feast on occasionally. But whenever I think of Sister Ambrose and her calling, I have no doubt that my going to Vietnam with the USO clubs was a calling, too. We all have our missions in life. We may live in a community, separated from others by language, philosophies, and customs, but we are still a community of man. Isn't it the right thing to serve that community with your talents and gifts? Fulfilling a mission, a calling? Sister Ambrose thought so. I still think so. Sister Ambrose deeply impressed me that April 13 day in 1970.

Wherever you are, Sister Ambrose, The Flying Nun, my hat's off to ya!

As much as I would like to deal with other topics, I have continued to write, talk, and dream about wars. When I am not, I am thinking, dreaming, taking pride, and remaining upset over the fact that I was born in one country, and now live in another. You can't undo the condition of exile. The moment I think I am done, I am right back to deciding where home is. Both Viet Nam and America are homes, but suffice it to say that the one book I have been working on, without hopes of ever finishing, is one tentatively called *Home Is Where You Hang Yourself, True Confessions of an Accidental Californian*. Now that I am returning to live in Viet Nam after thirty years in the United States, I think that life is full of strange accidents, and if you survive them, you accidentally meet your Buddha nature.

Grief

One day I swear
I will write a book
of blank pages.

I am tired of war.

War

They want war.
They want war.
They want war.

No one wants to read a book about peace.

Peace

Maxine Hong Kingston wrote
The Fifth Book of Peace
full of people
who will not stop talking
about war.

Words

Lời dối gian ai bỏ quên giữa đường,
em đi qua bị thương.

Lies someone left
in the middle of the road
wounding you.

Love

Today I found a lover's slippers
left so long ago
underneath where I sleep,
like empty jars
whose contents
I can no longer taste.

April

I lose one more day crossing
East, looking for home.

I gain one coming back.

But even thirty years in America
haven't amounted to much.

Language

You hear my native tongue
and think it liquid—a language
in which even wild grasses
reply in rhyme.

I don't know what's liquid
but here:

Năm đó hè về
Huế lặng lờ
Xác người
Nhiều hơn xác ve ve.

That year, summer came,
Huế turned quiet again.
Human bodies outnumbered
cicada shells.

In your native language
breath is word, is spirit.
In mine, breath is fragility.
Thều thào, thoi thóp.

In my tongue, death is constant.
I can't think of an adequate translation
for what remains: losses, losses.

In Huế, we say, *mất mát, mất mát.*

When I speak of suffering
you alone know I tire of it;
others want me to carry on
so they think they can learn
something of losses—

They could never.

They have stolen countless countries:
yours and mine, and are stealing them
still. They have stolen their own country
from their own people.

And they ask you and me about losses?

Listen: among the leaves, in the wind,
hear still the murmurs of the masses.
Quanh đây còn tiếng oan hồn nỉ non.

You learned how to say the rosary
with scented beads. I live still
with the scent of incense burning

at a thousand funerals
that summer in Huế.

I owe you more than apologies,
but no more words. I have talked always
of memory and suffering, given details
of where the skin was torn, the unbelievable,
unhealing scars. And I've talked until
I no longer know who you are.

I thank you, for times I couldn't see
that you remember, times I stayed blind.
My eyes still see nothing but what passed
long ago. I wait for some future that can put
my many parts back together.

But raindrops won't go back into clouds.
Mấy thuở mưa rơi nước ngược về trời.

September was when we last spoke—
but you no longer remember.

When we last spoke, it was of demons
that inhabit the space we exiles
keep out of sight.

*The language of exiles
has nowhere to go
but inside.*

There are two kinds of exiles—
those who insist on the illusions
of the new country, and those
who obsess over what was left behind:

Losses, losses—*mất mát.*

Your mother, in her house down south,
belongs to the first kind—the one with possibilities.
Your father, forever on a plane, hopeless,
back to his island, childhood home,
belongs nowhere.

You who knew this—how did you let yourself
plunge into me, my past?

I am sorry, we're stuck
between the two kinds: we're desperate
for a future, but would not make peace
with history. I am sorry
for the hopelessness that is us.

It's kind of you to have imagined us—
you, in southern sunlit Andalusian village
still in mourning, besieged by the ghost
of colonial cruelty and the vanquished.
Me, in my white stucco town
beyond Marrakesh, near the sea,
writing to you of desert and water.

Water, water —*Nước, nước, nước*

Water—in my language,
Nước: a word we use
to mean nation.

Write me another poem, to speak
of our nations, of how
they took yours and mine, water
cut from the source.

Write, even in this language
imposed on so many, but in which
there's no translation or truthful
words that speak of our condition:

Mất nước—nation lost.

Such is our obsession—we've been lost
without our countries, and there can be
no substitutes.

You, uprooted, anchorless,
are on to something: the sooner
you disassociate from me,

the sooner you end your sickness,
your obsession with war and losses.

It's brave of you to imagine us,
a separate but shared life: binding
our nations' histories together
to bind us together.

Mấy thuở mưa rơi nước ngược về trời.
Raindrops don't go back into clouds.

We make plans and rescind,
we are exiles—our lives
consist only of memories—*quá khứ.*

The language of exiles is spoken
in the past tense—*quá khứ.*

Sometimes, tired, I let it be:
things were the way they were.
Men act as they will, some
with kindness, some with cruelty.

We thought we could act with love,
the way I chose to sleep on the side
where the moon was luminous,
leaving you the darkness
I thought would soothe your nights.

In your sleep, you repaired to a language
I didn't understand. Your words,
like lovers intertwined, danced
with the rhythm of me
breathing, breathing—*thoi thóp.*
dancing in time with my sighs.

Outside, cactus flowers bloomed
on the fire escape—but I shielded you,
keeping quiet about how they reminded me
of flashing flares, exposing men in hiding,
exposing the killings of my youth.

But that part of history, even if I tried,
I cannot hide from you. You take it
inside, make my nightmares yours.

At some point, we became nomads.
We became nomads even in our sleep,
our roots yanked from us. *Mất nước.*

Conquistadors, men in green berets,
dark suits, stripped us—nation lost.

Afterward, you went from barrio
to barrio, trying to turn the language
of exiles into poetry. And me, from single
whitewashed rooms of cold cement
to terraced apartments far away,
alone to face my own solitude.

Homes that cannot be home.

We became nomads, modern cities
are the desert we cross, not so much
for salvation, nor for subsistence:
we cross our endless deserts, looking
for ourselves.

You who know this
should have known
love would have been impossible.

We would have been impossible.

The sky changes hues, the moon turns pale,
cactus flowers shrivel after their one night
and fall. My tongue has spoken every inch of
your skin, and I am ready to recede. Before dawn,
we go back to mute despair.

Neither love nor future is possible.

I can only see the past,
and would not see you
until you are no longer here.

We types of exiles live backwards.

Huế, to go backwards, is where
my mother was born. You would like
the Perfume River, although in Huế
we would always prefer its native self,
sông Hương: a river that flows
unrushed, out to sea, as if the town's
one thousand years of sorrow
never entered its currents.

Upon the sidewalks, in the shade
of the old flame trees, lovers whisper
lines they think original, unaware
of all the ghosts.

Huế is where mother met father,
fell in love, and I died my first death,
that spring, when it wasn't enough
for soldiers to kill in the battlefields.

My losses began then, and haven't ended.

I carry you still,
the way I carry Huế.

But you and I carry the things
we love as we do losses—*mất mát,*
deep in a place exiles
keep forever out of sight.

PAUL OCAMPO

I graduated from the University of California, Berkeley, with a B.A. in English literature in 2002. Maxine Hong Kingston was my professor in creative writing. My short stories and other writing projects deal with the theme of the struggle against disembodiment of identity and voice. I recently joined the Vietnam War Veteran Writers Group led by Maxine and have witnessed how writing and sharing stories can achieve peace.

I am a veteran of peace, and it is in this spirit that I wrote the short story "Butterfly."

Butterfly

A butterfly entered through the open window," I e-mailed my brother yesterday. "Nanay passed away. Come home. Love, Sophia."

Our grandmother would tell us Philippine folklore when we were young. One night, she told us that when a butterfly flies in and becomes trapped in the house, there will be a death in the family. I imagine a butterfly with thin tiger stripes coming in from the open window. She flutters around me and makes her presence known. Like a shy guest, she withdraws to the corner of the ceiling and rests her wings, unfurling her unparalled beauty to me.

It was three years ago when I last saw Kuya Raffi. Now he is on his way home.

———

"Could we stop by Nanay's?" Kuya Raffi whispered under his breath, preserving the delicate silence hanging on a thin thread that could crash without any warning.

"We're going to be late," I told Kuya. His eyes remained fixed on the barely visible road ahead of us. "Slippery When Wet" was a sign that I could not ignore. It had been raining fiercely for four days. The windshield wipers could barely clear the glass of water droplets. "You're going to be late. We don't have time to stop by Sylvan Glades."

"Sophia, please." His gaze could not be interrupted. His eyes kept their intensity on the glimmer and the shadows outside the refuge of our Camry. "I really need to. I don't know how long I'll be gone."

His words harkened me back to the night when he sat me on my bed to tell me his plan to leave home. I couldn't help but feel that his words came from pure selfishness. With or without my support, he would do it. It wasn't a threat. It sounded more like a warning. Remembering that night, I just wanted to slam on the accelerator and hit the next pole. At least then the scary sounds would be over.

"Sophia, thanks." The terseness held the floodgates. I turned right on Alighieri Street, passed two stop signs, and entered through the open gates of Sylvan Glades. The rain diminished to a drizzle. We could see the pastel-colored, two-story building with "Sylvan Glades" etched on the wall in elegant cursive writing. Ivy hung down and framed the arch of the entrance to the building. Rose and chrysanthemum petals littered the cement ground. I parked in a "Handicapped" space, turned the engine off, and pulled the handbrake up. I hung the azure Handicapped sign on the rearview mirror. I could hear Mama scolding me for improperly using the placard. We were supposed to take it out only when we drove Nanay home and back. I glanced at Kuya Raffi, hoping to catch his attention, but his mind remained absorbed. Not to make eye contact was both deliberate and warranted. He laid the backpack that had been sitting on his lap on the seat and left the car without an umbrella. I sighed, opened my door, and was catapulted back onto my seat, as I had forgotten to unfasten my seatbelt.

I ran to catch up with my brother, but he was nowhere to be seen in the main hallway. Bouquets of flowers adorned the makeshift waiting room. The overhead speakers softly played a piano concerto. And the waft of Lysol and potpourri made me conscious of where we were.

"Good evening. May I help you?" The receptionist, almost hidden by the piles of manila folders on the counter, greeted me with a dab of fatigue. She was on the final leg of her shift.

"My brother and I are here to visit my grandmother. I believe he's already in there." I searched for his name on the signup sheet. The receptionist asked me to log in the time of visit and reminded me of Nanay's room number. I walked down the empty hallways; the residents were in their rooms eating their dinners. Many, including our own grandmother, required the assistance of nurses and volunteers. I'd memorized the way to room 118 and, upon getting there, found my brother feeding Nanay. Nanay sat in her wheelchair, and while she chewed on her porridge, her hand grazed his face. She explored his face but didn't recognize her own grandson. Suffering from Alzheimer's, she was lost.

"Nanay, I know what you're going through. I understand. You knew it was going to happen." Kuya was kneeling in front of her. Nanay leaned her head closer to him as if she was about to say something but paused and looked up at the austere space. Kuya continued even if Nanay's eyes would not meet his. "You knew that when you came here, you had left your soul, just like the folklore that you once told us. I remember it, Nanay. I remember."

"*Sino ka? Hindi kita kilala.*" Her blank eyes welled up with fear.

"It's me, Nanay. It's Raffi. Remember? Nanay, you have to remember."

"*Umalis ka na. Aswang, umalis ka na.*"

"You must go. You cannot upset your grandmother like that," said the nurse who was feeding Rose, my grandmother's roommate. She put down the bowl of soup that she was holding and attended to Nanay. "We don't want her blood pressure to go up, now do we? You should just go." I approached Nanay and gave her a peck on the cheek, which felt soft to the touch. She was fragile. She had stopped her reproach of Kuya, pretended to ignore us, and stared at the newscast on television. Her hands strummed her lustrous white hair. My brother looked up at the TV monitor and froze, seeing footage of the most recent bombing and skirmish between American soldiers and the insurgents in Iraq. In his frown, I saw canyons of despair. When the news turned to the weather, the next segment, he awoke and turned to embrace Nanay. He quickly let go before she started to shake. His pace again was faster than mine when we walked out of Sylvan Glades. This time, his unmatched speed masked the tears that he let fall for Nanay. That was the last that Kuya Raffi saw Nanay. He knew that it was going to be the last time.

———

"I got my orders. I leave in a week."

The crash of the tea cup froze us in our spots as we were held captive by our anxieties, frustrations, hopelessness borne out of Kuya's news. The shards could not be made whole again. Mama collapsed under the weight of his announcement.

I was only thirteen years old then; my brother was a recent college graduate. He had received assistance from the ROTC while studying at UCSD, which was less than ten miles away. I couldn't fully grasp what was going on. But soon enough, my brother was gone for periods of time. Later I found out that he was headed toward Mindanao. He was to do his part for the War on Terrorism. To fight in a small, little-known war, one that nobody talked about. A war against the same enemies we'd fought before: the Muslims. Nobody explained the history, or cared to. It just seemed like we were always fighting the Muslims.

Nanay, who was in good health still, picked up the pieces. I put down my body board—my brother and I had planned on surfing at La Jolla Beach that afternoon—and helped our grandmother clean up the mess. Mama, Papa, and Kuya proceeded toward the living room, which had a view of the ocean.

The first time he came home, the changes were noticeable. I am not only talking about his crew-cut hair, his muscular build, or his coarser skin. The Army truly drained his youth and transformed him into a man we hardly knew.

At the Christmas Vigil Mass at St. Joseph's, Kuya seemed restless, impatient. He used to be attentive in church, reflecting his deep devotion to Catholicism. That night nothing would come out of him except for sighs. During the homily, he made paper airplanes of the envelopes for monetary contributions. After receiving Communion, he fidgeted, tapping his fingers on the newly polished pews. Papa had to grab his hand and tell him to cease the noise. He couldn't seem to pray, or even feign to. But the choir's singing that filled the vast yet contained space of St. Joseph's Cathedral soothed him. While the silent pauses between prayers and blessings and the droning sound of sustained unified voices irritated him, compelling him to lower his head close to his knees and cover his ears, the songs transformed him. He strained to hear something above the songs, something hidden; a deeper meaning was being revealed to him in the songs. I could see in his face that he understood the *Latin Mass in G major* that the full choir sang. He had taken Latin in college. He loved Latin. He knew it more than Tagalog. During the vigil, he would utter, *"Miserere nobis."*

At our *Noche Buena,* Christmas Vigil, dinner, everyone observed further silence. Nanay's Alzheimer's was beginning to set in. At the beginning of dinner, when she went to the kitchen to get knives for everyone, she didn't come back for such a long time that our papa had to fetch her. He found her under the table with the knives, not knowing where she was. She recognized her son and came out from under the table. In a few minutes, she remembered everything again. She blamed it on being homesick for her life in the Philippines.

We feasted at 1:30 in the morning, a Filipino tradition. Mama prepared and cooked everything that night, from rolling the *lumpia* to making the peanut-flavored oxtail stew called *kare-kare*. Papa, who seemed perplexed about how he should ask Kuya how the Army was going, got up to play Filipino Christmas jingles sung by Sharon Cuneta, Kuh Ledesma, and other Filipino celebrities. The music, played only once a year, livened the mood up a little.

"Let's all thank your mother for a wonderful Christmas meal. *Salamat,* Mama." Papa reached over to Mama on his left and planted a kiss on her soft complexion.

"Sophie, why don't you tell your Kuya your part in the play *The Christmas Carol? Sino ka ba?* Who were you again, the ghost of Christmas past?" Mama gleefully tried to continue the conversation.

I just nodded. Kuya turned to me and flashed a smile. "I wore chains," I added. I also wanted to tell him the eerie sound it made when I dragged them across the stage, but I just couldn't say it. There was a wall that couldn't be disavowed.

"So, Pa, why can't the Philippines take care of it themselves?" Kuya began to address what had clouded his mind since he'd returned.

"It's for the good of our country, *anak.* America is just helping us get rid of the rebels. They're causing the downfall of our country."

"Corruption at the highest levels is the downfall of the Philippines. I'm sorry, Papa, but America's my country. You, too. You're a citizen of this country. Why do we have to be involved? They can fend for themselves. Fix it themselves."

"Just leave it alone, *anak.* Accept it the way it is. It is what it is." Papa tried to end the discussion.

"I am not about to follow orders blindly, Pa. Not anymore."

"*Anak.* Don't shout at the dinner table," Mama interjected.

"Ma, I'm not."

"It's best that you do your part. Kids these days. They lose their respect for their elders. I was in the Army and I wasn't even a citizen yet. I fought hard so that our lives would be better. I followed my orders. It's best you should. We're fighting the terrorists around the world so all our lives would be better."

"Pa, if you haven't noticed...my life hasn't been better. The lives of our 'fellow' Filipinos in the Philippines are not any better. And our intervention is not making a difference. It's just worsened the situation."

"I followed my orders. It's best you should." At that, Papa stood up, took his glass of Scotch on the rocks, and sat in the living room. As he passed by Kuya and me, I heard him whisper, keeping his rage, "Who do you think you are?" Mama threw her napkin on the table and took her plate and Papa's untouched plate into the kitchen.

Kuya stood up and slammed the door of his room. I started to cry. I blamed him for ruining the dinner. I just didn't understand what had happened. All I wanted was for everyone to be together again. I suddenly felt a warm hand on my face. Nanay caught a tear on the net of her fingerprint. She then wiped the stream with her napkin.

The next time he came home, he locked himself in his room for most of that time. In the morning of the first day of his return, I wanted to invite him for a pickup game. I was about to knock but instead listened to a sound that I had never heard come out of his room. Kuya was sobbing. I thought it was best to leave him alone. I walked quietly away with my basketball. The following night, I woke to thumps on the wall that our two rooms shared. He seemed to be punching the wall. One of my picture frames fell hard. My brother heard it. Thereafter, a long pause. I would never hear the beating again.

On his third day, he finally left his room but was nowhere to be found in the house. Nanay was the only one to see him when he came home that day, as I was in school and Ma and Pa were at work. She was sewing in the living room when he stumbled inside the house. Drops of blood trailed on the floor. Nanay pursued him to the bathroom and found him pulling sheets of toilet paper as he wiped his nose. She quickly gathered ice cubes in a bag and handed the bag to Kuya to allay the flow of blood.

"It was just a stupid fight, Nanay. It's okay."

"*Anak,* what's going on?"

"What am I going to tell Mama and Papa? They're going to be so worried."

"I'm twenty-seven years old. I'm an adult. Just tell them I had to go. I will write to you and Mama. Not too sure about Papa."

"You are such a coward. You're a fuckin' coward," I yelled at my older brother. "You've not talked to Papa at all for what, four years! Don't you realize that it hurts him too?"

"Papa's ways are set. I've been away too long from home. He knows it's different now. *I'm* different now."

"You're a fuckin' coward."

"Sophie, don't let it end like this. You don't understand. The years that *I* lost. I have to somehow find a way to get it all back. To get myself back."

We only had less than a mile before reaching the Greyhound bus station. The rain would not let up. We passed by the mall where Kuya would take me to watch Pixar movies. When I was younger, I had wanted to be an animator for Pixar. College had blurred my ambitions. But I could still clearly map out my childhood with the memories of the time spent with my brother. He was my best friend, regardless of the fact that he was older by nine years. Mama would call me a "tomboy" and blame my brother for it. I thought, though, that he told me everything. There were some things that he hid very well. While I drove him to the Greyhound station, he revealed the depth of the emptiness in his shell. In that emptiness, there were only echoes of suffering.

"I didn't want to tell you this but I think I have to. So that you'll understand. Haven't you noticed that I haven't been going to church on Sundays with you and Ma and Pa? The last time was Christmas Vigil, about five years ago."

"I clearly remember that."

"During that mass, everything had lost its meaning. At first, I couldn't tell what it was. I thought I just lost my faith. Well, I guess that's a part of it. But I knew there was something more. The choir. It was the singing that revealed it all. But I didn't know what about the singing, the Latin phrases, that got to me."

I said, "You can tell me anything." We had arrived at the Greyhound station. As much as my anxiety worsened each passing second, my brother's confession brought me hope. The hope that I would be able to understand his decision. And the hope that his decision would be best for the family. I parked the car in an empty stall.

"The past couple of weeks, I've gone back to church on my own. I wanted to be alone. To give me some time to think. At the end of the mass, there was something in me that was afraid. Afraid of the silence that I strained to hear in the last echoes of the singing. It would get cold in the space. Quiet. Only shadows were there. I would grab the songbook in the pew and look up songs the choir would sing to death. But nothing would come out. Not from me. Not even a prayer. Certainly, not a song. I didn't know what I was doing there." My brother closed his eyes. He was suddenly in the space again. I could imagine the church, the cold, quiet, vast space. I, too, saw the shadows deeper than darkness.

"I could not get my feet to move. I wanted to leave. But I couldn't, until I knew what it was. The singing. There was something in the singing. When I was in church, it always made me aware of the technique to sing. Through the diaphragm, not the throat. 'Don't sing with your throat,' Miss Martin would say.

"I shot someone in the throat. Fuck, we were there just to train their army, not fight for them. We went into the jungle. Next thing you know, I'd shot a Filipino in the neck. This Muslim looked like he wanted to say something, but nothing could, or would, come out, because I fuckin' blew up his throat." Kuya suddenly pounded both of his fists on the dashboard. I jumped in my seat. "Sophia, it could've been a prayer. I took that away from him. After that, I just dropped my M-16. I dropped everything."

"Kuya, I'm sorry. I'm really sorry." I had begun to shake. I couldn't rely on the older brother who would embrace me on the edge of a whimper. He was nowhere to be found.

"Sorry? Sorry?" His voice started to rise. His face that would redden only when he drank alcohol, flushed crimson. "You don't know what it's like. You don't know what it's like. Nanay told us about the folklore that our people had. That when we enter into the woods, we must say a prayer so that our soul will come back to us. If we don't, the soul is forever lost in the forest. Sophia, that's what it feels like."

I let Kuya go. He bought his ticket at the station and boarded a bus to somewhere. I didn't want to know. I just made him promise to e-mail or call me to tell me he was safe.

After the first month of his departure, he wrote to me from San Francisco. After three months, he was in Baltimore to visit friends. Eight months later, he told me that he was e-mailing from Central Park. But exactly a year after I dropped him off at the Greyhound, I received an e-mail saying that he was in the Philippines. He said that he had saved enough money to go back to Mindanao. He told me that he went back to try to say sorry and offer a prayer to the earth for the blood that was spilled. And more important, for the brother who wasn't able to say his own prayer. He called this rebel his brother.

Kuya's flight from Seattle is a few minutes delayed. I sit just outside the terminal waiting for him, composing what I plan to say for Nanay's funeral. I try to remember the grace of a woman that my grandmother was. I scribble the word "Love."

Suddenly, I notice a familiar gait among many moving bodies. I look up and behold my brother's face. He carries his duffel over his shoulder. His hair is much longer than I remember, his countenance more delicate and youthful again. His eyes impart his affection in advance. I run up to him and give him the biggest kiss on his cheek. His skin feels softer and brighter since that stormy day when he left us. Suddenly, his arms close around my torso and he lifts me up. He holds me a little longer. It is a sign of peace.

A butterfly comes in from my open window. My grandmother meets the soul that she left behind. My brother brings his home.

Connections: Vermont Vietnam

Hot summer day
on the River Road
swimmers of the Ompompanoosuc
dust in my eyes
    oh
    it is the hot wind from Laos
    the girl in Nhe An covers her face with a straw hat
    as we pass   she breathes   through cloth
    she stands between two piles of stone

    the dust of National Highway 1 blinds

me
summertime
I drive through Vermont
my fist on the horn, barefoot
    like Ching

The Sad Story about the Six Boys about to Be Drafted in Brooklyn

I

There were six boys in Brooklyn and none of them wanted to be drafted.

Only one of them went to college. What could the others do?

One shot off his index finger. He had read about this in a World War I novel.

One wore silk underpants to his physical. His father had done that for World War II.

One went to a psychiatrist for three years starting three years earlier (his mother to save him had thought of it).

One married and had three children.

One enlisted and hoped for immediate preferential treatment. This is what happened next:

II

The boy who enlisted was bravely killed. There was a funeral for him at home. People sat on boxes and wore new sackcloth as it was one of the first of that family's bad griefs. They ate and wept.

Then, accidentally, due to a mistake in the filing system, the married father of three children was drafted. He lived a long time, maybe three months, and killed several guerrillas, two by strangulation, two by being a crack shot, and one in self-defense. Then he was killed as he slept in the underbrush for other people think they ought to act in self-defense too.

A couple of years later, the boy who had gone to the psychiatrist for three years and the boy in the silk underpants were reclassified. Because of their instabilities, they had always been against killing. Luckily, they never got farther than the middle air lane over the very middle of the Pacific Ocean. There, the mighty jet exploded, perhaps due to sabotage, distributing 133 servicemen in a blistery blaze to their watery graves.

As the war went on and on, the college boy became twenty-six years old. He was now in his eighth year in college. He could not remember the name of his high school when he applied for his first job. He could not remember his mother's maiden name, which is essential to applications. Nervousness ran in that family and finally reached him. He was taken to rest in a comfortable place in pleasant surroundings where he remained for twelve years. When he was about thirty-eight, he felt better and returned to society.

Now, the man with the shot-off index finger:

III

Even after four years, he didn't miss that finger. He had used it to point accusingly at guilty persons, for target shooting, for filing alphabetically. None of these actions concerned him anymore. To help him make general love, he still had his whole hand and for delicate love, his middle finger.

Therefore, he joyfully married and fathered several children. All of them had shot-off index fingers, as did their children.

That family became a peaceful race apart. Sickness and famine didn't devastate them. Out of human curiosity they traveled and they were stubborn and tough like the feathery seeds of trees that float over mountain barriers and railroad valleys. In far places, the children of the children of the man with the shot-off index finger gathered into settlements and cities and of course, they grew and multiplied.

And that's how at last, if you can believe it, after the dead loss of a million dead generations, on the round, river-streaked face of the earth, war ended.

MICHAEL PARMELEY

I'm almost sixty now. In 1968, I was a twenty-one-year-old infantry lieutenant, leading a combat platoon in Vietnam. I've been actively examining, creating, and recovering my life ever since. I live in a small cabin near the ocean in northern California and can see salt water from the window of my writing studio. I'm retired. I receive a small amount of money each month from the Veterans Administration for Post-Traumatic Stress difficulties. It helps and is a blessing. When I have worked in my life, it has often been as a window washer. This memoir is a more or less accurate account of one such workday. I have an eleven-year-old son who often hangs over my shoulder as I write. We talk about Vietnam and much else.

Three photos follow my poem. The first is of me as I looked in Vietnam, taken by a local Vietnamese photographer in his village studio. The second is a self-portrait, taken when I was thirty and just beginning to examine my life. The third was taken recently by my Vietnam vet friend, Ben Benet, and is how I look today. My window washing memoir comes next, followed by a short epilogue that addresses some of the memoir's deeper truths and how I hope, one day, to write about them. My next piece will deal with my father's World War II combat traumas and the way his war memories affected both of our lives. I've been a member of Maxine Hong Kingston's Veteran Writer's Group for almost ten years. It, too, is a blessing.

Meditation on Being a Baby Killer

We knew that we killed them
although no one had said it,
the terrified mother
clutching terrified child.

Big Sherman, my gunner,
said he couldn't continue.
He'd looked in the bunker.
He started to cry.

I tell him, "It happens.
No one had meant it.
It happens in war.
We have to move on."

Time passes, much later;
the bunker's behind me.
In my mind I revisit.
I try to move on.

Somewhere inside me
Big Sherman is crying.
I tell him it happens.
I tell myself too.

There's a myth of recovery,
that you put it behind you,
remember the good times,
let bad memories fade.

But memories aren't like that.
Like bones they help build you.
They stand up to be counted.
They're part of what's true.

And now I'm a writer.
I put words down on paper,
like baby and bunker
and terrified mother.

I know that we killed them.
No one need say it.
I know that they're dying
right now as I speak.

A mother and child,
alone in a bunker,
a war passing over,
right now as I speak.

As I looked in Vietnam,
self portrait at age thirty,
and how I look today.

The Art of Window Washing

Gently as a doting mother carefully tucking a soft, fleecy comforter around the body of her sleeping child, a billowing, white wave of fog floats in off the ocean, wraps itself around the ridgetops and waits for the sun to arrive. It dissolves familiar objects, makes them disappear, makes them seem out of reach but, at the same time, close at hand. The fog hides away a brilliant sunrise but lets the sun's warmth pass right through. It makes the air and everything the air touches glow. It feels both thick and thin, swallows up Tupper's high-on-the-ridge-line house and the lush meadow surrounding it. It makes the words *magical* and *electric* spring to mind to anyone who has been caught in its spell. It offers possibilities.

In town, far below the fog, I sit on a sidewalk bench outside Bridget's busy bakery, sipping coffee, reading the newspaper, and watching the day begin. Bright morning sunlight inches up the nearby hillsides, glints off east-facing windows at the Station House Cafe, and steadily advances up Main Street toward my bench. When I can no longer read because the sun's low glare hurts my eyes, I put my paper down, gulp the last of my coffee, and stand up. Bits of croissant and morning bun spill from my lap. Bold, black starlings quit their pretense of nonchalant sidewalk strutting and quickly dart between my feet to gather up my unwanted crumbs.

"I guess it's time to go to work," I say, quietly and mostly to myself, scattering the starlings at my feet as I walk toward my rusting white pickup parked at the curb. Squinting through my dirty windshield into the rising sun, I drive away. From Main Street I swing south, cross a bridge, and head out of town. Just beyond the bridge I turn right, drive a short way along a flat, bottom-of-the-bay road and turn again, left this time, and start up a long, narrow, winding lane that quickly gains altitude as it meanders into the hills where it will eventually dead-end near the top of the ridge.

Partway up the lane I round a curve in bright morning sunlight. But suddenly ambushed by thick, dark fog, I slow to a crawl. I begin peering through trees and brambles, searching for Tupper's driveway. I find it, turn left, bounce uphill into his meadow, and park below his house. Small, hunkered-down songbirds announce my arrival by flitting up, squawking their annoyance and settling back into their dry, protected roosts. I turn off my truck's engine and roll down my window. I breathe in the cool, wet air. The truck's rattle and vibration slowly fade away. I look around, listen, and hear only silence.

Tupper has already left for the day, and I have come alone. Reluctantly, I open my truck's door, break the stillness all around me, and step down onto the wet meadow. I walk around to the back of my truck, begin taking out my tools, and start to organize my workday. My plan is to spend the next five or six hours at Tupper's house, alone, washing windows.

The wet fog in the meadow weighs down head-high lupine bushes that line the gray brick path leading from my parking place up the hill to Tupper's house. Tiny droplets of water drip from their delicately drooping, bright-yellow blossoms. Spread out below the yellow-blossomed lupine, thick rosemary mats, festooned with a riot of tiny blue blossoms, more easily support the wet fog's weight. Together, they form a bright border along the edge of the brick path. Slender bunches of meadow grass seem not to notice the fog at all and wait patiently for any sign of a morning breeze.

If mornings at Tupper's house were bright and clear, as it still is at the busy bakery below, I would stand near my truck, gaze east over the crest of Tupper's meadow, past Tupper's house, and take in the vast Olema Valley, where endlessly repeating ridgelines stretch eastward to the horizon and hide away the nearby San Francisco skyline. I would imagine seeing in the distance an emerald city, its high-rise windows sparkling in bright, early-morning sunlight. The magnificence of the view would mesmerize me, hold me immobile and momentarily spellbound. But today the valley and rising sun, like so much else around me, lie hidden behind a curtain of fog, out of sight but intimately close at hand.

Unable to appreciate the view, I turn instead to look at Tupper's house. Even though the fog obscures it, I can tell it is handsome. Someone, maybe Tupper himself, built it by hand, with care, using straight, tight, old redwood and smooth river stones. For a moment I stop gathering up my tools and take another deep, cool breath. The day is young. I have left behind bright valley sunshine, early-morning routines, unfinished conversations, and the hurry-up of downtown, driven a few flat miles, turned left, and found myself in a mysterious, fog-shrouded, and quite possibly enchanted world. I return to gathering up my tools and organizing my day ahead. I will need the ladders on my truck to reach high windows but decide not to take them out just yet. I decide I will start slowly, work first outside, off decks, on low accessible windows.

Window washing is quiet, simple work. It requires no power tools, few tools at all really, but it does require skill. I gather up my squeegees with their sharp rubber edges, a soft absorbent window brush, a large blue plastic two-gallon water bucket, a small white plastic squeeze bottle filled with yellow Liquid Joy dishwashing soap, and a few 100 percent all-cotton white terry-cloth towels and follow the rough brick path, lined with its mix of lupine and rosemary, up to the front of Tupper's house. My tools dangle from my work belt. My small white soap bottle bounces noisily against the inside of my empty blue water bucket. The bucket swings easily from my arm. I notice, near Tupper's front door, a half-filled bird feeder with seeds scattered haphazardly on the ground, and I think about the songbirds, hunkered down nearby in the wet meadow grass. I walk past the feeder, past the house's front door, and stop at a hose bib attached to an outside wall between Tupper's front door and first deck. I fill my bucket, squeeze in a little yellow soap, snap the soap bottle lid closed, and toss the bottle into the water bucket where it will float for the rest of the day. Absentmindedly, I massage a towel that I have casually flipped over my shoulder while walking toward the first deck. I step onto the deck and begin to work.

Towels are my hardest tools to find. Window washers are very finicky about their towels. For years I bought towels at Hagel's Janitorial Supply House in San Rafael. Each towel I purchased was always exactly the same: white, small, thick, very soft, lint-free, very absorbent, and always, as the manufacturing label assured me, "Made in China." One day I stopped seeing those towels. The salesman at Hagel's told me that the British had returned Hong Kong to the Chinese, the rules for international textile trade had changed, and that I would never see those towels again. I looked aghast. "I know," he said. "But that's the way it is." He was right. Now I pick up almost as good towels whenever and wherever I can.

To wash windows I dip my window brush into my bucket of soapy water and wet the window in front of me. If I am working inside the house I must be very neat and avoid any water drops or spills. Every pet rock, crystal, flower, or *tchotchke* must be carefully cleared off the windowsill and then, after the window is washed, returned exactly as found. I return every chair leg to the depression in the rug from which it came. I can't bump, scratch, or disturb anything. When I leave the inside of someone's home, I must leave no sign of ever having been there, except of course for the clean windows. But today I am starting outside, off decks, on easy-to-reach windows, and can be more relaxed with my water, tools, and my body.

Inevitably, a little of the water I apply to the window with my window brush runs away from the glass, down my arm, and hides in my armpit. The rest of the water stays put and begins to do its work, loosening whatever *shmutz* has attached itself to the glass.

The water works at its own pace, and, while it works, I wait. This is the time I like best. I relax, catch my breath, and find my balance and rhythm. I look around. Sometimes I notice my reflection in the window glass in front of me and see myself working. Sometimes I don't. I think or daydream. But I can't wait too long. If I do, the soapy water that has loosened and now holds in delicate suspension days or years of accumulated shmutz will begin to evaporate and the shmutz will begin to rapidly and tenaciously reattach itself to the glass. That's why you usually see a good window washer working in the shade where the water evaporates more slowly and has more time to do its work, giving the window washer more time to enjoy the wait.

When the water has done its work, I begin to do mine. I touch one end of my squeegee to an edge of the window frame and begin a slow, deliberate herding of the soapy water and suspended shmutz off the glass. If my technique is right, in one continuous motion without ever lifting the squeegee's rubber edge off the glass, I round up every bit of soapy water and everything suspended in the water and drag it to one of the two lower corners of the window. I feel like an attentive sheepdog, carefully nipping at the heels of balky lambs. I constantly adjust wrist and squeegee, surround and coax my herd of water, shmutz, and lambs into a corner chute of the window-corral.

Then I inspect my work, looking for strays, streaks, or holidays. (*Holidays* is a wonderful housepainters' term for missed spots.) If I find any, I redip my brush into my bucket of soapy water, rewet the glass, and repeat the entire process. If I am impatient or restless I can find the work tedious and try to cut corners. But as any good craftsman or craftswoman can tell you, "Never time to do it right. Always time to do it over." Eventually I am satisfied that the glass is clean. Then I take my good towel, carefully wipe all four edges of the window frame, and in one last theatrical motion, pull my now damp towel the full length of my squeegee's rubber blade, wiping it clean, dry, and ready for the next window.

I'm washing windows at Tupper's house, high on a ridge, in the middle of a meadow, and surrounded by fog. Soapy water trickles down my arm and collects in my armpit. Below me, the Olema Valley stretches and slowly warms itself in bright morning sunshine, secure, nestled beneath its comforter of fleecy white fog. Behind the fog, the sun is strong and warm. Sweat begins to slide down my back and I can almost see my shadow. The thick fog surrounds me but the air is luminous.

Spanish speakers have a word for "to wait." *Esperar.* It also means "to hope" or maybe it means to blur the distinction between the two. Sometimes the fog acts like that. It hides the familiar, Tupper's house or the entire Olema Valley. It suggests that it is about to lift, and then it makes you wait. It offers the possibility, the hope, that when it does lift, something altogether new will emerge.

If my morning hadn't been shrouded in fog, I would have been able to look up from my work on Tupper's deck and see a grove of tall fir trees that mark the meadow's lower limit and I might have looked through the fir's sturdy branches and seen the outline of the high, arching dome of the Greek Orthodox retreat that stands below the cluster of trees just beyond the meadow.

A few years earlier, just beyond the same meadow, I almost killed one of the retreat's young monks. On a dark, moonless night, also shrouded in thick fog, he had been walking down the middle of the narrow lane that runs below both Tupper's house and the Greek Orthodox retreat. He was clad from head to toe in solid black cowl and robe, making him, on that night at least, all but invisible. I was behind the wheel of my pickup, rolling quietly downhill from a visit with friends who lived higher up on the ridge. As I silently glided out of the darkness, missing his ghostly figure by inches, he turned his cowled head toward me and I was amazed to see, in the faint glow of my already receding headlights, his startled and horrified face. Maybe the young monk was absorbed in prayer or walking meditation. Maybe he was just lost in his own thoughts. I doubt he heard me coming. Then my truck and I were gone, swallowed back into the black foggy night. It all happened so fast that I was a good forty yards down the road before I realized what had almost happened. I hit my brakes and stopped my truck. Then I just sat there in the dark, behind the wheel, alone, and shook for a long time.

I'm washing windows at Tupper's house. The water on the glass in front of me continues to do its work. I can now see through the fog to the grove of fir trees at the bottom of the meadow, but I can't yet see the domed retreat beyond. Patches of blue appear and disappear in the sky above me. I begin to play hide-and-seek with my shadow and occasionally I see my face looking back at me in the glass. The thinning fog makes the air even more luminous. Sweat slides more quickly down my body. My shirt begins to stick to my back. Both my armpits now feel wet.

I remember an older feeling of wetness, of heat and humidity, of never-ending sweat, of gravity continually dragging the sweat down my body, of sweat filling up my boots, soaking my socks, rotting my toes. I remember how the sweat stank, always stank, how it gave me away to anyone who could smell it and understand the meaning of its smell. No matter how hard I pretended otherwise, I was afraid. I stank of fear. I lived in a state of constant, stinking fear.

Memory is a real thing. The face of a monk, the feeling of sweat, the remembrance of the feeling of sweat live in unique places in the brain, surround and protect themselves with their own unique set of associations. I continue thinking about the young monk, remember his seemingly oblivious walk down the middle of the narrow, winding lane on a dark, foggy night, how the faint glow of my headlights allowed me to glimpse his startled and horrified face. The fog continues to thin. Sweat slides faster down my wet back. My armpits feel even wetter. Older memories of sweat invite me into their unique world.

I was swinging along on crutches, down an outdoor path, in the gardenlike grounds of a hospital in Da Nang, Vietnam. The year was 1968, and I was a young soldier who had temporarily stepped out of the war, who had been given time and a safe place to heal a bullet wound in his leg. I was waiting, relaxed, at ease. I'd caught my breath, found my balance and rhythm, and I was unarmed.

My knuckles weren't white from gripping my rifle. My trigger finger wasn't leaning nervously against my rifle's trigger guard. I wasn't trying to sleep with my rifle cradled next to me, nudging me in my dreams like a lover. I wasn't carrying my four hand grenades, divided into lethal pairs, loose, metal bouncing against metal, untethered and easily accessible in the two unbuttoned front pockets of my sweat-stained jungle jacket. My shoulders weren't supporting the weight of Zapata-like crossed bandoliers. I wasn't carrying my maps, my lists, my malaria pills, my salt tabs, my plastic-wrapped but still water-soaked novel, or my letters from home. I seemed so light; to need so little, to have so little that I needed to do. And I probably didn't stink. A nurse, a female nurse, would have given me a hospital sponge bath by then, would have wiped away my sweat and maybe even my fear.

It's hard to explain the way a soldier's mind adjusts to war, the way it finds comfort in, makes order out of, war's chaos and daily horrors. It's hard to explain any of it to someone who hasn't lived, day in and day out, with constant fear or internalized the reality that death and dying have become your intimate companions. The screaming and cry-ing, the odd mixture of love and hate, of excitement and boredom, of horror and comedy slowly overwhelm you. Consciously you begin to accept that what you are experiencing is normal. Over time you even lose track that any change in your sense of reality has occurred at all.

I hadn't figured any of that out yet. I was young, just swinging along on my crutches, healing the bullet wound in my leg. I might not even have been afraid. I had stepped out of the war and was therefore in an abnormal state. In my normal state there were a lot of things I didn't see. There were thousands of ways to let my attention slip, let the lit-tle horrors slide by. It helped me stay sane. But there were other times when I did see. Memory selects, holds on to its own odd collection of things, stores them away for future consideration, like the smell and feel of sweat or the frightened look on a young monk's face in a dark, foggy night. It stores them away in unique places in the brain and brings them out in ways you don't fully understand and at times and places you don't necessarily choose.

I was relaxed, swinging along on my crutches, outdoors, in a garden, in a hospital, in the late afternoon. I was seeing flowers in a new way, seeing how they formed colorful borders along the edge of my path. I was appreciating sunlight and long shadows as they filtered through bamboos I had never differentiated before. I was enjoying the relative coolness of the late afternoon, the interplay between light and shade. I wasn't scanning for the deadly, almost invisible trip wire. I heard birds sing. Had there been birds in Vietnam before that day?

Up ahead and on my left, just beyond a lush vine covered with bright blossoms I couldn't identify, I saw a courtyard, separated from the rest of the hospital grounds by multiple rows of thin wire. The low, afternoon sun filtering through the bamboo cast the courtyard in a gentle mottled light. One lone Vietnamese man stood in the courtyard, inside the wire, and looked out in the direction of my path. Like me, he supported himself on crutches. As I swung closer to him, I realized that, unlike me, he only had one leg. I decided not to look at him, out of courtesy. I continued to swing along the garden path as it meandered through the hospital grounds and neared the wired-off courtyard. I was trying not to look, but I saw that the wire surrounding the courtyard was barbed. I hadn't expected to see barbed-wire inside the hospital walls or the enemy enclosed by it. I saw the barbed-wire at first as something new, interesting. The whole unfolding scene caught me unprepared. I didn't see it as something necessarily dangerous, as something I should instinctually avoid.

The face I am remembering now, the face looking at me from behind the strands of barbed-wire, I probably never really saw. Memory is like that. It adds things, takes things away. It has its own reality, its own standards, and its own truth. I imagine the young Vietnamese man's piercing stare, his difficulty balancing himself on his crutches and his one leg, his body awkwardly turning so his eyes could follow me as I hurriedly swung along on my crutches, down the long, twisting hospital path, in the late afternoon, in order to disappear behind the next stand of bamboo.

I was trying not to look but I didn't swing fast enough. You can only move so quickly on crutches with a bullet hole in your leg. I'd been in Vietnam almost a year, been shot at and shot back many times, but I had never, knowingly, looked into the eyes of the enemy before. I was unarmed, in an abnormal state, trying not to see. But I wasn't prepared not to see, wasn't prepared to let one more little horror slide by. You can be wounded in many different ways in a war, on the battlefield, where a bullet can easily find its way into your leg, or within the sanctuary of a hospital garden, where you are relaxed and swinging along on crutches, unarmed, in the soft, cool, late-afternoon light.

Wounds can leave scars, can be invisible, can heal quickly, or can remain unhealed for a long time.

I am washing windows on Tupper's deck. Sweat slides down my body. I'm waiting. Waiting is the time I like best. Another face appears to me, replaces the unseen face of my one-legged enemy standing behind barbed-wire in the hospital at Da Nang, and I enter into its unique world for a while.

I was wounded and I stank. I still had the bullet in my leg that the doctors would remove later at the hospital in Da Nang. My whole body was shaking so badly that I had propped myself up against a wall to keep from collapsing. This new face, into whose world I had now slipped, I also probably never saw. It and the soldier's body attached to it came from out of sight, from around the corner of the building I was using to hold myself upright. The corner was close, maybe only ten feet away. I didn't have time to think. I saw movement. I shot. His momentum carried him forward for a few feet and then he fell to the ground. He didn't move. I knew he was dead. As he fell, his head and neck twisted away from me at an awkward angle so that I couldn't see his face or look into his now-blank eyes. I wanted to move, to go to him, to look at him, to say I was sorry, but I couldn't. I was too afraid. I just stood there with my back bracing me against the wall, alone, and shook for a long time.

This really happened, or maybe I had entered the dreamtime. *Esperar.* The long, thin stalks of meadow grass start to dry and wave gently in a newfound light morning breeze. Delicate yellow lupine blossoms stop dripping, lift up their heads, and turn to face the morning sun. Previously hunkered-down songbirds abandon their safe, protected roosts, flutter about, and begin to sing. Sweat slides even faster down my back. Both my armpits feel wet but they do not stink. I know that. I return to playing hide-and-seek with my shadow. The soapy water on the window glass begins to evaporate more quickly. My wait is coming to an end, and soon I will have to go back to work.

My mind returns memories to their proper and unique resting places. My body, with its long-healed leg, returns to Tupper's deck. Once again I am high on a ridge and surrounded by meadow. The fog begins to disappear, letting brilliant sunshine glint off freshly cleaned window glass. Blue sky opens up above me, and the most perfect sound human beings can create races toward me from beyond the grove of fir trees at the bottom of the meadow. The sound leaps and spins, mixes joyously with sparkling sunshine and the excited chirpings of meadow songbirds. The mixture of sounds fills in every space left vacant by the retreating fog. There must be a choir staying at the Greek Orthodox retreat below Tupper's meadow. I never see them. At the exact moment when the fog lifts, choral voices, perfect, harmonious, and a cappella, fill the air. I stand in silent amazement, unable to move, arms akimbo, my right hand holding my squeegee securely, as if it were tethering a long, multicolored prayer flag, fluttering in the new morning breeze, or a mad conductor's silver baton keeping time for the invisible chorus.

Soapy water continues to evaporate off the window glass. It is time to go back to work. Carefully I place one end of my squeegee against an edge of the window frame. As mysteriously as the singing began, it stops. Like an attentive sheepdog nipping at the heels of balky lambs, I herd soapy water and suspended shmutz off the glass toward a bottom corner of the window, toward the beckoning chute in its corral. I take my good towel, wipe all four edges of the window frame, and inspect the glass to make sure it is clean. I see my reflection in the window looking back at me. Behind my reflection, I see slender bunches of meadow grass, dry now, waving slowly in the soft morning breeze. The breeze feels good, moving gently under my wet armpits and across my wet back. Even more sweat, sweet-smelling sweat, slides down my body and is evaporated by the cooling breeze.

If I were to turn around on Tupper's deck, I would be able to look across Tupper's meadow, see down the ridge and far off into the Olema Valley, its fleecy white comforter secretly lifted and stored away for another day. I would sense the nearness of the San Francisco skyline, its gleaming high-rise windows sparkling in morning sunlight. I would be mesmerized, held spellbound, and unable to move. Instead I take one more look at the glass in front of me to make sure it is clean. I hesitate, breathe deep. Then with a theatrical motion I take my now damp towel and pull it the full length of my squeegee's rubber blade, reach down for my bucket of soapy water, step carefully to the window on my right, and begin again.

Epilogue

It's a story, memoir, a mixture of fact, fiction, and memory. It has its own truth. Here are two additional facts. The man I killed, the man whose face I didn't see, the man who came so unexpectedly from around the corner, was on our side. That's one of the assumptions of a war story, that there are sides. Fact two: I have been back to Vietnam. I'm not your usual kind of traveler. I went back on my own. I was there for three months. I traveled with a backpack. During my travels, I revisited the village where I killed the man who was on our side. Through a series of extraordinary coincidences, I had the chance to spend two days and one incredible night with the actual men I fought against in that village. One of the men I drank beer with may have been the man who shot me in the leg. We just looked at each other, shook our heads, and realized we were just old farts telling our old war stories. We realized we could be friends instead of enemies. I'd like to write my memoir again, include those facts, and exclude the whole idea of enemy. I won't be writing a war story. I'm glad that what I've written feels done. I'm glad that some people feel it is done well. Well isn't good enough, only the truth will do. Only the truth and love can make a difference. I'm trying to teach that to my boy. We're both starting to understand. *Esperar.*

TOM PATCHELL

The first thing I ever remember hearing about the Korean War, though I didn't know what it was I was hearing at the time, was the bodies. In matters of war, the bodies usually are the end product, but to me they were the beginning. I overheard a conversation between my dad and a priest about a battlefield of the dead. Sometimes it seems that the dead do not haunt the living, but that we haunt them. We worry about where they rest, how they rest, and if they are resting. Writing captures ghosts and makes them physical.

After a lot of different grinds of life, I find myself living back on the central coast of California with my two red-haired boys and my loving wife, Jennie. Many late nights working on these writings have passed; I have been preparing for them all my life.

During the late '80s and early '90s, I found myself in the Marine Reserves in Los Angeles in an artillery battery.

"Graves Reg" does not so much seek to honor the dead as much as those night-shifters who dug to bring them back home. Dig on.

Graves Reg

Six diggers working
The pinnacle of military efficiency
The Korean hills grayish blue at night could be anywhere
Even the green daylight hills of California so far away
Battalion wants a certain body
All the bodies here and they want one in particular
They want this one
And so they dig like methodical ghouls
Measure off the square
Every square borders on another square
Measure off the squares within the square
Make it neat and even
Corralling the bodies below the ground
Digging in silence
And in the dark
It was certainly for more than twenty-four hours that they had
    been going it was

The second night so many squares
So many holes
So many bodies
But battalion had to have this one
"You'll know it when you see it," the radio buzzes
"The unknown soldier!" jokes Jones between digging grunts
Nobody laughs
No seeing blisters in the dark, just feeling them
Even the driver digs sometimes out of boredom
The interpreter digs as if the digging can reveal the meaning
    behind the
Language of the earth
E-tools are page turners
Rocks and dirt, consonants and vowels
Interpret the signs beneath
Mechanistic *han ghul* symbols floating in the guarded speech of
    the old farmer
And even though this field grows his crops,
He alone doesn't dig
Just sits there
Eating a tin of that stinky food of theirs
Trying to keep his head from nodding
Farmer Kim; millions of Kims in Korea
The interpreter asking in that damned hing ding
"Was this the place the 187th buried their dead?"
though not like that in Korean
The whole place had become like some giant gray blue mystical
    hilly graveyard
And the young jazz kid with the name I can't pronounce
Who says digging means something totally different
Something black and cool
Back in the world
Brooklyn and all
Grumpy gravediggers
The corporal arguing with the driver about whether or not he has
    to dig
Those two entertaining the rest of us the squares moving and us
    like ants digging our way across that farmer's field

Maybe he just wants his earth tilled—the interpreter should be
  suspicious
And the moon—more light, but maybe too much light
We dig with a rhythm
We get into it like some sort of improvised cadence
Bring the truck around put the headlights behind us
Six silhouettes digging in the field
Get 'em up, get 'em out
Be gentle with them, they're ours
Turn the headlights off you nitwits
We work in the dark
Light discipline
They're everywhere
Bring 'em home again
But we still don't find that one body—
The one battalion says is so important.

Fragments of Bacon

PFC Pascal's narrative:

Our unit was crossing through another crummy field with broken walls running across and lots of junk all around. There was an old wagon wheel that looked like it could've rolled right out of a John Wayne movie and settled in its current location under what looked like some kind of oak tree. If oak trees grew in Korea: there weren't too many trees left, really. We had been on the march and hard at it since morning chow, but now we seemed to be running out of steam, though there was lots of smoke in the sky over the yellowish fields.

There was that smell too. The whole country was a land of smells: stinky sour smells, sweet *kimchee* smells, the stench only humans can make, and the garlic smell. Not the warm garlic smell mixed with the tomato and oregano of Italian kitchens, welcoming with red-and-white checked tablecloths, but an alien, almost putrid and sinister garlic smell. This particular hazy afternoon had a different smell. A smell that was at once familiar but also new. It gave the day a strange quality of phoniness, as if we were going to walk around a bunch of trees and find a

Hollywood movie crew with their cameras on us. We all had the quiet feeling that something strange was going to happen to us that day.

Most of the cheesedicks in the platoon were FNGs, but Moretti had been through some of the stuff with me. We were also both from Brooklyn and Catholic; I guess I trusted him a little bit. I watched him about eight feet from my right, his M-1 slung a way they told us not to have them, holding it steady with a dark arm grimy and tanned, but I could still see the dark green tattoo on his arm that read "San Guiseppe."

"Moretti!" I called over to him, not caring if I pissed off the green butter-bar Cornwall, our latest platoon leader.

The wiry dago's head turned to me and tossed the chin up in one smooth motion—beak nose and Army issue "birth-control glasses."

"How about this smell?"

"What smell?"

"This weird smell?"

"Like gasoline?"

"Different."

The second lieu looked back at us, and I glared back at him.

"Keep your noise discipline, PFC." I was thinking about shooting him when there was sudden action. We were coming up on some brush and Reinhardt, our shitbird point man, was just about touching it.

"Get down!" he yelled as he dropped to a crouch. I shouldered my M-1 as I got down on one knee. There was a lot of yelling, and then some people came running and screaming through the bushes.

"Don't shoot! Don't shoot!" Cornwall was yelling and so was someone else with a gook accent from behind the strangers running toward us. They were kids.

The moment was amazingly frozen in time, and no one shot, even more amazing. I looked at the kids. One was a teenage boy wearing clothes that didn't fit him well, and he was crying and flailing his arms around. There were a couple of small girls and a kid who looked like he was about five, all screaming and crying and running right toward us. Then there was another girl, about eight years old, skinny body stark naked, short cropped hair all skin and bones and no bush or breasts. At first I wasn't sure if she was a boy or a girl—she didn't look right and I felt something go wrong in my gut. I looked at her naked ribs over the sight of my rifle. Then the voice came, and I moved the sight onto him, an old gook man screaming and yelling and choking. Cornwall seemed frozen stiff like he was hypnotized or something, but the geezer broke the spell on me and Joe, and we tackled the old screwball before he got too far.

"What? What?" Joe was yelling and the guy was crying. He was missing one of his front teeth, which reminded me of the pain in my front tooth, bad pain.

"*Galbi! Galbi!*" were the only words I could make out from the guy. He was really going nuts, screaming and crying. We were all gathering around while Joe shook him trying to make sense of what he was saying.

"Where's Basin?" The lieutenant was yelling as he hustled back toward us, having got ahold of himself.

"*Galbi kook in!*" the man was yelling and screaming and then he just broke down into a bunch of blubbering snorting sobs. Basin, our RTO, fat guy, always sweating, came huffing over to us. I think Basin was supposed to have an MOS in admin, but they gave him the RTO job in boot as incentive training for losing weight. He didn't seem to be losing any.

"What the fuck is he screaming about? Don't you speak gook?" Cornwall was shaken up. Basin tried to get the old guy's undivided attention, but it wasn't working. We were getting the feeling that Basin's gook was not very good.

"I think he wants to go after the kids, Sir." We all looked together at where the kids had run off to. I thought about the girl running through the fields barefoot and naked, crying. I looked down at my own foot in its dirty boot. Something wasn't right about it, but I felt like it wasn't bothering me as much as it should have.

"Is he saying anything else?" The lieu was trying to stay calm, put on a good show for the men.

"Something about people having a barbecue—like a cookout or something." Basin looked like he had no idea what he or the old man was talking about.

"Are you sure? This doesn't look like a picnic party. You can't get anything else?" Basin shook his jowls, "No, Sir."

"Let him go—and call battalion; see if they know anything about this area."

Crying and wiping his eyes, the old man walked in the direction he thought the children had gone. He was calling something in Korean. It sounded like a ghost song on an old wooden cathedral radio like I'd seen in front of a junk shop in Sugamo once. The trees that he was walking toward were blowing around a little, as it had gotten breezy. The day had taken on a strange feel; it seemed silent, except for the old man calling and Basin's voice on the radio. I listened to the whispering sound of the leaves on the trees being blown together and apart, and it reminded me of a day during the summer when I was a young kid, and I walked to the nun's school that I went to and no one was there. It was breezy that day too, and time seemed to have stopped. Summers seemed endless when I was a little kid.

"It does smell kind of like cookout, hey John?" It was Moretti. I sniffed at the wind.

"Yeah—but weird, though."

"We smelled it before, remember?"

"Lieutenant! We've got something strange over in the meadow. I think you'll want to take a look: looks like troops, but there's something weird about them."

It was Reinhardt. He must have gone ahead a little bit, as a ridge and some bushes were blocking our view of the land beyond. He was holding out a pair of field glasses, and he looked more confused than usual.

Cornwall turned around.

"What do you mean troops, Reinhardt?" He looked scared now. "What type? How many? How far away?"

"You better take a look, sir."

We were supposed to be following a retreating Chinese unit that was heading north of Chunchin [perhaps Sunchon—Lt. Bloom's note]. We had been after them only for about a day since some heavy fighting in a crummy little town we captured a couple of days ago. Someone had the idea that there was a Chinese soldier in this unit who had some intelligence that would prove useful to the big wheels running this campaign. The lieutenant was frozen in time, like everything else. I felt a nervousness in my gut like we were going to go through that brush and over the ridge and into that valley. I started wondering who would die this time and how, and then started thinking that I was somehow wishing deaths on my buddies—that my thinking about it was going to cause it in some way. I started feeling sick and was surprised when I startled at Cornwall's signal to move.

Cornwall's log:

I gave the signal to move into that place, that shallow valley. There was a strange sensation inside of me like a glowing dread, like something unspeakably wrong and missing, and I had the thought of that little naked Korean girl, crying and running barefoot and naked across the cold harsh terrain. I realized that I had an agreement with her. That it was she who was leading us into this harsh place, that little completely vulnerable girl was our guide down into what was starting to form in my mind later than it had formed in my eye. She was leading us down there to reveal her secrets, to show us something about herself and Korea. Some part of me knew that what she would show us was going to be much more than the intelligence we were supposed to get from that mysterious Chinese soldier we had been told about. She was out there in front of Reinhardt, her little bare girl butt in front of us. Her tiny feet dancing across the rocky and weedy ground with no pain or discomfort. In my mind for a split second I could not recall if she had been singing or crying, for this phantom I had created before myself was doing both.

There was other singing. Pask was singing that "Lovesick Blues" song, while another soldier out of my sight was singing a new Hank Williams song, "Six More Miles to the Graveyard." All my tiredness came to mind, all the grief and death. I felt sick and lost in the world; it seemed that valley contained all fears and despair the human mind could contain. I thought about how the men cheered as the Marine Corsairs passed overhead this morning, fresh from a napalm run, how some of the men seemed to enjoy combat, but I kept following her into the valley and its inhabitants were becoming clear to me. It was the unit we were following.

PFC Pascal's narrative:

Cornwall was marching like some kind of zombie. He didn't even get mad at us for the Hank Williams tunes we were singing. Basin had stopped trying to call battalion and his radio was letting out a fuzzy whine mixing in with the singing. Nobody thought about setting up the BAR or other positions of defense or offense. We just walked through the brush and down the ridge like we were hypnotized.

The bodies were all over the field. Some of them were standing and some of them were sitting; some were crouching down and some were lying down. They were all in some shade of black and all burnt to a crisp. We hardly realized that we had stopped walking.

"Never seen anything like this." It was Hendricks—he'd been with me and Moretti and the unit for a while too. I looked over at him and the cold closed in on me. I'd been thinking about summer back in Brooklyn, as if I had forgotten it was November now. The afternoon was getting cold. I looked around at the guys in their field jackets and helmets, bundled up like fat green mummies. It was going to be a cold night. Hendricks walked up to one of the bodies, eyeballing it intently, and the spell was broken. We started to wander into the field. Cornwall was still in a silent daze.

"Here's your cookout, eh Basin?" Moretti smiled at the heavy RTO who looked like he was seeing ghosts or was a ghost himself. His cheeks had gone white and ashen as he approached a cooked Chinaman who seemed to be squatting by a radio that was not working.

I walked up to one of the bodies. I could see teeth white in a twisted mouth. The man didn't look real. I stared as if it would make it all more clear. They looked like dummies or something. Reinhardt walked up next to me and reached out and broke a piece of the arm off the body in front of me. It came away exactly like bacon. Rheiny looked like he was considering tasting it.

"Smells like bacon." He said it as if talking about breakfast. I looked around and everyone was looking at the dead bodies. There were weapons scattered around, some still in the hands of their owners, but everything was wrecked, burnt out of use. A low haze was across the field, and I thought the whole thing was like a scene in a monster movie. The sun was even getting low in the sky. The strangest thing of all was that none of this seemed to bother me, like none of it was real. The feeling was like we weren't really here, just watching it all.

Cornwall's log:

The burnt soldiers scattered around the hazy field like a child's toys. A big bag of toy soldiers. I once knew a kid who would set up all of his soldiers in intricate strategic arrangements and then set fire to them all, sometimes pouring gas or kerosene over the whole diorama. He would have made a great officer. The song that soldier was singing came to mind. It wasn't six miles, but this was certainly a graveyard.

The dead in this graveyard were their own dark and temporary grave-stones. There was a corpse in the center that for some reason struck me as their officer. The figure stood at roughly the center of his troops. He might have been looking up when he was torched. He had a pair of destroyed field glasses around his neck and a sidearm on his hip. His uniform seemed to be in better condition than those of the rest of the corpses and he even seemed to strike a rakish pose before me. There were twisted gold-rimmed eyeglasses hanging off the front of his burnt skull and what looked like a map bag protruding from the hip oppo-site the sidearm. Battalion didn't think the man we were after was a regular officer, so I didn't think this was the man with the intelligence we were seeking, but he looked like someone famous. As I looked around the field, this idea led to other strange ideas in my head.

PFC Pascal's narrative:

All along all I could think about was the girl. Naked, skinny, and hairless. She was the one who led us on to that gory stinking field that early fall day. Her screaming oriental face twisted and crying, her lanky black hair whipping around her head. She moved before us all the time leading us into that grim valley like she was some sort of weird guide. Like she'd made a deal with Cornwall to show us our future, the future that paraded in that valley, a future at once killing and dead and charred and stinking like centuries of death to come for us and our country.

Ghostly quiet, we drifted through that last line of brush. The oth-ers' faces seemed out of place. They were always faces I had a hard time thinking of as soldiers' faces, or even faces of people in a war. Soldiers seemed like they should have been more professional than us, or at least older. Soldiers should know more about the world than the young bunch of former prison guards that we were. The sudden silence fol-lowed by sounds of movement and concentration seemed to have taken our minds off of the never-ending war and had returned our thoughts to everyday life.

"This trenchfoot's killin' me," one of the boys said.

"I'm just so freakin' tired I feel like dyin'," whispered another in a yawn.

"Tired nothing; I'm starvin'. Seems like forever since we got chow."

All I felt was that I was completely alone in this war even though I was surrounded by all of my buddies.

The lieutenant put a fist in the air and then motioned us down. The word slowly made its way back.

"Troops in the open."

"Not moving, though."

I crouched in a bush wondering if anyone was going to die here. Someone was humming "Six More Miles to the Graveyard," just low enough so only the guys right around him could hear. The barbecue smell had grown thicker. Instead of smelling tasty, it had the stink of burnt hair or a drilled tooth in a dentist's shop. We were tense as hell, and then the lieu gave the signal and we went running out into the clearing with our M1s at shoulders.

The enemy troops were there. We all stopped dead and were once more silent. We were not as silent as they were. The Chinese soldiers stood and squatted all over the black field dead like giant cooked chess pieces on one of those huge chessboards like I used to watch them play games on in Central Park. We'd found the barbecue. I didn't think they'd show something like this in a John Wayne movie.

Rheiny was tall and lanky but wiry and hard too. I was listening to him talk, though he seemed to be talking too loud for this place.

"You see, the reason they'd never show this kind of scene in a John Wayne movie is because of dames." I watched and listened but said nothing. He was crouching by one of the bodies, which kind of looked like him. He was wiping the barrel of a charred rifle he had taken from the field. Very orderly, with an oily rag; he would swab it and then inspect it like a baseball bat he was thinking of swinging. "Dames." He looked up with a sort of a half-smile and one eye squinted in the sun.

"When a guy goes to the thee-ater (that's how Rheiny talked), sometimes he goes with his buddies, but most of the time he's taking a dame, right?" I continued to watch his swabbing motion. "Well, a guy takes his dame to have a nice time and maybe get a little kissy-kissy." He hefted the rifle and looked down its length like a telescope, cursing a little as a black chunk fell out of the stock. "I mean, *he* might not mind seeing something like this, but his dame—now that's different. Those Hollywood muckety-mucks know that selling two tickets is better than selling one ticket, right?" He looked up at me again intently.

"Face it, something like this could ruin a dame's night, and in kind, ruin a guy's night. Look at it this way: this is not like those monster movies." He was thinkin' like a professor. "You ever seen one of them?" He didn't wait for my answer. "They're kind of scary and they make you jump sometimes, but there's something different about them, I mean like, you know, Dracula and that kind of stuff. Here's something you should know." He looked around as if to see if anyone was listening. "Those movies—the horror ones—they get dames jazzed up." He studied me for dramatic effect. "I mean it; I took this dame Margaret to that *Creature from the Black Lagoon*—it got her all hot and stuff—something about that slimy monster carrying that lily-white babe in its arms—there's something sexy about that; it kind of got me turned on too, but this ain't like that, I mean burning meat just ain't sexy . . . that's got to be it." He took one last sharp look at the rifle and flung it away over his shoulder; it didn't hit any of the bodies. "Red junk."

Cornwall's story to the skipper [Lt. Cornwall claims to be writing a book]:

We were starting to get our shit together and CSMO when we heard a creepy noise. The noise sounded like keening—an old noise that Irish banshees made. The sound was growing and it seemed to be coming toward us. Keening meant that someone would die soon. I didn't want to die but sort of felt like I should; I don't know why. We should have all been dead after all that we'd seen and done. The real bastard about war is that you shouldn't feel sorry about all of the people that were annihilated and all; you should feel sorry for the morons that survive. For some bitch of a reason there are people who just go on living during war and after war. Wars are won by bastards who kill the people who try to kill them.

Anyway, we heard this noise and all. The noise was kind of like a screaming crowd—the way I always imagined first entry into hell would be. Suddenly I looked at the dummies. They were being punished for all of the crumby things they did and all. We were getting close to the field when I saw them. The strange thing being that it almost seemed like they came from right out of the crowd of torched stiffs. For a split second I had some really dumb ideas. Like we were the burned Chinese platoon and these banshees were us leaving; the only thing was they were coming right at us. They were women, but they looked like some kind of horrible ghosts. Some wore rags—they all wore rags, dressed in black rags, or so I remember. They were screaming at us in Korean—

they were like something out of books—too scary for movies; they were running at us, and they moved like angry spirits making a sound that was alien like. I almost remember it as some of them being naked, but I don't think that's right. Later, our translator said that they were yelling something about death. They were like a bunch of ragged witches flying at us in a fury.

Moretti and some of the guys were snapping rifles to their shoulders. The bastards wanted to shoot—they probably would have. I must have shouted, "Hold your fire! Hold your fire!" and time froze again. Goddamn time, whatever it is, it makes no sense. The hags were like a pack of tigresses. They wanted to tear us apart.

"Run!"

"Through the trees!"

It was more like a bunch of bushes.

In a rout, the men and I mobbed through the tree line. Jumping and running with my gear swinging all over the place. All I could hear was my own huffing breath and the sound of those women screaming. I didn't even realize I was still gripping the scorched satchel we recovered from the glasses-wearing torched Chinaman. Bastards.

The noise of a loud engine choked and grinded beyond the trees; I knew the sound as the men did also.

"Sounds like a five-ton!" Pask yelled as he ran wildly ahead.

The women didn't seem to be stopping behind us, but almost gaining. We broke the trees, huffing and puffing, equipment greenly swinging and banging all over our sore bodies. A U.S. Marine Corps five-ton shambled in the road ahead of us slow enough to catch if we got moving.

"Move it! Move it!" I yelled to the guys. The five-ton appeared like some sort of false dream. A Marine sat on the back open tailgate with his legs dangling—combat boots half laced up, no olive-drab top, just a wooly-pully; he wore Ray-Ban Wayfarer sunglasses and a Brooklyn Dodgers cap.

"Doggies in the open!" he shouted as we made the road. "Need a rideroo, fellas?" The truck's engine was making the deep metallic, throaty snorting sound before being gunned—just hovering between gears. I was almost at the tailgate as the women broke the trees and swept toward the road. Time moved slowly again.

"Holy shit! A bunch of gook bitches; didn't pay at the whore house, boys?" laughed the Dodger Marine. "Come on doggies—no run drops today; those bitches look hell-bent."

Our faces must have looked grim as we ran below this joker. Pask was catching onto the tailgate of this Marine Corps five-ton like a fake dream. It would take us away from the women in black rags. Another Marine appeared with a field jacket on and a backwards Pirates cap on his head—he was pulling Pask up onto the truck. Moretti was getting on and soon everyone was being pulled aboard by the two Marines. The other driver was wearing a Giants cap. I could not believe the lack of military regulation with these bastards. He yelled over his shoulder as he drove the truck, "No Yankees or their fans allowed aboard this five-ton—orders from Top!"

The last of the paratroopers aboard, the engine gunned and we all were jerked in our positions. I spread there on the metal floor and watched as the women faded away. It looked like they were crying, and I felt almost sorry for a moment that they didn't catch us.

We were all crouching and lying around panting and sweating like a pack of winded hounds. I focused on Dodger Marine.

"You fucking bastard," I wheezed, "I'll have your ass."

He smiled. "Hey, sir, everyone needs some good, motivating PT once in a while, even Army dogs." Then laughing, "Besides, we just saved your sorry cans."

The Pirates Marine was offering Moretti a cigarette with one hand and hefting an M-1 out the back of the five-ton with the other hand. Grinning. "I should have shot one of their pussies off."

My eyes closed. Green canvas and sweat—noise and dirt—the truck, the road, the Marines, my paratroopers. Some kind of garlic smell, sweet and thick. Those women in black, screaming and terrifying, fading away like ghosts on the radio.

REDLINE

Redline is a glancing blow poet. His days are numbered and so are his lines. He thanks you for reading his work. I wrote this poem at my first workshop with the vets. It took place on the University of Berkeley campus. I took a lot from these meetings; I hope that I gave some in return. Working for Peace is the most noble road on the map.

The Ride

Listening to the dull humm of the wide bicycle tires on the hot asphalt was a relief. Can't get too deep in the water though, the relaxing current will take you away. Just like that Mexican that drowned in the canal last week. Those tires sound like cool water flowing through the pine flat. I'm the generator. I'm PG&E. That dull humm is my grandfather's breath. How much longer can the humm, the flow, the relief last?

Too deep. Look around. Listen. I'm on Hamilton crossing Maple. Wide street, no cars. On the other side is the Vietnamese projects. Got to drown out the humm with dry silence. I've got to listen for their thoughts in English. I am not my father or my uncles, I can't speak their language. They listen to my tires humm. That's how we hear each other.

Two more blocks and it's Mexicans; eight more and it's blacks. Same kids playing similar games with the sticks and cardboard and plastic. Same cars that don't run. Same young people on the corners selling the same shit. Same food stamps, same guns, same dreams, same oppression. Different language. Same Humm.

My dad is a garbage man in Fresno. He likes to pick up the Vietnamese projects. He likes to speak the language. It is his relief. The children love the garbage man and his truck. They line up aluminum cans on the street, a whole block long, so that that green-eyed man can crush them with his truck tires. Children's relief from the humm. The children's laughter is my father's relief from the dry heat of his guilt.

One of my friends lost his arm to a Vietnamese gang from those projects. It was over heroin. I watch out for them. They want the neighborhood. They want our neighborhood. Marcell says "Butler Park is for the black man." My uncle says it's for the "Real Americans." My grandmother says it was for the hard-working good people that wanted better for their families, but now it has gone to shit. I say I got to get out of here.

MONICA ROSENTHAL

In 1957, at the age of three, I decided to become a doctor. I have now been practicing emergency medicine for more than twenty years. For much of my career, I worked in large county hospitals in Chicago, Los Angeles, and Oakland, California. My coming of age as an emergency physician paralleled the growing urban epidemics of drugs, AIDS, and interpersonal violence. I was trained to deal with witnessing such horror by detaching emotionally from myself and from the people I was treating. No one told me what the cost of that would be: I became progressively cynical, losing all my significant relationships and living as a smug, bitter, and lonely victim.

In 1994, an everyday encounter with an extraordinary patient woke me up. I saw for the first time how numb I had become, and how much pain that numbness had caused, both for me and for those around me. I developed a powerful desire to recapture my soul. Initially I thought I would have to stop practicing medicine to do so. I quit my career and fled to wander Europe. But my calling wouldn't let me go so easily. When a stranger collapsed on a train between Paris and Florence, I was thrust again into the role of physician, this time with my bare hands, with neither medical equipment nor backup. The joy of experiencing pure medical practice, without the trappings of the American health care system, shocked me into seeing how much I still love being a doctor. Since then, I have been searching for more openhearted ways to practice, and to teach, medicine.

My greatest satisfaction as an emergency physician these days lies less in mastering skills and more in the relational aspects of the job: listening to patients, meeting their families, even breaking difficult news. At the same time, after twelve years of working to undo my professional detachment, I still struggle during almost every shift. I have not had good role models.

I joined the Veterans' Writing Group in 1998, as a veteran of inner-city American urban warfare. With the support of the group, I am slowly writing a book illustrating my journey to numbness and then to wholeness. Through my writing, I hope to spare others the pain I have endured. I dream of someday breaking down the barriers between health care providers and the people they serve.

Close Call

I t's not my anxiety, Doc," he said. "I know my anxiety. I've been living with fucking anxiety since 'Nam. I'm telling you, this is different."

"Yeah, yeah," I tuned him out. I paged through his chart, even though I already knew what was there. An amputated leg. Homelessness, alcohol dependency. Chronic neck and back pain. Dozens, hundreds of visits to the emergency department for panic attacks, or for alcohol withdrawal. For being "found down" drunk on the street. For pain shots or refills of his pain medicine. All the ER doctors knew him, though he never recognized any of us. Often he would tear into civilians. "You just don't fucking *get it!*" he'd say. "You think you know about life. You don't know a *fucking thing.*"

Donald looked too old. Deep furrows lined his face. His eyes were glazed, hooded beneath tangled mats of graying hair. Most of his teeth were missing; the few remaining stumps stood out like popcorn kernels. His smell was pungent. Today he was wearing only a crumbling yellowed undershirt; his pants were too offensive to be tolerated and had been double-bagged and thrown away by the new young nurse assigned to him. He lay sprawled on the gurney, filth embedded so deeply in his pores that our hospital shower couldn't wash it away.

Donald signed out of treatment programs, one after another. He never kept the appointments we made, never seemed to last more than a day or two in any shelter before his anger exploded and he got bounced out on the street again. Despite their best efforts, even the nurses, champions of patient advocacy, became impatient with him, ground down by his hostility. He was always given the gurney at the end of the hall, as far away from the other patients as possible. That end of the hallway became an obstacle course, littered with empty juice cups, pieces of clothing, rinds of hospital sandwiches. "I need a *urinal,*" he always yelled. But most of the time he failed to use it properly when it was brought. He would decorate the walls and gurney with streams of piss, or somehow the full urinal would be overturned onto the newly cleaned floor. The housekeepers kept a safe distance from him, pushing mops beneath his gurney by the tips of their poles, their nostrils flared and their mouths compressed into thin lines. But the nurses and doctors didn't have the luxury of distance.

Stethoscope held in front of me as a talisman, I held my breath and moved in for a cursory physical examination. Left lung, right lung, heart sounds. My gloved hand pushed his belly up and down. "Hold your hand up like this," I directed him. "How long since your last drink?" I had treated Donald so many times over the years that my physical examinations of him had become sketchy, almost imaginary. After all, how many times did I need to listen to this man's heart?

I stepped carefully around the tattered plastic bags holding all his treasures: half-eaten food, balled-up clothing, stacks of ratty newspapers, and bottles with a swig or two left in the bottom. I made sure that the bottoms of my scrub pants didn't touch the floor as I walked back down the hall toward the nursing station. Even so, I felt dirty. I washed my hands with alcohol foam from the canister on the wall and waved them dry, grateful for the disinfectant sting. I sat at my desk, filling out his discharge papers. "Acute alcohol withdrawal and anxiety disorder," I wrote in the box marked "diagnosis," my handwriting large and confident. I wrote out a prescription for five tablets of Valium and reached for the dictation phone, issuing a staccato slurry of medicalese into the receiver, way too fast for anyone to comprehend without benefit of the pause and replay buttons. "S1, S2 normal," I intoned. "No S3, S4, murmur. Abdomen soft, nontender, bowel sounds active, no hepatosplenomegaly or mass." My mouth on autopilot, I gazed around the department. There were three new patient charts in the rack, waiting. I glanced down the hall and noticed the young new nurse rechecking Donald's blood pressure in preparation for discharging him. He reached up with a practiced hand and grabbed her wrist. "It was my fucking *birthday,*" he said. "My God-Damned Nineteenth Birthday." I winced. He told the story, or some version of it, every time he came in. I could almost recite it myself. The steamy jungle setting. Out on patrol. The VC birthday present lurking beneath the creeping vines. A glimpse of smoothness, the smallest click against his boot. By the time the "Boom!" came, he was unconscious. Suddenly it was two days later and he was lying in an air-conditioned room, in horrible pain. I saw the nurse lay a manicured hand on his shoulder, and I sighed. We had all been compassionate toward him, once upon a time. "She'll learn," I thought.

Pam, the triage nurse, came toward me waving an EKG. "Got a female, twenty-eight, chest pain. Doesn't sound cardiac to me. Think she can stay in the waiting room?"

"Sure," I said, signing the EKG.

"You know, Monica, I don't know about Donald today," she said, leaning a hand on the counter in front of me. "He just doesn't look right." Any good ER doctor learns very quickly that when an experienced nurse says something like that, it's a good idea to go take another look.

"OK," I said, trying not to roll my eyes too obviously; I was sure she was exaggerating.

I went back to the end of the hallway. Donald was fidgeting on the gurney. I looked at him a little more closely. He was covered with goose bumps. "Are you cold?" I asked.

"You nuts? It's a fucking oven in here."

Then I saw it—a faint quiver in his thigh muscles. I took out my reflex hammer. Sure enough, when I tapped on his patellar tendon, his leg jumped and shook like a wet dog. It was the same on the other side. And in both of his arms.

"Have you been doing speed?" I asked.

"Hell no. I hate speed—it makes me paranoid."

I looked at the medication list on his chart. "When did you get put on Prozac?" I asked.

"Oh, that shit does nothing! I've been taking it three months, and all I can see is it's fucked up my sex life."

I suppressed a snort, trying to picture someone peeling away his urine-soaked clothing for anything other than a medical purpose. "Has the dose changed recently?"

He looked away, then stared at his lap. "Well, it wasn't doing anything," he muttered. "How was I supposed to know it'd make me sick to take more?"

"How much more?" I demanded.

"I dunno, two or three a day."

"How long?"

"Maybe a week."

"Yeah, it can make you *very* sick," I told him, exasperated. I ordered an ICU bed and a hefty dose of Ativan and went into the corner for a minute to sit, fat textbook propped in front of me, riffling through the section on toxicology.

Pam came bustling in from triage with a stack of new charts. "Hey, you were right about Donald." I told her. "I think he may have Serotonin Syndrome. I'm admitting him to the ICU. Good thing we caught it early. Good call."

She beamed, pleased. "What's Serotonin Syndrome? I never heard of that."

"I'm not surprised you haven't heard of it; it's only recently been identified. It's a toxidrome. A kind of poisoning, from excess serotonin. Donald took too much of his antidepressant, that's one cause."

"Is it a big deal?"

"Hell, yeah. It can cause muscle twitching, fever, seizures, coma, even death, if it isn't diagnosed. Our Donald probably would have just kept on drinking to medicate the symptoms—and he probably would have been found dead in a doorway somewhere by morning."

"Not to exaggerate, or anything," she said, winking; "Well, no harm done, right? Thanks for letting me know. I just *knew* something was up with him."

She walked off, and I felt a little wave of relief at her pleasure.

But under the relief, I sensed a tight coil of discomfort. I looked over at Donald. I owed him an apology. I wanted to ask his forgiveness for missing the diagnosis, for being so dismissive, for erasing his humanity so completely. But my legs balked and wouldn't walk me over to him.

I watched him peeling open his second box lunch. He stuffed half a sandwich into his rancid mouth. My neck grew hot with revulsion as I thought of approaching him. I owed him nothing. After all, nothing bad had happened to him. It was a close call, nothing more. Donald tossed the corner of the sandwich onto the floor and yawned, gums caked with mashed tuna. I wondered how good the generic sandwich must taste to him, when it's soft and whole and not even starting to turn. I imagined the usual competition at the dumpster in back of the Safeway, ragged men and women clawing each other like ravens at a carcass. My chest hurt. Close call? No harm done? I almost let him die. I watched as he stretched out luxuriously on the sixteen-inch-wide gurney.

Was it just because he smelled so bad? If he were cleaner, handsomer, would I have listened differently? I looked down at my hands and swallowed hard. Donald's sticker sat on my log sheet, at the end of a line of fourteen other stickers, each bearing the name of a patient I had seen on that shift. Was Donald the only close call today? My palms felt slick, weak with fear. I thought I had grown beyond not listening to my patients. Donald had pleaded with me, damn it. *He* knew that there was something really wrong with him. And now the familiar demon of self-loathing draped an arm across my shoulders and said, "Hey, piece of shit, you think you can grow? You think you can change? Hah!!" I cringed, discouraged and fatigued to the bone; in that moment I agreed with her. My eyes stung. I stopped for a second and closed them. The demon's power faded as I sat, just feeling my aching heart. I picked up my pen and drew a line through the diagnosis I had written earlier on the chart. "Acute Serotonin Syndrome," I wrote, in a careful hand.

GREGORY ROSS

A psychic once told me I had been involved with war in many past lives. She also told me I had accrued a lot of karma that I needed to work off. I groaned at that statement, but she laughed and said, "Let me explain further; it is the accruing that is difficult—the killing and maiming and destruction and dying a bad death—but the payment is different; here you are an acupuncturist helping people heal." I hope her interpretation is correct.

This life, I was an R.E.M.F. (Rear Echelon M__ F__, officially known as support personnel). Actually, the in-country R.E.M.F.s would consider me an ultra R.E.M.F. U.S. Navy, Seventh Fleet, the Gun Line, a mile off the coast of Viet Nam, on a ship functioning as a floating artillery unit. About as close to combat as you can get and not be anywhere near it. Nonetheless, I carry my share of responsibility and therefore, guilt for the death and destruction caused by the 2,000-pound shells fired from that ship.

I joined the Navy in 1966 to try to avoid Vietnam and in some senses I did; I was never in direct combat, but was support—in my case, as a communications technician on board two cruisers on what the navy called the Gun Line. The whole Seventh Fleet sat about a mile off the coast of Vietnam and acted as a floating artillery unit. My work/living spaces were one deck below a set of sixteen-inch guns capable of throwing 2,000-pound shells up to twenty miles. Part of my job was to see they went to the right place; on target people died, off target people died.

There were weeks we fired twenty-four hours a day, seven days a week. That is a lot of death and destruction; a lot of energy to be absorbed.

To this day, I cannot tolerate the sound of two glass bottles clinking together, because it reminds me of the sound of the mechanism used to move the guns, and on the Fourth of July, I join our dog under the bed, waiting for the whole thing to end.

I Look at Him and Smile,
He Looks at Me with Concern

Nervously my hand, of its own volition, searches the lid as we talk. He has too much power, my only child. Just talking to him can cause my mind to race; my hands nervously to wander across the lid of this mustard jar and press down the "safety" button as we talk. It pushes down and remains down.

We are talking over food, lately one of the few things we share easily. The chasm between us, that of father and teenaged son, has been looming large lately. I realize he struggles to communicate with me as much as I with him, but he has much of his life in front of him and feels less pressured. We talk about cars: '66 Mustangs, while my mind remembers a time before his birth and my whole nervous system—I believe even my DNA—remembers a time further back.

As my only child and I struggle to communicate through superficial words, my mind remembers other male children I loved almost as much, years before his birth. Boys who are now men, perhaps fathers themselves. Old enough to have been in war. Old enough to have lived the frightening vision I had of them years ago. My child and I talk about cars and computers while my mind races through a memory of four boys, nine-year-olds, training for the next war in front of me. I struggled to communicate with these boys too, for months, for years with some. But, boys will play at war.

Leo didn't get it at all. He just ran out in the open, pointing his finger like a gun and smiling with the game. I want to yell at him that if he is going to do it, do it right. Stan, instinctively, knows. Stay out of sight and show no mercy. Survive.

My hand nervously reaches for my fork as I nod in response to what my son is saying, and the mustard jar lid pops up with a very loud click. Every cell in my body explodes, jumps, twitches as if I was aboard the USS *Newport News,* firing 2,000-pound shells at Viet Nam. My son is startled, not perplexed, he has seen me avoid loudness, he has seen my body react before, but usually to much more powerful stimuli. He is startled by the minuteness of the sound and the magnitude of the reaction.

We both laugh nervously, then resume talking, as my mind relives the vision I had of Stan as a young man in combat get hit and die. I could smell his blood, it was so real. I quit working child care shortly after that experience.

Nervously, my hand of its own accord, searches the lid as we talk. It finds the "safety" button and presses it down; it remains down. We continue to talk about cars and computers as every molecule in every cell of my body struggles to calm the response triggered by what to most would be an innocuous, insignificant sound. I push the vision of Stan out of my mind only to have the fears for my son's life rush in as we calmly talk and the jar lid pops again and I jump again, just as hard, taking my breath away again.

I look at him and smile; he looks at me with concern. I laugh and say, "Avoid war at all costs, it really fucks you up." He just looks at me. I laugh again and as I consciously push down the jar lid, I say, "Let's see if it happens again."

We sit in silence.

Dear George

Dear George,

I have been assigned to write a love letter to an "enemy." You immediately came to mind. I know you don't know me and could care less what I think or feel, but this exercise, I guess, is really for my benefit, so here goes:

When I see you on TV and open my heart to you, what I feel is sadness. I can see the pain in your eyes. George, I work with the chemically dependent and you have their eyes. Now, I'm extrapolating here, but a vast majority of the people I work with have been abused as children and, well, like I said, you make me sad.

You also make me angry, George. When I hear you talk, I wish I could say you disappoint me, but to be truthful, I didn't expect much from you to begin with. But you do make me angry. The same anger I used to feel toward the school-yard bully, until the day I realized how sad those bullies were; how much they felt unloved and inadequate.

You know, George, once I realized that those bullies were acting out of fear, I lost my fear of them and was no longer a target.

I feel I need to talk about that smirk of yours, George. You are fooling yourself: it is clear when you are lying and it seems most of the time you are lying.

To quote your predecessor, "I feel your pain." Here you are, the "Leader of the Free World," and if you look closely, you see the scared, scarred, insecure, damaged child you really are.

OK, this did not go the way I wanted it to. This really has just been a soft-spoken rant on my part: so I will try again.

You do seem to truly love your wife and children. I am betting you try to be a good father and husband: a difficult job at any time in history.

And, although I don't like the outcome of your organizational skills, you do seem to have a good work ethic. (Perhaps you do take a few too many vacations, but it is a high-stress job.)

Once again, I don't like those that you exhibit loyalty toward, but you do seem to have a goodly amount of that virtue.

I have run out of things to say to you, George, so my parting words are these, trite as they may be, yet still true: If you could learn to love yourself the world would be a better place.

Peace and Light
Gregory Ross

P. S. Just to make that National Security/FBI/CIA/Homeland Security search easier, my social security number is . . .

SANDY SCULL

I began writing bad haiku poetry in the spring of 1961, after removing everything but a mattress and a naked lightbulb from my room. In order to cultivate a more seasoned perspective, I took a thirty-three-year break from poetry. It also took me many years to thaw my imagination, frozen by my experience of war. I served as a lieutenant in the Marines in Vietnam during 1967–1968.

I hold a Ph.D. in transpersonal psychology. My internship was at the Center for Traumatic Stress (the Menlo Park Program). My dissertation dealt with transpersonal and existential themes in interviews with Vietnam veterans. During 1988 and 1989, I worked with Soviet veterans from their war in Afghanistan.

After being published in psychology, *Fathers, Son & Daughters: Exploring Fatherhood, Renewing the Bond,* and appearing on *Oprah,* I have kept my poetry a private affair—except when asked. Currently, I am assembling my poems under the title *Reaching Across.* I write for the gift of renewal that comes from getting underneath an experience, and the play of memory with the present.

I am a board member of the Marin Poetry Center and believe in promoting the poetic perspective to the wider culture. I have volunteered for ten years with The Living/Dying Project, which gives counsel to the life threatened. I enjoy improvisational dance as a practice and as an inspiration. Occasionally, I still surf. Living in western Marin County, I am married with two children and two golden retrievers.

Skewed

When I returned from war,
mother threw me a party
on the brick terrace ringed by
roses and pansies. From a balcony
I looked down on the guests.

My mother wore a miniskirt.
My ex-tennis partner, a beard
and pony tail. My brother
brought one of my old dates.

I gripped a gin and tonic,
grateful for ice to freeze-frame

something familiar. In my absence,
everything had skewed.

A friend suggested I take
his date home, an apology
for his not writing.
A WWII vet presented me
a dorky statue that said, "Our Hero."

Then, something from Vietnam
intruded. At first I thought it was
the off idea of an award for war.
Or the sound of the word "hero"
that I coupled with dead.

No, it was a smell.
In my brain, pungent orange napalm
devoured jungle green.
Father had sprayed gasoline
between the bricks to kill the grass.
His war with what grew wild.

Sea Salt

After the Vietnam War, I withdrew
to Nantucket: "faraway isle."
Hoping to glimpse the boy
before spirit fled the body.
Thirty-three miles of ocean exiling me
from a homeland offering little embrace.

Me and my dog Christopher. Christ-love
disguised as loyal canine. We combed beaches.
Working for the island newspaper connected me.
Tides soothed with ebb and flow.
A rhythm I could trust. Even eat by.
I fished the last three hours of the east tide.
Buried my toes in the sand, searching
for the texture of littleneck clam.

When water was warm, I sailed out solo.
Stripped then slid into the sound.
Looking up toward the surface light.
Christopher's gaze wavering with wind
and water between us. Breath bubbles
rose, bursting under his nose.

My body now embraced,
a ritual purification in salt.
Dismembered dreams floated closer.
Something dissolved in a solution
that held me. Breathing easier,
I could imagine again.

Mrs. Martinez

Dear Mrs. Martinez, regret to inform you
that your son PFC . . . First name forgotten,
yet his safety entrusted to me.
He was a good Marine. Sorry about your loss.

Though just past eighteen, he looked
haggard. Last week even ghostlike blue,
like some part of him already knew.
Wanted to finish high school and marry
the Houston girl. Carried a decayed photo
showing her pimples and bouffant hair.

Died when a sandbagged roof fell
under nine inches of rain. An engineering stake
pinned across his throat, eyes bulging.
No blood. Dubbed non-hostile casualty.
Us Marines don't know bunker building,
better at digging foxholes and latrines.

He had been drinking hot cocoa. I found his canteen cup.
And some C-4 explosive we burned for a quick boil.
It was during Monsoon rain. The other sentry
grabbing sandbags off in vain.

Maybe he was daydreaming of home,
sitting in your kitchen. Numb sentiment.
Whatever she wanted, I was unable . . .
Top Sergeant said, *Use the files, LT.*
And keep it brief. Fall back on a form letter,
don't need more grief.

War's Confession

I like my steak tartar, shrapnel-cut
and raw—my name spelled backwards.
I awake with the first stone cast,
slumber when the other cheek
gets turned. But my fire ignites
in an eye for an eye. Scorches
until skeletons lie limp in pits and caves.
A strip search gone berserk.

I am the shadow initiator of young men.
Carnage—cruel and kicking ass.
And all that male bonding, baby.
I have become the father of addiction
for those lacking the will to say, "enough."

If you want to hunt human flesh
not fur, then join my team.
Play the baddest endgame around.
The big bang without the theory.
I am so much larger than
your miserable, little life.

Replace me with an adrenaline rush?
Up-level my mean weenie by practicing
Kundalini? You think war a joke?
I'll cut you a deal though.
Make my belly laugh, I'll relent.
That's not spelled repent.
I have never apologized,
never will.

TED SEXAUER

I went to war to fight against war. I was already in the Army, having enlisted in the face of the draft, before I came to understand the moral ugliness of the war in Viet Nam. I felt betrayed. As a citizen of the offending nation, I felt I had an obligation to try to set right the wrong.

So I became a medic. I took the best training for field medics the Army had to offer, the Special Forces medics' course, and served two tours—first, with 571st Dust-Off (Helicopter Ambulance), operating all over I Corps, serving primarily U.S. Marines and MACV advisors, which meant transporting many injured and sick Vietnamese civilians; after that, as senior medic with a line company of the 173d Airborne Brigade, in northern Binh Dinh province, II Corps. (Eighteen months in all, in 1969 and '70.)

I did what I'd set out to do, but it cost a great deal. The moral clarity I'd acted on became clouded and confused. I saved some lives, and I helped the army machine do its work. I was accomplice to murder. I did a lot of medcaps (village clinics), and that was good, and the army used them as propaganda. Doing the right thing did not make me lighter—it gave me nightmares; it confused the hell out of me.

I went to war to fight against war. I do not recommend that course. To young people, I say: Work for peace before you get into a compromised position. Do not stand up for empire. There is humanity inside the machine, but any way you cut it, the military is about killing.

"The Well by the Trail to Mỹ An": This is a poem of compassion in retrospect. The second line of the poem is meant as a progression in terms of respect: The word Ông, meaning "grandfather," is the proper term of address toward a man older than oneself.

"Poem for Tết": I returned to Viet Nam in 1995. Tết is the ten-day celebration of the Lunar New Year. Following the tradition of writing a poem on the first day of Tết, I wrote these lines. I happened to be having a hard time on that day. The progression of the poem wasn't planned; it wrote itself line by line, drawing down in increments from a plea for a saving idea down to the essential. An instance of writing oneself out of trouble . . . A Buddha poem.

The Well by the Trail to Mỹ An

Bình Định Province, 1970

I think of you
papa-san, grandfather, Ông,
standing at your open well

there you are, smiling host
to a squad of well-armed foreigners, pulling up
red Folger's coffee cans of cool sweet water
dousing bowed teenaged heads
eight young men this time, huge, all hairy
like dogs, bearing strange black rifles
(they will not go away) wearing only
boots and floppy war-green undershorts
careless youth from a rich world, blind
to soap water spilling back down the well
your task of diplomacy to keep the soap out
without getting shot

for once
I could see clearly what you thought
as I watched you grin and nod non-stop
like an imbecile, disappearing in that grin
into a sea of caricature *papa-sans*
I saw something I knew in your eyes
I saw you calling on the god
of get me out of this
I saw in you myself
desperate
to preserve the healthful water

Poem for Tết

Lăng Cô village, Việt Nam
Lunar New Year, 31/1/1995

This is the poem
that will save my life
this the line that will cure me
this word, this, the word *word* the one

this   breath   the one I am

Two Squads

Two squads, routine patrol.
We will split into two groups
and set up night laagers
along the market trail,
to secure the trail
for elections tomorrow.

We're taking a break
before splitting up.
I'm talking with my cherry
third Platoon medic, who's about
to leave my wing for the first time.
He worries me. He's not ready.
I've been riding him hard to shape him up
for what he'll be seeing,
and he's beginning to chafe
under my hard edge.

To make it human for him,
I break a rule that has been in place
in armies forever, the one that says
no one may show a weakness or a doubt
in proximity of the enemy.
I figure we're medics, we're different,
it might be the way to get through.

I tell him, "We all started out
not knowing enough here." I say,
"The truth is, I don't feel qualified
to be Company Medic. I came here from Dust-Off,
I know more about trauma than field medicine.
Nobody showed me the ropes. I'm still
having to work out too many things for myself."

Big mistake.
One of the squad leaders steps up,
gives me a piercing look, says
"You are Special Forces-trained, right?"
I say "right." He says "Okay then"
and it's time to move out—he leading
the other squad. We part at a Y
in the trail. My skin squirms, I don't know
what he and the others have made of the exchange.
A reputation is such an insubstantial thing
and also, I wish I knew everything.

＊

No more than five minutes later,
we're filing along a rice paddy dike—
quiet, sundown's approaching . . .
an enormous explosion presents in the near distance,
off to our right, fills the air
with a surreal excess of sound.
We look at each other up and down the line—
no word is spoken—and we all jump into the paddy,
start running, on line,
and we run and we run in this parallel formation
through the knee-high water
knowing without thought
what we'll see, what we dread to see.

We see paddies and dikes and jungle trees,
and we see a cloud of brown
rising past the treetops, drifting
in a gentle lazy wind up and away from us;

we see a small clearing, a grassy mound;
we smell cordite and earth;
I hear, along with the pounding in my ears,
only a ringing on the other side of silence,
a shadow of sound.
We approach the grassy mound,
we see our other squad, some walking, some down.
I see chaos.

We do as we've been trained,
grunts set up perimeter, I sort the wounded;
I act as though independent of the rest;
this is my scene, I am in the spotlight now.
Loud in the back of my head is a prayer
shouting God don't let me fuck up,
let me keep my cool, let me make the right choices,
dear God, let me be seen not to fail . . .
I move through the wounded, eight of the nine—
traumatic amputation left hand, walking;
frag wounds, right eye and face, walking . . .
In correct triage protocol, I deal with those
less injured first, those who will be able to fight
if we come under attack now.
Some of my guys are assigned to help me,
I put them to applying tourniquets and dressings,
assemble the casualties at a landing zone—
radioman has done his job, Dust-Off is close on its way.

Then I come to the last two.
Blankenship, the new medic, is now seeing
his very first casualty, and it's him,
and he's blowing it bad.
He has a single fragmentation wound
to the lower right abdomen—
just a three-inch bright red triangle
as though superimposed on his jungle green fatigues.
Nothing I can do with that, and his screaming
sets off a rage in me
I feel to this very day.

In disgust as close to my center
as I ever want to bear,
I tell two guys to carry him off
to the chopper site, as I turn away,
to the man who must have been closest
to the blast. It's my friend,
my friend Jo-Jo—everyone's friend—
both his legs are shredded
above the knee;
I'm flying high on adrenalin,
I want him to be alive—no respiration,
I check his carotid artery
and I want so bad to feel a pulse,
I feel a pulse, and I'll never know
if I imagined it; and I tie off his legs
and slap in an IV and start CPR
and now I'm yelling, come on Jo-Jo,
come on let's go you can make it—
second chopper comes and takes him away.

Jo-Jo is dead and the new medic is dead,
and none of the others ever came back
to the field. As far as I know,
no one ever doubted my expertise
after that day. Except me.
And I never mentioned my doubt again,
until now.

Inside the Wire

We come in off a three-day patrol,
up to the company CP, our hilltop fort;
old French position, manned by Legionnaires
in the time when we were kids playing war
against imaginary Nazis. This is real.

Everybody's beat, humping hard wet Viet Nam
lowland heat, one hundred thirty degrees.
You never stop sweating and you better not.
No sleep. We are hard-core, we don't complain.
We always keep going.

Finally up home hill, through
our cleared fields of fire
(no man's land, but ours), over
hard-packed red clay, dust throat, step
by step past strangely normal scrub bushes
I know by heart still, having counted
each leaf in and out this way a hundred
hundred times. My bush rosary:
still here, still here, still here.

Through double razor concertina,
the Claymores, the berm, the outer trench.
Down knee-deep transverse trenches,
right, then left to the doc shack.
My load takes on its real weight,
inside the wire. Mercy lives inside
the wire. Mercy makes me suddenly old.

⸻

Doc Washington from 3rd Platoon,
reading in the dirt smell relative cool
of the medics' bunker, our sandbag sanctorum.
Doesn't look up. Something's up—
what he's reading's more interesting
than it is. "Hey Dub. What haps?"
Nothing. Five minutes, maybe less
I'm racked out, just fading into sleep:

"Yeah, Bateman got it.

"Hates to tell you, man.
Yesterday morning, down
by the pepper patch.
That quiet place. Yeah.
Sniper got him.

They was on a night laager,
nothin special, y'know, just a campout.
Jameson was there, he tol' me.
Say Doc Bateman was jus' the first
to get up an' stand in the morning,
Mr. Charles in a tree in the woodline
draws a bead, one round, and jammed.
They lit up the woods, you know they did,
but they never found nobody.

"One round in the head,
Bater he didn't had no chance.
Sorry, man."

I just turn away.

Fort Benning Return: 2000

November 19, 2000, a little after noon. We are gathered outside the front gate of Fort Benning, Georgia, a vigil of some ten thousand people from all over the United States, calling for the closing of the School of the Americas.

A bandstand has been erected just outside the entrance; speeches and music, call and response, have been going on all morning. The temperature is in the low forties and a steady light rain is falling.

Twelve of us in my affinity group have decided to enter the post together in a "high-risk" action, intending to be arrested, to carry our witness forward in a court trial and possibly into prison. The risk is not great compared with that faced by reform leaders in Latin America, where dissent is very much a matter of life and death. Here we face a lesser unknown, the possible loss of some liberty, some dignity, a police record.

In the weeks and months since I became involved in this movement, I've been wondering how it will feel to be at Fort Benning again. This place is a hinge-post in my personal history, the place where I changed my mind about the war in Vietnam and subsequently resigned from Officer Candidate School and resolved to serve as a medic instead.

Because of this history—the change of heart and the deadly events that followed—there are two things I contribute to this event, now, thirty-three years later. One is that I can speak to my fellow activists about how it feels to be a GI in time of protest, and about how conversion happens. The main thing I have to tell them is that it wasn't argumentation that won me over; if I'd been confronted directly, it only would have made it harder to find my way.

And so I encourage my friends now to see each soldier as a unique individual, and when talking to soldiers to ask them about their lives, their hopes and ideals, rather than press our agenda on them—to have faith in their intelligence and their instinct for the honorable.

The second contribution is more personal, something I will do for myself with the understanding that it will benefit others. I will practice awareness of the *feelings* I experience throughout the day. In the old days, in places like Fort Benning, Georgia, and Tam Quan district, Vietnam, I learned the necessity of shutting emotions down when engaged in "action." But this is a different kind of action. Here we're trying to save lives by our witness, not by direct intervention. Instead of isolated mind, this action requires full humanity, full aliveness; and this is what I need to give.

———

12:15 P.M. The main procession has already entered Fort Benning in a solemn funeral march, fifteen hundred strong. It is anticipated that they will be stopped by the military police, escorted onto buses, and driven a couple of miles off post and released, as has happened in past years. The plan for the high-risk groups—approximately two hundred of us—is to wait for the procession to completely enter the post, so as not to detract from its solemnity, and then to enter and penetrate as far as possible overland toward the School of the Americas, until we are arrested. It really isn't much of a plan. Although I can articulate the difference between heart action and military execution, I repeatedly catch myself reflecting how skimpy our preparation *feels* compared with . . . serious soldiering.

I experience a certain nostalgia, not for the regimentation nor the stupid class system of the army, but for the security in working with a tested group—I miss the closeness we had in my company, knowing teammates' tendencies and reactions down to a T. Our affinity group is disciplined and positive, but we have no real history together.

Also, increasingly now, I note similarities with old times. The long wait for engagement . . . how unreal the near future seems, or any other time but this very moment . . . how surreal this generic waiting for action . . . waiting . . . the tension . . . the odd sense of recognition: this is the universal moment of standing still, of mindfulness induced by extremity. There's nothing to do but wait and be, be in the stillness.

Finally the signal is given. Right away, we're moving fast. We file through the entrance, walking at a rapid pace—constrained from running by the nonviolence guidelines—then form a line, holding hands, as we take a diagonal uphill route, on slippery wet grass . . . There are six or eight lines like ours ahead of us, maybe the same number behind. Somehow there's a big gap, fifty to seventy-five meters between us and the groups both ahead of us and behind us—we're oddly apart, not sure whether to speed up or slow down. At first we're trying to catch up with the groups ahead; then we slow down to try to keep continuity with those behind, and we continue like this, absurdly linking the two groups, yet distinctly alone . . .

I'm in the far right position in our formation; because of a gimpy hip joint, I carry a cane in my right hand. Halfway up the hill, I slip and fall. Fortunately, my hand-partner, Derrlyn, who isn't very big, proves very strong and pulls me to my feet without slowing down.

As we approach a road at the top of the hill, we encounter a handful of policemen, led by a tall black man who is a uniformed Department of Defense police officer; the rest are military police in civilian clothes, presumably so that there will be no photographs of soldiers forcibly subduing protesters. Oddly, since the military is so well integrated, this group is all male and all white. These people have been put in a bad position, as there are too few of them to physically stop us; they become angry when they order us to stop and we simply pass them by.

The feeling atmosphere is rarefied here: I'm aware mainly of a great momentum to push forward, to do the thing we came to do. Fueled by the pace, the difficult footing, the company (still hand in hand)— social pressure to keep up, leadership pressure to keep order—I entertain an image of "feelings" (those things I'd intended to mind) flapping behind me like a Civil War battle flag. I'm vaguely aware—a self-generating loop—of an obscuring of vision, the famous "fog of battle" comprised not of gunsmoke but of time compacted. Encountering the lone DOD man, I'm alternately saying "Sorry, man" to him and "Let's go!" to my friends. I feel the need to press on. I remember college days, before the army, a game, fraternity brothers dragging me to a pool, throwing me in the water: you were supposed to resist, but not too hard; I could never figure out how hard . . . I empathize with the officer—he's getting frustrated . . . At the same time I'm annoyed that he thinks we should stop just because he says so . . . and I'm beginning to wonder whether we're really being nonviolent, because we're actually pressing against him now and he's really getting angry. Something deep inside is telling me that hurting someone's feelings is violence.

Finally enough of the plainclothes MPs are in place to stop our progress. People start falling in a heap, slipping on the wet grass. So here comes my moment of truth: my personal "endgame" plan has been to engage a pair of officers and try to make a deal with them—if they'll take the same time with me as if I were going limp or otherwise resisting, I'll cooperate by walking with them to the bus. I'm hoping they'll appreciate saving some sweat, I'll keep some dignity, and we'll be friends, or friendly. Surely it's a naive plan, but I've always found a limited naiveté helpful in dealing with the police. Anyway, I've never done anything like this before; the documentaries I've seen make it look fairly easy.

I approach the nearest policeman and I say, "I came here to be arrested"—not just to get a ban-and-bar letter—"and I want to cooperate with you if you can guarantee I'll be arrested."

The MP says, "You'll be arrested—just get on the bus."

Too easy; I don't trust him. I say, "You have to guarantee."

He says, "Guaranteed—now get on the bus."

I say, "Okay, but you have to take me."

Then he pushes me, and someone I can't see has hold of my ankles. The first man says, "This one wants to be manhandled," and I'm tossed onto the steps of the bus. I haven't lost my cane, I'm not hurt at all—except now *my* feelings are hurt, because I didn't make myself understood.

What I hadn't taken into account was momentum; I hadn't foreseen that it would be faster for them to throw me than to walk with me. They don't move that fast in the movies.

This is one of the two things I feel badly about in the whole exercise: that I couldn't manage to keep it friendly between us and still get arrested. The other is that, as it turned out, we couldn't even get arrested. Even with the impressive (I thought at the time) yellow "Resisting Arrest" ID band on my wrist, I only got a ban-and-bar letter: I'm not to return within five years, or *then* I'll be arrested. The "low-risk" group on the lower road was lied to as well: they were told they'd be let go if they got on the buses, but they were all processed and got ban-and-bar letters, too.

And that was the "action." It probably lasted no more than fifteen minutes. Once we were on the bus, there was no further unpleasantness. We had completed our objective and there was no more need for obstruction. We were taken to a hangar at Lawson Army Airfield, where the uniformed MPs who processed us—males and females, black and white—were as friendly and human as the plainclothes apprehenders had been abrupt.

After four hours of detention and processing, a last piece of drama rounds out the day: an impromptu audience with General LeMoyne, the commanding general of Fort Benning. I'm sitting in another bus waiting to be taken off post. A two-star general passes by the bus, doing a walk-through. He looks up through the open door, sees the Combat Medic's Badge pinned to my field jacket. He says, "Hey, Combat Medic." I say, "Hey, General," and he climbs up and we talk for about five minutes. He tells me where he'd been in Vietnam, around Tay Ninh, and I tell him where I'd been. I tell him I'd served as a medic as a form of protest; he says he'd gone with an open mind; he'd wanted to see for himself. When I ask him his conclusion, he says he'd been appalled, and he'd "determined that it would never happen again."

(We leave it at that, but the word *Iraq* hangs like smoke in the air—147 Americans killed in action compared with 150,000 Iraqis, in 100 hours. One man's job well done is another's war crime. See the Seymour Hersh article, "Overwhelming Force," in *The New Yorker,* May 22, 2000, in which then-Colonel John LeMoyne, as commander of the 1st Brigade, 24th Infantry Division, is implicated in the massacre of a large number of retreating Iraqis who were traveling under protection of the negotiated ceasefire.)

He asks me what I'm doing now, how I'm getting on. I say, "That would be a long story. I better give you my poem." And he is quite patient and generous, I feel, as I fumblingly search all my pockets for the one copy I have left. I actually like him for that. I harbor no illusion that he'll be persuaded by the poem, but I'm grateful for the symmetry, for the sense of having gotten to say my piece.

Progress Report

For Charles Liteky

To know is arrogance; to not know, stupidity.
The vibrant mystery of life lies somewhere between.
—NORMAN FISHER

1967 and already in the Army
I became aware of the untoward nature
of the war then going on and
I received a calling to become a medic,
to act directly in the face of the evil
and, unfortunately for me, this calling
was composed of an unhealthy mix
of Buddha-like compassion and a young man's
impatience and, more damning,
a young man's desire to be tested,
all without benefit of any real spiritual base—
I said I was a humanist, I said "right's right,"
"now's now," and "put it on the line"

and I did some good there in that country
and I tested out okay and I survived
except to the extent that my friends did not
and so many in that country did not
and I became overwhelmed by the suffering
that passed through my hands my heart my mind
and I was benumbed and I was lost
for many years.

Now thirty years have passed,
thirty years, and in these last few years
I have, at last, returned to life.
I taught myself to feel by writing out
narratives of those times I remembered
becoming numb in increments,
and by reading the writings to citizens.
I found perspective in the Dharma,

in the Dharma I found soul sufficient
to inform the heat of spirit.

And now at peace, I am become
human. I let go
the dread story, survivor's identity.
I am here
now. I don't want more.

And now I am called back.
At a gathering of veterans,
a strong man stood and said these words:

"The Vietnam war is not over.
It is being carried on in other places
by other means. The policy of the United States
is to keep the third world
third. We take what is not ours.
And the United States is
us, each of us responsible."

I have known this all along.
And now I become one with the good Americans
who will to turn their ears away . . .

I do not wish to forgo my easy life so long in coming.
I can't deny my responsibility.

I wonder what I'll do.

Charles Liteky is a former Roman Catholic priest and U.S. Army chaplain who was awarded the Medal of Honor during the Vietnam War. He is currently serving a one-year prison sentence at Lompoc Federal Prison for repeatedly bearing witness/trespassing at Fort Benning. Before he reported to prison, I heard him speak at a commemoration of the twenty-fifth anniversary of the fall of Saigon. His presentation of the parallel between the war in Vietnam and the "war on the poor" in Latin America was so clear to me that I couldn't turn away.

MICHAEL SHUVAL

A draft board pulled me into the U.S. Army during the Vietnam conflict. I served in the Fort Ord military hospital. Afterward I grabbed a graduate degree and set off for Israel, where I became a citizen and a soldier. Annually, for a month each time, I hunted for infiltrators along the northern borders, working mostly at night. At forty-four, I had seen and smelled too much, so I quit. The demobilizing officer sought to keep me in. It would enhance my masculinity, he said. When I retire from my university job, I will become a certified chef ministering to children suffering from digestive tract diseases. Yes, I'll be in uniform again: this time clean, hospital white.

In "February on the Jordan Rift," I wrote about helmeted soldiers put on solitary guard duty and left to their own devices. An infantryman's initial alertness (mine) is followed by flight to Roman foot soldiers of yore, and to Terminus, a god I love. It, though armless and legless, retains immense power to this day. Terminus is a spirit calling to men who have lost limbs in battle, and to the emotionally wounded. Terminus is the god of getting along together, of community no matter how difficult it is to reach and sustain accord.

And Her Chicks

A pheasant and her chicks
stir up dust on cleared earth
between two fences
set twelve feet apart.
Her brood swerves as we
draw near, the mother scrawling
on clay and flashing past
pint-sized cartons, mines
sealed in rectangles of tar
and wax. She flattens her
feathers, feints, tumbles down
a chute made by mice,
clears the fence bottom
and leaves the bald earthen strip
for sagebrush
and sheltering rosemary,
her brood scurrying after her.

470

What's their hurry?
Even birds should know I'm too
old to soldier.
I may look like a killer,
my vest fruited with cloth pods
over dormant grenades,
straps and buckles quivering,
bandoliers, cartridges in clips,
a canteen slapping my leg;
but I'm a moron in a helmet,
near blind, plugged and shut down,
capped like a rogue oil well
streaked with salt, and sour.

In truth I move heavily
by the twin chain-link fence
and stoop in search of footprints.
I clank and wheeze,
my armpits drip,
and though I tolerate
the wild plants that mount me
with their smells,
I may blast them,
use my M-16 to rout and shatter
their prickly stems.

What else should I shoot?
Ticks and midges and snakes,
along with tracker Malben,
who naps at night on the hood
of our Land Rover
while we shiver near it,
waiting for footfalls
and the firefight.

I scour the gullies five hours straight,
earning hot soup and a nod
on my back in a cot so mean
it saps the spines of troops
who keep their boots
laced while napping.

On honeymoon against theft,
I hump my rifle between the sheets
till my tongue lolls on
the pillow.

One black wax carton blew its top
while I was snoozing
yesterday, shearing the rump off
a wild boar, tossing teeth,
tusks, and muscles over fences.
I slept through the blast
and the squealing of piglets,
but twitched, they say,
to the grim patter of
gravel and gristle
settling back to earth.

February on the Jordan Rift

From a bunker I scan date palm groves
then gauge the wadi far off
where smugglers hide.
A trail copying a kite's
        cloth knotted tail
    clings to a cliff
        the color of red smoke sky.
I note a granite wishbone lodged north
of brown and
    yellow hills,
beyond shoals of oak which edge plantations
in leaf shadow.

Night is gathering its wits now, pulling low
its black cap to bird cries,
casting its cape
at a flash of antelope rump.
Sounds sign
their names in cold ink

on my skin:
    grass being cropped;
a doe's turds, which drop and spill
drumming on crisp leaves.
    Are antlers being honed on the bark
of a tree by a buck,
or is an evil hill edging closer
stalking me?
A vixen yammers at her brood,
    bats
    crisscross
  overhead,
and I step
from the bunker to walk the border
until morning.

War veterans held this land twice-one-thousand
years ago, with pensions fit
for gimpy fools.
Each got an ass and goats,
seed and simple tools, a cord of wood,
and farms of ten *acti* for tilling.
    How to counter
  a neighbor's greed,
    and obviate
        seasons
           of senseless killing?
These Romans kept the peace
by cradling a Terminus
in the fleeces of sacrificed sheep
and lowering the stone Boss
into a herb-scented pit
dug where farmers' fences crossed.
    It had no eyes, legs
    or arms, the God of Boundaries,
    but it turned around
the charms and chants
of those who cursed a neighbor,
and brought the sinners harm.

Flowers

Driver was nodding off as
a land mine took feet, license,
and jeep
away.
He'd spilled soldiers in the field.
One breathed and bled;
two others lay broken;
a third, wrestling barbed-wire roses
on a stem,
jerked and hollered.
"Who's that?" Driver's soul asked.
"Your wife without you," Death replied.

BARBARA SONNEBORN

On the morning of my twenty-fourth birthday, March 2, 1968, I was awakened by the sound of the doorbell. A young man with a sad face, dressed in a military officer's uniform, was standing outside. "I regret to inform you that your husband, Lieutenant Jeff Gurvitz, is missing in action in Vietnam." The next afternoon, the same young man came to tell me that Jeff was dead. He had been killed in a mortar attack. There are events in our lives that change us on a cellular level and color the way we see the world from then on. A few years after it happened, I realized that Jeff's death was either going to destroy me or make me stronger. I had a choice, and his death became my teacher.

I'd always wanted to be a writer, but from the moment I learned about Jeff's death, I was unable to write. Words were too painful, they made me too angry. So, in 1973, I began working as a visual artist, primarily with photography. For a couple of years, I made self-portraits filled with war, death, and pain. I had a one-person show in New York, and many other shows around the country. I did installations, resulting in a set design for a Jean-Claude van Itallie play, *Bag Lady,* in New York.

For twenty years after Jeff was killed, I avoided meeting Vietnam veterans. I didn't see movies or TV specials. My own imagery of Jeff's death was as much as I could handle.

On January 1, 1988, I awoke feeling compelled to transform Jeff's death into a powerful statement against war. What had happened to all the widows in the U.S. and also in Vietnam? What could be learned about war through their stories? I wanted everyone in the U.S. to understand what it is like to have somebody you love come home in a flag-draped coffin. The result is the documentary film, *Regret to Inform,* which looks at the Vietnam War, and at the idea of war itself, through the stories of widows. The film is coproduced by my wonderful husband, Ron Greenberg.

I have been a student of Buddhism since the early '70s. In 1989, I attended a retreat for veterans led by Thich Nhat Hanh. Thich Nhat Hanh's refusal to take sides in the war—his compassion—resonated profoundly for me. This was another life-changing event.

At Thich Nhat Hanh's second retreat for veterans, in 1991, I met Maxine Hong Kingston, as she was beginning to conceive the idea for our writing group. I joined the group in 1994. The encouragement, support, and challenging questions of Maxine and my fellow writers helped shape my ideas and give birth to the film. Although composed of very distinct individuals, the group has a life of its own, offering healing, refuge, encouragement, pure energy, and deep friendship. My heart fills with great gratitude to Maxine and to all my fellow writers as we walk the path together.

Regret to Inform opened in 1999 at the Sundance Film Festival, where it received Best Director and Best Cinematography awards. It was nominated for an Academy Award, received the Peabody Award, the Independent Spirit Award, the Human Rights Watch Film Festival Award, the Courage of Conscience Award from The Peace Abbey, and numerous other awards. Regret to Inform continues to be shown nationally and internationally, and is used in this and other war-torn countries as a vehicle for healing and reconciliation, to look at how war creates profound suffering on all sides.

Last Time

It is New Year's Day 1968, a gray, misty day, damp and cold, about one in the afternoon. We walk to the car holding hands. I wait, notice that I'm tapping my foot, my hand clenched in a fist. You are biting your lip as you load your army duffle and my small bag, afraid to be late, and not wanting to go at all. We are just leaving our hotel, the San Francisco Hilton. The streets are deserted.

In the weeks before, as this day grew closer, I contemplated shooting you in the leg. You had, after all, taught me to shoot a .22-caliber pistol. I just wanted to stop you from going. But I couldn't do it. I didn't have the courage of my convictions and I couldn't interfere with your integrity. Besides, you keep telling me you'll be all right and I just want to believe you. I have to believe you.

At six o'clock this evening, January 1, 1968, you are leaving for Vietnam. You are to report at three o'clock to Travis Air Force Base, across the Bay Bridge and then to Fairfield, an hour and a half northeast.

Now is the hour to drive across the Bay Bridge. You open the car door, and then pull me toward you, hugging me hard, and saying, "I love you so much. I can't imagine being away from you for a whole year." We cling to each other outside the hotel for a long time.

Driving across the Bay Bridge in the fine gray mist, we head north on Interstate 80. Conversation doesn't come easily. I fumble with the radio, but everything sounds jarring. We talk about mundane things: our younger brothers in school, our friends Bonnie and Neal who are about to have a baby, the weather. We've talked about everything else, even our terror.

Suddenly I see the sign for Fairfield, Travis Air Force Base. My heart pounds and sinks. Exiting the freeway, we drive through a thickening fog, past gas stations, motels, and drive-ins, all colorless and gray in the mist. I feel as though I am in a movie of somebody else's life, a movie I don't like but can't turn off.

Yesterday we were in our rented Volkswagen on Van Ness Avenue. I was driving. As I moved away from a traffic light, I shifted into first gear, then second, passing Green Street. I noticed the cars parked along the curb, and suddenly I thought I'd just jerk the wheel and hit this car or that one, cause an accident, not a major one, but hopefully enough to injure you. But I didn't do it. Once you got your orders in September we argued. I begged you to leave the country or go to jail. But you said, "No, if I don't go, someone will go in my place. I can't do that."

A small sign, the entrance to Travis Air Force Base suddenly looms large out of the fog. You show your orders and are directed to a two-story, grayish-white building. The pavement is wet and I can barely see across the street, the fog is so heavy. Another soldier, tall and gangly, walks into the building. It's about 2:30 in the afternoon.

You're dressed in full uniform; an infantry officer, trained at Fort Benning, Georgia, and Fort Ord, California. The Army even sent you for jungle training in Panama. You called from there on Thanksgiving morning to tell me that the night before you had been startled awake in the darkness. You looked out and saw a leopard next to your tent. I'm holding my breath.

"I'll just check in and be right back."

"Sure, fine, I'll wait here." I don't want to see anybody but you now. I can't bear polite conversation with anyone.

Just a few minutes pass. I realize I'm clutching the door handle. You get back in the car.

"Good news, honey. I'm not leaving until 11:30."

I'm happy. Yet I don't know if I can handle a long good-bye.

We look at each other. "Let's get a motel room." We drive off the base back to the main street, pick up some fried chicken and biscuits, fries, and Cokes from Colonel Sanders, drive past a couple of motels all looking the same, pull into one and take my small bag and our dinner into the room.

A double bed, a faded orange quilted bedspread, two chairs with nubby gold fabric, a worn colorless carpet. The light in the bathroom flickers. You pull the curtains and we stand there looking at each other, just looking for a long time. I put my arms around you and ruffle your crewcut, stroke your face with both hands, running my fingers over your skin, thinking how much I love your honey-brown eyes, your long eyelashes, your ears, the little scar on your right cheekbone. You kiss my face, my eyes softly, so softly.

"Let's just get in bed . . ." We undress, looking at each other, memorizing each other. Lying down, entwined, kissing we realize we're too nervous, too upset to make love. We just want to hold each other. Stroking your back I feel the warmth of your skin, the pulse of young life in you. You're so, so alive, Jeff, so full of life, how could you be any other way? You have to come home.

You lie on your back, your right arm around me. I'm on my left side, pressed up against you, our legs entwined. You occasionally smoke a cigarette, Benson & Hedges, with your left hand, stub it out, and roll back toward me, and we just hold on tight, touching, not talking much. We listen to the sounds the cars and trucks make on the wet pavement.

"You know, Barbara, I want to tell you something . . ."

"Don't tell me, I don't want to hear it. You've already told me. Please . . . hush."

"No, listen to me. If I don't come back, I want you to have a good life, get married, be happy."

"Don't say that." I start to cry. "If you don't come back I'll die. I can't imagine living without you. I've loved you since I was fourteen."

"No, you won't die. You'll live and be happy. You'll do that for me."

"Jeff, please don't talk like that. Please, please."

"Just promise me. Promise me."

"Okay, okay, okay. I promise."

For a long time we lie pressing our bodies together, tears wetting both our faces, each other's shoulders. Finally it is almost 10 P.M. You have to report back at 11. We kiss, a long sweet, sweet kiss.

"Hmm, love you, baby."

"Love you too, sweetheart."

Dressing quickly, you suddenly get practical—instructions about the car, the bank.

"Okay, I get it. We already did this." You smile, the smile fades. You grab me, hugging me tightly, burying your face in my neck, you whisper, "I'm scared. I'm so scared."

"Please be careful. Be so careful."

We pick at our dinner. Now it is time. We throw my things together, trying to be ordinary. Finally we get back into the car. It all feels like slow motion. Driving, it is very dark and very foggy. We move carefully down the road, the only car, streetlights in pools of white, wet light in between the darkness. We enter the base and follow the signs to the terminal. It's all happening too fast now.

Walking in, there are lots of people in the waiting room, but it's quiet, very quiet. In the dim light, couples are embracing, women are crying, nobody is smiling. We stand there waiting for your flight to be called, our arms around each other, leaning on each other. I've cried too much. I can't cry any more. Everything we want to say has been said. We just hang on to each other.

I hear the number of your flight. My heart pounds out of control. I walk you to a door into a long hallway, and it is clear that I can go no further.

I kiss your lips, your eyes, your forehead. You squeeze me so hard, tell me to write every day, twice even, and then you walk down that hall. I stand there. You turn at the end and wave and walk out of my life forever.

The experiences of war and travel and exotic new peoples were so intense that they begged expression. I found taking up the pen to be one of the most satisfying exercises in life. My mother would read my letters to the family, and they begged for more. My younger sister would take them to school, where her history and geography teachers would read them to their classes. A few were published in the local newspaper. I later took my degree in English and have plied the trade of scribe ever since.

I joined the navy. I haven't dropped anchor since. And when I die, I'll be buried at sea. It's already arranged with the navy. Not that I'll die any time soon, mind you. Hey, I've got a lot of living to do! And a lot of beer to drink!

Death's Journeyman

I wonder how that son of Cain, Manuel, went about the business of death. I cannot imagine that he killed in cold blood using a knife. Such an act, so close that you could feel your victim's last breath on your face, is too intimate for cold blood, for calculating thought. To stab a man in the heart would take blood that boils. And though men might not absolve you of it, it would be a deed for which you could go to the priest, or pray to God, and say, "Forgive me. I have sinned. I burned with a passion so hot that I surrendered to my raging desire to quench it."

But what of deathly works done coldly: planned, practiced, done again and again. Done on a massive scale? Done in the comfort of the notion that while the death of one is a human tragedy, the death of a million is mere statistics? What do you say to the priest then? What then is your prayer of contrition? Do you say, "Forgive me. I banked the fire"?

Dealers of Death: the name we gave ourselves. That was a good name, Dealers of Death. And we sailed a ship known as the Gray Ghost of the Nam Coast. God, that was a good name! And we were death to the gooks. Man, we killed some gooks.

I don't know the name of the place we were at that day. Somewhere south of Haiphong. The gooks know the name of the Gray Ghost in

Haiphong, from the time we steamed into the fortified harbor. We went in early in the morning with the sun at our back, battleflags flying like medieval knights, guns announcing our name. We shot the place to pieces, leaving it all smoke and chaos. All a part of Operation Linebacker II. A good American name for a good American operation. You've got to have good names. LBJ's Operation Rolling Thunder was a flop and its name was too pretentious for Americans. But Richard Nixon's Linebacker had a good name, and dealt the gooks a serious blow.

So it was somewhere south of Haiphong. And we were pumped, because we were some gook-killing sons of bitches. And we were Dealers of Death, and we sailed in a ghost ship and now we were linebackers as well. And we all had cool-sounding nicknames like Chopper, the Bear, Doobie, Radar Love, and Petty Officer Monsoon. We had such good names.

So there were these gooks in a bunker on the shore south of Haiphong and we blasted 'em. We hit 'em with four triple salvos from the heavy turret with its six-inch-bore guns. Twelve rounds of heavyweight frag. Then we used the five-inch dual mount and fired a few incendiary rounds, just to flame their gook ass.

And we cheered. We could see 'em. They were close. "Yaaah! Fuckin' gooks! Ha! Look at their gook arms and legs fly like matchsticks." Yeah, that's what they looked like; tossed and burning matchsticks. And we sent 'em all to their gook hell.

And we all worked at it together. Black guys, white guys, guys in between, even guys who looked like the gooks. People have trouble understanding that. There were a lot of tensions between us in those days, and sometimes they spilled over into fighting. I guess it was mainly black versus white, but there were tensions between us all, over lots of things. But not when it came to killing. Killing transcended things. Race, religion, class, education, hometown; these distinctions had no meaning in the business of killing, for Death respects none of them.

That night we killed some more. We found a target we had been looking for at the time we came upon the bunker. The gooks had a surface-to-air missile battery hidden away in some hills and they were giving the Air Force a bad time. And the Air Force couldn't seem to pinpoint it, or they couldn't hit it, so they called the Ghost Ship. And we found it, electronically. Because you don't hide from the Ghost.

We didn't know at first if it was the site we were looking for, but we had a language officer on board who could speak gook, so he patched into their radio traffic and identified them. "Yeah," he said. "These are those bad boys."

We launched two of our homing missiles at them. They were well over the horizon so we couldn't see, and it was a trick shot, but our telemetry seemed to confirm we'd done the job.

Then we sailed away to rest up. Because maybe I make it sound easy, killing gooks, because of the way I tell it; but it's not easy. It's hard. You've got to have skill, and know-how, and teamwork. Everybody has got to be good at his job, and do it right all the time. When the moment comes to close the firing key and send those projectiles or those missiles off to their target, there's no turning back. There's no chance to correct errors, change your mind, or lose your nerve.

And it's hard to kill gooks because your days are full of labors and your nights are so often sleepless. It seemed like the gooks never slept. And you had to hit 'em when you could, day or night. And they would make it all the harder. They would run. And they would hide. And they would shoot back, too. Cocky little fucks. So don't think it's easy.

A day or so after the missile launch we heard from the Air Force's aerial reconnaissance operation, known as Operation Big Look. The Bear brought the news down from the radio shack to the weapons control shack where some of us were maintaining our gear.

"Hey, I just got the skinny from Big Look," he said. And we dropped everything.

"Wha'd they say? Wha'd they say?"

"They say we kill taksan gooksan."

"No shit!?"

"Fuckin' aye! They said there were so many they couldn't count 'em all. That makes taksan in my Japanese dictionary!"

"The Gray Ghost kicks ass!" we all cheered. "She's the ass-kickin'est ship in the whole fucking navy." And we chanted our pride in our ship: "Haze gray and under weigh, this motherfucker is a-OK!"

Then we imitated the marines and said "Uuragh!" a few times. Man, we were pumped. We were some death-dealing, ghost-riding, linebacking, taksan-gook-killing sons of bitches. And when the cheering died down we were flushed and quiet a minute, and Gunner Rodino said, "Gentlemen, that was a difficult shot. But attaboys all around. You've all done a good piece of work."

You see, that's what we called what we did. That was the name we gave to the thing we practiced. It was work. It was your job. And you remembered that, because sooner or later it would happen. It was like it was inevitable. Some civilian you met on the beach would ask you. Or some high school friend who went to college when you joined up would send you a letter from campus and demand to know. "How does it feel?" You know what I mean? "Do you have any objections to killing people?" Jeeze! And there were the real pain-in-the-ass types who would put it in terms like "angst," and "taking of human life," and "gestalt." Gestalt!? Jeeze. Assholes.

So what do you tell 'em? What can you tell 'em? You tell 'em the truth: Just doing your job. You tell 'em there's a war on, and this is your job in wartime. You tell 'em you're a highly skilled individual. The U.S. Navy has put a lot of time and money into you, to train you, and bring you up to do this job. You're a petty officer of the line, that's the name you bear, and this is what you do. And you make sure those civilians know that the line we're talking about is the battle line. Like in "ship of the line." Because you're the man. You're the one who operates these weapons. You close the firing key. When you take the rest of the whole U.S. Navy and you put it all together, it has one task. And that is to get you to the place where the work is done. And you make sure to tell 'em you do good work.

So that was my job. See? That was my work. Like people have work everywhere, military and civilian too. Like, say a guy is a carpenter, that's his work, and you call him a worker. If he's good, maybe you call him "a hard-working man." That's a good compliment, "hard-working man." Or say a guy's a preacher. You could call him a worker in God's vineyard, or say that he does "good works."

· Well I never worked to build anybody a house to live in. And I never worked in the vineyard. But I worked. I worked hard, and I was good at my work. I did good work. I did. I was a hard-working man. You can't say I wasn't!

RICHARD L. STEVENS

I was born in Chicago in 1939, grew up in way-rural Prairie City, Iowa, and joined the Marines soon out of high school, mostly for adventure. I was in Vietnam three years during the war in military and civilian roles, was wounded twice, and came home wiser. I've been a gardener, Foreign Service Officer, refugee worker, university professor, and hunter of ancient trails for the state of Hawai'i. I've written two books on organic gardening and two on the Ho Chi Minh Trail and the role of nature in the Vietnam War. I'm a hiker, camper, and passionate tree planter, and I work on native-species restoration projects, including the "Arlington of the Pacific," the West Hawai'i Veterans' Cemetery.

In 1969, I was the *Chieu Hoi* ("Open Arms") Advisor in Quang Tri Province. Chieu Hoi was the program to induce communist guerrillas to defect; Quang Tri bordered North Vietnam. On the night of the midsummer full moon, a Vietnamese Buddhist holiday called the Night of Wandering Souls, I met and helped capture the "goddess" of this story. What I saw her do that night and what she endured after changed my mind about what humans are capable of, and about the war. In 1995, I returned to Vietnam to search for her. The title of this account, "Meeting with the Goddess," is taken from Joseph Campbell's *The Hero with a Thousand Faces,* in which the mythic hero's journey is understood to be the life journey of us all.

Meeting with the Goddess
True Story of the Vietnamese Annie Oakley

Thence entered I the recesses of my memory . . .
and I considered, and stood aghast . . .
—ST. AUGUSTINE, *CONFESSIONS*

It's already hot at 8 A.M. as I leave my house in Quang Tri City and head for the Chieu Hoi Center. The empty road ahead bakes on a Vietnamese holiday, something about "Wandering Souls." My counterpart, the South Vietnamese government official I advise, is staying home with his family. I had nothing better to do, I was longing for adventure, and I wanted to practice Vietnamese with the ex-guerrillas guarding the Center. They, as "ralliers" to the South Vietnamese and

U.S. side, and *traitors* to their former comrades, got no holiday from threat of attack to their sandbag fort on the edge of town.

I ease my Scout down my narrow driveway. The wrinkled old Vietnamese veteran who guards the front of my house comes out of his sandbag bunker and drags open the iron and barbed-wire gate, gouging a trench in the dirt. I turn east toward the sea. Behind me, the hot dry wind that blows all summer from Laos sweeps past, stirring dead leaves at the side of the road.

I parallel the river, then swing south past the broad, mossy moat and high stone walls of Quang Tri Citadel, an ancient feudal castle now with M-60 machine guns mounted in the narrow slits, and the yellow-and-red flag of South Vietnam flying in the hot Lao wind. At a narrow, bamboo-framed dirt lane, I turn left and bump along between thatched houses and packed-earth rice-drying yards, the bamboo reaching, scraping my Scout as it growls along in low gear, dropping into holes cut by winter rains, dust bowls now in summer heat. Chickens scratch, low-slung pigs root, women in conical hats pass rocking with carrying poles and big tins full of sloshing water.

Gun towers rise ahead, and I pass through the barbed-wire gate of the Chieu Hoi Center, the ralliers' fortress-island at the edge of the rice-paddy sea. The guard, an ex-Viet Cong guerrilla with a Chinese-made AK-47 slung across his back, calls, *"Ong Co-Van! Mr. Advisor! Working on the Wandering Souls holiday?"*

I wonder what "Wandering Souls" is about as I cross the dusty compound and park outside my tin-roofed office. Suddenly, a motor scooter zooms through the gate, and Ong Ba, "Mr. Three," one of our district agents, pulls up in a cloud of smoke and dust. Ba, who I don't like and definitely don't trust, breathes stale black tobacco and rancid *nuoc mam* fish sauce directly into my face and says in Vietnamese, "We have to talk, Co-Van. Call Dang-Sy. Very important!"

Dang-Sy, Commander of the Chieu Hoi Armed Propaganda Team, 105 ex-VC guerrillas and North Vietnamese soldiers, comes in wearing dark sunglasses, tailored Marine camouflage, brown beret, and a .45 pistol hanging to his knee. Tall, slim, and superintelligent, Dang-Sy is a former VC schoolteacher. He looks at Ba with distaste: besides smelling bad, Ba is a South Vietnamese government official, *not* an ex-VC.

Ba sits in my chair, lights up a Gauloise, and fills the room with tobacco smoke and foul breath. Dang-Sy stays at the door; I lean on the open window. Ba talks fast, and I only catch a few words: "Moun-tains . . . forest . . . midnight . . . girl."

Dang-Sy gets excited at the word *"co"*—"girl." He sits on my desk almost in Ba's face, and fires rapid questions. Ba answers in a torrent of words. I get: "Old man . . . nephew . . . house . . . rally." I have no idea what's going on.

Dang-Sy turns to me. "We have to go *now,* Co-Van! Very important!"

"Duoc," I say. "Good."

Go where? I think.

Outside, I pull Dang-Sy aside. "Tell me again where we're going?"

Dang-Sy looks surprised. "I thought you understood, Co-Van. Hai Lang District, to meet the old man."

"Duoc," I say.

Who's the old man? I think. And what about the girl?

I drive fast down Highway 1, the old Mandarin Road, dodging holes, buses, jeeps, and trucks. Ba sits in back, smoking and picking his yellow, broken teeth.

I lean over to Dang-Sy and say, "Tell me the story again—slowly."

Dang-Sy slowly, in basic Vietnamese, tells the story. I catch a few more words: "Guerrilla . . . ambush . . . capture . . . tonight."

I still don't get it. Who's the girl? Why do they get so excited about her?

We enter Hai Lang District Town, dusty open markets and ramshackle tin-roof buildings. We go in Ba's stifling-hot, windowless office. There are no chairs, just a battered desk and a hanging, burned-out lightbulb. It looks like no one *ever* comes here.

Ba cracks the back door and a sliver of light slices the room, illu-minating golden, floating dust. Ba calls sharply into the alley, "You! Old man! Come!"

An old farmer squeezes in and stands looking scared, blinking watery eyes and turning his rice-straw hat in gnarled, trembling hands.

"Tell us the story!" Ba barks. "Talk fast!"

Half-hidden in the gloom, I sweat and struggle to breathe and under-stand. The old man speaks country dialect in a phlegm-filled, quavering voice. I catch only, "My house . . . midnight . . . girl." Again the girl!

Ba puffs and offers one to Dang-Sy. Dang-Sy doesn't smoke, but he lights up, too, as he questions the old man. The room fills with hot, stinking haze. The old man turns his conical hat round and round and stammers. They discuss the girl and *dong*—Vietnamese money—lots of *dong*. My lungs and head are bursting to get out.

Dang-Sy turns to me. "Now we go to Major Ngoc, the District Chief. Co-Van, you talk to him. He won't listen to me, I'm ex-VC; and Ba has no standing."

"Duoc," I say.

Talk about *what?* I think. Ba pushes the old man into the alley.

We drive to the District Headquarters: gun towers, barbed-wire, and sandbags. Fat and greasy Major Ngoc, the District Chief, invites us to his office. We sit in stuffed chairs around a low glass table, while Ngoc's sergeant pours tea into small porcelain cups.

Ngoc ignores Ba and Dang-Sy, and speaks to me in French: "Remember the good old days in Hue? Now we're in this outpost of desolation!"

"Major," I say in French, "I'm going to ask Dang-Sy to tell you why we're here."

"Non!" Ngoc explodes, his belly bumping the table and rattling the teacups. "Not VC! Ba will tell me!"

Ba leans forward eagerly, sweat shining on the back of his chair. He tells the story. When he says, "Girl," Ngoc belly-bumps the table and they discuss *dong*. Ngoc even talks to Dang-Sy; they seem to be planning a night operation.

Ngoc leans back grinning, his jowls shining. *"Bon plan, eh, Monsieur Chieu Hoi?"*

"Très bon plan," I say. *"Formidable."*

What plan? I think. And what about the girl?

Ngoc giggles and calls for more tea. *"Bon,* we go tonight!" he says. "Big operation! Big success! Big *reward!"*

I ask in French, "Tell me again about the girl?"

Ngoc laughs. *"Vous n'avez pas compris?* You didn't understand? I thought you were studying Vietnamese! Go ask 'Captain Rose,' my Intelligence Advisor. He'll tell you all about the girl!"

I leave them sipping tea and cross the baking compound to the air-conditioned U.S. Advisors' Hut. My friend "Rosie" Rosenberg's not around; he won't be back till chow time.

I drive fast through blazing heat to Quang Tri City. Dang-Sy gets off at his number two wife's house; I drop Ba at his scooter.

"Be here at five, Co-Van," Ba breathes in my face. "We need your Scout."

I go to my house and try to sleep. My alarm clock ticks, and two words beat in my mind: Ambush-Trap. The whole thing is a setup! The girl, whoever she is, probably planned it, using herself as bait! And the possibility for leaks and betrayal is *everywhere*. Ba—I don't trust him at all—he'd sell his soul for *dong*. Major Ngoc could be a VC, except he's absurd, though he could be acting. The old farmer *looked* scared, but maybe he's a great actor, too, maybe he's the mastermind! And Ngoc's sergeant, so interested in our conversation! Dang-Sy could *definitely* still be a VC, sharp as he is. They *all* could be VC, all but me! I saw our plan, whatever it was, flowing like a river out to the mountains and forests of Indian Country, and the VC coming to kill us.

I get up, dress in Marine camouflage, and load my M-16. It's almost five o'clock. I drive to the Center. It's still hot as Hell.

Dang-Sy stands frowning in my office. "*Buon lam, Co-Van!* Very sad! I can't go with you tonight; I have to stay here on guard. Since I'm sending the best APT with you maybe the VC will attack *here* tonight!"

My stomach drops into empty space. Dang-Sy's not going! He knows the plan, and he's not going! This *is* a trap! *He's* the one!

"Luc-Thanh will command the APT," Dang-Sy says. "He'll take care of you, Co-Van."

Luc-Thanh! I think. I'm going on night ambush with Luc-Thanh!

Luc-Thanh was our most famous former VC, a longtime guerrilla with one of their highest medals for "destroying a tank and killing many enemy." Luc-Thanh looked like a pirate, with one bad, "rolling" eye from a wound he got fighting U.S. Marines.

Luc-Thanh looks in and says, "*Minh di.* We go."

We drive fast down Highway 1, my Scout loaded with ex-VC and the APT pickup behind filled with more ex-guerrillas. We bristle like porcupines with AKs and '16s poking out the windows, and Chinese RPD machine guns on the pickup's cab. Highway 1 is empty: *no one* drives the roads this late. Night, like underground, forests, and mountains, is Indian Country.

"This is the life, eh, Co-Van!" Luc-Thanh laughs, thrusting his AK into the hot wind. "Go on night operation! Night is the best! *Nhung dung ban co gai!* But don't shoot the girl!"

I look at him and slam into a hole. "I would never shoot a girl!"

We pull up to Ngoc's office in a cloud of dust. Ngoc comes out in white T-shirt and plastic slippers! He's not going! *He* planned this!

"Quel dommage!" he says. "What a pity I can't go! I have to stay here and wait for an important call from my colonel. But I'm sending Lieutenant Tuan, my Intelligence Officer, and my whole Intelligence Squad, my best men!"

Slim, hard-faced Lt. Tuan steps out of Ngoc's office, then six Intel Squad soldiers, equally tough-looking. Tuan looks at Luc-Thanh and snarls, "Those guys are VC! We're not going on operation with them!"

Captain Rosie Rosenberg, the Intelligence Advisor, comes out of Ngoc's office, and in dazzlingly fluent Vietnamese says, "Those are *ex*-VC, Lieutenant Tuan. And I thought you Intel Squad boys weren't afraid of anything!"

"Once a VC, *always* a VC," Tuan growls, not taking his eyes off Luc-Thanh.

Ngoc pushes forward with his belly rolling. "My Intelligence Squad *is* going—to represent me in the reward!"

Sgt. Jones, the Advisory Team's radio operator and medic, comes out with a PRC-25 radio hulking up on his back, and a big medic's bag hanging from his shoulder.

I pull Rosie aside. "Tell me what's going on, especially about the girl. I don't like the sound of this."

Rosie laughs. "Girl can kill you dead as a man! And this is no ordinary girl, this is Annie Oakley!"

Vietnam was full of the American frontier. In Quang Tri we had Indian Country, the Oregon Trail, Kit Carson Scouts, Daniel Boone Teams, and more—but Annie Oakley?

Rosie draws me in his office and opens her file. "Her real name is Hoang Thi Nu. She's twenty-eight, and a *very* important VC: several high positions, and on the province's 'Most Wanted' list. 'Nu'—her given name—means 'woman.' She's unmarried, so the Vietnamese still call her 'co'—'girl': 'Miss Woman.' We call her 'Annie Oakley' for the two guns she carries, and her magical ways. We've tried to catch her before, my man, but she never shows, gets away, or ambushes us! And look at this—several times she's been reported in two places at the same time! She's magic, I tell you! And she's from a long tradition of Vietnamese women warriors."

I flip through Annie's file, agents' reports of her trips down from the mountains and forests, and her night missions in the paddylands. According to the reports, she carries a folding-stock AK-47, and a Soviet officer's K-54 pistol. "How reliable is all this?"

Rosie grins and pats his pocket. "Best intelligence money can buy."

"Have you ever thought this could be a trap?"

"I *always* think that," Rosie says. "I'm from New York, remember?"

We load up. Lt. Tuan leads with the Intel Squad jammed in Ngoc's jeep. Rosie drives his jeep, with Jones in the shotgun seat. I follow in my Scout; then the APT pickup, Chinese machine guns rattling on the cab. This is already crazy: it's far too late to drive, with the sun dropping behind the mountains along the Laos border, and a big shadow spreading across the land. Even the wind is dead, the flag of South Vietnam hanging limply on its pole as we rumble out the barbed-wire gate and head east into the paddy-sea.

My mind whirls as we fly through the darkening countryside, ditches tuning black beside the road. Annie—I'm starting to think of her like that—Annie Oakley. Co Nu—Miss Woman. It's bad to give your enemy a name.

"This is good, eh, Co-Van?" Luc-Thanh laughs with his eye rolling, and pats his AK butt. "Night ambush! But when we meet the girl, *bat song! Capture alive! Dung ban!* Don't shoot, don't kill her!"

"*Khong bao gia!*" I say, squinting into Rosie's dust. "Never! I would *never* kill a girl!"

"*Nguy hiem!*" Luc-Thanh says, staring at me with his good eye. "Very dangerous! When the shooting starts—*nguy hiem!*"

We cross a rumbling, wooden-plank bridge, turn into the ruins of an old French church, and get out beside a dark, slow-flowing stream. From bush-grown, broken church walls, Popular Forces—Ngoc's men—emerge and surround us.

"Hey, I know those guys!" a sharp-faced PF sergeant says, pointing at Luc-Thanh. "They're VC! What are they doing out here?"

Rosie fires back in fast Vietnamese, "*Ex*-VC, Sergeant! Anyway, you 'roughpuff' are not going on operation with us! You will stay here and fall asleep on ambush like you *always* do!"

The sergeant steps forward with an M-16 in his hand. "Maybe if you get in a fight with the VC tonight, 'Captain Rose,'" he sneers, using a popular Vietnamese girl's name, "those *ex*-VC will fight *you!*"

"At least they fight!" Rosie shoots back, and we duck under the bridge.

More enemies, I think, as we sit beside the dark water.

Above, Ba struts among the PF—probably telling them our plan! Tuan and the PF lieutenant stand talking and staring across a fallow paddy at a black treeline. They could be VC, I think, *all* of them! Maybe me, Rosie, and Jones are the only non-VC here!

Annie, I think, Miss Nu—did she lead us out here? Is she waiting in the gathering night?

Tuan looks under the bridge and says, *"Minh di.* We go."

He forms us into a line beside the stream, Americans in the middle, APT at the end; the PF watch from the bank.

The PF sergeant calls, "Be careful, 'Captain Rose'! Watch your big ass!"

For once Rosie stays silent, and with Tuan and the Intel Squad leading, we step off at five-meter intervals, and float like ghosts beside the stream.

Luc-Thanh moves up behind me and whispers, "We have to go faster, Co-Van! The moon will rise soon!"

We stop and crouch by the stream. Luc-Thanh fumes: "The moon!"

Annie's out there, I think. The moon will rise and she'll get us all: best of the APT, the Intel Squad, District Advisory Team, and me! Dead on the Night of Wandering Souls!

Tuan lies on the stream bank studying the broad paddy and the distant treeline.

Why is he waiting? I agonize. To give the moon more chance to rise?

Tuan goes over the bank and down into the paddy. We flow behind him like a snake across the giant chessboard of dikes and elevated paths. At the paddy's far end, trees rise like tall, black kings and queens.

Here's where it will come, I think. Ambush! Here's where Annie will get us!

Crunching stubble, we race the moon down the river of night. Ahead, near the base of the dark trees, white sand mounds of a cemetery roll, and a path leads to them. Tuan takes the path and weaves among the sandy mounds.

Why is Tuan taking us here? I think. I picture Annie and her men lying at the base of the grave-mounds shooting, and our bodies falling, twitching, blood streaking the white sand. I see her hiding like a leopard, her legs drawn up, ready to spring.

Light breaks through the trees, the moon rising huge from the South China Sea. It shines on us as we snake among the graves. *Now* Annie will get us, I think. *Now!*

Our shadows float behind us like our spirits, armed on the path among the graves. Tuan steps up on the main hamlet trail. It's a tunnel through tall, overhanging trees and we join him in a spaced-out line, sweating and breathing hard. Left are tree-shrouded, thatched houses with spirit houses on poles in rice-drying yards, and the smell of incense floating in the air. Right, through jumbled bamboo, the stream shines in moonlight.

We walk quietly down the trail-tunnel. At the first house, an old man stands before his spirit house, rocking, praying, and clutching incense. Suddenly, he *senses* us, his eyes pop open, he spins, and goes in his house. I picture him descending into the bunker dug into his packed-earth floor, lowering the wooden door, and lying in close, damp dark. I feel my heart sink as my boots hit the trail: how quickly he changed when he saw us, from lost in his prayers to terror. I see a sudden image of boots crushing a lotus. We flow on through the trail-tunnel, soft sounds coming from the stream.

Before the open window of the next house, two women and two girls laugh, their faces illuminated by a candle. Outside in their spirit house, incense sticks glow like tiny, golden eyes, and smoke wafts off to guide the Wandering Souls. The girls and women don't see us; they keep talking and laughing as if nothing bad is about to happen.

Tuan kneels at a trail junction, and Ba creeps up to whisper. We crouch in the bamboo. Over the shimmering, moonlit stream, a spider-leg bamboo bridge crosses into sinister darkness. Ba points to a house across the trail junction, where a candle burns in an open window.

Ba whispers along our line: "The old man's house—the girl will come here at midnight."

Tuan leads us into a shallow, grassy ditch outside the old man's house. Tuan and Ba whisper under a mango tree, then call Luc-Thanh and point east, where a trail runs toward the ocean.

Tuan talks and Rosie translates: "The APT will ambush along the trail to the east. She may come from there, from the dunes along the beach. The Intel Squad will watch the old man's house; Americans stay here in the ditch."

"What?" I whisper to Rosie. "They're isolating us here! One grenade, one burst will get us all!"

"Hey, it's a Vietnamese show," Rosie whispers, and he lies back in the grazed grass. "We're just Advisors, remember? Relax and enjoy the night."

"Like Hell," I whisper. I hurry to catch up with the APT, and fall in behind Bon, the young ex-guerilla at the end of their fast-moving line.

Luc-Thanh leads us out the back of the hamlet to the top of a high dike overlooking a broad, fallow paddy. We lie in soft grass and moonlight, and look out at one of the most beautiful sights I've ever seen: moon-flooded fields, dikes, paths, distant treeline. Beyond, though I can't see them from here, are the rolling, ghostly-white dunes, the long, empty, golden beaches of Quang Tri, and the sea. I realize again how much I love Vietnam.

"Khong duoc!" Luc-Thanh whispers, staring into the field. "No good for ambush! Lying out there with only a few small bushes! This was *Ba's* idea, and he stays at the old man's house!"

Luc-Thanh rises and leads us down the steep bank into the paddy. We walk fast, weaving among small, dark, curled shapes scattered on moon-glowing stubble. A bad smell blows in the dying breeze. Luc-Thanh quickly places us in ambush positions watching the trail, motioning for me to lie beside a bush.

"Watch this stretch of trail," he whispers, pointing. "Remember, *bat song!* Capture alive! *Dung ban co gai!* Don't shoot the girl!"

"I won't!"

I point my rifle at the path and picture Annie and her men walking. I don't think we can distinguish man from woman on that trail, all wearing baggy clothes and carrying AKs. How will we ever capture her? What will *they* do when they see us here?

Luc-Thanh lies on the other side of my bush, pointing his AK at the trail. The faint breeze dies, and an overwhelming stench fills the night. I twist back, looking for the source. The small, dark, curled shapes lie close to my boots. I flash on the high dike across the back of the hamlet, the scattered bushes, and the dark shapes on the stubble. Of course! This is the hamlet toilet! *Ba* sent us here!

"It stinks here, Co-Van," Luc-Thanh whispers forlornly. "It stinks real bad!"

No shit, Luc-Thanh! I want to say, but I don't know how.

"*Ba,*" Luc-Thanh mutters through gritted teeth. "Ba sent us out here!"

We lie rigid, afraid to move, shallow-breathing, and staring at the trail. No VC come to relieve us. *Hours* of foul stench pass. There's no shit-smell like human shit-smell, I think. Nothing even close.

I stare at the trail, and try not to breath. I can't imagine Annie coming here.

At midnight, a shadow comes from the hamlet, creeps among us, whispering, and finds Luc-Thanh. "Lieutenant Tuan wants everybody back at the old man's house. *Truoi oi,* it stinks here!"

We walk carefully, like crossing a minefield. Back at the ditch, Rosie and Jones look pretty casual, lying in soft grass with fresh breezes blowing.

"Where've you *been?*" Rosie whispers. "You guys stink!"

The old man's house is dark; the whole hamlet lies in heavy silence. Nearby, Tuan and Ba question a young, scared VC. Behind the chunky, wild-haired VC, his AK lies radiating power. It's just come from "out there," the mountains and forests of Indian Country.

"Annie's bodyguard," Rosie whispers. "He wants to rally, but for us to make it look like he's being captured. He's scared to death of her."

I sit on the trail behind the VC.

"Where is she now!" Ba breathes and the VC flinches. "You know!"

"No, I don't! She doesn't tell us anything!"

"Who helps her here?" Tuan demands. "You know that!"

The VC looks wildly toward the bamboo bridge. "I don't know, she doesn't tell us! Please, get me away from here! She's coming soon!"

Tuan and Ba call Luc-Thanh and they whisper. Tuan talks and Rosie translates: "She's coming soon. Intel Squad will watch the bridge and this side of the house; APT the trail and the other side. Advisors stay here in the ditch."

"Like Hell," I whisper. "I'm not missin' this."

I hurry after the APT, and catch up with Bon in the trail-tunnel. In front of the old man's house, Luc-Thanh places Bon and me. "You two watch the door," he whispers. "*Bat song!* Capture alive! Don't shoot her!"

"Khong bao gia!" I whisper. "Never!"

Luc-Thanh vanishes down the trail, and we lie with young bamboo rising all around us, our rifles low and pointed at the old man's house. I aim at the door, deep in shadow under shaggy thatch. Could I tell Annie from a man there?

Bon reaches over and shoves my muzzle to the ground. *"Dung ban co gai! "* he whispers savagely. "Don't shoot the girl!"

"I *won't!* " I whisper. *Damn,* why do they think I'm going to *shoot* her?

Overhead, the bamboo creaks, sighs, and falls silent. Something goes "Plop!" in the stream. Across the trail, the old man's house looms black and deathly still. Suddenly, a wave of energy, unseen and powerful, surges through the bamboo, hits Bon and me, and passes on, leaving the bamboo shivering. Bon and I rise up on our elbows and look at each other big-eyed, slack-jawed. An electric, invisible force has just swept through the bamboo and us.

"It's her!" Bon whispers. "She's coming!"

We squirm low into leaves and dirt, hearts hammering, rifles trembling. Adrenaline starts to rule the night.

A black phantom shape—not solid, but vibrating waves of energy—silently floats across the old man's rice-drying yard and enters the house!

"Dung ban co!" Bon gasps. "Don't shoot her!"

Two *more* phantoms cross the rice-drying yard, and disappear inside the house! *Three* people in there! But who?

Low voices, then Luc-Thanh's shout from the house shatters the night: "Miss Nu! Come out and rally! You don't have to be a prisoner!"

The night tumbles back into silence. All around the house men lie rigid and ready to shoot.

Luc-Thanh shouts again: "Miss Nu! We know you're down there! The house is surrounded! Come out and rally! You don't have to be a prisoner!"

The house explodes, and everything begins happening at such speed that time melts into itself, and sanity starts to lose its grip. Crashing, grunts, shouts, a table overturning, someone running through a wall! More shouts! Shots! *Bam! Bam!*

Wild thrashing erupts in the banana patch at the corner of the house, and Bon and I jump up and stand on the trail staring. A black phantom bursts out of the bamboo, flashes across the trail, and smashes into the bamboo bordering the stream. Like a wild deer, the phantom fights its way toward the water.

"The girl!" Bon says. "She's running away!"

Bon runs up the path and I follow, boots and heart pounding. All around the night comes alive with running shadows. More shots! *Bababam!*

"Dung ban!" Luc-Thanh shouts. *"Bat song!"*

Bon turns into the bamboo where Annie flashed across the path and I follow, plowing ahead, whiplashed. Sudden silence ahead—she's stopped! We freeze. Now *she* ambushes *us!*

A big "Splash!" in the stream!

"She jumped!" Bon says. "She's in the water!"

He pushes forward and I follow, gouged, panting, sweating. We force our way to the bank and stare stunned. Annie's already at midstream, *throwing* herself toward the opposite side, moonlight and water streaming from her pants, shirt, and hair. She's getting away!

Bababam! Bon begins shooting into the water ahead of her.

Bababam! Bababam! Deadly bullet-fountains spring up in her path, and she *throws* herself toward them. She looks like a sea lion lunging through moonlit water, fighting for darkness and escape.

Bababam! More APT and Intel Squad fight their way to the bank and fire, shooting up more bullet-fountains. She throws herself *eagerly* toward them. *Bababam!*

"Dung ban!" Luc-Thanh shouts from the shaking bridge. *"Co Nu!* Stop! You don't have to be a prisoner!"

All around the night writhes like a great glowing snake. Blood pounds in brains, guns explode, flames burst from barrels. I begin to shoot with everybody else, *ahead* of her, trying to make her stop, turn, anything, just don't get away. *Babababam!* It's the first time I've fired at a visible person, and she's a *girl,* she's Annie Oakley! *Bababam!* My damn '16 jams, and I drop to one knee, fumble, clear it, rise, and shoot again: *Babababam!* Fountains spout all across Annie's path, and she lunges forward as if she wants to *bathe* in them.

She's getting away! I think. No, stop, you *can't* get away! *Bababababam!*

"Co Nu!" Luc-Thanh shouts. "Stop! Rally! Join us!"

Babababam!

"Dung ban! Bat song!"

Tuan shoots up a parachute flare, which arches over the stream and comes down hissing, burning, and making giant shadows dance. Trees, houses, the bridge, men sway and dance in yellow chemical light; everything seems beyond human scale. Annie streams flare-lit water as she hurls herself toward the bullet-fountains. *Bababam! Bababam!* She'd rather *die* than be captured or join us! Everyone runs for the bridge. I'm the only one left here to stop her!

"Dung ban! Bat song!"

Annie suddenly begins to lunge downstream! I see her face in desperate profile, *and* where she's heading, a dry ditch directly across the stream from me that comes in from the darkness like an arrow. If she can get there, she can run up it and escape! Only I can stop her! "Oh, God," I hear myself say, "I'm going to have to kill her."

Rocked by shooting and lit by adrenaline, my mind shouts more dark words: We're going to fail. We *can't* fail. Oh, God, I'm going to have to kill her!

"Dung ban! Bat song!"

Bababam!

I see her eye, like a wild animal trying to escape. I point my muzzle at her head. Oh, God, I'm going to kill her!

Bababam!

Bullet-fountains fly up on both sides of her head. She falls to one knee near the bank. Oh God, I hit her!

She staggers up and begins sprinting down the ditch, soles of her bare feet flying. She's getting away! We can't *fail,* we can't *lose!* I aim at her back and pull the trigger.

Babababam!

Dirt-fountains shoot up on both sides of her flying feet. She pitches forward and is swallowed by the night.

Oh God, I've killed her! screams in my mind. I killed Annie, I killed Miss Nu! I shot her in the back!

I turn to the bridge and start to sink. I don't know if I can live with this.

Shouts and shots explode across the stream! A grenade! Another!

I run to the quaking bridge and cross fast. If I could bring her back, I would. I dash across a stubble field to ghostlike figures gathering around a still form. Pushing through APT, I look down in horror at Annie, crumpled on the ground, head shining with blood. I reel back; I want the earth to swallow me.

I killed her! I think. I shot her!

Luc-Thanh looks up with his bad eye rolling. "Why did you shoot, Co-Van?" he demands. "You didn't hear me shout, *'Dung ban!'*?"

"*Xin loi,*" I say. "I'm sorry." It sounds so pitiful. "I'm sorry she's dead."

"*Khong chet!*" Luc-Thanh laughs in my face. "*Bi thuong!* Not dead! Wounded! Lucky for you!"

I come alive again, and whirl to look at her head. "But how bad?"

Luc-Thanh grins and pulls his ear lobe. "Only her ear! Ear bleeds a lot, and not you! APT got her with grenades, knocked her out and cut her ear! Lucky for *them* they didn't kill her!"

Sgt. Jones parts the circle and kneels behind Annie's head. He gently pulls back her bloody hair, peers at her ear, and wraps her head round and round with a long bandage.

"Earlobe bleeds a lot," he says, looking up. "I don't see any other wounds. *Maybe* she's unconscious—I'd say it's fifty-fifty she's faking."

"We have to go *now,* Co-Van!" Luc-Thanh says, pulling my sleeve. "We're making too much noise! The VC will try to get her back!"

Rosie squats and picks Annie up, cradling her in his arms, her hair and head hanging, her bare feet dangling, bouncing. We walk back toward the bridge like a holy procession. I follow a little to the side of Rosie, where I can see her head, her face mostly hidden by the long bandage. Rosie walks solemnly, like a knight bearing a queen. What is it like to hold that wet, dark power?

I stand aside at the bridge as Rosie approaches with Annie. Rosie walks like he's in a trance. He steps onto the trembling, loosened bamboo, sways, uses her body as a balance, and flows across to the other side.

Crossing, I hear my rifle exploding again, and see my bullet-fountains, and the way she *threw* herself toward them. The way she ran, jumped, swam—the courage, the determination—where does she get the power? And what happens to her now?

Rosie carries her into a water buffalo shed beside the trail, and lays her gently on a pile of straw. Everyone crowds in under the thatch, buzzing and staring at Annie. The tethered buffalo pulls back in a corner, eyes terror-struck, nose running, horns swinging. Annie lies curled on the straw in a fetal position. Suddenly I think of Mary, and Bethlehem.

Luc-Thanh pulls my sleeve. "We have to keep moving, Co-Van! We're making too much noise!"

Tuan whispers and two of his men disappear down the trail. Ba pushes in and stares at Annie, breathing hard. The Intel men return with two scared-looking peasant women carrying a long, thick bamboo pole. Tuan spits words at the women, and they put the bamboo down.

"Annie's aunts," Rosie whispers. "They raised her."

She's listening, I think, glancing at Annie. She knows everything.

Tuan snarls at the aunts and jerks his head at Annie. The women come in the shed, passing through us all as if we were invisible. They grasp Annie's shoulders and feet, and half carry, half drag her out and stretch her by the pole. Tuan tosses them rope, and they tie Annie's wrists and ankles to the big bamboo. As they crouch and work near her feet and head, I see something passing between them and Annie!

Tuan sees it too. *"Mao di!"* he snaps. "Hurry up!"

The aunts squat at the ends of the pole, struggle it onto their shoulders, and stand, weaving under Annie's dead weight.

"Di!" Tuan orders, and the women stagger off bent-legged, Annie hanging from the pole.

What must the pain be like, I think, to her head, ankles, wrists? How can she keep feigning unconsciousness?

We pass back through the sand-mound graveyard, then take a roundabout route across the field toward the church ruins. I walk just to the side and a little behind Annie, unable to tear my eyes from her, wanting to be close to her power. Her hair hangs, her body rocks; the aunts stumble and strain across the broad field. We look like we're on safari: Annie's our captured lion, swaying beneath the pole.

Now comes the ambush, I think. Annie's men will rise up from underground, race after us as the moon goes down, and catch up to the aunts' painfully slow gait. Annie! Who is she? Where does she get the courage, the power?

Luc-Thanh walks beside me, and we watch her long hair brush the earth. I want to ask where she gets the power, but I don't know how.

I try, "You know how she ran, swam, didn't care if we killed her, but wasn't going to stop?"

Luc-Thanh seems to know what I want, and he turns toward me, his war-ravaged face dark and his bad eye rolling. *"Khong co co gai o trong nay,"* he says sadly. "There are no girls like that on this side."

I wonder in a flash what side *is* he on, then I think of all the Vietnamese girls I know. I know amazingly beautiful, strong, brave women, but I don't know one who could have done what Annie did, or bear what she's enduring now. I think through *all* the people I know, but I don't know *anyone* who could have done what she did, who has that kind of power—and I almost killed her.

The moon sinks behind the western mountains as we approach the dark church ruins. Wandering souls crossing the field, we bear our wild being into captivity.

Postscript

Over the next few weeks, I was able to keep some contact with Annie. Then she disappeared into the higher hells of the Vietnamese interrogation system, and my knowledge of her was cut. Over the years, I told her story, as far as I could follow it, to help teach about the war. In 1995, I went back to Vietnam to look for her in the time of Wandering Souls.

After that visit, I received the following letter:

> June 10, 1996
>
> Dear Mr. Richard Stevens,
>
> I received your letter more than half a year ago, but never got a chance to respond to you. That has been bothering me. However, I do hope you'll understand and ignore the time to "enjoy" my letter now!
>
> According to me, time is not important. It's not something that you and I can use to blame each other for. It is the heart that counts. Our Vietnamese famous writer, Nguyen Du, in his "Kim Van Kieu," wrote, "The heart is worth three times more than the talent." You are American, yet you do have the heart. You are so far away, with time, everything stays in the past. In other words,

the war has separated hundreds of families, children from their fathers and wives from their husbands. At the same time, thousands of people sacrifice their lives for their country's independence and freedom. I am a Vietnamese woman, born and raised in that spirit. As I remember, when my secret cave was discovered, armed soldiers surrounded me and gunshots were all over me. Yet I don't understand why I have survived until now. Maybe, as you said, "everything is God's will." That's also why we are able to see each other again. After more than 25 years, you still have the heart to visit an enemy! In a war, there will always be winners and losers. However, I always respect you for your love of human beings. Time to weep over our losses has gone. What's now important is the present. That's why you don't hold grudge for the past, for what happened more than one fourth a century ago. And, the bottom line, if you have a love for your fellow humans, you will always feel the closeness of hearts no matter how far away we are from each other.

After your visit to Vietnam, you've left us with love and compassion. You admire our country and our people. To tell you the truth, the Vietnamese are very enduring and hard-working. Vietnamese women, particularly, are always devoted and loyal to their families and their works. That's why, to me, my courage and loyalty are just part of being a Vietnamese woman. It's not noble, it's just normal, if not trivial. In Vietnam, during the war, you could see heroes everywhere. And thanks to that war, you and I had a chance to meet with each other.

Have you achieved your dream? Has your book published? I am not sure if the main character is myself. Very humbly, let me introduce you the Vietnamese woman, whom beloved Uncle Ho has called "heroic, courageous, loyal, and defiant." Inherited from heroic blood of the Trung sisters and Trieu Ai, the Vietnamese women consider fighting against foreign invasion natural and normal.

The time I met you and received your letter has been in the past, but never will I forget you with your caring love of our family. Please accept our gratitude and also give our best regards to your family. I hope you don't mind my mistakes in this letter. That's what it means to have a human heart!

I wish you health, luck and success in everything. And of course, like you, I am looking forward to hearing from you.

Affectionately,
Hoang Thi Nu

LEE SWENSON

I was born in Minnesota in 1939, of Norwegian and Swedish farmer parents, and migrated with my family to California two years later for the post–Pearl Harbor shipyard jobs. As a teenager, fascinated by the labor struggles of the postwar unions, I searched out the Wobblies (Industrial Workers of the World), but Gandhi's nonviolent ideas captured my imagination and life path. As a draft resister in the early '60s, I dropped out of Stanford University to join the antifallout shelter, atomic testing ban, and blossoming civil rights movements.

I met Joan Baez and Ira Sandperl in 1959 at the Peninsula School in Menlo Park, and in 1969 became director of their Institute for the Study of Nonviolence, a great crossroads of draft and war tax resistance, AWOL soldiers seeking refuge, farmworker boycott staff, and Buddhist monks and nuns.

At the end of the Vietnam War, I edited the *Simple Living Newsletter* for the Quakers, then became the executive director of the catalytic Farallones Institute. I met my wife, Vijaya Nagarajan, through Ivan Illich in 1982, and since 1985 we've worked in the Recovery of the Commons Project and our Institute for the Study of Natural and Cultural Resources. Our twin girls, Jaya and Uma, were born in 2000.

During the Vietnam War, some 6,000 draft resisters did time in federal prisons, mostly serving two-year sentences. During World War II nearly the same number served prison time—up to four years in federal prison. Each prisoner had a visitor-and-correspondence list of eight people. As one of them, I would make the monthly trip to visit the Safford Federal Prison in southeast Arizona to see Randy Kehler and David Harris. Then they were transferred to La Tuna Maximum Security Prison on the Rio Grande River near El Paso, where the pigpens were air-conditioned and inmates' cells were not. Visiting hours were 9 A.M. to 5 P.M. Saturday and Sunday, once a month. I drove a thousand miles each way in my noisy Volkswagen Bug. My ears still ring.

Two years before his federal prison sentence began, while the Tet offensive was ramping up in South Vietnam, Randy Kehler and I spent twenty days in Santa Rita Jail (along with 150 other draft resisters and demonstrators) over Christmas and New Year's, 1967 into 1968. Randy and I paced endlessly up and down the caged-in sidewalk of the rundown World War II barracks, Alameda County's dumping ground for demonstrators.

Dr. Martin Luther King, Jr., and Andy Young came cross-country to visit Joan Baez at Santa Rita, over on the women's side. King would be killed three months later, in the spring of that superheated year. The following is an imaginary letter to Randy Kehler while he was in prison for draft resistance from 1970 to 1971. Gurney Norman was a writer living in Menlo Park in the '60s and '70s. Gurney went on to a fleeting moment of fame with his hilarious novel *Divine Rights Trip: Our Story Thus Far,* published on the right-hand side of the pages in *The Last Whole Earth Catalogue.* He moved back to Kentucky and is, to this day, a legendary, local hero.

Composting America

Lee Swenson
440 Oakdale Avenue
East Palo Alto, California

Saturday April 2, 1970

To:
Randy Kehler, #1146
Safford Federal Prison
Safford, Arizona

Dear Randy,

Just back from Gurney Norman's compost party. I have the paper cup he gave us as we left, filled with compost and two worms—male and female, not sure which is which, but I guess they know best.

At a time when the Vietnam War body count is so high, Westmoreland ups the troop levels in Vietnam again, and Kissinger keeps lying, Gurney hosts a compost party. Twenty of us gathered this morning in Chloe's dance studio just off Perry Lane. In his slow, beautifully cadenced country-hollow Kentucky voice, Gurney sings the praises of compost—of the necessity, inevitability, and sweetness of compost. Then he takes us out back to his compost heap, gets us all down on our hands and knees to feel the compost pile, and tells some Kentucky-hill-country Jack-in-the-Beanstalk stories about how you've gotta have a compost pile outside the window so when your mother—who had sent you out to get some food and you trade away the cow for some magical beans—throws the beans out the window in disgust, and overnight they grow into this sky-high beanstalk and Jack takes off.

Gurney just makes you weep, he's such a fine storyteller. He scoops down, fills a Dixie cup full of compost, making sure you get your two worms to bring home. "Let's compost America, one pile at a time," he says.

Halfway through the party, gnarly old Howard comes in with twenty one-pound coffee cans of homemade whole wheat bread. You remember Howard, forever in his workman overalls. He lives just three houses up from our land-trust cottage here on Oakdale Avenue and keeps on cranking out loaves of bread. Ever since Stop-the-Draft Week in October '67, he's been baking bread for every demonstration and celebration. He's really got it down; he takes his 200 dinged coffee cans, fires up his two ovens, uses Ed Brown's *Tassajara Bread Book* recipe times 100 for the big demonstrations, and brings warm loaves of wheat bread oozing out like mushroom caps. He takes a can, turns it over, and with a sharp rap, out comes a loaf of bread. He's got to get the multiplying fishes part of it down, too!

After I stowed the loaf of bread and cup of worms and compost in the VW Bug, rolling down the window to be sure the worms could breathe (how *do* worms breathe?), I walked around the old Perry Lane neighborhood, Little Carmel, an oasis of one-lane, no-sidewalk streets, with grand old gnarly oak trees in the middle of the street—this postage stamp of unincorporated area, just north of Sand Hill Road, on San Francisquito Creek and the Stanford Golf Course in Menlo Park. I lived there, just around the corner in the early '60s, before moving cross-town to East Palo Alto, where I bought my six-thousand-dollar 500-square-foot shack.

Perry Lane, an as yet unimproved, bohemian world, goes back to the turn of the century, the early 1900s, when Thorstein Veblen was fired from Stanford for his affairs with other professors' wives. Veblen's great *Theory of the Leisure Class* was and still is right-on about conspicuous consumption as the driving force of the consumer juggernaut. More relevant than ever—money is riding into town and stealing everything. Another old cottage on Perry Lane has been torn down and a humungous house and two-car garage blasts in there. Ken Kesey and the Merry Pranksters are now long gone from Perry Lane, up to La Honda, but the memories linger.

Menlo Park must seem like a long way from your cell. What is it now? Five hundred forty-nine days and you'll be back here. But who's counting? Probably you are!

I'll drive down again the last week of April to see you and David. I can't believe it was just last week I saw you at Safford Prison, your desert home. Best thing on the way home was camping in the California desert—Joshua Tree—no rain in eighteen months. I pumped the campground pump handle, washed my hair and felt the water evaporate right off my head.

Well, short hair, write when you can. Keep on trucking 'til the wheels fall off.

Love ya,
Lee

Salt

Jaywalking across Beacon Street, I felt a firm but light hand on my shoulder. I looked up at his handsome, clean-shaven face towering over me, his slight smile sharp and focused, his other huge hand gesturing in front of me.

"Hi, I'm Chris. I'm from Lompoc, and I hear the antiwar movement in Santa Barbara is going to build a monument to itself. If they do, I'm gonna blow it up."

We were walking along the Boston Common, to the Red Line MBTA train out to the Joiner Center for the Study of War and Social Consequences's annual writing workshop. It was June 1999. Chris seemed to know who I was—an anarchist-pacifist from the long-gone Institute for the Study of Nonviolence in Palo Alto. Did he want to blow me up, too?

Then I saw his eyes. One eye moved, twinkled, and searched. The other, still and glassy. Then I saw the wide scar running jaggedly down his throat, going down into his immaculate white T-shirt. Not like my cancerous thyroid surgery, the thin scar tucked into a horizontal neck wrinkle. Ah, a Vietnam veteran, probably in-country while students were burning down the Santa Barbara Bank of America.

"Chris," I said, sliding my token into the coin box, "There are a lot of issues to untangle here. It's much easier to hate the rich than it is to love the poor—and a lot of those kids were hating the rich then." My old tapes started playing. I stopped and asked him where the scar was from.

"Nineteen sixty-seven, twenty-eight days in-country, walking point in the Delta, three hand grenades hanging on a trip wire—we walked into a booby trap. Tore up three of us. I got a fragment in the throat, another in the eye."

I blinked.

"How long was it 'til you were medevacked out?" I asked.

"Ten minutes. Saved my life. Great medics. Choppered out, into the OR in less than half an hour, blood transfusions flowing. Then years of rehab. Now I'm a high school teacher in Lompoc."

Ah, Lompoc, I thought, where some of the draft resisters were locked up, a small joint you passed through on your way to bigger pens. Santa Barbara, a tony town with its dense little student ghetto of cemented-over sand dune, a high-rise plantation, inappropriately named Isla Vista.

Quite a ride on the train.

"Let's talk later," I said, as our U. Mass stop rolled up.

That Saturday we met at the Harvard Garden Pub, a Vietnam veteran hangout for drinking and talk. The big-gun writers were there, Larry Heinemann with his award-winning *Paco's Story,* and Bao Ninh, the North Vietnamese author of *The Sorrow of War.* On the book's jacket it says, "Bao Ninh served with the Glorious 27th Youth Brigade. Of the five hundred who went to war with the Brigade in 1969, he is one of the ten who survived. He lives in Hanoi." Black market copies of his classic antiwar novel were sold along with a shoeshine by street kids all over Hanoi. Others joined in. Nguyen Muu, also from Hanoi, a prolific novelist and poet, served thirteen years with the Viet Cong in South Vietnam. The rest of us were more occasional writers—using the Writers Workshop as an anvil to hammer our stories. Some of the faces still carried the war—scars, twitches, and tics. And a silent one, with a long gaunt face, an officer on 100 percent disability, glided up in a taxi. He couldn't ride the subway. Whiskey with beer chasers for some, others stuck with straight whiskey. Tongues loosened slowly, following the serious business of drinking.

A lotta weight sittin' 'round the table. American draftees, North Vietnamese regulars, a draft resister peace veteran. A quiet deference to the elder writers—Heinemann, whose *Paco's Story* fifteen years before had scooped the National Book Award from Toni Morrison's *Beloved*. Son of a bus driver, he was back in Chicago in the summer of 1969 after his year in Vietnam; driving his bus through the police riots at Hubert Humphrey's shit-eating-grin-nominating convention, he picked up tear-gassed demonstrators, driving them out of baton's reach.

I remembered sitting on a wooden crate in the so-called club car on the Danang-to-Hue train in 1997. Larry and I swapped stories about 1967 and 1968. We were traveling with a small gang of American and Vietnamese writers, celebrating the fortieth anniversary of the Vietnamese Writers' Association, traveling from Hanoi in the north to Ho Chi Minh City in the south. Larry was writing a book on train travel in Vietnam and was in hog heaven, flicking cigarette butt after butt out the open-air barred windows, a can of beer between his feet. As we talked, three scruffy Vietnamese kids were dragged into the car, caught sneaking on board the train without tickets, fear written all over their faces. We weren't sure if they were going to be thrown off the moving train, but they were left to huddle in the corner till the next stop.

Slowly it unfolded that on New Year's Eve, that last night of 1967, Larry's unit, in the shadow of Nui Ba Den, Black Virgin Mountain, would kill 500 Viet Cong regulars. Oliver Stone portrayed that firefight in the film *Platoon*. That same evening, 150 of us, including Randy Kehler, were in Santa Rita Jail for a sit-in at the Oakland Army Induction Center.

My thoughts came back to the Harvard Garden Pub, when through our translator, Nguyen Ba Chung, Heinemann asked the North Vietnamese veterans, "What was the hardest thing about the war?"

"Burying our dead," Muu replied. "Finding all the body parts. The B-52 bombing raids were vicious. The whole earth trembled; everything was blown apart. We stitched our names into our shirts and our pant legs, so when a blast blew us apart, they could try to put the body back together again. To go on to the next world, you need to have your whole body together. B-52s held a special terror for us."

Then Muu asked, "Did any of you bury your dead?"

The table was still. Finally, a response: "They were choppered out—in body bags, refrigerated, shipped back stateside ice cold."

Another lull. More pints polished off.

"How long did it take to get from Hanoi down to the South?" I asked.

"Six months," Bao Ninh replied. "Sometimes by train, sometimes a lorry, mostly on foot."

"Did you get back home?"

"Not once."

"Did you write?"

"No pen or paper. Paper went for cigarettes."

"What happened when you were wounded?"

"Four women carried me in a string hammock, a day-and-a-half walk. I had a rocket fragment in my hip. I begged them not to squat down when the American aircraft came overhead. If they did, my hip would hit the ground, and the pain would shoot through me. The Americans controlled the air; we had the ground. Two months of rehab in a tunnel hospital, underground. Then back with my unit. Six of the bloodiest years of the war."

Another round of drinks. Steve, sloppy and loud, throwing his total-disability money around trying to order more rounds, kept busy interrupting everyone while drowning himself in drink. I didn't know it then, but he was so ill he would die a few months later. Agent Orange, drugs, and booze didn't mix well. Chris, big and strong, stood behind him, his sure hands holding Steve upright. Chris's flare-up, his bomb threat to me had eased away. Such were the volatile feelings about the antiwar movement and the war itself. When the street demonstrators threw burning Molotov cocktails at the Isla Vista Bank of America branch and the American government ordered GIs to napalm Vietnamese villages, things began to blur.

Now Chris was the peacemaker.

The Irish waitress refused to serve the obnoxious ones. Tempers flared and subsided.

Bao Ninh quietly sipped his whiskey. We talked daily life, cooking, food, supplies. Some little things were hard, he said. Hard to get enough salt to cook with. They would try to scrape up the salt traces from evaporated water in the dried-out bomb craters.

Heinemann responded, "And there we were, maybe half a mile away, our half-track carrying gallon jugs of salt tablets. Handfuls of salt. You had no salt, and we had more salt than we could ever use."

Heinemann and Bao Ninh understood a bit of each other. Two things they knew. They hated the army. And they especially hated the god-damn lifers.

"Let's get a smoke," Heinemann said, and the table cleared out, leaving a forest of empties.

I teach English and business, and am dean of the Language Arts Division at De Anza College in Cupertino, California. I took my undergraduate degree in engineering at the United States Military Academy at West Point. After two tours of duty in Vietnam, including a year in Cu Chi, above the tunnels, and a year in Saigon at the American headquarters, I took a graduate degree in English at the University of Virginia, and later, a graduate degree in business systems from the University of Northern Colorado.

A retired Army officer, I have lived in Asia, Europe, and Africa. I have extensive experience in sales and marketing, including Internet marketing, and have cowritten and coproduced a Hollywood movie, *Fire Birds,* starring Nicolas Cage, Tommy Lee Jones, and Sean Young. I am past president of the De Anza College Faculty Senate, and have been on six Campus Abroad trips to Paris, London, and Vietnam. I recently returned to Vietnam (my fourth trip back) with 440 wheelchairs from the Wheelchair Foundation and the Santa Clara Valley Vietnamese Chamber of Commerce. My wife, Susan, and I live in Saratoga, California.

The Chicopee Flash

Last night at about midnight, I went to The Wall to visit our twenty-three West Point classmates who were killed in Vietnam. They were all there: our first captain, Bob Arvin; our class comic, Patrick O'Toole; our first fatality, Gary Kadetz, whose death had been a great personal shock when I tripped over his body bag at the airstrip at Cu Chi. But I went, mostly, to see my roommate from senior year, "The Chicopee Flash."

Bob's nickname was a deliberate misnomer. He was from Chicopee, Massachusetts, but he was no flash. Like Patton, it took him five years to get through West Point. Unlike Patton, Bob was slow and laid back, in part because of his natural inclinations, and in part because he was overweight. He was seldom on time, seldom had his shoes shined, and was at the bottom of the class in both academics and military aptitude. He was "Mr. No Sweat," and he loved to play cribbage.

The perspectives now are changing as we change and get older. I started to cry and turned away from The Wall. Finally smoked a cigarette

Ranger School style between cupped hands, and I found a new perspective as I faced out from The Wall that Jack Wheeler, the freshman across the hall, had built. God, what a contribution he has made to our country and the Long Gray Line of our alumni.

The perspective of The Chicopee Flash looks out from The Wall at the Hart statue of the three soldiers and the Women's Memorial. To the left is the Washington Monument, to the right the Lincoln Memorial. The Chicopee Flash shares the National Mall with two of our finest presidents and our other classmates, the other members of the Long Gray Line who gave their lives in Vietnam—and the 58,000 other soldiers, men and women, whose service The Wall honors.

I thought, my God, what a privilege, what an honor, to have roomed with The Chicopee Flash, the Corps of Cadets' finest cribbage player, who was also one of our country's finest soldiers.

When I was a child, I climbed the steps of the Washington Monument and the Lincoln Memorial and dreamed of attending West Point. And in my life it was my great privilege to play cribbage with a man who now has a monument alongside those two presidents. The radiators banged, the minute callers yelled the number of minutes remaining until formation, and we still played cribbage, oblivious to the legacy that would be ours, the shared service to country, or the monument that would be his, The Chicopee Flash.

He graduated before the weight rules were strictly enforced, and he weighed 260 when he got to Fort Benning. He ate only one steak and drank only water each day of jump school and still lost nothing. Despite that, he made it through, earned his parachute wings, and then soldiered on through Ranger School, losing only 5 pounds in the process. It took guts, but he made the mark and went on to lead our soldiers in Vietnam.

It was the weight that finally got him. It complicated a stomach wound from a small-caliber rifle bullet that wouldn't heal, and things got worse. After thirteen days, there was no more cribbage, here, for The Chicopee Flash.

We miss him. And Bob Arvin and Patty O'Toole and Gary Kadetz, and all the others. We mourn their loss. We each deal with those losses in various ways. A trip to The Wall, as Jack Wheeler intended, really will help heal the nation—and the individual.

Bob was an unlikely hero, but he was a hero. How fortunate we were to have known him, how much richer our lives for his sacrifice, and our collective service. And now his name is on the Mall, on The Wall, next to the monuments with the names of Washington and Lincoln. And I suspect this midnight, in Heaven, it's after taps and Bob Gagne's got the blanket over the windows and he's running the biggest cribbage tournament up there. And I'll bet they still call him "The Chicopee Flash."

CLAUDE ANSHIN THOMAS

I served in Vietnam from 1966 to 1967 as a helicopter crew chief. During my tour of duty, I was shot down five times and wounded once, receiving the Purple Heart. Since then, I have been working to heal the emotional, mental, and spiritual wounds from that war and to find a way to use these experiences to help others. As part of this process, I lived and studied at a Vietnamese monastery and retreat center, Plum Village, founded and guided by the Venerable Thich Nhat Hanh, and I was later ordained as a Zen Buddhist monk by Roshi Bernie Glassman.

Writing has been a crucial tool in my journey to come to peace with the devastation of war. In 2005, my book *At Hell's Gate: A Soldier's Journey from War to Peace* was published by Shambhala, and as a result, I've received many invitations to speak about violence and how to heal it. I facilitate mindfulness-meditation retreats that give participants tools to aid them in the process of healing. I have led retreats for veterans, the homeless, and prisoners, and taught in jails, schools, nursing homes, and hospitals. I also practice pilgrimage, walking in my Buddhist robes and carrying all my belongings on my back. In 1994 and 1995, I took part in an interfaith pilgrimage from Auschwitz, where I was ordained, to Vietnam. In 1998, I walked across the United States, and in 1999, I walked through many sites of concentration camps, prisoner-of-war camps, prisons, and other places of suffering connected to World War II. In 2002, I walked from Budapest to the site of the Bergen-Belsen concentration camp in Germany, following the paths that many Jews had to take to their imprisonment and death. In 2007, I will walk from California to Texas, along the Mexican border.

I now divide my time between the U.S., Europe, South America, and Asia, sharing with people that violence is not a solution.

10)

A
bullet
slams
into
my body,
I feel

no
pain,
I
cannot
see,
the
sounds
of war
disappear—
I
must be
dead
for all
is
peaceful,
then suddenly,
the medics,
a poncho,
mortars,
flesh
being ripped
from
legs,
I
snap upright
in
my bed
soaked
in perspiration—
should
I
be glad
that
now
it's
only
a dream?

12)

The
surf's
up
in
Panama City,
I watched
the
previews
for
Quicksilver
and
climbed
Monadnock
on
my own—
my
heart pace
is lonely
but
more regular
this
way—
maybe
this has nothing
to do
with
war—
the sounds,
the smells,
that steal
my sleep
dead eyes
starin'
at me
everywhere,

maybe I'm
just
allergic
to
perfume
and
body oils.

A Soldier's Prayer

I am here on retreat with veterans for the eighth consecutive year, a critical piece of my practice. An essential component of these gatherings is the exercise of writing. I have asked those in attendance to write about an experience they thought they could never write about.

Where does that leave me? What will I write about? Sitting in meditation this morning—November 19, 2005—I had the memory of meeting my father on my first leave from the hospital, the first time we'd seen each other after my return from Vietnam.

My father was a schoolteacher at Fort LeBouef High School in Waterford, Pennsylvania. He was a good man, and I loved him as well as I could. He always provided the necessities—food, shelter, clothes, and some money—but he was not able to provide the emotional support a young man needs from his father. I can see now the effects his war, World War II, had on him. In his efforts to distance himself from the war, he distanced himself from me.

It was a Friday afternoon in 1968. I'd come home unexpectedly and gone to the high school where he taught American History and Driver's Education, walked into the office, and spoke with the school secretary, who didn't recognize me, even though it was just two years since I was in this office often. When she finally figured out who I was, she seemed shocked. Her reaction confirmed what I'd sensed, that I had changed profoundly in Vietnam.

She told me that my father was in his room, the same room he taught in year after year until he died in July 1973 at the age of fifty-three of a massive heart attack. I told her I wanted to surprise him and asked if she would invite him to come to the office without saying I was there. She agreed, and I waited inside the principal's office.

When my father knocked on the door, I said, "Come in." I was standing there in my khaki uniform, the shirt wrapped around the body cast that was supporting my left shoulder under reconstruction. He was visibly shaken. He looked as though he'd been hit by an unseen energy field, and tears welled up in his eyes, if only for a moment. Then he quickly composed himself and we were on to business as usual. He shook my hand.

Today while sitting in meditation, I realized that I never considered what he might have been thinking or feeling while I was in Vietnam fighting, that I might have ended up like the dead or wounded soldiers and sailors who were his World War II buddies, and I felt a twinge of remorse that I'll never have this conversation with him.

I miss my father, Benson Mac Thomas, himself a casualty of war.

⸺

I grew up in northwestern Pennsylvania in a small farming community. My father was a teacher and my mother took in laundry, cleaned houses, and sometimes worked as a waitress or a barmaid to make ends meet. Throughout my childhood, I was taught to block out pain and trust no one. And that love equals violence and violence is a necessary response to problems.

One day when I was five, I wanted to ride my bicycle and my mother didn't want me to. I was excited and probably a bit too persistent, and my mother's response was to push the bicycle, with me on it, down a flight of stairs. Another time, for no apparent reason, she placed her hand on the back of my neck and smashed my face into the wall, telling me that if I were a better person, she wouldn't have to do that.

My father was emotionally hidden. Alcohol and tobacco held the walls of his repression in place. But what's hidden will surely find its way out, and one day when I was eight, I got back home late from playing with my friends, and he immediately took me to the bathroom, pulled down my pants, and beat me with his leather belt until I was black and blue and bleeding. Then he realized how much he was hurting me, and he began to doctor the wounds with Mercurochrome and told me that he did it because he loved me.

I excelled in sports and was offered an athletic scholarship to college. But my father urged me to turn it down. "You're too wild," he said, and that was true. I stole cars from the local used car lot, for example, just for fun. My dad suggested that instead of college I enter the military. Through sports I'd developed a warrior's romantic vision of competition and battle, and from an early age I'd learned that if you love your country, you have to be ready to fight and maybe even die for it. So I signed up.

My father and his World War II friends often sat around and, drunk, told stories that made war seem glamorous, exciting, and even romantic. They didn't speak truthfully. They spoke of war as a great adventure. I drank their stories up and longed to be a part of them. I was extremely insecure, and I envisioned war as a game in which I could fight and receive a lot of medals and be loved and admired. "The military," my father told me," will help make a man out of you."

———

The day I left for military service, my father drove me to the bus station twenty-five miles from home. I had my Boy Scout suitcase with my name written on it in Magic Marker. My father bought my ticket and left me there—no hug, handshake, or parting words. The bus took me to Buffalo, where I was going to be inducted. When I got there, they gave me a voucher to stay in a hotel, and instead I went out and got drunk. The next morning, sick, I went back to the induction center, took the physical, filled out a lot of forms, and took an oath. I was a soldier.

We got off a bus that took us to Fort Dix, and a staff sergeant greeted us with humiliating obscenities. Right then I knew that my father had lied. I wanted to go home, but couldn't. My life had changed forever.

During basic training I was taught to kill human beings. On the firing range, our targets resembled people. When we were done, we were supposed to stack our weapons in a particular way. One day, I dropped my rifle, and the drill instructor screamed and cursed that I wasn't looking after my rifle properly, that it was the most important thing in my life because whether I lived or died depended on it. This six-foot three-inch sergeant first class stood in front of me, his chest jammed against my face, stabbing me with his finger and screaming obscenities. Then he pulled out his penis and urinated on me in front of everyone.

I wasn't allowed to wash for two days. I felt shame at such a deep level that I couldn't handle it. All I could feel was rage and I knew I couldn't act it out. So I focused my rage on the enemy—which was everyone unlike me. This kind of conditioning is essential in creating a soldier. Soldiers see everything "other" as threatening and potentially deadly. You dehumanize a whole race of people, and you dehumanize yourself. But if I hadn't been prepared for this by my whole life, it wouldn't have taken hold.

Basic training was an emotional struggle for me. I excelled at the physical training, but I had a tremendously difficult time with the discipline. It was bizarre and arbitrary and it didn't make any sense.

One day, I was feeling so desperate I punched out every window in the barracks. My hands cut and bleeding, I went upstairs into a room, closed the door, pushed a wall locker in front of it, climbed out the window, and sat on the roof.

An angry, aggressive first lieutenant in his early twenties managed to get out to where I was. I was crying and I didn't know what to do. His response was to slap my face and punch me repeatedly.

Later a staff sergeant who seemed to care genuinely about me told me, "Listen, you're not going to go home, so you might as well make the best of it."

There was something in the way he said it that made me just shut down to everything I was feeling and say to myself, Okay, I'll just do this thing. I'll be the best soldier that I can be. I'll turn off my feelings and do the best I can.

I was drinking a lot by then, and my paycheck would be gone long before the next one came. My life was in a tailspin, and, to escape my troubles, I volunteered for Vietnam. At first they said I was too young, but I persisted. They said I had to write an essay explaining why I wanted to go. I can't remember what I wrote, but whatever it was, it worked.

—

During my tour in-country I was directly responsible for the deaths of many, many people. But I didn't recognize what I was doing as killing. The enemy was simply the enemy, not human.

My first assignment was in Long Binh with the Ninetieth Replacement Battalion. I had been there for about ten days when I was randomly assigned to an assault helicopter company as a door gunner. There was no time to think about it or to realize what was happening.

In Phu Loi, near Saigon, I was assigned to the 116th Assault Helicopter Company. I was taken to the barracks and given a bunk and a place to put my things, and then I was introduced to Richie, the crew chief I would fly with. He showed me where the gun shack was, where the tools of my new trade were kept: the M60 (7.62 mm) machine guns. He showed me how to clean the guns and took me out to the helicopter to demonstrate how to mount and load them.

Then he introduced me to the pilots and told me that we'd begin with a simple day, just flying pass runs and mail runs. I didn't have any idea what he meant. Everything was new and I was scared to death. When we took off, my job was to tell the pilot we were clear on the right and to watch for approaching aircraft. I was essentially the pilot's rearview mirror. I had no clue what I was doing. I didn't really even understand that I could get shot. I just felt scared and confused, and I knew that I wasn't supposed to be either.

We made several trips to pick up and deliver mail and take soldiers to Saigon on pass. The weather was great, the air was cool and dry, and I remember feeling a sense of wonder about this thing called war.

We were just finishing up our runs as night approached. We returned to Phu Loi, where we ate. Then I went to my barracks and lay down on my bunk. I noticed that there weren't many people around, but I didn't think much about it. Then Richie came running in and told me excitedly to get my things together, that the unit had gotten into a mess, some ships were down, and we needed to fly. I got dressed, grabbed my flight gloves, flak jacket, and flight helmet, and rushed down to the gun shack where I grabbed clean M60s and ran them out to the bunker where the helicopter was parked.

I mounted the guns, and as I waited for the rest of the crew, I saw that there was a lot of activity around some helicopters sitting on the flight line. When I walked closer, I saw that men with water trucks were hosing blood out of the crew compartments. Richie grabbed me by the arm and told me to get to the helicopter because it was time to go. I climbed into the right-side crew compartment, put on my flight helmet, and plugged in my microphone cord. We did a radio check and then Richie gave the clear-left and I gave the clear-right announcement to the pilots. We hovered into the blackness above the airfield and took off.

Soon we arrived at a staging location where there were several other helicopters. This was my first experience flying with the whole unit. Troops were loaded into the helicopters and we took off again into the night. As we approached the landing zone (LZ), the sky was lit up with parachute flares that gave the darkness a bright yellowish tint. Though you could hardly see, everything seemed in silhouette. Forms were identifiable but not clear. As we began to descend into the LZ, I sensed a tense and exciting energy in the air, the feeling of unspoken fear. The pilot gave the order to open fire. The next thing I knew we were on the ground and all of the troops were off the helicopter. Other ships were taking off all around us but we weren't. We'd been shot down.

Richie yelled at me to get the pilot out and grab the guns. I ran to the pilot's door, opened it, and unlocked a sliding piece of body armor designed to protect the side of the pilot's head. We had been instructed to be cautious when sliding this piece back because we could easily push it off its track and damage the helicopter floor. Well, I did exactly what I was not supposed to do. Wrapped up in my guilt, I didn't notice at first that the pilot had been shot. When I realized he was seriously wounded, I didn't know what to do. I ran for Richie. He told me to unbuckle the pilot and get him out of the ship if he wasn't able to get himself out. I had to pull the pilot out of his seat and over my shoulder, because he was unconscious. I laid him down and then I grabbed my machine gun and then Richie's and laid them down next to the pilot. I didn't realize until the next morning that the pilot was dead.

Richie told me the company would send in a helicopter to get us out. We ended up spending the night in the LZ. So my first day ended in heavy combat. Emotionally, I went numb. All around me, I saw, heard, and felt the wounded. I had been trained as an infantryman, trained in small arms and heavy weapons, trained in first aid. But none of the training prepared me for what was happening when I was actually on the ground in heavy fighting. So I fell back on childhood experiences of playing war and cowboys and Indians, and I played well.

There was one dead and two wounded, and I decided to be quiet because I didn't know what else to do. Once you expose your position, you're vulnerable. It was just like playing cowboys and Indians in the woods, except the bullets were real.

During that time, waiting to be evacuated, I heard a lot of men, really scared, crying for their mothers or somebody, or praying. I was proud of myself. "I'm not crying, I'm not praying. Who would I pray to?" It didn't make sense to believe in God. If there was a God, how could this happen? Finally the intense fighting quieted and in the morning we were evacuated.

I went on to become a very good soldier. I received awards and decorations, and I enjoyed my job, not in the way you might enjoy a hike in the mountains, but in the sense that I felt useful and could function well. Imagine—the chaos and insanity of war was where I felt most comfortable. The vulnerable eighteen-year-old boy scared to death was gone, just like that. You can't have access to your feelings and function in a situation like that.

In Vietnam I wasn't fighting for democracy or any ideal. That died within weeks. What was left was just to be the best soldier I could be so I could help myself, and as many of the other soldiers as possible, stay alive. That was the reality.

Later I became a crew chief on helicopters. I crewed slick ships (the helicopters that carried soldiers into battle, did medical evacuations and resupplies) and gunships (helicopters that were used to provide close fire support for the soldiers on the ground). From the time I became a crew chief, nearly every day I was in combat. To get an Air Medal, you had to fly twenty-five combat missions and twenty-five combat hours. By the end of my tour, I had been awarded more than twenty-five Air Medals, which amounts to about 625 combat hours and combat missions. During those combat missions people were killed, but I never saw them as people.

I flew on many operations. On one, we were near the Duc Hua rubber plantation, which was on the Saigon River about an hour's flight north of Saigon, where the river served as a border with Cambodia. I hated flying in this area. I had been shot down twice in this vicinity and shot up numerous other times. This place was too dangerous.

Our mission was to pick up a group of "Kit Carson Scouts," Vietcong soldiers who had surrendered and then agreed to work for us as double agents. They were used to infiltrate enemy groups of all types; they would then desert and be picked up by U.S. forces at a prescribed place and time to report what they had learned. The whole concept seemed so bizarre to me. How could these men be trusted?

As we approached our pickup point, we hovered at the side of a tree line. Suddenly there was a loud sound, and I knew it wasn't good. In my peripheral vision, I saw that the helicopter next to ours was upside down and burning.

Events unfolded quickly, and somehow it seemed as if this hadn't just happened but had always been. The space around us filled with the orange-red glow of tracer rounds crackling like storm-downed electric wires. I could feel the rounds hitting the ship—thump . . . thump, thump, thump. Our pilots immediately lifted the tail of the helicopter, pointing the nose down, and rotated from side to side in a 180-degree arc, as we opened up with all of the firepower we had. We positioned ourselves between the incoming fire and the downed ship as best we could, spinning and whirling, digging into our airspace, acting like a giant mechanical badger protecting its den.

The Special Forces sergeant who was riding with us started yelling, "Get out, get out of here, get out!"

I remember turning my focus toward him while I continued to fire, yelling at him at the top of my lungs to shut up and shoot. I fired my M60 machine gun until the barrel glowed red. I stopped firing for an instant, changed the barrel, then began firing again. The pilot maneuvered our helicopter around and behind the downed ship, and I jumped out to assist the crew on board. Amazingly, they had all survived.

We beat it back to the rubber plantation, dropped off the boys, and flew back to our main base, Cu Chi, where our company maintenance facility was located. We could not operate this helicopter any longer. It was leaking fuel and hydraulics; it was out of action. We knew we were shot up, we just didn't know how badly. We didn't really want to know, or care. Indifference and terror were completely intermingled.

We flew over to the maintenance area, landed, went through the usual procedures of shutting down. Then I headed up to the hooch (barracks) to pack up my stuff because I was supposed to be leaving the country at 0800 hours the next morning. It seemed I had survived my tour of duty and it was time to rotate back to the states.

I packed up, had some beers, went to sleep, woke up, ate breakfast, and headed out to the airstrip for my last helicopter ride in Vietnam. This one took me to Bien Hoa Air Base to begin my trip home. When we landed, I grabbed my stuff and started to walk away from the helicopter. I turned around to wave good-bye or something, but the helicopter was already hovering to a position for takeoff, so I just walked over to a Quonset hut with my orders. In a blink, I was walking up a set of portable steps to board a jumbo jet to the states.

During the flight back I didn't talk to anyone. I had absolutely nothing to say. It was as though my mind was frozen, held in stasis. Conversation, unless functional, was simply not important. I didn't want to bother getting to know anyone, because then, when they rotated or were wounded or killed, there was no connection, no person to lose. This was true in Vietnam, and flying back I had even less reason to talk to anyone.

The flight went from Bien Hoa to Tokyo to Anchorage to Travis Air Force Base in California. We deplaned and boarded buses with blackened windows so that we would not be exposed to the protesters waiting outside the gate, and we were transported to Oakland Army Depot, and then to Newark, New Jersey.

At Newark Airport, I had to change planes to fly home to Pennsylvania, I vividly remember walking through the airport in uniform with all my ribbons, insignias, unit patches, and flight wings.

As I was making my way through the airport, I noticed a beautiful young girl across the transit hall looking directly at me. She began to walk toward me, and I thought she was coming to greet me, to thank me. With these thoughts running through my mind, our eyes met, and with one deft movement, she spit on me. I stood there stunned, frozen in place. Before I could move again, she turned and walked away.

I was flooded with the urge to annihilate the enemy. She had committed an act of violence against me, and she had become the enemy. Desperately confused and in unbearable, inaccessible pain, I went to the nearest bar and got drunk. And I stayed self-medicated until I checked into rehabilitation in 1983.

The war was ever-present in my thoughts. I couldn't sleep. When I tried to talk to people, they'd say, "The war is over now. Try and forget it. You survived. Now just get on with your life." But I wasn't able to. So I kept using drugs to cover my pain and loneliness, to cover my rejection, to dull the memories, to hide from the sounds, the faces, the smells that clung to me like skunk spray.

From the time I came home until a month before I went into drug and alcohol rehabilitation, I carried a gun everywhere. I didn't feel safe without a gun. I slept with a gun, ate with a gun, went to school with a gun, and kept a gun in my car. My sense of safety was completely dependent on having a gun.

One night in 1978, I found myself sitting with an unloaded shotgun under my chin, pulling the trigger—click, click, click—screaming and crying, because the pain was so overwhelming. I wanted to die—but at the same time, I didn't really want to die, I just didn't know how to live with all the suffering. I kept looking for something to fix me, to make it better, and nothing was working.

Now, twenty-three years after rehab, after quite some time in therapy, and after subsequent training as a Buddhist monk, I finally know that, first of all, we need to find ways to heal from the wounds of the endless wars that rage within us, in our families, schools, and society. The answer to this question does not rest externally. This awareness begins by being willing to recognize the conditioning that supports repeating cyclical patterns of destructive behavior and allowing ourselves to feel the powerful feelings that rise when becoming conscious of this. I had to stop running away from and denying what is uncomfortable. In this process I discovered that the truth of who we are begins to become clear and we can begin to live our own lives, not that of others' fears and expectations.

We each have our own unique path. Mine was to be born in a small town, to go through the hell of war, to exist trapped in addiction for nearly twenty years, and eventually to find peace, to find healing and transformation after a lifetime of war. This did not happen without the support and help of many people, including Vietnamese (my conditioned enemy) Buddhists. While it is true that something positive can be garnered out of the most horrifying of experiences, while I have come to a position of acceptance of this path, my path to peace, I want to be cautious that my experiences are not taken as an indirect validation of war or violence—trauma or suffering. Every day I am aware that there is something to be done, that healing is possible, and that the world can be different. That violence, hatred, and greed only lead to more violence, hatred, and greed, and that the solution is not an intellectual matter and does not exist in blaming or in being against something. I have learned that the roots of healing and transformation from the consequences of our uninformed life rests in an understanding that *violence on any level is never a solution.* So, every day I do whatever I am able to do to share the fruit of my experience with others, especially those who are still convinced that violence is the way to peace, to healing and transformation. I share the fruits of an experience that has helped me more than I can express.

I served two tours with the 5th Special Forces in Viet Nam and was assigned to MACV SOG, CCN, Forward Operations Base 4, next to Marble Mountain. I returned to Da Nang in 1994 to more fully understand the essence of the mountain in its historical, spiritual, and geological sense. Afterward, I engaged a Vietnamese scholar to translate the book *Ngu Hanh Son (Water Mountain,* one of the five element mountains) into English. This piece is an excerpt from *Marble Mountain.* After returning from Da Nang in 1995, I wrote *aNAMnesis (A Viet Nam Journal).* In addition to the novel *Marble Mountain,* I have written *Sleeping Soldiers, The Snake Pit (Death at Walter Reed),* and numerous short stories. It is with the help and encouragement of Maxine Hong Kingston, the Veterans Group, my beautiful wife, Mary, and the Richmond Men's Group, that I have organized a cohesive remembrance of war. I am blessed with three children, Elizabeth, Daniel, and Alexandra, and a grandson, Isaiah.

Marble Mountain

Icarus fell out of the sky at infinite leisure,
long after his cry had fallen . . .
slowly pinwheeling among the feeble stars
and was wrapped in a pall of smoke
which seemed to muffle him against the cold
on his journey out of heat.
—MICHAEL AYRTON,
THE MAZE MAKER

Looks like a Saturn V rocket," said Lieutenant Hiroshi Kinch, U.S. Army Reserve. He finished chiseling a field expedient stove from a C-ration can, inhaled, and admired his handiwork. He scuffed his thumb across the razorlike fins and fingered the holes at the base of the stove. He guided his K-bar knife into its sheath, which was taped upside down on the left suspender of his LBE, and snapped the strap. A grenade dangled from the D-ring below for quick access.

"Hole placement is key. Fins feed air to the C-4," said Kinch. He found the sergeant's outstretched hand. Buck Sergeant Mulligan closed his hand and felt the fins cut into his palm.

"Fine piece of work," said Sergeant Mulligan. "Where'd you learn that?"

Mulligan studied its symmetry, intricate as a swan folded from paper. "Tin-can origami," he said. He pushed the tripod into the dirt floor and nodded. He lifted a P-38 can opener from a chain around his neck and gave it the obligatory kiss, like dice before a roll. He ratcheted open a can of cheddar cheese and set it on the B-4 crackers. "Check the door, sir."

"Is that an order, sergeant?" Kinch did not move.

"Don't play games, sir," said Mulligan. "Monsoon, no moon. Charlie come very soon. I'm a poet, my feet show it. They're Longfellows."

The lieutenant's eyes slid sideways toward the bunker's forward gun port and stretched wide as he scanned the Asian darkness. Cloud-covered stars, which at sunset glittered with pinpricks of possibility, were hidden from sight. Kinch strained to memorize this reality. Nothing more than a dream, he thought, then felt a throb of pain in his right leg.

"Move out, troop," said Mulligan, "and tape that grenade to your LBE before you kill both of us."

"Yes, Sergeant." The unrelenting heat sapped Kinch like a steam-bath. Lack of sleep and food eroded his capacity to repair. Diarrhea flooded his GI tract like the muddy Mekong. He leaned closer to the aperture and scraped his cheek on a sandbag. An illumination round backlit the low-hanging clouds. They spun like a kaleidoscope.

Lieutenant Kinch leaned back, shifted his compact frame, and kneaded his thigh. His cramped legs stretched out on the dank bunker floor. He checked the luminescent dial on his Seiko watch, 0333 hours. He surveyed the surroundings. An olive-drab speaker, somewhere behind Mulligan, discharged a steady rush of squelch. A cable snaked along the parapet ledge and connected to the PRC-25 radio. Decay leaked from ripped sandbags. The smell of humus collapsed about him. His lungs labored to discharge the wet air. A hot breeze passed through the gun port that offered no relief. It bore a perfume of putrefied fish and feces from the Cua Ba River.

The Cua Ba snaked from north to south along Nha Trang's western perimeter past the rickety patchwork of bunkers. The sandbagged vaults defended 5th Special Forces Headquarters and Nha Trang Airfield. Further south along the coast, its brown effluence spread like an oil stain into the China Sea.

Under this vale of darkness Kinch did not see flowers wend through the watery maze, past his bunker, lotus petals offered to the river by grieving widows for the freshly dead ARVN soldiers. Nor did he see them pass a second time, when the current slackened. Lily stems straightened in midstream, then tilted backwards in the opposite direction, their faces lifted toward the giant white Buddha and the Bridge of Sorrow, three kilometers north at the edge of town.

Kinch detected no movement through the portal. The sleepless hours and endless watch provoked a thin vibration in his bowels. The sting of mosquitoes on his arm was a reminder to take his pills.

Kinch found two chloroquine primaquine tablets in his pants pocket. He removed a plastic canteen from his web belt and swallowed the orange horse pills with gulps of grape Kool-Aid. Moments passed. The prophylactic prodded a sharp cramp in his empty stomach. He bared his teeth and released a low dithyrambic fart.

"Put a cork in it, El-Tee," said Sergeant Mulligan. "One match and we'd go up like a drum of *fugas*." He shook his head like a dog with a burr in his snout. "Eleven months and twenty-nine days in–country and I have to put up with this shit."

Kinch stretched his arms against the sagging ceiling. Another hot gust of wind blew through the portal.

"Give me a break, El-Tee. Go up top while I fix Jane Fondue. Daybreak in a couple hours and we're all done," said Mulligan. "You go to the delta and I fly home on the big iron bird."

Kinch pretended to gather himself up. He was exhausted from tedious hours of guard duty, patrolling, and classes, interposed with cycles of fear and relief. He squeezed his arms. His biceps were flaccid.

Nightly, when not on ambush patrol, newbies like Kinch were paired with veteran boonie rats like Mulligan, troopers at the end of their tour of duty. The grizzled veterans taught the uninitiated more how to survive than to fight. The only thing Kinch fought now was sleep.

Mulligan hit the safety strap of his K-bar and the leather handgrip slid into his palm. He sawed a packet of stringy meat bartered from the mess hall cook for a fake Montagnard crossbow. He removed a brass bell from his rucksack, felt the smooth baseball curve of its bottom in the palm of his hand. Like a pitcher after the seventh–inning stretch, he eyed the lieutenant.

"Once upon a time, Nungs from A-503 provided security around Nha Trang," said Mulligan. "But they were absorbed by the projects."

"Projects?"

"Black ops. Sneak and Peek. SOG, Alpha, Omega, Delta, it's all Greek to me." Mulligan laughed. He broke off a piece of white plastique from a loaf of C-4, rolled it into a ball and dropped it midpoint between the rocket's fins. His palms glittered with flecks of nitrate.

"A regular Lenny Bruce."

"Take my life, please . . ."

"You mean wife."

"Life . . . if you don't get your ass up top and look around. I got caterpillars crawling all tingly on my neck." Mulligan flicked open a Zippo and lit the ball of plastique. He balanced the brass bowl on the circular rim of the stove as blue flame ignited like an afterburner. "We have lift off."

Kinch grabbed his rifle and duck-walked to the exit. The thought of eating caused his stomach to hitch. The door opened to a wall of corrugated tin. He shook his head and blinked to clear the cobwebs. He aimed one ear toward the perimeter. Pebbles jangled in a C-ration can that hung from razor wire.

The lieutenant stepped into the narrow trench that zigzagged toward the next bunker twenty-five meters on his left and a guard tower fifty meters to the right. He scaled the sandbagged wall to the top and sat in a makeshift lookout made of two-by-fours with a plywood roof. The ends of the rotted board splayed into thin strips that hung like fruit. Its top curved like a bowed tree.

The wind swirled as he scanned the valley; a vast array of paddies connected to the far ridgeline. A zephyr carried the delicate scent of cinnamon that drifted from Mt. Thein Thai, ten kilos west. He savored the aroma, a reprieve from the mold, wet earth, the Cua Ba, and his own stink.

Two days ago he had patrolled the mountain. Along the ridgeline the lush jungle had a sweet bouquet like Eden; at its base were stagnant pools of jungle heat that smelled of death.

"Easy, up there," called Mulligan. "Shit's falling in my fondue."

Kinch watched a flare blossom to the north of Na Trang. A bone-white statue of Buddha materialized from the dark. The three-story statue triggered a vague memory of youth. His mind could not grip the fleeting image.

He checked for movement along the river between the white fluorescent statue and the Recondo School water tower, then lowered his gaze to the defensive perimeter in front of the guard tower. To the left the bunkers curved out of sight. The red-tipped glow of a cigarette cupped in a hand lit the face of a guard.

Kinch checked his watch and listened for the high-pitched whine of a jeep as it banged along the potholed road behind him. Security patrol was late. He searched the road that curled north like a question mark behind the guard tower but saw nothing.

A second wind, laden with the smell of incense from the Van Gia Forest, found his nose. It was driven harder now by a ragged curtain of thermals that loomed like Everest on the horizon. The thunderheads were further fueled by heated air that rose from jungles and flooded paddies. A sheet of lightning spread its thin fingers across the sky. Cool air from the China Sea brushed Kinch's neck and sent a chill down his spine.

Kinch lowered his eyes and scanned the base of the guard tower and the glint of razor wire. Something moved at its base—a guard taking a piss?

Kinch swiveled on his haunches and faced the airstrip. Helicopter gunships lined the cement runways, their sharklike profiles with sleek metallic dorsal fins extended from the sandbagged revetments. Rotor blades, thin black brims, were tethered to tapered tail booms. Lead pipes, twenty-millimeter gun barrels, extended from their noses. Along the sandy apron, fuel bladders of JP-4 collapsed like stranded whales. Nothing stirred except the wind, now gathering its nightly head of steam.

Kinch slid down the sandbags and into the trench. "No sign of the jeep," he said, stepping through the bunker door. He failed to judge the height of the steel header and clipped the top of his skull.

"God!" said Kinch. He dropped his weapon, cradled his head and fell forward into the dirt. The blow set off a sprinkle of flashbulbs behind his eyes. Kinch locked his jaw and growled through his teeth.

"That's using your head," said Mulligan. A machine gun further down the line fired a burst of rounds. Mulligan looked out the portal.

A lazy stream of tracers arced over the river and was swallowed by blackness.

Kinch lay fetaled, covered his head with both hands, and squeezed. The distant sound of machine-gun fire filtered through the portal with smooth refrain. *Tat-tat-tat-tat-tat.* Each burst of sound crossed the Cua Ba, the valley, then bounced off the distant mountains. As the echoes returned, they collided with each new report. The sound became garbled like a 45 record switched to 33. *Tat-hag-at-ag-ar-bra.* The odd sputter of sounds matched the throb in his head.

"Trigger-happy fools," said Mulligan.

Kinch lifted his left leg like a dog and let slip a rancid burp.

"Sweet Jesus." Mulligan gagged, untied a cravat from around his neck, and held his breath. He shined a red-filtered flashlight on the bloody hole on the lieutenant's crown.

"Should have guessed," said Mulligan. "Empty as a five-gallon jerry can."

He fit the flap of hair and meat into the hole. Mulligan stretched the cravat beneath the lieutenant's jaw and cinched the sod in place with a square knot. The ends stood out like rabbit ears. Mulligan inspected his handiwork. He retrieved a canteen and two Darvon from his aid kit. "Take two and call someone in the morning that gives a shit." Kinch rose to his knees and braced against the wall.

Pain spiked through his head. He popped the pills to the back of his throat and drank. His eyelids grew weighted. Blood trickled down his forehead into his eyes. He blinked and wiped it away. Tomorrow he graduated COC, Special Forces In-Country Combat Orientation Course. Graduated from the two-week cycle of PT, indoctrination, guard duty, and ambush patrols. A certified COC.

"Glad it's your last night," said Mulligan. "Any better trained and they'd send you home in a body bag." He studied the lieutenant's outline, coughed a wad of phlegm into his fist and wiped it on his pants. He checked the stove, then dumped the leathery meat onto a crinkled swatch of tin foil. He spooned the cheddar cheese into the bowl. "Good shit."

Kinch returned the gaze. Even after two weeks it still felt awkward. He outranked the sergeant, yet Mulligan was in charge. If anything went wrong the buck sergeant, six years in SF and three tours in

Vietnam, would take the hit. A trickle of blood eased across the lieutenant's lips and dripped from his chin. A stain shaped like Florida grew on his T-shirt.

"No time, no time . . . I got, got, got, got, got, no time," sang Mulligan as he placed another marble of plastique between the fins and lit it.

"I'm so short," said Mulligan, "I can walk under doors." He licked the melted cheese from his K-bar.

"Sixty-two, sixty-four, we did good work," said Mulligan, "but after Tet, the bombing halt, Paris Peace Talks . . . just do the time, El-Tee." He speared a piece of meat and dipped it into the bowl of bubbling cheese. "Nothing like munching on Jane Fondue, if you get my drift."

"Going home to little mama and the princess," said Mulligan. "Sell in-showance for her daddy, race dirt track on weekends."

"Give up all this?"

Mulligan dipped another piece of meat into the melted cheese. He leaned attentively toward the side portal and listened. The distant drone of a twin-engine plane drifted into the bunker.

"Spooky," he said, "C-47." Mulligan distinguished sounds of war like a bird watcher listening to a rare call. Kinch was a quick study. He knew the difference between an eighty-one and four-deuce mortar, a 105 Howitzer and a 155. He knew the metallic "chunk" of the Russian Dsh K38 heavy machine gun from the .50 caliber, and the "pop" of an AK-47 from the "crack" of the SKS assault rifle.

Mulligan pulled the radio from the ledge below the front portal. He cocked his ear like a thief cracking a safe. His bony fingers spun the dial. The sound of lumbering aircraft engines faded to a muted hum.

"Somebody holed up in the Dien Khanh Wall. Probably trainees from Recondo School," said Mulligan. "Nothing but four walls and four doors. Charlie been using it for a thousand years."

Kinch turned toward the forward gun port as a string of flares lit the mantle of clouds at the far end of the valley. Green tracers rose toward the invisible plane that circled the embattled team.

"Mighty low ceiling for Spooky," said Mulligan. "Somebody's ass is in a crack."

Kinch checked his watch, 0354, then looked back at the portal, a

TV screen of sorts. A waterfall of red tracers poured from the apex of the invisible plane. The rounds hit the ground and corkscrewed skyward like sparks from a blast furnace.

"Got it," said Mulligan, as he found Spooky's radio frequency. He turned up the volume.

The shrill sound of Gatling guns bore into Kinch like a dentist's drill.

"Panther Six, this is Spooky, over," said the pilot.

"This is Panther, over," said the recon team leader.

"Sit-rep, over," said Spooky. The crackle of ground fire filtered through the speaker.

"One Whiskey-India-Alpha, two Kilo-India-Alpha. Surrounded and taking heavy small arms fire, over," said the RTO.

"Roger, I copy. I'll be acting as forward air-control. Fast movers inbound, do you copy?"

"Roger."

"Whiskey X-ray closing in. Don't know how long I can stay on station, over."

"Roger."

"Sure you don't want any Fondue?" said Mulligan. "Sorry you didn't taste my Rat Roulade or Barbecue Bunker Beef." He looked down the valley.

"Some Recondo team gettin' their ass chewed," said Mulligan. "LuRP. Stands for Low Retention Probability. Same old program. Put them in, take 'em out from the same LZs. Comes a point when Charlie sets his watch by what we do."

Kinch drifted into a dull reverie. The night sounds faded. He saw a sign with a slogan that hung over the hanger at Fryer Field, Fort Benning. "Through these doors pass the best-trained fighting men in the world." Was that true? Was he better trained than NVA soldiers? How did he measure up against the enemy, his peers, and most of all, against his father?

At the infantry school, Kinch and his roommate Matt Wolf excelled in night tactics: patrol and ambush. He learned to use the night. The TAC officer dubbed Wolf and him Nightwalkers. Here in Viet Nam he did not relish defending a static position.

Kinch winced as he remembered his first night in-country at the 90th Repo Depot.

Kinch wedged himself into The Club, at Long Binh, nothing more than a double-wide trailer, doors flung wide open at each end, men packed six deep. He braced his elbows against the plywood bar and locked his legs. He studied the plywood counter and metal bookshelves stacked beneath a wall mirror. He stared at his reflection. His lip was covered with dried ice cream. What would the specialist who handed him the cone say to his son when asked, "What did you do in the war, Daddy?"

Kinch feigned a cough and wiped off the mustache. His black, stubbled hair was even as a brush. His almond eyes and dark eyebrows hinted at his ancestry, yet high cheekbones and hazel eyes suggested the odd splice of DNA, east meets west. His compact torso was disproportionate to his long arms and legs. The reflection was curious, like a trick mirror at the carnival.

Kinch sucked on a can of tepid beer. His neck and shoulders were smaller than during his football days at Virginia Tech. He would start an exercise regimen when he arrived at his permanent station.

Kinch braced his shoulder against an unshaven soldier in soiled fatigues that smelled like urine. As he glanced at the mirror, he spotted a raw-boned major barking commands at the bartender. The weathered officer wore a Screaming Eagle shoulder patch. Kinch studied his image. He calculated how his voice would reach the major: angle of incidence equals angle of reflection. His mind formulated the equation as he calibrated the distance. Kinch yelled at the major's smoky reflection, then waved his hand. The sergeant beside him turned.

"I thee oou," said the grunt. He waved a limp wrist. The grunt laughed, turned to his buddies and continued talking. Kinch ignored him.

"Lieutenant Matt Wolf," yelled Kinch. Perhaps the major knew his friend. The sunburned officer found Kinch's reflection in the mirror.

"Do you know a Lieutenant Matt Wolf?" asked Kinch. He formed his lips precisely like speaking to the deaf.

"Dead," said the major. He looked down at his beer. "Dead three weeks."

"Dead?"

The grunt sergeant turned and looked hard at Kinch. He glanced down the bar at the crowd. He could not see the major. The grunt stared at the lieutenant, shook his head, and turned around. Kinch found the major's sunken eyes.

"Turd?"

"That's it, the turd rule," said Mulligan. He gulped a deep breath and felt beneath his arm. "Some captain will come at first light and want to know what happened. He doesn't really want to know what happened. Uncle Sam wants a goat. That's why they made you an officer." His face slackened and he winced as he gripped his side.

"What happened?"

Mulligan scanned the perimeter, "Charlie's long gone." He moved inside the bunker and sat. Kinch got to his knees and crawled through the door on all fours. He leaned back against the bunker wall.

"You hear anything when the illum 'popped' and lights came on? Whispers, sweet like a blues number?" said Mulligan.

"What?"

"People hear things is all I'm saying."

"Music?"

"Couldn't say." Mulligan held up a bent metal flange as light from a flare streamed through the gun port. "It's a copper counterweight from a four-duce illumination round." He tossed the heavy metal disc like a Frisbee. It hit Kinch in the chest with a hollow thud.

"You know time's up when you hear it," said Mulligan. "I remember one night we got hit in our R-O-N. Found a Montagnard striker the next morning, head hanging to one side. Dead as a rooster ready for pickin'." Mulligan shook his head and coughed. "Lotta ways you can die in this country. Trouble is, just when you think you've seen everything…goddamn if they don't come up with another way to kill you."

"You all right?" said Kinch.

"Two days and a duffle bag drag. Two fucking days." He removed his hand from beneath his armpit. His fingers were wet and sticky. "Like a tuning fork, you hear? Time's up."

Kinch pressed the gauze between his eyes and juggled the copper counterweight in his right hand. He lay back. The cool, damp dirt pressed against him. Light from a flare poured into the bunker. Dust, suspended like fine talcum, reflected the light and split the room in two, atoms dancing. Kinch removed the K-bar from his sheath and held the cold blade to his lip. He grew tired and stabbed it into the dirt like an aiming stake. A sharp pain split his skull. Chatter from the base net spilled from the radio.

"Bees," said Mulligan, "buzzing round the hive and NO-body to

"Bad way to die," said the major. He slammed an empty can on the bar and signaled the bartender to hit him again. "Took a round here." The major tapped his middle finger on the center of his forehead, leaving a white spot between his eyes. He paid the bartender and drank. "Friendly fire."

The major's voice lowered. Kinch leaned forward to hear and pushed into the grunt's back.

"He set out an L-P and got turned around. Didn't come back through the same spot in the perimeter. Poor execution, end of story." The major nodded. "Always that 10 percent that don't get the word."

Kinch closed his eyes and saw Wolf's head recoil from the sleek copper jacketed 5.56 round that bore a pencil-size hole between the eyes, tumble erratically, collect into a ball of soft brain tissue, and explode like a water balloon out the back of his head.

"God," said Kinch.

"You talking to me?" said Grunt, as he turned.

Kinch opened his eyes and pointed toward the mirror. The major was gone.

"You'd better get a grip, Lieutenant," said the Grunt. He turned back to his comrades. "Goddamn newbie already talking to himself."

Kinch snapped awake. A machine gun fired a long burst from the adjacent bunker. Mulligan quickly scrambled to reset the radio frequency to Base Net. A siren gave a long low lament that grew into a caterwaul.

"Show time, El-Tee!" said Mulligan. "Gooks in the wire." Kinch anticipated Mulligan's next order and moved toward the door.

"Check the airfield," said Mulligan. "If it moves, fire. We'll sort it out later."

Kinch stepped into the trench and caught movement next to a revetment across the field. An explosion split the air and lit the tarmac. He ducked as debris from a second and third blast swept over him. The lieutenant raised his head slowly above the wall. He scanned the open ground. Black-clad figures ran from one revetment to another, ahead of the explosions. The sappers slid satchel charges into the steel cocoons. *Ka-Rump! Ka-Rump!* The blasts shattered the sleeping sharks.

Illumination lit the adjacent tower. Kinch shielded his eyes with his hand. On the road sat the patrol jeep, its driver slumped at the wheel. There was no sign of the gunner.

The black-clad figures walked upright together, their hands swinging by their sides, as though out for an evening stroll. Light reflected from their shaved heads.

"Monks on the apron?" said Kinch, haltingly. He blinked, and they were gone. He adjusted the blood-soaked cravat on top of his skull and realized he'd forgotten his hat.

"Why doesn't the tower fire?" Mulligan jacked back the operating handle of the M-60 machine gun and chambered a round.

Kinch shouldered his rifle and hit the safety switch. He looked away from the burning aircraft and eyed the trench and bunkers down the line. A runaway machine gun sprayed the paddies with tracers.

"They've got an exfil point around here somewhere!" said Mulligan. He keyed the handset. "This is Bravo, two, two. Request two rounds of Whiskey-Lima, over." He waited.

"Shot over," said the radio.

"Shot out," said Mulligan as he heard the hollow *K-thunk, K-thunk* from the distant mortar pit. "Illumination on the way!"

Kinch sighted down his barrel as two illumination rounds popped above him. *Ploop, Ploop.* He looked skyward.

"If it moves, fire," yelled Mulligan.

Kinch looked into a blaze of white light, then down. Too late. His rods were fried. Shadows danced at the corner of his eyes.

Kinch lifted his hand to his forehead and made a brim. His rabbit ears stood erect. He leaned forward and searched for movement, like Custer's scout. He shifted his eyes left to right. Ghostly images trailed wherever he looked.

Kinch heard a fluttery moan above. He steadied the M-16 rifle on a sandbag. He pressed his cheek against the butt of the rifle and formed a good spot weld. He waited for the pop-up target. Fire center mass, he told himself.

Secondary explosions cooked off from the intense heat of the burning choppers. The hollow twirl of metal, melodic like an Andean flute, grew louder. Shadow blended with shadow as they crossed the road behind the guard tower. Kinch blinked and rubbed his watery eyes. They wore black smocks like the monks he'd seen at the giant white Buddha. He could not make out any weapons.

"Monks behind the tower!" The whirling sound grew louder.

"Fire," yelled Mulligan.

"Monks!" said Kinch, straining to make sure.

"Shoot, El-Tee!"

Kinch aimed his rifle as a metallic hum filled his ears. He felt the tension of his finger against the trigger and was aroused by a warm vibration that spread to his crotch. A metal band sliced past him and hit the wall with a slap-thud, then ricocheted violently as he raised his head. It struck Kinch square between the eyes. He heard the hollow clunk of something dense like a lead pipe striking a barrel, saw a brilliant flash, then all went dark.

Kinch awoke and looked up. Mulligan stood spread-eagle over him and squeezed off controlled bursts from the M-16 rifle. Kinch lifted his head and wiped blood from a gash between his eyes.

Green tracers flashed past like lasers and slammed into the wall beside his head. Mulligan crouched and returned fire at the tower. "The fucking tower!"

Mulligan hit the eject button. An empty ammo clip fell from its chamber toward the lieutenant's face and struck his mouth. Kinch heard the sound of cracking ice, then blacked out.

Kinch felt the smack of Mulligan's hand against the side of his face. He opened his eyes. A pink snake licked at his swollen lip, then disappeared behind his clotted teeth. His front tooth felt ragged, like a band saw.

Mulligan looked down and smiled. "You all right, El-Tee?"

"Jesus."

Mulligan pulled a field dressing from the lieutenant's first aid pouch on his LBE. He propped a sandbag behind the lieutenant's head and pressed a gauze pad on the deep laceration between his eyes.

"You are one snake-bit trooper," said Mulligan.

Kinch reached into his shirt and felt for his chain and the familiar shape of a cross. He retrieved it and then kissed it.

"Lay still," said Mulligan as he wrapped the lieutenant's head. "First rule. If you see the Buddha, kill him."

"Yeth, sergeant" said Kinch. He tentatively touched the balloon lip with a finger.

"Second. React, don't think. You kill some gook in a firefight that wasn't in the right spot, *xin loi*, motherfucker," said Mulligan. "Better to have twelve men try you than six men plant you. Understand?"

"Third," said Mulligan. "Shit flows downhill."

sting." Mulligan grunted and changed the radio frequency. He looked through the portal down the valley. "Spooky's still working those LuRPs at the wall."

Kinch looked through the front aperture. A stream of tracers fell from an invisible point on the horizon, an angel with Gatling guns. He smiled. Spooky talked calmly to Black Cat One-Seven, flight leader of the inbound F-4's.

"Roger, Black Cat, I have you inbound," said Spooky.

"Spooky's mic must be keyed open," said Mulligan. He fumbled in his medical kit and removed a gauze bandage. He opened his shirt and stuffed it under his arm.

"Roger, Black Cat, I have friendlies in the pagoda," said Spooky.

"It ain't a pagoda," said Mulligan. "Those Recondo School trainees survive tonight and they'll be on the first available to one of the projects in the morning."

"Roger, Black Cat, friendlies in the pagoda. Do NOT hit the pagoda," said Spooky.

"You're lucky you're going to the delta, El-Tee," said Mulligan. "Nothing like a happy ending." "Cavalry arrives in the nick of time." He coughed hard and spit a plug.

A scream broke from the radio, "Abort! Abort!" said Spooky. The horizon lit with the glow of orange. The boiling flame licked at the low-hanging clouds.

"Abort, Black Cat, abort!" said Spooky. "You hit the pagoda! I say again, you hit the fucking pagoda!"

Mulligan changed the radio frequency back to base net and slumped against the wall. "Friendly fire."

"Friends like that...," said Kinch. "Who needs enemies?"

I was born in Whitefish, Montana, entered the U.S. Air Force in 1964, served in Vietnam from November 1967 to September 1968, and was awarded the Air Force Commendation Medal. I left the military in 1968 as one of only two men in the Air Force in Vietnam to reach the rank of staff sergeant (E5) with fewer than four years of service.

I entered the University of Montana ten days after returning from Vietnam and within a month assaulted and almost killed an anti-draft protester. This was the first indication of my PTSD, although it took more than twenty years to diagnose it. I started treatment at the local vet center in 1988.

I obtained an M.B.A. from the University of Oregon, and spent thirty years working as a forestry consultant and real estate broker. Then I went from this successful career to becoming an alcoholic, a drug user, and came within three days of homelessness due in a large part to PTSD. Family, writing, Native American spirituality, and friends have helped me to come to terms with my Vietnam experience.

I returned to Vietnam in May 2006 and came home knowing I left "my" war behind. Following my return, I attended the first Native American ceremony during which I was completely free of any of my Vietnam "shit." I have been clean and sober since 1997 and currently do some freelance writing and photography. I've been published by Harley-Davidson, *Easyriders,* and *Biker Magazine.*

from *To Touch*

A Vietnam War Medic's Diary

Sunday, November 8, 1992

My journey to the Vietnam Veterans Memorial began Thanksgiving Day 1967, when I departed for Vietnam. I had no idea then how thoroughly the war would affect the rest of my life.

I visited the Wall for the first time on its tenth anniversary, which was also the day of groundbreaking for the Vietnam Women's Memorial. Although I'd served in Vietnam with nurses, I'd more or less forgotten about them, and I wanted to be there to apologize for my forgetfulness. To symbolize that this trip was a new start for me, I bought all new clothes—shirts, jeans, shoes, socks, and even under-wear.

We arrived in D.C. without problems and were bussed to our hotel. As I physically became closer to the Wall, I noticed that my own walls—my "medic shield"—were going up to protect me from what I might feel. I kept busy being outgoing, helping others, taking pictures, doing whatever I could to block out my feelings and keep from facing what would inevitably be ahead of me.

In 1992, the Native American veterans were going to lead the Veterans Day parade to honor their military contributions. As part of this honoring, a Native American pow-wow was scheduled the evening we arrived and I wanted to attend because, according to my mother, I am part Cherokee and Choctaw. Chris and Rick, a couple I'd just met, also wanted to attend, and they accompanied me to the pow-wow, where the Vietnam veterans were honored by dances and tobacco. Here, I started to feel at home, not totally but more than anyplace else.

I had resolved that when I reached Washington, D. C., and the Wall, I wasn't going to put anything off or be tentative. I'd always wanted a neck choker, and a Native American Vietnam veteran was selling them at the pow-wow. I looked at them and selected one but decided not to buy it right away.

As the pow-wow progressed, I decided to go ahead and buy the choker, because I didn't want to look back and say, "Gee, I wish . . ." as I have for so long with my other Vietnam experiences. Attending the pow-wow with the dancing and buying the choker started me on a path toward my spiritual healing, connecting me to my Native American heritage.

After the pow-wow, Chris, Rick, and I went looking for a place to eat and stumbled onto a really good Chinese restaurant. Other veterans, as well as a couple of volunteers who help at the Wall each Veterans Day, were having dinner there, and they recognized that we were veterans by the pins and other items we were wearing. The volunteers told us that in honor of the tenth anniversary of the Wall, all 58,000-plus names were going to be read. I mentioned I wanted to read some names but all the time slots were taken, and one of the volunteers offered to share some of the names she was going to read.

After dinner, Rick and Chris decided to walk to the Wall and asked if I wanted to go. I really didn't want to go to the Wall this early in my visit, but I also did not want to go there by myself the very first time. They said if I didn't want to go they would understand, but I said yes, I would try. As we were walking toward the Wall, I put up my "photographer's shield," taking pictures to protect myself, hiding behind the lens, seeing the Wall as a photograph, looking at it in any way but what it is and what it represents.

My first sight of the Wall was through the trees bordering it. The Wall was lit in an unreal sort of way, and I couldn't walk any closer. I just stopped and started to cry, shaking so much I couldn't even stand. So I sat on a bench, and then I got up and began walking toward the Wall again. Chris and Rick said I didn't need to go any closer, but I *needed* to. Little by little, I walked closer, stopping and starting, crying as I went.

As I viewed the Wall, I saw solders—grunts—emerging from it. Their spirits were walking toward me. They wanted to ask why I left them, why I didn't just tell my commander, Fuck you! and fly the Army gunship missions that might have saved their lives, why did I stay in my "safe" dispensary while they boarded the helicopters and were getting shot up in ambushes and firefights. Those ghosts wanted to ask why I couldn't or wouldn't help them. A fellow Air Force medic and friend, Mac, was one of them. He'd received a head wound the day he was going home, and I couldn't help him. I let him die and now I saw him. God, what your fears will do to you. "Fuck," I kept saying, but the men kept walking out from the Wall.

I saw the statues of the three soldiers and they were real men but not whole. One had a chest wound, black and sucking; another one's intestines lay open. Parts of their bodies were gone—an arm wasn't there, just the bone, muscle, and tissue. Blood was flowing down their muscles, tracing their veins in the bronze and then dripping off their arms and fists, black and sticky. I saw the blood clearly—it was black, not red; "old" blood, not fresh. I wanted to touch it to see if it was real, but I was afraid it might be. I couldn't have that blood on me again, the blood of the men I didn't help.

In Vietnam, when I lay on my bed in the barracks, I thought of the men who were in the field without medics. I watched them from across the road as they boarded the helicopters and I wondered: Do they have a medic? If they don't, shouldn't I go? As I sat in my base, safe and secure, I saw the blood of those who lay out in the field, and those in the black rubber bags in the morgue next to our clinic at Ton Son Nhut. I had watched the Graves Registration men washing the blood from those bags with hoses, and the blood was always black. That scene and that smell were still with me. I still haven't washed that blood off my hands or out of my soul. I didn't need more of it, not now. Christ, not now.

I saw the pain in the faces on these bronze soldiers, the same pain I'd seen in the emergency ward at the base during Tet of '68 and sometimes on the wards and sometimes in my imagination and dreams. God, please let me run away from here. The memories are too real, my guilt too overpowering. I hear their screams: "Mamma!" "Am I going to be all right?!" "God! It hurts!" "Jesus, man, the pain! Give me something for the pain, Doc, please!" I heard these words—not in the field, not in the wards, not at the terminal when the rocket hit—but as I lay in my bed on the base safe and secure, and in my thoughts and dreams. I heard them when I came home and started to think about what I could and should have done. I heard them in my bed at college, alone in the dorm. A car backfired, and I huddled in a fetal position on my bed, scared because I had no weapon, guilty because I was home, because I wanted to live and be safe while they were over there dying without the medic who could have saved them.

———

Rick and Chris kept close to me, letting me move at my own pace. They asked if I wanted to go back. "No," I said. I needed to see if the people walking in front of the Wall were real or if they were ghosts coming out of the Wall. When you are afraid of facing something, your legs are weak and your feet move like lead. But your mind keeps you going; you know what to do.

I walked closer, and then I couldn't go any further. I just knelt there and cried, not the deep cry I needed, but a cry of relief. I had faced one of my deepest fears and made it. It was a cry of, *Look at me. I am hurting. I am the veteran. I need your help. I need your acceptance.* When I looked more closely, I saw that the men were not coming out of the Wall. They were real men and women, themselves looking at the Wall. I was crying out of relief that I'd finally made it here, past my fears and my own personal wall, but not out of grief. I was also crying for help. Right there, on the Wall, were my fears, my pain, my sadness, my guilt. The coldness of my fears sent a shiver though my very being.

———

Chris and Rick came back several times to check on me. They touched me and asked if I was all right. They said that everything is okay and I will be all right. Several people touched me that night and some hugged me. It was a good touch, an "I know what you are feeling and I care about you" touch. Not the complete healing touch I needed, but a good touch.

I wanted to walk the rest of the way down to the Wall to look for the names of three other medics I knew, so I put up the medic shield to protect myself. I soon found two of their names, but not the third.

———

It was nearly midnight when Ruth, the volunteer who'd agreed to share her names with me, took me to an area where other readers were rehearsing—to be sure they pronounced the names correctly, with feeling and respect. At the Wall, some were reading without breaking down. Others couldn't. Some even read the names of their own relatives and friends.

President Bush came and read some names. I wonder why presidents generally are afraid of being here openly, sending their vice president instead. Perhaps it's the shame of having left our men behind.

The volunteer and I finally read our names at 0145. I started in "medic mode," shutting off my feelings, but by the second page, I started to cry, for them and also for me. I needed to be seen and helped and comforted. I needed respect and acceptance, to know that what I did and didn't do in Vietnam was all right. I walked Ruth back to her room and got to bed at four in the morning. I don't know what time sleep actually came.

Reflections

At the end of our week in D.C., I told Rick and Chris that our meeting hadn't been an accident. I had actually picked them out, because I didn't want to face this alone. They understood. Along the way since 1992 I have also made my amends to the women veterans of the Vietnam War, the nurses and the Red Cross volunteers.

My journey along the Red Road of Native American spirituality started in 1992 when I marched with the Navajo veterans, and later in 1993 with the Walk of the Warriors. While at their campsite, I received my first traditional Navajo healing. I have continued to follow the Red Road and heal in the Native American way. Sometimes, I feel good about my spirituality; at other times, I struggle.

My Navajo friends are much more accepting of my feelings than I am. I have been told many times by Navajos and other Native Americans that as long as your heart walks the Red Road, the color of your skin is not important. I am working more on following the Red Road and not worrying about exact details of my ancestry.

Some veterans may not be able to physically reach the Wall, and they stop at the line of trees I spoke of. During one visit, I was able to help a veteran who was standing there reach the Wall. He was ready to go but he didn't want to do it alone. By having a "medic" with him, he wasn't. Later in our conversations, he laughed and called himself a "Tree Vet." I listened and then shared some of my own turmoil.

I explained to him my ritual for leaving the Wall. I would touch the wrist of the grunt whose blood was flowing to reassure myself that the blood wasn't real, and then I would walk along the front of the Wall. I asked if he would like to join me, and after some thought, he said yes. We started to walk together. I kept a short distance away, so he could have his own time at the Wall. He stood there crying while touching the Wall. When he'd collected himself, I went to talk to him and he started to cry again so I held him until he quit. Then I asked if he had made his peace, and he said "Yes," so we walked up the sidewalk and he went on his way.

After he left, I went back to the Wall and spent some time reaffirming my commitment to myself. My name isn't on that Wall because I failed to put myself at risk when my help was needed. After a couple of hours, crying a little and working on self-reassurance, I left.

The night before the Wall was first dedicated in 1982, a veteran came to it and committed suicide. Now the veterans and volunteers at the Wall want to make sure that doesn't happen again. So, on Veterans Day and Memorial Day, there is someone at the Wall at all hours to be sure no one is alone. When you are at the Wall, even when you aren't accompanied by anyone, you know you are not alone. Someone is there watching over you. Some of the volunteers at the Wall are Vietnam veterans, but others are just people with a heartfelt desire to help.

When you go to the Wall with all that pain, you are very vulnerable, and when your need for being there is met, that memory becomes a significant part of your life. When I tell the people I've met at the Wall how much they've meant to me, they are surprised. It has been the same for me; when someone tells me how much I helped him, I find it hard to believe. When I help someone heal, there is a feeling of deep satisfaction and peace within me. But until I healed myself, there was no real fulfillment giving this help. Now, with the bulk of my healing completed, there is fulfillment.

To help other veterans, I sometimes use traditional Native American prayers. At other times, it's just hugs and listening. I used to seek out those in emotional need but now I wait for them to ask.

My Navajo friends spent a lot of time teaching me about healing prayers and how and when to perform them. They told me not to go to the rescue but to wait for the person to ask for help, unless he is immediately hurting and needs help. Medicine people from other nations have also given me their blessings to do prayers in this same manner. I have never represented myself as a medicine man. I just offer prayers from me for them.

Many veterans who return from Vietnam feel they didn't do enough. It doesn't matter if you are a combat veteran, a rear echelon one, a nurse, or a Red Cross worker. We always feel we could have done more—we could have saved one more life, flown one more mission, done one more patrol, held one more hand, stayed one more day, worked one more hour, and if we had, maybe there would be one less name on the Wall. Inside of each of us is that "one more name because we didn't," and we carry that name with us our whole lives.

Even Medal of Honor recipients have to resolve the same issues the rest of us are dealing with—guilt, anger, pain. They are just us with the added responsibility of being a "hero." To some, this responsibility is more than they can deal with. If you ever hear the barroom bravado of a Vietnam vet, knowing that what he's saying isn't true, he is probably driven by his shame. I know I was when my "stories" were better.

I visited the Wall as part of my healing and wrote the diary to explain the visit to my family. I wrote with my raw feelings, being as honest as

I could, and the writing itself evolved into an emotional catharsis. For the next thirteen years, I returned to each day's entry and noted how an event or emotion was being resolved in the present. Writing this way has been an important part of my path toward healing PTSD. Over the years, I have come to peace in large part thanks to the writing of this diary.

Even more significant has been the way the diary has helped my ex-wife and my children understand me. My wife divorced me after twenty-five years, directly due to my Vietnam "stuff," and my kids were certainly embarrassed by my behavior at times. Since then, my ex-wife has read the complete diary and we have become closer than ever before.

My kids also read parts of it, but the main thing that helped us was visiting the Wall together. After spending a week with me there, meeting many of my friends, my eighteen-year-old daughter gave me a big hug and said, "Dad, you're not so weird after all. Everyone here is like you." I just held her and cried.

I was born in 1946, in Würzburg, Germany. After graduating high school in Montana, I joined the Army and did a tour in Vietnam 1966 to 1967, as a recon and rifle company medic with the 1st Infantry Division.

I remember suggesting to a friend's father (a Mormon elder) over a convivial family dinner, but in a pugnacious way given to untactful youth, that Christ's death "wasn't so significant in the way of pain and suffering considering the Resurrection." He asked me to explain myself. I told him an embellished tale of a soldier dying on the Cambodian border. He stood up at the table and screamed at me, "Get thee behind me, Satan!" This also meant, "Get the hell out of my house."

I went back to Vietnam in 1994 and poked around Tan Son Nhut Airport and the location of the old MACV compound. I knew that the American mortuary was located in the MACV compound and realized that an autopsy was a more convivial way to say that some young soldiers' sacrifices are so great in pain and suffering that they are Christs. I think my feelings all through the war, and after, about the conflict between religion and war put the Christian tale of the Crucifixion up as fair game to be mocked, or challenged.

Saigon Passional

Then to the third—a face nor child
nor old, very calm, as of
Beautiful yellow-white ivory;
Young man I think I know you—
I think this face is the face
Of the Christ himself,
Dead and divine and brother of all,
and here again he lies.
—"A SIGHT IN CAMP IN THE DAYBREAK
GRAY AND DIM," WALT WHITMAN

The United States Army mortuary was encompassed by a slat-and-beam fence and housed in the sprawling Personnel Property Depot, USA Support Command, Saigon, erected by Raymond International and Morrison-Knudsen. It stood at the southeast end of Tan Son Nhut Air Base and away from the larger MACV annex. The mortuary was built of wood and corrugated tin finished in Arctic green and double-thick insulation with a gray ventilation weasand running the length of the roof, rising above eaves level. Hooded air-conditioning vents poked from ducts like the communication funnels of a large merchant ship.

Entering the mortuary at Area A from the 80 percent humidity of Saigon, Myrtle Jones was burnt by a freezing wind. Area A was a refrigeration unit cooling more than a hundred bodies awaiting transportation back to the U.S. She walked from the refrigeration unit into the embalming chamber scattered with ten embalming tables and then entered the abdomen of the building: an atrium of wall shelves holding newly embalmed bodies on general support litters. The bodies glowed from a sheen of hexaphene MA37 recently applied in preserving cocoons. The graveyard shift had all but disappeared to morning chow and the bunk.

She entered the WDMET area where wounds data indicating munitions effectiveness was collected and saw the body on the solitary pathology table in the center of the room. A calendar featuring Bireley's orange pop, "A Drink for Good Health and New Vitality," was pinned to the far wall. The odor of hexaphene and formaldehyde cloyed.

Picking up and reading from a collection of field reports, eyewitness statements, and operation records in an ochre file folder, Myrtle saw that the body on the porcelain pathology table belonged to the former Cooper, Felix A., Sergeant. The body had been flown by Caribou from the mortuary collection point at Quon Loi on the Cambodian border. Three hours earlier, under the cover of darkness, the plane had taxied down one of the northeast runways of Tan Son Nhut barely a thousand meters from the entrance to the mortuary off Quang Trung Road. Myrtle looked at the face of the Seiko watch on her left wrist. The hands showed 0845 hours.

An olive-drab body bag with one carrying handle exposed was unzipped, folded back on the floor, and propped against a duralumin leg of the mortuary table. It looked like the abused leaf of a giant

Moses-in-the-Cradle plant: dark green on the topside, dark purple on the underside. A large piece of masking tape marked HOLD FOR POST hung from the zipper closure. The chilled room was redolent with the sweet, nasty smell of brackish waters of the Saigon River pushed in by opening and closing doors shunting cooled air out.

Myrtle looked momentarily to the east window, where the river, unseen for the seven-foot slat fence, meandered a scant distance away in its sluggish progress northward to Bien Hoa. Mortuary supplies and equipment lined the east wall of the WDMET area in metal-shelved inventory: fifteen-gallon drums of embalming fluid (cavity and arterial), dermasurgery wax in one-pound cans, gooseneck embalming tubes (brass and steel), hardening compound in five-gallon metal pails, injector and embalming needles, trocars of varying lengths, replacement mortuary headrests of molded semihard rubber fabrication and an electric portable sealer. A vertical mirror measuring three by six feet with a wood veneer frame was fastened by punched tin brackets to a shelf post of the supply case directly across from the pathology table.

Myrtle walked to it and, standing on tiptoes, reached to the top shelf to turn on a small, brown radio dialed to 99.9 FM, Armed Forces Radio Vietnam. Stepping back, Myrtle looked at her reflection in the mirror, luminous on the edges from the ceiling arc of a 1,000-watt floodlight jerry-rigged above the table. She lifted her right hand to her short auburn hair, running her plain-nailed fingers gently from front to back, returning with middle finger to her lips. She wiped with downward pull a discernment of sun-shimmering Max Factor UltraLucent Crème Iridescent lipstick in California Coral from the left corner of her mouth.

She turned ten degrees to her left and lifted the right heel of her Panama-soled tropical boot, posing her right knee in front of her left, her hands pushing her hair up from the back of her neck. Her short hair corresponded with a regulation that required it be neat and well groomed yet not extend below the bottom edge of the collar nor be cut so short as to present an unfeminine appearance. The corpse materialized under her absent gaze. She saw that it had already begun swelling, characteristic of the decomposition occurring so quickly with too long exposure to the noonday sun in Vietnam—already the surprising odor of rot.

Myrtle took from an open brown wrapper on a trundle cabinet a blue surgical smock off a pile of autoclaved smocks and pulled its three-holed bag over her head, covering her fatigues to midthigh. She turned from these preparations and made her first observation of the corpse. DD 891, Record of Identification-Dental Chart, positively identified Sergeant Cooper. Attached to the right wrist was a paper and wire tag reading in part:

MACV-SOG, 5th SFG.
LOCATION—CLASSIFED/TOP SECRET

The thumb and fingers were oddly contracted into the palm and a blood-caked wound covered most of the wrist above the palm. Turning the hand, Myrtle could see the same wound on the posterior wrist. A glance at the left wrist revealed an identical wound, identical crabbing of the hands. The bones of the feet and ankles protruded from below the ruined and macerated flesh of the legs. The tibia and fibula of the left leg were exposed, as were parts of the femur up to the symphysis pubis face of the pubis, and at the center of this path, instead of a penis, a ripped and dark vesicle of flesh.

Myrtle still did not look into the face of the dead soldier. It remained clouded in the periphery of her vision as she kept her eyes to the wreckage of the young body resting with clenched palms ceilingward. She observed the acronyms for Top Secret, and sensed that terrible wounds had something to do with the U.S. Army Green Berets. With the remains was a tightly rolled green felt trademark, which opened revealed an orange, black, and white shield with a metal crest of arrows crossed upon a sword surrounded by a scroll inscribed in Latin, *De Oppresso Liber*. She began to sing softly and hum where she did not know the words a stanza from a ballad that had reached the top of American pop music charts three months earlier:

Fighting soldiers from the sky,
Those brave men who jump and die.
Duh-duh-duh-daaaa, Duh-duh-duh-day,
But only three wear the Green Beret.

It was rumored that the composer, a Green Beret sergeant, had written it in a whorehouse in Mexico.

The address for the effects inventory was Thu Duc, 5th Special Forces Group (ABN). The records revealed that Cooper had been a member of a six-man recon team, otherwise unidentified, found in a spot on the Cambodia–Vietnam border and near a geographic location given on the map as Bao Menk Key. The remnant uniform attached to the remains was a camouflage ERDL stripped of unit signifiers and personal identification. Turning away from the face of the corpse, Myrtle began to read from the Report of Recovery Activities:

> Remains found at 1845 hours 18 August 1966, at XT 872666, Map Sheet 6332-III, AMS Vietnam 1:50,000, were recovered in two hours. Search party included elements of the 1st Inf Div, 2nd Bde, located at Quon Loi. Remains found nailed through the hands to a mangrove stump in approx. 3–4 ft. of water. Remains mutilated with gunshot wounds, impalement wounds and environmental damage. Nails were not recovered.

She flipped further to the DA Form 2773-R, searching for the circumstances of death:

> *Circumstances:* Recon Team in area XT 872666, Dong Menk Key, 3 kilometers due south Srok Chala on Quan An Loc, Quan Loc Ninh border; nipa and mangrove swamp located between elevations NW and SE of the Tonle Trou river.

Page two noted other personnel killed in the action:

> SGT FRYE, William R.   TSN 2467-66
> SGT DUTREMBLE, Robert   TSN 2468-66
> Nguyen Ai Quoc, *Trung Si*   _____
> Lui Van Toom, *Trung Si*   _____
> Boun Blech, Ha Si   _____

The circumstances of death were not given for the other members of the patrol. She read on. The weaponry list on DD 890 caught her eye:

> Recovered:
> 1 K-Bar Knife, 7 1/2"; 2 rifle magazines (empty).

> Unrecovered:
> 3 Swedish K submachine guns, 9mm M-45; 2 XM177ESZ submachine guns; 1 sawed-off Ithaca 12-gauge pump shot gun w/24 rounds 00 buckshot; 10 'flechette' rounds, Browning high power; 6 claymores; 8 lbs. C-4 plastic; 18 M61A frag grenades; 6 M59 concussion grenades; 6 M34 WP grenades; 5 K-Bar knives, 7 1/2"; 114 rifle magazines.

Myrtle pulled from the file a rag of paper torn page-size with tattered edges from the grid squares of an artillery map. The map side was stained through. The reverse was hand-printed semilegibly in what appeared to be blood:

WE GET BACK
YOUR X RAY
& THINK WE
KNOW PROBLEM

The map note had a slash hole through the words *X RAY* and *THINK*. Myrtle shuffled to DA 10-249, Certificate of Death. In addition to the several primary traumatic causes given for death, the form listed under "Other Significant Conditions" a further explanation:

> KIA had note fashioned from patrol map fragment
> reading WE GET BACK YOUR X RAY AND THINK
> WE KNOW PROBLEM impaled in chest at sternum
> with a knife having a 7 1/2" blade.

She looked quickly to the breast of the body, seeing the gash of the knife amid other blackened and purple wounds. "Other Significant Conditions" was footnoted with the number 2 explaining that such condition, or conditions, while contributing to the death, was not related to the disease or condition causing death. Two notes of Vietnamese piasters, also bloody and ragged, were included in the file. A soiled envelope corner poked from the amassed paperwork. Myrtle opened the torn, addressed envelope, peeling the contents apart, and began to read.

> August 17, 1966
>
> Dear Andrea,
>
> I am sorry I haven't written since July. I haven't been
> convenient to a mail drop of late. Cherokee country.
> Things have been hectic and I'll explain hectic later. Yes.
> I still carry the crucifix you gave me at graduation. I
> don't use the chain it came with but   it taped in an
> ammo pouch. I don't wear anything around my nec
> is carrying some kind of token, medal, lucky rabbit's foot.
> Thes   a special meaning here in tough times. One of
> my buds wears a   Sig Heil. You know how I

bounced the ball 3 times before shooting freet   not
2, not 7, just 3. Same here. I put a lot of emphasis on
brushing my teeth these days, no matter the time. In June
Graydon got hit in both legs, severed his femoral artery in
the right leg. Harper (I've told you about him) worked on
him and ran a bottle of albumin. Graydon was gasping
and going into shock. I started giving him mouth to
mouth. He vomited in my mouth. I couldn't help
gagging and crawled away to vomit myself. You can guess
the rest. It was more the leg wounds. I could taste and
smell the LRRP ration he had eaten an hour earlier, or so
back on the trail and noticed later a kind of green
on his teeth. My thoughts went I don't want to die with
green scum on my tee   Crazy, Huh? So, over 3
months the need to have teeth if I should get zapped,
brushing, has taken on a different meaning. Now if I
brush my teeth *I won't die*. Cleanest teeth in Vietnam.
Vooodoooo. Wooooooo. I hope you aren't disturbed by
these confessions. As always, if I can't tell you, who can I
tell. Will send you the team picture I promised.
Tell Diana, Chloe, and Jurnee HI and Kisses. I love you.
F.

She stared at the blotched erasures of the letter and then looked for
the first time at the dead soldier's face. It was swollen and pocked.
Some mandibular and maxillary bones with teeth were exposed by
missing lips. The recesses of the mouth were clotted with blood or
other materials. Myrtle looked closely at the gaping smile of teeth and
saw a bile-colored vestige. The eyes were open, but a large patch of
flesh was torn down from the left temporal area eroding partially over
the left eye. The hair from the sidewall gave the upper eyelid the appearance of having an ill-fitted and grotesque toupee and, paired with the
pale furrows of exposed skull, the face a frown.

Myrtle sorted DD Form 894 from a filing of blank forms to provide fingerprint documentation from the corpse in testimony of the
dental identification already completed. Without washing her hands,
she pulled on a pair of surgical gloves. She then took into her hands
the right hand of Sergeant Cooper and began to work at the tightly
clenched fingers and thumb, attempting to break the rigor of the death-
stiffened muscles. She noticed that the thumbnail was fractured to the

cuticle and the index finger lacked a fingernail. Two fingers appeared misshapen. The right wrist was abraded and bruised extending about to the elbow.

Myrtle drew a bowl of warm water from a scrubbing tub tap, placed the hand in it, and bathed and massaged it, attempting to coax the rigor from it. The hand would not open, and further bathing only wrinkled the fingerprints. To get to the ridge detail, she would have to cut the hand. Myrtle took a scalpel from a line of scalpels on the presentation table and made a cut at the second joint on the inner side of each of the four fingers. She repeated this between the thumb and index finger. She then pressed the fingers and thumb to the pallet top and pressed the weight of her fist to the back of the hand. This straightened the hand. After drying and inking the fingers she placed Form 894 in a spoon cardholder and rolled the encircled form over the cutaneous whorls of Sergeant Cooper's fingers, the motion identical to that of her middle finger in the adjustment of her lipstick.

An Armed Forces DJ announced the AFRVN morning show, *Small World,* and music by somebody, vocals by Frank Sinatra:

> This night could be be - yond for - get - ting
> If the two of us were here.

—Good morning, Specialist Jones. Myrtle turned. Captain Neil Runberg, the forensic pathologist, his longer than regulation hair in morning disarray, stood eyeing the body of Felix Cooper over her left shoulder.

—Good morning, Captain Runberg. Myrtle closed the file and replaced it on a table of equipment trays and surgical instruments.

—He sniffed. You can bathe a decomposing cadaver in good perfume and it still smells like rotting meat on a bed of roses. Ain't helped by two million Vietnamese shitting in the river next door.

—I must have acclimated. Have you seen this yet? She picked up the file and offered it to Runberg.

—Yeah, Captain Runberg said, nodding. Jarvis gave it to me at Property Depot when I came in this morning. Hearing Sinatra on the radio, he held his hands up and began singing in an exaggerated baritone:

> Full moon and emp - ty arms . . .
> To - night I'll use the mag - ic moon to wish up - on . . .

—You know this tune was lifted from Rachmaninoff's Piano Concerto Number Two? The *meno mosso* passage in the finale. He hummed the same tune that had accompanied the phrase "Full moon and emp - ty arms":

Dah–duh–dah–dah–duh–dah.

—Yeh. A beautiful piece of music, Rachmaninoff's Second. You read the file?

—Myrtle nodded. This one's really messed up. Makes you wonder what he was up to. There were six of them and six died.

—He was a snake eater. A volunteer for suicide, Runberg said, as he picked up an autoclaved smock.

—Suicide?

—Green Berets. They drop 'em in small units deep in enemy territory to collect intelligence and maybe more. When they're detected in the middle of an enemy force of hundreds, even thousands, bad things happen. This soldier, what's left of him, and his buddies are the real idealists in this war. No mission too difficult, no sacrifice too great, duty first. You know what I mean?

—Is there something wrong with that? Myrtle asked.

—Apparently. Look what it got him.

—But he died for an honorable cause? Myrtle looked at Runberg for an affirmation. Didn't he?

—Runberg turned toward Myrtle with a frown. You think they look worse than this for a dishonorable one?

—Myrtle shrugged her shoulders and nodded her head indecisively. August 17th. He wrote that letter Wednesday. This letter. She picked up the file jacket again and pulled the blotched sheaf written by Cooper from the file. Some strange stuff about brushing his teeth. I understand the basketball thing though. Like avoiding a crack in the sidewalk in hopscotch.

—Step on a crack and break your mother's back?

—Yes. Something like that.

—You were seeking the fortunate event. Calling on the gods. Myrtle looked at Runberg.

—Two unrelated events occur. You wear a charm or brush your teeth. The grenade going off next to you hits everybody but you. You make connections. The fastening onto the fortunate event associated with the object or behavior is the start of superstition or religion. Where chance and circumstances are not fully controlled by knowledge, man is more likely to resort to magic. There are certain types of occupations involving risk, uncertainty, or fear, that are particularly liable to superstition. Soldier, sailor, athlete, actor, to name a few.

—Brush your teeth and live longer?

—Yes. Wearing protective charms and amulets, performing ritual preparations.

—Myrtle frowned. How does all that start?

—Someone making meaning out of meaningless coincidence.

A business card fell to the tabletop from the file containing the letter. It was embossed with a skull bearing a Green Beret and a scroll advertising *Murphy's Rules of Combat.*

—Myrtle scanned the contents and said. Listen. Murphy's rules of combat:

1. When in doubt, empty your magazine.
2. Never share a foxhole with anyone braver than you are.
3. If your attack is going well, it's an ambush.
4. If you are forward of your position, the artillery will fall short.
5. Incoming fire has the right of way.
6. Friendly fire—isn't.
7. Radios will fail as soon as you need fire support desperately.
8. The only thing more accurate than incoming enemy fire is incoming friendly fire.
9. Make it tough for the enemy to get in and you can't get out.
10. Professional soldiers are predictable, but the world is full of amateurs.

—Sounds like someone taking notice of meaningful coincidence, Runberg said. We got our tape recorder?

—Right here. She fingered the voice-activated CIA Continental Uher 4,000L tape recorder and switched it to the foot trundle for start and stop. Are you ready?

—Not yet. Captain Runberg pulled a green rubber apron from a clotheshorse peg and welding goggles from an adjoining peg.

—Want an apron? As he said this, he handed one over to Myrtle. He fitted himself, pulling the inner tube strap of the goggles behind his head and snapping it several times. He put on a pair of surgical gloves snapping all powdered latex fingers on each hand, repeated this exercise with another pair, and picked up a scalpel. Myrtle pulled at the fingers of her gloves, having donned the green butcher's apron with rubber straps that tugged down in the ellipses of her shoulders.

—Captain Runberg cleared his throat over the beveled face of the corpse. This guy was, what? Twenty years old?

—1946. Yes, twenty. Myrtle answered.

—Uhh. We're a day late, Runberg said.

—A day late?

—The psychologist knows everything and does nothing. The surgeon knows nothing and does everything. The dermatologist knows nothing and does nothing. The pathologist knows everything but is always a day late.

—You don't have a high regard for dermatologists.

—That was a medical school ditty. I don't know why they picked on dermatologists.

—Are you ready? Myrtle looked at her watch.

—What time is it? Runberg asked.

—Saigon Standard Time. 9:15, Myrtle said.

—Okay. I am identifying the body by the tag tied around the right wrist. The name is Felix Cooper, Sergeant, U.S. Army. Runberg snipped the tag wire with surgical scissors, letting it drop to the floor. Date of death, Thursday, August 18, 1966.

He described the superficial appearance of the body, naming the various wound types and locations. He probed the torn and drawn flesh pulling down from the orbit arch, the mandible, and maxillary exposure, and noted the names of each wound. He reached a finger into the mouth and pulled at its contents, removing a shard of black flesh. He handed this to Myrtle and she placed it on the dissection table to the head of the platform.

—Looks like a penis. We'll have it analyzed. Make sure. He caught a load of shrapnel in the upper chest and neck from a grenade.

Runberg draped a blue hand towel over the face of Cooper. He described the knife wound in the center of Cooper's chest and the gunshot wound entrance high right of his umbilicus.

—Man, they did him a job. He looked at the pit of flesh marking the site of the genitalia and perfunctorily noted the excision by blunt instrument of Cooper's penis and testes.

—They must have used his knife to do this surgery. He reached to the wrists of the body and rubbed his gloved thumbs along the punctured and swollen contours, gently tracing the black and blue on Cooper's forearms.

—Runberg looked at Myrtle. Did the records use the word *crucifixion?*

—I don't think so, Myrtle said.

—This guy was crucified, you know. Someone went to a lot of trouble to nail him to a mangrove stump. I wonder why.

—And why him and not one of the others, or one of the three Vietnamese? Myrtle asked.

—I don't know about nailing him up but picking him out of the lineup had something to do with natural selection. He was the tallest, blondest.

—The others *were* Vietnamese, weren't they?

—Maybe. Might have been tribe folk. Runberg placed a finger on the scabbed chest wound. How about that map note piked in his chest?

—We get your X-rays and we think we know the problem. Jesus. Sick, Myrtle said.

—A monstrous sense of humor for a monstrous war, but probably just paybacks. Some American units have special-made card decks containing fifty-two aces of spades with the unit's patch. They impale these cards in the bodies of the dead enemy after battle.

—Why?

—The ace of spades has some symbolic meaning for the Vietnamese, or I think it does, and it degrades the victim.

He inserted the head of the scalpel at the head of the left humerus and cut to below the left nipple medially, repeated this from the right shoulder to right nipple, then finished the letter *Y* down the midline through the belly button to the empty pubis. He pulled back the skin and muscle tissue, exposing the costochondral cartilage on the ribs, and removed the chest plate with a small saw taken from the presentation table. Taking up a new scalpel, he began to cut connectors from all the organs, removing them in a mass from the thyroid down to the urinary bladder and rectum, dictating as he went. As he did this, Myrtle began scooping the organs from the cavities, placing them on the dissecting table. She stopped and shook her head.

—God must be dead, she murmured.

—Dead? Runberg asked. Well, not quite as popular as He once was, according to the Beatles.

—You read that? In the *Saigon Post* yesterday about John Lennon apologizing for saying the Beatles were more popular than Jesus. They're burning their records back home.

—Yeah. Well, it ain't quite as bad as Nietzsche saying God is dead, and now...Myrtle Jones? The edges of Runberg's eyes crinkled behind the welding goggles.

—I didn't mean dead so much as, as, well, I can't see God associated with these things. Not the God I was brought up knowing, Myrtle explained.

Runberg moved to the dissection table to inspect the organs, which were in the pathway of the projectile that entered Cooper's belly; then he returned to the corpse.

—Cooper was shot from some distance. He pointed to about five centimeters below the transpyloric plane on Cooper's right side, where a coarse wound opening was evident on the abdominal sheath before he pulled it back. He cut quickly through the right lateral border of the rectus sheath on both sides of the wound.

—The projectile lost some speed. See the flattening effect here. It also entered at a trajectory from ten or more degrees below the victim. Runberg was cutting along the wound line on a trail through the fatty deposits of the greater omentum.

—The bullet died here in the right renal cortex, severing the right ureter. With a hemostat, he pulled a flattened piece of blackened metal from the right kidney.

—That's what took him down. The grenade must have come later. For the others. If they crucified him after this, he wouldn't have felt anything. Where the hell did they find nails in the middle of a swamp? Runberg looked up at Myrtle. He stroked his chin with the back of a gloved hand. Strange you should have said that.

—What?

—That God must be dead.

—What?

—He did die. Two thousand years ago. The servants of some Roman physicians who believed it might have special properties stole his body. An autopsy was done in the doctors' dissecting rooms. Would be interesting to know exactly what they were looking for.

—Oh, bullshit, Neil. Myrtle said.

—You know what they found?

—What?

—A hemohidrosis on the body. A rare condition caused by extreme stress. Ruptured capillaries. Looked like a ruby flush, the one you see around the neck in spinal meningitis. Remember that Vietnamese baby? The body had deep stripes like lacerations on the back and buttocks with an inferomedial direction of the wounds. From a beating with a short whip with several braided leather thongs of various lengths in which sharp pieces of sheep bones were tied at intervals. Deep contusions where the bones cut into the skin and subcutaneous tissues, finally tearing into the skeletal muscles. Fragments of the bone were embedded in His wounds. An examination of the head revealed lacerations of the face, fracture of the nasal cartilage and back of the head with minute imbedded fragments of the Zizyphus spina.

—Jesus.

—Yeah. If you've ever read the three or four versions of it, you'd have to say that it sounds close, wouldn't you? Runberg said, continuing to inspect the corpse.

He did an arc midline incision, exposing multiple metallic fragments in the subcutaneous tissue of the chest and in the pectoral muscles. He noted fragments 1 to 3 mm in diameter and that the clavicles were fragmented bilaterally and that the left chest had approximately 200 cc's of blood and the right chest 600 cc's.

—There are fractures of the following ribs; left anterior 3,4,5; right 3rd anteriorly with metallic fragments 2 to 3 mm in diameter. The right transverse process of the 6th, or is it 7th thoracic vertebra, make it 6th, is chipped. Tip of knife lodged in spine, pierced the spinous process and nicked the ventral ramus of the 6th.

Curious about the heart from the state of the cavity, he moved to the dissecting table and picked it up. He placed it on a gram scale. The radio announced the time: 10:30 A.M. Saigon Standard Time; introduction of a vocal by Laurindo Almeida.

—Who the hell's that?

—Never heard of him, her, Myrtle answered.

—The heart weighs 250 grams. The knife passage missed the heart entirely. There are two perforations in the left ventricle from metal fragments. They are 1 and 2 mm in diameter on the anterior surface and 2 and 3 mm in diameter posteriorly. Opening the left ventricle demonstrates a traumatic rupture of the papillary muscles. The heart valves are delicate. Look at this. Early atherosclerosis of the anterior descending branch of the left coronary artery. Damn. Wouldn't expect that.

—Myrtle began weighing the lungs and liver. I wonder if Christ had atherosclerosis of the anterior descending branch of the left coronary artery?

—Yeah? Runberg hesitated. Now that would be interesting. Christ facing a different death if he hadn't faced Golgotha. I never thought about the gods suffering from disease, or old age. He was now inspecting the lungs of Cooper.

—The trachea and bronchi are filled with gastric contents and there are small metallic fragments beneath the pleura.

—Wonder what Christ was eating at the last supper? Myrtle asked as she stared at the excised respiratory tree.

—Probably fig cake, gum arabic, a few cc's of wine mixed with myrrh given as a mild analgesic before His hands and feet were nailed to the cross. And a big helping of crow.

—Crow?

—For the big mistake. Joke. Just a joke.

—You said hands. Was he nailed through the hands?

—No. A Frenchman named Barbet working with amputated arms demonstrated that the only way the weight of a nailed body could be supported was by nailing it through the wrists. Place called the space of Destot. The nailed hands were impaled at the wrist between carpal bones and radius. The nail transected the median nerve and impaled the flexor longus without breaking the wrist bones. Barbet also discovered that the nail hitting the median nerve caused the thumb to contract into the palm.

—The Vietnamese knew something about Barbet and crucifixion then, Myrtle said, touching Cooper's right wrist. They hit Destot's space and the median nerve right on the head.

—Yeah. There were also fractures in two or three fingers on both hands from the smashing effect of an off-mark mallet. The feet were impaled in the second intermetatarsal space with one foot nailed on top of the other. The right foot must have been the top foot because there was chipping of the cuboid and a fracture of the 3rd metatarsal from the force of the mallet.

—Cooper?

—No. Christ.

—God. That's a detail you wouldn't think of. Smashed hands and feet. She pointed at Cooper's hands. He had smash injuries, didn't he?

—Yeah. Whatever they used to hammer the spikes home busted him a couple of times in the hands. Christ had crabbed thumbs. I saw a picture of a shroud, the Shroud of Turin. They say it was the burial cloth that covered Christ. The thumbs were crabbed into the palms.

—What explains his legs? Myrtle pointed to the denuded leg bones.

—There's a small snapping crab indigenous to the marsh waters of Vietnam called *ca ro*. They've eaten the flesh of the feet and legs. Would have had a hard time nailing his feet under water.

—Jesus. They may as well have, Myrtle said.

—Runberg touched the adductor magnus, femoral vessels, rectus femoris, and vastus medialis as he inspected Cooper's right leg above the knee. He picked up the bladder and turned it over.

—Empty. Self-drained at death.

Blowwwwww, illllllllllll wind, blow away.

Runberg started humming over the strong and pure voice of Ella Fitzgerald.

— Goddamn. That lady can sing.

The *Small World* host announced: And that was Ella Fitzgerald with the Billy May Orchestra from *Ella Fitzgerald Sings the Harold Arlen Song Book*. The time is 11:15 A.M. Saigon Standard.

The wound to Cooper's groin had shaved the genitalia flat with the adductor longus to the raphe. Runberg noted the exposure of the posterior scrotal vessels and nerves as well as the bulbospongiosus overlying the bulb of the penis and remarked that the anus was intact. A flower of cotton batting protruded from it as well as from the rectum on the now visible, excised, inner wall. He gave a low whistle.

—He could have died for a lot of different reasons, Myrtle said. She began to replace the cut and inspected viscera back into the body cavities.

—Cooper? Runberg asked.

—No, Christ.

—Huh-uh. Two ways. Suffocation and a spear wound to the heart. When they crucify you, you can't breathe. The weight of the body hanging from the cross hinders passive exhalation. To blow out you have to lift your body by pushing up on the feet and by flexing the elbows and adducting the shoulders.

Myrtle raised her arms and bounced up and down on her toes.

—We don't usually have to think about breathing, but hanging fixes the intercostal muscles in an inhalation state and that interferes with passive exhalation. Having to physically assist breathing on a cross causes extreme pain in the feet and the damaged median nerves in the wrists. Every respiration requires flexing and adducting, which leads to fatigue. When you can't lift up any longer, you can't exhale. *Voilà*. Suffocation.

—Do you think Cooper was alive when they nailed him to the tree? Myrtle asked.

—No. The North Vietnamese, or whoever, reversed the Passion Play. Killed him, then crucified him.

—The knife wound to his chest alone could have killed him.

—True, but that was an afterthought.

—What about the spear to Christ's side?

—That finished the job. An eyewitness said there was a spurt of blood and water from the wound. The blood would have been from the blood-distended, thin-walled right ventricle when the spear entered the thorax, piercing the right lung and pericardium. The water was from pleural and pericardial effusions. Just on that testimony alone I can tell you that Christ was in hypovolemia and acute heart failure.

Runberg placed the heart back into the body of Cooper, and pulled the goggles from his face and head, removed his gloves and lab clothing, finishing the nearly three hours of autopsy.

—Who's the civilian embalmer on duty?

—Mr. Arnold, Myrtle said. She threw her butcher's apron and smock to the floor.

—He can repair this damage. Runberg placed his apron and goggles on the specimen table. I'm getting hungry. I didn't eat breakfast. You?

—Just coffee.

—Myrtle and Runberg walked one after the other to the embalming atrium and entered the refrigeration unit, threading around other members of the mortuary company who had filtered into the mortuary sometime after their arrival.

—How about that Buddhist restaurant on Hung Vuong Street? Get some of that vegetarian *Pho*.

—Vietnamese soup. I don't think so.

—They make American too.

—You know, Neil. I can't help thinking that Cooper's death was more terrible than Christ's.

—The manner of death. Yeah.

—I'm suddenly feeling like I'm missing something here. Two thousand years of a religion depends on this sacrifice, the greatest sacrifice of all. But sacrifice seems to be a relative thing.

—Or a symbolic thing. But there is a big difference, said Runberg. He pulled on his baseball cap with two silver bars before stepping from the darkened mortuary into a tropical sun.

—What would that be? Myrtle said, reaching her right forearm to her eyes to shield them from the brightness of the light.

—Christ was resurrected.

When Saigon fell, my parents fled together by helicopter and boat, and I was born in the United States the following year. My father was an American civilian contractor servicing Huey helicopters in Viet Nam. Before their marriage, my Cham–French Vietnamese mother had lost her first husband, a lieutenant in the Army of the Republic of Viet Nam. She had left behind five children in the evacuation, whom she did not see for sixteen years. One died, and another was imprisoned for two years in Cambodia during an attempted escape. After my parents' marriage ended, my mother wed a U.S. Army captain who'd spent six years in Viet Nam as a combat helicopter pilot. I negotiated an inheritance of ghosts and regret, while living in a culture of theatrical cinema, hushed tones, and conspicuous silences about Viet Nam.

In 1999, I traveled with siblings to Viet Nam to finally meet our maternal kin and dying grandmother. The next year I interviewed my mother and stepfather in Texas about their war memories, before returning to Viet Nam for a touring seminar over the war's historical, geopolitical, and psychological aspects. In 2001, I began making *Crossing Fire: Salvadoran and Vietnamese Women After War,* a film about surviving, organizing, and healing. In 2002, I visited El Salvador to interview women and photograph sites of remembrance. My oral history with U.S. Army veteran Robert Cagle, prefacing our visit to My Lai, was in *Takin' It to the Streets: A Sixties Reader.* I often exhibit my Viet Nam portraits, and I was included in NPR's *Crossing East,* a May 2006 documentary on Asian Americans.

I returned to Viet Nam in 2006 to photograph and film my Cham grandmother's *Second Burial.* My mother, extended family, and I exhumed her skeleton, prayed, atoned regrets, feasted, and reburied her by tradition. Through a fellowship at the William Joiner Center for the Study of War and Social Consequences at the University of Massachusetts, Boston, I have researched how conquest, colonialism, and war have affected the cultural survival of the Cham, whose 1,500-year-old kingdom the Vietnamese destroyed.

Spanning eight years, these dreams are allegories revealing my vulnerability and culpability about witnessing, remembering, and healing war's atrocities and sorrows.

My web address is www.jthiunderhill.com.

war dream i

i am crossing water on a boat
with refugees when it capsizes
close to shore. i dive beneath
the water to save two children,
both under the age of six. one at a time.
yet even after bringing them to a pier
& expelling water from their lungs
they each died. almost everyone
sank to ocean's bottom.
then fast forward
to years later, when i get
a letter from someone
whom i'd thought had drowned
that day.
i read it
uncomprehending.

war dream ii

i am working in a country
in central Africa that's suffering
famine, ethnic cleansing, disease
& civil war, when i am assigned
by my supervisors to dig
a mass grave on the outskirts
of town. i go to the town's edge
to assess the area.
yet when i begin to dig,
i hit skulls, only to realize
that i am digging
into a preexisting mass grave.
i move & discover more of the same.
nearly every scrap of dirt
was stretched thin over piles of bodies;
i never find a place to begin
again.

CHRISTOPHER UPHAM

I was born in New York City, lived over my grandfather's bar in East Newark, New Jersey, and was raised in the desert near Tucson with my five sisters. My father had navigated a B-25 bomber in the South Pacific and courted my mother, an Army nurse. Growing up during the 1950s, I heard the adults speak about "the war" over cocktails like a secret society, while on television, John Wayne, detectives, and cowboys battled evil, inspiring me and my friends to run endless raids through the Arizona desert, throwing rocks, shooting BB guns, and dying beautiful deaths.

In 1968, ambivalent and uninformed about Vietnam, I dropped out of college and was drafted immediately. I ended up in the 299th Combat Engineers near the Cambodian and Laotian border, serving as an ambulance driver and medic. During the 1969 siege at Dak To, all that television blood and movie dying became real and the world changed forever. After my war, no one wanted to listen to our stories or try to understand where America had gone. The Left called us baby killers, the Right called us losers, and everyone else just ignored us.

After college, I could only bear to work out under the open sky, exploring for minerals all over the Rocky Mountains. I spent sixteen months in Europe running away from the war and nearly ended it all in a rowboat on a cold Norwegian lake. Afterward, I lived in Laguna Beach, California, thinking that law school, the ocean, and a family might be the solution. But the war would not go away. So I began writing about it. I got married, raised a stepdaughter, and got divorced.

In 1992, I journeyed to Hanoi with the poet Bruce Weigl to photograph for the "Poems from Captured Documents" project. In 2004, I took four veterans I had fought with back to Dak To for my first documentary film, *War Within*. I live in San Francisco and work as a writer, actor, producer, and story consultant.

Nothing to Crow About

The war was still on television, but we had come home to Flagstaff and didn't watch it anymore. In the mornings we walked to college along the highway past Ruff's Liquor where hunters hung their deer carcasses by the horns to weigh, so the dead animals, dusted with snow, swayed stiffly in the wind.

It felt good to walk in the cold with the wind whipping across Route 66, crowded with tractor trailers and hunters down from the Uncompaghres and the Sangre de Cristos. Gray ice stained the pavement beneath the railroad underpass as freight trains roared past the bars and the curio shops, the windblown gas stations, the cheap motels and the empty hamburger joints.

The sidewalks were deserted except for a lone Navajo in a ragged black coat; he was collecting trash blown into the chain-link fences around motel pools with logs thrown in the ice to keep the pool walls from cracking.

Under the neon mess of signs at Five Points, we crossed 66 with cinders grating under our feet. Then we walked through the red sandstone gates and into the College Union. We found our table near the fireplace and drank coffee and watched the C-U lawn turn white until the snow quit and the wind blew drifts off the spruce and the aspen.

There were three of us: me, big Durk, who had been an L-T, and Claver, a flat-faced guy with a bushy mustache and a purple scar on his neck from Hue, where his fire team went hand-to-hand with North Vietnamese regulars. If anyone asked about his scar, Claver always said, "Got overrun, outa ammo, scared shitless. This dink fell on me and cut me badass so I greased him."

"What's our mission today, L-T?" Claver asked.

"Shoot down the Command and Control bird, Sergeant," Durk said.

"That's a rog," Claver said.

"Then business as usual," Durk said, as a tight grin crept across his face. "Kill dinks. Kick ass and take names."

Claver's eyes glittered and the scar on his neck throbbed.

"Hey, Claver," I said, "Remember. We're back in the world."

"Like anyone fucking cares," he said, dragging his cigarette and sipping his coffee.

Durk pointed outside at crows huddled on a snow-covered spruce.

"Looks like your bird escaped," he said.

"What do you know, L-T?"

"Gotta be your crow," Durk said. "Second from the left. I heard him talk."

"Yeah? What did he say?" Claver asked.

Durk sipped his coffee.

"Nevermore," he said, laughing.

Claver fingered his scar and squinted hard at the tree.

"For your infor-fucking-mation, Lieu-tenant," he said, "That ain't my crow. Top's way bigger than them."

My coffee was cold, so I got up and left. Durk caught up with me outside. The ground was hard under a thin layer of snow. We walked into the wind to an ugly brick building with no trees. Durk studied engineering with an English minor so we had this rhetoric class together on the Sophists. Sometimes this blond with a deep voice and an afghan coat would smile at me. She had bright blue eyes and beautiful hands.

Claver always wore Levi's, a field jacket, and scuffed jungle boots. He collected his green VA checks and rarely went to class. You could usually find him in the C-U lounge playing somebody's guitar. Claver wasn't bad, but his habits were. He could consume anything until it was gone or he fell down, whichever came first. His girlfriends rarely could take him for more than a couple of weeks. "Don't mean nothing,'" he always said. Claver couldn't imagine anything turning out worse than Vietnam.

The three of us shared an old sheepherder's cabin beneath a grove of ponderosas on a ridge overlooking Flagstaff and the mainline Santa Fe tracks. We never spoke directly about the war; we communicated through a shorthand of gallows Vietnam slang. I was a medic with the engineers, and Durk had been an artillery forward observer. Claver's ground war was written in his hard, watery eyes that never missed a thing. Like that crow Durk had pointed out.

At night we lounged on an old brown sofa in front of our fireplace and watched the records go around until the beer and the tequila and the weed killed our dreams, which was all right. We had seen our share of bad dreams. All we wanted to do now was watch the fire burn down.

Sometimes there were women and sometimes there weren't. Eventually the blond with the afghan coat showed up at our cabin and broke my streak of bad luck. Her name was Debbie Jarvis. Her laugh was quick, and her hair and her legs were long, and her deep, musical voice almost made me forget all those dead faces. If it wasn't for Claver's crow, things might even still be the same.

Claver really did have a crow. Every morning it perched on a dead pine limb outside his window—the first thing he saw in the morning. Not that he slept all that much. Claver called the crow "Top" after his first sergeant, and fed him with raw hamburger. Eventually, he lured the crow into the house and it hopped up on our brown sofa.

"So what's your opinion of that son of a bitch Nixon?" Claver asked the crow.

Top cocked his head and flapped his wings. "CAW! CAW CAW!"

Claver laughed like hell and gave the bird the meat.

One night, in the darkness of my small bedroom, Debbie Jarvis stiffened in the crook of my arm and woke me. Out in the living room Claver muttered as Top's sharp claws clacked back and forth across our stone mantel. Sometimes it got so bad for Claver that even the beers and the shots and the joints didn't work.

Claver's dull voice rose above the crackling fire.

"Remember Hue, Top? Hue. Fucking Hue. We should be dead. Maybe we are dead, Top. Maybe all this is just a bad motherfuckin' dream. Just like Hue."

The crow rasped and cawed once quietly, then paced those bony feet back and forth across the mantelpiece.

"Who's Hue?" Debbie whispered.

"It's a place. In Vietnam."

Outside, an icy wind rattled our windows.

"Just you and me now, Top," Claver droned. "Pinocchio bought it on Dak To airstrip. Calhoun—greased, *friendly* fire. Minh Thi Tanh, *xin loi,* sorry 'bout that. Fremo, blown clean away—ambush out on Highway 14, dumb shit. And Delta Roger sucked away by malaria . . ."

"What's he talking about?" Debbie whispered.

"Nothing."

I ran my hand across Debbie's cheek and traced her sweet full lips with my index finger. The wind began to howl.

"Joyce, poor sweet fucker, that was one badass tree line. Fuckin' Perfume River. Jesus—rocket-propelled grenade right in the chest. K-I-fuckin' A, M-O-U-S-E, *MICKEY MOUSE.* Then dipshit Thomas got himself sniped taking a dump up at LZ Lincoln. 'Member that, Top?"

The crow croaked long and deep.

"Nobody left in first platoon. Not one swingin' Richard. And all them fuckin' new guys after 8-6-1? Even you didn't have time to learn their names, Top. Don't tell me you did. I seen you tryin' to match up body bags and dog tags. Oh man, man. And then the Cake flamed out with all them silly-assed officers in the C and C bird two clicks west of An Khe, and freaky Newman had the brass goddamn balls to *cheer . . ."*

"SHUT THE FUCK UP, CLAVER!" Durk shouted.

Claver shut up, but the crow panicked. Wings fluttered the air and scraped the walls, banging and thrashing all over the living room, horrible sounds like men when they're drowning in their own blood. Beer bottles crashed down and the fireplace screen fell over, as Debbie Jarvis wrapped around me like a snake, but that crow kept on squawking.

Claver walked over to Durk's door. Over the crow, we heard him say, "Hey. L-T. You know, I fragged me an officer once."

The horrible cawing stopped. The crow's wings fluttered a few times, then went silent. Claver's footsteps walked past my bedroom.

We sat up in bed. We could see the crow perched on Claver's shoulder as he opened and closed the front door with a rattle of glass. As they crunched across the frozen ground, Claver whispered to the crow. Debbie Jarvis shivered uncontrollably, until the shrieking wind rose and drowned out everything, and she threw herself all over me.

In the morning Claver was gone, but the crow was outside, sitting on that dead limb, picking at his feathers. When Debbie Jarvis and I left for class, the crow swiveled his head around, gave us a long, slow look, whistled once and slowly flew off. He flapped up from our tree, sailed out from the grove of ponderosas and over the snowy rooftops, soaring down the steep ridge toward the railroad tracks until he became a hard black speck in the sky above the college.

After class, I went into the Union. Claver was drinking coffee. He hadn't shaved and his eyes were red and wild.

"You ever been in an Indian bar, man?" he asked.

I shook my head.

"Them Indian dudes know how to party. They live the true worth of 'don't mean nothin,'" he said. He spread his hands to include everything around us.

"Plus, most Indian's done honest grunt time in the green killin' machine."

Claver stared at me with those bad watery eyes he usually reserved for Durk.

"You need anything, Claver?" I asked.

"Naw. Them bars open at six A.M. I'm feelin' goood."

"Your crow was waiting for you."

"Fuck that crow," Claver said. "This Hopi dude told me stay away from that crow. Says it's a badass spirit."

"Well, he's still there."

As I walked to English class, a line of blackbirds perched on the roof of the Union building, silhouetted against the gray sky. When the noon sawmill whistle blew, the blackbirds lifted as one, soaring and wheeling in a thin feathery cloud that grew smaller and nearly vanished. Only three blackbirds came back to settle on the roof.

Claver didn't show up for two weeks. One afternoon I drove Debbie Jarvis to buy art supplies near the mainline Santa Fe railroad tracks.

"Jack," Debbie said, gripping my arm. "There's Jimmy Claver."

He was leaning against a derelict brick building beside the tracks, passing a green bottle of applejack wine back and forth with three Indians.

We parked in the train station lot and crossed the double set of tracks. Claver's field jacket was ripped in three places and his greasy hair was plastered to his skull. It was so cold we could see our breath, but at least they were out of the wind. Claver's mustache was frozen and his eyes were on fire, darting every which way.

"Hey, brother," he said.

"How 'ya doing?" I asked.

"Fine, man, really fine."

Nobody gave Debbie Jarvis a glance. The three Indians stared straight ahead, their large brown faces pudgy with bruises, their deerlike eyes flecked with red.

"Hit?" Claver asked, tilting the bottle toward me.

"No thanks."

Claver wouldn't look at me.

"Anything I can do?" I asked.

Claver hooted a laugh, and said, "Not unless you got the codes to call an arc light in on this place."

An arc light was a B-52 bombing strike. Claver grinned viciously, and then his eyes lost themselves in the distance, like he was dismissing us. I said good-bye, took Debbie Jarvis's hand, and walked back across the tracks to my car.

We left them drinking beneath a big red circle painted on a wall with peeling yellow letters that said: CHEW RED MAN.

The one-ten freight train roared in from Gallup and blocked our view. Flocks of swallows off the train station roof soared and wheeled together, their tiny fluttering shadows streaking black against the snow-capped San Francisco Peaks.

"Shouldn't we do something?" Debbie Jarvis shouted over the passing train.

I started the car. My eyes felt like ice.

"What?"

"Bring him home."

"Home? He is home."

"On the railroad tracks?"

"He's back in the world."

"What does that mean?" Debbie demanded. "You always say that. What does it mean, 'back in the world'?"

"As opposed to Vietnam."

"What are you talking about, Jack?" she said.

"This is a great country. Nobody's shooting at you. We're back in the world. It's wonderful to be home."

But when I kissed Debbie, her whole face went rigid—the tip of her nose, her flushed cheeks—even her lips. When the freight train was gone, the tracks were empty. Claver and his friends had moved on.

A week later, after the snow had been plowed into muddy banks overflowing our yard, Claver pounded on the front door. His unshaven face was cut and he was broke, and dirty, and stank, but he was back. The crow was perched outside on that widowmaker pine limb dripping with icicles, but Claver didn't look at it as he marched into the bathroom for a shower. I was frying him some eggs when Durk came back from class.

"Sergeant Claver! Your bird wants a word."

"I ain't got nothing to say to no bird," Claver answered.

"You could shoot it," Durk said.

"Not me, Lieutenant. I've done all the shootin' I'm ever gonna do."

"Then request yourself a fire mission, Sergeant," Durk said. "I got a new four-ten shotgun."

All that winter, the crow perched outside his window. Claver discovered some uncashed VA checks in a drawer, so he was flush. Nearly every afternoon for two months, Claver camped out on our brown sofa, so I guess he'd given up on school. Every afternoon, he played the Doors and Led Zeppelin over and over, while he burned a fire down to coals, then roasted hot dogs and buns and marshmallows on coat hangers.

He grew his hair into a ponytail and somehow acquired a girlfriend. Marina Marie Silver was a skinny girl with stringy hair who wore black and only showed up at night. Neither Marina nor Claver talked as much as they drank, but things were better than before. Marina claimed to be a poet, so Durk took to mouthing "Nevermore."

In the spring, Claver bought a Harley-Davidson motorcycle and two black leather jackets. Marina and Claver were gone for days, camping on the Indian reservations, at the Grand Canyon or down on the Mogollon Rim. When they came back, the crow was always waiting outside on the dead pine limb, but Claver never had anything to do with him.

For Durk's graduation, we threw a party with two-pound Mormon Lake Lodge steaks, a keg of Michelob, and plenty of good dope, so the cabin overflowed with people and smoke. Durk wore his cap and gown and leaned against the mantel, beer in hand, telling stories. He mentioned to somebody who told somebody else how Claver had tamed a crow. Somebody else called bullshit, so Claver snorted once, got that glint in his eye, set his wine down, and stomped outside.

The crow hopped right up on Claver's shoulder. They marched back through all the people and the smoke and the loud music, and everyone cheered and drank toasts to Claver and to the crow and to Durk. The bird seemed to examine every face carefully, mechanically flitting its eyes back and forth.

When Claver persuaded the crow to hop down and drink out of a saucer of beer, Marina ran outside crying. Claver set the crow on his shoulder and shoved his way through the party after her.

All that night, Marina and Claver sat on his chrome Harley-Davidson in our driveway, drinking Spañada out of a big jug and laughing and crying on each other until streaks of tears and wine ran shining down their black leather in the moonlight. When we finally went to bed, they were still there, and the crow was perched on the chrome handlebars.

Sometime during the night, the motorcycle kicked over and roared off.

The next morning, when Debbie Jarvis and I dragged ourselves awake to clean up, we found Marina sleeping on the sofa in her black jacket. She never budged while we threw away the cups and the plates and emptied the ashtrays and dragged the trash can away.

Finally, when Debbie ran the vacuum, Marina bolted straight up, her straggly black hair like a bird's nest. She coughed once, lit a cigarette, and threw the match into the fire I had started with the trash. Then she stared into the flames like someone was in there burning.

"Where's Claver?" I asked.

"California," Marina said slowly.

"California?"

She nodded and studied her cigarette. "L-A," she said.

"Claver went to California?"

Marina looked at me like I was crazy.

"For good?"

"For weal or woe I will not flee," she muttered into the fire.

"Oh, Jesus," a hungover Durk said, lurching out of his bedroom wearing underwear. "Spare me fucking poetry."

Marina grimaced, and shut her eyes tight and pulled on her boots. She stood up and pushed her hair around.

"Claver's really gone?" Durk asked.

"Yeah," Marina said.

"So why didn't you go with him?"

Marina shrugged, then dragged on her cigarette.

Durk scratched his stomach, ambled to the front door, wiped condensation off the glass, and looked out. Suddenly, Durk whirled around, ran to his bedroom, got something, and disappeared out the front door.

A shotgun blast shook the windows.

Durk returned with a stupid grin and smoke pouring out of the gleaming four-ten's breech.

"Done," he said.

Nobody moved as the sharp smell of cordite invaded the room.

"I only scared him away," Durk explained. "I have to live here all summer."

Beer cartons roared in the fireplace. We sat on the sofa. No one spoke for a long time.

"I should go," Debbie Jarvis said.

She got up, touched my shoulder, and kissed the back of my head. I started to say something, but she slipped quickly away and out the back door. Marina threw on her jacket, ran out, and caught up with Debbie.

"Chicks," Durk said, coming out of his room and running a cleaning patch down the barrels of his shotgun.

It was a long summer. Debbie Jarvis went home to her parents' house in Phoenix and then decided to transfer. I got a letter postmarked from Berkeley.

In the beginning of November, there was a letter from Hutch. I opened it as Durk and I walked down Highway 66 to school. Inside was a newspaper clipping from the Riverside paper. The headline read: "Decorated Veteran Jimmy Earl Claver, 24, Killed In Motorcycle Accident."

"Shit," Durk said. "Must have been drunk. Or stoned."

"Gentlemen," Hutch's letter read, "I saw Claver in the hospital after the accident. He said he was accelerating his bike out of a corner when a big bird flew up and hit him in the chest so his Harley jumped across the center divide and smashed into a palm tree. Claver only broke his leg, so everything seemed OK. But the next day when I came back, his bed was empty. The nurse returned with a doctor, who told me an embolism—an air bubble—somehow got into Claver's veins, went straight to his heart and killed him. 'It's unusual,' the doctor said, 'but it happens.'"

"Jesus," Durk said, "Claver had no luck at all."

We walked through the railroad underpass past Ruff's Liquor Store. Underneath Ruff's big sign, a hunter stood in the bed of a red pickup truck, wrapping a rusty chain around the hooves of a white-tailed deer.

The Riverside paper printed a photograph of Claver before the war—just a kid, grinning in a green Army dress uniform.

"That's not our Claver," Durk said.

"What do you mean?"

"That kid," Durk said, "died a long time ago."

Snow began to fall.

Beneath Ruff's sign, the hunter jerked the chain. The deer carcass lifted up out of the pickup bed, slowly rising and swaying stiffly in the wind, the sleek noble head and great antlers pointing down, the golden fur all dusted with snow.

Durk and I turned our backs on the dead deer and headed for the College Union.

MICHAEL L. WONG

I once was a first lieutenant in high school Army ROTC who believed fervently in the Army and our government leaders. Then came the real Army. My story, "Honor's Death," tells of my Army experience and why I turned against the Viet Nam War and deserted to Canada. The next story, "To Take a Street," tells of one small protest.

What these stories don't tell you is that in Toronto, Canada, I was a member of a hippie counterculture community known as Rochdale College. An Internet search will produce over 800 entries about this experiment that happened in an eighteen-story apartment building. I wrote in Maxine Hong Kingston's *Fifth Book of Peace:* "We were a world unto ourselves, with our own government, a free medical clinic, a movie theater, a library, a health food restaurant, a store, a dance studio, and a host of other features of a community. We even had our own hippie 'police force,' Rochdale Security . . . "

A war of attrition by the Canadian government and police against Rochdale formed for me a counterpoint to the war in Viet Nam. The war hawks lost the war to control South Viet Nam. We hippies lost the war to save Rochdale College. I deserted the U.S. Army, only to serve on Rochdale Security. I never faced the guns of the Viet Cong, but I faced—unarmed—the guns of the Toronto Police Department. My closest comrade, Cindy Lei, was one of those who died for Rochdale. I was never the same.

There is, however, also healing. During a protest against the first Gulf War, I met a group of Viet Nam veterans who welcomed me home with open arms. I have been a member of Veterans for Peace and the Veterans Writing Group ever since. Together, we continue to heal. The journey never ends, but friends make all the difference. To all who have helped me along the way, thank you, thank you, thank you. Peace be with you.

Honor's Death

The bright summer sun shone down on the long line of young men in olive-drab fatigues and black spit-shined combat boots. Olive drab, our normal clothes. We were in the U. S. Army's medic training school at Fort Sam Houston, Texas. The year was 1969. The Viet Nam War was raging, and so was antiwar protest. It was still early morning, but the bright sun and the rapidly warming air told us it would be another hot day. We stood in the chow line talking casually, patiently waiting for our turn to enter the mess hall and eat breakfast. I liked meals here, I liked the chance to be with my friends and socialize. My platoon was tight. Many of us questioned the Army and the war, a few of us didn't, but whatever our opinions, we all supported each other. I was feeling relaxed and easy. This was a quiet time, a time when the sergeants left us alone and we had nothing to do but stand in a long line.

Suddenly the guy directly in front of me said, "Hey, Wong, something's going on down there." We could see a small commotion at the front of the line. Guys were talking to each other excitedly, and one soldier gestured toward the single newspaper rack. Then the whisper started up the line toward us. One soldier would turn to the next and whisper something, who then would turn to the fellow behind him and pass on the whisper. I watched anxiously, wondering what it could be. Finally the guy in front of me got the whisper from the guy in front of him, and he turned around to tell me.

"They're killing women and children in Viet Nam," he said.

"What?" I was stunned, confused. I couldn't quite get what he was talking about. "Who's killing women and children?" I asked. "The Viet Cong?"

"No, we are," he said loudly. His voice broke the whisper, with a suddenness that jarred me to the core. I was speechless. I couldn't grasp this somehow, it just seemed beyond me. As I stood there stunned, the guy passed the news on to the soldier behind me.

When we got down to the front of the line, we saw. We saw the headlines on the paper in the rack. The My Lai massacre. Over 300 Vietnamese civilians—old men, women, children, and babies—slaughtered by American soldiers. American soldiers, just like us.

My buddies saw the paper, I could hear the murmur of their voices all around me. But I just stood in front of the newspaper rack in shock. I didn't want to see. In my mind's eye, I don't see the newspaper, I don't see the headlines, I don't see the pictures. I don't see anything. I just see a plain newspaper rack. I don't even know the color of the rack. I only know how I feel. I feel my world in shock, reality not in place, not being able to make sense, not understanding anything. Not understanding.

Later we would see the photographs. We, I, could not avoid them. They would haunt us for days, for months, for years, for decades, staring out at us from the pages of newspapers, magazines, and books. Marching in front of us across TV screens. Horrible pictures. Pictures of the soldiers herding the Vietnamese into groups at gunpoint. Pictures of the women and children huddled together, terrified. The women holding the children desperately to them, their eyes and mouths wide open in fear. Pictures of women and children literally down on their knees begging the soldiers for mercy. And then pictures of their dead bodies piled in heaps, after they were shot by the soldiers. American soldiers. American soldiers, just like us.

We were stunned. We had heard about smaller atrocities, and the peace movement had been telling us for some time that atrocities were going on, but now we saw it. We saw the pictures, solid and real. Our men were killing women, children, and babies.

Overnight, everything was different. Morale dropped, for we could no longer be proud of being American, or of being soldiers. Our honor died at My Lai. In the days that followed, guys walked around muttering, "They can't do this to us," meaning, They can't make us do these things. We were in shock. The shock sank down into our gut. Then something inside of us turned, and the shock became action.

If we had questioned the Army and the war before, now the questioning became the focus for our anger and our outrage. The antiwar militants in the platoon became point men against the officers. In Army indoctrination classes, the officers would try to convince us that the war was right, and that we should fight. The militants would question the officers, asking, "Wasn't our intervention illegal under international law? Didn't the CIA set up the Saigon regime as a puppet government? What about the atrocities?" The officers acted like macho straight men in a bad comedy. A typical exchange went like this:

Militant: "Sir, why should we fight when this is an illegal and immoral war of capitalist imperialism?"

Lieutenant: "Because we're fighting for freedom and democracy against Communist aggression, and as an American fighting man, you ought to understand that."

Militant: "Sir, if we're fighting for freedom and democracy, then why, after the French left, did we support the Saigon regime in blocking internationally supervised free elections to reunite Viet Nam?"

Sergeant: "Shut up, troop! Don't talk to the lieutenant like that!"

Militant: "Sir, does this mean you can't answer my question?"

Sergeant: "Shut up, troop! You're a soldier, you follow orders. You're just saying this shit 'cause you're afraid to fight!"

Lieutenant: "You are American soldiers. It is your duty to be loyal, to obey, and to fight. You represent the honor of the U.S. Army. You fight because you are American soldiers, and because you are MEN!"

The Army's arguments amounted to: We had a moral duty to kill babies because we were men. International law and foreign free elections mean nothing to us because we are American soldiers. We had to ask ourselves, "Is this what being a soldier means? Is this what being a MAN means? What do loyalty, duty, and honor really mean?" The Army gave us guns, orders, and so-called manhood, and the hippie counterculture offered us the ideals of "peace, love, and groovy." Some of the guys in our platoon had been in the counterculture before being drafted. One guy was an SDS (Students for a Democratic Society) organizer who had joined the Army to organize from within. In various ways, they told us of the dream.

In the '60s, the hippies had a dream, a vision. A dream of a world in which all people lived in peace, love, freedom, equality, and happiness. A world in which there was no war, no hunger, no hatred; no killing, no oppression, and no poverty. A world in which every person has enough food, clothing, shelter, education, and opportunity. A world in which humanity lives at peace with the earth, the wind, the water, the plants, the animals, and most of all, itself.

We heard stories of that dream, and some of us began to feel that peace, love, and groovy was the higher standard.

One weekend, a bunch of us changed into our civvies (civilian clothes), rented a car, and drove to Houston. We toured the university and the downtown area, looking for a piece of the dream. Off a major square in the downtown area we found a small bookshop, very simple, with wood construction, a long-haired clerk, and books, wonderful books, on everything from politics to literature to spirituality. It was the kind of place I might have imagined Jack Kerouac, Allen Ginsberg, or Gary Snyder hanging out if they were ever to visit Texas. We walked in and explored the plain wooden shelves full of books just waiting to be discovered by our eager eyes. We went back and forth excitedly telling each other of books we had found. In the end, I bought only one book, Hermann Hesse's *Siddhartha*. It was enough.

Back in the barracks, I devoured the book, a story about a monk in

India who gives up status, wealth, power, and privilege to wander the world alone, seeking truth. Truth, the one vital thing the Army seemed unable to come to grips with. After I finished the book, a friend borrowed it. He passed it to another guy, who passed it to another guy, who passed it to another guy, until finally it made it around the barracks, and eventually returned to me battered and worn, but happy. It spoke something to us, something we desperately missed, deep in our souls. I knew I had to pursue it. Truth.

About this time, a story came through our barracks. The story went like this:

A guy is in Viet Nam, trying to survive to make it back to "the world." He dreams every day of returning home and reuniting with his girlfriend. In his mind, he sees himself getting off the plane, dropping his duffel bag, and running toward her with outstretched arms. She runs toward him as well, and they come closer and closer. Finally, they meet and embrace and kiss with passionate love. Hanging on to his dream, he finds the strength to keep going even in the most terrible of times. Then, the big day comes. His tour ends, and he gets on that plane to come back to "the world." When his plane finally lands in the United States, he gets out, and there waiting for him are his parents, and most of all, his girlfriend. He calls out her name, and just like in his dream, he drops his duffel bag and runs toward her with all his might, arms outstretched. She runs toward him. They come closer and closer. Then, just at the instant before they meet, she stops dead in her tracks and looks him hard in the face. "Murderer!" she shouts, "How many people did you kill over there, you murderer?" Then she turns her back on him, and walks out of his life forever.

I never knew where the story came from, who it happened to, or even if it was true or not. But the story ran from barracks to barracks like wildfire. Overnight, any morale we had left just crashed, like a huge rock slamming into the earth from high above. I felt overwhelmed with fear, anger, and confusion. I didn't know what to think, or what I should do. There was no escape, no honorable way out, no right course of action. If we went and fought, half the country would call us murderers. If we refused to go and fight, the other half of the country would call us cowards. It was the devil's choice: Damned if you do, damned if you don't.

As we neared the end of our ten-week training cycle, we came closer to the day our training would end and we would each get our individual orders assigning us as medics to units anywhere in the world. We knew most of us would probably get orders for Viet Nam. We debated what we should do, what we would do. The officers told us that we would serve by healing people rather than hurting people. But they also kept repeating the medics' motto, "To preserve the fighting strength," and telling us how important we were to keeping the war machine operating. Without us, the troops wouldn't be able to keep fighting, they said. It was the ultimate irony—by saving lives, we enabled the killing to go on. Baby killers by proxy. The tension grew as the day for our orders approached.

The day was, as usual, hot and sunny. I had an Army truck driver's license, so instead of being with my unit, I was out running errands in a deuce-and-a-half (a two-and-a-half-ton truck). I finally finished the day and got back to the barracks about an hour after everybody else.

I walked in to the usual busy routine of men cleaning the barracks, arranging their stuff, taking showers, and so on. As I walked by, one of the guys said to me, "Hey, Wong, we got our orders." I felt a tinge of fear in my heart, and my adrenaline went up immediately. "Oh yeah," I said, "what happened?"

"Half our platoon's goin' to 'Nam."

"Oh, fuck!"

Almost as if on signal, other guys crowded around, starting to tell me about it.

"They had us all in a classroom and announced that they got our orders. Then they started reading them out, one by one."

"They'd call a guy's name, he'd answer 'Yo!' and then they they'd name the place he was going."

"When they told people they were going to 'Nam, some guys broke down and cried. The officers and sergeants tried to order us not to cry, but it didn't work." They described how one man after another would start tearing up, then some just started crying outright. As each additional man cried, more men felt able to do so. The crying gained its own momentum. It became a statement. The momentum grew.

"Finally, enough guys were crying that they called the whole platoon to attention. Then they got up in guys' faces and started yelling at them to stop crying. They started giving us all this shit again about we're American fighting men, and American fighting men don't cry, and this is 'conduct unbecoming an American soldier,' and all the rest of that shit. But nobody cared. What more could they do to us?"

Then somebody said a phrase that I would hear over and over in the months to come, "Yeah, what're they gonna do, *send us to 'Nam?*"

The classroom degenerated into chaos, until the officers finally finished reading the list of orders, and just moved the platoon out of there.

That Friday night, everybody went into town on pass. Most of the guys planned to get very drunk, but I wasn't a drinker. I simply took in a movie and came back to the barracks. I walked slowly up the stairs to my bay on the second floor, aware that most everyone else would probably come in totally smashed. At the top of the stairs I turned the corner to the left, and walked down the rows of double bunk beds on each side of the bay. At the far end of the bay I could see several of the guys, all white, standing or sitting around talking to a black soldier I'll call Jackson. This was unusual, because Jackson had always remained very distant from the white guys, and usually talked only with other blacks. Jackson was tall and well built, a strong soldier who worked hard and always did well at any task, but never said very much. As I got closer, I saw something even more unusual. Jackson was crying. More than just crying, he was bawling. Tears were rolling down his cheeks, as he put his face down in his hands and began sobbing horribly. As I got closer, I could smell everybody's alcohol, and I heard his words.

"Please don't die, guys, don't die," he sobbed. "I never wanted any of you to die."

The white guys tried to comfort him. "We're all in this together," one of them said, "none of us can do anything about it."

"But you guys are white!" Jackson exclaimed. I couldn't tell if he was screaming or sobbing. "I always thought white guys would have some kind of special pull, and could get out of going to 'Nam! I couldn't believe it when all you guys got orders."

"No, man," another guy replied, "we're just like you. We can't get out of it, either. None of us want to go."

I was astounded. At the time I didn't know that a disproportionately large number of blacks were being sent to Viet Nam, but I did know that whites were among the troops being sent. It never occurred to me that anyone would think that whites were immune to going to 'Nam. If Jackson had thought that white soldiers wouldn't get sent to 'Nam but black soldiers would go instead, no wonder he had kept his distance from the whites for almost ten weeks.

"I wanted equal rights," Jackson said, "but I didn't want anyone to die. I'd be willing to die if it would save all you guys from dying!" He started sobbing again. Now some of the white guys started crying, too. One guy hugged Jackson, and they cried together.

Antiwar sentiment in the platoon continued rising until it became an explosive rage. A week later, we were all sitting or standing around outside our barracks waiting for an afternoon formation. A small street ran down the side of our barracks, and I was sitting on the grass right by the street. A platoon of new guys just entering the training cycle marched down toward us, straight and tall, boots spit-shined, uniforms squared away. They were loudly chanting their cadence calls and looking proud.

One of our guys yelled, "Fuck the Army!" I heard someone in the new platoon yell something back at us. Instantly, our whole platoon was on their feet, and like a mob, we moved in toward the new platoon.

Though no command had been given, the new platoon came to a complete halt. A few of their guys broke ranks and moved out to face us. I hadn't been aware of getting to my feet, but I was standing facing the new platoon, as our guys moved up behind me and the new troops moved in toward me. Because I had been sitting right at the edge of the street, I suddenly found myself in the very front of what was now a dangerous confrontation. As I looked down the street, the two lines came almost together.

At the front of the line, one of our guys was arguing with a large guy from the new platoon. I tensed, and as I faced the line of troops, an image flashed in my mind, the image of a soldier jabbing me with a knife-hand thrust to the throat as we'd all been taught in basic training. I didn't want to kill anybody and I didn't want to die, certainly not in a riot that didn't make any sense to me.

A trainee leader from the new platoon stepped in between the two arguing men. He looked his man directly in the eyes, covered the man's hands with his, and spoke words I couldn't hear. Then he seemed to move his man back almost by sheer force of will. When the two men were separated, a sergeant yelled the command, "Forward, MARCH!!" Half the new platoon stepped forward. Some men scrambled to get back in formation. The new platoon continued to march down the street, as more men ran back into formation. Then they marched off. It was over.

I turned to one of my comrades. "That was close," I said, "I was afraid somebody might get killed, and for what?"

My comrade looked straight at me and replied, "If we die here, or die in Viet Nam, what's the difference?"

To kill or be killed, and for what? We each had to look deeply into our own souls, and decide.

A couple of weeks later, the platoon was gone. New orders assigned every man to different units, over half in Viet Nam. I went to William Beaumont General Hospital, near El Paso, Texas. But I knew that wouldn't last forever.

Seven months later, my Viet Nam orders came, bringing to a head my intense moral crisis. Should I go and fight? Or should I refuse and be branded a coward for the rest of my life? Where did duty lie? If I obeyed orders and went, would I become a murderer? Murderer or coward, what was right? I feared being a murderer, I feared death, and I feared being a coward. I didn't know which I feared more. I struggled with these questions. Thinking and thinking, I finally decided that if the choice was between being a coward or being a murderer, it was better to be a coward. At least I would be the only one hurt; I would not hurt innocent women and children. I was twenty-one. Both the Army and the peace movement had framed these questions in black and white. It was damned if you do, damned if you don't. Either way, half the country would love you and the other half would hate you. You just got to choose which half. It would be many years before I would learn to understand shades of gray and the complex colors of life, and see that it was not as simple as coward or murderer. It was a no-win situation, and every possible decision we could make would damn us in some way and save us in another. We were all afraid of something, and we all killed something in our choices. We also all saved something.

I decided to resist orders.

I went home on leave to San Francisco, got a lawyer, and wrote up a limited conscientious objector case. This meant I was objecting only to a specific war, not to legitimate national defense. I wasn't a pacifist, but I wasn't an aggressor either. Individuals or a nation may have the right to defend themselves from a mugger, but that doesn't give them the right to go out and mug others. Viet Nam did not attack us, we attacked them. The Army did not recognize this kind of case, but pressing it meant that while I might not win my case, I would be held in the stockade rather than being shipped overseas. I planned to refuse

Viet Nam orders and go to prison, rather than fight in an illegal and immoral war.

Then, with my lawyer, I turned myself in at the Army's stockade in the Presidio (an Army base in San Francisco). I refused Viet Nam orders, requested limited conscientious objector status, and pleaded guilty to the charges of AWOL, refusing a direct order, refusing to serve in a combat zone, and missing an overseas shipment. The last three were felonies, each worth five years in prison, for a total of fifteen years. I was mentally preparing myself to go to prison, but this didn't happen. Instead the Army dropped all charges, released me, and put me back on Viet Nam orders. As we drove out the main gate of the stockade, I said to my lawyer, "I don't get it. I'm guilty, I'm pleading guilty, all the evidence proves I'm guilty, how can they just release me?" My lawyer answered, "Mike, the Constitution guarantees you the right to be found innocent if you're innocent, but it says nothing about guaranteeing you the right to be found guilty if you're guilty."

I split from my lawyer and hid out. I realized that I had only two choices left: desert to Canada or go to Viet Nam. For me, the honor of this war was dead. This was the hardest decision of my life. It meant giving up everything I had ever known, but I made the choice. I decided to desert to Canada. When I got there, I discovered that at least two other soldiers from my medic training platoon had arrived before me. Everyone had to choose.

We choose peace.

To Take a Street

Toronto, Canada. It is the early 1970s, and the Viet Nam war is raging. I'm a U.S. Army deserter, wanted by the FBI. But like most draft dodgers and deserters, I don't just hide in a safe haven, I continue to actively oppose the war. This day I'm going to an antiwar demonstration. As is the custom of American deserters, I wear my Army field jacket with my name, "U.S. Army," and unit patches still on. It's called flying your colors, letting the enemy know who you are.

Being Chinese-American, I have made friends with a small group of Vietnamese students. Today I am going with about five or six of them to the demo. I don't speak Vietnamese and I stand about five inches taller than the others, but we share being Asian. Along with the students there is one illegal immigrant, who is in the country hiding from the Vietnamese draft. He's the smallest one of us all, a head shorter than me, and probably weighing less than ninety pounds. We tell him he shouldn't be here, that it's too dangerous for him. It's dangerous for us all, and he repeats the phrase, "One man in a demonstration is worth ten VC in the field."

When we arrive at the demonstration, the cops are there in force. They have row upon row upon row of cops on motorcycles, backed up by many more rows of cop infantry. They are dressed in full riot gear: helmets, sticks, guns, and motorcycle jackboots. I feel intimidated by this show of force, but I came here to do my duty—to march against the war. We join the demonstration.

As we march, the cops order us to stay on the sidewalk, and we do so. But as we continue along, a small group of protesters dance down the line chanting, "Take the street, take the street!" I've seen these guys before at other demos, and friends have warned me that they're a local Marxist group known particularly for inciting others to break the law, then splitting and letting others take the bust. I've been told they excuse this by saying that they're the "revolutionary cadre," and their job is to survive and lead while the "masses" die. I've never seen any Marxist group before (or since) that had such a philosophy, but it matched this particular group's behavior.

A few Canadians hear the chants and step into the street. Immediately, the first row of motorcycle cops gun their engines and charge. They come in a half flying wedge formation, and the Canadians turn and run back to the safety of the curb. The Marxists run back along the crowd, again chanting, "Take the street!" and clapping their hands. Another group of Canadians step out into the street. The next row of motorcycles charges, again sweeping the people back onto the sidewalk.

The one illegal immigrant among us, I'll call him Dinh, looks around. Then he steps off the curb and walks out into the middle of the street. As I watch, stunned, he just stands there facing the cops, a ninety-pound David facing an army of Goliaths.

The students with me are screaming at him in Vietnamese to come back. He just stands there. Then he looks over and waves for us to come out and join him.

A million thoughts race through my head in a jumbled instant.

"He'll be deported and the South Vietnamese government will torture him to death or they'll send him to the front and keep him there until he's killed. If I get arrested, they'll deport me and hand me over to the FBI or the Army, then I'll go to prison or Viet Nam." My head whirls in confusion and fear. I know that if Dinh gets arrested, his death is certain. For me, death is only one possibility. I don't know what to do. Then a voice in my head says very clearly, "This man is your brother."

I step into the street. I walk out to the middle, and I stand beside my brother.

I look over at the Vietnamese. They are still screaming, now in Vietnamese and English. I wave to them to come out and join us.

They hesitate, look at each other. Then they step out into the street, walk over, and join us. Because I am the tallest, they instinctively cluster around me. I find myself looking over the heads of my friends at the rows and rows of huge cops, with their motorcycles, their helmets, their guns, and their three-foot riot sticks. I don't know what is going to happen. I don't know if I will live or die, if I'll be taken in shackles to Viet Nam or to prison. I feel intense fear in my stomach, and I try to push it down.

Suddenly, something shifts. In fact, it seems as if the world itself has shifted. Time stops. I see the cops, immobile in space. I look over at the crowd. I can feel the energy of their yelling, but there is no sound, no movement. It is as if the whole world is frozen, except me. Everything is silence. I no longer feel any fear. Instead, I feel perfectly calm. I know I have made the right decision, and that whatever happens, I can accept it. I feel a vast euphoria and deep peace.

Suddenly, time snaps back to normal. The crowd surges out into the street. In an instant, we are surrounded by hundreds of singing, chanting demonstrators. The police motorcycles charge. But the crowd is too dense to be moved, and the motorcycles have to stop. We have taken the street!

We hold the street all the way to the American Consulate. The police can only follow. We have our demonstration in front of the consulate, and we have it on our own terms.

Later, when it is all over, the other Vietnamese ask Dinh why he did such a crazy thing. He answers, "I did it for my country."

PAUL WOODRUFF

Born in New Jersey and raised in western Pennsylvania, I joined the Army through ROTC at Princeton in 1965. I took a few years at Oxford and then served as a junior officer with MACV at Chau Doc in the Delta of Vietnam from June 1969 to June 1970. My brother had been a Marine in I Corps the previous year.

I have been teaching at the University of Texas since 1973. I have written plays, opera libretti, poetry, and short fiction, as well as a number of translations and scholarly works. My novella set in Vietnam won an Austin Book Award, and my play on returning veterans won a B. Iden Payne Award for best new play of 1983 in Austin. A play I wrote at Oxford was produced as a radio play by the BBC in 1968. I have written philosophical works on reverence and democracy, and I am currently writing a book called *The Necessity of Theater*.

I began writing poetry about my Vietnam experience during Operation Desert Storm. In 2002, I revisited Vietnam and found the tall pagoda described in "Sanctuary." It was built as a prayer for peace, and it still stands, although in need of restoration. Like most veterans, I found that Vietnam cut across past relationships like a fire. Hence "Walking Across a Burnt Field, I Feel a Puff of Ashes Up My Jeans." Luckily, however, Lucia and I renewed our relationship and married in 1973. We have two daughters and one granddaughter.

Sanctuary

Translate the pagoda. Forget
my odd internal rhyme,
the three-stress line.

But the pagoda, tall as two
palm trees, touched in blue
and gold, half-built, bamboo

crane still swinging, workmen
running for their huts, me
huddling with them. Where the

one-eyed warlord made
his servant call me out
to his safe ditch and said

this was friendly fire. Translate
the shining narrow white
tall-as-two-palms pagoda,

the wrinkled men who built
up, painting as they went,
unsurprised by war.

And the walls I dumbly prayed
would save me when I saw
such misplaced beauty: machine-

gun fire, pagoda rising
white and tall as two palms.
The hope of builders. Translate that.

Walking across a Burnt Field, I Feel a Puff of Ashes up My Jeans

I remember loving fire,
toasting marshmallows
till they flared. Did you know,
the night before I flew to Saigon,

that the fire was lit across our past?
We lay on the red sofa,
my wet cheek brushed yours,
my mother made a tactful exit.

We parted in the kitchen.
Mother drove me to the airport.
I remembered you in pictures,
letters, songs you taped for me.

But mainly in the pulse between my legs.
I didn't know, when I flew home
next year, that everything was ashes.
Books looked like books, home home,

and you looked every inch yourself.
Or so we thought, enacting love on the false
leather sofa, remembering tears.
The emergency had passed unnoticed.

No one broke the glass or sounded
the alarm. There were no sirens.
You never saw my blackened thigh,
or the clouds of dark ash, spreading.

I was born in China at the very beginning of the Cultural Revolution. For the first ten years of my life, tens of millions people were persecuted by the Chinese government and many died. The United States was identified as the enemy. I never imagined one day I would come to this country and write in its language stories about China. My first book, *Little Green: Growing Up During the Chinese Cultural Revolution*, a memoir in verse, has been published by Simon and Schuster (March 2005). It is the first book of a trilogy. "The Petition" is intended for the third book in the trilogy.

When I was a child, my grandma used to tell me about the wars she had lived through. At a time when all children's books were burned, those stories, told in vivid detail, were my bedtime stories. For many years, it didn't make sense to me why she chose to tell those stories, until I wrote "Lullaby," a prayer for peace.

The Petition

On April 22, 1989, three student representatives knelt on the stairs outside the People's Great Hall in Tiananmen Square. They held above their head the petition for an equal conversation between the students and the government. In the Great Hall, the Central Government leaders were holding a farewell ceremony for Yaobang Hu, the former Secretary of the Party, who had passed away a week earlier. Many of those present for the ceremony had themselves been student leaders in the first half of the century. I was a student at Peking University at that time.

You look down at me from behind thick windows,
high above.
Here I am, below steep stairs, down on my knees.

How did this happen?

Years ago, you were the one, right here
where I am now,
your youth pure, your heart unstained,
like this one I hold in my chest.
You must understand how it feels,
you must remember what it was like.

The cause you fought for,
we fight for:
Everyone shall be born to be equal and free—
including us to be equal to you,
and us to be free from you.

What happened?

Is it just life? Or shall we blame time?
Or human nature?

But it can't be you who should show me
how a heart would change over the years
and how one's eyes would change
the world that's coming upon them.

It can't be you who should show me
what should become
of a person,
let alone a nation—
now that you stand high above
me
who kneel down low.

I know that day by day,
I will also grow older, as you have.
All I want is really
just to stand,
not above and not below.

Lullaby

For my grandma and the war stories she told me when I was a child.

Good night
In war and peace

Sleep in peace
Wake up in peace
Beautiful peaceful human dreams

On the East Sea
An empire floods out
To see your angel's face

And I
Will be the phoenix
Spreading wings of clouds
Over your sleeping beauty

Sleep in peace
Wake up in peace
Beautiful peaceful human dreams

Good night
In war and peace.

DOUG ZACHARY

I was born in 1949 in Pixley, California (the setting of *Of Mice and Men*), to Texas-Okie migrants who had not been informed of the end of the Depression. My childhood included nine years in a Southern Baptist orphanage on the outskirts of Dallas, Texas, and four years of public school in San Bernardino, California. I also spent a year embedded with a group of families from Mexico moving about Texas building highways; I lived briefly in an especially kind foster home in Odessa, Texas.

I joined the Marines in 1968 and won discharge as a conscientious objector in 1970. I have since earned a B.S. in political theory from the University of Texas and an M.A. in culture and spirituality from the Sophia Center at Holy Names College in Oakland, California. I work for Veterans for Peace as a fund raiser.

I want to dedicate these stories to my friend with whom I joined the military, thinking that we would serve our country and our people. John suffered an unimaginably severe beating while we were in Marine boot camp in San Diego. The rest of our platoon almost literally carried him through the remaining weeks of training, but John never regained his emotional balance, and he committed suicide a few weeks after we completed our training. Brother, I am seeking, and I will find, the courage to tell your story.

I have profound karmic debts to each of my children: Billy, Krickett, Isabelle, and Elisa. Their unnecessary suffering at my hands has taught me much about the destructiveness of anger and the value of tenderness. I am eternally grateful to each of the three women with whom I have parented children; Phyllis Blevins, Helene Dreyfus, and Gina Sconza have each made significant contributions to my healing from early childhood trauma. To my friend Meg Patterson and to Mary "Magdalene" Mulligan, who, meeting me at the door of an open tomb, assured me that ALL things can heal, I will forever be grateful.

As described accidentally in a newspaper article, I am a "*former* ex-Marine" (my emphasis). Don't buy that jive about "Once a Marine always a Marine" till you've talked to me. Having been brought up on Christian parables and the Sermon on the Mount, like Bill Moyers I learned everything I needed to know about politics and war in Sunday School. The Bodhisattva Jesus is my secretary of state, the Beatitudes my national security doctrine.

Christmas at Grandma's

This story takes place in the mid-1950s on the Zachary farm some seventy-odd miles northeast of Dallas and nine miles east of Blue Ridge, Texas (population 300), when I was eight or nine years old. My grandparents were second-generation settlers from Tennessee and Kentucky whose fathers had seized the area by killing Mexicans, Indians, wolves, and most indigenous flora; when done with those chores, they turned their violence upon each other, their wives, and their children.

Men in my family were lean and hard bodied; they burned every calorie they ate working or fighting. Their vices were alcohol, illicit sexual adventures, and fistfighting. They owned nothing they did not need; their wardrobes consisted of two or three sets of overalls and maybe half a dozen Western-style work shirts. One full set of clothing was referred to as "Sunday go-to-meeting clothes." They were rarely worn, saved for Easter and Christmas church services and the one day each month when the family would travel nineteen miles to Farmersville to cash their Social Security checks and obtain provisions.

Grandma's place was a frontier house (built circa 1840s) made out of rough-cut planks nailed vertically and whitewashed infrequently. It had neither running water in the kitchen nor any indoor toilets; indeed, the Zacharys didn't even have an outhouse. It was understood that there were 160 acres, two barns, a hen-house, and plenty of dung beetles to take care of our business.

My brothers and I spent rare weekends and long weeks during the summer there. We were often working in the fields, chopping weeds, hauling hay or picking cotton. Unsatisfactory work performance meant a switching from Grandma.

As a young child I never understood why my father was the outcast in the Zachary family, but I did understand that his lack of status was transferable to his children. I don't imagine that his siblings respected him a lot for having abandoned his sons to an orphanage. I suspect that in their eyes he drank too much and earned way too little money.

"Christmas at Grandma's" is written in the voice of an eight-year-old boy. It recalls my impressions on a very scary day in the life of my family. I have noticed that my brothers' memories often differ significantly from mine; I would expect that to be true of my other relatives as well. In no way is this little "memoir" meant to reflect the "objective truth" concerning these events; instead, these are my stories and mine alone.

It's Christmas at Grandma's house. Daddy's come to get us at Buckner Orphuns Home and we're up at Grandma's agin! Nigh on four years now, me and my brothers been stayin' in the Orphuns Home down in Dallas, gettin' out only on holidays and for a few weeks in the summer to chop Grandma's cotton. But this here visit is for a holiday, meanin' there won't be no fieldwork. My very favorite people in the world, all my cousins, are here at the farm. I'm so happy to be here, with Sissy and Randy especially, that I cain't help but expect that someday soon we'll git outa Buckners's and come back here an' live among our aunts, uncles, and cousins agin. This here, Christmas at Grandma's, is as good as life gits.

We've eaten our holiday feast in three separate sittings, the men first of course, then the children, and last of all, the women. The men are out drinkin' and working on the tractor and us younguns are in the kitchen helpin' the women with the cleaning.

The lingering smells of fresh-killed-country-fried chicken, mashed potatoes, cream gravy, and home-made soda biscuits mix with the cheap, heavy perfumes worn by my aunts and the hot smoky soapy smells of cleaning up in a primitive Northeast Texas kitchen. Hot water for rinsing dishes boils noisily on the rear burners of Grandma's old wood-burning stove. My aunts Ola, Tessie, and May are scraping plates into the enameled slop bucket next to the rear door and braggin' on each others' home-made pies. Me and Randy are busy dryin' dishes and soaking up their praise.

Suddenly, screams and shouts from outside interrupt the peace and harmony of the kitchen. Dishes clatter noisily to the floor and Randy and me are soaked with hot soapy water as Aunt Tessie upsets the dishpan and tramples us in her wild rush to the porch. We follow fearfully in her wake.

There, in the front yard, between the cistern and an old broken-down tractor, lies my Daddy, and he ain't movin' one little bit. Randy's dad, my Uncle Roby, stands tall over him, gripping a bloodstained tire iron. Up and down, up and down—like one of them East Texas oil field pumps. Again and again the tire iron reaches for the sky and plummets into Daddy's head and shoulders; he still aint movin'.

Randy and me, we're afraid; quietly we move toward each other and, shoulder to shoulder, seek safety. Then, suddenly, I am sinking, falling away.

"Kill the son of a bitch! Hit him, hit him again!"

"'Bout time someone killed that asshole!" The cheers, the jeers bypass my ears and sink directly into my heart. Everyone in the family, aunts, uncles, cousins, even my Daddy's mama, is urging Roby to destroy my Daddy.

I look into the faces of first one aunt and then another, desperately seeking some hint of compassion or connection. No one meets my eyes. Suddenly I know that my Daddy is about to die and that these people will probably kill his boys too.

From out of nowhere comes the plan. My brothers and I will have to fight our way out of this place. I turn to my best friend in the whole world, my constant playmate Randy, and begin attacking his face with both my fists. He is younger and smaller and caught by surprise so I soon gain the advantage. Then we are both bleeding and weeping and throwing punches as fast as we can.

In the background, I can sense some change. Someone grabs me from behind and pulls us apart. The jeers and angry shouts have turned to laughter.

"Ain't that the sweetest damn thang, how that boy fought for his no-good ol' Daddy?"

"Boy might be a Zachary after all, with all that fight in him!"

Then they're putting us in the back seat of Daddy's car, where we wait, tearfully and fearfully, till he's on his feet and stumbles, half-blind and unaided, into the car. He's covered with blood—red—red from head to waist so totally red and draggin' a wet smell I have only known from slaughter-time. My stomach starts to turn on me, it feels like I just had my face stuffed into a slop bucket; I move away and my innards begin to quiet down. He cranks the car and we drive away.

As we come to the end of the white rock road and draw to a stop, he spits bloodily out the window, turns toward us, and asks, "Now what'd y'all boys thank 'bout that?" I cannot meet his gaze. I am repulsed, ashamed that he cannot stand his ground. I hate him and I despise his offspring.

I swear to myself that no one will ever whup me in the way I have seen my Daddy beaten. Within a week I will challenge Kenny Isaacs to a knock-down drag-out fistfight for second place in Pires dormitory.

As for my Daddy, soon his eye falls to the lonely road ahead. That evening, he returns us to the Orphuns Home and drives away again.

Last Call on the Farm

In 1983, after a lengthy exile, I returned to Collin County, Texas, for the double funeral of my father and my favorite uncle, Leslie. My father's status as the family outcast was confirmed at his death at the hand of his brother; those who felt a need to point the finger of blame held that my father was responsible for his own death and that of his murderer. I did not vigorously disagree.

Uncle Leslie, the triggerman, was everyone's favorite uncle. He had an emotional genius that endeared him to all the children in his life. Whenever we visited the farm, I awaited with anticipation, as did every child, the moment when this gentle giant would turn to me and say, "Well, Doug Martin, I'm needing a pilla about, let's see now, shore nuff 'bout your size!" He'd then grab me and tickle me fiercely as he positioned me on the porch planks to gleefully act as his new pillow while the other children eagerly waited for their turn.

To this day I do not know whether Uncle Leslie was actually retarded or whether his "simple" status was some kind of fraud engineered to ensure that Grandma and Grandpa would have someone to care for them in their dotage. When I returned from the University as a sophomore Forestry student, I learned that Leslie was the only person on the farm who could distinguish, without failure, every tree and every bush along the creek bed one from another. He also knew the names, habits, and family histories of each of the dozens of cattle on the farm.

Leslie also spoke with the cattle and taught the children to do so. Each day he called them up from the creek bottom to be milked and fed. This involved hollering at the top of one's lungs, loud enough to be heard a mile and a half away, using a variety of heavily accented, country takes on two words: "here" and "cow." "HEAH COW, HEAH HEAH HEAH, HEAH COW HEAH! The calls had changing rhythms and combinations of the words. The seemingly impossible volume and the cattle's eager response never changed. It was my first opera.

My dear Uncle Leslie never left home and became a permanent fixture on the Zachary farm. He lived on and served the Zachary Quarter-Section till the day that he, my Daddy, and the farm died.

On a beautiful spring morning in 1983 Leslie Zachary, my dear simple Uncle Pie, as he was called because of his love of pecan pie, woke up at the break of dawn, as he had for seventy-two years, walked through the sweet morning air to the crest of the hill, and called the cows. Three dozen head of mixed Angus and Herefords trotted up the hill expecting to be milked and fed and stroked, their sense of entitlement having grown steadily over the years because of the tender loving kindness shown them by my retarded uncle.

Upon successfully corralling the herd, Uncle Pie drew his .22 automatic and proceeded to shoot and kill each and every one of the herd, whose mother's mother's mother he had known by sight, name, and personality.

When he had finished the gruesome task, I am sure weeping and suffering through every moment, Leslie walked back to the house and fought his way into the room in which my Daddy had barricaded himself. There in the same room where they and all their siblings had been born, Leslie and Daddy struggled mightily until Uncle Pie was able to put several bullets through my Daddy's head.

He then walked covered in blood two miles to Clyde McDonald's place, where he borrowed the phone and called my Uncle Willie over at Princeton and told him, "I have hurt Troy. You need to come to the farm."

Twenty-odd minutes later, Willie drove up to the house and found Leslie sitting in a cane chair on the porch. Seeing all the cattle dead on the ground and Leslie soaked in blood, Willie cautiously stepped around Leslie and found Daddy dead on the floor. He returned to the porch to ask, "Now Leslie, what in the hell did you go and do that for?"

Leslie gave a reply that in the eyes of most of the Zachary clan and for that matter most of Collin County might have justified his actions. My Daddy had been rustling, as we say in Texas, selling Leslie's beloved herd off one by one to pay his debts to the used-car dealers, pimps, and bootleggers over at the county seat. Leslie, in his mind, had taken enough, too damned much.

At this point, Uncle Pie looked Willie straight in the eye and declared, "I have lived on this farm all of my seventy-two years and I am not going to die in jail." Willie's instant and unthinking reply: "Now Leslie, everyone in Collin County knows you for a simple man. No judge or jury would think of sending you to jail. You will be taken care of over at Rusk for the rest of your life." Willie was referring to Rusk State Hospital for the Criminally Insane, for many years America's poster child for mismanaged, cruel, and dangerous facilities for the mentally ill. A simple man like my uncle would have been assaulted, brutalized, raped even, and, perhaps mercifully, murdered at Rusk State Hospital.

Willie reported that a look of sheer terror passed over Leslie's face, then one of sheer determination and resolve. "Like hell I will!" he said to Willie before leaning back in the cane chair, placing the pistol between his eyes, and pulling the trigger.

Later that morning, 300 miles away, as I was sitting at my desk I heard on the radio that two eccentric brothers had died by murder-suicide in northeast Collin County. (In Texas, "eccentric" is a classist euphemism for old, poor, illiterate sub-proletarians). I knew instantly that it was Daddy and Leslie and reached for the phone to call my brother and confirm my intuition.

Too alienated to give a damn, I had not been going to Zachary funerals. I was very busy building my business, providing for my wife and children, and medicating myself with pot, cocaine, and tequila in an effort to deal with the Post-Traumatic Stress Disorder I had known for my entire life, and which I now attribute to my family's habits of violence. In fact, the two men who were now dead had, in a drunken rage in the summer of 1970, attempted to murder me. However, I had also known the sweet and gentle sides of Leslie and Daddy. Now that they were dead and no longer dangerous, I felt that I needed to go to the double funeral in Blue Ridge and bury them in peace, forgiveness, and honor. I further believed that the entire family, and the whole county for that matter, would be busy projecting their own meanness and hatefulness into the situation, and that I was called to go home, so to speak, and to make and to be peace.

Sure enough, on the day of the funeral, I found the Zacharys lining up on one side or the other of the fierce arguments, speaking on behalf of or against one or the other of the dead brothers. The more "successful" members of the clan were denouncing my Daddy for his degenerate way of life that had brought about this sad day. Hell, the man had even abandoned his children to an orphanage so that he could follow his dick through four (was it five, or six?) failed marriages and countless bars and whorehouses, ending up at sixty-two years old back on the farm and exploiting Leslie.

On the other side coalesced my brothers and I, my Aunt Tessie, who glared at Leslie's corpse as if she wished to resurrect him so she could kill him again, and Daddy's unwashed friends. These were people who had known Dad in the fields or in the bars. They were too smelly or too dirty or too drunk to enter the church; they had no Sunday go-to-meeting overalls. These folks knew Daddy as a man who lived among them in drunken poverty and sweet humility. He was known among them as a man who would give away anything he had to anyone in need. They stood with his boys.

Things really began to heat up when someone announced that Grandma's will read that poor simple Leslie, who had cared for her and Grandpa till their deaths at home on the farm, would be allowed to live on the farm till he died, after which the farm would be divided evenly among the surviving siblings. The argument went that since Daddy died a few minutes before Leslie, he was not a surviving sibling and therefore my brothers and I would be excluded from any share of the proceeds from the sale of the farm.

Things began to get really ugly: my brothers and I lining up with Daddy's untouchable friends, and the rest of the family on the other side of the issue with the patriarchs. People began to talk of "goin' to their trunks," a Texas euphemism for more gunplay.

At this point I found myself being drawn into the fight, thirteen years after fighting for and winning a discharge from the Marines as a conscientious objector. Hell, I had endured ten years in a tough-ass orphanage, four years on the streets, and one and a half years among Marines. I wanted to whip all these bastards who were talking trash about my Daddy and gain revenge for our many years of exile as the outcasts in this white-trash family

Reason prevailed somehow; it must have been the women. Willie agreed to write a $4,000 check for each of Troy's boys on the condition that we would agree to leave Collin County and promise never to return. Not wanting to trust the Zacharys for a day to honor the check, I drove directly to Citizen's State Bank in Princeton, got my two hundred twenty-dollar bills, and hit the road for Central Texas.

What continues to blow my mind about this story is how after gaining such blessed insights from LSD and the spiritual and political counterculture, after receiving an honorable discharge from the Marines as a conscientious objector, I came so close to getting into some serious violence, all for the sake of $4,000 and my Daddy's totally unredeemable reputation. To this day, I am shook up, fearful, and uncertain about my behavior in a potentially violent situation. Too often I have awakened to find myself way up in the face of a red-faced cop at a demonstration, putting me and him and others in danger's path. Having recently moved from my blessed Alameda County in California to rural Texas, far behind enemy lines, I find myself at war with my new neighbors because of their right-wing bumper stickers. I want to make and to be peace, but I know that within me lurks a mindless, violent, possibly even murderous impulse.

Most of my folks are dead now—those that still live are old and feeble and not much danger to anyone. Yet I have returned to Collin County only once in the past twenty-five years, sneaking in under the cover of darkness (without my black daughter) to visit with my cousin Sissy and to recall how all the children once loved each other. I have been so lonely.

Now I am returning to the scene of the crime. Collin County lies in the Blackland Prairie; a few miles south is Crawford, Texas, where Veterans for Peace, the organization I have worked for in recent months, set up Camp Casey to honor Cindy Sheehan's honest and profound suffering of the loss of her son Casey in the war against Iraq. The same soil, the same Scots-Irish-Appalachian-derived Texas plains culture I had come up in. "The Blackest Soil and the Whitest People in Texas," the folk proclaimed proudly.

Returning from my lengthy exile, I have gone three times to Camp Casey, accompanied by my Wiccan daughter Krickett, my youngest daughter Elisa, my granddaughter Katriana, and Genevieve Vaughn, a sweet and powerful feminist ally. Three times I went to Camp Casey to reclaim the soil I was brought up on, to renounce my Exile, and to deepen my faith in Peace and in Love. Camp Casey has been a healing miracle in my life.

My sad, confused, and violent family life was always a war zone. It was not necessary for me to go somewhere like Vietnam to know violence and its aftermath. The fear and violence I have witnessed throughout my entire life led me to become first, a Marine, then a conscientious objector. It is dawning on me that having been present at such chaos has somehow been a gift, and I pray that I might fully comprehend the message and respond with lovingkindness toward myself, my family, and my misguided culture.

About the Editor

Maxine Hong Kingston began writing at the age of nine ("I was in the fourth grade and all of a sudden this poem started coming out of me"). She won her first writing award—a journalism contest at UC Berkeley—when she was sixteen. In 1976 *The New York Times* praised her first book, *The Woman Warrior,* comparing it to Joyce's *Portrait of the Artist as a Young Man,* saying, "It is an investigation of soul . . . Its sources are dream and memory, myth and desire. Its crises are crises of the heart in exile from roots that bind and terrorize it." At the age of thirty-six, she was a celebrity, winning the National Book Critic's Circle Award. Other books would follow, and the praise would continue to be unstinting. In 1980, she was named a Living Treasure of Hawai'i by the Honpa Hongwanji Mission of Hawai'i.

In 1991, following a massive fire in the Oakland-Berkeley hills that consumed Maxine's house and the only copy of her manuscript-in-process, *The Fourth Book of Peace,* and as the first President Bush was ordering the invasion of Iraq, she began offering writing and meditation workshops for veterans, to help them give voice to their experiences and work toward personal peace. As she'd hoped, the writing became a process of healing and renewal not just for the veterans but also for Maxine. She drew on the experience of these workshops in *The Fifth Book of Peace.*

In 1997, Maxine Hong Kingston was awarded the National Humanities Medal by President Bill Clinton. In March 2003, she was arrested for crossing a police line at the White House as part of a CODEPINK action to protest the Iraq War.

She retired last year from her career teaching literature and creative writing, mostly at UC Berkeley, where she was known for offering personalized instruction to each student, even in auditorium-sized classes, encouraging "real communication." She and her husband, actor Earll Kingston, live in Oakland, California. Their son, Joe Kingston, is a musician in Honolulu.

MICHAEL L. WONG

Afterword

The Veteran Writers Group

*V*eterans of War, Veterans of Peace is a harvest of creative, redemptive
storytelling—fiction and nonfiction, poetry and prose—that
grew out of a community of veterans and others profoundly affected
by war.

The group's first gathering was a daylong workshop led by Maxine Hong Kingston in June 1993, held at the University of California,
Berkeley. Organized by the Community of Mindful Living, it was the
beginning of a three-year project for healing the wounds of war through
writing in community, supported by the Lila Wallace-Reader's Digest
Fund. Most of those who came to the first session were Viet Nam War
veterans. We began the day with introductions, followed by sitting
meditation, writing instruction, and then a long period of writing.
After lunch, taken partly in silence, each veteran read his work aloud
while the group listened. Midway through the readings, we went outdoors for walking meditation, and ended the day with another period
of silent sitting.

The days and the stories never stopped. We continued to meet
month after month, and veterans from other wars and even from other
armies began joining the group. At one meeting, North Vietnam Army
veterans wrote about their experiences on the opposite side of the war.
Resisters and other peace activists joined, more and more women came
to participate, and people caught in drug wars, gang violence, and
domestic abuse also found their way to us. We were neither a peace
group nor a war group, but a place where people of different backgrounds could meet and share their experiences.

We met monthly from 1993 to 1996, when the project was supposed to end. We had a "last session" at Green Gulch Farm Zen Center. But it didn't end. We couldn't end. We began as an experiment
and had become a community. To this day, we continue meeting four
times a year at a private home in Northern California.

Veteran Writers' gathering, Sebastopol, California, March 2006

Enormous creative expression has emerged from these gatherings. Maxine has chronicled the history of our group in *The Fifth Book of Peace*. Stories and poems started in community were published, including John Mulligan's *Shopping Cart Soldiers,* which received the 1998 PEN/Oakland/Josephine Miles Award for Literary Excellence in Fiction; Richard Sterling's *The Fire Never Dies: One Man's Raucous Romp Down the Road of Food, Passion & Adventure;* James Janko's *Buffalo Boy and Geronimo;* Pauline Laurent's *Grief Denied: A Vietnam Widow's Story;* Carroll Parrott Blue's *The Dawn at my Back: Memoir of a Black Texas Upbringing;* Ted Sexauer's *Mercy Lives Inside the Wire;* Claude AnShin Thomas' *At Hell's Gate: A Soldier's Journey from War to Peace;* and Clare Morris' *In Transit: Love Poems to the City.*

Other forms of expression have included film, art, and activism. Barbara Sonneborn, a war widow, interviewed American and Vietnamese widows and coproduced the Academy Award-nominated documentary *Regret to Inform.* Roman "Hopper" Martinez is featured in the film, *The Two Faces of Roman Martinez,* produced by Erik Pauser and the Swedish Film Institute. Keith Mather and I are featured in the film *Sir! No Sir!* Tom Currie had a one-man show at the Berkeley Art

Center. Sharon Kufeldt became national vice president of Veterans for Peace. Ted Sexauer went to Iraq during the runup to war to bear witness to the anticipated suffering. Many veterans have returned to Viet Nam to help build schools, hospitals, and other works of social service.

Much healing has occurred. Healing is a never-ending process, and together we continue to find new insights and deeper levels of healing. Through our pain and anger, our understanding and joy, the skills of writing, speaking, and deep listening have enabled members of the Veteran Writers Group to become a transformative resource for many people and a model for engaging creative expression to help the trauma of war heal.

For further information or to contact the Veteran Writers Group, please visit www.vowvop.org.

Permissions

The following works are used with permission:

Carroll Parrott Blue, from *The Dawn at My Back: Memoir of a Black Texas Upbringing,* © 2003. By permission of Carroll Parrott Blue and the University of Texas Press.

George Evans, "A Walk in the Garden of Heaven," from *The New World,* Curbstone Press, Willimantic, Connecticut, 2002.

Dennis Fritzinger, "Charlie Don't Surf," from *Vietnam Generation Newsletter 3.3.,* www3.iath.virginia.edu/sixties/HTML_docs/Texts/Poetry/Fritzinger_poems_3&3.html

Gary Gach, "opera patrons pass by," originally published in *San Francisco Reader #7.*

Gary Gach, "kept from playing with toy guns," originally published in *Turning Wheel,* Winter 2005.

Larry Heinemann, "The Geese," translated by Nguyen Quang Thieu, originally published in *Van Nghe,* Hanoi, Vietnam, 1997.

Ho Anh Thai, from *The Women on the Island,* University of Washington Press, Seattle, 2000.

James Janko, "Buffalo Boy," from *Buffalo Boy and Geronimo,* Curbstone Press, Willimantic, Connecticut, 2006.

Wayne Karlin, "The American Reader," from *War Movies: Journeys to Vietnam: Scenes and Out-takes,* Curbstone Press, Willimantic, Connecticut, 2005. Also published in *Youth Magazine,* Ho Chi Minh City, 2004.

Joe Lamb, "Reuniting Gondwanaland," originally published in *Five Fingers Review 7,* 1989.

Pauline Laurent, "Shattered Dream," from *Grief Denied: A Vietnam Widow's Story,* Catalyst for Change, Santa Rosa, California, 1999.

Le Minh Khue, "Fragile as a Sunray," from *The Stars, The Earth, The River: Short Fiction by Le Minh Khue,* Curbstone Press, Willimantic, Connecticut, 1997.

Fred Marchant, "C.O." and "Elephants Walking," from *Tipping Point,* The Word Works, Washington, D.C., 1994.

Photo Credits

The Vietnamese font used in the poetry of Nguyen Qui Duc is Vtopia, designed by James Do.

Koa Books

Koa Books publishes works on personal transformation, progressive politics, and native cultures. Our recent and forthcoming titles include:

Cindy Sheehan, **Not One More Mother's Child** (available in stores everywhere)
"If anyone wonders why Cindy Sheehan has emerged as the single most galvanizing figure in the antiwar movement, they have but to hear her speak or better yet read her new book . . . one quickly understands the magnetism, the electricity she has generated in the peace movement. She speaks with a clarity, directness, and authenticity that remind us of how hungry we are for such voices in American politics."
—LEWIS KLAUSNER, BLACK OAK BOOKS, BERKELEY, CALIFORNIA

Ann Wright and Susan Dixon, **Dissent in a Democracy** (Spring 2007)
A collection of profiles of officials who leaked documents, resigned, or otherwise confronted the Bush administration, compiled by Army Col. (ret.) and former State Department diplomat Ann Wright, with UH–Manoa lecturer Susan Dixon. *"Revealing lies, cover-ups, and abuses is not disloyal. . . . It is a courageous and patriotic act."* —DANIEL ELLSBERG

Manulani Aluli Meyer, **Hawaiian Ways of Knowing** (Spring 2007)
In lyrical, expressive language, UH–Hilo Professor Manu Meyer shows how the Hawaiian's world is spiritually alive, physical, and relational, and she offers insights to help the reader understand it. *"Manu Meyer is able to capture the essence of what it means to be Hawaiian."* —LUANA BUSBY–NEFF

Robert A. Johnson, **Inner Gold: Understanding Psychological Projection** (Fall 2007)
The author of the bestselling *He, She, We,* and other psychology classics, brings together teachings from medieval alchemy, Jungian psychology, early Christianity, and myth to explore projection, loneliness, fundamentalism, and the spiritual dimensions of psychology.

Lama Surya Das, **Words of Wisdom** (Fall 2007)
Renowned Buddhist teacher and author of the bestselling *Awakening the Buddha Within,* Lama Surya Das expresses his depth of understanding in this book of pithy and witty wisdom sayings: *"There are too many Only Ways." "Every step is the Great Way. Practice being there while getting there." "Meditate as fast as you can."*

Koa Books • P.O. Box 822 • Kihei, HI 96753 • www.koabooks.com